P9-CEL-102

Cognitive Psychology and Its Implications

Seventh Edition

Cognitive Psychology and Its Implications

Seventh Edition

John R. Anderson

Carnegie Mellon University

Worth Publishers

To Gordon Bower

Senior Publisher: Catherine Woods
Acquisitions Editor: Erik Gilg
Marketing Manager: Amy Shefferd
Development Editor: Valerie Raymond
Supplements Editor: Christine Ondreicka
Assistant Editor: Jaclyn Castaldo
Associate Managing Editor: Tracey Kuehn
Project Editors: Dana Kasowitz
Leo Kelly, Macmillan Publishing Solutions
Art Director: Babs Reingold
Cover Designer: Kevin Kall
Text Designer: Lissi Sigillo
Photo Editor: Ted Szczepanski
Production Manager: Sarah Segal
Composition: Macmillan Publishing Solutions
Printing and Binding: Quebecor
Cover Painting: Waiting © Ryoko Tajiri 2009

Library of Congress Cataloging-in-Publication Number: 2009928920

ISBN-13: 978-1-4292-1948-8
ISBN-10: 1-4292-1948-3

Printed in the United States of America

First Printing 2009

Worth Publishers
41 Madison Avenue
New York, NY 10010
www.worthpublishers.com

John Robert Anderson is Richard King Mellon Professor of Psychology and Computer Science at Carnegie Mellon University. He is known for developing ACT-R, which is the most widely used cognitive architecture in cognitive science. Anderson was also an early leader in research on intelligent tutoring systems, and computer systems based on his cognitive tutors currently teach mathematics to about 500,000 children in American schools. He has served as President of the Cognitive Science Society, and has been elected to the American Academy of Arts and Sciences, the National Academy of Sciences, and the American Philosophical Society. He has received numerous scientific awards including the American Psychological Association's Distinguished Scientific Career Award, the David E. Rumelhart Prize for Contributions to the Formal Analysis of Human Cognition, and the inaugural Dr. A. H. Heineken Prize for Cognitive Science. He is the incoming editor of the prestigious Psychological Review.

Brief Contents

Contents

Preface

This is the seventh edition of my textbook—a new edition has appeared every 5 years. Each time I sit down to write the preface for a new edition, I feel that I have gained more perspective on progress in the field of cognitive psychology. When I wrote the first edition in 1980, the field of cognitive psychology had gone through 30 years of amazing development. In the 1950s, a number of true pioneers broke with the behaviorist tradition and laid the foundations for cognitive psychology. In the 1960s, psychologists worked hard to establish experimental paradigms and theoretical models for the new discipline. Their achievements are often (and properly) referred to as the "cognitive revolution." When I entered the field at the beginning of the 1970s, I was able to take full advantage of the two preceding decades of effort. In the 1970s, there was an amazing blossoming of research. By the end of the decade, it became apparent that the field had a larger, more developed, and coherent structure that could be communicated in a textbook.

The first edition appeared in 1980, halfway between the beginning of the cognitive revolution in 1950 and the publication of this seventh edition in 2010. From the perspective of 2009 (when I am writing this preface), it is abundantly clear that there has been accelerated scientific progress in the field. There is no subject of psychological research covered in this textbook for which the level of knowledge has not dramatically increased since the first edition. There is an unfortunate tendency to use adversarial terms to describe the evolution of the field— "Theory 1 claimed one thing, but Theory 2 said it was wrong, and a critical experiment was done that showed Theory 2 was right, but then it was shown that Theory 1. . . ." This textbook tries not to focus on this "clash of theories," although there is no way to honestly report the field without mentioning some of this. While not ignoring the disagreements, the text tries to emphasize what is much more compelling—the enormous cumulative progress in how we understand the mental workings of humans.

Textbooks in this field tend to rely heavily on specific experimental studies from the literature to illustrate the emerging understanding of the human mind. This textbook is no exception. Thus, the references in this textbook provide a measure of the growth of knowledge in our field. The figure on the next page shows the number of references from various decades. Noting that the reporting from the last decade (the 2000s) is still incomplete in this edition, this graph nicely illustrates what is happening in cognitive psychology. Knowledge in the field began to grow in the 1950s and has accelerated. I have not felt the need to throw out references to classic studies that still serve their purpose. Therefore, the fact that most of the citations are to research that appeared after the first edition is a testimony to the acceleration of knowledge.

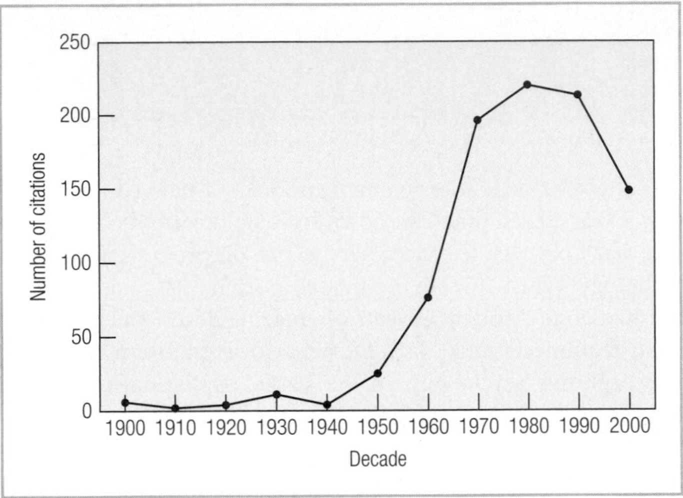

There have been two major dimensions of development in cognitive psychology since 1980, and they have been reflected in the changes to successive editions. The first involves elaboration and deepening of the understanding of the different domains of human cognition, including in many cases substantial corrections to earlier ideas that had been proposed. The second dimension is the dramatic growth in the ability of cognitive neuroscience to use research on the brain to understand the mind. Now, looking over the seventh edition of this book, it seems to be a work that is dramatically different from the first edition. I would never have imagined in 1980 some of the things I can report on in the current edition.

The seventh edition adds a good number of things to the sixth. For instance:

- Research on new neuroscience applications to topics like visual attention, mental imagery, and decision making
- New conclusions on a variety of subjects such as memory and emotion, scientific discovery, and second language acquisition
- The renewed comparisons between artificial intelligence and human intelligence in fields like vision, game playing, and language processing
- Separate chapters on decision making and reasoning, a change that reflects the new research in these fields, including the contributions from cognitive neuroscience

It should be noted that with the last change, Chapters 2 through 13 now organize themselves into six thematic pairs on perception and attention, knowledge representation, memory, problem solving, reasoning and decision making, and language. Although different instructors will find their own ways through the material, I find these pairings useful for organizing my course into a small number of units so that students can keep track of where they are.

I would like to highlight the inclusion of two new features that served to enliven my engagement as a writer and which I hope will increase the reader's engagement:

- Implication boxes make one of the original goals of the book more transparent: the demonstration of how cognitive psychology has relevance to many aspects of our life and to our conceptions of ourselves as humans.
- End-of-chapter questions offer an opportunity to challenge the reader to work out the lessons of the chapter for many topics, including issues that are at the frontier of the field.

There are a number of other features that have been added to the book at the suggestions of my editor Erik Gilg, and the development editor, Valerie Raymond. For instance, we have added color inserts to illustrate things that really require color. If you have the book in hand (and I don't yet), most of those changes should be transparent. They have done a lot to move the format of the textbook into the 21st century.

In addition to Erik and Valerie, Worth has provided a well-coordinated team to carry this book through to publication. Jaclyn Castaldo, Assistant Editor, was the linchpin in coordinating many of the activities undertaken by others in producing the manuscript and illustrations. Ted Szczepanski managed the photograph program by obtaining the new photographs that elucidate the latest findings in the field. Dana Kasowitz, Project Editor, with the help of Leo Kelly of Macmillan Publishing Solutions, oversaw and coordinated the later editorial stages and scrutinized the manuscript to promote clarity and eliminate inconsistency. Amy Shefferd and Jennifer Bilello, Marketing Manager and Marketing Assistant, respectively, have done a very fine job pre-marketing the new edition. Finally, Sarah Segal, Production Manager, worked hard to make sure that the production of this book was consistent with the highest publishing standards.

Two people at Carnegie Mellon have also helped me. My research associate, Jennifer Ferris, kept track of all the new permissions. Also, Abe Anderson has read over the many drafts of the book, keeping me informed about what things the new generation of students know and don't know, various instances of awkward language, and potential opportunities to better communicate with my readers.

A particularly valuable editorial activity carried out by Worth was an extensive set of reviews of the sixth edition. I am grateful for the many comments and suggestions of these reviewers: Ann Sloan Devlin, *College Marshall;* Alyse C. Hachey, *Borough of Manhattan Community College;* Jay Schumacher, *Texas A&M University;* Lumei Hui, *Humboldt State University;* Martha J. Hubertz, *Florida Atlantic University;* Mike Dodd, *University of Nebraska-Lincoln;* Nancy Alvarado, *California State Polytechnic University–Pomona;* Robert J. Hines, *University of Arkansas, Little Rock;* K. Anders Ericsson, *Florida State University;* Dominic W. Massaro, *University of California, Santa Cruz;* Murray Singer, *University of Manitoba;* and Daniel L. Schacter, *Harvard University.*

I would also like to thank the people who read the first six editions of my book, because much of their earlier influence remains: Chris Allan, Jim Anderson,

James Beale, Irv Biederman, Liz Bjork, Stephen Blessing, Lyle Bourne, John Bransford, Bruce Britton, Tracy Brown, Gregory Burton, Robert Calfee, Pat Carpenter, Bill Chase, Nick Chater, Micki Chi, Bill Clancy, Chuck Clifton, Lynne Cooper, Gus Craik, Bob Crowder, Thomas Donnelly, David Elmes, K. Anders Ericsson, Martha Farah, Ronald Finke, Ira Fischler, Susan Fiske, Michael Gazzaniga, Ellen Gagné, Rochel Gelman, Barbara Greene, Dorothea Halpert, Lynn Hasher, Geoff Hinton, Kathy Hirsh-Pasek, Buz Hunt, Louna Hernandez-Jarvis, Robert Hoffman, Laree Huntsman, Lynn Hyah, Earl Hunt, Andrew Johnson, Philip Johnson-Laird, Marcel Just, Stephen Keele, Walter Kintsch, Dave Klahr, Steve Kosslyn, Al Lesgold, Clayton Lewis, Beth Loftus, Marsha Lovett, Maryellen MacDonald, Michael McGuire, Brian MacWhinney, Dominic Massaro, Jay McClelland, Karen J. Mitchell, John D. Murray, Al Newell, E. Slater Newman, Don Norman, Gary Olson, Allan Paivio, Thomas Palmieri, Nancy Pennington, Jane Perlmutter, Peter Polson, Jim Pomerantz, Mike Posner, Roger Ratcliff, Lynne Reder, Steve Reed, Russ Revlin, Phillip Rice, Lance Rips, Roddy Roediger, Miriam Schustack, Terry Sejnowski, Bob Siegler, Ed Smith, Kathy Spoehr, Bob Sternberg, Roman Taraban, Charles Tatum, Joseph Thompson, Dave Tieman, Tom Trabasso, Henry Wall, Charles A. Weaver, Patricia de Winstanley, Larry Wood, and Maria Zaragoza.

1

The Science of Cognition

Our species is called *Homo sapiens,* or "human, the wise." This term reflects the general belief that our superior thought processes are what distinguishes us from other animals. Today we all know that the brain is the organ of the human mind, but the connection between the brain and the mind was not always known. For instance, in a colossal misassociation, the Greek philosopher Aristotle localized the mind in the heart. He thought the function of the brain was to cool the blood. **Cognitive psychology** is the science of how the mind is organized to produce intelligent thought and how it is realized in the brain. This chapter introduces fundamental concepts that set the stage for the rest of the book by addressing the following questions:

- Why do people study cognitive psychology?
- Where and when did cognitive psychology originate?
- How to the cells in the brain process information?
- What parts of the brain are responsible for different functions?
- What new research methods have expanded the field of cognitive psychology?

Motivations

Intellectual Curiosity

One impetus for studying cognitive psychology is the same one that motivates any scientific inquiry: the desire to know. In this respect, the cognitive psychologist is like the tinkerer who wants to know how a clock works. The human mind is a particularly fascinating device that displays a remarkable intelligence and ability to adapt. We are often unaware of the extraordinary aspects of human cognition. Just as we can underestimate the enormous accumulation of technology that allows a news event to be broadcast live on television from anywhere in the world, so too can we forget how sophisticated our mental processes must be to enable us to understand that news event. Cognitive psychologists strive to understand the mechanisms that make such intellectual sophistication possible.

The inner workings of the human mind are far more intricate than the most complicated systems of modern technology. Researchers in the field of **artificial intelligence (AI)** have been attempting to develop programs that will enable computers to display intelligent behavior. Although this field has been an active one for over half a century and there have been many notable successes, AI researchers still do not know how to create a program that matches human intelligence. No existing program can recall facts, solve problems, reason, learn, and process language with human facility. This failure of AI to achieve human-level intelligence has become the cause of a great deal of soul-searching by some of the founders of artificial intelligence (e.g., McCarthy, 1996; Nilsson, 2005). There is a resurging view that AI needs to pay more attention to how human thought functions.

There does not appear to be anything magical about human intelligence that would make it impossible to model it on a computer. Consider scientific discovery, for instance. This endeavor is often thought to reflect the ultimate feats of human intelligence: Scientists supposedly make great leaps of intuition to explain a puzzling set of data. To formulate a novel scientific theory is supposed to require both great creativity and special deductive powers. Herbert Simon, who won the 1978 Nobel Prize for his theoretical work in economics, spent the last 40 years of his life studying cognitive psychology. Among other things, he focused on the intellectual accomplishments involved in "doing" science. He and his colleagues (Langley, Simon, Bradshaw, & Zytkow, 1987) built computer programs to simulate the problem-solving activities involved in such scientific feats as Kepler's discovery of the laws of planetary motion and Ohm's development of his law for electric circuits. These computer programs are among the most impressive accomplishments of AI. Simon also examined the processes involved in his own now-famous scientific discoveries (Simon, 1989). In all cases, he found that the methods of scientific discovery could be explained in terms of the basic cognitive processes that we study in cognitive psychology. He wrote that many of these activities are just well-understood problem-solving processes (we will study them in Chapters 8 and 9). He adds:

> Moreover, the insight that is supposed to be required for such work as discovery turns out to be synonymous with the familiar process of recognition; and other terms commonly used in the discussion of creative work—such terms as "judgment," "creativity," or even "genius"—appear to be wholly dispensable or to be definable, as insight is, in terms of mundane and well-understood concepts. (p. 376)

Thus, Simon concluded that when we look in detail at human genius, we find that it involves basic cognitive processes operating together in complex ways to produce the brilliant results.[1] Most of this book will be devoted to describing what we know about those basic processes.

[1] Weisberg (1986) comes to a similar conclusion.

Great feats of intelligence, such as scientific discovery, are the result of basic cognitive processes.

Implications for Other Fields

Students and researchers interested in other areas of psychology or social science have another reason for following developments in cognitive psychology. The basic mechanisms governing human thought are important in understanding the types of behavior studied by other social sciences. For example, an appreciation of how humans think is important to understanding why certain thought malfunctions occur (clinical psychology), how people behave with other individuals or in groups (social psychology), how persuasion works (political science), how economic decisions are made (economics), why certain ways of organizing groups are more effective and stable than others (sociology), and why natural languages have certain features (linguistics). Cognitive psychology is thus the foundation on which all other social sciences stand, in the same way that physics is the foundation for the other physical sciences.

Nonetheless, much social science has developed without a grounding in cognitive psychology. Two facts account for this situation. First, the field of cognitive psychology is not that advanced. Second, researchers in other areas of social science have managed to find other ways to explain the phenomena in which they are interested. An interesting case in point is economics. Neo-classical economics dominated the last century. It completely ignored the cognitive processes of individuals and assumed that one could predict the behavior of markets by assuming that individuals simply behaved in a way to maximize their wealth. However, more recently the field of behavioral economics has developed, which emphasizes that economists need to pay attention to the flawed decision-making processes of individuals (the topic of Chapter 11) if they want to understand the behavior of markets. So, for instance, people are more willing to pay more for something when they use a credit card than when they use cash (Simester & Drazen, 2001). In recognition of the importance of the psychology of decision making to economics, two cognitive psychologists, Daniel Kahnemann and Amos Tversky, were awarded the Nobel Prize for economics in 2002.

Cognitive psychology is the foundation for many other areas of social science.

Practical Applications

Practical implications of the field constitute another key incentive for the study of cognitive psychology. If we really understood how people acquire knowledge and intellectual skills and how they perform feats of intelligence, then we would be able to improve their intellectual training and performance accordingly.

The knowledge of the mind that cognitive psychologists are developing will prove beneficial to both individuals and society. Many of our problems derive from an inability to deal with the overload of cognitive demands made on us. These problems are being exacerbated by the current information explosion and the technological revolution. Cognitive psychology is just beginning to make headway on these issues, but some clear and positive insights with direct application to everyday life have already emerged. There have been applications of cognitive psychology to law (e.g., Loftus, 1996, on the reliability of eyewitness testimony); to the design of computer systems (e.g., Card, Moran, & Newell, 1983, on using word processors, or Pirolli & Card, 1999, on surfing the Web); and to instruction (Gagné, Yekovich, & Yekovich, 1993; Mayer, 2008). Cognitive psychology is also making important contributions to our understanding of brain disorders that reflect abnormal functioning, such as schizophrenia (Cohen & Servan-Schreiber, 1992) or autism (Baron-Cohen, 1995).

At many points in this book, we will see that research in cognitive psychology has implications for our daily lives. In various places throughout the text, Implication boxes will reinforce these connections. The first such box discusses study skills.

○ *The results from the study of cognitive psychology have practical implications for our daily lives.*

● The History of Cognitive Psychology

Cognitive psychology today is a vigorous science producing many interesting discoveries. However, this productive phase was a long time coming, and it is important to understand the history of the field that led to its current form.

Early History

In Western civilization, interest in human cognition can be traced to the ancient Greeks. Plato and Aristotle, in their discussions of the nature and origin of knowledge, speculated about memory and thought. These early philosophical discussions eventually developed into a centuries-long debate. The two positions were **empiricism,** which held that all knowledge comes from experience, and **nativism,** which held that children come into the world with a great deal of innate knowledge. The debate intensified in the 17th, 18th, and 19th centuries, with such British philosophers as Berkeley, Locke, Hume, and Mill arguing for the empiricist view and such continental philosophers as Descartes and Kant propounding the nativist view. Although these arguments were philosophical at their core, they frequently slipped into psychological speculations about human cognition.

During this long period of philosophical debate, such sciences as astronomy, physics, chemistry, and biology developed markedly. Curiously, however, no attempt was made to apply the scientific method to the understanding of human cognition; such an undertaking did not take place until the end of the 19th century. Certainly, there were no technical or conceptual barriers preventing the study of cognitive psychology earlier. In fact, many cognitive psychology experiments could have been performed and understood in the

Implications

What does cognitive psychology tell us about how to study effectively?

Cognitive psychology has identified methods that enable one to read and remember a textbook like this one. This research will be described in Chapters 6 and 13. I will give you the gist of these techniques now, however, so that you can apply them to your study of this book. The key idea is that it is crucial to identify the main points of each section of a text and to understand how these main points are organized. I have tried to help you do this by ending each section with a short summary sentence identifying its main point. I recommend that you use the following study technique to help you remember the material. This approach is a variant of the PQ4R (Preview, Question, Read, Reflect, Recite, Review) method discussed in Chapter 6.

1. Preview the chapter. Read the section headings and summary statements to get a general sense of where the chapter is going and how much material will be devoted to each topic. Try to understand each summary statement, and ask yourself whether this is something you knew or believed before reading the text.

Then, for each section of the book, go through the following steps:

2. Make up a study question. From the section heading, think of a related question that you will try to answer while you read the text. For instance, in the section Intellectual Curiosity, you might ask yourself, "What is there to be curious about in cognitive psychology?" This will give you an active goal to pursue while you read the section.
3. Read the section to understand it and answer your question. Try to relate what you are reading to situations in your own life. In the section Intellectual Curiosity, for example, you might try to think of scientific discoveries you have read about that seemed to require creativity.
4. At the end of each section, read the summary and ask yourself whether that is the main point you got out of the section and why it is the main point. Sometimes you may need to go back and reread some parts of the section.

At the end of the chapter, engage in the following review process:

5. Go through the text, mentally reviewing the main points. Try to answer the questions you devised in step 2 plus any other questions that occur to you. Often, when preparing for an exam, it is a good idea to ask yourself what kind of exam questions you would make up for the chapter.

As we will learn in later chapters, such a study strategy improves one's memory for the text.

time of the ancient Greeks. But cognitive psychology, like many other sciences, suffered because of our egocentric, mystical, and confused attitude about ourselves and our own nature. Before the 19th century, it had seemed inconceivable that the workings of the human mind could be subjected to scientific analysis. As a consequence, cognitive psychology as a science is less than 150 years old. We have spent much of the first 100 years freeing ourselves of the misconceptions that can arise when people engage in such an introverted enterprise as a scientific study of human cognition. Such research seems like the mind studying itself.

Only in the last 150 years has it been realized that human cognition could be the subject of scientific study rather than philosophical speculation.

Psychology in Germany: Focus on Introspective Observation

The date usually cited as marking the beginning of psychology as a science is 1879, when Wilhelm Wundt established the first psychology laboratory in Leipzig, Germany. Wundt's psychology was cognitive psychology (in contrast to other major divisions, such as comparative, clinical, or social psychology), although he had far-ranging views on many subjects. Wundt, his students, and a large number of the early psychologists used a method of inquiry called **introspection.** In this method, highly trained observers reported the contents of their own consciousnesses under carefully controlled conditions. The basic belief was that the workings of the mind should be open to self-observation. Drawing on the empiricism of the British philosophers, Wundt and others believed that very intense self-inspection would be able to identify the primitive experiences out of which thought arose. Thus, to develop a theory of cognition, a psychologist had only to account for the contents of introspective reports.

Let us consider a sample introspective experiment. Mayer and Orth (1901) had their participants perform a free-association task. The experimenters spoke a word to the participants and then measured the amount of time they took to generate responses to the word. Participants then reported all their conscious experiences from the moment of stimulus presentation until the moment of their response. To get a feeling for this method, try to come up with an association for each of the following words; after each association, think about the contents of your consciousness during the period between reading the word and making your association.

coat
book
dot
bowl

In Mayer and Orth's experiment, many participants reported rather indescribable conscious experiences. Whatever was in consciousness, it did not always seem to involve sensations, images, or other concrete experiences that participants in these laboratories were accustomed to reporting. This result started a debate over the issue of imageless thought—whether conscious experience could really be devoid of concrete content. As we will see in Chapters 4 and 5, modern cognitive psychology has made real progress on this issue, but not by using introspective methods.

At the turn of the 20th century, German psychologists tried to use a method of inquiry called introspection to study the workings of the mind.

Psychology in America: Focus on Behavior

Wundt's introspective psychology was not well accepted in America. Early American psychologists engaged in what they called "introspection," but it was not the intense analysis of the contents of the mind practiced by the Germans. Rather, it was largely an armchair avocation in which the only self-inspection was casual and reflective rather than intense and analytic. William James's *Principles of Psychology* (1890) reflects the best of this tradition, and many of the proposals in this work are still relevant today. The mood of America was determined by the philosophical doctrines of pragmatism and functionalism. Many psychologists of the time were involved in education, and the demand was for an "action-oriented" psychology that was capable of practical application. The intellectual climate in America was not receptive to a psychology focused on such questions as whether or not the contents of consciousness were sensory.

One of the important figures of early American scientific psychology was Edward Thorndike, who developed a theory of learning that was directly applicable to classrooms. Thorndike was interested in such basic questions as the effects of reward and punishment on the rate of learning. To him, conscious experience was just excess baggage that could be largely ignored. As often as not, his experiments were done on animals such as cats. Research on animals involved fewer ethical constraints than research on humans. Thorndike was probably just as happy that such participants could not introspect.

While introspection was being ignored at the turn of the century in America, it was getting into trouble on the continent. Various laboratories were reporting different types of introspections—each type matching the theory of the particular laboratory from which it emanated. It was becoming clear that introspection did not give one a clear window into the workings of the mind. Much that was important in cognitive functioning was not open to conscious experience. These two factors—the "irrelevance" of the introspective method and its apparent contradictions—laid the groundwork for the great behaviorist revolution in American psychology that occurred around 1920. John Watson and other behaviorists led a fierce attack not only on introspectionism but also on any attempt to develop a theory of mental operations. **Behaviorism** held that psychology was to be entirely concerned with external behavior and was not to try to analyze the workings of the mind that underlay this behavior:

> Behaviorism claims that consciousness is neither a definite nor a usable concept. The Behaviorist, who has been trained always as an experimentalist, holds further that belief in the existence of consciousness goes back to the ancient days of superstition and magic. (Watson, 1930, p. 2)

> The Behaviorist began his own formulation of the problem of psychology by sweeping aside all medieval conceptions. He dropped from his scientific vocabulary all subjective terms such as sensation, perception, image, desire, purpose, and even thinking and emotion as they were subjectively defined. (Watson, 1930, pp. 5–6)

The behaviorist program and the issues it spawned pushed research on cognition into the background of American psychology. The rat supplanted the human as the principal laboratory subject, and psychology turned to finding out what could be learned by studying animal learning and motivation. Quite a bit was discovered, but little was of direct relevance to cognitive psychology. Perhaps the most important lasting contribution of behaviorism is a set of sophisticated and rigorous techniques and principles for experimental study in all fields of psychology, including cognitive psychology.

Behaviorism was not as dominant in Europe. Psychologists such as Frederick Bartlett in England, Alexander Luria in Russia, and Jean Piaget in Switzerland were pursuing ideas that are important in modern cognitive psychology. Cognitive psychology was an active research topic in Germany, but much of it was lost in the Nazi turmoil. A number of German psychologists immigrated to America and brought **Gestalt psychology** with them. Gestalt psychology claimed that the activity of the brain and the mind was more than the sum of its parts and as such conflicted with much of the introspectionist program in Germany. In America, Gestalt psychologists found themselves in conflict with behaviorism on this point but also because they were concerned with mental structure at all. In America, Gestalt psychologists received the most attention for their claims about animal learning, and they were the standard targets for the behaviorist critiques, although some Gestalt psychologists became quite prominent. For example, the Gestalt psychologist Wolfgang Kohler was elected to the presidency of the American Psychological Association. Although not a Gestalt psychologist, Edward Tolman was an American psychologist who did his research on animal learning and anticipated many ideas of modern cognitive psychology. Again, his ideas were frequently the target for criticism by the dominant behaviorist psychologists, although his work was harder to dismiss because he spoke the language of behaviorism.

In retrospect, it is hard to understand how American behaviorists could have taken such an anti-mental stand and clung to it for so long. Just because introspection proved to be unreliable did not mean that it was impossible to develop a theory of internal mental structure and process. It meant only that other methods were required. In physics, for example, a theory of atomic structure was developed, although that structure could only be inferred, not directly observed. But behaviorists argued that a theory of internal structure was not necessary to an understanding of human behavior, and in a sense they may have been right (see Anderson & Bower, 1973, pp. 30–37). A theory of internal structure, however, makes understanding human beings much easier. The success of modern cognitive psychology shows that understanding mental structures and processes is critical to understanding human cognition.

In both the introspectionist and behaviorist programs, we see the human mind struggling with the effort to understand itself. The introspectionists held a naïve belief in the power of self-observation. The behaviorists were so afraid of falling prey to subjective fallacies that they refused to let themselves think about mental processes. Modern cognitive psychologists seem to be much more at ease with their subject matter. They have a relatively detached attitude toward human cognition and approach it much as they would any other complex system.

- *Behaviorism, which dominated American psychology in the first half of the 20th century, rejected the analysis of the workings of the mind to explain behavior.*

The Cognitive Revolution: AI, Information Theory, and Linguistics

Cognitive psychology, as we know it today, took form in the two decades between 1950 and 1970 in the cognitive revolution that overthrew behaviorism. Three main influences account for its modern development. The first was research on human performance, which was given a great boost during World War II, when governments badly needed practical information about how to train soldiers to use sophisticated equipment and how to deal with such problems as the breakdown of attention under stress. Behaviorism offered no help with such practical issues. Although the work during the war had a very practical bent, the issues it raised stayed with psychologists when they went back to their academic laboratories after the war. The work of the British psychologist Donald Broadbent at the Applied Psychology Research Unit in Cambridge was probably the most influential in integrating ideas from human performance research with new ideas that were developing in an area called information theory. Information theory is an abstract way of analyzing the processing of information. Broadbent and other psychologists, such as George Miller, Fred Attneave, and Wendell Garner, initially developed these ideas with respect to perception and attention, but such analyses soon pervaded all of cognitive psychology.

Second, and closely related to the development of the information-processing approach, were developments in computer science, particularly AI, which tries to get computers to behave intelligently. Allen Newell and Herbert Simon at Carnegie Mellon University spent 40 years educating cognitive psychologists about the implications of AI (and educating workers in AI about the implications of cognitive psychology). The direct influence of computer-based theories on cognitive psychology has always been minimal. The indirect influence, however, has been enormous. A host of concepts have been taken from computer science and used in psychological theories. Probably more important, observing how we can analyze the intelligent behavior of a machine has largely liberated us from our inhibitions and misconceptions about analyzing our own intelligence.

The third influence on cognitive psychology was **linguistics,** which studies the structure of language. In the 1950s, Noam Chomsky, a linguist at the Massachusetts Institute of Technology, began to develop a new mode of analyzing the structure of language. His work showed that language was much more complex than had previously been believed and that many of the prevailing behaviorist formulations were incapable of explaining these complexities. Chomsky's linguistic analyses proved critical in enabling cognitive psychologists to fight off the prevailing behaviorist conceptions. George Miller, at Harvard University in the 1950s and early 1960s, was instrumental in bringing these linguistic analyses to the attention of psychologists and in identifying new ways of studying language.

Cognitive psychology has grown rapidly since the 1950s. A milestone was the publication of Ulric Neisser's *Cognitive Psychology* in 1967. This book gave a new legitimacy to the field. It consisted of 6 chapters on perception and attention and 4 chapters on language, memory, and thought. This chapter division contrasts sharply with this book's, which has only 2 chapters on perception and attention and 11 on language, memory, and thought. My chapter division reflects the growing emphasis on higher mental processes. Following Neisser's work, another important event was the beginning of the journal *Cognitive Psychology* in 1970. This journal has done much to define the field.

In the 1970s, a related new field called cognitive science emerged that attempts to integrate research efforts from psychology, philosophy, linguistics, neuroscience, and AI. This field can be dated from the appearance of the journal *Cognitive Science* in 1976, which is the main publication of the Cognitive Science Society. The fields of cognitive psychology and cognitive science overlap. Speaking generally, cognitive science makes greater use of such methods as logical analysis and the computer simulation of cognitive processes, whereas cognitive psychology relies heavily on experimental techniques that grew out of the behaviorist era for studying behavior. This book draws on all methods but makes most use of cognitive psychology's experimental methodology.

Cognitive psychology broke away from behaviorism in response to developments in information theory, AI, and linguistics.

Information-Processing Analyses

The various factors described in the previous section converged in a particular approach to studying human cognition—the **information-processing approach**—that became the dominant approach in cognitive psychology. It attempts to analyze cognition as a set of steps in which an abstract entity called "information" is processed. Probably the best way to explain this approach is to describe a classic example of it.

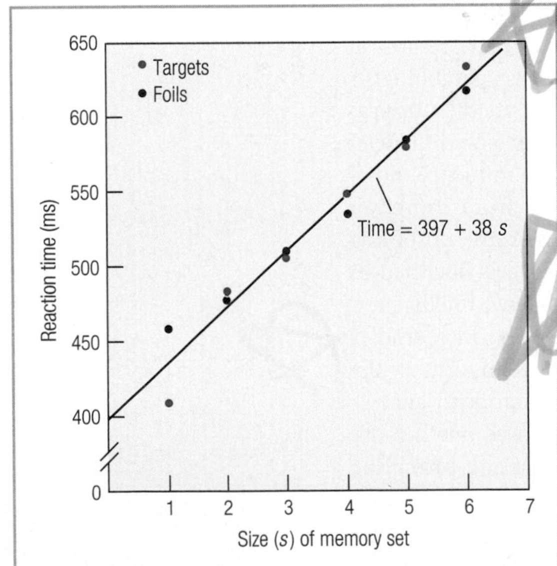

FIGURE 1.1 The time needed to recognize a digit increases with the number of items in the memory set. The straight line represents the linear function that fits the data best.
(From S. Sternberg, 1969. Reprinted by permission of the publisher. © 1969 by *American Scientist*.)

In 1966, Saul Sternberg described an experimental paradigm and proposed a theoretical account of it that proved to be quite influential. In what has come to be called the **Sternberg paradigm**, participants were shown a small number of digits, such as "3 9 7," to keep in mind. Then they were shown a probe digit and asked whether it was in the memory set, and they had to answer as quickly as possible. For example, 9 would be a positive probe for the "3 9 7" set; 6 would be a negative probe. Sternberg varied the number of digits in the memory set from 1 to 6 and measured how quickly participants could make this judgment. Figure 1.1 shows his results as a function of the size of the memory set. Data are plotted separately for positive probes, or targets, and for negative probes, or foils. Participants could make these judgments quite quickly; latencies varied from 400 to 600 milliseconds (ms)—a millisecond is a thousandth of a second. Sternberg found a nearly linear relationship between judgment time and the size of the memory set. As shown in Figure 1.1, participants took about 38 ms extra to judge each digit in the set.

Sternberg developed a very influential account of how participants made these judgments. This account exemplifies what an abstract information-processing

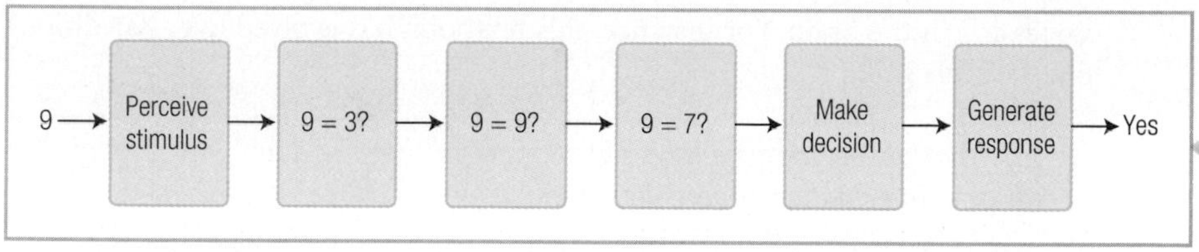

9 → Perceive stimulus → 9 = 3? → 9 = 9? → 9 = 7? → Make decision → Generate response → Yes

FIGURE 1.2 Sternberg's analysis of the sequence of information-processing stages in his task.

theory is like. His explanation is illustrated in Figure 1.2. Sternberg assumed that when participants saw a probe stimulus such as a 9, they went through the series of information-processing stages illustrated in that figure. First the stimulus was encoded. Then the stimulus was compared to each digit in the memory set. Sternberg assumed that it took 38 ms to complete each one of these comparisons, which accounted for the slope of the line in Figure 1.1. Then the participant had to decide on a response and finally generate it. Sternberg showed that different variables would influence each of these information-processing stages. Thus, if he degraded the stimulus quality by making the probe harder to read, participants took longer to make their judgments. This did not affect the slope of the Figure 1.1 line, however, because it involved only the stage of stimulus perception in Figure 1.2. Similarly, if he biased participants to say yes or no, the decision-making stage, but not other stages, was affected.

It is worth noting the ways in which Sternberg's theory exemplifies a classic abstract information-processing account:

1. The information processing that is going on is discussed without any attempt to conceptualize it in terms of brain location or brain processes.
2. The processing of the information has a highly symbolic character. Thus, we speak of the system as comparing the symbol 9 against the symbol 3. There is no consideration of possible neural representations of these symbols.
3. Sternberg called upon the computer metaphor in justifying his theory of information processing. He thought that information processing in this task could be compared to the way computers do high-speed scanning.
4. The measurement of time to make a judgment is a critical variable, because the information processing is conceived to be taking place in discrete stages. Flowcharts such as the one in Figure 1.2 have been a very popular means of expressing the steps of information processing. Flowcharts are themselves imported from computer science.

Each of these four features listed reflects a kind of narrowness in the classic information-processing approach to human cognition. Cognitive psychologists have gradually broadened their approach as they dealt with more complex phenomena and as they began to pay more attention to the nature of information processing in the brain. For instance, this textbook has evolved over its editions to reflect this shift.

- *Information-processing analysis breaks a cognitive task down into a set of abstract information-processing steps.*

Cognitive Neuroscience

The field of cognitive psychology is in the midst of a change that may turn out to be as significant as the cognitive revolution. This change is the infusion of considerations of brain processes into almost all analyses of human cognition. There is a field called **cognitive neuroscience** that is devoted to the study of how cognition is realized in the brain. The rise of cognitive neuroscience feels less like a revolution because most cognitive psychologists are welcoming it. For instance, in my own psychology department at Carnegie Mellon, the cognitive program and the cognitive neuroscience program merged as we all find ourselves concerned with the same issues.

The study of perception (see Chapter 2) always had a strong basis in physiology, but the other elements of cognition seemed too complex to be studied by physiological methods. The steady development of knowledge about the brain and methods for studying brain activity, however, has slowly eroded this complexity barrier. Even for the most complex thought processes, there are exciting new findings related to their realization in the brain. I will describe new techniques for imaging brain activity later in this chapter. In various ways (and with various limitations), we are now able to see how cognition unfolds in the brain. As an example of the new power of cognitive neuroscience techniques, I will describe a study of the neural processes that are involved as one solves a mathematical equation.

Until recently, the information-processing approach described in the previous section was viewed as having little to do with cognitive neuroscience, but we are now seeing a developing synergy between cognitive neuroscience and information-processing analysis. Neuroscience data can be used to discriminate between alternative information-processing models, and information-processing models can be used to organize neuroscience data. We will see an example of the latter when we talk about the brain imaging of equation solving.

- *Cognitive neuroscience is developing methods that enable us to understand the neural basis of cognition.*

Information Processing: The Communicative Neurons

The brain is just one part of the nervous system. The full nervous system includes the various sensory systems that gather information from parts of the body and the motor systems that control movement. In some cases, considerable

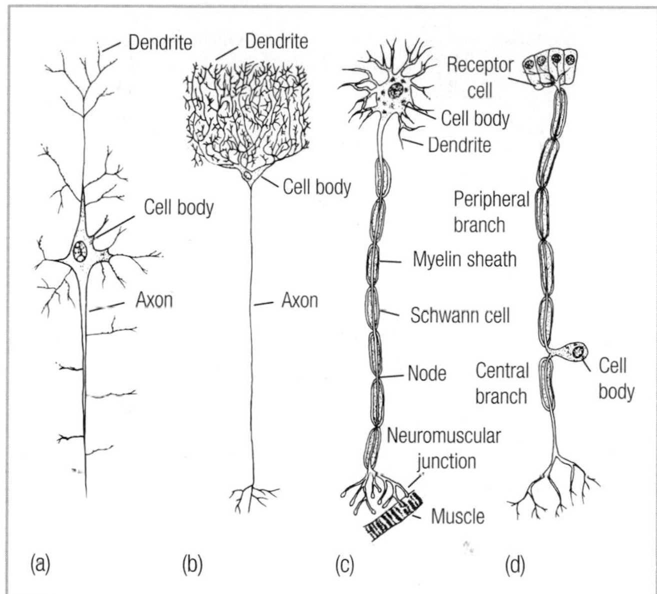

FIGURE 1.3 Some of the variety of neurons: (a) pyramidal cell; (b) cerebellar Purkinje cell; (c) motor neuron; (d) sensory neuron. (From Keeton, 1980. Reprinted by permission of the publisher. © 1980 by W. W. Norton.)

information processing takes place outside the brain. From an information-processing point of view, the most important components of the nervous system are the neurons.[2] A **neuron** is a cell that accumulates and transmits electrical activity. The human brain itself contains approximately 100 billion neurons, each of which may have roughly the processing capability of a small computer.[3] A considerable fraction of the 100 billion neurons are active simultaneously and do much of their information processing through interactions with one another. Imagine the information-processing power in 100 billion interacting computers! According to this view of the brain, there is more computational power in one 3-pound brain than in all the computers in the world. Lest you become overwhelmed by contemplating the brain, however, we must point out that it is not good at doing some things the computer does well. There are many tasks, such as finding square roots, at which a simple hand calculator can outperform all 100 billion neurons. Comprehending the strengths and weaknesses of the human nervous system is a major goal in understanding the nature of human cognition.

The Neuron

Neurons come in a wide variety of shapes and sizes, depending on their exact location and function. (Figure 1.3 illustrates some of this variety.) There is, however, a generally accepted notion of what the prototypical neuron is like,

[2] Neurons are by no means the majority of cells in the nervous system. There are many others, such as glial cells, whose main function is thought to be supportive of the neurons.

[3] For instance, according to one view, each neuron computes on the order of 1,000 multiplications and additions of real numbers every 10 ms.

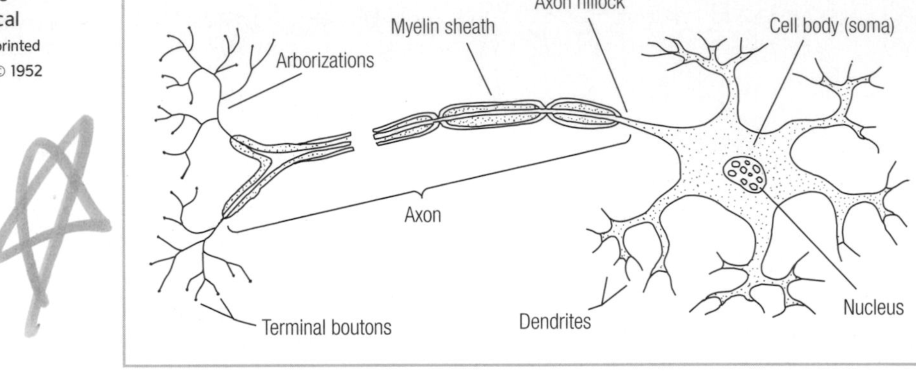

FIGURE 1.4 A schematic representation of a typical neuron. (From Katz, 1952. Reprinted by permission of the publisher. © 1952 by *Scientific American*.)

and individual neurons match up with this prototype to greater or lesser degrees. This prototype is illustrated in Figure 1.4. The main body of the neuron is called the **soma**. Typically, the soma is 5 to 100 micrometers (μm) in diameter (a micrometer is a millionth of a meter). Attached to the soma are short branches called **dendrites**, and extending from the soma is a long tube called the **axon**. The axon can vary in length from a few millimeters to a meter.

Axons provide the fixed paths by which neurons communicate with one another. The axon of one neuron extends toward the dendrites of other neurons. At its end, the axon branches into a large number of **arborizations**. Each arborization ends in **terminal boutons** that almost make contact with the dendrite of another neuron. The gap separating the terminal bouton and the dendrite is typically in the range of 10 to 50 nm (a nanometer (nm) is one billionth of a meter). This near contact between axon and dendrite is called a **synapse**. Typically, neurons communicate by releasing chemicals, called **neurotransmitters**, from the axon terminal on one side of the synapse that act on the membrane of the receptor dendrite to change its polarization, or electric potential. The inside of the membrane covering the entire neuron tends to be 70 mV more negative than the outside, due to the greater concentration of negative chemical ions inside and positive ions outside. The existence of a greater concentration of positive sodium ions on the outside of the membrane is particularly important to understanding the functioning of the neuron. Depending on the nature of the neurotransmitter, the potential difference can decrease or increase. Synapses that decrease the potential difference are called **excitatory**, and those that increase the difference are called **inhibitory**.

The average soma and dendrite have about 1,000 synapses from other neurons, and the average axon synapses to about 1,000 neurons. The change in electric potential due to any one synapse is rather small, but the individual excitatory and inhibitory effects will accumulate. If there is enough net excitatory input, the potential difference in the soma can drop sharply. If the reduction in potential is large enough, a **depolarization** will occur at the **axon hillock**, where the axon joins the soma (see Figure 1.4). This depolarization is caused by a rush of positive sodium ions into the inside of the neuron. The inside of the neuron momentarily (for a millisecond) becomes more positive than the outside. This sudden change, called an **action potential** (or spike), will propagate down the axon. That is, the potential difference will suddenly and momentarily change down the axon. The rate at which this change travels can vary from 0.5 to 130 m/s, depending on the characteristics of the axon—such as the degree to which the axon is covered by a myelin sheath (the more myelination, the faster the transmission). When the nerve impulse reaches the end of the axon, it causes neurotransmitters to be released from the terminal boutons, thus completing the cycle.

To review: Potential changes accumulate on a cell body, reach a threshold, and cause an action potential to propagate down an axon. This pulse in turn causes neurotransmitters to be sent from the axon terminal to the body of a different neuron, causing changes in that neuron's membrane potential. I should emphasize that this sequence is almost all there is to neural information processing, yet intelligence arises from this simple system of interactions. A major challenge for cognitive neuroscience is to understand how.

The time required for this neural communication to complete the path from one neuron to another is roughly 10 ms—definitely more than 1 ms and definitely less than 100 ms; the exact speed depends on the characteristics of the neurons involved. This is much slower than the billions of operations that a modern computer can perform in one second. There are, however, billions of these activities occurring simultaneously throughout the brain.

- *Neurons communicate by releasing chemicals, called neurotransmitters, from the axon terminal on one side of the synapse and these neurotransmitters act on the membrane of the receptor dendrite to change its electric potential.*

Neural Representation of Information

Two quantities are particularly important to the representation of information in the brain. First, the membrane potential can be more or less negative. Second, the number of nerve impulses an axon transmits per second, called its **rate of firing,** can vary. It is generally thought that it is the number, not the pattern, of impulses along a single axon that is important. There can be upward of 100 nerve impulses per second. The greater the rate of firing, the greater the effect the axon will have on the cells to which it synapses. We can contrast information representation in the brain with information representation in a computer, where individual memory cells, or bits, can have just one of two values—off (0) or on (1). A typical computer cell does not have the continuous variation of a typical neural cell.

There is a general way to conceptualize the interactions among neurons that captures the many specific variations of information transfer in the nervous system. We can think of a neuron as having an activation level that corresponds roughly to the firing rate on the axon or to the degree of depolarization on the dendrite and soma. Neurons interact by driving up the activation level of other neurons (excitation) or by driving down their activation level (inhibition).

All neural information processing takes place in terms of these excitatory and inhibitory effects; they are what underlies human cognition.

Just how neurons represent information is an interesting question. There is evidence that individual neurons respond to specific features of a stimulus. For instance, Chapter 2 will describe neurons that are most active when there is a line in the visual field at a particular angle. There is evidence that some neurons respond to more complex sets of features. For instance, there are neurons in the monkey brain that appear to be most responsive to faces (Bruce, Desimone, & Gross, 1981; Desimone, Albright, Gross, & Bruce, 1984; Perrett, Rolls, & Caan, 1982). It is not possible, however, that single neurons encode all the concepts and shades of meaning we possess. Moreover, the firing of a single neuron cannot represent the complexity of structure in a face.

If a single neuron cannot represent the complexity of our cognition, how are our complex concepts and experiences represented? How can the activity of neurons represent our concept of baseball; how can it result in our solution of an algebra problem; how can it result in our feeling of frustration? Similar questions can be asked of computer programs, which have been shown to be capable of answering questions about baseball, solving algebra problems, and displaying frustration. Where in the millions of off-and-on bits in a computer program does the concept of baseball lie? How does a change in a bit result in the solution of an algebra problem or in a feeling of frustration? The answer in every case is that these questions fail to see the forest for the trees. The concepts of a sport, a problem solution, or an emotion occur in large patterns of bit changes. Similarly, human cognition is achieved through large patterns of neural activity. One study (Mazoyer et al., 1993) compared participants who heard random words to participants who heard words that made nonsense sentences, to participants who heard words that made coherent sentences. Using methods that will be described shortly, the researchers measured brain activity. They found activity in more and more regions of the brain as participants went from hearing words to hearing sentences, to hearing meaningful stories. This result indicates that our understanding of a meaningful story involves activity in many regions of the brain.

It is informative to think about how the computer stores information. Consider a simple case: the spelling of words. Most computers have codes by which individual patterns of binary values (1s and 0s) represent letters. Table 1.1 illustrates the use of one coding scheme, called ASCII; it contains a pattern of 0s and 1s that codes the words *cognitive psychology.*

Similarly, the brain can represent information in terms of patterns of neural activity rather than simply as cells firing. The code in Table 1.1 includes redundant bits that allow the computer to correct errors should certain bits be lost (note that each column has an even number of 1s, which reflects the added bits for redundancy). As in a computer, it seems that the brain codes information redundantly, so that even if certain cells are damaged, it can still determine what the pattern is encoding. It is generally thought that the brain uses schemes for encoding information and achieving redundancy very different from the ones a computer uses. It also seems that the brain uses a much more redundant

TABLE 1.1

Coding of the Words *COGNITIVE PSYCHOLOGY* in 7-Bit ASCII with Even Parity

1	1	0	0	1	1	1	0	1	
1	1	1	1	1	1	1	1	1	
0	0	0	0	0	0	0	0	0	
0	0	0	0	0	1	0	1	0	
0	1	0	1	1	0	1	0	0	
0	1	1	1	0	1	0	1	1	
1	1	1	1	0	0	0	1	0	
1	1	1	0	1	0	1	0	1	
0	0	0	1	0	1	1	1	0	0
1	1	1	1	1	1	1	1	1	1
0	0	0	0	0	0	0	0	0	0
1	1	1	0	0	0	0	0	0	1
0	0	1	0	1	1	1	1	0	1
0	0	0	0	0	1	1	1	1	0
0	1	0	1	0	1	0	1	1	0
0	1	1	1	0	1	0	1	1	1

code than a computer does because the behavior of individual neurons is not particularly reliable.

So far, we have talked only about patterns of neural activation. Such patterns, however, are transitory. The brain does not maintain the same pattern for minutes, let alone days. This means that neural activation patterns cannot encode our permanent knowledge about the world. It is thought that memories are encoded by changes in the synaptic connections among neurons. By changing the synaptic connections, the brain can enable itself to reproduce specific patterns. Although there is not a great deal of growth of new neurons or new synapses in the adult, the effectiveness of synapses can change in response to experience. There is evidence that synaptic connections do change during learning, with both increased release of neurotransmitters (Kandel & Schwartz, 1984) and increased sensitivity of dendritic receptors (Lynch & Baudry, 1984). We will discuss some of this research in Chapter 6.

- *Information is represented in patterns of activation across many neurons and in the synaptic connections among neurons that allow these patterns to be reproduced.*

Organization of the Brain

Now that we have reviewed some of the basic principles of neural information processing, let us look at the overall structure of the central nervous system, which consists of the brain and the spinal cord. The major function of the

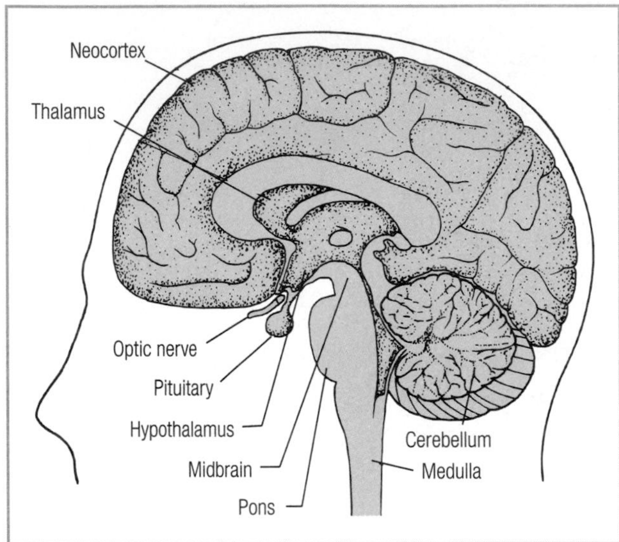

FIGURE 1.5 A cross-sectional view of the brain showing some of its major components. (From Keeton, 1980. Reprinted by permission of the publisher. © 1980 by W. W. Norton.)

spinal cord is to carry neural messages from the brain to the muscles, and sensory messages from the body back to the brain. Figure 1.5 shows a cross section of the brain with some of the more prominent neural structures labeled. The lower parts of the brain are evolutionarily more primitive. The higher portions are well developed only in the higher species.

Correspondingly, it appears that the lower portions of the brain are responsible for more basic functions. The medulla controls breathing, swallowing, digestion, and heartbeat. The hypothalamus regulates the expression of basic drives. The cerebellum plays an important role in motor coordination and voluntary movement. The thalamus serves as a relay station for motor and sensory information from lower areas to the cortex. Although the cerebellum and thalamus serve these basic functions, they also have evolved to play an important role in higher human cognition, as we will discuss later.

The **cerebral cortex, or neocortex,** is the most recently evolved portion of the brain. Although it is quite small and primitive in many mammals, it accounts for a large fraction of the human brain. In the human, the cerebral cortex can be thought of as a rather thin neural sheet with a surface area of about 2,500 cm^2. To fit this neural sheet into the skull, it has to be highly convoluted. The large amount of folding and wrinkling of the cortex is one of the striking physical differences between the human brain and the brains of lower mammals. A bulge of the cortex is called a **gyrus,** and a crease passing between gyri is called a **sulcus.**

The neocortex is divided into left and right hemispheres. One of the interesting curiosities of anatomy is that the right part of the body tends to be connected to the left hemisphere and the left part of the body to the right hemisphere. Thus, the left hemisphere controls motor function and sensation in the right hand. The right ear is most strongly connected to the left hemisphere. The neural receptors in either eye that receive input from the left part of the visual world are connected to the right hemisphere (as the next chapter will explain with respect to Figures 2.5 and 2.6).

Brodmann (1909) identified 52 distinct regions of the human cortex (see Color Plate 1.1), based on differences in the cell types in various regions. Many of these regions proved to have functional differences as well. The cortical regions are typically organized into four lobes: frontal, parietal, occipital, and temporal (Figure 1.6). Major folds or sulci on the cortex separate the areas. The **occipital lobe** contains the primary visual areas. The **parietal lobe** handles some perceptual functions, including spatial processing and representation of the body. It is also involved in control of attention, as we will discuss in Chapter 3. The **temporal lobe** receives input from the occipital area and is

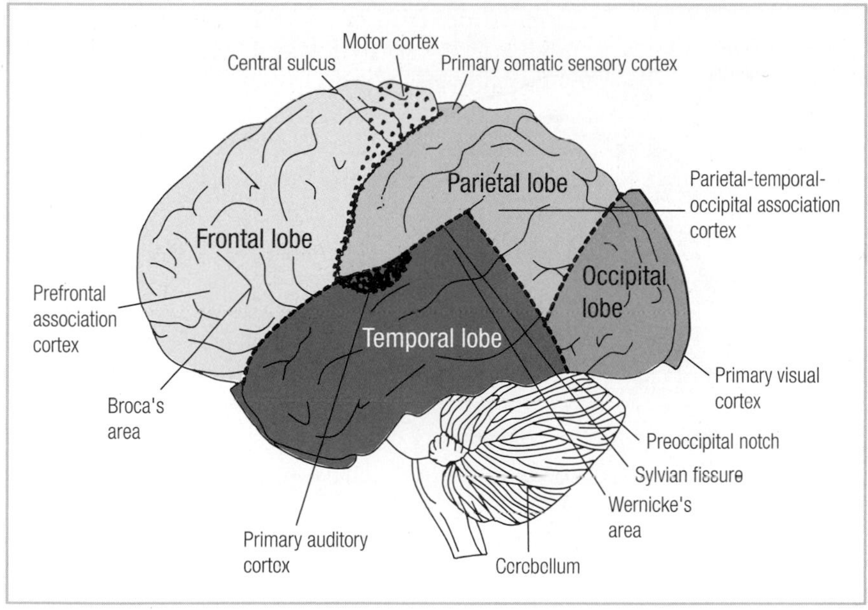

FIGURE 1.6 A side view of the cerebral cortex showing the four lobes—frontal, occipital, parietal, and temporal—of each hemisphere (red-shaded areas) and other major components of the cerebral cortex. (From Kandel & Schwartz, 1984. Reprinted by permission of the publisher. © 1984 by Elsevier.)

involved in object recognition. It also has the primary auditory areas and Wernicke's area, which is involved in language processing. The frontal lobe has two major functions: The back portion of the frontal lobe is involved primarily with motor functions. The front portion, called the **prefrontal cortex**, is thought to control higher level processes, such as planning. The frontal portion of the brain is disproportionately larger in primates than most mammals and among primates humans are distinguished by having disproportionate increases in the most anterior portions of the prefrontal cortex (Area 10 in Color Plate 1.1—Semendeferi, Armstrong, Schleicher, Zilles, & Van Hoesen, 2001). Figure 1.6 will be repeated at the start of many of the chapters in the text, with an indication of the areas relevant to the topics in those chapters.

One should not conclude that only the neocortex plays a significant role in higher level cognition. There are many important circuits that go from the cortex to subcortical structures and back again. A particularly significant area for memory proves to be the limbic system, which is at the border between the cortex and the lower structures. The limbic system contains a structure called the **hippocampus** (which is inside the temporal lobes), which appears to be critical to human memory. Unfortunately, it is not possible to show the hippocampus in a cross section like Figure 1.5 because it is a structure that occurs in the right and left halves of the brain between the surface and the center. Figure 1.7 illustrates the hippocampus and related structures. Damage to the

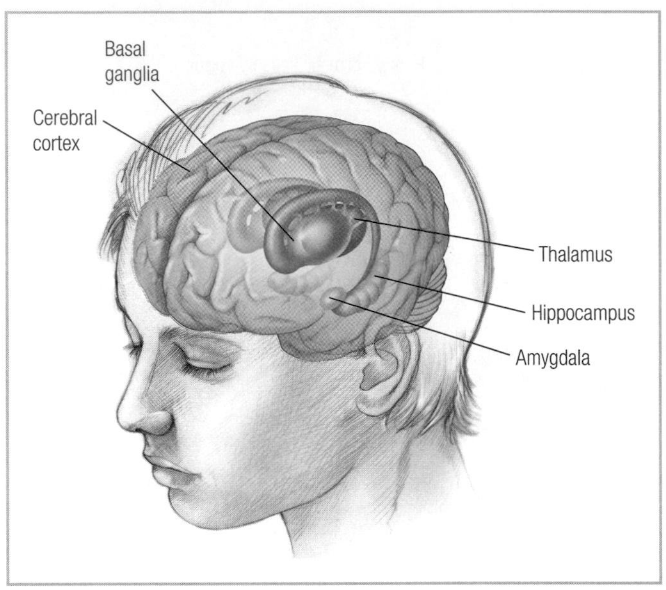

FIGURE 1.7 Structures under the cortex that are part of the limbic system, which includes the hippocampus (shaded in red). Related structures are labeled. (From Gluck, Mercado, & Myers, 2008, Figure 2.3.)

hippocampus and to other nearby structures produces severe amnesia, as we will see in Chapter 7.

Another important collection of subcortical structures is the **basal ganglia.** The critical connections of the basal ganglia are illustrated in Figure 1.8. The basal ganglia are involved both in basic motor control and in the control of complex cognition. These structures receive projections from almost all areas of the cortex and have projections to the frontal cortex. Disorders such as Parkinson's disease and Huntington's disease result from damage to the basal ganglia. Although people suffering from these diseases have dramatic motor control deficits characterized by tremors and rigidity, they also have difficulties in cognitive tasks. The cerebellum, which has a major role in motor control, also seems to play a role in higher order cognition. Many cognitive deficits have been observed in patients with damage to the cerebellum.

- *The brain is organized into a number of distinct areas, which serve different types of functions.*

Localization of Function

We are now beginning to understand where higher level cognitive functions occur in the brain. It appears that the two hemispheres are somewhat specialized for different types of processing. In general, the left hemisphere seems to be associated with linguistic and analytic processing, whereas the right hemisphere is associated with perceptual and spatial processing. The left and right hemispheres are connected by a broad band of fibers called the **corpus callosum.** The corpus callosum has been surgically severed in some patients to

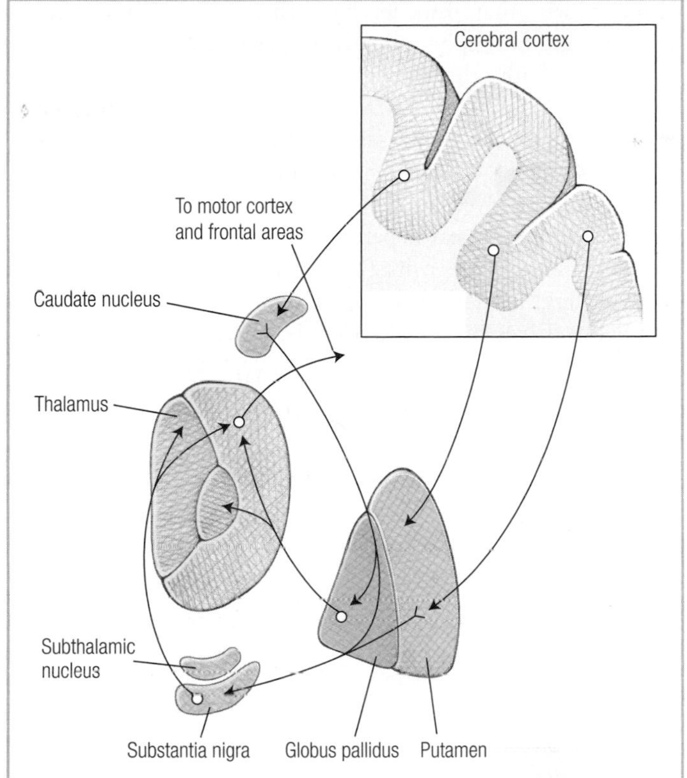

FIGURE 1.8 The major structures of the basal ganglia (red-shaded areas) include the caudate nucleus, the subthalamic nucleus, the substantia nigra, the globus pallidus, and the putamen. The critical connections (inputs and outputs) of the basal ganglia are illustrated. (From Gazzinga, Ivry, & Mangun, 2002. Reprinted by permission of the publisher. © 2002 by W. W. Norton.)

prevent epileptic seizures. Such patients are referred to as **split-brain patients.** The operation is typically successful, and patients seem to function fairly well. Much of the evidence for the differences between the hemispheres comes from research with these patients. Careful psychological research has found profound differences between split-brain patients and participants who have not had this surgery. In one experiment, the word key was flashed on the left side of a screen the patient was viewing. Because it was on the left side of the screen, it would be received by the right, nonlanguage hemisphere. When asked what was presented on the screen, the patient was not able to say because the language-dominant hemisphere did not know. However, his left hand (but not the right) was able to pick out a key from a set of objects hidden from view.

Studies of split-brain patients have enabled psychologists to identify the separate functions of the right and left hemispheres. The research has shown a linguistic advantage for the left hemisphere. For instance, commands can be presented to these patients in the right ear (and hence to the left hemisphere) or in the left ear (and hence to the right hemisphere). The right hemisphere can comprehend only the simplest linguistic commands, whereas the left hemisphere displays full comprehension. A different result is obtained when the ability of the right hand (hence the left hemisphere) to perform manual tasks is compared with that of the left hand (hence the right hemisphere). In this situation, the right hemisphere clearly outperforms the left hemisphere.

Research with other patients who have had damage to specific brain regions indicates that there are areas in the left cortex, called **Broca's area** and **Wernicke's area** (see Figure 1.6), that seem critical for speech, because damage to them results in **aphasia**, the severe impairment of speech. These may not be the only neural areas involved in speech, but they certainly are important. Different language deficits appear depending on whether the damage is to Broca's area or Wernicke's area. People with Broca's aphasia (i.e., damage to Broca's area) speak in short, ungrammatical sentences. For instance, when one patient was asked whether he drives home on weekends, he replied:

> Why, yes . . . Thursday, er, er, er, no, er, Friday . . . Bar-ba-ra . . . wife . . . and, oh, car . . . drive . . . purnpike . . . you know . . . rest and . . . teevee. (Gardner, 1975, p. 61)

In contrast, patients with Wernicke's aphasia speak in fairly grammatical sentences that are almost devoid of meaning. Such patients have difficulty with their vocabulary and generate "empty" speech. The following is the answer given by one such patient to the question "What brings you to the hospital?"

> Boy, I'm sweating, I'm awful nervous, you know, once in a while I get caught up, I can't mention the tarripoi, a month ago, quite a little, I've done a lot well. I impose a lot, while, on the other hand, you know what I mean, I have to run around, look it over, trebbin and all that sort of stuff. (Gardner, 1975, p. 68)

Different specific areas of the brain support different cognitive functions.

Topographic Organization

In many areas of the cortex, information processing is structured spatially in what is called a **topographic organization**. For instance, in the visual area at the back of the cortex, adjacent areas represent information from adjacent areas of the visual field. Figure 1.9 illustrates this fact (Tootell, Silverman, Switkes, & De Valois, 1982). Monkeys were shown the bull's-eye pattern represented in Figure 1.9a. Figure 1.9b shows the pattern of activation that was recorded on the occipital cortex by injecting a radioactive material that marks locations of maximum neural activity. We see that the bull's-eye structure is reproduced with only a little distortion. A similar principle of organization governs the representation of the body in the motor cortex and the somatosensory cortex along the central fissure. Adjacent parts of the body are represented in adjacent parts of the neural tissue. Figure 1.10 illustrates the representation of the body along the somatosensory cortex. Note that the body is distorted, with certain areas receiving a considerable overrepresentation. It turns out that the overrepresented areas correspond to those that are more sensitive. Thus, for instance, we can make more subtle discriminations among tactile stimuli on the hands and face than we can on the back or thigh. Also, there is an overrepresentation in the visual cortex of the visual field at the center of our vision, where we have the greatest visual acuity.

It is thought that topographic maps exist so that neurons processing similar regions can interact with one another (Crick & Asanuma, 1986). Although there

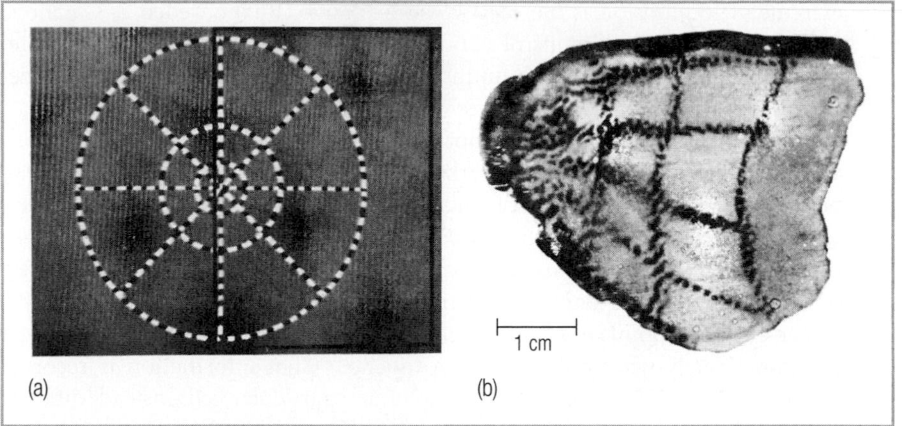

FIGURE 1.9 Evidence of topographic organization. A visual stimulus (a) is presented to a monkey. The stimulus produces a pattern of brain activation (b) in the monkey that closely matches the structure of the stimulus. (From Tootell et al., 1982. Reprinted by permission of the publisher. © 1982 by the American Association for the Advancement of Science.)

are fiber tracks that connect different regions of the brain, the majority of the connections among neurons are to nearby neurons. This emphasis on local connections is driven to minimize both the communication time between neurons and the amount of neural tissue that must be devoted to connecting them. The

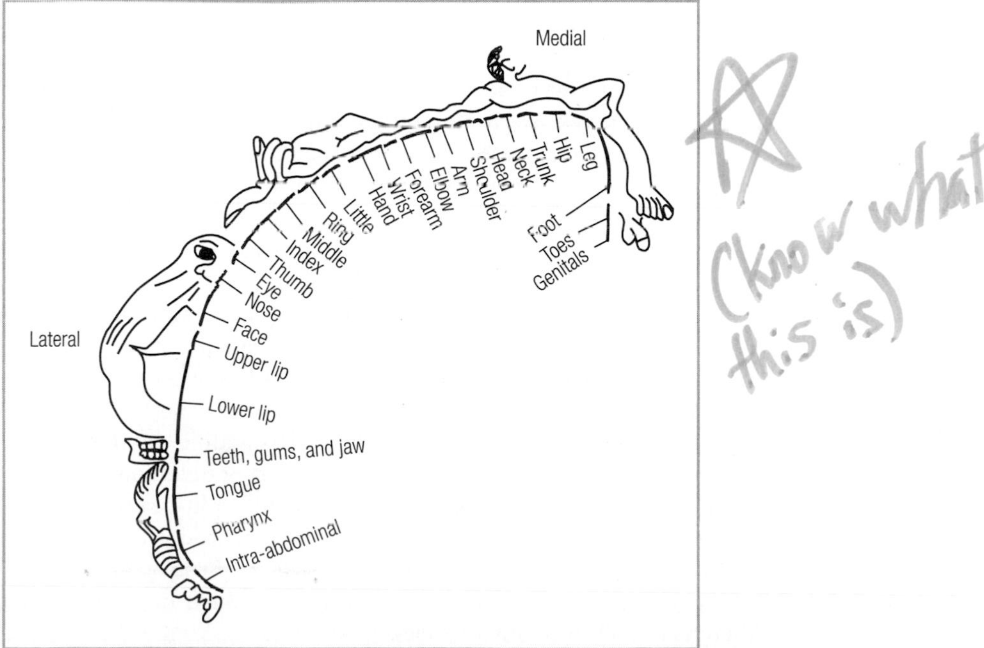

FIGURE 1.10 A cross section of the somatosensory cortex, showing how the human body is mapped in the neural tissue. (From Kandel & Schwartz, 1984. Reprinted by permission of the publisher. © 1984 by Elsevier.)

extreme of localization is the cortical minicolumn (Buxhoeveden & Casanova, 2002)—tiny vertical columns of about 100 neurons that have a very restricted mission. For instance, cortical columns in the primary visual cortex are specialized to process information about one orientation, from one location, in one eye.

Neurons in a mini-column do not represent a precise location with pinpoint accuracy but rather a range of nearby locations. This is related to another aspect of neural information processing called coarse coding. Single neurons seem to respond to a range of events. For instance, when the neural activity from a single neuron in the somatosensory cortex is recorded, we can see that the neuron does not respond only when a single point of the body is stimulated, but rather when any point on a large patch of the body is stimulated. How, then, can we know exactly what point has been touched? That information is recorded quite accurately, but not in the response of any particular cell. Instead, different cells will respond to different overlapping regions of the body, and any point will evoke a different set of cells. Thus, the location of a point is reflected by the pattern of activation, which reinforces the idea that neural information tends to be represented in patterns of activation.

- *Adjacent cells in the cortex tend to process sensory stimuli from adjacent areas of the body.*

Methods in Cognitive Neuroscience

How does one go about understanding the neural basis of cognition? Much of the past research in neuroscience has been done on animals. Some research has involved the surgical removal of various parts of the cortex. By observing the deficits these operations have produced, it is possible to infer the function of the region removed. Other research has recorded the electrical activity in particular neurons or regions of neurons. By observing what activates these neurons, one can infer what they do. However, there is considerable uncertainty about how much these animal results generalize to humans. The difference between the cognitive potential of humans and that of most other animals is enormous, however. With the possible exception of other primates, it is difficult to get other animals even to engage in the kinds of cognitive processes that characterize humans. This has been the great barrier to understanding the neural basis of higher level human cognition.

Until recently, the principal basis for understanding the role of the brain in human cognition has been the study of patient populations. We have already described some of this research, such as that with split-brain patients and with patients who have suffered strokes that cause language deficits. It was research with patient populations that showed the brain is lateralized, with the left hemisphere specialized for language processing. Such hemispheric specialization does not occur in other species.

More recently, there have been major advances in noninvasive methods of imaging the functioning of the brains of normal participants engaged in various cognitive activities. These advances in neural imaging are among the most exciting developments in cognitive neuroscience and will be referenced throughout the text. Although not as precise as recording from single neurons, which can be done only rarely with humans (and then as part of surgical procedures), these methods have achieved dramatic improvements in precision.

Electroencephalography (EEG) records the electric potentials that are present on the scalp. When large populations of neurons are active, this activity will result in distinctive patterns of electric potential on the scalp. In the typical methodology, a participant wears a cap of many electrodes. The electrodes detect rhythmic changes in electrical activity and record them on electroencephalograms. Figure 1.11 illustrates some recordings typical of various cognitive states. When EEG is used to study cognition, the participant is asked to respond to some stimulus, and researchers are interested in discovering how processing this stimulus impacts general activity on the recordings. To eliminate the effects not resulting from the stimulus, many trials are averaged, and what remains is the activity produced by the stimulus. For instance, Kutas and Hillyard (1980a) found that there was a large dip in the wave about 400 ms after participants heard an unexpected word in a sentence (I will discuss this further in Chapter 13). Such averaged EEG responses aligned to a particular stimulus are called **event-related potentials (ERPs).** ERPs have very good temporal resolution, but it is difficult to infer the location in the brain of the neural activity that is producing the scalp activity.

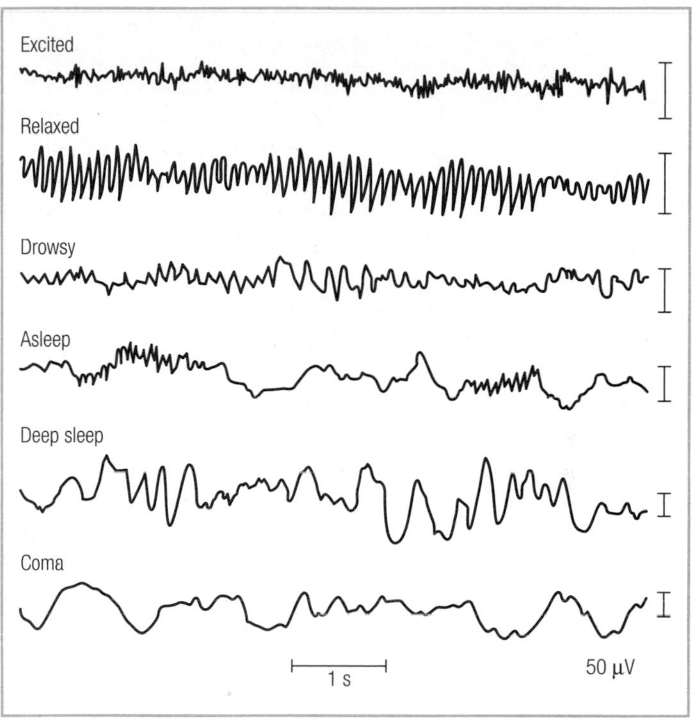

FIGURE 1.11 EEG profiles obtained during various states of consciousness. (From Kolb & Whishaw, 1996; after Penfield & Jasper, 1954. Reprinted by permission of the publisher. © 1996 by W. H. Freeman.)

A recent variation of ERP that offers better spatial resolution is **magnetoencephalography (MEG)** that records magnetic fields produced by the electrical activity. Because of the nature of the magnetic fields it measures, it is best at detecting activity in the sulci (creases) of the cortex and is less sensitive to activity in the gyri (bumps) or activity deep in the brain.

The next two methods we talk about, **positron emission tomography (PET)** and **functional magnetic resonance imaging (fMRI)**, are relatively good in terms of their ability to localize neural activity but rather poor in their ability to trace out the time course of that activity. Neither PET nor fMRI measures neural activity directly. Rather, they measure metabolic rate or blood flow in various areas of the brain, relying on the fact that more active areas of the brain require greater metabolic expenditures and have greater blood flow. They can be conceived as measuring the amount of work a brain region does.

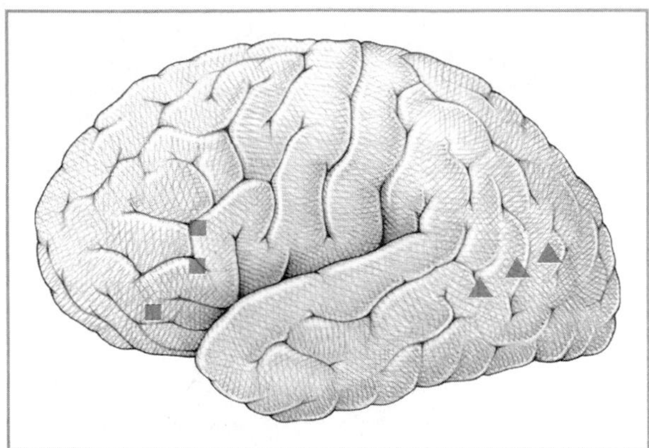

FIGURE 1.12 Areas in the lateral aspect of the cortex activated by visual word reading. Triangles mark locations activated by the passive visual task, squares the locations activated by the semantic task. (From Posner et al., 1988. Reprinted by permission of the publisher. © 1988 by the American Association for the Advancement of Science.)

In PET, a radioactive tracer is injected into the bloodstream (the radiation exposure in a typical PET study is equivalent to two chest X rays and is not considered dangerous). Participants are placed in a PET scanner that can detect the variation in concentration of the radioactive element. Current methods allow a spatial resolution of 5 to 10 mm. For instance, Posner, Peterson, Fox, and Raichle (1988) used PET to localize the various components of the reading process by looking at what areas of the brain are involved in reading a word. Figure 1.12 illustrates their results. The triangles on the cortex represent areas that were active when participants were just passively looking at concrete nouns. The squares represent areas that became active when participants were asked to engage in the semantic activity of generating uses for these nouns. The triangles are located in the occipital lobe; the squares, in the frontal lobe. Thus, the data indicate that the processes of visually perceiving a word take place in a different part of the brain from the processes of thinking about the meaning of a word.

The fMRI methodology has largely replaced PET. It offers even better spatial resolution than PET and is less intrusive. fMRI uses the same MRI scanner that hospitals now use as standard equipment to image various structures, including patients' brain structures. With minor modification, it can be used to image the functioning of the brain. fMRI does not require injecting the participant with a radioactive tracer but relies on the fact that there is more oxygenated hemoglobin in regions of greater neural activity. (One might think that greater activity would use up oxygen, but the body responds to effort by overcompensating and increasing the oxygen in the blood—this is called the **hemodynamic response.**) Radio waves are passed through the brain, and these cause the iron in the hemoglobin to produce a local magnetic field that is detected by magnetic sensors surrounding the head. Thus, fMRI offers a measure of the amount of energy being spent in a particular brain region: The signal is stronger in areas where there is greater activity. Among its advantages over PET are that it allows measurement over longer periods because there is no radioactive substance injected and that it offers finer temporal and spatial resolution. I will describe an fMRI study in detail in the next section to illustrate the basic methodology and what it can accomplish.

Neither PET nor fMRI are what one would call practical, everyday measurement methods. Even the more practical fMRI uses multimillion-dollar scanners that require the participant to lie motionless in a noisy and claustrophobic space. There is hope, however, that more practical techniques will become available. One of the more promising is near-infrared sensing (Strangman, Boas, & Sutton, 2002). This methodology relies on the fact that light penetrates tissue (put a flashlight to the palm of your hand to demonstrate this) and is reflected back. In near-infrared sensing, light is shined on the skull, and the instrument senses the spectrum of light that is reflected back. It turns out that near-infrared light tends not to be absorbed by oxygenated tissue, and so by measuring the amount of light in the near-infrared region (which is not visible to human eyes), one can detect the oxygenation of the blood in a particular area of the brain. This methodology promises to be much cheaper and less confining than PET or fMRI and does not require movement restriction. Even now it is used with young children who cannot be convinced to remain still and with Parkinson's patients who cannot control their movements. A major limitation of this technique is that it can only detect activity 2 or 3 centimeters into the brain because that is as far as the light can effectively penetrate.

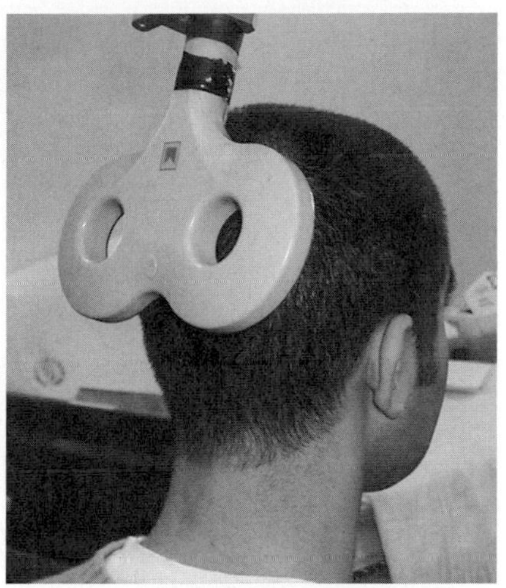

FIGURE 1.13 TMS is delivered by a coil on the surface of the head, which generates a brief but powerful magnetic pulse that induce a temporary current in a small area on the surface of the brain. This current can interfere with processing of the brain with high temporal and fair spatial precision. (Courtesy of Sabine Kastner.)

Although these various imaging techniques have revolutionized our understanding of human cognition, they have their limitations. Beyond their different limitations in temporal and spatial resolution, they have limitations in making causal inferences. Just because activity is detected in a region of the brain during a task does not mean that the region of the brain is critical to the execution of the task. Until recently we have had to study patients with strokes, brain injuries, and brain diseases to get some understanding of how critical a region is. However, there are now methods available that allow one to briefly incapacitate a region. Principal among these is a method called **transcranial magnetic stimulation (TMS),** in which a coil is placed over a particular part of the head and a pulse or pulses are delivered to that region (see Figure 1.13). This will disrupt the processing in the region under the coil. If properly administered, TMS is safe and has no lasting effect. It can be very useful in determining the role of different brain regions. For instance, there is activity in both prefrontal and parietal regions during study of an item that a participant is trying to remember. Nonetheless, it has been shown that TMS to the prefrontal region (Rossi et al., 2001) and not the parietal region (Rossi et al., 2006) disrupts the memory formation. This implies a more critical role of the prefrontal region in memory formation.

- *Techniques like EEG, MEG, fMRI, and TMS are allowing researchers to study the neural basis of human cognition with a precision starting to approach that available in animal studies.*

Using fMRI to Study Equation Solving

Most brain-imaging studies have looked at relatively simple cognitive tasks, as is still true of most research in cognitive neuroscience. A potential consequence of the rise of cognitive neuroscience is that we will come to believe that the human mind is capable only of the simple things that are studied with these neuroscience techniques. There have been forays into examining more complex processes, however, and the results have been quite successful. I will describe a study of ours (Qin, Anderson, Silk, Stenger, & Carter, 2004) that looked at equation solving by children aged 11 to 14 who were just learning to solve equations. This research illustrates the profitable marriage of information-processing analysis and cognitive neuroscience techniques.

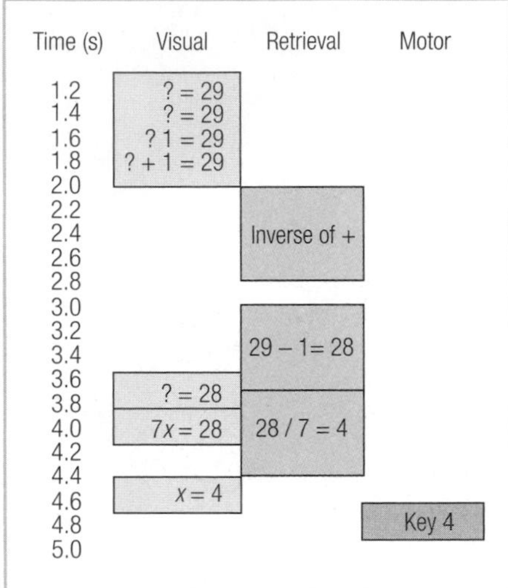

FIGURE 1.14 The steps of an information-processing model for solving the equation $7x + 1 = 29$. The model includes imagined transformations of the equations (visual processing), retrieval of arithmetic and algebraic facts, and programming of the motor response.

Qin et al. (2004) studied eighth-grade students as they solved equations at three levels of complexity, in terms of the number of steps of transformation that were required:

0 step: $1x + 0 = 4$

1 step: $3x + 0 = 12$ or $1x + 8 = 12$

2 steps: $7x + 1 = 29$

Note that the 0-step equation is rather unusual, with the 1 in front of the x and the $+\ 0$ after the x. This format reflects the fact that the visual complexity of different conditions must be controlled to avoid obtaining differences in the visual cortex and elsewhere just because a more complex visual stimulus has to be processed. Students kept their heads motionless while being scanned. They wore a response glove and could press a finger to indicate the answer to the problem (thumb = 1, index finger = 2, middle finger = 3, ring finger = 4, and little finger = 5).

Qin et al. (2004) developed an information-processing model for the solution of such equations that involved imagined transformations of the equations, retrieval of arithmetic and algebraic facts, and programming of the motor response. Figure 1.14 shows the sequencing of these activities. In line with existing research, it was postulated that

1. Programming of the hand would be reflected in activation in the left motor and somatosensory cortex. (See Figure 1.10; participants responded with their right hands, and so the left cortex would be involved.)
2. The imagined transformations of each equation would activate a region of the left parietal cortex involved in mental imagery (see Chapter 4).
3. The retrieval of arithmetic information would activate a region of the left prefrontal cortex (see Chapters 6 and 7).

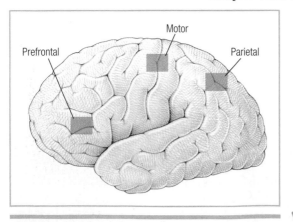

FIGURE 1.15 Regions of interest for the fMRI scan in the equation-solving experiment. The imagined transformations would activate a region of the left parietal cortex; the retrieval of arithmetic information would activate a region of the left prefrontal cortex; and programming of the hand's movement would activate the left motor and somatosensory cortex.

Figure 1.15 shows the locations of these three regions of interest. Each region is a cube with sides of approximately 15 mm, about the size of the end of your finger. fMRI is capable of much greater spatial resolution, but our application did not require this level of accuracy.

The times required to solve the three types of equation were 2.0 s for 0 step, 3.6 s for 1 step, and 4.8 s for 2 steps. However, after students pressed the appropriate finger to indicate the answer, a long rest period followed to allow brain activity to return to baseline for the next trial. Qin et al. (2004) obtained the data in terms of the percentage increase over this baseline of the **blood oxygen level dependent (BOLD) response.** In this particular experiment, the BOLD response was obtained for each region every 1.2 s. Figure 1.16a shows the BOLD response in the motor region for the three conditions. The percentage increase is plotted from the time the equation was presented. Note that even though students solved the problem and keyed the answer to the 0-step equation in an average of 2 s, the BOLD function did not begin to rise above baseline until the third scan after the equation was solved, and it did not reach peak until after approximately 6.6 s. This result reflects the fact that the hemodynamic response to a neural activity is delayed because it takes time for the oxygenated blood to arrive at the corresponding location in the brain. Basically, the hemodynamic response reaches a peak about 4 to 5 s after the event. In the motor region (see Figure 1.16a), the BOLD response for a 0-step equation reached a peak at approximately 6.6 s, for a 1-step equation at approximately 7.8 s, and for a 2-step equation at approximately 9.0 s. Thus, the point of maximum activity reflects events that were happening about 4 to 5 s previously.

The peak of a BOLD function allows one to read the brain and see *when* the activity took place. The height of the function reflects the *amount* of activity that took place. Note that the functions in Figure 1.16a are of approximately equal height in the three conditions because it takes the same amount of effort to program the finger press, independent of the number of transformations needed to solve the equations.

Figure 1.16b shows the BOLD responses in the parietal region. Like the responses in the motor region, they peaked at different times, reflecting the differences in time to solve the equations. They peaked a little earlier, however, because the BOLD responses reflected the transformations being made to the mental image of the equation, which occurred before the response was emitted. Also, the BOLD functions reached very different heights, reflecting the different number of transformations that needed to be performed to solve the equation. Figure 1.16c shows the BOLD responses in the prefrontal region, which were quite similar to those in the parietal region. The important difference is that there was no rise in the function in the 0-step condition because it was not necessary to retrieve any

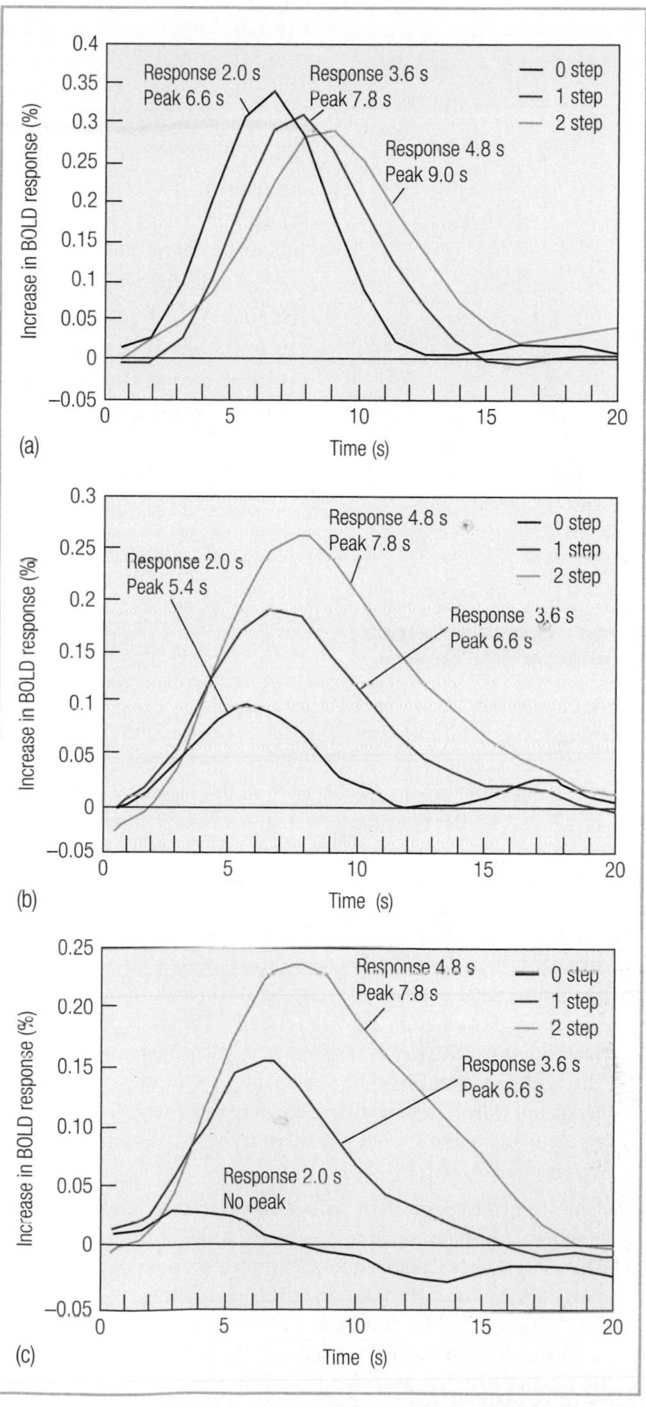

FIGURE 1.16 Responses of the three regions of interest shown in Figure 1.14 for different equation complexities: (a) motor region; (b) parietal region; (c) prefrontal region.

information in that condition. Students could just read the answer from the mental representation of the original equation.

This experiment shows that researchers can separately track different information-processing components involved in the solution of a complex task. The fMRI methodology is especially appropriate for the study of complex cognition. Its temporal resolution is not very good, and so it is difficult to study very brief tasks such as the Sternberg task (see Figures 1.1 and 1.2). On the other hand, when one is looking at a task that takes many seconds, it is possible to distinguish the timing of processes, as we see in Figure 1.16. Because of its high spatial resolution, fMRI enables one to separate out different components of the overall processing. For brief cognition, ERP is often a more appropriate brain-imaging technique because it can achieve much finer temporal resolution

- *fMRI allows researchers to track activity in the brain of different information-processing components of a complex task.*

Questions for Thought

The Web site for this book contains a set of questions (see Learning Objectives and also FAQ) for each chapter. These can serve as a useful basis for reflection—for executing the reflection phase of the PQ4R method discussed early in the chapter. The chapter itself will also contain a set of questions designed to emphasis the core issues in the field. For this chapter consider the following questions:

1. Research in cognitive psychology was described as the mind studying itself. Is this really an accurate characterization of what cognitive psychologists do in studies like those described in Figures 1.1 and 1.16? Does the fact that cognitive psychologists study their own thought processes create any special opportunities or challenges? Is there any difference between a scientist studying a mental system like memory versus a bodily system like digestion?
2. The scientific program of reductionism tries to reduce one level of phenomena into a lower level. For instance, this chapter has discussed how complex economic behavior can be reduced to the decision making (cognition) of individuals and how this can be reduced to the actions of individual neurons in the brain. Reductionism does not stop here. The activity of neurons can be reduced to chemistry, and chemistry can be reduced to physics. When does it help and when does it not help to try to understand one level in terms of a lower level? Why is it silly to go all the way in a reductionist program and attempt something like explaining economic behavior in terms of particle physics?
3. Humans are frequently viewed as qualitatively superior to other animals in terms of their intellectual function. What are some ways in which humans seem to display such qualitative superiority? How would these create problems in generalizing research from other animals to humans?
4. New techniques for imaging brain activity have had a major impact on research in cognitive psychology, but each technique has its limitations. What are the limitations of the various techniques? What would the properties be of an ideal brain-imaging technique? How do studies that actually go into the brain (almost exclusively done with nonhumans) inform the use of brain imaging?
5. What are the ethical limitations on the kinds of research that can be performed with humans and nonhumans?

Key Terms

This chapter has introduced quite a few key terms, most of which will reappear in later chapters:

action potential
aphasia
artificial intelligence (AI)
axon
basal ganglia
behaviorism
blood oxygen level dependent (BOLD) response
Broca's area
cognitive neuroscience
cognitive psychology
corpus callosum
dendrite
electroencephalography (EEG)
empiricism
event-related potential (ERP)
excitatory synapse
frontal lobe
functional magnetic resonance imaging (fMRI)
Gestalt psychology
gyrus
hemodynamic response
hippocampus
information-processing approach
inhibitory synapse
introspection
linguistics
magnetoencephalography (MEG)
nativism
neuron
neurotransmitter
occipital lobe
parietal lobe
positron emission tomography (PET)
prefrontal cortex
rate of firing
split-brain patients
Sternberg paradigm
sulcus
synapse
temporal lobe
topographic organization
transcranial magnetic stimulation (TMS)
Wernicke's area

2

Perception

Our bodies are bristling with sensors that detect sights, sounds, smells, and physical contact. Billions of neurons process sensory information and deliver what they find to the higher centers in the brain. This enormous information-processing system creates a problem for higher-level cognition: how to decide what to attend to from all the sensory information being processed. Chapter 3 will address this problem. First, this chapter focus on how our sensory systems identify what is in the world outside our bodies, concentrating on visual perception and, to a lesser extent, on the perception of speech—the two most important perceptual systems for the human species.

This chapter will address these questions:

- How does the brain extract information from the visual signal?
- How is visual information organized into objects?
- How are visual and speech patterns recognized?
- How does context affect pattern recognition?

Visual Information Processing

Visual Perception in the Brain

Figure 2.1 shows the cortical regions devoted to processing information from the senses of vision and hearing. The illustration makes clear that humans have a big neural investment in processing visual information. This investment in vision is part of our "inheritance" as primates, who have evolved to devote as much as 50% of their brains to visual processing (Barton, 1998). The enormous amount of processing in the brain underlies the human ability to recognize what we see.

Damage to certain brain regions results in conditions where one is able to register visual information but unable to recognize anything. **Visual agnosia** is an inability to recognize objects that results neither from general intellectual loss nor from a loss of basic sensory abilities. One case of visual agnosia involved

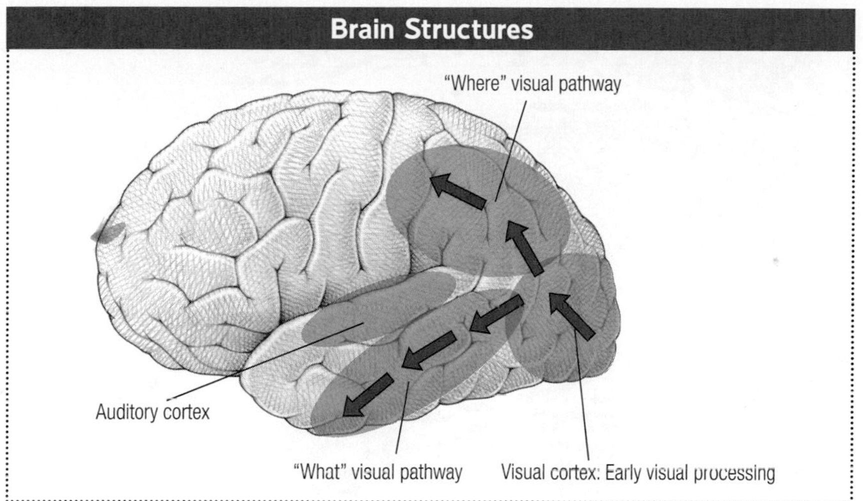

FIGURE 2.1 Some of the cortical structures involved in vision and audition: the visual cortex, the auditory cortex, the "where" visual pathway, and the "what" visual pathway. (Ungerleider & Mishkin, 1982.)

a soldier who suffered brain damage resulting from accidental carbon monoxide poisoning. He could recognize objects by their feel, smell, or sound, but he was unable to distinguish a picture of a circle from that of a square or to recognize faces or letters (Benson & Greenberg, 1969). On the other hand, he was able to discern light intensities and colors and to tell in what direction an object was moving. Thus, his sensory system was able to register visual information, but the damage to his brain resulted in a loss of the ability to transform visual information into perceptual experience. This case shows that perception is much more than simply the registering of sensory information.

Generally, visual agnosia is classified as either **apperceptive agnosia** or **associative agnosia** (for a review, read Farah, 1990). Benson and Greenberg's patient is described as having apperceptive agnosia. Such patients are unable to recognize simple shapes such as circles or triangles or to draw shapes they are shown. Patients with associative agnosia, in contrast, are able to recognize simple shapes and can successfully copy drawings, even of complex objects. However, they are unable to recognize the complex objects. Figure 2.2 shows the original drawing of an anchor and a copy of it made by a patient with associative agnosia (Ratcliff & Newcombe, 1982). Despite being able to produce a relatively accurate drawing, the patient could not recognize this object as an anchor (he called it an umbrella). It is generally believed that patients with apperceptive agnosia have problems with **early processing** of information in the visual system, whereas patients with associative agnosia have intact early processing but have difficulties with **pattern recognition**, which occurs later. It is common to distinguish between early processing of information in the visual stream and later processing of the information. This distinction will be one of the organizing principles of this chapter.

FIGURE 2.2 A patient with associative agnosia was able to copy the original drawing of the anchor at left (his drawing is at right), but he was unable to recognize the object as an anchor. (From Ellis & Young, 1988. Reprinted by permission of the publisher. © 1988 by *Quarterly Journal of Experimental Psychology*.)

FIGURE 2.3 A scene in which we initially perceive just low-level visual details (blobs); only after viewing the scene longer does the pattern of a dog emerge. (Courtesy of Ronald James.)

Figure 2.3 offers an opportunity for a person with normal perception to appreciate the distinction between early and late visual processing. If you have not seen this image before, it will strike you as just a bunch of ink blobs. You will be able to judge the size of the various blobs and reproduce them, just as Ratcliff and Newcombe's patient could, but you will not see any patterns. If you keep looking at the image, however, you may suddenly see a dog in the center of the picture. Now your pattern perception has succeeded, and you have interpreted what you have seen. We will discuss how visual information is processed before patterns are recognized, and then move on to the discussion of the processes of pattern recognition.

- *Visual perception can be divided into an early phase, in which shapes and objects are extracted from the visual scene, and a later phase, in which the shapes and objects are recognized.*

Early Visual Information Processing

We know a fair amount about the neural underpinnings of very early visual information processing. Figure 2.4 is a schematic representation of the eye. Light passes through the lens and the vitreous humor and falls on the retina at the back of the eye. The retina contains the photoreceptor cells, which are made up of light-sensitive molecules that undergo structural changes when exposed to light. Light is scattered slightly in passing through the vitreous humor, so the image that falls on the back of the retina is not perfectly sharp. One of the functions of early visual processing is to sharpen that image.

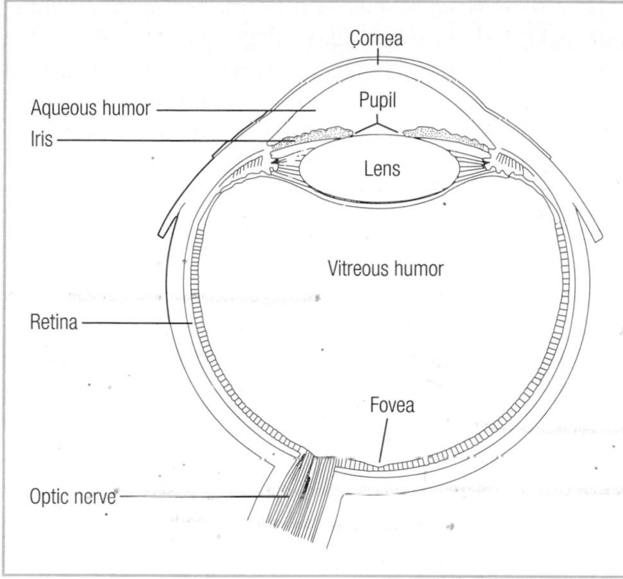

FIGURE 2.4 A schematic representation of the eye. Light enters through the cornea; passes through the aqueous humor, pupil, lens, and vitreous humor; then strikes and stimulates the retina. (From Lindsay & Norman, 1977. Reprinted by permission of the publisher. © 1977 by Academic Press.)

A photochemical process converts light into neural energy. There are two distinct types of photoreceptors in the eye: **cones** and **rods**. Cones are involved in color vision and produce high resolution and acuity. Less light energy is required to trigger a response in the rods, but they produce poorer resolution. As a consequence, they are principally responsible for the less acute, black-and-white vision we experience at night. Cones are especially concentrated in a small area of the retina called the **fovea**. When we focus on an object, we move our eyes so that the object falls on the fovea. This enables us to maximize the high resolution of the cones in perceiving the object. Foveal vision detects fine details, whereas the rest of the visual field—the **periphery**—detects more global information, including movement.

The receptor cells synapse onto bipolar cells and these onto ganglion cells, whose axons leave the eye and form the optic nerve, which goes to the brain. Altogether there are about 800,000 ganglion cells in the optic nerve of each eye. Each ganglion cell encodes information from a small region of the retina. The neural firing on a ganglion axon will typically encode the amount of light stimulation in that region of the retina.

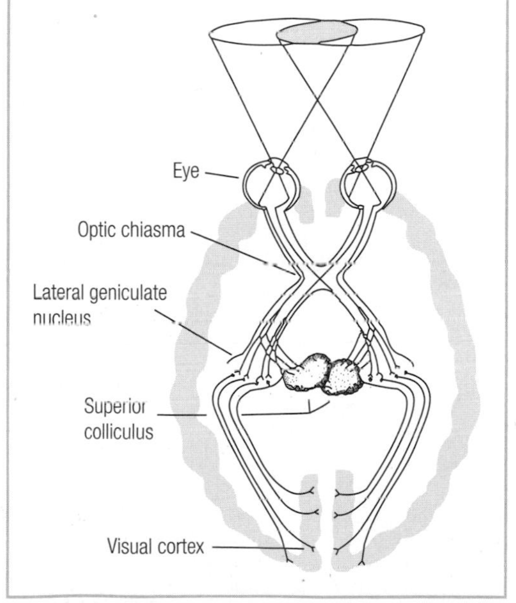

FIGURE 2.5 Neural pathways from the eye to the brain. The optic nerves from each eye meet at the optic chiasma. Information about the left part of the visual field goes to the right brain, and information about the right side of the visual field goes to the left brain. Optic nerve fibers synapse onto cells in subcortical structures, such as the lateral geniculate nucleus and superior colliculus. Both structures are connected to the visual cortex. (From Keeton, 1980. Reprinted by permission of the publisher. © 1980 by W. W. Norton.)

Figure 2.5 illustrates the neural pathways from the eyes to the brain. The optic nerves from both eyes meet at the **optic chiasma**, and the nerves from the inside of the retina (the side nearest the nose) cross over and go to the opposite side of the brain. The nerves from the outside of the retina continue to the same side of the brain as the eye. This means that the right halves of both eyes are connected to the right brain. As Figure 2.5 illustrates, the lens focuses the light so that the left side of the visual field falls on the right half of each eye. Thus, information about the left part of the visual field goes to the right brain, and information about the right side of the visual field goes to the left brain. This is one instance of the general fact, discussed in Chapter 1, that the left hemisphere processes information about the right part of the world and the right hemisphere processes information about the left part.

Once inside the brain, the fibers from the ganglion cells synapse onto cells in various subcortical structures. ("Subcortical" means that the structures are located below the cortex.) Two of these structures are the lateral geniculate nucleus and the superior colliculus (see Figure 2.5). It is thought that the lateral geniculate nucleus is important in perceiving details and recognizing objects, whereas the superior colliculus is involved in locating objects in space. This division is referred to as the "what-where" distinction. Both neural structures are connected to the primary visual cortex (Brodmann area 17 in figure on the inside front cover). The primary visual cortex is the first cortical area to receive visual input, but there are many other visual areas, including Brodmann areas 18 and 19, surrounding it.

Figure 2.6 illustrates the representation of the visual world in the primary visual cortex. It shows that the visual cortex is laid out topologically, as discussed in Chapter 1. The fovea receives a disproportionate representation and

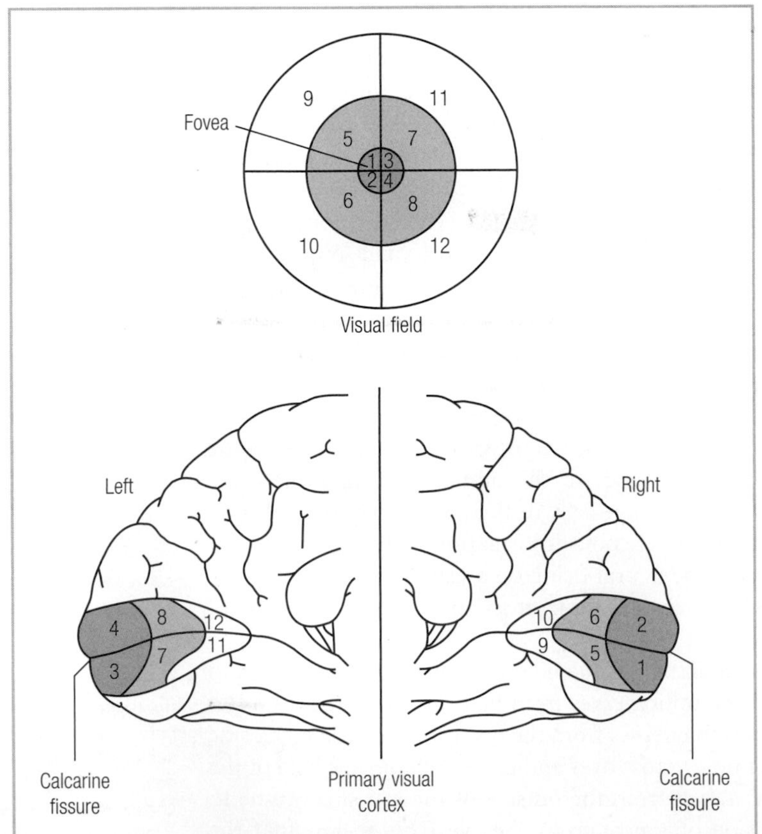

FIGURE 2.6 The orderly mapping of the visual field (above) onto the cortex. The upper fields are mapped below the calcarine fissure and the lower fields are mapped above the fissure. Note the disproportionate representation given the to fovea, which is the region of greatest visual acuity. (From Figure 29-7 in Kandel et al., 1991.)

the peripheral areas, less representation. Figure 2.6 shows that the left visual field is represented in the right cortex and the right in the left. It also illustrates another "reversal" of the mapping—the upper part of the visual field is represented in the lower part of the visual cortex and the lower part, in the upper region.

As Figure 2.1 illustrates, after visual information is projected to the primary visual cortex, it tends to follow two pathways. The information that progresses along the "where" pathway goes to parietal regions of the brain that are specialized for spatial information and for coordinating vision with action. Information that progresses along the "what" pathway goes to the temporal cortex, which is concerned with identifying objects. Monkeys with lesions in the "where" pathway have difficulty learning to identify specific locations, whereas monkeys with lesions in the "what" pathway have difficulty learning to identify objects (Pohl, 1973; Ungerleider & Brody, 1977). Other researchers (e.g., Milner & Goodale, 1995) have argued that the "where" pathway is really a pathway specialized for action. They point out that patients with agnosia because of damage to the temporal lobe, but with intact parietal lobes, can often take actions appropriate to objects they cannot recognize. For instance, one patient (see Goodale, Milner, Jakobson, & Carey, 1991) could correctly reach out and grasp a door handle that she could not recognize.

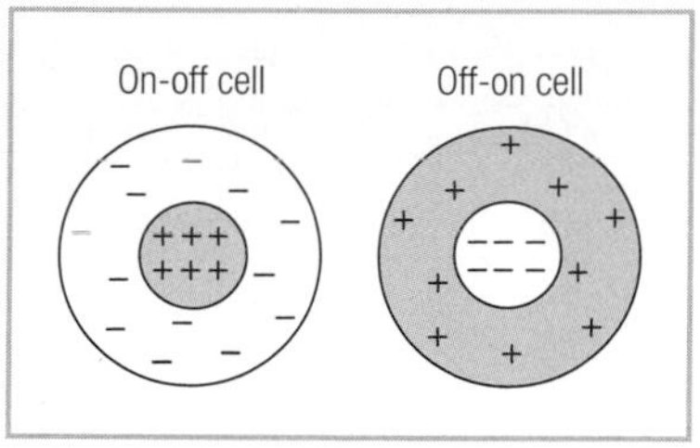

On-off cell

Off-on cell

FIGURE 2.7 On-off and off-on receptive fields of ganglion cells and the cells in the lateral geniculate nucleus.

A photochemical process converts light energy into neural activity. Visual information progresses by various neural tracks to the visual cortex and from there, along "what" and "where" pathways through the brain.

Information Coding in Visual Cells

Kuffler's (1953) research showed how information is encoded by the ganglion cells. These cells generally fire at some spontaneous rate even when the eyes are not receiving any light. For some ganglion cells, if light falls on a small region of the retina, these spontaneous rates of firing will increase. If light falls in the region just around this sensitive center, however, the spontaneous rate of firing will decrease. Light farther from the center elicits no change from the spontaneous firing rate—neither an increase nor a decrease. Ganglion cells that respond in this way are known as on-off cells. There are also off-on ganglion cells: Light at the center decreases the spontaneous rate of firing, and light in the surrounding areas increases that rate. Cells in the lateral geniculate nucleus respond in the same way. Figure 2.7 illustrates the receptive fields of such cells.

Hubel and Wiesel (1962), in their study of the primary visual cortex in the cat, found that visual cortical cells respond in a more complex manner than ganglion cells and cells in the lateral geniculate nucleus. Figure 2.8 illustrates four patterns that have been observed in cortical cells. These receptive fields all have an elongated shape, in contrast to the circular receptive fields of the on-off and off-on cells. The types shown in Figures 2.8a and 2.8b are **edge detectors.** They respond positively to light on one side of a line and negatively to light on the other side.

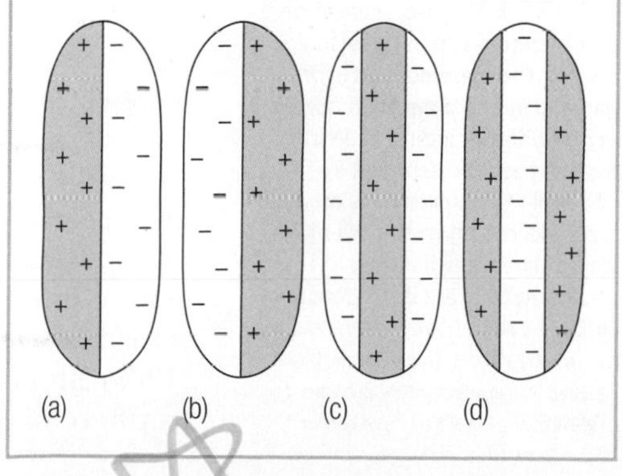

FIGURE 2.8 Response patterns of cells in the visual cortex. (a) and (b) are edge detectors, responding positively to light on one side of a line and negatively to light on the other side. (c) and (d) are bar detectors; they respond positively to light in the center and negatively to light at the periphery, or vice versa.

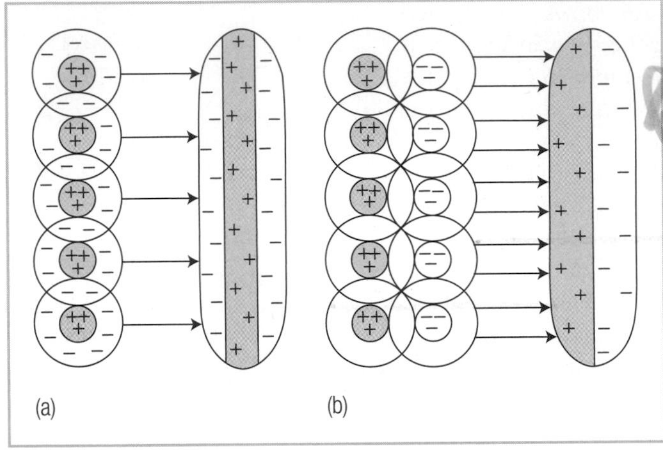

FIGURE 2.9 Hypothetical combinations of on-off and off-on cells to form (a) bar detectors and (b) edge detectors.

They respond most if there is an edge of light lined up so as to fall at the boundary point. The types shown in Figures 2.8c and 2.8d are **bar detectors.** They respond positively to light in the center and negatively to light at the periphery, or vice versa. Thus, a bar with a positive center will respond most if there is a bar of light just covering its center. Figure 2.9 illustrates how a number of on-off and off-on cells might combine to form a bar or edge detector. Note that no single cell is sufficient to stimulate a detector; instead, the detector responds to *patterns* of the cells. Even at this low level, we see the nervous system processing information in terms of patterns of neural activation, a theme emphasized in Chapter 1.

Both edge and bar detectors are specific with respect to position, orientation, and width. That is, they respond only to stimulation in a small area of the visual field, to bars and edges in a small range of orientations, and to bars and edges of certain widths. Different detectors seem to be tuned to different widths and orientations, however, and so some subset of bar detectors would be most stimulated by any bar or edge in the visual field.

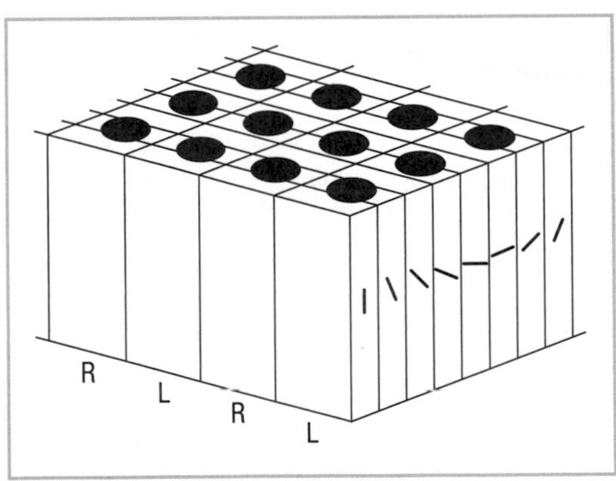

FIGURE 2.10 Representation of a hypercolumn in the visual cortex. The hypercolumn is organized in one dimension according to whether input is coming from the right eye or left eye. In the other dimension, it is organized according to the orientation of lines to which the receptive cells are most sensitive. Adjacent regions represent similar orientations. (After Horton, 1984. Adapted by permission of the publisher. © 1984 by the Royal Society of London.)

Figure 2.10 illustrates Hubel and Wiesel's (1977) hypercolumn representation of cells in the primary visual cortex. They found that the visual cortex is divided into 2 × 2 mm regions, which they called hypercolumns. Each hypercolumn represents a particular region of the receptive field. As noted in Chapter 1, the organization of the visual cortex is topographic, and so adjacent areas of the visual field are represented in adjacent hypercolumns. Figure 2.10 shows that each hypercolumn itself has a two-dimensional (2-D) organization. Along one dimension, alternating rows receive input from the right and left eyes. Along the other dimension, the cells vary in the orientation to which they are most sensitive. Adjacent regions represent similar orientations. This organization should impress upon us how much information about the visual array is encoded. Hundreds of regions of space are represented separately for each eye, and within these regions many different orientations are represented. Also, although this aspect of visual coding is not shown by the illustration, different cells will code for different sizes and widths of line. Thus, an enormous amount of information has been extracted from the visual signal by the time it reaches the first cortical areas.

In addition to this rich representation of line orientation, the visual system extracts other information from the visual signal. For instance, we can also perceive the colors of objects and whether they are moving. Livingstone and Hubel (1988) proposed that the visual system processes these various dimensions (form, color, and movement) separately. Many different visual pathways and many different areas of the cortex are devoted to visual processing (32 visual areas in the count by Van Essen & DeYoe, 1995). Different pathways have cells that are differentially sensitive to color, movement, and orientation. It seems that the visual system analyzes a stimulus into many independent features and represents the locations of these features. Such spatial representations of visual features are called **feature maps** (Wolfe, 1994). Thus, if a vertical red bar is moving at a particular location, there are separate feature maps representing that it is red, vertical, and moving in that location, and these maps may be in different visual areas of the brain.

- *The ganglion cells encode the visual field by means of on-off and off-on cells, which are combined by higher visual processing to form various features.*

Perceiving Depth and Surfaces

Even after the visual system has identified edges and bars in the environment, a great deal of information processing must still be performed before that system is able to perceive the world. One of the problems it must solve is deciding where those edges and bars are located in space. The fundamental problem is that the information laid out on the retina is inherently 2-D, whereas we need to construct a three-dimensional (3-D) representation of the world. The visual system processes a number of cues to infer distance. One of these cues is **texture gradient**, which is the tendency of elements to appear more closely packed together as the distance from the viewer increases. Consider Gibson's (1950) classic examples, shown in Figure 2.11. Even though the lines

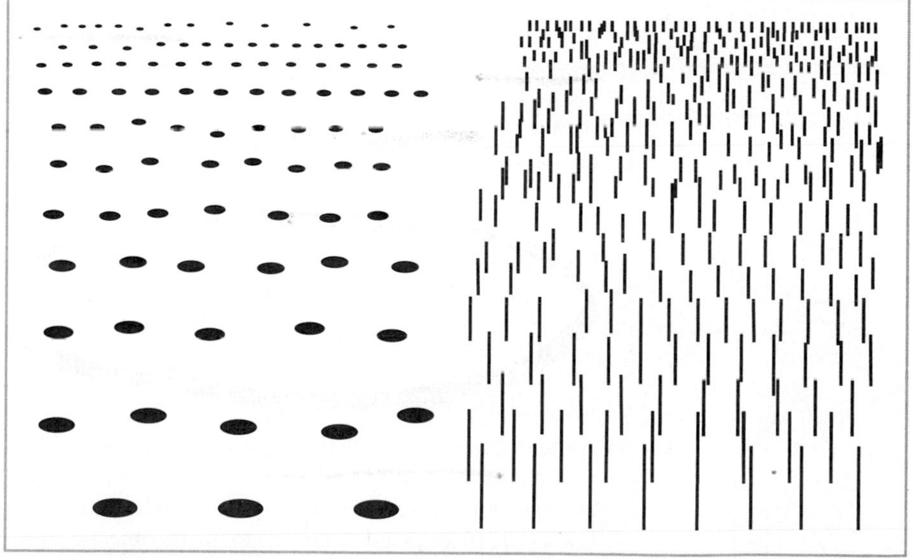

FIGURE 2.11 Examples of texture gradient. Elements appear to be further away when they are more closely packed together. (From Gibson, 1950. Reprinted by permission of the publisher. © 1950 by Houghton Mifflin.)

and ovals are rendered on a flat page, the change in the texture gives the appearance of distance. Another cue to depth is stereopsis, the ability to perceive 3-D depth because each eye receives a slightly different view of the world. Stereopsis is utilized by the 3-D glasses found in a few movies and some exhibits such as at Disney World. They filter the light coming from a single 2-D source (say, a movie screen) so that different light information reaches each eye. The perception of a 3-D structure resulting from stereopsis can be quite compelling.

A third source of information about 3-D structure comes from motion parallax. As more distant points move, they move across the retina more slowly than closer points. Similarly, as one moves one's head, objects that are more distant will move across the retina more slowly than closer objects. For an interesting demonstration, look at the leaves of a nearby tree or bush with one eye closed. Denied stereopic information, you will have the sense of a very flat image in which it is hard to see the position of the many leaves relative to one another. Then move your head. Suddenly, the 3-D structure of the tree becomes clear, and you can readily perceive the relative positions of leaves and branches.

Although it is easy to demonstrate the importance of such cues as texture gradient, stereopsis, and motion parallax to depth perception, it has been a challenge to understand how the brain actually processes such information. A number of researchers in the area of computational vision have worked on the problem. For instance, David Marr (1982) has been influential in his proposal that these various sources of information work together to create what he calls a **$2^1/_2$-D sketch** that identifies where various visual features are located relative to the viewer. He recognized, however, how far this representation is from an actual perception of the world. In particular, such a sketch represents only parts of surfaces and does not yet identify how these parts go together to form images of objects in the environment (the problem we had with Figure 2.3). He used the term **3-D model** to refer to a representation of objects in a visual scene.

FIGURE 2.12 An example of how we aggregate the perception of many broken lines into the perception of solid objects. (From Winston, 1970. Reprinted by permission of the publisher. © 1970 by Massachusetts Institute of Technology.)

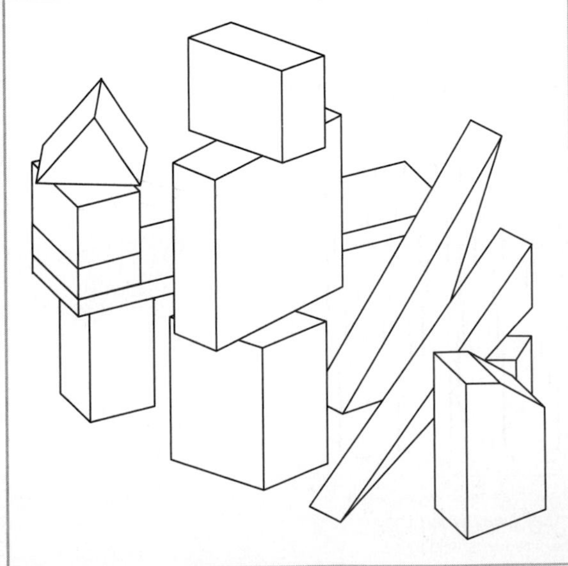

Cues such as texture gradient, stereopsis, and motion parallax combine to create a representation of the locations of surfaces in 3-D space.

Object Perception

A major problem in calculating a representation of the world is object segmentation. Knowing where the lines and bars are located in space is not enough; we need to know which ones go together to form objects. Consider the scene in Figure 2.12. Many lines go this way and that, but somehow we put them together to come up with the perception of a set of objects.

We tend to organize objects into units according to a set of principles called the **gestalt principles of organization** after the Gestalt psychologists who first proposed them (e.g., Wertheimer, 1912/1932). Consider Figure 2.13. In Figure 2.13a, we perceive four pairs of lines rather than eight separate lines. This picture illustrates the principle of proximity: Elements close together tend to organize into units. Figure 2.13b illustrates the principle of similarity. We tend to see this array as rows of o's alternating with rows of x's. Objects that look alike tend to be grouped together. Figure 2.13c illustrates the principle of good continuation. We perceive two lines, one from *A* to *B* and the other from *C* to *D*, although there is no reason why this sketch could not represent another pair of lines, one from *A* to *D* and the other from *C* to *B*. However, the line from *A* to *B* displays better continuation than the line from *A* to *D*, which has a sharp turn. Figure 2.13d illustrates the principles of closure and good form. We see the drawing as one circle occluded by another, although the occluded object could have many other possible shapes.

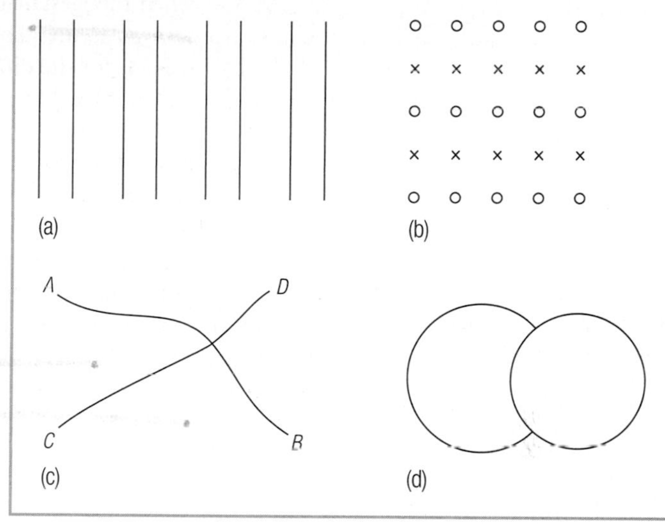

FIGURE 2.13 Illustrations of the gestalt principles of organization: (a) the principle of proximity, (b) the principle of similarity, (c) the principle of good continuation, (d) the principle of closure.

These principles will tend to organize even completely novel stimuli into units. Palmer (1977) studied the recognition of shapes such as the ones shown in Figure 2.14. He first showed participants stimuli (e.g., Figure 2.14a) and then asked them to decide whether the fragments depicted in Figures 2.14b through 2.14e were part of the original figure. The stimulus in Figure 2.14a tends to organize itself into a triangle (principle of closure) and a bent letter *n* (principle of good continuation). Palmer found that participants could recognize the parts most rapidly when they were the segments predicted by the gestalt principles. So the stimuli in Figures 2.14b and 2.14c were recognized more rapidly than those in Figures 2.14d and 2.14e. Thus, we see that recognition depends critically on the initial segmentation of the figure. Recognition can be impaired

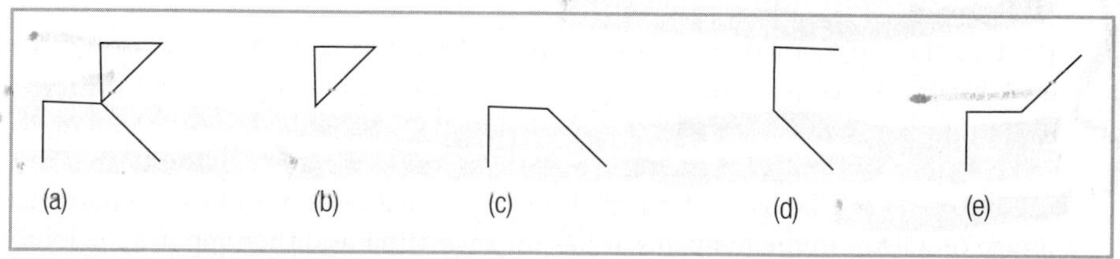

FIGURE 2.14 Examples of stimuli used by Palmer (1977) for studying segmentation of novel figures. (a) is the original stimulus that participants saw; (b) through (e) are the subparts of the stimulus presented for recognition. Stimuli shown in (b) and (c) were recognized more rapidly than those shown in (d) and (e).

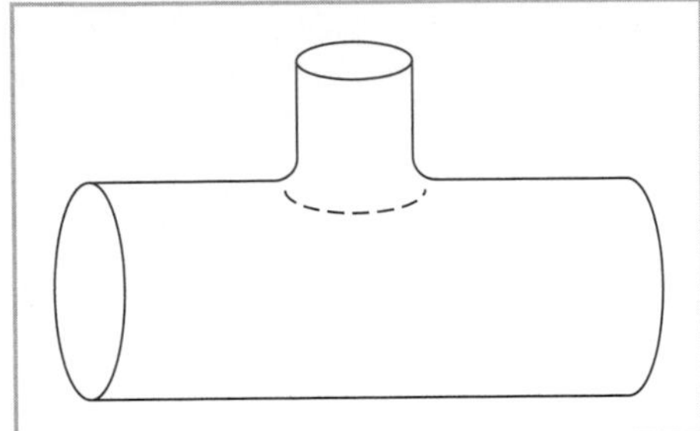

FIGURE 2.15 Segmentation of an object into subobjects. The part boundary can be identified with a contour that follows points of maximum concave curvature (dashed line). (From Stillings et al., 1987; based on Hoffman & Richards, 1985. Reprinted by permission of the publisher. © 1987 by Massachusetts Institute of Technology.)

when this gestalt-based segmentation contradicts the actual pattern structure. FoRiNsTaNcEtHiSsEnTeNcEiShArDtOrEaD. The reasons for the difficulty are that the gestalt principle of similarity makes it hard to perceive adjacent letters of different case as units and that removing the spaces between words has eliminated the proximity cues.

These ideas about segmentation can be extended to describe how more complex 3-D structures are divided. Figure 2.15 illustrates a proposal by Hoffman and Richards (1985) for how gestalt-like principles can be used to segment an outline representation of an object into subobjects. They observed that where one segment joins another, there is typically a concavity in the line outline. Basically, people exploit the gestalt principle of good continuation: The lines at the points of concavity are not good continuations of one another, and so viewers do not group these parts together.

The current view is that the visual processing underlying the ability to identify the position and shape of an object in 3-D space is largely innate. Young infants appear to be capable of recognizing objects and their shapes and of appreciating where these objects are in 3-D space (e.g., Granrud, 1986, 1987).

- *Gestalt principles of organization explain how the brain segment visual scenes into objects.*

Visual Pattern Recognition

We have now discussed visual information processing to the point where we organize the visual world into objects. There still is a major step before we see the world, however: We also must identify what these objects are. This task is pattern recognition. Much of the research on this topic has focused on the question of how we recognize the identity of letters. For instance, how do we recognize a presentation of the letter *A* as an instance of the pattern A? We will first discuss pattern recognition with respect to letter identification and then move on to a more general discussion of object recognition.

Template-Matching Models

Perhaps the most obvious way to recognize a pattern is by means of **template matching.** The template-matching theory of perception proposes that a retinal image of an object is faithfully transmitted to the brain, and the brain attempts to compare the image directly to various stored patterns. These patterns are called templates. The basic idea is that the perceptual system tries to compare the image of a letter to the templates it has for each letter and then reports the template that gives the best match. Figure 2.16 illustrates various examples of successful and unsuccessful template matching. In each case, an attempt is made to achieve a correspondence between the retinal cells stimulated and the retinal cells specified for a template pattern for a letter.

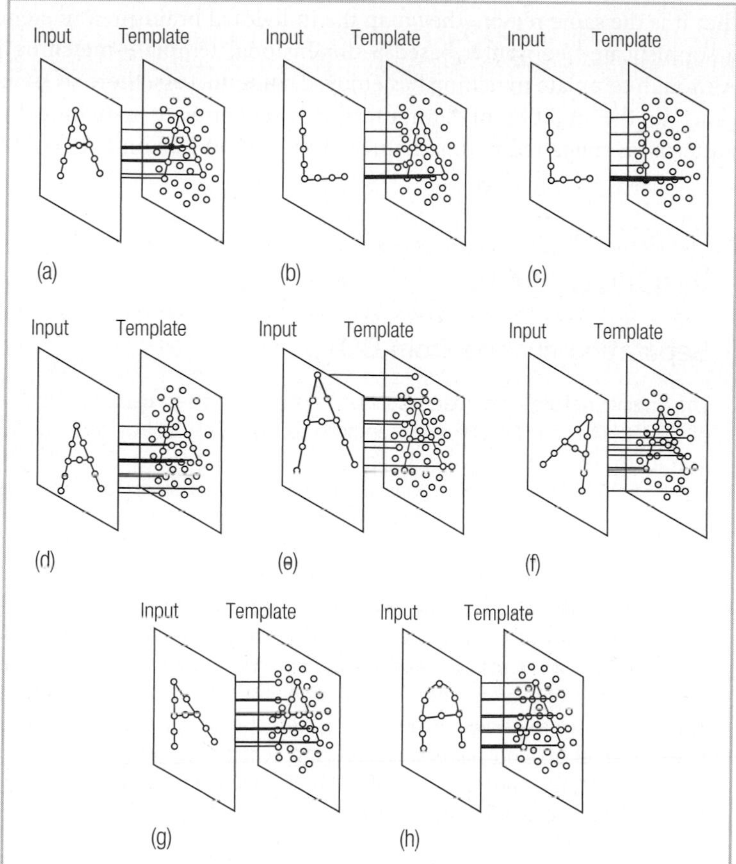

FIGURE 2.16 Examples of attempts to match templates to the letters *A* and *L*. (a) and (c) are successful template-matching attempts; (b) and (d) through (h) are failed attempts. (After Neisser, 1967. Adapted by permission of the publisher. © 1967 by Appleton.)

Figure 2.16a shows a case in which a correspondence is achieved and an *A* is recognized. Figure 2.16b shows a case in which no correspondence is reached between the input of an *L* and the template pattern for an *A*. But *L* is matched in Figure 2.16c by the *L* template. However, things can very easily go wrong with a template. Figure 2.16d shows a mismatch that occurs when the image falls on the wrong part of the retina, and Figure 2.16e shows the problem when the image is the wrong size. Figure 2.16f shows what happens when the image is in a wrong orientation, and Figures 2.16g and 2.16h show the difficulty when the images are nonstandard *A*'s.

Although there are these difficulties with template matching, it is one of the methods used in machine vision (see Ullman, 1996). Procedures have been developed for rotating, stretching, and otherwise warping images to match. Template matching is also used in fMRI brain imaging (see Chapter 1). Each human brain is anatomically different, much as each human body is different. When researchers claim regions like those in Figure 1.15 display activation patterns like those in Figure 1.16 they typically are claiming that the same region in the brains of each of their participants displayed that pattern. To determine that it is the same region, they map the individual brains to a reference brain by a sophisticated computer-based 3-dimensional template-matching procedure. Although template matching has enjoyed some success, there seem to be limitations to the abilities of computers to use template matching to recognize patterns, as suggested in this chapter's Implication Box on CAPTCHAS.

Implications

Separating humans from BOTS

The special nature of human visual perception has been used in the development of CAPTCHAs (von Ahn, Blum, & Langford, 2002). CAPTCHA stands for "Completely Automated Public Turing Test to Tell Computers and Humans Apart." The motivation for CAPTCHAs comes from such real world problems as faced by YAHOO, which offers free email accounts. The problem is that automatic BOTs will sign up for such accounts and then use them to send SPAM. To test that it is a real human, the system can present a figure like that in Figure 2.17. Although template-based approaches may fail on recognizing such figures, one should not count computers out. Some computer scientists have taken their appearance as an intellectual challenge, and an "arms race" is appearing in which more sophisticated recognition programs are appearing and more challenging CAPTCHAs are being developed. The successful methods being used have little to do with template matching, however, and attempt to extract defining features of these items (e.g., Mori & Malik, 2003). You can visit the CAPTCHA Web site and contribute to the research at http://recaptcha.net/captcha.html.

FIGURE 2.17 Examples of CAPTCHAs that humans can read but template-based computer programs have great difficulty with. Courtesy of Luis von Ahn.

- *Template matching is a way to identify objects by aligning the stimulus to a template of a pattern.*

Feature Analysis

Partly because of the difficulties posed by template matching, psychologists have proposed that pattern recognition occurs through **feature analysis.** In this model, stimuli are thought of as combinations of elemental features. Table 2.1 from Gibson (1969) shows her proposal for the representation of the letters of the alphabet in terms of features. For instance, the capital letter *A* can be seen as consisting of a horizontal, two diagonals in opposite orientations, a line intersection, symmetry, and a feature she called vertical discontinuity. She considered some of these features like the straight lines to be outputs of the edge and bar detectors in the visual cortex (discussed earlier—see Figure 2.8).

You might wonder how feature analysis represents an advance beyond the template model. After all, what are the features but minitemplates? The feature-analysis model does have a number of advantages over the template model, however. First, because the features are simpler, it is easier to see how the system might try to correct for the kinds of difficulties faced by the template-matching model in recognizing full patterns as in Figure 2.16. Indeed, to the extent that features are just line strokes, the bar and edge detectors we discussed earlier can extract such features. A second advantage of feature analysis is that it is possible to specify those relationships among the features that are most important to

TABLE 2.1

Gibson's proposal for the features underlying the recognition of letters

Features	A	E	F	H	I	L	T	K	M	N	V	W	X	Y	Z	B	C	D	G	J	O	P	R	Q	S	U
Straight																										
Horizontal	+	+	+	+		+	+								+				+							
Vertical		+	+	+	+	+	+	+	+	+				+		+		+				+	+			
Diagonal/	+							+	+		+	+	+	+	+											
Diagonal\	+							+	+	+	+	+	+	+									+	+		
Curve																										
Closed																+		+			+	+	+	+		
Open V																				+						+
Open H																	+		+	+					+	
Intersection	+	+	+	+			+	+					+			+						+	+	+		
Redundancy																										
Cyclic change		+							+			+				+									+	
Symmetry	+	+		+	+		+	+	+		+	+	+	+		+	+	+			+					+
Discontinuity																										
Vertical	+		+	+	+		+	+	+	+				+								+	+			
Horizontal		+	+			+	+								+											

the pattern. Thus, for *A*, the critical point is that there are three lines, two diagonals (in different directions) and one horizontal, and that these intersect. Many other details are unimportant. Thus, all the following patterns are *A*'s: A, A, A, A. Finally, the use of features rather than larger patterns reduces the number of templates needed. In the feature-analysis model, we would not need a template for each possible pattern but only for each feature. Because the same features tend to occur in many patterns, the number of distinct entities to be represented would be reduced considerably.

There is a fair amount of behavioral evidence for the existence of features as components in pattern recognition. For instance, if letters have many features in common—as *C* and *G* do, for example—evidence suggests that people are particularly prone to confuse them (Kinney, Marsetta, & Showman, 1966). When such letters are presented for very brief intervals, people often misclassify one stimulus as the other. So, for instance, participants in the Kinney et al. experiment made 29 errors when presented with the letter *G*. Of these errors, there were 21 misclassifications as *C*, 6 misclassifications as *O*, 1 misclassification as *B*, and 1 misclassification as *9*. No other errors occurred. It is clear that participants were choosing items with similar feature sets as their responses. Such a response pattern is what we would expect if a feature-analysis model were used. If participants could extract only some of the features in the brief presentation, they would not be able to decide among stimuli that shared these features.

Another kind of experiment that yields evidence in favor of a feature-analysis model involves stabilized images. The eye has a very slight tremor, called psychological nystagmus, which occurs at the rate of 30 to 70 cycles per second. Also, the eye's direction of gaze drifts slowly over an object. Consequently, the retinal image of the object on which a person tries to focus is not perfectly constant; its position changes slightly over time. There is evidence that this retinal movement is critical for perception. When techniques are used to keep an image on the exact same position of the retina regardless of eye movement, parts of the object start to disappear. If the exact same retinal and nervous pathways are used constantly, they become fatigued and stop responding.

The most interesting aspect of this phenomenon is the way the stabilized object disappears. It does not simply fade away or vanish all at once. Instead, different portions drop out over time. Figure 2.18 illustrates the fate of one of the stimuli used in an experiment by Pritchard (1961). The leftmost item was the image presented; the four others are various fragments that were reported. Two points are important. First, whole features such as a vertical bar seemed to be lost. This finding suggests that features are the important units in perception. Second, the stimuli that remained tended to constitute complete letter or number patterns. This result indicates that these features are combined to define the recognized patterns. Thus, even though our perceptual system may extract features, what we perceive are patterns composed from these features. The feature-extraction and feature-combination processes that underlie pattern recognition are not available to conscious awareness; all that we are aware of are the resulting patterns.

FIGURE 2.18 The disintegration of an image that is stabilized on the eye. At far left is the original image displayed. The partial outlines to the right show various patterns reported as the stabilized image began to disappear. (From Pritchard, 1961. Reprinted by permission of the publisher. © 1961 by *Scientific American*.)

> ○ *Feature analysis involves recognizing first the separate features that make up a pattern and then their combination.*

Object Recognition

Although feature analysis does a satisfactory job of describing how we recognize such simple objects as the letter *A*, one might wonder how it explains our recognition of more complex objects that might seem to defy description in terms of a few features. There is evidence that the same processes might underlie the recognition of familiar categories of objects such as horses or cups. The basic idea is that a familiar object can be seen as a known configuration of simple components. Figure 2.19 illustrates a proposal by Marr (1982) about how familiar objects can be seen as configurations of simple pipelike components. For instance, an ostrich has a horizontally oriented torso attached to two long legs and a long neck.

Biederman (1987) put forward the **recognition-by-components theory.** It proposes that there are three stages in our recognition of an object as a configuration of simpler components:

1. The object is segmented into a set of basic subobjects. This process reflects the output of early visual processing, discussed earlier in the chapter.
2. Once an object has been segmented into basic subobjects, one can classify the category of each subobject. Biederman (1987) suggested that

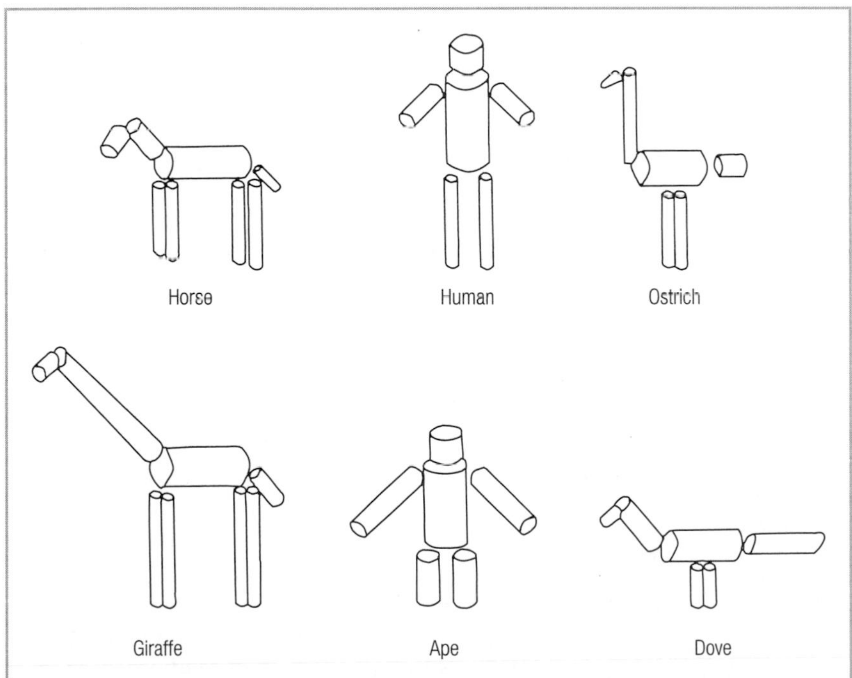

FIGURE 2.19 Segmentation of some familiar objects into basic cylindrical shapes. Familiar objects can be recognized as configurations of simpler components. (After Marr & Nishihara, 1978. Adapted by permission of the publisher. © 1978 by the Royal Society of London.)

there are 36 basic categories of subobjects, which he called **geons** (an abbreviation of *geometric ions*). Figure 2.20 shows some examples. We can think of the cylinder as being created by a circle as it is moved along a straight line (the axis) perpendicular to its center. We can generalize this basic cylinder shape to other shapes by varying some of the properties of its generation. We can change the shape of the object we are moving. If it is a rectangle rather than a circle that is moved along the axis, we get a block instead of a cylinder. We can curve the axis and get objects that curve. We can vary the size of the shape as we are moving it and get objects like the pyramid or wine glass. Biederman proposed that the 36 geons that can be generated in this manner serve as an alphabet for composing objects, much as letters serve as the alphabet for building up words. Recognizing a geon involves recognizing the features that define it, which describe elements of its generation such as the shape of the object and the axis along which it is moved. Thus, recognizing a geon is like recognizing a letter.

3. Having identified the pieces from which the object is composed and their configuration, one recognizes the object as the pattern composed from these pieces. Thus, recognizing an object is like recognizing a word.

As in the case of letter recognition, there are many small variations in the underlying geons that should not be critical for recognition. For example, one need only determine whether an edge is straight or curved (in discriminating, say, a brick from a cylinder) or whether edges are parallel or not (in discriminating, say, a cylinder from a cone). It is not necessary to determine precisely how curved an edge might be. Only edges are needed to define geons. Color, texture, and small detail should not matter. If this hypothesis is correct, schematic line drawings of complex objects that allow the basic geons to be identified should be recognized just as quickly as detailed color photographs of the objects. Biederman and Ju (1988) confirmed this hypothesis experimentally: Schematic line drawings of such objects as telephones provide all the information needed for quick and accurate recognition.

The crucial assumption in this theory is that object recognition is mediated by recognition of the components of the object. Biederman, Beiring, Ju, and Blickle (1985) performed a test of this prediction with objects such as those shown in Figure 2.21. Whole components of some objects were deleted; in other objects, all the components were present, but segments of the components were deleted. They presented these two types of degraded figures to participants for various brief intervals and asked them

FIGURE 2.20 Examples of Biederman's (1987) proposed geons, or basic categories of subobjects. In each object, the dashed line represents the central axis of the object. The objects can be described in terms of the movement of a cross-sectional shape along an axis. *Cylinder:* A circle moves along a straight axis. *Cone:* A circle contracts as it moves along a straight axis. *Pyramid:* A square contracts as it moves along a straight axis. *Football:* A circle expands and then contracts as it moves along a straight axis. *Horn:* A circle contracts as it moves along a curved axis. *Wine glass:* A circle contracts and then expands, creating concave segmentation points, marked by arrows. (From Biederman, Beiring, Ju, & Blickle, 1985. Reprinted by permission of the authors.)

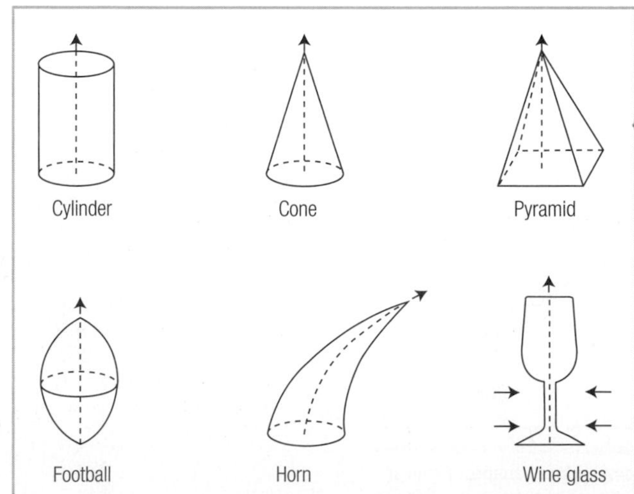

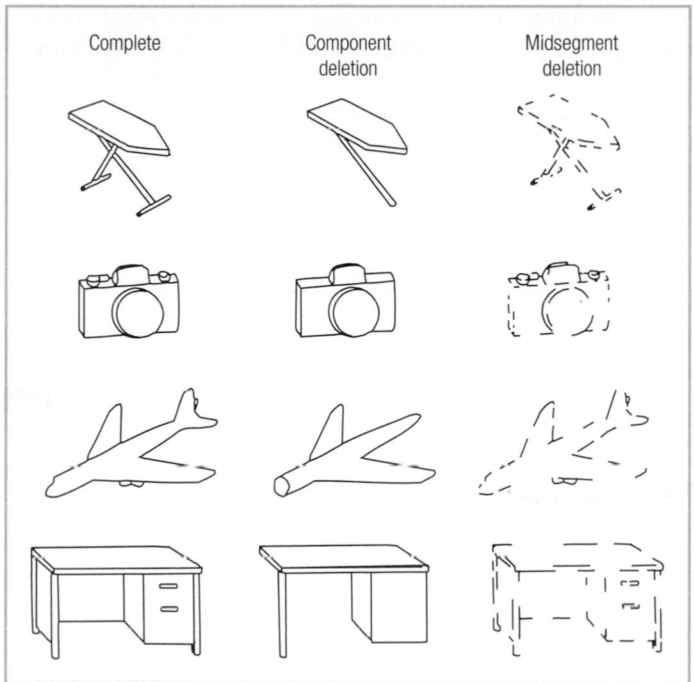

FIGURE 2.21 Sample stimuli used by Biederman et al. (1985) to test the theory that object recognition is mediated by recognition of components of the object. Equivalent proportions either of whole components or of contours at midsegments were removed. Results of the experiment are shown in Figure 2.22. (After Biederman, 1987. Adapted by permission of the publisher. © 1987 by the American Psychological Association.)

to identify the objects. The results are shown in Figure 2.22. At very brief presentation times (65 to 100 ms), participants recognized figures with component deletion more accurately than figures with segment deletion; the opposite was true for the longer, 200-ms presentation. Biederman et al. reasoned that at the very brief intervals, participants were not able to identify the components with segment deletion and so had difficulty in recognizing the objects. With 200-ms exposure, however, participants were able to recognize all the components in

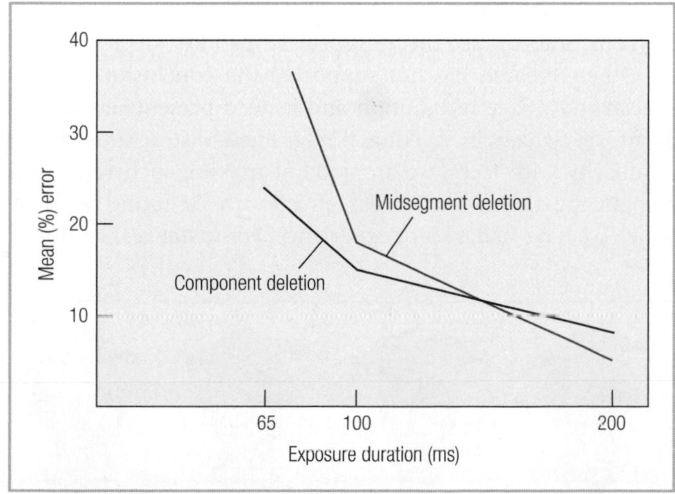

FIGURE 2.22 Results from the test conducted by Biederman, Beiring, Ju, and Blickle (1985) to determine whether object recognition is mediated by recognition of components of the object. Mean percentage of errors of object naming is plotted as a function of the type of contour removal (deletion of midsegments or of entire components) and of exposure duration. (After Biederman, 1987. Adapted by permission of the publisher. © 1987 by the American Psychological Association.)

either condition. Because there were more components in the condition with segment deletion, they had more information about object identity.

Objects such as horses and cups are recognized as configurations of a set of subobjects defined by simple features.

Face Recognition

Faces make up one of the most important categories of visual stimuli, and it has been argued that we have special mechanisms to recognize faces. Special cells that respond preferentially to the faces of other monkeys have been found in the temporal lobes of monkeys (Baylis, Rolls, & Leonard, 1985; Rolls, 1992). Damage to the temporal lobe in humans can result in a deficit called **prosopagnosia**, in which people have selective difficulties in recognizing faces. Brain-imaging studies using fMRI have found a particular region of the temporal lobe, called the **fusiform gyrus**, that responds when faces are present in the visual field (e.g., Ishai, Ungerleider, Martin, Maisog, & Haxby, 1997; Kanwisher, McDermott, & Chun, 1997; McCarthy, Puce, Gore, & Allison, 1997).

One piece of evidence that the processing of faces is special comes from research that examined the recognition of faces turned upside down. In one of the original studies, Yin (1969) found that people are much better at recognizing faces when the faces are presented in their upright orientation than they are at recognizing other categories of objects, such as houses, presented in the upright orientation. When a face is presented upside down, however, there is a dramatic decrease in its recognition; this is not true of other objects. Thus, it appears that we are specially attuned to recognizing faces. Studies have also found somewhat reduced fMRI response in the fusiform gyrus when inverted faces are presented (Haxby et al., 1999; Kanwisher, Tong, & Nakayama, 1998). In addition, we are much better at recognizing parts of a face (a nose, say) when it is presented in context, whereas there is not the same context dependency in recognizing parts of a house (for example, a window) (Tanaka & Farah, 1993). All this evidence leads some researchers to think that we are specifically predisposed to identify whole faces, and it is sometimes argued that this special capability was acquired through evolution.

Other research has not supported the conclusion that there is something special about face recognition and instead presents evidence that the fusiform gyrus specializes in making fine-grained distinctions. Because of our great familiarity with faces, we are good at making such fine-grained judgments in recognizing them, but similar effects can be found with other stimuli with which we have had a lot of experience. For instance, Gauthier, Skudlarski, Gore,

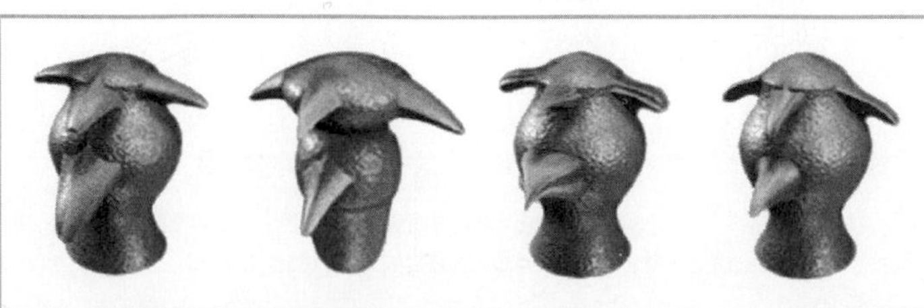

FIGURE 2.23 "Greeble experts" use the face area when recognizing these objects. (From Gauthier, Tarr, Anderson, Skudlarski, & Gore, 1999. Reprinted by permission of the publisher. © 1999 by *Nature Neuroscience*.)

and Anderson (2000) found that bird experts or car experts showed high activation in the fusiform gyrus when they made judgments about birds or cars. In another study, people given a lot of practice at recognizing a set of unfamiliar objects called greebles (Figure 2.23) showed activation in the fusiform gyrus.

- *The fusiform gyrus, located in the temporal lobe, becomes active when people recognize faces.*

Speech Recognition

Up to this point, we have considered only visual pattern recognition. An interesting test of the generality of our conclusions is whether they extend to speech recognition. Although we will not discuss the details of early speech processing, it is worth noting that similar issues arise. A major problem for speech recognition is segmentation of the objects to be recognized. Speech is not broken into discrete units the way printed text is. Although well-defined gaps between words seem to exist in speech, these gaps are often an illusion. If we examine the actual physical speech signal, we often find undiminished sound energy at word boundaries. Indeed, gaps in sound energy are as likely to occur within a word as between words. This property of speech is particularly compelling when we listen to someone speaking an unfamiliar foreign language. The speech appears to be a continuous stream of sounds with no obvious word boundaries. It is our familiarity with our own language that leads to the illusion of word boundaries.

Within a single word, even greater segmentation problems exist. These intraword problems involve the identification of **phonemes.** Phonemes are the basic vocabulary of speech sounds; we recognize words in terms of phonemes.[1] A phoneme is defined as the minimal unit of speech that can result in a difference in the spoken message. To illustrate, consider the word *bat.* This word is composed of three phonemes: /b/, /a/, and /t/. Replacing /b/ with the phoneme /p/, we get *pat;* replacing /a/ with /i/ we get *bit;* replacing /t/ with /n/, we get *ban.* Obviously, a one-to-one correspondence does not always exist between letters and phonemes. For example, the word *one* consists of the phonemes /w/, /e/, and /n/; *school* consists of the phonemes /s/, /k/, /ú/, and /1/; and *knight* consists of /n/, /ī/, and /t/. It is the lack of perfect letter-to-sound correspondence that makes English spelling so difficult.

A segmentation problem arises when the phonemes composing a spoken word need to be identified. The difficulty is that speech is continuous, and phonemes are not discrete in the way letters are on a printed page. Segmentation at this level is like recognizing a written (not printed) message, where one letter runs into another. Also, as in the case of writing, different speakers vary in the way they produce the same phonemes. The variation among speakers is dramatically clear, for instance, when a person first tries to understand a speaker with a strong and unfamiliar accent—as when an American listener

[1] Massaro (1996) presents an often proposed alternative that the basic perceptual units are consonant-vowel and vowel-consonant combinations.

tries to understand an Australian speaker. Examination of the speech signal, however, will reveal that even among speakers with the same accent, considerable variation exists. For instance, the voices of women and children normally have a much higher pitch than those of men.

A further difficulty in speech perception involves a phenomenon known as coarticulation (Liberman, 1970). As the vocal tract is producing one sound—say, the /b/ in *bag*—it is moving toward the shape it needs for the /a/. As it is saying the /a/, it is moving to produce the /g/. In effect, the various phonemes overlap. This means additional difficulties in segmenting phonemes, and it also means that the actual sound produced for one phoneme will be determined by the context of the other phonemes.

Speech perception poses information-processing demands that are in many ways greater than what is involved in other kinds of auditory perception. Researchers have identified a number of patients who have lost just the ability to hear speech, as a result of injury to the left temporal lobe (see M. N. Goldstein, 1974, for a review). Their ability to detect and recognize other sounds and to speak is intact. Thus, their deficit is specific to speech perception. Occasionally, these patients have some success if the speech they are trying to hear is very slow (e.g., Okada, Hanada, Hattori, & Shoyama, 1963), which suggests that some of the problem might lie in segmenting the speech stream.

Speech recognition involves segmenting phonemes from the continuous speech stream.

Feature Analysis of Speech

Feature-analysis and feature-combination processes seem to underlie speech perception, much as they do visual recognition. As with individual letters, individual phonemes can be analyzed as consisting of a number of features. It turns out that these features refer to aspects of how the phoneme is generated. Among the features of phonemes are the consonantal feature, voicing, and the place of articulation (Chomsky & Halle, 1968). The **consonantal feature** is the consonant-like quality of a phoneme (in contrast to a vowel-like quality). **Voicing** is the sound of a phoneme produced by the vibration of the vocal cords. For example, compare the ways you speak the words *sip* and *zip*. The /s/ in *sip* is voiceless, but the /z/ in *zip* is voiced. You can detect this difference by placing your fingers on your larynx as you generate these sounds. The larynx will vibrate for the voiced consonant.

Place of articulation refers to the location at which the vocal tract is closed or constricted in the production of a phoneme. (It is closed at some point in the utterance of most consonants.) For instance, /p/, /m/, and /w/ are considered bilabial because the lips are closed while they are being generated. The phonemes /f/ and /v/ are considered labiodental because the bottom lip is pressed against the front teeth. Two different phonemes are represented by /th/—one in *thy* and the other in *thigh*. Both are dental because the tongue presses against the teeth. The phonemes /t/, /d/, /s/, /z/, /n/, /l/, and /r/ are all alveolar because the tongue presses against the alveolar ridge of the gums just behind the upper front teeth.

The phonemes /sh/, /ch/, /j/, and /y/ are all palatal because the tongue presses against the roof of the mouth just behind the alveolar ridge. The phonemes /k/ and /g/ are velar because the tongue presses against the soft palate, or velum, in the rear roof of the mouth.

Consider the phonemes /p/, /b/, /t/, and /d/. All share the feature of being consonants. The four can be distinguished, however, by voicing and place of articulation. Table 2.2 classifies these four phonemes according to these two features.

TABLE 2.2

The Classification of /b/, /p/, /d/, and /t/ According to Voicing and Place of Articulation

Place of Articulation	Voicing	
	Voiced	Unvoiced
Bilabial	/b/	/p/
Alveolar	/d/	/t/

Considerable evidence exists for the role of such features in speech perception. For instance, Miller and Nicely (1955) had participants try to recognize phonemes such as /b/, /d/, /p/, and /t/ when presented in noise.[2] Participants exhibited confusion, thinking they had heard one sound in the noise when in reality another sound had been presented. The experimenters were interested in what sounds participants would confuse with which other sounds. It seemed likely that they would most often confuse consonants that were distinguished by just a single feature, and this prediction was confirmed. To illustrate, when presented with /p/, participants more often thought that they had heard /t/ than that they had heard /d/. The phoneme /t/ differs from /p/ only in place of articulation, whereas /d/ differs both in place of articulation and in voicing. Similarly, participants presented with /b/ more often thought they heard /p/ than /t/.

This experiment is an earlier demonstration of the kind of logic we saw in the Kinney et al. (1966) study on letter recognition. When the participant could identify only a subset of the features underlying a pattern (in this case, the pattern is a phoneme), the participant's responses reflected confusion among the phonemes sharing the same subset of features.

○ *Phonemes are recognized in terms of features involved in their production, such as place of articulation and voicing.*

● Categorical Perception

The features of phonemes refer to properties by which they are articulated. What properties of the acoustic stimulus encode these articulatory features? This issue has been particularly well researched in the case of voicing. In the pronunciation of such consonants as /b/ and /p/, two things happen: The closed lips open, releasing air, and the vocal cords begin to vibrate (voicing). In the case of the voiced consonant /b/, the release of air and the vibration of the vocal cords are nearly simultaneous. In the case of the unvoiced consonant /p/, the release occurs 60 ms before the vibration begins. What we are detecting when we perceive a voiced versus an unvoiced consonant is the presence or absence of a 60-ms interval between release and voicing. This period of time is referred to as the voice-onset time. The difference between /p/ and /b/ is illustrated in

[2]Actually, participants were presented with the sounds *ba*, *da*, *pa*, and *ta*.

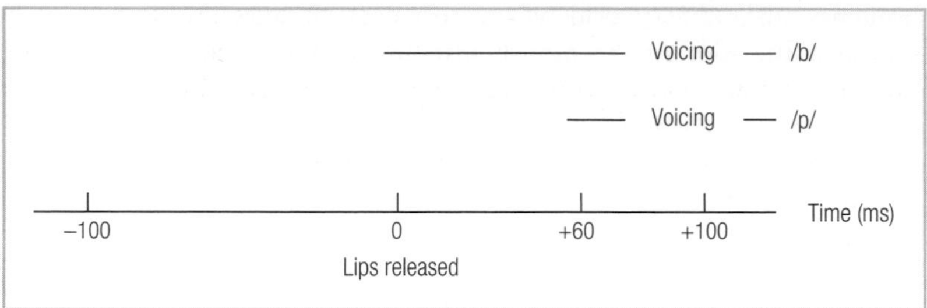

FIGURE 2.24 The difference between the voiced consonant /b/ and the unvoiced consonant /p/ is the delay in the case of /p/ between the release of the lips and the onset of voicing. (From H. H. Clark & E. V. Clark, 1977. Reprinted by permission of the publisher. © 1977 by Harcourt Brace Jovanovich.)

Figure 2.24. Similar differences exist in other voiced-unvoiced pairs, such as /d/ and /t/. Again, the factor controlling the perception of a phoneme is the delay between the release of air and the vibration of the vocal cords.

Lisker and Abramson (1970) performed experiments with artificial (computer-generated) stimuli in which the delay between the release of air and the onset of voicing was varied from –150 ms (voicing occurred 150 ms before release) to +150 ms (voicing occurred 150 ms after release). The task was to identify which sounds were /b/'s and which were /p/'s. Figure 2.25 plots the percentage of /b/ identifications and /p/ identifications. Throughout most of the continuum, participants agreed 100% on what they heard, but there was a sharp switch from /b/ to /p/ at about 25 ms. At a 10-ms voice-onset time, participants were in nearly unanimous agreement that the sound was a /b/; at 40 ms, they were in nearly unanimous agreement that the sound was a /p/. Because of this sharp boundary between the voiced and unvoiced phonemes, perception of this feature is referred to as categorical. **Categorical perception** is the perception of stimuli as belonging in distinct categories and the failure to perceive the gradations among stimuli within a category.

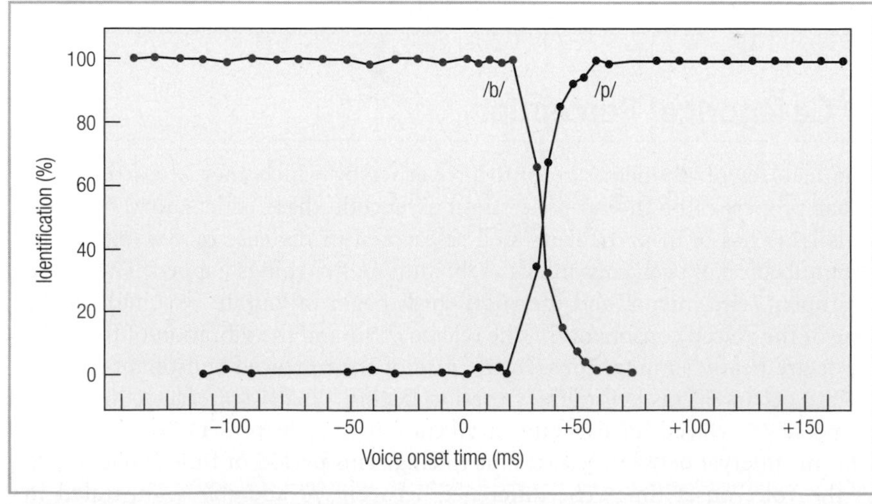

FIGURE 2.25 Percentage identification of /b/ versus /p/ as a function of voice-onset time. A sharp shift in these identification functions occurred at about +25 ms. (From Lisker & Abramson, 1970. Reprinted by permission of the publisher. © 1970 by Academia.)

Other evidence for categorical perception of speech comes from discrimination studies (see Studdert-Kennedy, 1976, for a review). People are very poor at discriminating between a pair of /b/'s or a pair of /p/'s that differ in voice-onset time. However, they are good at discriminating between pairs that have the same difference in voice-onset time but one of the pair is a /b/ and the other is a /p/. It seems that people can identify only the phonemic category of a sound and are not able to make acoustic discriminations within that phonemic category. Thus, people are able to discriminate two sounds only if they fall on different sides of a phonemic boundary.

There are at least two views of exactly what is meant by categorical perception, which differ in the strength of their claims about the nature of perception. The weaker view is that we experience stimuli as coming from distinct categories. There seems to be little dispute that the perception of phonemes is categorical in this sense. A stronger viewpoint is that we cannot discriminate among stimuli within a category. Massaro (1992) has taken issue with this viewpoint, and he has argued that there is some residual ability to discriminate within categories. He further argues that findings of poor discrimination within a category may reflect a bias of participants to say that stimuli within a category are the same even when there are discriminable differences.

Another line of research that provides evidence for use of the voicing feature in speech recognition involves an adaptation paradigm. Eimas and Corbit (1973) had their participants listen to repeated presentations of the sound *da*. This sound involves a voiced consonant /d/. The experimenters reasoned that the constant repetition of the voiced consonant might fatigue, or adapt, the feature detector that responds to the presence of voicing. Then they presented participants with a series of artificial sounds that spanned the acoustic continuum—such as the range between *ba* and *pa* (as in the Lisker & Abramson, 1970, study mentioned earlier). Participants were to indicate whether each of these artificial stimuli sounded more like *ba* or like *pa*. (Remember that the only feature difference between *ba* and *pa* is voicing.) Eimas and Corbit found that some of the stimuli participants would normally have called the voiced *ba*, they now called the voiceless *pa*. Thus, the repeated presentation of *da* had fatigued the *voiced* feature detector and raised the threshold for detecting voicing in *ba*, making many former *ba* stimuli sound like *pa*.

Although there is general consensus that speech perception is categorical in some sense, there is considerable debate about what the mechanism is behind this phenomenon. Anticipating a theme that will occupy much of Chapters 12 and 13, some researchers (e.g., Liberman & Mattingly, 1985) have argued that this reflects special speech perception mechanisms that enable people to perceive how the sounds were generated. Consider, for instance, the categorical distinction between how voiced and unvoiced consonants are produced—either the vocal cords vibrate during the consonant or they do not. This has been used to argue that we perceive voicing by perceiving how the consonants are spoken. However, there is evidence that categorical perception is not tied to humans processing language but rather reflects a general property of how certain sounds are perceived. For instance, Pisoni (1977) created nonlinguistic tones that had a similar distinguishing acoustic feature as present in voicing—a low-frequency tone that is either simultaneous with a high-frequency tone or lags it by 60 msec. His participants showed abrupt boundaries like those in Figure 2.24 for speech signals. In another study, Kuhl (1987) trained chinchillas to discriminate between a voiced "da" and an unvoiced "ta." Even though these animals do not have a human vocal track, they showed the sharp boundary between these stimuli that humans do. Thus, it seems that categorical perception depends on neither the signal being speech (Pisoni, 1977) nor the perceiver having a human vocal system (Kuhl, 1987). Diehl, Lotto, and Holt (2004) have argued that the phonemes we use are chosen so that they exist across categorical boundaries that occur in our auditory perception of speech. So it is more a case of our perceptual system determining our speech behavior than vice versa.

- *Speech sounds differing on continuous dimensions are perceived as coming from distinct categories.*

Context and Pattern Recognition

So far, we have considered pattern recognition as if the only information available to a pattern-recognition system were the information in the physical stimulus to be recognized. This is not the case, however. Objects occur in context, and we can use context to help us recognize objects. Consider the example in Figure 2.26. We perceive the symbols as *THE* and *CAT*, even though the specific symbols drawn for *H* and *A* are identical. The general context provided by the words forces the appropriate interpretation. When context or general knowledge of the world guides perception, we refer to the processing as **top-down processing,** because high-level general knowledge contributes to the interpretation of the low-level perceptual units. A general issue in perception is how such top-down processing is combined with the **bottom-up processing** of information from the stimulus itself, without regard to the general context.

One important line of research in top-down effects comes from a series of experiments on letter identification, starting with those of Reicher (1969) and Wheeler (1970). Participants were presented very briefly with either a letter (such as *D*) or a word (such as *WORD*). Immediately afterward, they were given a pair of alternatives and instructed to report which alternative they had seen. (The initial presentation was sufficiently brief that participants made a good many errors in this identification task.) If they had been shown the letter *D*, they might be presented with *D* and *K* as alternatives. If they had been shown *WORD*, they might be given *WORD* and *WORK* as alternatives. Note that both choices differed only in the letter *D* or *K*. Participants were about 10% more accurate in identifying the word than in identifying the letter alone. Thus, they discriminated between *D* and *K* better in the context of a word than as letters alone—even though, in a sense, they had to process four times as many letters in the word context. This phenomenon is known as the **word superiority effect.**

THE CAT

FIGURE 2.26 A demonstration of context. The same stimulus is perceived as an *H* or an *A*, depending on the context. (From Selfridge, 1955. Reprinted by permission of the publisher. © 1955 by the Institute of Electrical and Electronics Engineers.)

Figure 2.27 illustrates an explanation given by Rumelhart and Siple (1974) and Thompson and Massaro (1973) for why people are more accurate when identifying the letter in the word context. The figure illustrates the products of incomplete perception: Certain parts of the word cannot be detected—in part (a) just the last letter is obscured, whereas in part (b) multiple letters are obscured. If the last letter was all that a participant was shown, the participant would not be able to say whether that letter was a K or an R. Thus, the stimulus information is not enough to identify the letter. On the other hand, the context is not enough by itself either—although it is pretty clear in part (a) that the first three letters are *WOR*, there are a number of four-letter words consistent with a *WOR* beginning: *WORD, WORE, WORK, WORM, WORN, WORT.* However, if the participant combines the information from the stimulus with the information from the context, the whole word must be *WORK,* which implies *K* was the last letter. It is not that participants see the *K* better in the context of *WOR* but that they are better able to infer that *K* is the fourth letter. The participants are not conscious of these inferences, however; so they are said to make unconscious inferences in the act of perception. Note in particular that the participants in this example do not have conscious access to specific features such as the target letter having a lower right diagonal or it would have been possible to choose correctly whether they saw that letter alone and were given the alternatives *D* and *K*. Rather, the participants have conscious access only to the whole word or whole letter that the perceptual system has perceived. Note that this analysis is not restricted to the case where the context letters are unambiguous. In part (b), the second letter could be an O or a U and the third letter could be a B, P, or R. Still, WORK is the only possible word.

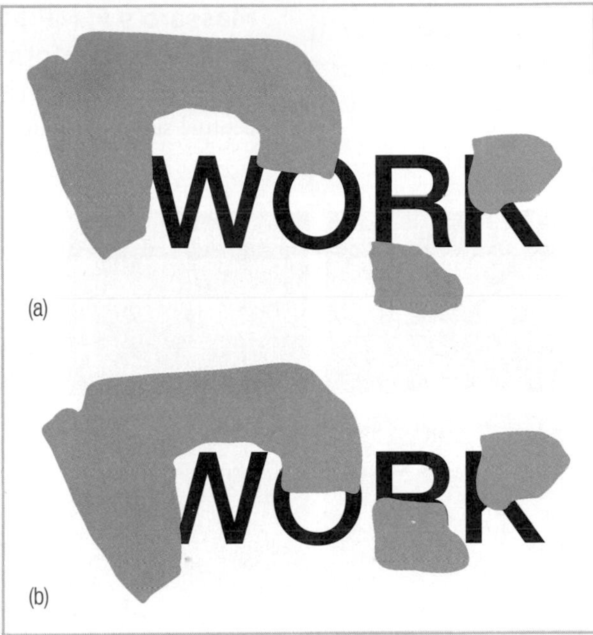

FIGURE 2.27 A hypothetical set of features that might be extracted on a trial in an experiment of word perception: (a) when only the last letter is obscured; (b) when multiple letters are obscured.

This example illustrates the redundancy present in many complex stimuli such as words. These stimuli consist of many more features than are required to distinguish one stimulus from another. Thus, perception can proceed successfully when only some of the features are recognized, with context filling in the remaining features. In language, this redundancy exists on many levels besides the feature level. For instance, redundancy occurs at the letter level. We do not need to perceive every letter in a string of words to be able to read it. To xllxstxatx, I cxn rxplxce xvexy txirx lextex of x sextexce xitx an x, anx yox stxll xan xanxge xo rxad xt—ix wixh sxme xifxicxltx.

Word context can be used to supplement feature information in the recognition of letters.

Massaro's FLMP Model for Combination of Context and Feature Information

We have reviewed the effects of context on pattern recognition in a variety of perceptual situations, but the question of how to interpret these effects conceptually still remains. Massaro has argued that the stimulus and the context provide two independent sources of information about the identity of the stimulus and that they are just combined to provide a best guess of what the stimulus might be. Figure 2.28 shows examples of the material he used in a test of recognition of the letter *c* versus the letter *e*. The four quadrants represent four possibilities in the amount of contextual evidence: Only an *e* can make a word, only a *c* can make a word, both letters can make a word, or neither can make a word. As one reads down within a quadrant, the image of the ambiguous letter provides more evidence for letter *e* and less for letter *c*. Participants were briefly exposed to these stimuli and asked to identify the letter. Figure 2.29 shows the results as a function of stimulus and context information. As the image of the letter itself provided more evidence for an *e*, the probability of the participants' identifying an *e* went up. Similarly, the probability of identifying an *e* increased as the context provided more evidence.

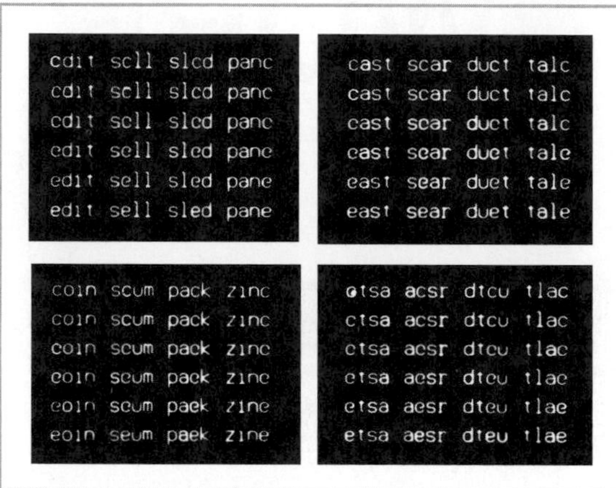

FIGURE 2.28 Contextual clues used by Massaro (1979) to study how participants combine stimulus information from a letter with context information from the surrounding letters. (From Massaro, 1979. Reprinted by permission of the publisher. © 1979 by the American Psychological Association.)

Massaro argued that these data reflect an independent combination of evidence from the context and evidence from the letter stimulus. He assumed that the letter stimulus represents some evidence L_c for the letter *c* and that the context also provides some evidence C_c for the letter *c*. He assumed that these evidences can be scaled on a range of 0 to 1 and can be thought of basically as probabilities, which he called "fuzzy truth values." Because probabilities sum to 1, the evidence for *e* from the letter stimulus is $L_e = 1 - L_c$, and the evidence from the context is $C_e = 1 - C_c$. Given these probabilities, then, the overall probability for a *c* is

$$p(c) = \frac{L_c \times C_c}{(L_c \times C_c) + (L_e \times C_e)}$$

The lines in Figure 2.29 illustrate the predictions from his theory. In general, Massaro's theory (called **FLMP** for **fuzzy logical model of perception**) has done a very good job of accounting for the combination of context and stimulus information in pattern recognition.

- *Massaro's FLMP model of perception proposes that contextual information combines independently with stimulus information to determine what pattern is perceived.*

Other Examples of Context and Recognition

Word recognition is one case for which there have been detailed analyses (for example, Massaro addressed how context influences perception), but contextual influences are ubiquitous. For instance, equally good evidence exists for the role of context in the perception of speech. A nice illustration is the **phoneme-restoration effect,** originally demonstrated in an experiment by Warren (1970). He asked participants to listen to the sentence "The state governors met with their respective legislatures convening in the capital city," with a 120-ms tone replacing the middle *s* in *legislatures*. Only 1 in 20 participants reported hearing the pure tone, and that participant was not able to locate it correctly.

An interesting extension of this first study was an experiment by Warren and Warren (1970). They presented participants with sentences such as the following:

It was found that the *eel was on the axle.
It was found that the *eel was on the shoe.
It was found that the *eel was on the orange.
It was found that the *eel was on the table.

In each case, the * denotes a phoneme replaced by nonspeech. For the four sentences above, participants reported hearing *wheel, heel, peel,* and *meal,* depending on context. The important feature to note about each of these sentences is that they are identical through the critical word. The identification of the critical word is determined by what occurs after it. Thus, the identification of words often is not instantaneous but can depend on the perception of subsequent words.

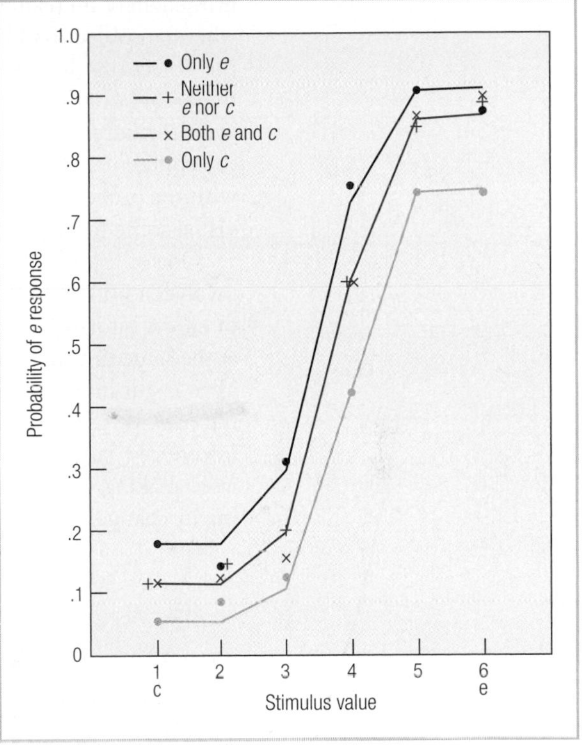

FIGURE 2.29 Probability of an *e* response as a function of the stimulus value of the test letter and of the orthographic context. The lines reflect the predictions of Massaro's FLMP model. The leftmost line is for the case where the context provides evidence only for *e*. The middle line is the same prediction when the context provides evidence for both *e* and *c* or when it provides evidence for neither *e* nor *c*. The rightmost line is for the case where the context provides evidence only for *c*. (From Massaro, 1979. Reprinted by permission of the publisher. © 1979 by the American Psychological Association.)

Context also appears to be important for the perception of complex visual scenes. Biederman, Glass, and Stacy (1973) looked at the perception of objects in novel scenes. Figure 2.30 illustrates the two kinds of scenes presented to their participants. Figure 2.30a shows a normal scene; in Figure 2.30b, the same scene is jumbled. Participants viewed one or the other scene briefly on a screen, and

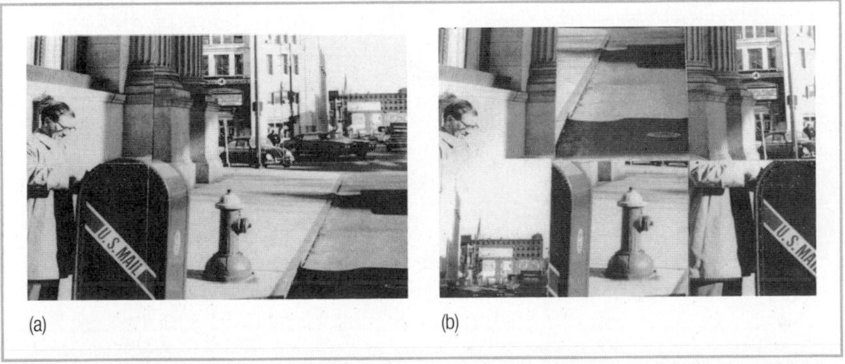

FIGURE 2.30 Scenes used by Biederman, Glass, and Stacy (1973) in their study of the role of context in the recognition of complex visual scenes: (a) a coherent scene; (b) a jumbled scene. It is harder to recognize the fire hydrant in the jumbled scene. (From Biederman, Glass, & Stacy, 1973. Reprinted by permission of the publisher. © 1973 by the American Psychological Association.)

immediately thereafter an arrow pointed to a position on the now-blank screen where an object had been moments before. Participants were asked to identify the object that had been in that position in the scene. So, in the example scene, the arrow might have pointed to the location of the fire hydrant. Participants were considerably more accurate in their identifications when they had viewed the coherent picture than when they had viewed the jumbled picture. Thus, as with the processing of written text or speech, people are able to use context in a visual scene to help in their identification of an object.

One of the most dramatic examples of the influence of context on perception involves a phenomenon called **change blindness.** People are unable to keep track of all the information in a typical complex scene. If elements of the scene change at the same time as there is some retinal disturbance (such as an eye movement or a scene-cut in a motion picture), they often fail to detect the change if it matches the context. The original studies on change blindness (McConkie & Currie, 1996) introduced large changes in pictures that participants were viewing while they were making an eye movement. For instance, the color of a car in the picture might change. These changes were usually not detected. Figure 2.31 illustrates a

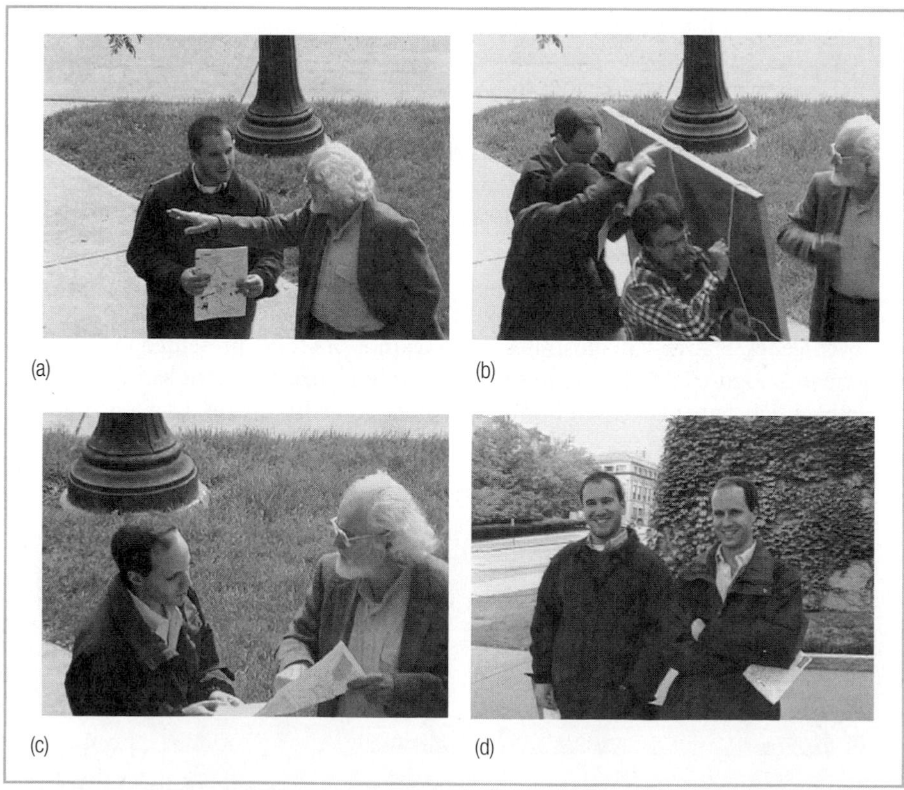

FIGURE 2.31 An example of change blindness. Frames from a video showing how one experimenter switched places with an accomplice as workers carrying a door passed between the experimenter and an unwitting participant. Only 7 of the 15 participants noticed the change. (a) through (c) show the sequence of the switch; (d) shows the two experimenters side by side. (From Simons & Levin, 1998. Reprinted by permission of the publisher. © 1998 by *Psychonomic Bulletin and Review.*)

dramatic instance of change blindness (Simons & Levin, 1998). The experimenter stopped pedestrians on Cornell University's campus and asked for directions. While the unwitting participant was giving the directions, workers carrying a door passed between the experimenter and the participant. An accomplice took the place of the experimenter. Only 7 of the 15 participants noticed the change. In the scene shown in Figure 2.31, the participants thought of themselves as giving instructions to a student, and as long as the changed experimenter fit that interpretation, they did not process him as different. In a laboratory study of the ability to detect changes in people's faces, Beck, Rees, Frith, and Lavie (2001) found greater activation in the fusiform gyrus (see the earlier discussion of face recognition) when face changes were detected than when they were not.

Contextual information biases perceptual processing in a wide variety of situations.

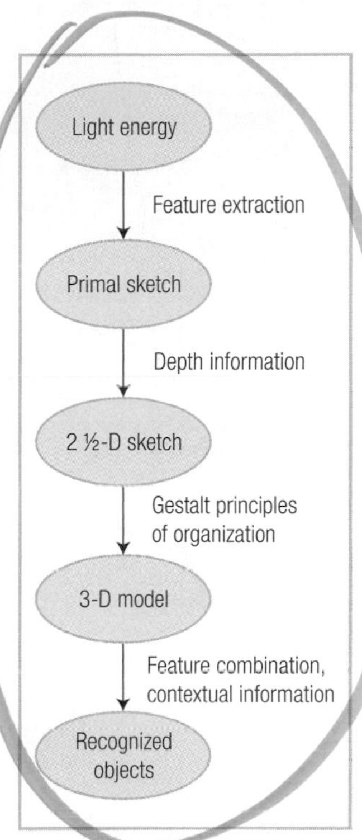

FIGURE 2.32 How information flows from the environment and is processed into our perceptual representation of it. The ovals represent different levels of information in Marr's (1982) model and the lines are labeled with the perceptual processes that transform one level of information into the next.

Conclusions

This chapter discusses how the neurons process sensory information, deliver it to the higher centers in the brain, and how the information becomes recognizable as objects. Figure 2.32 depicts the overall flow of information processing in the case of vision perception. Perception begins with light energy from the external environment. Receptors, such as those on the retina, transform this energy into neural information. Early sensory processing makes initial sense of the information. Features are extracted to yield what Marr called the **primal sketch.** These features are combined with depth information to get a representation of the location of surfaces in space; this is Marr's $2^1/_2$-D sketch. The gestalt principles of organization are applied to segment the elements into objects; this is Marr's 3-D model. Finally, the features of these objects and the general context information are combined to recognize the objects. The output of this last level is what we are consciously aware of in perception, which is a representation of the objects and their locations in the environment. This information is the input to the higher level cognitive processes. Figure 2.32 illustrates an important point: A great deal of information processing must take place before we are consciously aware of the objects we are perceiving.

Questions for Thought

1. Figure 2.33a illustrates an optical illusion called Mach Bands after the Austrian physicist and philosopher, Ernst Mach, who discovered them. Each band is a uniform shade of gray and yet it appears lighter on the right side near the darker adjacent band, and it appears darker on the left side near the lighter band. Can you explain why, using on-off cells, edge detectors, and bar detectors (see Figures 2.7 & 2.8)?
2. Use the Gestalt principles to explain why we tend to see two triangles in Figure 2.33b.
3. Rather than Biederman's geon proposal (see Figure 2.20), which involves recognizing objects by recognizing abstract features of their components, Ullman (2006) proposes we recognize objects by recognizing concrete fragments like those in Figure 2.33c. What might be the relative strengths

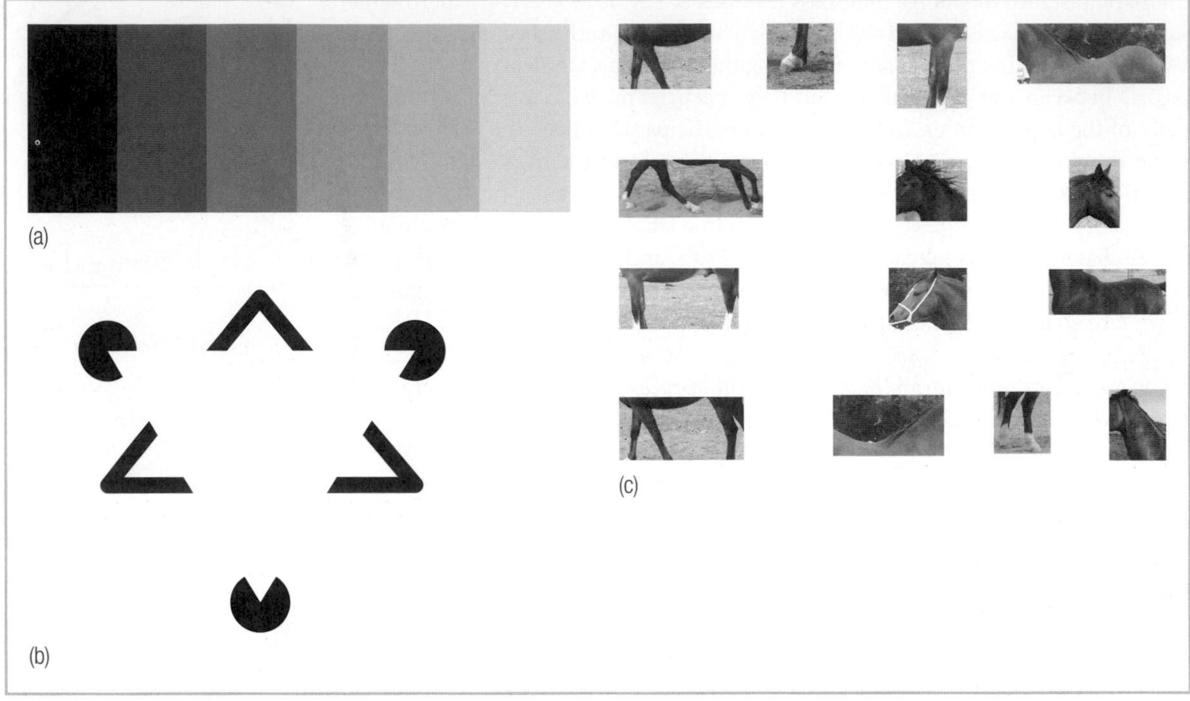

FIGURE 2.33 Figures for Questions for Thought. (a) Mach bands; (b) demonstration of Gestalt principles of organization; (c) fragments for recognizing a horse from Ullman (2006).

of the geon theory versus the fragment-based theory?

4. In Figure 2.21, we see that presented with the stimulus "cdit," there is an increased tendency for participants to say that they have seen "edit," which makes a word. Some people describe this as a case of context distorting perception. Do you agree that this is a case of distortion?

Key Terms

2½-D sketch
3-D model
apperceptive agnosia
associative agnosia
bar detectors
bottom-up processing
categorical perception
change blindness
consonantal feature
edge detectors
feature analysis
feature maps
fovea
fusiform gryrus
fuzzy logical model of perception (FLMP)
geons
gestalt principles of organization
phonemes
phoneme-restoration effect
place of articulation
primal sketch
prosopagnosia
recognition-by-components theory
template matching
top-down processing
visual agnosia
voicing
word superiority effect

3

Attention and Performance

Chapter 2 described how the human visual system and other perceptual systems simultaneously process information from all over their sensory fields. However, there are limits on how much we can do in parallel. There are points at which we can attend to only one spoken message or one visual object at a time. This chapter addresses how higher level cognition determines what to attend to

In this chapter, we will address these questions:

- In a busy world filled with sounds, how do we select what to listen to?
- How do we find meaningful information within a complex visual scene?
- What role does attention play in putting visual patterns together as recognizable objects?
- How do we coordinate parallel activities like driving a car and holding a conversation?

Serial Bottlenecks

Psychologists have proposed that there are **serial bottlenecks** in human information processing, points at which it is no longer possible to continue processing everything in parallel. For example, it is generally accepted that there are limits to parallelism in the motor systems. Although most of us can perform separate actions simultaneously when the actions involve different motor systems (such as walking and chewing gum), we have difficulty in getting one motor system to do two things at once. Thus, even though we have two hands, we have only one system for moving our hands, so it is hard to get our two hands to move in different ways at the same time. Think of the familiar problem of trying to pat your head while rubbing your stomach. It is hard to prevent one of the movements from dominating—one tends to wind up rubbing one's head or patting one's stomach.[1] The many human motor systems—one for moving feet, one for moving hands, one for moving eyes, and so on—can and do work independently and separately, but it is difficult to get any one of these systems to do two things at the same time.

One question that has occupied psychologists is how early do the bottlenecks occur: before we perceive the stimulus, after we perceive the stimulus but before we think about it, or only just before motor action is required? Common sense suggests that there must be a certain amount of serial thinking before motor action can occur. For instance, we find it basically impossible to add two digits and multiply them simultaneously. Still, there remains the question of just where the bottlenecks in information processing lie. Various theories about when they happen are referred to as **early-selection theories** or **late-selection theories,** depending on when they propose that bottlenecks take place. This question is one of those examined by psychologists who are interested in studying **attention.** Wherever there is a bottleneck, our cognitive processes must select which pieces of information to attend to and which to ignore. A related research question concerns *how* we select what to attend to.

In addition to the question of where information selection takes place in the information-processing stream, researchers have asked the question of what factors determine what we attend to. A major distinction is made between goal-directed factors (sometimes called endogenous control) and stimulus-driven factors (sometimes called exogenous control). To illustrate the distinction, Corbetta and Shulman (2002) ask us to imagine ourselves at the El Prado Museum in Madrid, looking at Bosch's painting *The Garden of Earthly Delights* (see Color Plate 3.1). Initially, our eyes will be probably be drawn to large, salient objects like the instrument in the center of picture. This would be an instance of stimulus-driven attention—it is not that we wanted to attend to this; it just grabbed our attention. However, our guide may start to comment on a "small animal playing a musical instrument." Now we have a goal and will direct our attention over the picture to find the object being described. Continuing their story, Corbetta and Shulman ask us to imagine that we hear an alarm system starting to ring in the next room. Now a stimulus-driven factor has intervened, and our attention will be drawn away from our goal of understanding our guide and the picture and switch to the adjacent room. Corbetta and Shulman argue that somewhat different brain systems control **goal-directed attention** versus **stimulus-driven** attention. For instance, neural imaging evidence suggests that the goal-directed attentional system is more left lateralized, whereas the stimulus-driven system is more right lateralized.

The brain regions that select information to process can be distinguished (to an approximation) from those that process the information selected. Figure 3.1

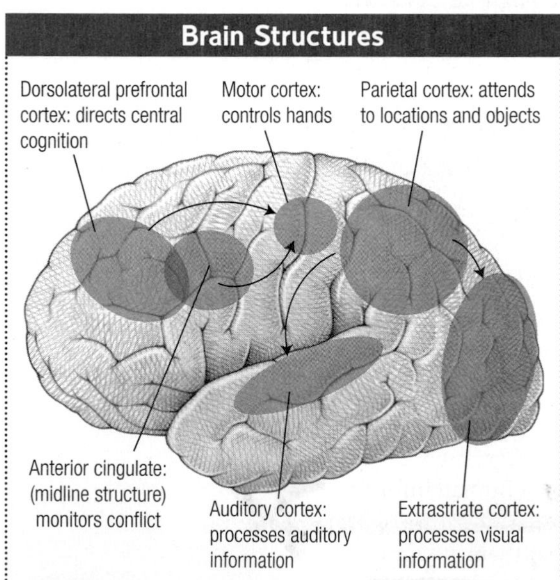

FIGURE 3.1 A representation of some of the brain areas involved in attention and some to the perceptual and motor regions they control. The parietal regions are particularly important in directing perceptual resources. The prefrontal regions (dorsolateral prefrontal cortex, anterior cingulate) are particularly important in executive control.

[1] Drummers (including my son) are particularly good at doing this—I definitely am not a drummer. This suggests that the real problem might be motor timing.

highlights the parietal cortex, which influences information processing in regions such as the visual cortex and auditory cortex. It also highlights prefrontal regions that influence processing in the motor area and more posterior regions. These prefrontal regions include the dorsolateral prefrontal cortex and, well below the surface, the anterior cingulate cortex. The regions that do the selecting and direct the processing are responsible for attentional control. As this chapter proceeds, it will elaborate on the research involving the various brain regions in Figure 3.1.

- *Attentional systems select information to process at serial bottlenecks where it is no longer possible to do things in parallel.*

Auditory Attention

Some of the early research on attention was concerned with auditory attention. Much of this research centered on the **dichotic listening task.** In a typical dichotic listening experiment, illustrated in Figure 3.2, participants wear a set of headphones. They hear two messages at the same time, one entering each ear, and are asked to "shadow" one of the two messages (i.e., repeat back the words from one message only). Most participants are able to attend to one message and tune out the other.

Psychologists (e.g., Cherry, 1953; Moray, 1959) have discovered that very little information about the unattended message is processed in a dichotic listening task. After hearing the messages, participants report that they can tell whether the unattended message was a human voice or a noise; whether

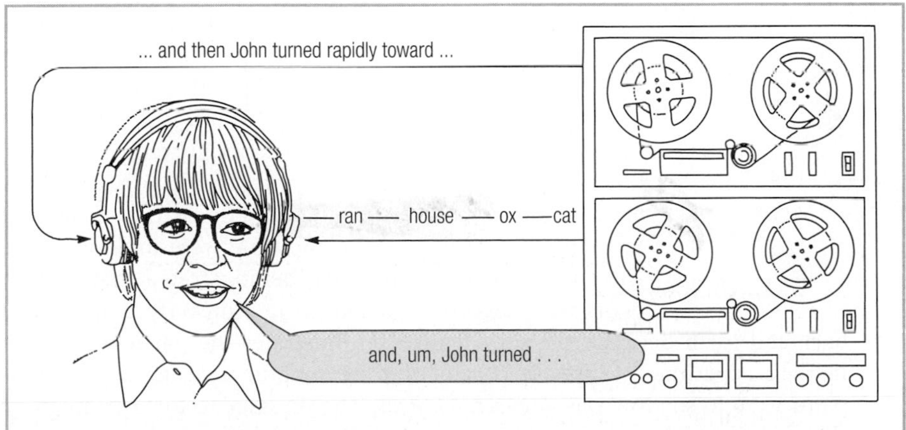

FIGURE 3.2 A typical dichotic listening task. Different messages are presented to the left and right ears, and the participant attempts to "shadow" the message entering one ear. (From Lindsay & Norman, 1977. Reprinted by permission of the publisher. © 1977 by Academic Press.)

the human voice was male or female; and whether the sex of the speaker changed during the test. This limited information is often all that they can report. They cannot tell what language was spoken or remember any of the words, even if the same word was repeated over and over again. An analogy is often made between performing this task and being at a cocktail party, where a guest tunes in to one message (a conversation) and filters out others. This is an example of goal-directed processing—the listener selects the message to be processed. However, to return to the distinction between goal-directed and stimulus-driven processing, important stimulus information can disrupt our goals. We have probably all experienced the situation in which we are listening intently to one person and hear our name mentioned by someone else. It is very hard in this situation to keep your attention on what the original speaker is saying.

The Filter Theory

Broadbent (1958) proposed a particular early-selection theory called the **filter theory** to account for these results. His basic assumption was that sensory information comes through the system until some bottleneck is reached. At that point, a person chooses which message to process on the basis of some physical characteristic. The person is said to filter out the other information. In a dichotic listening task, it was assumed that the message to each ear was registered but that at some point the participant selected one ear to listen with. At a cocktail party, we pick which speaker to follow on the basis of physical characteristics, such as the pitch of the speaker's voice.

FIGURE 3.3 An illustration of the shadowing task in the Gray and Wedderburn (1960) experiment. The participant follows the meaningful message as it moves from ear to ear. (After Klatzky, 1975. Adapted by permission of the publisher. © 1975 by W. H. Freeman.)

A crucial feature of Broadbent's original filter model is its proposal that we select a message to process on the basis of physical characteristics such as ear or pitch. This hypothesis made a certain amount of neurophysiological sense. Messages entering each ear arrive on different nerves. Nerves also vary in which frequencies they carry from each ear. Thus, we might imagine that the brain, in some way, selects certain nerves to "pay attention to."

People can certainly choose to attend to a message on the basis of its physical characteristics. There is evidence, however, that we can also select messages to process on the basis of their semantic content. In one study, Gray and Wedderburn (1960), who at the time were undergraduate students at Oxford University, demonstrated that participants were successful in following a message that jumped back and forth between the ears. Figure 3.3 illustrates the participants' task in their experiment. Suppose part of the meaningful message that participants were to shadow was *dogs scratch fleas.* The message to one ear might be *dogs six fleas,* whereas the message to the other might be *eight scratch two.* Instructed to shadow the meaningful message, participants would report *dogs scratch fleas.* Thus, participants can shadow a message on the basis of meaning rather than on the basis of what each ear physically hears.

Treisman (1960) looked at a situation in which participants were instructed to shadow a particular ear (Figure 3.4). The message in the ear to be shadowed was meaningful up to a certain point; then it turned into a random sequence of words. Simultaneously, the meaningful message switched to the other ear—the one to which the participant had not been attending. Some participants switched ears, against instructions, and continued to follow the meaningful message. Others continued to follow the shadowed ear. Thus, it seems that sometimes people use the physical ear to select which message to follow, and sometimes they choose semantic content.

I SAW THE GIRL/Song was wishing . . .
. . . me that bird
JUMPING IN THE STREET.
The to-be-shadowed ear
I SAW THE GIRL JUMPING . . .

FIGURE 3.4 An illustration of the Treisman (1960) experiment. The meaningful message moves to the other ear, and the participant sometimes continues to shadow it against instructions. (After Klatzky, 1975. Adapted by permission of the publisher. © 1975 by W. H. Freeman.)

Broadbent's filter model proposes that we use physical features, such as ear or pitch, to select one message to process, but it has been shown that people can also use the meaning of the message as the basis for selection.

The Attenuation Theory and the Late-Selection Theory

To account for these kinds of results, Treisman (1964) proposed a modification of the Broadbent model that has come to be known as the **attenuation theory.** This model hypothesized that certain messages would be weakened but not filtered out entirely on the basis of their physical properties. Thus, in a dichotic listening task, participants would minimize the signal from the unattended ear but not eliminate it. Semantic selection criteria could apply to all messages, whether they were attenuated or not. If the message were attenuated, it would be harder to apply these selection criteria, but it would still be possible, as in the Gray and Wedderburn (1960) experiment. Treisman (personal communication, 1978) emphasized that in her 1960 experiment, most participants actually continued to shadow the prescribed ear. It was easier to follow the message that is not being attenuated than to apply semantic criteria to switch attention to the attenuated message.

An alternative explanation was offered by J. A. Deutsch and D. Deutsch (1963) in their **late-selection theory.** They proposed that all the information is processed completely without attentuation. Their hypothesis was that the capacity limitation is in the response system, not the perceptual system. They claimed that people can perceive multiple messages but that they can shadow only one message at a time. Thus, people need some basis for selecting which message to shadow. If they use meaning as the criterion (either according to or in contradiction to instructions), they will switch ears to follow the message. If they use the ear of origin in deciding what to attend to, they will shadow the chosen ear.

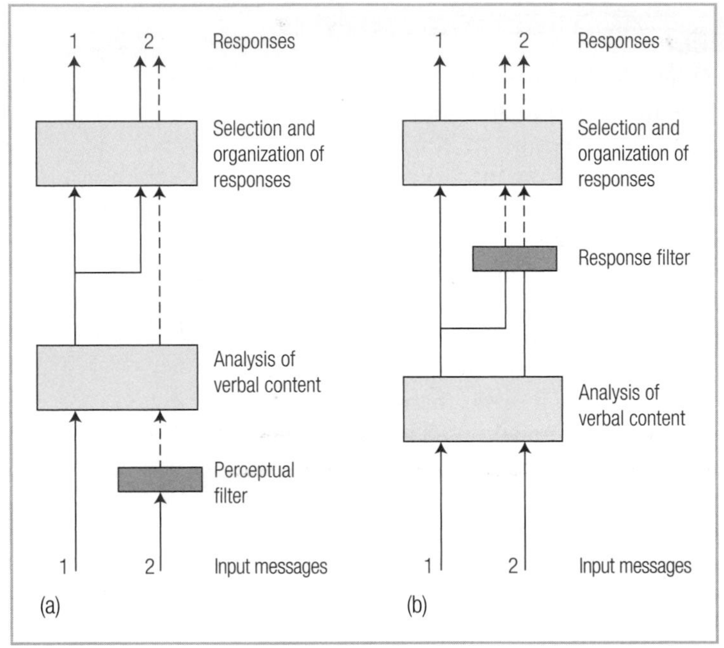

FIGURE 3.5 Treisman and Geffen's illustration of attentional limitations produced by (a) Treisman's (1964) attenuation theory and (b) Deutsch and Deutsch's (1963) late-selection theory. (From Treisman & Geffen, 1967. Reprinted by permission of the publisher. © 1967 by the *Quarterly Journal of Experimental Psychology*.)

The difference between the two theories is illustrated in Figure 3.5. Both models assume that there is some filter or bottleneck in processing. Treisman's theory (Figure 3.5a) assumes that the filter selects which message to attend to, whereas Deutsch and Deutsch's theory (Figure 3.5b) assumes that the filter occurs after the perceptual stimulus has been analyzed for verbal content. Treisman and Geffen (1967) tried to address the difference between these two theories. They used a dichotic listening task in which participants had to shadow one message and also had to process both messages for a target word. If they heard the target word, they were to signal by tapping. According to the Deutsch and Deutsch late-selection theory, messages from both ears would get through and participants should have been able to detect the critical word equally well in either ear. In contrast, the attenuation theory predicted much less detection in the unshadowed ear because the message would be attenuated. In the experiment, participants detected 87% of the target words in the shadowed ear and only 8% percent in the unshadowed ear. Other evidence consistent with the attenuation theory was reported by A. M. Treisman and Riley (1969) and by Johnston and Heinz (1978).

There is neural evidence for a version of the attenuation theory that asserts that there is both enhancement of the signal coming from the attended ear and attenuation of the signal coming from the unattended ear. The primary auditory area of the cortex (see Figure 3.1) shows an enhanced response to auditory signals coming from the ear the listener is attending to and a decreased response to signals coming from the other ear. Through ERP recording, Woldorff et al. (1993) showed that these responses occur between 20 and 50 ms after stimulus onset.

The enhanced responses occur much sooner in auditory processing than the point at which the meaning of the message can be identified. There is also evidence for enhancement of the message in the auditory cortex on the basis of features other than location. For instance, Zatorre, Mondor, and Evans (1999) found in a PET study that when people attend to a message on the basis of pitch, there is similar enhancement (registered as increased activation) in the auditory cortex. This study also found increased activation in the parietal areas that direct attention.

Although auditory attention can enhance processing in the primary auditory cortex, there is no evidence of reliable effects of attention on earlier portions of auditory processing, such as in the auditory nerve or in brain-stem processing (Picton & Hillyard, 1974). The various results we have reviewed suggest that the primary auditory cortex is the earliest area to be influenced by attention. It should be stressed that the effects at the auditory cortex are a matter of attenuation and enhancement. Messages are not completely filtered out and so it is still possible to select them at later points of processing.

○ *Attention can enhance or reduce the magnitude of response to an auditory signal in the primary auditory cortex.*

● Visual Attention

The bottleneck in visual information processing is even more apparent than the one in auditory information processing. As we saw in Chapter 2, the retina varies in acuity, with the greatest acuity in a very small area called the fovea. Although the human eye registers a large part of the visual field, the fovea registers only a small fraction of that field. Thus, in choosing where to focus our vision, we also choose to devote most of our visual processing resources to a particular part of the visual field, and we attenuate the resources allocated to processing other parts of the field. Usually, we are attending to that part of the visual field on which we are focusing. For instance, as we read, we move our eyes so that we are fixating the words we are attending to.

The focus of visual attention is not always identical with the part of the visual field being processed by the fovea, however. People can be instructed to fixate on one part of the visual field (making that part the focus of the fovea) and attend to another, nonfoveal region of the visual field.[2] In one experiment, Posner, Nissen, and Ogden (1978) had participants focus on a constant point and then presented them with a stimulus 7° to the left or the right of the fixation point. In some trials, participants were told on which side the stimulus was likely to occur; in other trials, there was no such warning. When there was a warning, it was correct 80% of the time—but 20% of the time the stimulus appeared on the unexpected side. The researchers monitored eye movements and included only those trials in which the eyes had stayed on the fixation

[2] This is what quarterbacks are supposed to do when they pass the football, so that they don't "give away" the position of the intended receiver.

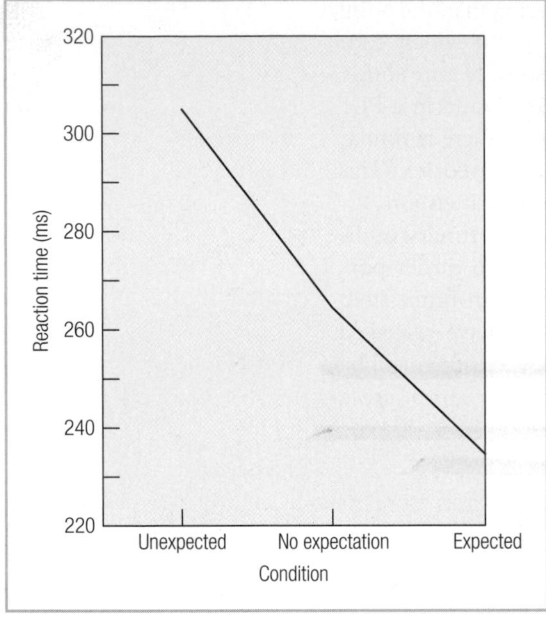

FIGURE 3.6 The results of an experiment to determine how people react to a stimulus that occurs 7° to the left or right of the fixation point. The graph shows participants' reaction times to expected, unexpected, and neutral (no expectation) signals. (From Posner et al., 1978. Reprinted by permission of the publisher. © 1978 by Erlbaum.)

point. Figure 3.6 shows the time required to judge the stimulus if it appeared in the expected location (80% of the time), if the participant had not been given a cue (50% of the time), and if it appeared in the unexpected location (20% of the time). Participants were able to shift their attention from where their eyes were fixated: Their responses to the stimuli were faster when the stimulus appeared in the expected location and slower when it appeared in the unexpected location.

Posner, Snyder, and Davidson (1980) found that people can attend to regions of the visual field as far as 24° from the fovea. Although visual attention can be moved without accompanying eye movements, people usually do move their eyes, so that the fovea processes the portion of the visual field to which they are attending. Posner (1988) pointed out that successful control of eye movements requires us to attend to places outside the fovea. That is, we must attend to and identify an interesting nonfoveal region so that we can guide our eyes to fixate on that region to achieve the greatest acuity in processing it. Thus, a shift of attention often precedes the corresponding eye movement.

To process a complex visual scene, we must move our attention around in the visual field to track the visual information. This process is like shadowing a conversation. Neisser and Becklen (1975) performed the visual analog of the auditory shadowing task. They had participants observe two videotapes superimposed over each other. One was of two people playing a hand-slapping game, the other of some people playing a basketball game. Figure 3.7 shows how the situation appeared to the participants. They were instructed to pay attention to one of the two films and to watch for odd events such as the two players in the hand-slapping game pausing and shaking hands. Participants were able to monitor one film successfully and reported filtering out the other. When asked to monitor both films for odd events, the participants experienced great difficulty and missed many of the critical events.

FIGURE 3.7 Frames from the two films used by Neisser and Becklen in their visual analog of the auditory shadowing task. (a) The "hand-game" film; (b) the basketball film; and (c) the two figures superimposed. (From Neisser & Becklen, 1975. Reprinted by permission of the publisher. © 1975 by Academic Press.)

As Neisser and Becklen (1975) noted, this situation involved an interesting combination of the use of physical cues and the use of content cues. Participants moved their eyes and focused their attention in such a way that the critical aspects of the monitored event fell on their fovea and the center of their attentive spotlight. On the other hand, the only way they knew how to move their eyes to follow an event was by making reference to the content of the event they were processing. Thus, physical cues facilitated their processing of the critical film, which in turn facilitated extracting content so they would know where to move their eyes.

FIGURE 3.8 An example of a picture used in the study of O'Craven et al. (1999). When the face is attended, there is activation in the fusiform face area, and when the house is attended, there is activation in the parahippocampal place area.

Figure 3.8 shows examples of the overlapping stimuli used in an experiment by O'Craven, Downing, and Kanwisher (1999) to study the neural consequences of attending to one object or the other. Participants in their experiment saw a series of pictures that consisted of faces superimposed on houses. They were instructed to either look for repetition of the same face in the series or repetition of the same house. Recall from Chapter 2 that there is a region of the fusiform gyrus, the fusiform face area, which becomes active when people are observing faces. There is another area within the temporal cortex, the parahippocampal place area, which becomes more active when people are observing places. What is special about these pictures is that they consisted of both places and locations. Which region would become active—the fusiform face area or the parahippocampal place area? As the reader might suspect, the answer depended on what the participant was attending to. When participants were looking for repetition of faces, the fusiform face area became more active; when they were looking for repetition of places, the parahippocampal place area became more active. Attention was able to select which region of the temporal cortex was engaged in the processing of the stimulus.

People can focus their attention on parts of the visual field and move their focus of attention to process what they are interested in

The Neural Basis of Visual Attention

It appears that the neural mechanisms underlying visual attention are very similar to those underlying auditory attention. Just as auditory attention directed to one ear enhances the cortical signal from that ear, visual attention directed to a spatial location appears to enhance the cortical signal from that location. If a person attends to a particular spatial location, a distinct neural response (detected using ERP records) in the visual cortex occurs within 70 to 90 ms after the onset of the stimulus. On the other hand, when a person is attending to a particular object (attending to chairs and not tables, say), rather than to a particular location in space, we do not see a response for more than 200 ms. Thus, it

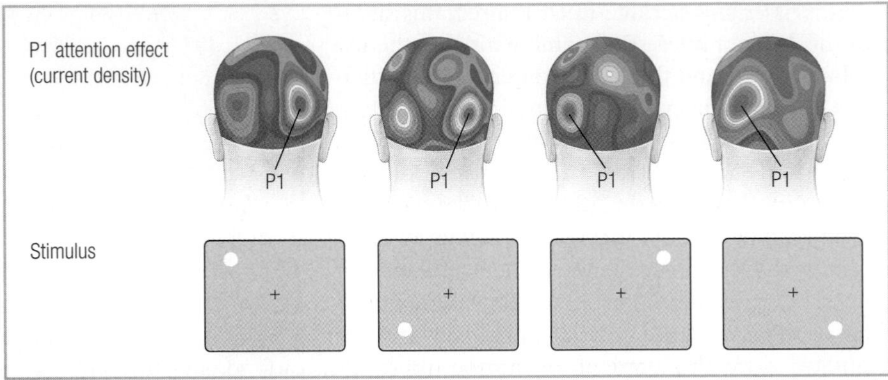

FIGURE 3.9 Results from an experiment by Mangun, Hillyard, and Luck. Distribution of scalp activity recorded by ERP when a participant was attending to one of the four different regions of the visual array depicted in the right-hand column while fixating on the center of the screen. The greatest activity was recorded over the side of the scalp opposite the side of the visual field where the object appeared, confirming that there is enhanced neural processing in portions of the visual cortex corresponding to the location of visual attention. (After Mangun et al., 1993. Adapted by permission of the publisher. © 1993 by MIT Press.)

appears to take more effort to direct visual attention on the basis of content than on the basis of physical features, just as is the case with auditory attention.

Mangun, Hillyard, and Luck (1993) had participants fixate on the center of a computer screen, then judge the lengths of bars presented in positions different from the fixation location (upper left, lower left, upper right, and lower right). They documented how much an ERP recording was affected at various locations across the back of the scalp. Figure 3.9 shows the distribution of scalp activity when a participant was attending to one of the four different regions of the visual array (while fixating on the center of the screen). Consistent with the topographic organization of the visual cortex, there was greatest activity over the side of the scalp opposite the side of the visual field where the object appeared. Recall from Chapters 1 and 2 (see Figure 2.6) that the visual cortex (at the back of the head) is topographically organized, with each visual field (left or right) represented in the opposite hemisphere. Thus, it appears that there is enhanced neural processing in the portion of the visual cortex corresponding to the location of visual attention.

FIGURE 3.10 The experimental procedure in Roelfsema et al. (1998): (a) The monkey fixates the start point. (b) Two curves are presented, one of which links the start point to a target point. (c) The monkey saccades to the target point. The box represents the receptive field in the primary visual cortex V1.

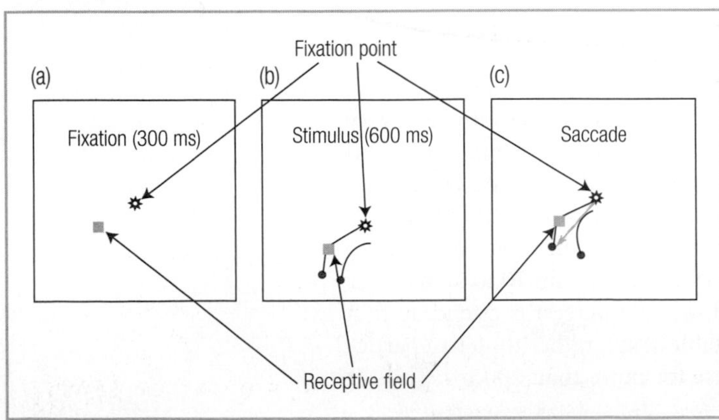

A study by Roelfsema, Lamme, and Spekrejse (1998) illustrates the impact of visual attention of information processing in the primary visual area of the macaque monkey. They trained monkeys to perform the rather complex task illustrated in Figure 3.10. A trial in the experiment would begin with the monkey fixating on a particular stimulus in the visual field, as in part (a) of the figure. Then two curves would appear, as in part (b), only one of which connected the original object to the fixation point. The monkey had to remain fixated on this point for 600 ms and then perform a saccade (an eye movement) to the end of the curve that connected the original point (part c). While monkeys performed this task, Roelfsema et al. recorded from cells in the monkey's primary visual cortex (where cells with receptive fields like those in Figure 2.8 are found). Indicated by the square in Figure 3.10 is a receptive field of one of these cells. It shows increased response when a line falls on that part of the visual field and so responds when the curve appears that crosses it. The cell responds more during the 600-ms waiting period when the receptive is on the curve that connects the fixation point to the destination than when it is on the other curve. The monkey must shift its attention along this curve to determine where to saccade to, and this shift of attention causes the line detectors in V1 to respond more strongly.

When people attend to a particular spatial location, there is greater neural processing in portions of the visual cortex corresponding to that location.

Visual Search

People are able to select stimuli to attend to, either in the visual or auditory domain, on the basis of physical properties and, in particular, on the basis of location. Although selection based on simple features can occur early and quickly in the visual system, not everything people look for can be defined in terms of simple features. How do they find an object with particular higher order properties, such as the face of a friend in a crowd? In such cases, it seems that they must search through the faces in the crowd, looking for one that has the desired properties. Much of the research on visual attention has focused on how people perform such searches. Rather than study how people find faces in a crowd, however, researchers have tended to use simpler material. Figure 3.11, for instance, shows a portion of the display that Neisser (1964) used in one of the early studies. Try to find the first *K* in the set of letters displayed.

TWLN
XJBU
UDXI
HSFP
XSCQ
SDJU
PODC
ZVBP
PEVZ
SLRA
JCEN
ZLRD
XBOD
PHMU
ZHFK
PNJW
CQXT
GHNR
IXYD
QSVB
GUCH
OWBN
BVQN
FOAS
ITZN

FIGURE 3.11 A representation of lines 7–31 of the letter array used in Neisser's search experiment. (After Neisser, 1964. Adapted by permission of the publisher. © 1964 by *Scientific American*.)

Presumably, you tried to find the *K* by going through the letters row by row, looking for the target. Figure 3.12 graphs the average time it took participants in Neisser's experiment to find the letter as a function of which row it appeared in. The slope of the best-fitting function in the graph is about 0.6, which implies that participants took about 0.6 s to scan each line. When people engage in such searches, they appear to be allocating their attention intensely to the search process. For instance, brain-imaging experiments have found strong activation in the parietal cortex during such searches (see Kanwisher & Wojciulik, 2000, for a review).

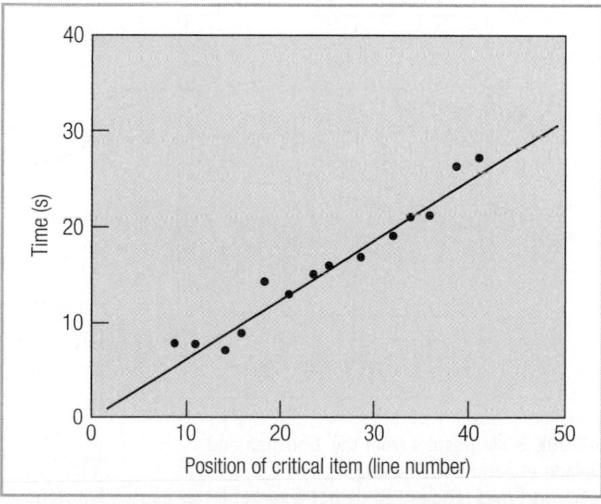

FIGURE 3.12 The time required to find a target letter in the array shown in Figure 3.9 as a function of the line number in which it appears. (After Neisser, 1964. Adapted by permission of the publisher. © 1964 by *Scientific American*.)

Although a search can be intense and difficult, it is not always that way. Sometimes we can find what we are looking for without much effort. If we know that

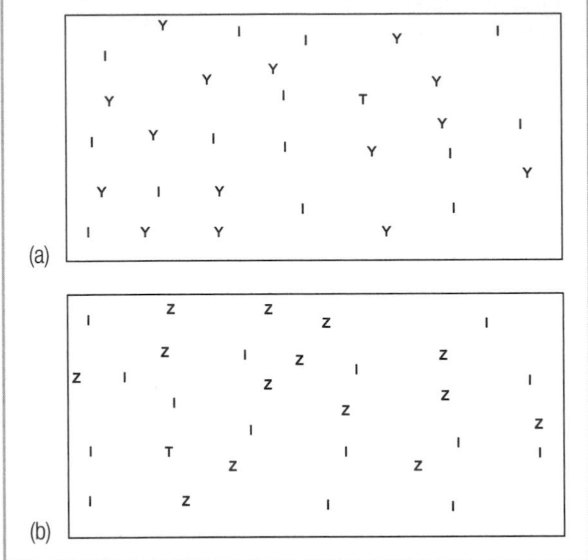

FIGURE 3.13 Stimuli used by Treisman and Gelade to determine how people identify objects in the visual field. They found that it is easier to pick out a target letter (*T*) from a group of distracter letters (*I*'s and *Y*'s) if (a) the target letter has a feature that makes it easily distinguishable from the distracters than if (b) the same target letter is in an array of distracters (*I*'s and *Z*'s) that offer no obvious distinctive features. (After Treisman & Gelade, 1980. Adapted by permission of the publisher. © 1980 by Cognitive Psychology.)

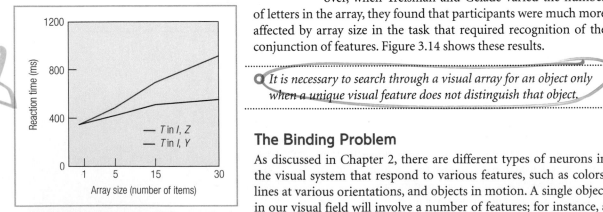

our friend is wearing a bright red jacket, it can be relatively easy to find him or her in the crowd, provided that no one else is wearing a bright red jacket. Our friend will just pop out of the crowd. Indeed, if there were just one red jacket in a sea of white jackets it would probably pop out even if we were not looking for it—an instance of stimulus-driven attention. It seems that if there is some distinctive feature in an array, we can find it without a search.

Treisman studied this sort of pop-out. For instance, Treisman and Gelade (1980) instructed participants to try to detect a *T* in an array of 30 *I*'s and *Y*'s (Figure 3.13a). They reasoned that participants could do this simply by looking for the crossbar feature of the *T* that distinguishes it from all *I*'s and *Y*'s. Participants took an average of about 400 ms to perform this task. Treisman and Gelade also asked participants to detect a *T* in an array of *I*'s and *Z*'s (Figure 3.13b). In this task, they could not use just the vertical bar or just the horizontal bar of the *T*; they would have to look for the conjunction of these features and perform the feature combination required in pattern recognition. It took participants more than 800 ms, on average, to find the letter in this case. Thus, a task requiring them to recognize the conjunction of features took about 400 ms longer than one in which perception of a single feature was sufficient. Moreover, when Treisman and Gelade varied the number of letters in the array, they found that participants were much more affected by array size in the task that required recognition of the conjunction of features. Figure 3.14 shows these results.

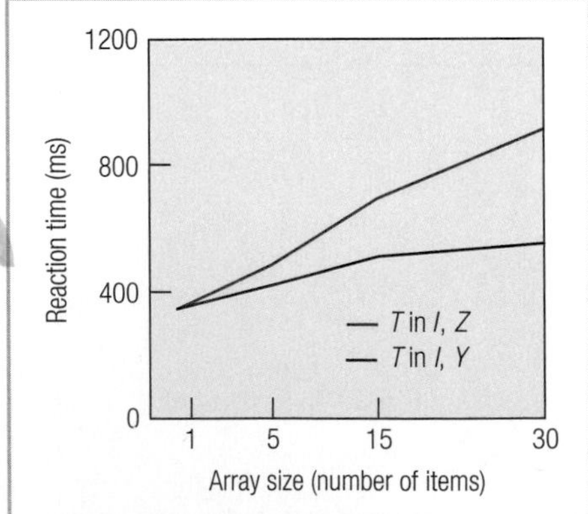

FIGURE 3.14 Results from the Treisman and Gelade experiment. The graph plots the average reaction times required to detect a target letter as a function of the number of distracters and whether the distracters contain separately all the features of the target. (After Treisman & Gelade, 1980. Adapted by permission of the publisher. © 1980 by *Cognitive Psychology*.)

It is necessary to search through a visual array for an object only when a unique visual feature does not distinguish that object.

The Binding Problem

As discussed in Chapter 2, there are different types of neurons in the visual system that respond to various features, such as colors, lines at various orientations, and objects in motion. A single object in our visual field will involve a number of features; for instance, a red vertical line combines the vertical feature and the red feature. The fact that different features of the same object are represented by different neurons gives rise to a logical question: How are these features put back together to produce perception of the object? This would not be much of a problem if there were a single object in the visual field. We could assume that all the features belonged to that object. But what if there are multiple objects in the field? For instance, suppose there were just two objects: a red vertical bar and a green horizontal bar. These two objects might result in the firing of neurons for red, neurons for green, neurons for vertical lines, and neurons for horizontal lines. If these firings were all that occurred, though, how would the visual system know it saw a red vertical bar and a green horizontal bar rather than a red horizontal bar and a green vertical bar? The question of how the brain puts together various features in the visual field is referred to as the **binding problem.**

Treisman (e.g., Treisman & Gelade, 1980) developed her **feature-integration theory** as an answer to the binding problem. She proposed that people must focus their attention on a stimulus before they can synthesize its features into a pattern. For instance, in the example just given, the visual system can first direct its attention to the location of the red vertical bar and synthesize that object, then direct its attention to the green horizontal bar and synthesize that object. According to Treisman, people must search through an array when they need to synthesize features to recognize an object (for instance, when trying to identify a *K*, which consists of a vertical line and two diagonal lines). When there is a single unique feature, such as a red jacket or a line at a particular orientation, we can move our attention directly to the object and recognize it, thus avoiding the need to search.

The binding problem is not just a hypothetical dilemma—it is something that humans actually suffer from. One source of evidence comes from studies of **illusory conjunctions** in which people report combinations of features that did not occur. For instance, Treisman and Schmidt (1982) looked at what happens to feature combinations when the stimuli are out of the focus of attention. Participants were asked to report the identity of two black digits flashed in one part of the visual field. This was their primary task, and it was where their attention was focused. In another part of the visual field, letters in various colors were presented. Thus, participants might be presented with a pink *T*, a yellow *S*, and a blue *N* in the unattended portion of the field. After they reported the numbers, participants were asked to report any letters they had seen and the colors of these letters. They reported seeing illusory conjunctions of features (e.g., a pink *S*) almost as often as they reported seeing correct combinations. Thus, it appears that we are able to combine features into an accurate perception only when our attention is focused on an object. Otherwise, we perceive the features but may well combine them into a perception of objects that were never there. Although rather special circumstances are required to produce illusory conjunctions in an ordinary person, there are certain patients with damage to the parietal cortex who are particularly prone to such illusions. For instance, one patient studied by Friedman-Hill, Robertson, and Treisman (1995) confused which letters were presented in which colors even when shown the letters for as long as 10 seconds.

A number of studies have been conducted on the neural mechanisms involved in binding together the features of a single object. The neurons in visual area V4 have large receptive fields (several degrees of visual angle), and multiple objects in a display may be within the visual field of a single neuron. Luck, Chelazzi, Hiillyard, and Desimone (1997) trained macaque monkeys to fixate on a certain part in the visual field and recorded neurons around this region. They found neurons that were specific to particular types of objects. For instance, they found a cell that responded to a blue vertical bar. What happens when a blue vertical bar and a green horizontal bar are presented both within the receptive field of this cell? If the monkey attended to the blue vertical bar, the rate of response of the cell will remain at the same level as it would have had there been only a blue vertical bar alone. On the other hand, if the monkey focused on the green horizontal bar, the rate of firing of this same cell will be greatly depressed. Thus, the same stimulus (blue vertical bar plus green horizontal bar) can evoke different responses depending on which object is attended to. It is speculated that this phenomenon occurs because attention suppresses responses to all features in the receptive field except those at the attended location.

FIGURE 3.15 Single frame from the movie used by Simons and Chabris to demonstrate the effects of sustained attention. When participants were intent on tracking the ball passed among the players dressed in T-shirts, they tended not to notice the black gorilla walking through the room. (From Simons & Chabris, 1999. Reprinted by permission of the publisher. © 1999 by *Perception*.)

Similar results have been obtained in fMRI experiments with humans. Kastner, DeWeerd, Desimone, and Ungerleider (1998) measured the fMRI signal in visual areas that responded to stimuli presented in one region of the visual field. They found that when attention was directed away from that region, the fMRI response to stimuli in that region decreased; but when attention was focused on that region, the fMRI response was maintained. These experiments indicate enhanced neural processing of attended objects and locations.

A striking demonstration of the effects of sustained attention was reported by Simons and Chabris (1999). They asked participants to watch a video in which a team dressed in black tossed a basketball back and forth and a team dressed in white did the same (Figure 3.15). Participants were instructed to count either the number of times the team in black tossed the ball or the number of times the team in white did so. Presumably, in one condition participants were looking for events involving the team in black and in the other for events involving the team in white. Because the players were intermixed, the task was difficult and required sustained attention. In the middle of the game, a person in a black gorilla suit walked through the room. When participants were tracking the team in white, they noticed the black gorilla only 8% of the time; when they were tracking the team in black, they noticed it 67% of the time. They were so fixed on searching the video for events involving team members dressed in white that they completely missed an event involving a black object. People passively watching the video never miss the black gorilla. The actual video is currently available from the demonstrations page of Simons's Visual Cognition Lab:

http://viscog.beckman.uiuc.edu/djs_lab/demos.html

For feature information to be synthesized into a pattern, it must be in the focus of attention.

Neglect of the Visual Field

We have discussed the evidence that visual attention to a spatial location results in enhanced activation in the appropriate portion of the primary visual cortex. The neural structures that control this shift of attention, however, appear to be located elsewhere. Three areas of the monkey brain have been shown to be involved in controlling attention (S. E. Peterson, Robinson, & Morris, 1987; Wurtz, Goldberg, & Robinson, 1980). These areas are the superior colliculus, the posterior parietal lobe, and a midbrain area known as the pulvinar. Damage to these areas in human patients, particularly to the parietal lobe (see Figure 3.1), has been shown to result in deficits in visual attention. For instance, Posner, Walker, Friedrich, and Rafal (1984) showed that patients with parietal lobe injuries have difficulty in disengaging attention from one side of the visual field.

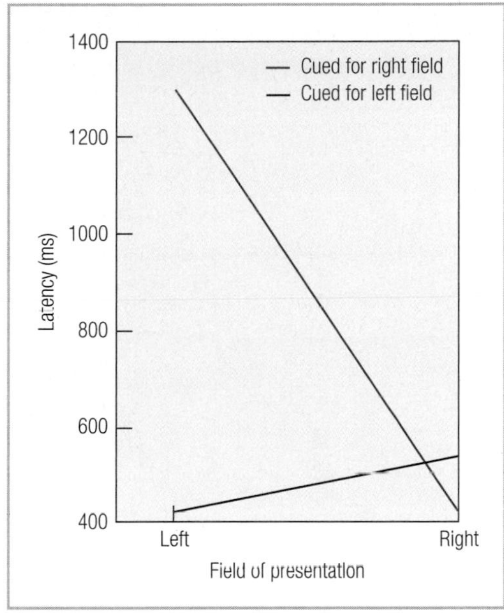

FIGURE 3.16 The attention deficit shown by a patient with right parietal lobe damage when switching attention to the left visual field. (From Posner, Cohen, & Rafal, 1982. Reprinted by permission of the publisher. © by the Royal Society of London.)

Damage to right parietal regions produces distinctive patterns of deficit. Posner, Cohen, and Rafal (1982) studied the attention deficit in one such patient. The patient was cued to expect a stimulus to the left or right of the fixation point, and 80% of the time that is where the stimulus was present. However, 20% of the time the stimulus appeared in the unexpected field. Figure 3.16 shows the time required to detect the stimulus as a function of which visual field it was presented in and which field had been cued. When the stimulus was presented in the right field, the patient showed only a little disadvantage if inappropriately cued. If the stimulus appeared in the left field, however, the patient showed a large deficit if inappropriately cued. Because the right parietal lobe processes the left visual field, damage to the right lobe impairs its ability to draw attention back to the left visual field once attention is focused on the right visual field. This sort of one-sided attentional deficit can be temporarily created in normal individuals by presenting TMS to the parietal cortex (Pascaul-Leone et al., 1994—see Chapter 1 for discussion of TMS).

A more extreme version of this attentional disorder is called unilateral visual neglect. Patients with damage to the right hemisphere completely ignore the left side of the visual field, and patients with damage to the left hemisphere ignore the right side of the field. Figure 3.17 shows the performance of a patient with damage to the right hemisphere, which caused her to neglect the left visual field (Albert, 1973). She had been instructed to put slashes through all the circles. As can be seen, she ignored the circles in the left part of her visual field. Such patients will often behave peculiarly. For instance, one patient failed to shave half of his face (Sacks, 1985).

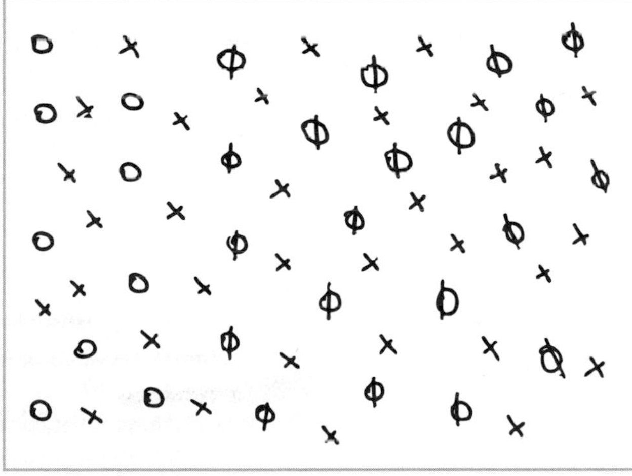

FIGURE 3.17 The performance of a patient with damage to the right hemisphere who had been asked to put slashes through all the circles. Because of the damage to the right hemisphere, she ignored the circles in the left part of her visual field. (From Ellis & Young, 1988. Reprinted by permission of the publisher. © 1988 by Erlbaum.)

It seems that the right parietal lobes are involved in allocating spatial attention in many modalities, not just the visual (Zatorre et al., 1999). For instance, when one attends to the location of auditory or visual stimuli, there is increased activation in the right parietal region. It also appears that the right parietal lobes are

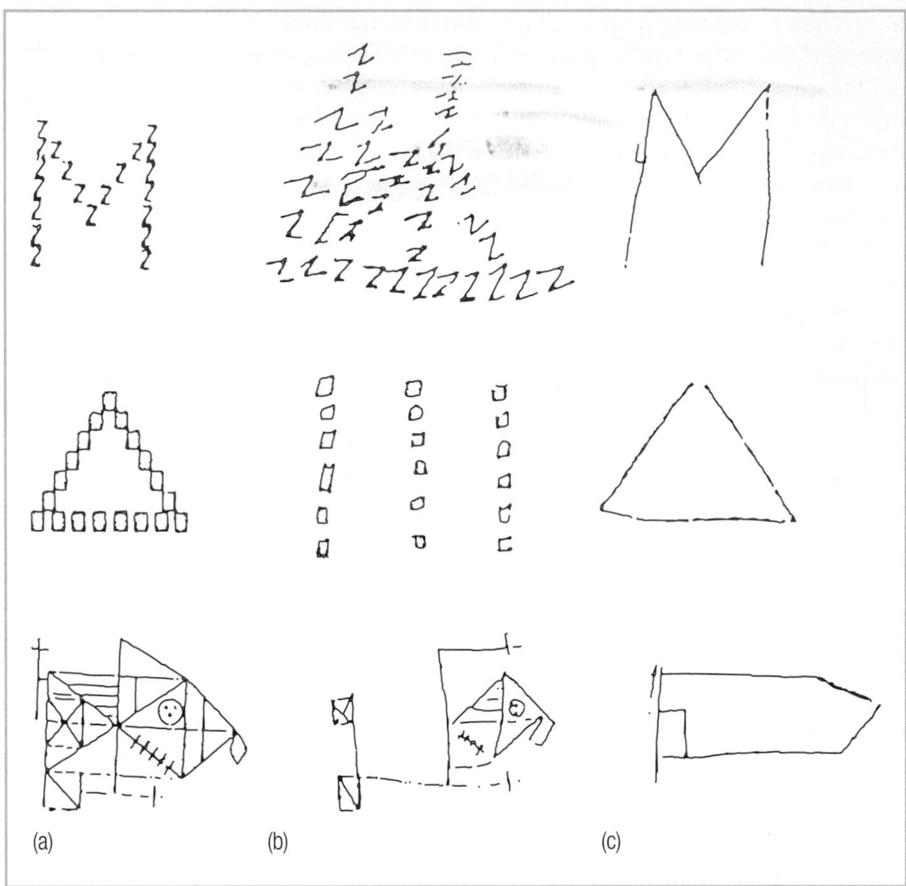

FIGURE 3.18 (a) The pictures presented to patients with parietal damage. (b) Examples of drawings made by patients with right-hemisphere damage. These patients could reproduce the specific components of the picture but not their spatial configuration. (c) Examples of drawings made by patients with left-hemisphere damage. These patients could reproduce the overall configuration but not the detail. (After Robertson & Lamb, 1991. Adapted by permission of the publisher. © 1991 by *Cognitive Psychology*.)

more responsible for the spatial allocation of attention and that this is why right parietal damage tends to produce such dramatic effects. Left parietal damage tends to produce a subtler pattern of deficits. Robertson and Rafal (2000) argue that the right parietal lobe is responsible for attention to such global features as spatial location, whereas the left parietal region is responsible for directing attention to local aspects of objects. Figure 3.18 is a striking illustration of the different types of deficits associated with left and right parietal damage. Patients were asked to draw the objects in Figure 3.18a. Patients with right parietal damage (Figure 3.18b) were able to reproduce the specific components of the picture but were not able to reproduce their spatial configuration. In contrast, patients with left parietal damage (Figure 3.18c) were able to reproduce the overall configuration, but not the detail. Similarly, brain-imaging studies have found more activation of the right parietal region when a person is responding to global patterns and more activation of the left hemisphere when a person is attending to local patterns (Fink et al., 1996; Martinez et al., 1997).

- *Parietal regions are responsible for the allocation of attention, with the right hemisphere more concerned with global features and the left hemisphere with local features.*

Object-Based Attention

So far we have talked about space-based attention, where people allocate their attention to a region of space. There is also evidence, though, for object-based attention, where people focus their attention on particular objects rather than regions of space. An experiment by Behrmann, Zemel, and Mozer (1998) is an example of the research that shows people sometimes find it easier to attend to an object than to a location. Figure 3.19 illustrates some of the stimuli used in the experiment. Participants were asked to judge whether the numbers of bumps on the two ends of objects were the same. The left column shows instances in which the numbers of bumps were the same, the right column instances in which the numbers were not the same. Participants made these judgments faster when the bumps were on the same object (top and bottom rows in Figure 3.19) than when they were on different objects (middle row). This result occurred despite the fact that when the bumps were on different objects, they were located closer together, which should have facilitated judgment. Behrmann et al. argue that participants can shift attention to one object at a time, but not one location at a time. Therefore, when the bumps were all on the same object, participants did not need to shift their attention between objects.

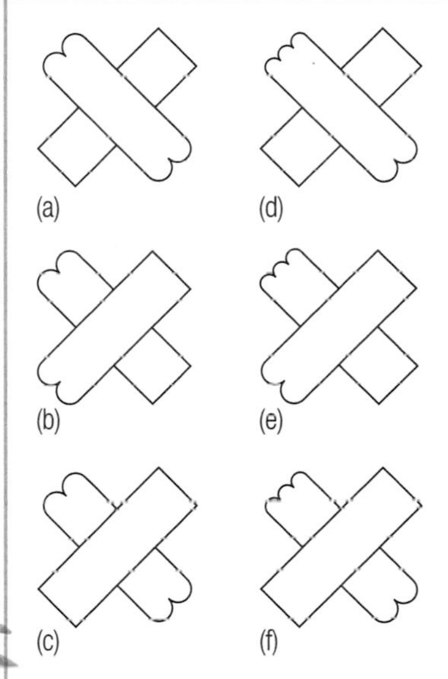

FIGURE 3.19 Stimuli used in an experiment by Behrmann, Zemel, and Mozer to demonstrate that it is sometimes easier to attend to an object than to a location. The left and right columns indicate same and different judgments, respectively; and the rows from top to bottom indicate the single-object, two-object, and occluded conditions, respectively. (From Behrmann, Zemel, & Mozer, 1998. Reprinted by permission of the publisher. © 1998 by the *Journal of Experimental Psychology: Human Perception and Performance*.)

Other evidence for object-centered attention involves a phenomenon called **inhibition of return.** If we have looked at a particular region of space, we find it harder to return our attention to that region. This phenomenon also makes sense. If we are searching for something and have already looked at a location, we would prefer our visual system to find other locations to look at rather than return to an already searched location. If we move our eyes to location A and then to location B, we are slower to return our eyes to location A than to some new location C. This is also true when we move our attention without moving our eyes (Posner, Rafal, Chaote, & Vaughn, 1985).

Tipper, Driver, and Weaver (1991) performed one demonstration of the inhibition of return that also provided evidence for object-based attention. In their experiments, participants viewed three squares in a frame, similar to what is shown in each part of Figure 3.20. In one condition, the squares did not move (unlike the moving condition illustrated in Figure 3.20, which we will discuss in the next paragraph). The participants' attention was drawn to one of the outer squares by making it flicker. Attention was drawn back to the center square 200 ms later by making that square flicker. A probe was then presented in one of the two outer positions, and participants were instructed to press a key indicating that they had seen the probe. On average, they took 420 ms to

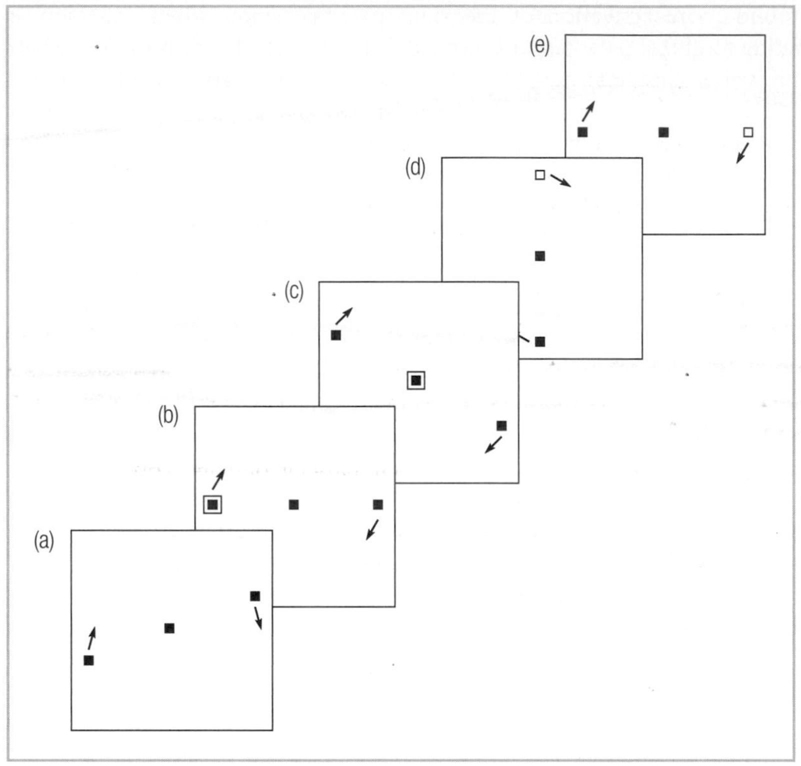

FIGURE 3.20 Examples of frames used in an experiment by Tipper, Driver, and Weaver to determine whether inhibition of return would attach to a particular object or to its location. Arrows represent motion. (a) Display onset, with no motion for 500 ms. After two moving frames, the three filled squares were horizontally aligned (b), whereupon the cue appeared (one of the boxes flickered). Clockwise motion then continued, with cueing in the center for the initial three frames (c–e). The outer squares continued to rotate clockwise (d) until they were horizontally aligned (e), at which point a probe was presented, as before. (From Tipper, Driver, & Weaver, 1991. Reprinted by permission of the publisher. © 1991 by the *Quarterly Journal of Experimental Psychology*.)

see the probe when it occurred at the outer square that had not flickered and 460 ms when it occurred at the outer square that had. This 40-ms advantage is an example of a spatially defined inhibition of return. People are slower to move their attention to a location where it has already been.

Figure 3.20 illustrates the other condition of their experiment, in which the objects were rotated around the screen after the flicker. By the end of the motion, the object that had flickered on one side was now on the other side—the two outer objects had traded positions. The question of interest was whether participants would be slower to detect a target on the right (where the flickering had been—which would indicate location-based inhibition) or on the left (where the flickered object had ended up—which would indicate object-based inhibition). The results showed that they were about 20 ms slower to detect an object in the location that had not flickered but that contained the object that had flickered. Thus, their visual systems displayed an inhibition of return to the same object, not the same location.

Another example of object-based attention comes from studies of visual neglect. Earlier, we noted that some patients with damage to the right parietal lobe have difficulty detecting information in the left side of the visual field (see Figure 3.17). Researchers have identified a number of patients who neglect the left side of objects regardless of which visual field these objects occur in (Behrmann & Moscovitch, 1994; Driver, Baylis, Goodrich, & Rafal, 1994).

It seems that the visual system can direct attention either to locations in space or to objects. Experiments like those just described indicate that the visual system can track objects. On the other hand, there are many experiments in which people direct their attention to regions of space where there are no objects (see Figure 3.6 for the results of such an experiment). It is interesting that the left parietal regions seem to be more involved in object-based attention and the right parietal regions in location-based attention. Patients with left parietal damage appear to have deficits in focusing attention on objects (Egly, Driver, & Rafal, 1994), unlike the location-based deficits that I have described in patients with right parietal damage. Also, when participants without brain damage attend to objects rather than locations, there is greater left parietal activation, as revealed by fMRI (Arrington, Carr, Mayer, & Rao, 2000). This seems consistent with the earlier research we reviewed (see Figure 3.18) showing that the right parietal region is responsible for attention to global features and the left for attention to local features.

- *Visual attention can be directed either toward objects independent of their location or toward locations independent of what objects are present.*

Central Attention: Selecting Lines of Thought to Pursue

So far, this chapter has considered how people allocate their attention to process stimuli in the visual and auditory modalities. What about cognition after the stimuli are attended to and encoded? How do we select which lines of thought to pursue? Suppose we are driving down a highway and encode the fact that a dog is sitting in the middle of the road. We might want to figure out why the dog is sitting there, we might want to consider whether there is something we should do to help the dog, and we certainly want to decide how best to steer the car to avoid an accident. Can we do all these things at once? If not, how do we select the most important problem of deciding how to steer and save the rest for later? It appears that people allocate central attention to competing lines of thought in much the same way they allocate perceptual attention to competing objects.

In many (but not all) circumstances, people are able to pursue only one line of thought at a time. This section will describe two laboratory tasks: one in which it appears that people have no ability to overlap two tasks and another pair in which they appear to have almost total ability to do so. Then we will address how people can develop the ability to overlap tasks and how they select among tasks when they cannot or do not want to overlap them.

The first experiment, which Mike Byrne and I did (Byrne & Anderson, 2001), illustrates the claim made at the beginning of the chapter about it being impossible to multiply and add two numbers at the same time. Participants in this experiment saw a string of three digits, such as "3 4 7." There were two tasks they might be asked to do:

- Task 1: Judge whether the first two digits add up to the third and press a key with the right index finger if they do and another key with the left index finger if they do not.
- Task 2: Report verbally the product of the first and third numbers. In this case, the answer is 21, because $3 \times 7 = 21$.

Participants either performed these two tasks individually or tried to do both at once. Figure 3.21 compares the time required to do each task in the single-task condition versus the time required for each task in the dual-task condition. Participants took almost twice as long to do either task when they had to perform the other as well. The illustration also displays the time participants took to complete both tasks in the dual-task condition. (They answered the multiplication problem first 59% of the time and the addition problem first 41% of the time.) The horizontal black line near the top of Figure 3.21 represents the time they took to give the second answer, whichever it was. This line reflects the mean time required to complete both tasks (1.99 s). Note that this time is greater than the sum of the time for the verification task by itself (0.88 s)

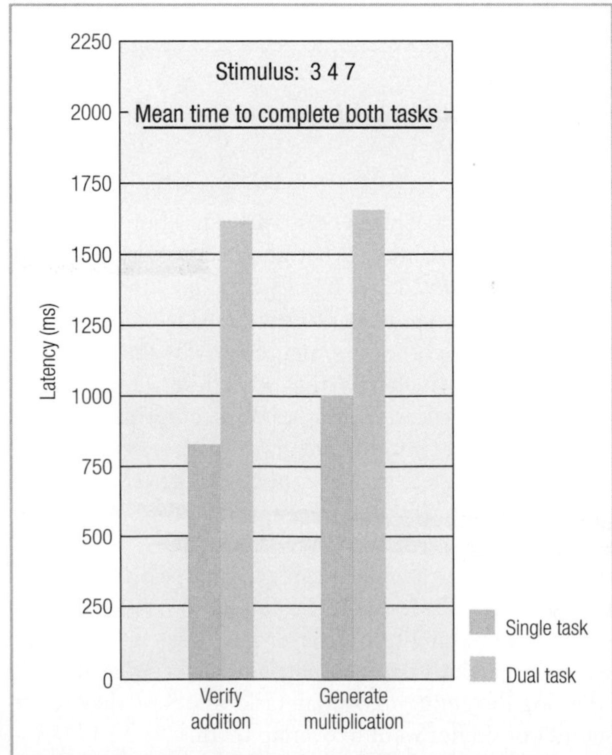

FIGURE 3.21 The results of an experiment by Byrne and Anderson to see whether people can overlap two tasks. The bars show the response times required to solve two problems—one of addition and one of multiplication—when done by themselves and when done together. The results indicate that the participants were not able to overlap the addition and multiplication computations. (From Byrne & Anderson, 2001. Reprinted by permission of the publisher. © 2001 by *Psychological Review*.)

and the time for the multiplication task by itself (1.05 s). The extra time probably reflects the cost of shifting between tasks (for a review, see Monsell, 2003). In any case, it appears that the participants were not able to overlap the addition and multiplication computations at all.

The second experiment, reported by Schumacher et al. (2001), illustrates what is referred to as **perfect time-sharing.** The task was much simpler than the Byrne and Anderson (2001) experiment. Participants simultaneously saw a single letter on a screen and heard a tone. As in the first experiment, they had to perform two tasks:

- Task 1: Press a left, middle, or right key according to whether the letter occurred on the left, in the middle, or the right.
- Task 2: Report "One," "two," or "three" according to whether the tone was low, middle, or high in frequency.

Figure 3.22 compares the times required to do each task in the single-task condition and the dual-task condition. As can be seen, these times are nearly unaffected by the requirement to do the two tasks at once. There are many differences between this task and the Byrne and Anderson task. Perhaps the most apparent is the complexity of the tasks. Participants were able to do the individual tasks in the second experiment in a few hundred milliseconds, whereas the individual tasks in the first experiment took around a second. Thus, there was significantly more thought required in the first experiment, and it is apparently harder for people to engage in both streams of thought simultaneously. Also,

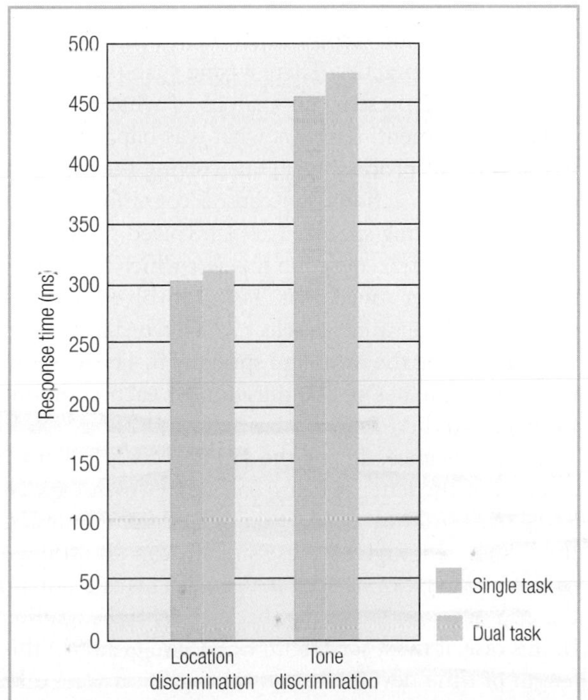

FIGURE 3.22 The results of an experiment by Schumacher et al. illustrating perfect time-sharing. The bars show the times required to perform two tasks—a simple location discrimination task and a tone discrimination task—when done by themselves and when done together. The times were nearly unaffected by the requirement to do the two tasks at once, indicating that the participants achieved almost perfect time-sharing. (From Schumacher et al., 2001. Reprinted by permission of the publisher. © 2001 by *Psychological Science*.)

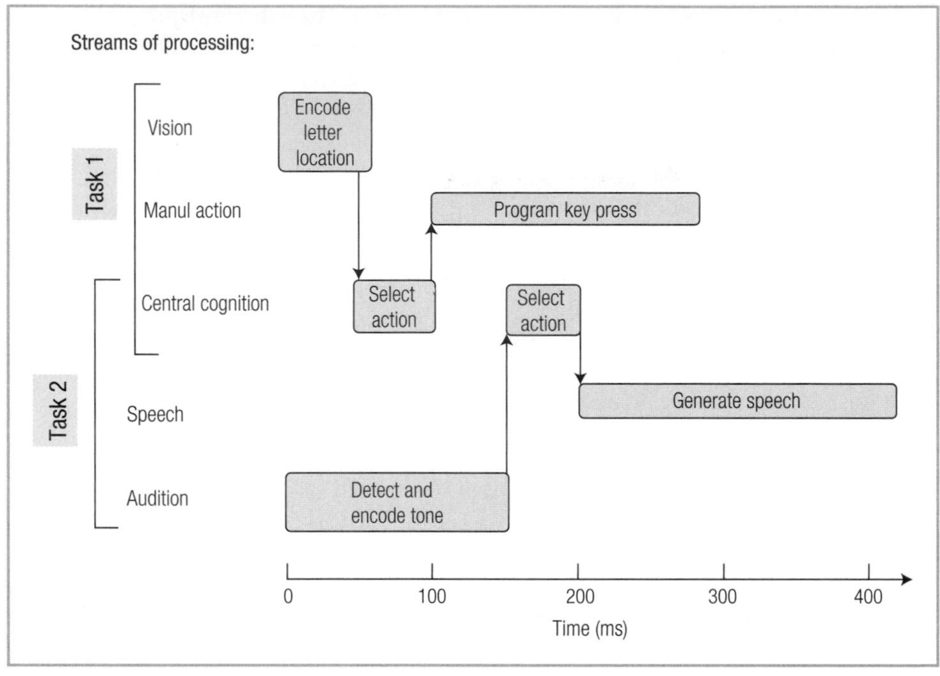

FIGURE 3.23 An analysis of the timing of events in five streams of processing during execution of the dual task in the Schumacher et al. (2001) experiment: (1) vision, (2) manual action, (3) central cognition, (4) speech, and (5) audition.

participants in the second experiment achieved perfect time-sharing only after five sessions of practice. There was no such practice in the first experiment.

Figure 3.23 presents an analysis of what occurred in the Schumacher et al. (2001) experiment. It shows what was happening at various points in time in five streams of processing: (1) perceiving the visual location of a letter, (2) generating manual actions, (3) central cognition, (4) perceiving auditory stimuli, and (5) generating speech. Task 1 involved visually encoding the location of the letter, using central cognition to select which finger to press, and then performing the actual finger movement. Task 2 involved detecting and encoding the tone, using central cognition to select which word to say ("one," "two," or "three"), and then generating the word and speaking it. The lengths of the boxes in Figure 3.23 represent estimates of the duration of each component based on human performance studies. Each of these streams can go on in parallel with the others. Thus, for instance, during the time the tone is being detected and encoded, the location of the letter is being encoded (which happens much faster), a finger is being selected by central cognition, and the motor system is starting to program the action. Although all these streams can go on in parallel, within each stream only one thing can happen at a time. This is a potential problem in the case of the central cognition stream because central cognition must direct all activities. In this case, it must serve both task 1 and task 2. In this experiment, however, the length of time devoted to central cognition was so brief that the two tasks did

Implications

Why is cell phone use and driving a dangerous combination?

Bottlenecks in information processing can have important practical implications. A study by the Harvard Center for Risk Analysis (Cohen & Graham, 2003) estimates that cell phone distraction results in 2,600 deaths, 330,000 injuries, and 1.5 million instances of property damage in the United States each year. Strayer and Drews (2007) review the evidence that people are more likely to miss traffic lights and other critical information while talking on a cell phone. Moreover, these problems are not any better with hands-free phones. In contrast, listening to a radio or books on tape does not interfere with driving. Strayer and Drews suggest that the demands of participating in a conversation place more requirements on central cognition. When someone says something on the cell phone, they expect an answer and are unaware of the driving conditions. Strayer and Drews note that participating in a conversation with a passenger in the car is not as distracting because the passenger will adjust the conversation to driving demands and even point out things like exits to the driver.

not contend for the resource. The five days of practice in this experiment played a critical role in reducing the amount of time devoted to central cognition.

Although the discussion here has focused on bottlenecks in central cognition, there can be bottlenecks in any of these modalities. People cannot attend to two locations at once. Earlier, we reviewed evidence that they must shift their attention across locations in the visual array serially if they must attend to more than one location. Similarly, they can process only one speech stream at a time, move their hands in one way at a time, or say one thing at a time. Even though all these peripheral processes have bottlenecks, it is generally thought that bottlenecks in central cognition can have the most significant effects, and they are the reason we seldom find ourselves thinking about two things at once. This bottleneck in central cognition is referred to as the **central bottleneck.**

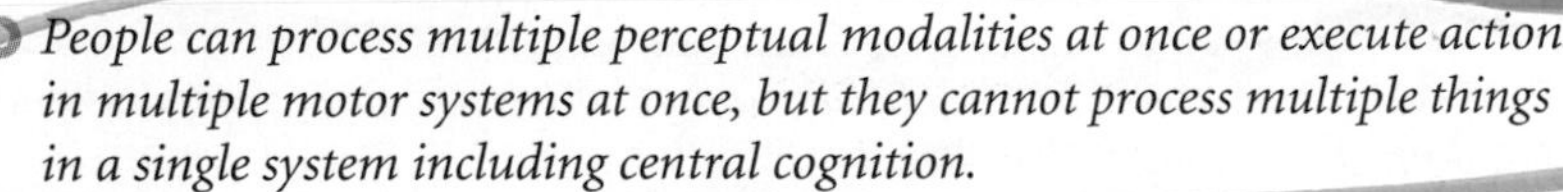

People can process multiple perceptual modalities at once or execute actions in multiple motor systems at once, but they cannot process multiple things in a single system including central cognition.

Automaticity: Expertise Through Practice

In Chapter 9, we will discuss at some length how people become expert with practice. The general effect of practice is to reduce the central cognitive component of information processing. When one has practiced the central cognitive component of a task so much that the task requires little or no thought, we say that doing the task is automatic. Automaticity is a matter of degree. A nice example is driving. For experienced drivers in unchallenging conditions, driving has become so automatic that they can carry on a conversation while driving with little difficulty. Experienced drivers are much more successful at doing secondary tasks like changing the radio (Wikman, Nieminen, & Summala, 1998). Experienced drivers also often have the experience of traveling long stretches of highway with no memory of what they did.

There have been a number of dramatic demonstrations in the psychological literature of how practice can enable parallel processing. One demonstration of the way practice affects attentional limitations is the study reported by Underwood (1974) on the psychologist Neville Moray, who had spent many years studying shadowing. During that time, Moray practiced shadowing a great deal. Unlike most participants in experiments, he was very good at reporting what was contained in the unattended channel. Through a great deal of practice, the process of shadowing had become partially automatic for Moray, and he had capacity left over to attend to the unshadowed channel.

Spelke, Hirst, and Neisser (1976) provided an interesting demonstration of how a highly practiced skill ceases to interfere with other ongoing behaviors. (This was a follow-up of a demonstration pioneered by the writer Gertrude Stein when she was at Harvard University.) Their participants had to perform two tasks: read a text silently for comprehension while simultaneously copying words dictated by the experimenter. At first, these tasks were extremely difficult to do simultaneously. Participants read much more slowly than normal. After six weeks of practice, however, the participants were reading at normal speed. They had become so skilled that their comprehension scores were the same as for normal reading. For these participants, reading while copying had become no more difficult than reading while walking. It is of interest that participants reported no awareness of what it was they were copying. Much as with driving, the participants lost their awareness of the automated activity.[3]

Another example of automaticity is transcription typing. The typist is simultaneously reading the text and executing the finger strokes for typing. In this case, we have three systems operating in parallel: perception of the text to be typed, central translation of the earlier perceived letters into keystrokes, and the actual typing of still earlier letters. Skilled transcription typists often report little awareness of what they are typing, because this task has become so automated. Skilled typists also find it impossible to stop typing instantaneously. If suddenly told to stop, they will hit a few more letters before quitting (Salthouse, 1985, 1986).

As tasks become practiced, they become more automatic and require less and less central cognition to execute.

The Stroop Effect

Automatic processes not only require little or no central cognition to execute but also appear to be difficult to prevent. A good example is word recognition for

[3] When given further training with the intention of remembering what they were transcribing, participants were also able to recall this information.

practiced readers. It is virtually impossible to look at a common word and not read it. This strong tendency for words to be recognized automatically has been studied in a phenomenon known as the **Stroop effect,** after the psychologist who first demonstrated it, J. Ridley Stroop (1935). The task requires participants to say the ink color in which words are printed. Color Plate 3.2 provides an illustration of such a task. Try naming the colors of the words in each column as fast as you can. Which column was easiest to read? Which was hardest?

The three columns illustrate three of the conditions in which the Stroop effect is studied. The first column illustrates a neutral, or control, condition in which the words are not color words. The second column illustrates the congruent condition in which the words are the same as the color. The third column illustrates the conflict condition in which there are color words but they are different from their colors. A typical modern experiment, rather than having participants read a whole column, will present a single word at a time and measure the time to name that word. Figure 3.24 shows the results from an experiment on the Stroop effect by Dunbar and MacLeod (1984). Compared to the control condition of a neutral word, participants could name the ink color somewhat faster in the congruent condition—when the word was the name of the ink color. In the conflict condition, when the word was the name of a different color, they named the ink color much more slowly. For instance, they had great difficulty in saying that the ink color of the word *red* is green. Figure 3.24 also shows the results when the task is switched and participants are asked to read the word and not name the color. The effects are asymmetrical; that is, individual participants experienced very little interference in reading a word as a function of its ink color. This reflects the highly automatic character of reading. Additional evidence for its automaticity is that participants could also read a word much faster than they could name its ink color. Reading is such an automatic process that not only is it unaffected by the color, but participants are unable to inhibit reading the word, and that reading can interfere with the color naming.

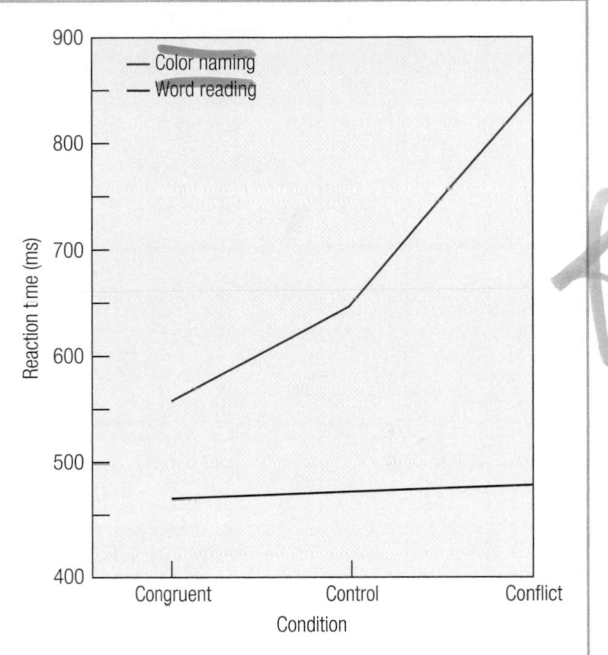

FIGURE 3.24 Performance data for the standard Stroop task. The curves plot the average reaction time of the participants as a function of the condition tested: congruent (the word was the name of the ink color); control (the word was not related to color at all); and conflict (the word was the name of a color different from the ink color). (From Dunbar & MacLeod, 1984. Reprinted by permission of the publisher. © 1984 by the *Journal of Experimental Psychology: Human Perception and Performance.*)

MacLeod and Dunbar (1988) looked at the effect of practice on performance in a Stroop task. They used an experiment in which the participants learned the color names for random shapes. Part (a) of Color Plate 3.3 illustrates the shape-color associations they might learn. The experimenters then presented the participants with test geometric shapes and asked them to say either the color name associated with the shape or the actual ink color of the shape. As in the original Stroop experiment, there were three conditions, and these are illustrated in part (b) of Color Plate 3.3:

1. Congruent: The random shape was in the same ink color as its name.
2. Control: White shapes were presented when participants were to say the color name for the shape; colored squares were presented when they were

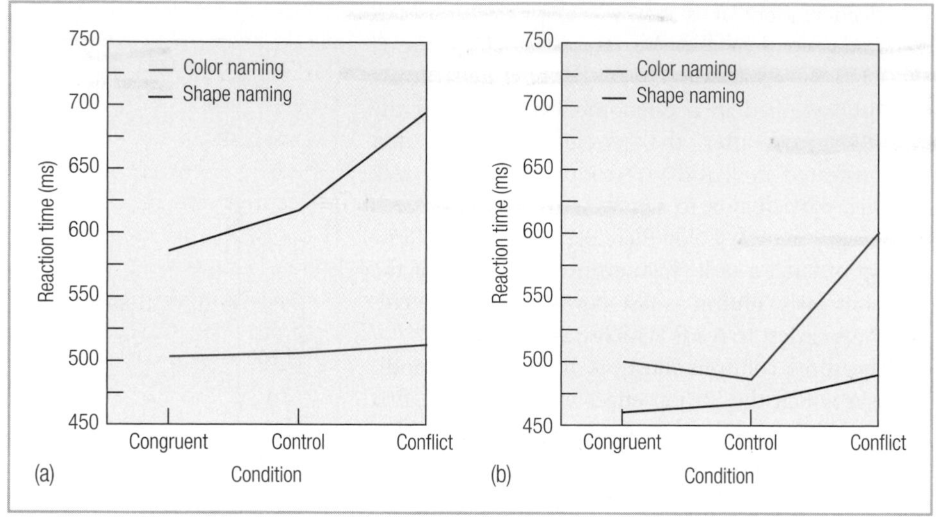

FIGURE 3.25 Results from the experiment created by MacLeod and Dunbar (1988) to evaluate the effect of practice on the performance of a Stroop task. The data reported are the average times required to name shapes and colors as a function of color-shape congruence: (a) initial performance (note correction); (b) after 20 days of practice. The practice made shape naming automatic, like word reading, so that it affected color naming.

to name the ink color of the shape. (The square shape was not associated with any color.)

3. Conflict: The random shape was in a different ink color from its name.

Figure 3.25 shows the results from this experiment. Color naming was much more automatic than shape naming and was relatively unaffected by congruence with the shape, whereas shape naming was affected by congruence with the ink color (Figure 3.25a). Then MacLeod and Dunbar gave the participants 20 days of practice at naming the shapes. Participants became much faster at naming shapes, and now shape naming interefered with color naming rather than vice versa (Figure 3.25b). Thus, the consequence of the training was to make shape naming automatic, like word reading, so that it affected color naming.

Reading a word is such an automatic process that it is difficult to inhibit, and it will interfere with processing other information about the word.

Prefrontal Sites of Executive Control

We have seen that the parietal cortex is important in the exercise of attention in the perceptual domain. There is evidence that the prefrontal regions are particularly important in direction of central cognition, often known as **executive control.** The prefrontal cortex is that portion of the frontal cortex anterior to the premotor region (the premotor region is area 6 in Color Plate 1.1). Just as damage to parietal regions results in deficits in the deployment of perceptual attention, damage to prefrontal regions results in deficits of executive control. Patients with such damage often seem totally driven by stimulus and fail to control their behavior according to their intentions. A patient who sees a comb on the table may simply pick it up and begin combing her hair; another who sees a pair of glasses will put them on even if he already has a pair on his face. Patients with damage to prefrontal regions show marked deficits in the Stroop task and often cannot refrain from reading the word rather than naming the color (Janer & Pardo, 1991).

Two prefrontal regions seem particularly important in executive control. One is the **dorsolateral prefrontal cortex (DLPFC)**, which is the upper portion of the prefrontal cortex (see Figure 3.1). It is called dorsolateral because it is high (dorsal) and to the side (lateral). The second region is the **anterior cingulate cortex (ACC)**, which is a structure below the surface of the brain along the midline. It is part of the cortex that is folded under its visible surface. The DLPFC seems particularly important in the setting of intentions and the control of behavior. For instance, it is highly active during the simultaneous performance of dual tasks such as those whose results are reported in Figures 3.19 and 3.20 (Szameitat, Schubert, Muller, & von Cramon, 2002). The ACC seems particularly active when people must monitor conflict between competing tendencies. For instance, brain-imaging studies show that it is highly active in Stroop trials when one must name the color of a word printed in an ink of conflicting color (J. V. Pardo, P. J. Pardo, Janer, & Raichle, 1990).

There is a strong relationship between the ACC and cognitive control in many tasks. For instance, it appears that children develop more cognitive control as their ACC develops. The amount of activation in the ACC appears to be correlated with the performance by children in tasks requiring cognitive control (Casey et al., 1997a). Developmentally, there also appears to be a positive correlation between performance and sheer volume of the ACC (Casey et al., 1997b). A nice paradigm for demonstrating the development of cognitive control in children is the "Simon says" task. In one study, Jones, Rothbart, and Posner (2003) had children receive instructions from two dolls—a bear and an elephant. The instructions were things like "Elephant says, 'Touch your nose.'" The children were to follow the instructions from one doll (the act doll) and ignore the instructions from another (the inhibit doll). All children successfully followed the act doll but many had difficulty ignoring the inhibit doll. From the age of 36 to 48 months children progressed from 22% success to 91% success in ignoring the inhibit doll. A few children used regulatory self-speech to control their behavior, as famously proposed by Luria (1961), but they also used strategies such as sitting on their hands or distorting their actions—pointing to their ear rather than their nose.

Another way to appreciate the importance of prefrontal regions to cognitive control is to compare performance of humans with other primates. As reviewed in Chapter 1, a major dimension of the evolution from primates to humans has been the increase in the size of prefrontal regions. Primates can be trained to do many tasks that humans do and so permit careful comparison. One such task involving a variant of the Stroop task presents participants with a display of numerals (e.g., five 3's) and pits naming the number of objects against indicating the identity of the numerals. Figure 3.26

5 5 5
1 1 1 1
2
3 3 3 3 3
4 4
5 5 5
4 4 4 4 4
5 5 5 5
3
4 4 4
2 2 2 2
3 3
4 4 4
1 1 1 1
3
2 2 2

FIGURE 3.26 A numerical Stroop task comparable to the color Stroop task (see Color Plate 3.2).

TABLE 3.1

Mean Response Times and Accuracy Levels as a Function of Species and Condition

Condition	Accuracy (%)	Response Time (ms)
	Rhesus Monkeys (*N* = 6)	
Congruent numerals	92	676
Baseline (letters)	86	735
Incongruent numerals	73	829
	Human Subjects (*N* = 28)	
Congruent numerals	99	584
Baseline (letters)	99	613
Incongruent numerals	97	661

provides an example of this task in the same form as the original Stroop task (Color Plate 3.2): trying to count the number of numerals in each line versus trying to name the numerals in each line. The stronger interference in this case is from the numeral naming to the counting (Windes, 1968). This paradigm has been used to compare Stroop interference in humans versus rhesus monkeys who had been trained to use the numerals (Washburn, 1994; see Table 3.1). Both groups of participants were shown two arrays and were required to indicate which had more numerals independent of the identity of the numerals. Compared to a baseline where they had to judge which array of letters had more objects, both humans and monkeys performed better when the numerals agreed with the difference in cardinality and performed worse when the numerals disagreed (as they do in Figure 3.26). Both populations showed similar reaction time effects, but whereas the humans made 3% errors in the incongruent condition, the monkeys made 27% errors. The level of performance observed of the monkeys was like the level of performance observed with patients with damage to their frontal lobes.

- *Prefrontal regions, particularly DLPFC and ACC, play a major role in executive control.*

Conclusions

There has been a gradual shift in the way cognitive psychology has perceived the issue of attention. For a long time, the implicit assumption was captured by this famous quote from William James (1890) over a century ago:

> Everyone knows what attention is. It is the taking possession by the mind, in a clear and vivid form, of one out of what seem several simultaneously possible objects or trains of thought. Focalization, concentration of consciousness are of its essence. It implies withdrawal from some things in order to deal effectively with others. (pp. 403–404)

Two features of this quote reflect conceptions once held about attention. The first is that attention is strongly related to consciousness—we cannot attend to one thing unless we are conscious of it. The second is that attention, like consciousness, is a unitary system. More and more, cognitive psychology is coming to recognize that attention operates at an unconscious level. For instance, people often are not conscious of where they have moved their eyes. Along with this recognition has come the realization that attention is multifaceted (e.g., Pashler, 1995). We have seen that it makes sense to separate auditory attention from visual attention and attention in perceptual processing from attention in executive control from attention in response generation. The brain consists of a number of parallel processing systems for the various perceptual systems, motor systems, and central cognition. Each of these parallel systems seems to suffer bottlenecks—points at which it must focus its processing on a single thing. Attention is best conceived as the processes by which each of these systems is allocated to potentially competing information-processing demands. The amount of interference that occurs among tasks is a function of the overlap in the demands that these tasks make on the same systems.

Questions for Thought

1. The chapter discussed how listening to one spoken message makes it difficult to process a second spoken message. Do you think that listening to a conversation on a cell phone while driving makes it harder to process other sounds like a car horn honking?
2. Which search should produce greater parietal activation: searching Figure 3.13a for a *T* or searching Figure 3.13b for a *T*?
3. Describe circumstances where it would be advantageous to focus one's attention on an object rather than a region of space, and describe circumstances where the opposite would be true.
4. We have discussed how automatic behaviors can intrude on other behaviors and discussed how some aspects of driving have become automatic. Consider the situation in which a passenger in the car is a skilled driver and has automatic aspects of driving evoked by the driving experience. Can you think of examples where automatic aspects of driving seem to affect a passenger's behavior in a car? Might this help explain why having a conversation with a passenger in a car is not as distracting as having a conversation over a cell phone?

Key Terms

anterior cingulate cortex (ACC)
attention
attenuation theory
automaticity
binding problem
central bottleneck
dichotic listening task
dorsolateral prefrontal cortex (DLPFC)
early-selection theories
executive control
feature-integration theory
filter theory
goal-directed attention
illusory conjunction
inhibition of return
late-selection theories
object-based attention
perfect time-sharing
serial bottleneck
space-based attention
stimulus-driven attention
Stroop effect

4

Mental Imagery

Try answering these two questions:

- How many windows are in your house?
- How many nouns are in the American Pledge of Allegiance?

Most people who answer these questions have the same experience. For the first question they imagine themselves walking around their house and counting windows. For the second question, if they do not actually say the Pledge of Alliance out loud, they imagine themselves saying the Pledge of Allegiance. In both cases they are creating mental images of what they would have perceived had they actually walked around the house or said the Pledge of Allegiance.

Use of visual imagery is particularly important. As a result of our primate heritage, a large portion of our brain functions to process visual information. Therefore, we use these brain structures as much as we can, even in the absence of a visual signal from the outside world, by creating mental images in our heads. Some of humankind's most creative acts involve visual imagery. For instance, Einstein claimed he discovered the theory of relativity by imagining himself traveling beside a beam of light.

A major debate in this field of research has been the degree to which the processes behind visual imagery are the same as the perceptual and attentional processes that we considered in the previous two chapters. Some researchers (e.g., Pylyshyn, 1973, in an article sarcastically titled "What the mind's eye tells the mind's brain") have argued that the perceptual experience that we have while doing an activity such as picturing the windows in our house is an **epiphenomenon;** that is, it is a mental experience that does not have any functional role in information processing. The philosopher Daniel Dennett (1969) also argued that mental images are epiphenomenal—that is, that the perceptual components of mental images are not really functional in any way:

> Consider the Tiger and his Stripes. I can dream, imagine or see a striped tiger, but must the tiger I experience have a particular number of stripes? If seeing or imagining is having a mental image, then the image of the tiger *must*—obeying the rules of images in general—reveal a definite number of stripes showing, and one should be able to pin this down with such questions as "more than ten?", "less than twenty?" (p. 136)

Dennett's argument is that if we are actually seeing a tiger in a mental image, we should be able to count its stripes just like we could if we actually saw a tiger. Because we cannot count the stripes in a mental image of a tiger, we are not having a real perceptual experience. This argument is not considered decisive, but it does illustrate the discomfort some people have with the claim that mental images are actually perceptual in character.

This chapter will review some of the experimental evidence showing the ways that mental imagery does play a role in information processing. We will define **mental imagery** broadly as the processing of perceptual-like information in the absence of an external source for the perceptual information. We will consider the following questions:

- How do we process the information in a mental image?
- How is imaginal processing related to perceptual processing?
- What brain areas are involved in mental imagery?
- How do we develop mental images of our environment and use these to navigate through the environment?

Verbal Imagery versus Visual Imagery

There is increasing evidence from cognitive neuroscience that several different brain regions are involved in imagery. This evidence has come both from studies of patients suffering damage to various brain regions and from studies of the brain activation of normal individuals as they engage in various imagery tasks. In one of the early studies of brain activation patterns during imagery, Roland and Friberg (1985) identified many of the brain regions that have been investigated in subsequent research. They had participants either mentally rehearse a word jingle or mentally rehearse finding their way around streets in their neighborhoods. The investigators measured changes in blood flow in various parts of the cortex. Figure 4.1 illustrates the principal areas they identified. When participants engaged in the verbal jingle task, there was activation in the prefrontal cortex near Broca's area and in the parietal-temporal region of the posterior cortex

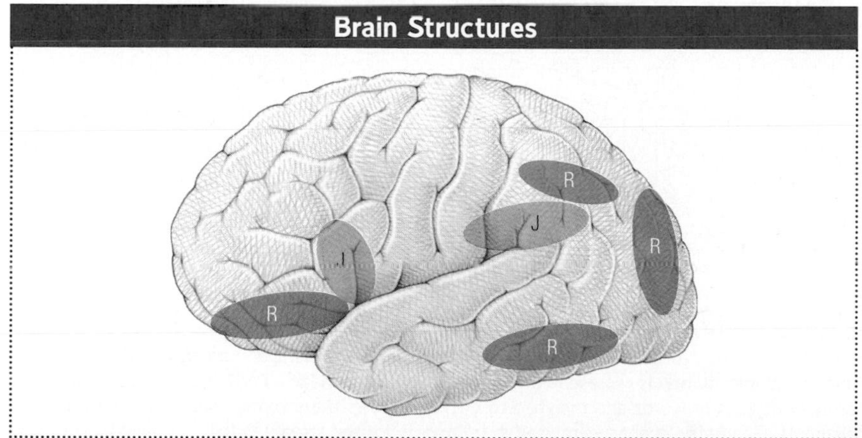

FIGURE 4.1 Results from Roland and Friberg's (1985) study of brain activation patterns during mental imagery. Regions of the left cortex showed increased blood flow when participants imagined a verbal jingle (J) or a spatial route (R).

near Wernicke's area. As discussed in Chapter 1, patients with damage to these regions show deficits in language processing. When participants engaged in the visual task, there was activation in the parietal cortex, occipital cortex, and temporal cortex. All these areas are involved in visual perception and attention, as we saw in Chapters 2 and 3. When people process imagery of language or visual information, some of the same areas are active as when they process actual speech or visual information.

An experiment by Santa (1977) demonstrated the functional consequence of representing information in a visual image versus representing it in a verbal image. The two conditions of Santa's experiment are shown in Figure 4.2. In the geometric condition (Figure 4.2a), participants studied an array of three geometric objects, arranged with one object centered below the other two. This array had a facelike property—without much effort, we can see eyes and a mouth. After participants studied the array, it was removed, and they had to hold the information in their minds. They were presented with one of several different test arrays. The participants' task was to verify that the test array contained the same elements as the study array, although not necessarily in the same

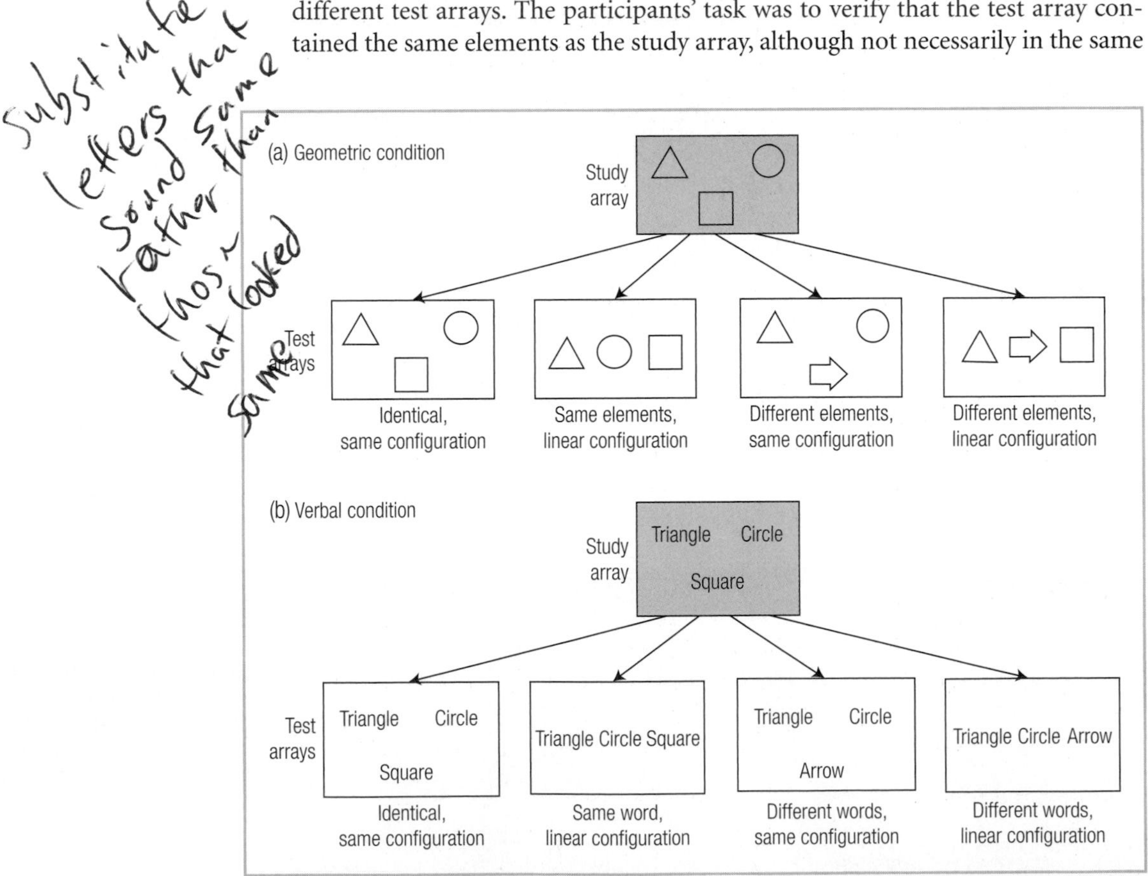

FIGURE 4.2 The procedure followed in Santa's (1977) experiment demonstrating that visual and verbal information is represented differently in mental images. Participants studied an initial array of objects or words and then had to decide whether a test array contained the same elements. Geometric shapes were used in (a), words for the shapes in (b).

spatial configuration. Thus, participants should have responded positively to the first two test arrays and negatively to the last two. Santa was interested in the contrast between the two positive test arrays. The first was identical to the study array (same-configuration condition). In the second array, the elements were displayed in a line (linear-configuration condition). Santa predicted that participants would make a positive identification more quickly in the first case, where the configuration was identical—because, he hypothesized, the mental image for the study stimulus would preserve spatial information. The results for the geometric condition are shown in

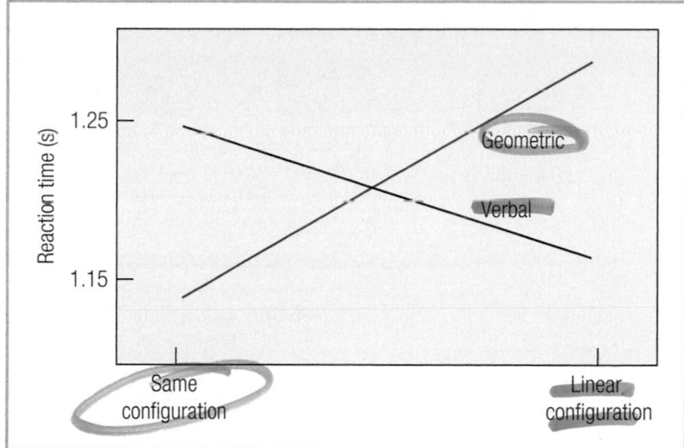

FIGURE 4.3 Results from Santa's (1977) experiment. The data confirmed two of Santa's hypotheses: (1) In the geometric condition, participants would make a positive identification more quickly when the configuration was identical than when it was linear, because the visual image of the study stimulus would preserve spatial information. (2) In the verbal condition, participants would make a positive identification more quickly when the configuration was linear than when it was identical, because participants had encoded the words from the study array linearly, in accordance with normal reading order in English.

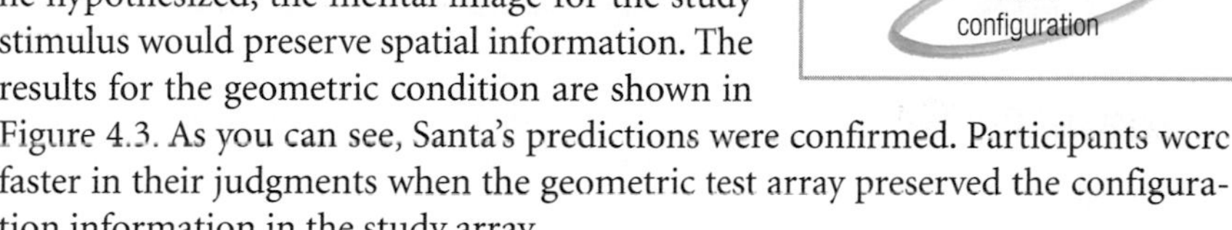

Figure 4.3. As you can see, Santa's predictions were confirmed. Participants were faster in their judgments when the geometric test array preserved the configuration information in the study array.

The results from the geometric condition are more impressive when contrasted with the results from the verbal condition, illustrated in Figure 4.2b. Here, participants studied words arranged exactly as the objects in the geometric condition were arranged. Because it involved words, however, the study stimulus did not suggest a face or have any pictorial properties. Santa speculated that participants would read the array left to right and top down and encode a verbal image with the information. So, given the study array, participants would encode it as "*triangle, circle, square.*" After they studied the initial array, one of the test arrays was presented. Participants had to judge whether the words were identical. All the test stimuli involved words, but otherwise they presented the same possibilities as the test stimuli in the geometric condition. The two positive stimuli exemplify the same-configuration condition and the linear-configuration condition. Note that the order of words in the linear array was the same as it was in the study stimulus. Santa predicted that, unlike the geometric condition, because participants had encoded the words into a linearly ordered verbal image, they would be fastest when the test array was linear. As Figure 4.3 illustrates, his predictions were again confirmed.

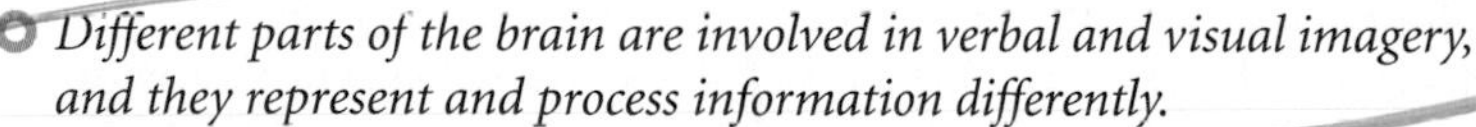

Different parts of the brain are involved in verbal and visual imagery, and they represent and process information differently.

Visual Imagery

Most of the research on mental imagery has involved visual imagery, and this will be the principal focus of this chapter. One function of mental imagery is to anticipate how objects will look from different perspectives. People often have the impression that they rotate objects mentally to achieve perspective. Roger Shepard and his colleagues have been involved in a long series of experiments

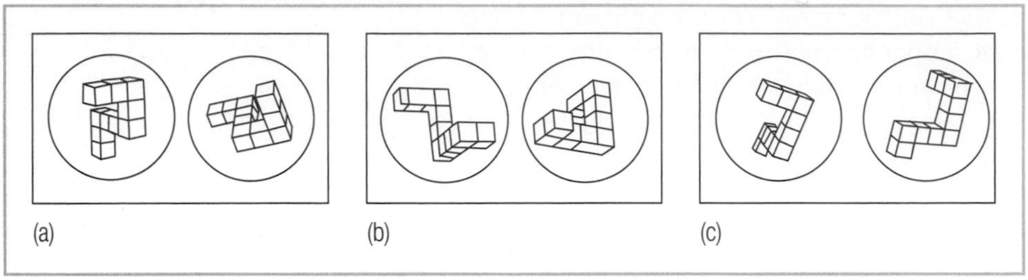

(a) (b) (c)

FIGURE 4.4 Stimuli in the Shepard and Metzler (1971) study on mental rotation. (a) The objects differ by an 80° rotation in the picture plane (two dimensions). (b) The objects differ by an 80° rotation in depth (three dimensions). (c) The objects cannot be rotated into congruence. (From Metzler & Shepard, 1974. Reprinted by permission of the publisher. © 1974 by Erlbaum.)

on **mental rotation.** Their research was among the first to study the functional properties of mental images, and it has been very influential. It is interesting to note that this research was inspired by a dream (Shepard, 1967): Shepard awoke one day and remembered having visualized a 3-D structure turning in space. He convinced Jackie Metzler, a first-year graduate student at Stanford, to study mental rotation, and the rest is history.

Their first experiment was reported in the journal *Science* (Shepard & Metzler, 1971). Participants were presented with pairs of 2-D representations of 3-D objects, like those in Figure 4.4. Their task was to determine whether the objects were identical except for orientation. The two objects in Figure 4.4a are identical, as are the two objects in Figure 4.4b, but in both cases the pairs are presented at different orientations. Participants reported that to match the two shapes, they rotated one of the objects in each pair mentally until it was congruent with the other object. There is no way to rotate one of the objects in Figure 4.4c so that it is identical with the other.

The graphs in Figure 4.5 show the times required for participants to decide that the members of pairs were identical. The reaction times are plotted as a function of the angular disparity between the two objects presented. The angular disparity is the amount one object would have to be rotated to match the other object in orientation. Note that the relationship is linear—for every increment in amount of rotation, there is an equal increment in reaction time. Reaction time is plotted for two different kinds of rotation. One is for 2-D rotations (Figure 4.4a), which can be performed in the picture plane (i.e., by rotating the page); the other is for depth rotations (Figure 4.4b), which require the participant to rotate the object into the page. Note that the two functions are very similar. Processing an object in depth (in three dimensions) does not appear to have taken longer than processing an object in the picture plane. Hence, participants must have been operating on 3-D representations of the objects in both the picture-plane and depth conditions.

These data might seem to indicate that participants rotated the object in a 3-D space within their heads. The greater the angle of disparity between the two objects, the longer participants took to complete the rotation. Though the participants were obviously not actually rotating a real object in their heads, the mental process appears to be analogous to physical rotation.

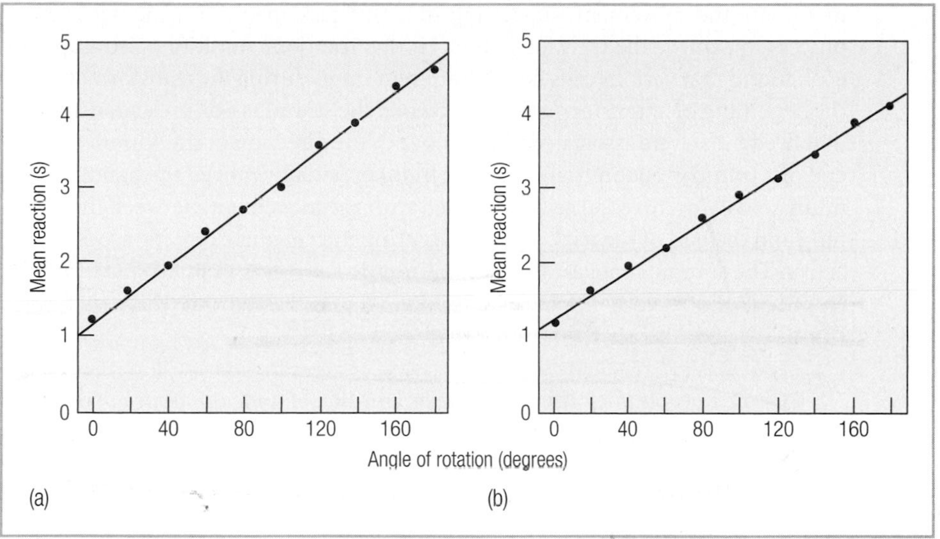

FIGURE 4.5 Results of the Shepard and Metzler (1971) study on mental rotation. The mean time required to determine that two objects have the same 3-D shape is plotted as a function of the angular difference in their portrayed orientations. (a) Plot for pairs differing by a rotation in the picture plane (two dimensions). (b) Plot for pairs differing by a rotation in depth (three dimensions). (From Metzler & Shepard, 1974. Reprinted by permission of the publisher. © 1974 by Erlbaum.)

There has been a great deal of subsequent research examining the mental rotation of all sorts of different objects. The typical finding is that the time required to complete a rotation does vary with the angle of disparity. In recent years, there have been a number of brain-imaging studies that looked at what regions are active during mental rotation. Consistently, the parietal region (roughly the region labeled R at the upper back of the brain in Figure 4.1) has been activated across a range of tasks. This finding corresponds with the results we reviewed in Chapter 3 showing that the parietal region is important in spatial attention. Some tasks involve activation of other areas. For instance, Kosslyn, DiGirolamo, Thompson, and Alpert (1998) found that imagining the rotation of one's hand produced activation in the motor cortex.

Neural recordings of monkeys have provided some evidence about neural representation during mental rotation involving hand movement. Georgopoulos, Lurito, Petrides, Schwartz, and Massey (1989) had monkeys perform a task in which they moved a handle at a specific angle in response to a given stimulus. In the base condition, monkeys just moved the handle to the position of the stimulus. Georgopoulos et al. found cells that fired for particular positions. So, for instance, there were cells that fired most strongly when the monkey was moving to the 9 o'clock position and other cells that responded most strongly when the monkey moved to the 12 o'clock position. In the rotation condition, the monkeys had to move the handle to a position rotated some number of degrees from the stimulus. For instance, if the monkeys had to move the handle 90° counterclockwise and the stimulus appeared at the 12 o'clock position, they would have to move the handle to 9 o'clock. If the stimulus appeared at the 6 o'clock position, they would have to move to 3 o'clock. The greater the angle, the longer it took the monkeys to initiate the movement, suggesting that this task involved a mental rotation process to achieve the transformation. In this rotation condition, Georgopoulos et al. found that various cells fired at different times during the transformation. At the beginning of a transformation trial, when the stimulus was presented, the cells that fired most were associated with a move in the direction of the stimulus. By the end of a transformation trial, when the monkey actually moved the handle, maximum activity occurred in cells associated with the movement. Between the beginning and the end of the trial, cells representing intermediate directions were most active. These results suggest that mental rotation involves gradual shifts of firing from cells that encode the initial stimulus to cells that encode the transformed stimulus or, in this case, the transformed response.

When people must transform the orientation of a mental image to make a comparison, they rotate its representation through the intermediate positions until it achieves the desired orientation.

Image Scanning

Something else we often do with mental images is to scan them looking for some critical information. For instance, when people are asked how many windows there are in their houses (the task described at the beginning of this chapter), many report mentally going through the house visually as they count the windows. Researchers have been interested in the degree to which people are actually scanning perceptual representations in such tasks, as opposed to just retrieving abstract information. For instance, are we really "seeing" each window in the room or are we just remembering how many windows are in the room?

Brooks (1968) performed an important series of experiments on the scanning of visual images. He had participants scan imagined diagrams such as the one shown in Figure 4.6. For example, the participant was to scan around an imagined block *F* from a prescribed starting point and in a prescribed direction, categorizing each corner of the block as a point in the top or bottom (assigned a yes response) or as a point in between (assigned a no response). In the example (beginning with the starting corner), the correct sequence of responses is yes, yes, yes, no, no, no, no, no, no, yes. For a nonvisual contrast task, Brooks also gave participants sentences such as "A bird in the hand is not in the bush." Participants had to scan the sentence while holding it in memory, deciding whether each word was a noun or not. A second experimental variable was how participants made their responses. Participants responded in one of three ways: (1) said yes or no; (2) tapped with the left hand for yes and with the right hand for no; or (3) pointed to successive *Y*'s or *N*'s on a sheet of paper such as the one shown in Figure 4.7. The two variables of stimulus material (diagram or sentence) and output mode were crossed to yield six conditions.

FIGURE 4.6 An example of a simple block diagram that Brooks used to study the scanning of mental images. The asterisk and arrow show the starting point and the direction for scanning the image. (From Brooks, 1968. Reprinted by permission of the publisher. © 1968 by the Canadian Psychological Association.)

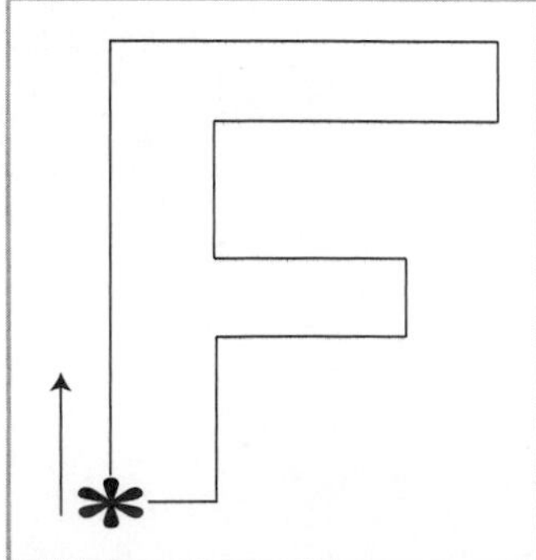

Table 4.1 gives the results of Brooks's experiment in terms of the mean time spent in classifying the sentences or diagrams in each output condition. The important result for our purposes is that participants took much longer for diagrams in the pointing condition than in any other condition, but this was not the case when participants were working with sentences. Apparently,

scanning a physical visual array conflicted with scanning a mental array. This result strongly reinforces the conclusion that when people are scanning a mental array, they are scanning a representation that is analogous to a physical visual array. Requiring the person simultaneously to engage in a conflicting scanning action on an external physical visual array disrupts the mental scan.

One might think that Brooks's result was due to the conflict between engaging in a visual pointing task and scanning a visual image. Subsequent research makes it clear, however, that the interference is not a result of the visual character of the task per se. Rather, the problem is spatial and not specifically visual; it arises from the conflicting directions in which participants had to scan the physical visual array and the mental image. For instance, in another experiment, Brooks found evidence of similar interference when participants had their eyes closed and indicated yes or no by scanning an array of raised *Y*'s and *N*'s with their fingers. In this case, the actual stimuli were tactile, not visual. Thus, the conflict is spatial, not specifically visual.

Baddeley and Lieberman (reported in Baddeley, 1976) performed an experiment that further supports the view that the nature of the interference in the Brooks task is spatial rather than visual. Participants were required to perform two tasks simultaneously. All participants performed the Brooks letter-image task. However, participants in one group simultaneously monitored a series of stimuli of two possible brightnesses and had to press a key whenever the brighter stimulus appeared. This task involved the processing of visual but not spatial information. Participants in the other condition were blindfolded and seated in front of a swinging pendulum. The pendulum emitted a tone and contained a photocell. Participants were instructed to try to keep the beam of a flashlight on the swinging pendulum. Whenever they were on target, the photocell caused the tone to change frequency, thus providing auditory feedback. This test involved the processing of spatial but not visual information. The spatial auditory tracking task produced far greater impairment in the image scanning task than did the brightness judgment task. This result also indicates that the nature of the impairment in the Brooks task was spatial, not visual.

Y *N*
Y *N*
Y *N*
Y *N*
Y *N*
Y *N*
Y *N*
Y *N*
Y *N*
Y *N*
Y *N*
Y *N*

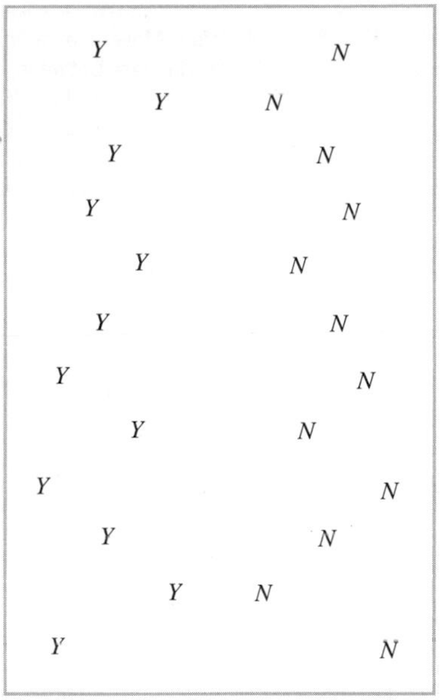

FIGURE 4.7 A sample output sheet of the pointing condition in Brooks's study of mental image scanning. The letters are staggered to force careful visual monitoring of pointing. (From Brooks, 1968. Reprinted by permission of the publisher. © 1968 by the Canadian Psychological Association.)

TABLE 4.1

Results of Brooks's (1968) Experiment Showing Conflict Between Mental Array and Visual Array Scanning

	Mean Response Time (s) by Output Mode		
Stimulus Material	**Pointing**	**Tapping**	**Vocal**
Diagrams	28.2	14.1	11.3
Sentences	9.8	7.8	13.8

From Brooks, 1968. Reprinted by permission of the publisher. © 1968 by the Canadian Psychological Association.

People suffer interference in scanning a mental image if they have to simultaneously process a conflicting perceptual structure.

Visual Comparison of Magnitudes

A fair amount of research has focused on the way people judge the visual details of objects in their mental images. One line of research has asked participants

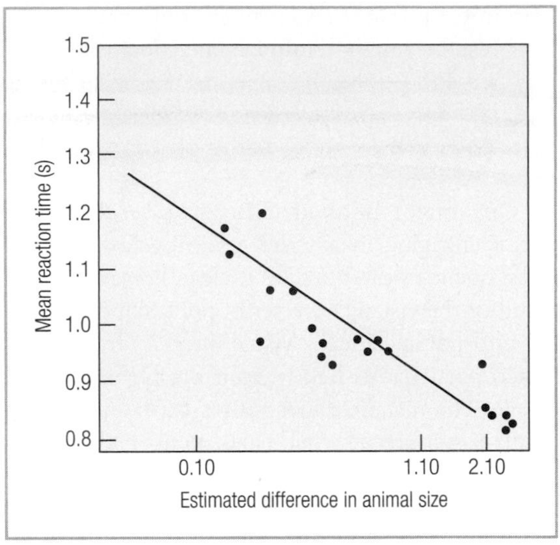

FIGURE 4.8 Results from Moyer's experiment demonstrating that when people try to discriminate between two objects, the time it takes them to do so decreases as the difference in size between the two objects increases. Participants were asked to compare the imagined sizes of two animals. The mean time required to judge which of two animals is larger is plotted as a function of the estimated difference in size of the two animals. The difference measure is plotted on the abscissa in a logarithmic scale. (From Moyer, 1973. Reprinted by permission of the publisher. © 1973 by *Perception and Psychophysics.*)

to discriminate between objects based on some dimension such as size. This research has shown that when participants try to discriminate between two objects, the time it takes them to do so decreases continuously as the difference in size between the two objects increases.

Moyer (1973) was interested in the speed with which participants could judge the relative size of two animals from memory. For example, "Which is larger, moose or roach?" and "Which is larger, wolf or lion?" Many people report that in making these judgments, particularly for the items that are similar in size, they experience images of the two objects and seem to compare the sizes of the objects in their images.

Moyer also asked participants to estimate the absolute size of these animals. He plotted the time required to compare the imagined sizes of two animals as a function of the difference between the two animals' estimated sizes. Figure 4.8 reproduces these data. The individual points represent comparisons between pairs of items. In general, the judgment times decreased as the difference in estimated size increased. The graph shows that judgment time decreases linearly with increases in differences in the size of the animals. Note, however, that the differences have been plotted logarithmically. A log-difference scale makes the distance between small differences large relative to the same distances between large differences. Thus, the linear relationship in the graph means that increasing the size difference has a diminishing effect on reaction time.

FIGURE 4.9 Results from the D. M. Johnson (1939) study demonstrating that making mental comparisons involves difficulties of discrimination similar to those involved in making perceptual comparisons. Participants compared the lengths of two lines. The mean time required to judge which line was longer is plotted as a function of the difference in line length. The difference measure is plotted on the abscissa in a logarithmic scale.

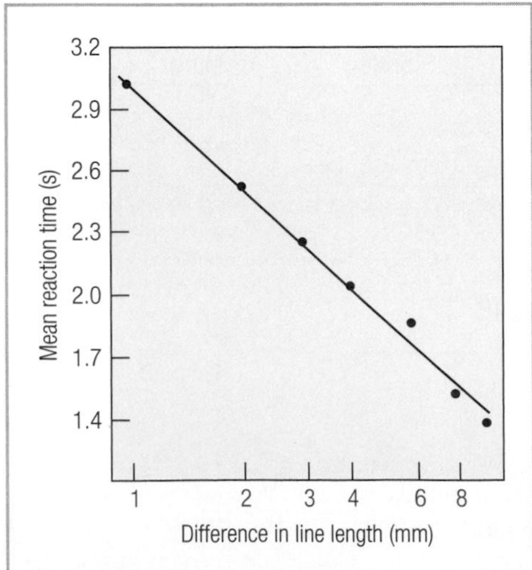

Significantly, very similar results are obtained when people visually compare physical size. For instance, D. M. Johnson (1939) asked participants to judge which of two simultaneously presented lines was longer. Figure 4.9 plots participant judgment time as a function of the log difference in line length. Again, a linear relation is obtained. It is reasonable to expect that the more similar the lengths being compared are, the longer perceptual judgments will take, because telling them apart is more difficult under such circumstances. The fact that similar functions are obtained when mental objects are compared indicates that making mental comparisons involves the same process as those involved in perceptual comparisons.

People experience greater difficulty in judging the relative size of two pictures or of two mental images that are similar in size.

Are Visual Images Like Visual Perception?

Research has been done to determine to what degree visual imagery is like perception. In one experiment, Finke, Pinker, and Farah (1989) set out to determine the degree to which people were able to recognize the images they constructed in the same way they would be able to recognize objects they saw. These researchers asked participants to create mental images and then engage in a series of transformations of those images. Here are two examples of the problems that they read to their participants:

- Imagine a capital letter *N*. Connect a diagonal line from the top right corner to the bottom left corner. Now rotate the figure 90° to the right. What do you see?
- Imagine a capital letter *D*. Rotate the figure 90° to the left. Now place a capital letter *J* at the bottom. What do you see?

Participants closed their eyes and tried to imagine these transformations as they were read to them. The participants were able to recognize their composite images just as if they had been presented with them on a screen. In the first example, they saw an hourglass; in the second, an umbrella. The ability to perform such tasks illustrates an important function of imagery: It enables us to construct new objects in our minds and inspect them. It is just this sort of visual synthesis that structural engineers or architects must perform as they design new bridges or buildings.

The Finke et al. (1989) study shows that we can make judgments about imagined objects and come to the same conclusions as we would about seen objects. But are these imagined objects really the same as seen objects? Researchers have been doing studies to see whether subtle properties associated with visual perception are also reproduced in mental images. For instance, Wallace (1984) did an experiment to study the Ponzo illusion (Berbaum & Chung, 1981) illustrated in part (a) of Figure 4.10: Even though the two horizontal lines have the same length, the upper one seems longer. In the experiment, participants were first shown the converging lines in part (b) and then shown the two horizontal lines in part (c) and asked to imagine them together so that the top horizontal line touched the two diagonals. They were asked to compare the length of the two horizontal lines in their mental images. Participants rated as high in imagery ability reported as strong an illusion for their mental image as for the actual stimulus in part (a). Thus, it appears

FIGURE 4.10 The Ponzo illusion is illustrated in part (a): Even though they have the same length, the upper horizontal line seems longer. Parts (b) and (c) illustrate the material Wallace (1984) used to study the illusion in imagery. Participants imagined the parts superimposed so that the diagonal lines in (b) just touched the horizontal lines in (c). (From Wallace, 1984. Reprinted by permission of the publisher. © 1984 by the Psychonomic Society.)

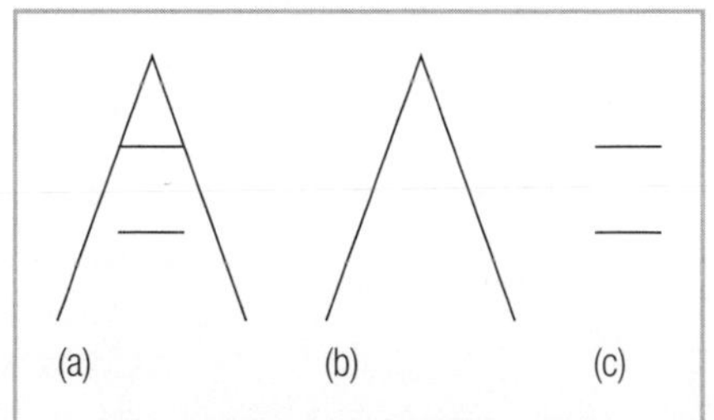

FIGURE 4.11 The ambiguous duck-rabbit figure used in Chambers and Reisberg's study of the processing of reversible figures. (From Chambers & Reisberg, 1985. Reprinted by permission of the publisher. © 1985 by the American Psychological Association.)

that the imagery system can reproduce a detailed visual illusion, supporting the apparent equivalence between imagery and perception.

Chambers and Reisberg (1985) reported a study that seemed to indicate differences between a mental image and visual perception of the real object. Their research involved the processing of reversible figures, such as the duck-rabbit shown in Figure 4.11. Participants were briefly shown the figure and asked to form an image of it. They had only enough time to form one interpretation of the picture before it was removed, but they were asked to try to find a second interpretation. Participants were not able to do this. Then they were asked to draw the image on paper to see whether they could reinterpret it. In this circumstance, they were successful. This result suggests that visual images differ from pictures in that one can interpret visual images only in one way, and it is not possible to find an alternative interpretation of the image.

Subsequently, Peterson, Kihlstrom, Rose, and Gilsky (1992) were able to get participants to reverse mental images by giving them more explicit instructions. For instance, participants might be told how to reverse another figure or be given the instruction to consider the back of the head of the animal in their mental image as the front of the head of another animal. Thus, it seems apparent that although it may be more difficult to reverse an image than a picture, both can be reversed. In general, it seems harder to process an image than the actual stimulus. Given a choice, people will almost always choose to process an actual picture rather than imagine it. For instance, players of Tetris prefer to rotate shapes on the screen to find an appropriate orientation rather than rotate them mentally (Kirsh & Maglio, 1994).

- *It is possible to make many of the same kinds of detailed judgments about mental images that we make about things we actually see, though it is more difficult.*

Visual Imagery and Brain Areas

Brain imaging studies indicate that the same regions are involved in perception as in mental imagery. As already noted, the parietal regions that are involved in attending to locations and objects (last chapter) are also involved in mental rotation. A study by O'Craven and Kanwisher (2000) illustrates how closely the brain areas activated by imagery correspond to the brain areas activated by perception. Recall from Chapter 2 that the fusiform region of the temporal cortex responds preferentially to faces. There is another region of the temporal cortex, the **parahippocampal place area (PPA)**, that responds preferentially to pictures of locations. O'Craven and Kanwisher asked participants either to view faces and scenes or to imagine faces and scenes. The same areas were active when the participants were seeing as when they were imagining. Figure 4.12 compares activation in the **fusiform face area (FFA)** with activation in the PPA. Every time the participants viewed or imagined a face, there was increased activation in the FFA, and this activation went away when they processed places. Conversely, when they viewed or imagined scenes, there was activation in the

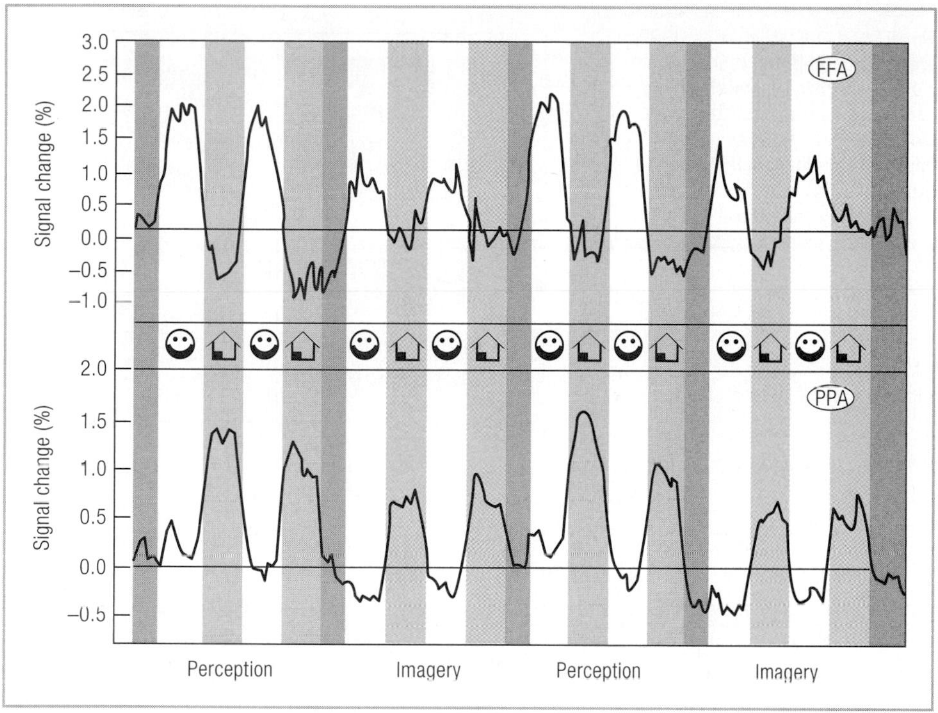

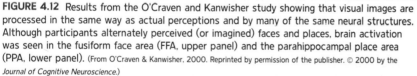

FIGURE 4.12 Results from the O'Craven and Kanwisher study showing that visual images are processed in the same way as actual perceptions and by many of the same neural structures. Although participants alternately perceived (or imagined) faces and places, brain activation was seen in the fusiform face area (FFA, upper panel) and the parahippocampal place area (PPA, lower panel). (From O'Craven & Kanwisher, 2000. Reprinted by permission of the publisher. © 2000 by the *Journal of Cognitive Neuroscience.*)

PPA that went away when they processed faces. The responses during imagery were very similar to the responses during perception, although a little weaker. The fact that the response was weaker during imagery is consistent with the behavioral evidence we have viewed suggesting that it is more difficult to process an image than a real perception.

There are many studies like these that show the involvement of cortical regions that are further along in the visual processing stream, but the evidence is less clear about activation in the primary visual cortex (areas 17 and 18) where visual information first reaches the brain. The O'Craven and Kanwisher study found activation in the primary visual cortex during imagery. Such results are important because they suggest that visual imagery includes relatively low-level perceptual processes. However, activation has not always been found in the primary visual cortex. For instance, the Roland and Friberg study illustrated in Figure 4.1 did not find activation in this region (see also Roland, Eriksson, Stone-Elander, & Widen, 1987). Kosslyn and Thompson (2003) reviewed 59 brain-imaging studies that looked for activation in early visual areas. About half of these studies find activation in early visual areas and half do not.

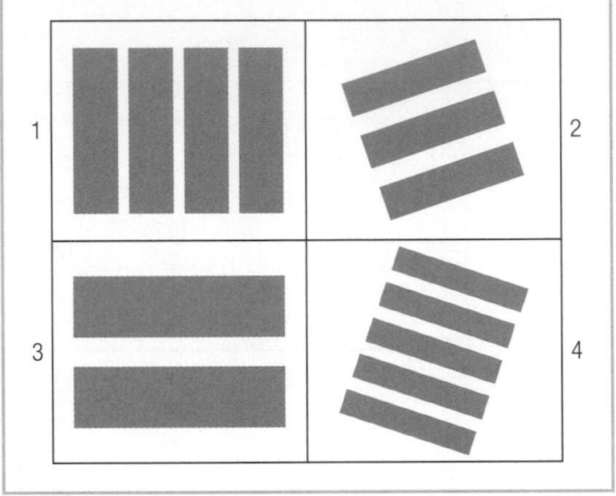

FIGURE 4.13 Illustration of stimuli used in Kosslyn et al. (1999). The numbers 1, 2, 3, and 4 were used to label the four quadrants, each of which contained a set of stripes. After memorizing the display, the participants closed their eyes, visualized the entire display, heard the names of two quadrants, and then heard the name of a comparison term (for example, "length"); the participants then decided whether the stripes in the first-named quadrant had more of the named property than those in the second.

Their analysis suggests that the studies that find activation in these early visual areas tend to emphasize high-resolution details of the images and tend to focus on shape judgments. As an instance of one of the positive studies, Kosslyn et al. (1993) did find activation in area 17 in a study where participants were asked to imagine block letters. In one of their experiments, participants were asked to imagine large versus small letters. In the small-letter condition, activity in the visual cortex occurred in a more posterior region closer to where the center of the visual field is represented (recall that the visual field is topographically organized—see Figure 2.6). This would make sense because a small image would be more concentrated at the center of the visual field.

Imaging studies like these show that perceptual regions of the brain are active when participants are engaged in mental imagery, but they do not establish whether these regions are actually critical to imagery. To return to the epiphenomenon critique at the beginning of the chapter, it could be that the activation plays no role in the actual tasks being performed. A number of experiments now have used transcranial magnetic stimulation (TMS—see Figure 1.13) to investigate the causal role of these regions in the performance of the underlying task. For instance, Kosslyn et al. (1999) presented participants with 4-quadrant arrays like those in Figure 4.13 and asked them to form a mental image of the array. Then, with the array removed, participants had to use their image to answer questions like "Which has longer stripes: Quadrant 1 or Quadrant 2?" or "Which has more stripes: Quadrant 1 or Quadrant 4?" Application of TMS to primary visual area 17 significantly increased the time they took to answer these questions. Thus, it seems that these visual regions do play a causal role in mental imagery, and temporarily deactivating them results in impaired information processing.

- *When performing a visual imFagery task, there is activation in brain regions involved in visual perception, and disruption of these regions results in disruption of the imagery task.*

Imagery Involves Both Spatial and Visual Components

We have reviewed the Brooks (1968) research indicating that people are sensitive to the spatial structure of their mental images and the Moyer (1973) research indicating that people process visual details such as size in their mental images. The distinction between the spatial and visual attributes of imagery has proved important in recent research. We can encode the position of objects in space by seeing where they are, by feeling where they are, or by hearing where they are. Such encodings use a common spatial representation that integrates information that comes in from any sensory modality. On the other hand, certain aspects of visual experience, such as color, are unique to the visual modality and seem separate from spatial information. Thus, imagery involves both spatial and visual components. In the discussion of the visual system in Chapter 2, we reviewed the evidence that there is a "where" pathway for processing spatial information and a "what" pathway for processing object information (see Figure 2.1). Corresponding to this distinction, there is evidence that the parietal regions support the spatial component of visual imagery, whereas the temporal lobe supports the visual aspects (see Figure 4.1). We have already noted that mental rotation, a spatial task, tends to produce activation in the parietal cortex. Similarly, temporal structures are activated when people imagine visual properties of objects (Thompson & Kosslyn, 2000).

Patient studies of imagery also support this association of spatial imagery with parietal areas of the brain and visual imagery with temporal areas. Levine, Warach, and Farah (1985) compared two patients, one who suffered bilateral parietal-occipital damage and the other who suffered bilateral inferior temporal damage. The patient with parietal damage could not describe the locations of familiar objects or landmarks from memory, but he could describe the appearance of objects. The patient with temporal damage had an impaired ability to describe the appearance of objects but could describe their locations.

Farah, Hammond, Levine, and Calvanio (1988) carried out more detailed testing of the patient with temporal damage. They compared his performance on a wide variety of imagery tasks to that of normal participants. They found that he showed deficits on only a subset of these tasks: ones in which he had to judge color ("What is the color of a football?"), sizes ("Which is bigger, a popsicle or a pack of cigarettes?"), the lengths of animals' tails ("Does a kangaroo have a long tail?"), and whether two states in the United States had similar shapes. In contrast, he did not show any deficit in performing tasks that seemed to involve a substantial amount of spatial processing: mental rotation, image scanning, letter scanning (as in Figure 4.7), or judgments of where one U.S. state was relative to another state. Thus, temporal damage seemed to affect only those imagery tasks that required access to visual detail, not those that required spatial judgments.

- *Neuropsychological evidence suggests that imagery of spatial information is supported by parietal structures, and imagery of objects and their visual properties is supported by temporal structures.*

Cognitive Maps

Another important function of visual imagery is to help us figure out and remember the spatial structure of our environment. Our imaginal representations of the world are often referred to as cognitive maps. The connection between imagery and action is particularly apparent in cognitive maps. We often find ourselves imagining our environment as we plan how we will get from one location to another.

An important distinction can be made betweeen **route maps** and **survey maps** (Hart & Moore, 1973). A route map is a path that indicates specific places but contains no 2-D information. It can even be a verbal description of a path ("Straight until the light, then turn left, two blocks later at the intersection . . ."). Thus, with a pure route map, if your route from location 1 to location 2 were blocked, you would have no general idea of where location 2 was, and so you would be unable to construct a detour. Also, if you knew (in the sense of a route map) two routes from a location, you would have no idea whether these routes formed a 90° angle or a 120° angle with respect to each other. A survey map, in contrast, contains this information, and is basically a spatial image of the environment. When you ask for directions from typical online mapping services, they will provide both a route map and a survey map to support both mental representations of space.

Thorndyke and Hayes-Roth (1982) investigated workers' knowledge of the Rand Corporation Building (Figure 4.14), a large, maze-like building in Santa

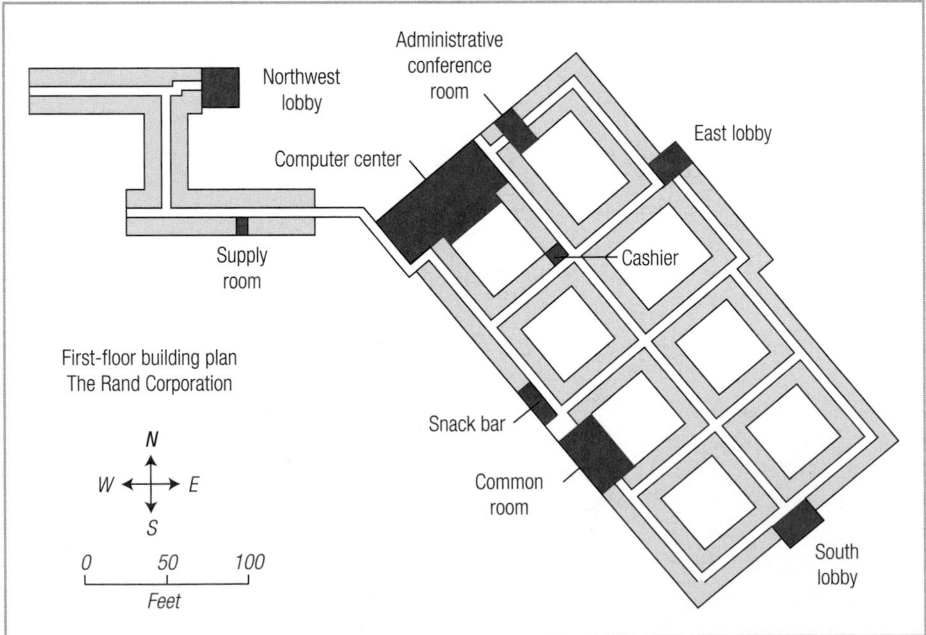

FIGURE 4.14 The floor plan for part of the Rand Corporation Building in Santa Monica, California. Thorndyke and Hayes-Roth studied the ability of secretaries to find their way around the building. (From Thorndyke and Hayes-Roth, 1982. Reprinted by permission of the publisher. © 1982 by *Cognitive Psychology*.)

Monica, California. People in the Rand Building quickly acquire the ability to find their way from one specific place in the building to another—for example, from the supply room to the cashier. This knowledge represents a route map. Typically, though, workers had to have years of experience in the building before they could make such survey-map determinations as the direction of the lunch-room from the photocopy room.

Hartley, Maguire, Spiers, and Burgess (2003) looked at the different brain activity when people used these two types of representations. They had participants navigate virtual reality towns under one of two conditions. In one condition, called route-following, participants learned to follow a fixed path through the town. In the other condition, called way-finding, participants first freely explored the town and then had to find their way between locations. The fMRI activation was compared when engaged in the route-following or way-finding tasks. The results on the experiment are illustrated in Color Plate 4.1. In the way-finding task, participants showed greater activation in a number of regions found in other studies of visual imagery including the parietal cortex. Also, they found greater activation in the hippocampus (see Figure 1.7), a region that has been implicated in navigation in many species. In contrast, in the route-following task participants showed greater activation in more anterior regions motor regions. It would seem that the survey map is more like a visual image and the route map is more like an action plan. This is a distinction that is supported in other fMRI studies of route maps versus survey maps (e.g., Shelton & Gabrieli, 2002).

Our knowledge of our environment can be represented in either survey maps that emphasize spatial information or route maps that emphasize action information.

Egocentric and Allocentric Representations of Space

Navigation becomes difficult when we must tie together multiple different representations of space. In particular, we often need to relate the way space appears as we perceive it to some other representation of space, such as a cognitive map. The representation of "space as we see it" is referred to as an egocentric representation. Figure 4.15 illustrates an egocentric representation that one might have upon entering Camp Snoopy at the Mall of America in Bloomington, Minnesota. Even young children have little difficulty understanding how to navigate in space as they *see* it—if they see an object they want, they go for it. Problems arise when one wants to relate what one sees to such representations of the space as cognitive maps, be they route maps or survey maps. Similar problems arise when one wants to deal with physical maps, such as the map of Camp Snoopy shown in Figure 4.16. This kind of map is referred to as an allocentric representation because it is not specific to a particular viewpoint, though, as is true of most maps, north is oriented to the top of the image. Try to identify which building on the map corresponds to the circled building in Figure 4.15, assuming

FIGURE 4.15 An egocentric representation of Camp Snoopy at the Mall of America. (Courtesy of Camp Snoopy/Bob Cole.)

that the viewpoint is the one of the stick figure illustrated in Figure 4.16. When people try to make such judgments, the degree to which the map is rotated from their actual viewpoint has a large effect. Indeed, people will often rotate a physical map so that it is oriented to correspond to their point of view. The map in Figure 4.16 would have to be rotated approximately 90° counterclockwise to be oriented with the representation shown in Figure 4.15.

When it is not possible to rotate a map physically, people show an effect of the degree of misorientation that is much like the effect we see for mental rotation (e.g., Boer, 1991; Easton & Sholl, 1995; Gugerty, deBoom, Jenkins, & Morley, 2000; Hintzman, O'Dell, & Arndt, 1981). Figure 4.17 shows a recent result from a study by Gunzelmann and Anderson (2002), who looked at the time required to find an object on a standard map (i.e., north oriented to the top) as a function of the viewer's location. When the viewer is located to the south, looking north, it is easier to find the object than when the viewer is north looking south, just the opposite of the map orientation. Some people describe imagining themselves moving around the map, others talk about rotating what they see, and still others report using verbal descriptions ("to the left of Snoopy, before the Ferris wheel"). The fact that the angle of disparity in this task has as great an effect as it does in mental rotation has led many researchers to believe that the processes and representations involved in such navigational tasks are similar to the processes and representations involved in mental imagery.

Physical maps seem to differ from cognitive maps in one important way: Physical maps show the effects of orientation, and cognitive maps do not. For

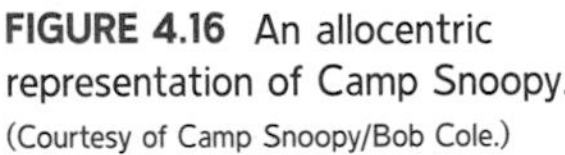

FIGURE 4.16 An allocentric representation of Camp Snoopy. (Courtesy of Camp Snoopy/Bob Cole.)

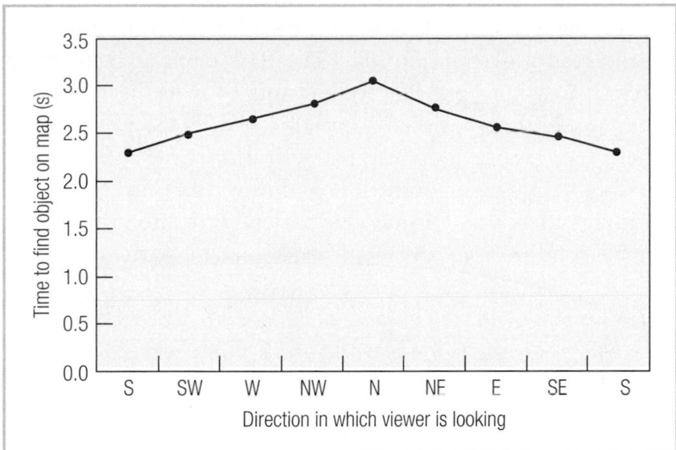

FIGURE 4.17 Results from Gunzelmann and Anderson's study to determine how much effect the angle of disparity between a standard map (looking north) and the viewer's viewpoint has on people's ability to find an object on the map. The time required for participants to identify the object is plotted as a function of the difference in orientation between the map and the egocentric viewpoint. (After Gunzelmann & Anderson, 2002. Adapted by permission of the publisher. © 2002 by Erlbaum.)

example, imagine yourself standing against various walls of your bedroom, and point to the location of the front door of your home or apartment. Most people can do this equally well no matter which position they take. In contrast, when given a map like the one shown in Figure 4.16, people find it much easier to point to various objects on the map if they are oriented in the same way the map is.

Recordings from single cells in the hippocampal region (inside the temporal lobe) of rats suggest that the hippocampus plays an important role in maintaining an allocentric representation of the world. There are place cells in the hippocampus that fire maximally when the animal is in a particular location in its environment (O'Keefe & Dostrovsky, 1971). Similar cells have been found in recordings from human patients in a procedure to map out the brain before surgery to control epilepsy (Ekstrom et al., 2003). Brain-imaging studies have shown that when humans are navigating their environment, there is high hippocampal activation (Maguire et al., 1998). Another study (Maguire et al., 2000) showed that the hippocampal volume of London taxi drivers was greater than that of people who didn't drive taxis and increased with the length of time they had been taxi drivers. It takes about 3 years of hard training to gain a knowledge of London streets adequate to become a successful taxi driver, and this training appears to have an impact on the structure of the brain. The amount of activation in hippocampal structures has also been shown to correlate with age-related differences in navigation skills (Pine et al., 2002) and may relate to gender differences in navigational ability (Gron, Wunderlich, Spitzer, Tomczak, and Riepe, 2000). These regions include the PPA, which O'Craven and Kanwisher (2000) found active when participants imagined places (see Figure 4.12).

Although it appears that the hippocampus is important in supporting allocentric representations, it seems that the parietal cortex is particularly important in supporting egocentric representations (Burgess, 2006). In one fMRI imaging study comparing egocentric and allocentric spatial processing (Zaehle et al., 2007), participants where asked to make judgments that emphasized either an allocentric or an egocentric perspective. In the allocentric conditions, participants would read a description like "The blue triangle is to the left of the green square. The green square is above the yellow triangle. The yellow triangle is to the right of the red circle." Then they would be asked a question like "Is the blue triangle above the red circle?" In the egocentric condition, they would read a description like "The blue circle is in front of you. The yellow circle is to your right. The yellow square is to the right of the yellow circle." They would then be asked a question like "Is the yellow square to your right?" There was greater hippocampal activation when participants were answering questions in the allocentric condition than in the egocentric condition. Although there was considerable parietal activation in both conditions, the egocentric condition was distinguished by greater parietal activation.

Our representation of space includes both allocentric representations of where objects are in the world and egocentric representations of where they are relative to ourselves.

Map Distortions

Our mental maps often have a hierarchical structure in which smaller regions are organized within larger regions. For instance, the structure of my bedroom is organized within the structure of my house, which is organized within the structure of my neighborhood, which is organized within the structure of Pittsburgh. Consider your mental map of the United States. It is probably divided into regions, and these regions into states, and cities are presumably pinpointed within the states. It turns out that certain systematic distortions arise because of the hierarchical structure of these mental maps. Stevens and Coupe (1978) documented a set of common misconceptions about North American geography. Consider the following questions taken from their research:

- Which is farther east: San Diego or Reno?
- Which is farther north: Seattle or Montreal?
- Which is farther west: the Atlantic or the Pacific entrance to the Panama Canal?

The first choice is the correct answer in each case, but most people hold the wrong opinion. Reno seems to be farther east because Nevada is east of California, but this reasoning does not account for the westward curve in California's coastline. Montreal seems to be north of Seattle because Canada is north of the United States, but the border dips south in the east. And the Atlantic is certainly east of the Pacific—but consult a map if you need to be convinced about the location of the entrances to the Panama Canal. The geography of North America is quite complex, and people resort to abstract facts about relative locations of large physical bodies (e.g., California and Nevada) to make judgments about smaller locations (e.g., San Diego and Reno).

Stevens and Coupe were able to demonstrate such confusions with experimenter-created maps. Different groups of participants learned the maps illustrated in Figure 4.18. The important feature of the incongruent maps is that the relative locations of the Alpha and Beta counties are inconsistent with the locations of the X and Y cities. After learning the maps, participants were asked a series of questions about the locations of cities, including "Is X east or west of Y?"

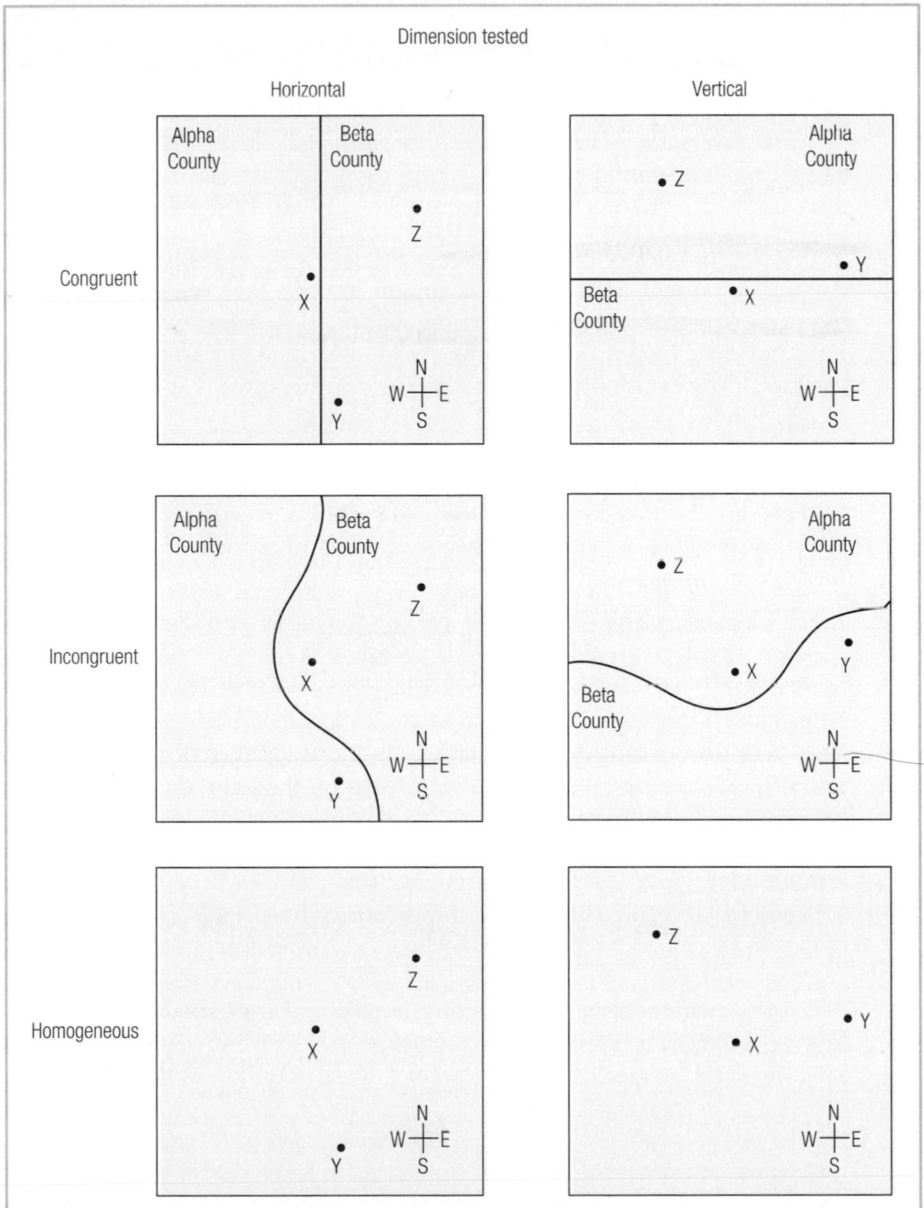

FIGURE 4.18 Maps studied by participants in the experiments of Stevens and Coupe, which demonstrated the effects of higher order information (location of county lines) on participants' recall of city locations. (From Stevens & Coupe, 1978. Reprinted by permission of the publisher. © 1978 by *Cognitive Psychology*.)

for the left-hand maps and "Is X north or south of Y?" for the right-hand maps. On these questions, participants were in error 18% of the time for the congruent maps and 15% percent of the time for the homogeneous maps—but 45% of the time for the incongruent maps. Participants were using information about the locations of the counties to help them remember the city locations. This reliance on higher order information led them to make errors, just as similar reasoning can lead to errors in answering questions about North American geography.

When people have to work out the relative positions of two locations, they will often reason in terms of the relative positions of larger areas that contain the two locations.

Translating Words to Images

Another important use of spatial cognition involves the creation of a mental image when we hear a word description of a spatial structure. This happens, for instance, when we process directions, read a description of an event, or hear a sportscast. The British psychologist Alan Baddeley reported that he was not able to drive while trying to follow an American football game on the radio because of the conflicting imagery. To get an idea of how difficult it can be to construct a spatial image from words, try reading the description in Table 4.2.

Franklin and Tversky (1990) presented participants with such stories. After the participants read the stories, they were asked to reorient themselves based on descriptions such as

> As you remain where you are on the balcony, you turn your body 90 degrees to your right, and you now face the lamp. You look again at the short, rigid pole by which it is fixed to the wall. Perhaps this is a precautionary feature in case of earthquake.

Then they were asked to judge what was in a specific direction. For instance, on different trials they would be asked what is on the right, on the left, above, below, behind, or in front of them.

TABLE 4.2

Description Read by Participants in Franklin and Tversky's (1990) Experiment
You are hob-nobbing at the opera. You came tonight to meet and chat with interesting members of the upper class. At the moment, you are standing next to the railing of a wide, elegant balcony overlooking the first floor. Directly behind you, at your eye level, is an ornate lamp attached to the balcony wall. The base of the lamp, which is attached to the wall, is gilded in gold. Straight ahead of you, mounted on a nearby wall beyond the balcony, you see a large bronze plaque dedicated to the architect who designed the theatre. A simple likeness of the architect, as well as a few sentences about him, are raised slightly against the bronze background. Sitting on the shelf directly to your right is a beautiful bouquet of flowers. You see that the arrangement is largely composed of red roses and white carnations. Looking up, you see that a large loudspeaker is mounted to the theatre's ceiling about 20 feet directly above you. From its orientation, you suppose that it is a private speaker for the patrons who sit in this balcony. Leaning over the balcony's railing and looking down, you see that a marble sculpture stands on the first floor directly below you. As you peer down toward it, you see that it is a young man and wonder whether it is a reproduction of Michelangelo's *David*.

Figure 4.19 shows the times required for participants to make their judgments in the various directions. Participants made the above-below judgments fastest and the right-left judgments slowest. Franklin and Tversky point out that such results make sense if we assume that participants are constructing a spatial framework while reading the description. Both the up-down vertical axis and the front-back horizontal axis are relevant when we navigate in the real world. In contrast, we suffer many left-right confusions because of the bilateral symmetries of the body. We have similar confusions about left and right in our imagery.

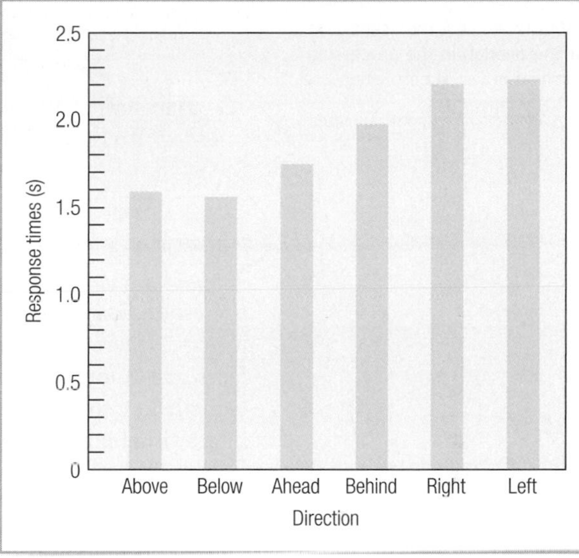

FIGURE 4.19 Results from Franklin & Tversky's experiment demonstrating that we create mental images from a word description of a spatial structure. Participants read stories that required them to orient themselves in an imaginary environment, then were asked to identify the locations of objects in the environment. The results are the times required to identify objects in various directions. (From Franklin & Tversky, 1990. Reprinted by permission of the publisher. © 1990 by *Journal of Experimental Psychology: General*.)

In another experiment, H. A. Taylor and Tversky (1992) compared the relative effectiveness of three types of spatial information: route descriptions, survey descriptions, and actual maps. The route descriptions were a mental tour through the environment, whereas the survey descriptions gave a bird's-eye view of the environment. After studying the descriptions or the actual map, participants had to verify route or survey statements about the environment. A route statement might be

Driving from the Town Hall to the gas station, you pass Maple Street on your right.

A survey statement might be

Horseshoe Drive runs along the northern shore of Pigeon Lake.

Participants were asked to judge whether these sentences were true of the environment they studied. They were equally fast at judging such questions whether they had studied route descriptions, survey descriptions, or actual maps. From this result, Taylor and Tversky concluded that people can construct cognitive maps from verbal descriptions as effectively as from actual maps.

We can convert verbal descriptions into cognitive maps of our environment.

Conclusions: Visual Perception and Visual Imagery

This chapter has also reviewed some of the evidence that the same brain regions that are involved in visual perception are also involved in visual imagery. Such research has presumably put to rest the issue raised at the beginning of the chapter that the visual imagery experiences are purely epiphenomenal. However, although it seems clear that perceptual processes are involved in visual imagery, it remains an open question to what degree the mechanisms of visual imagery are the same as the mechanisms of visual perception. Evidence for a substantial overlap comes from neuropsychological patient studies (see Bartolomeo, 2002, for a review). Many patients who have cortical damage leading to blindness have corresponding deficits in visual imagery. As Behrmann (2000) notes, the

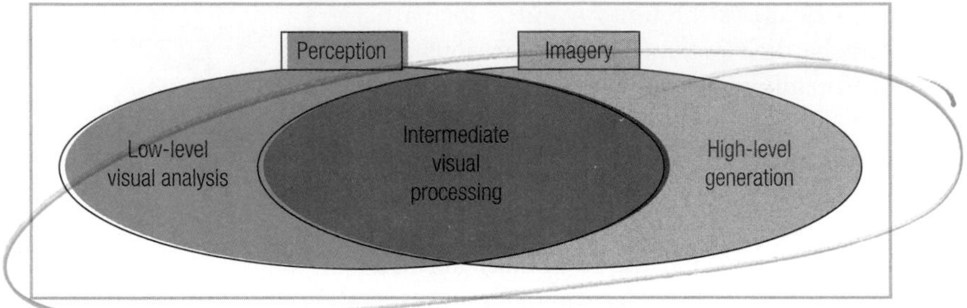

FIGURE 4.20 A representation of the overlap in the processing involved in visual perception and visual imagery.

correspondences between perception and imagery can be quite striking. For instance, there are patients who are only unable either to perceive or to image faces and colors, but are otherwise unimpaired in either perception or imagery. Nonetheless, there exist cases of patients who suffer perceptual problems but have intact visual imagery and vice versa. Behrmann argues that visual perception and visual imagery are best understood as two processes that overlap but are not identical, as illustrated in Figure 4.20. To perceive a kangaroo requires low-level visual information processing that is not required for visual imagery. Similarly, to form a mental image of a kangaroo requires generation processes that are not required by perception. Behrmann suggests that patients who suffer only perceptual losses have damage to the low-level part of this system, and patients who only suffer imagery losses have damage to the high-level part of this system.

Questions for Thought

1. It has been hypothesized that our perceptual system regularly uses mental rotation to recognize objects in nonstandard orientations. In Chapter 2 we contrasted template and feature models for object recognition. Would mental rotation be more important to a template or feature model?
2. Consider the following problem:

   Imagine a wire-frame cube resting on a tabletop with the front face directly in front of you and perpendicular to your line of sight. Imagine the long diagonal that goes from the bottom, front, left-hand corner to the top, back, right-hand one. Now imagine that the cube is reoriented so that this diagonal is vertical and the cube is resting on one corner. Place one fingertip about a foot above the tabletop and let this mark the position of the top corner on the diagonal. The corner on which the cube is resting is on the tabletop, vertically below your fingertip. With your other hand, point to the spatial locations of the other corners of the cube.

   Hinton (1979) reports that almost no one is able to perform this task successfully. In light of the successes we have reviewed for mental imagery, why is this task so hard?
3. The chapter reviewed the evidence that many different regions are activated in mental imagery tasks—parietal and motor areas in mental rotation, temporal regions in judgments of object attributes, and hippocampal regions in reasoning about navigation. Why would mental imagery involve so many regions?
4. Consider the map distortions such as the tendency to believe San Diego is west of Reno. Are these distortions in an egocentric representation, an allocentric representation, or something else?

Key Terms

allocentric representation
cognitive maps
egocentric representation
epiphenomenon
fusiform face area
mental imagery
mental rotation
parahippocampal place area
route maps
survey maps

5

Representation of Knowledge

Recall a wedding you attended a while ago. Presumably, you can remember who married whom, where the wedding was, many of the people who attended, and some of the things that happened. You would probably be hard pressed, however, to say exactly what all the participants wore, the exact words that were spoken, the the way the bride walked down the aisle, and so on—although you probably registered many of these details. It is not surprising that after time has passed, our memories lose some of the information of the original experience. What is interesting is that our loss of information is selective: We tend to remember the gist (that which is most meaningful or useful) and forget the detail (that which is not important).

The previous chapter was about our ability to form visual images of the detail of our experiences. It might seem that it would be ideal if we had the capacity to always represent information in such detail and remember the detail. However, the histories of the few individuals who have such detailed memories suggest that this might be a curse rather than a blessing. Luria (1987) describes the story of a Russian journalist who lived in the first half of the 20th century, who had very vivid imagery and the ability to remember a great many perceptual details of his experience. He had problems with many aspects of ordinary life, including reading:

> As he put it: "Other people *think* as they read, but I *see* it all." As soon as he began a phrase, images would appear; as he read further, still more images were evoked, and so on. . . . If a passage were read to him quickly, one image would collide with another in his mind; images would begin to crowd in upon one another and would become contorted. (p. 112)

Such problems caused him great difficulties in many aspects of life, including keeping his job. Parker, Cahill, and McGaugh (2006) describe a current case of an individual with highly detailed memory.[1] She is able to remember many details from years ago in her life but had difficulty in school and seems to perform poorly on tasks of abstract reasoning such as processing analogies. There are many situations when we need to rise above the details of our experience and get to their true meaning and significance.

[1] She has written her own biography, *The Woman Who Can't Forget* (Price, 2008).

In this chapter we will address the following questions:

- What happens to our memories for gist versus detail with the passage of time?
- How do we represent the gist of an experience?
- Are there representations of knowledge that are not tied to specific perceptual modalities?
- What is the nature of our representation of categorical knowledge and how does this affect the way we perceive the world?

Knowledge and Regions of the Brain

Figure 5.1 shows some of the brain regions involved in the abstraction of knowledge. Some prefrontal regions are associated with extracting meaningful information from pictures and sentences. The left prefrontal region is more involved in the processing of verbal material and the right prefrontal region is more involved in the processing of visual material (Gabrielli, 2001). Part of the processing is to represent events in terms of general categories such as *bride* or *wedding*. This categorical information is represented in posterior regions of the temporal, parietal, and occipital cortices. As we will see, there is evidence that different posterior regions represent different types of concepts.

We will review neuroscience data on the localization of processing and information in the brain, but much of the most striking evidence comes from behavioral studies that examine what people remember or forget after an event.

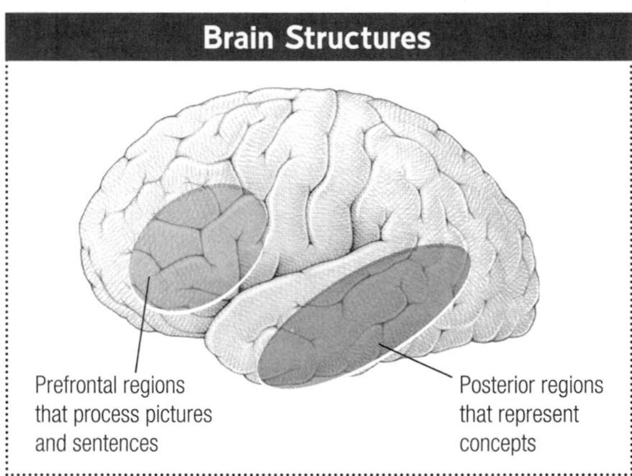

FIGURE 5.1 Cortical regions involved in the processing of meaning and the representation of concepts.

Prefrontal regions of the brain are associated with meaningful processing of events, whereas posterior regions are associated with representing concepts.

Memory for Meaningful Interpretations of Events

Memory for Verbal Information

An experiment by Wanner (1968) illustrates circumstances in which people do and do not remember information about exact wording. Wanner asked participants to come into the laboratory and listen to tape-recorded instructions. For one group of participants, the warned group, the tape began this way:

> The materials for this test, including the instructions, have been recorded on tape. Listen very carefully to the instructions because you will be tested on your ability to recall particular sentences which [sic] occur in the instructions.

The participants in the second group received no such warning and so had no idea that they would be responsible for the verbatim instructions. After this point, the instructions were the same for both groups. At a later point in the instructions, one of four possible critical sentences was presented:

1. When you score your results, do nothing to correct your answers but mark carefully those answers which are wrong.
2. When you score your results, do nothing to correct your answers but carefully mark those answers which are wrong.
3. When you score your results, do nothing to your correct answers but mark carefully those answers which are wrong.
4. When you score your results, do nothing to your correct answers but carefully mark those answers which are wrong.

Immediately after one of these sentences was presented, all participants (warned or not) heard the following conclusion to the instructions:

> To begin the test, please turn to page 2 of the answer booklet and judge which of the sentences printed there occurred in the instructions you just heard.

On page 2, they found the critical sentence they had just heard plus a similar alternative. Suppose they had heard sentence 1. They might have to choose between sentences 1 and 2 or between sentences 1 and 3. Both pairs differ only in the ordering of two words. However, the difference between 1 and 2 does not contribute critically to the meaning of the sentences; the difference is just stylistic. On the other hand, sentences 1 and 3 clearly do differ in meaning. Thus, by looking at participants' ability to discriminate between different pairs of sentences, Wanner was able to measure their ability to remember the meaning versus the style of the sentence and to determine how this ability was affected by whether or not they were warned.

The relevant data are presented in Figure 5.2. The percentage of correct identifications of sentences heard is displayed as a function of whether participants had been warned. The percentages are plotted separately for participants who were asked to discriminate a meaningful difference in wording and for those who were asked to discriminate a stylistic difference. If participants were just guessing, they would have scored 50% correct by chance; thus, we would not expect any values below 50%.

FIGURE 5.2 Results from Wanner's experiment to determine circumstances in which people do and do not remember information about exact wording. The ability of participants to remember a wording difference that affected meaning versus one that affected only style is plotted as a function of whether or not the participants were warned that they would be tested on their ability to recall particular sentences. (After Wanner, 1968. Adapted by permission of the author.)

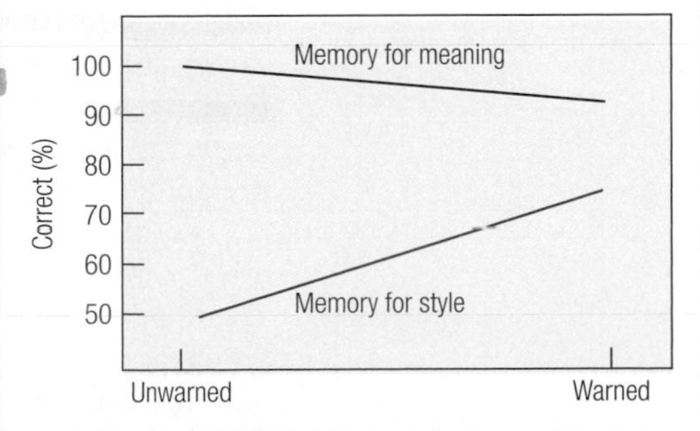

The implications of Wanner's experiment are clear. First, memory is better for changes in wording that result in changes of meaning than for changes in wording that result just in changes of style. The superiority of memory for meaning indicates that people normally extract the meaning from a linguistic message and do not remember its exact wording. Moreover, memory for meaning is equally good whether people are warned or not. (The slight advantage for unwarned participants does not approach statistical significance.) Thus, participants retained the meaning of a message as a normal part of their comprehension process. They did not have to be cued to remember the sentence.

The second implication of these results is that the warning did have an effect on memory for the stylistic change. The unwarned participants remembered the stylistic change at about the level of chance, whereas the warned participants remembered it almost 80% of the time. This result indicates that we do not normally retain much information about exact wording, but we can do so when we are cued to pay attention to such information. Even with a warning, however, memory for stylistic information is poorer than memory for meaning.

After processing a linguistic message, people usually remember just its meaning and not its exact wording.

Memory for Visual Information

On many occasions, our memory capacity seems much greater for visual information in a picture or a scene than for verbal information (whether that verbal information is presented auditorially by speech or visually by text). Shepard (1967) reported an experiment in which he had participants study a set of magazine pictures, one picture at a time. Then they were presented with pairs of pictures consisting of one they had studied and one they had not. The task was to recognize which picture of each pair had been studied. This task was contrasted with a verbal condition in which participants studied sentences and were similarly tested on their ability to recognize those sentences when they were presented in pairs containing one new and one studied sentence. Participants made errors 11.8% of the time in the sentence condition but only 1.5% of the time in the picture condition. In other words, recognition memory was fairly high in the sentence condition but was virtually perfect in the picture condition. There have been a number of experiments like Shepard's, which involved 600 pictures. Perhaps the most impressive demonstration of visual memory is the experiment by Standing (1973), who showed that participants had only a 17% error rate after studying 10,000 pictures.

Although people can show very good memory for pictures under some circumstances, what they seem to be remembering is some interpretation of the picture rather than the exact picture itself. That is, it proves useful to distinguish between the meaning of a picture and the physical picture, just as it is important to distinguish between the meaning of a sentence and the physical sentence. A number of experiments point to the utility of this distinction with respect to picture memory and to the fact that we tend to remember an interpretation of the picture, not the physical picture.

For instance, consider an experiment by Mandler and Ritchey (1977). They asked participants to study pictures of scenes, such as the classroom scenes in Figure 5.3. After studying eight such pictures for 10 s each, participants were tested for their recognition memory. They were presented with a series of pictures and instructed to identify which pictures they had studied. The series included the exact pictures they had studied as well as distracter pictures. A distracter such as the one shown in Figure 5.3b was called a token distracter. It differed from

FIGURE 5.3 Pictures similar to those used by Mandler and Ritchey in their experiment to demonstrate that people distinguish between the meaning of a picture and the physical picture itself. Participants studied the target picture (a). Later they were tested with a series of pictures that included the target (a) along with token distracters such as (b) and type distracters such as (c). (After Mandler & Ritchey, 1977. Adapted by permission of the publisher. © 1977 by the American Psychological Association.)

the target only in the pattern of the teacher's clothes, a visual detail relatively unimportant to most interpretations of the picture. The distracter shown in Figure 5.3c, by contrast, involves a type change—from a world map to an art picture used by the teacher. This visual detail is relatively more important to most interpretations of the picture because it indicates the subject being taught. All eight pictures shown to participants contained possible token changes and type changes. In each case, the type change involved a more important alteration to the picture's meaning than did the token change. There was no systematic difference in the amount of physical change involved in a type change versus a token change. Participants were able to recognize the original pictures 77% percent of the time and to reject the token distracters only 60% of the time, but they rejected the type distracters 94% of the time.

The conclusion in this study is very similar to that in the Wanner (1968) experiment reviewed earlier. Wanner found that participants were much more sensitive to meaning-significant changes in a sentence; Mandler and Ritchey (1977) found that participants were more sensitive to meaning-significant

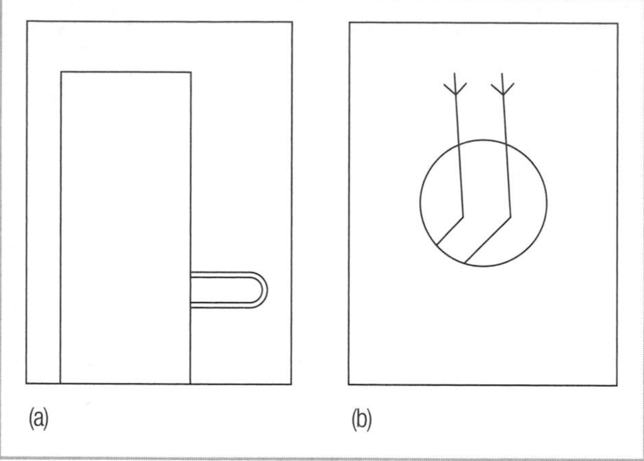

FIGURE 5.4 Recalling "droodles." (a) A midget playing a trombone in a telephone booth. (b) An early bird who caught a very strong worm. (From Bower, Karlin, & Dueck, 1975. Reprinted by permission of the publisher. © 1975 by *Memory & Cognition*.)

changes in a picture. It may be that people have better memory for the meanings of pictures than for the meanings of sentences, but they have poor memory for the physical details of both.

Bower, Karlin, and Dueck (1975) reported an amusing demonstration of the fact that people's good memory for pictures is tied to their interpretation of those pictures. Figure 5.4 illustrates some of the material they used. These investigators had participants study such drawings, called droodles, with or without an explanation of their meaning. Then they were given a memory test in which they had to redraw the pictures. Participants who had been given an explanation when studying the pictures showed better recall (70% correctly reconstructed) than those who were not given an explanation (51% correctly reconstructed). Thus, memory for the drawings depended critically on participants' ability to place a meaningful interpretation on the pictures.

- *When people see a picture, they tend to remember a meaningful interpretation of it.*

Retention of Detail versus Meaning

There is evidence that people initially encode many of the perceptual details of a sentence or a picture but tend to forget this information quickly. Once the perceptual information is forgotten, people retain memory for their interpretation of the picture. Memory for the orientation of a picture is one of the visual details that appear to decay rapidly, as demonstrated in an experiment by Gernsbacher (1985). Participants were shown pictures such as the ones illustrated in Figure 5.5. After studying one of these pictures, the participants were asked to judge which of the pair they had seen. After 10 s, participants made their judgments with 79% accuracy, showing considerable retention of information about left–right

FIGURE 5.5 Example picture from an experiment by Gernsbacher, displayed in one orientation (*left*) and the reverse (*right*). The experiment showed that memory for the orientation of a picture is a visual detail that appears to decay rapidly. (From Gernsbacher, 1985. Original illustration from Mercer and Mariana Meyer, *One Frog Too Many*. © 1975 by Mercer and Mariana Meyer. Reprinted by permission of the publisher, Dial Books for Young Readers, New York.)

orientation. After 10 min, however, their accuracy in judgment had fallen to 57% (50% percent would reflect chance guessing). On the other hand, their memory for what the picture was about remained high over that period of time.

When I was a graduate student, I performed an experiment (Anderson, 1974b) that made the same point in the verbal domain. Participants listened to a story that contained various critical sentences that would be tested; for instance:

The missionary shot the painter.

Later, participants were presented with one of the following sentences and asked whether it followed logically from the story they had heard. They were also asked to judge which sentence they had actually heard.

1. The missionary shot the painter.
2. The painter was shot by the missionary.
3. The painter shot the missionary.
4. The missionary was shot by the painter.

The first two sentences require a positive response to the logical judgment, and the last two require a negative response. Participants were tested either immediately after hearing the sentence or after a delay of about 2 min. The delay had little effect on the accuracy of their logical judgments (e.g., 1 versus 3 above)—98% were correct immediately and 96% were correct after a delay. However, when they were asked to judge which sentence they had heard (e.g., 1 versus 2 above), the delay had a dramatic effect. Participants were 99% correct immediately after hearing the sentence but only 56% correct after a delay.

Memory for detail is available initially but is forgotten rapidly, whereas memory for meaning is retained.

Implications of Good Memory for Meaning

We have seen that people have relatively good memory for meaningful interpretations of information. So when faced with material to remember, it will help if they can give it some meaningful interpretation. Unfortunately, many people are unaware of this fact, and their memory performance suffers as a consequence. I can still remember the traumatic experience I had in my first paired-associates experiment. It happened in a sophomore class in experimental psychology. For reasons I have long since forgotten, we had designed a class experiment that involved learning 16 pairs, such as DAX-GIB. Our task was to recall the second half of the pair when prompted with the first half. I was determined to outperform the other members of my class. My personal theory of memory at that time, which I intended to apply, was that if you try hard and focus intensely, you can remember anything well. In the impending experimental situation, this meant that during the learning period I should say (as loud as was seemly) the paired associates over and over again, as fast as I could. I believed that this method would burn the paired associates into my mind forever. To my chagrin, I wound up with the worst score in the class.

My theory of "loud and fast" was directly opposed to the true means of improving memory. I was trying to memorize a meaningless verbal pair. But the material discussed in this chapter so far suggests that we have the best memory for meaningful information. I should have been trying to convert my memory task into something more meaningful. For instance, DAX is like *dad* and GIB is the first part of *gibberish*. So I might have created an image of my father speaking some gibberish to me. This would have been a simple **mnemonic** (memory-assisting) **technique** and would have worked quite well as a means of associating the two elements.

We do not often need to learn pairs of nonsense syllables outside the laboratory. In many situations, however, we do have to associate various combinations of terms that do not have much inherent meaning. We have to remember shopping lists, names for faces, telephone numbers, rote facts in a college class, vocabulary items in a foreign language, and so on. In all cases, we can improve memory if we associate the items to be remembered with a meaningful interpretation.

Implications

Mnemonic techniques for remembering vocabulary items

One domain where we seem to have to learn arbitrary associations is foreign language vocabulary. For instance, consider trying to learn that the Italian *formaggio* (pronounced "for modge jo") means *cheese*. There is a memorization technique, called the keyword method, for learning vocabulary items, which some students are taught and others discover on their own. The first step is to convert the foreign word to some sound-alike in one's native language. For example, one might convert *formaggio* into "for much dough." The second step is to create a meaningful connection between the sound-alike and the meaning. For example, we might imagine expensive cheese being sold for much money or "for much dough." Or consider the Italian *carciofi* (pronounced "car-choh-fee"), which means *artichoke*. We might transform "car-choh-fee" into "car trophy" and imagine a winning car at an auto show with a trophy shaped like an artichoke. The intermediate (e.g., *for much dough* or *car trophy*) is called the keyword, although in both of these examples they are really key phrases. There has been extensive research on the effectiveness of this technique (for a review, read Kroll & DeGroot, 2005). The research shows that, like many things, one needs to take a nuanced approach in evaluating the effectiveness of the keyword technique. There is no doubt that it results in more rapid vocabulary learning in many situations, but there are potential costs. One might imagine that having to go through the intermediate keyword slows down speed of translation, and the keyword method has been shown to result in slower retrieval times compared to retrieval of items that are directly associated without an intermediate. Moreover, one might wonder about the implications of having to go through the intermediate for long-term retention, and again it has been shown to result in poorer long-term retention. Finally, there is evidence that suggests that although the method may help in passing the immediate vocabulary test in a class and hurt in a delayed test that we have not studied for, its ultimate impact on achieving real language mastery is minimal. Chapter 12 will discuss issues involved in foreign language mastery.

It is easier to commit arbitrary associations to memory if they are converted into something more meaningful.

Propositional Representations

We have shown that in many situations people do not remember the exact physical details of what they have seen or heard but rather the "meaning" of what they have encountered. In an attempt to become more precise about what is meant by "meaning," cognitive psychologists developed what is called a **propositional representation.** The concept of a **proposition,** borrowed from logic and linguistics, is central to such analyses. A proposition is the smallest unit of knowledge that can stand as a separate assertion, that is, the smallest unit one can meaningfully judge as true or false. Propositional analysis applies most clearly to linguistic information, and I will develop the topic here in terms of such information.

Consider the following sentence:

Lincoln, who was president of the United States during a bitter war, freed the slaves.

The information conveyed in this sentence can be communicated by the following simpler sentences:

A. Lincoln was president of the United States during a war.

B. The war was bitter.

C. Lincoln freed the slaves.

If any of these simple sentences were false, the complex sentence also would be false. These sentences correspond closely to the propositions that underlie the meaning of the complex sentence. Each simple sentence expresses a primitive unit of meaning. One condition that our meaning representations must satisfy is that each separate unit composing them must correspond to a unit of meaning.

However, the theory of propositional representation does not claim that a person remembers the simple sentences such as the three just presented. Past research indicates that people do not remember the exact wording of such simple sentences any more than they remember the exact wording of the original complex sentence. For instance, in another study I did as a graduate student (Anderson, 1972), I showed that participants demonstrated poor ability to remember whether they had heard sentence C or the sentence:

The slaves were freed by Lincoln.

Thus, it seems that we represent information in memory in a way that preserves the meaning of the primitive assertions but does not preserve any information about specific wording. A number of propositional notations represent information in this abstract way. One, used by Kintsch (1974), represents each proposition as a list containing a **relation** followed by an ordered list of **arguments.** The relations organize the arguments and typically correspond to the verbs (in this case, *free*), adjectives (*bitter*), and other relational terms (*president of*). The arguments refer to particular times, places, people, or objects, and typically correspond to the nouns (*Lincoln, war, slaves*). The relations assert connections among the entities these nouns refer to. Kintsch represents each proposition by a parenthesized list consisting of a relation plus arguments. As an example, sentences A through C would be represented by these lists:

a. (president-of: Lincoln, United States, war)

b. (bitter: war)

c. (free: Lincoln, slaves)

Note that each relation takes a different number of arguments: *president of* takes three, *free* takes two, and *bitter* takes one. Whether a person heard the original complex sentence or heard

The slaves were freed by Lincoln, the president during a bitter war,

the meaning of the message would be represented by lists a through c.

Bransford and Franks (1971) provided an interesting demonstration of the psychological reality of propositional units. In this experiment, participants studied 12 sentences, including the following:

The ants ate the sweet jelly, which was on the table.

The rock rolled down the mountain and crushed the tiny hut.

The ants in the kitchen ate the jelly.

The rock rolled down the mountain and crushed the hut beside the woods.

The ants in the kitchen ate the jelly, which was on the table.

The tiny hut was beside the woods.

The jelly was sweet.

All these sentences are composed from two sets of four propositions. One set of four propositions can be represented as

1. (eat: ants, jelly, past)
2. (sweet: jelly)
3. (on: jelly, table, past)
4. (in: ants, kitchen, past)

The other set of four propositions can be represented as

1. (roll down: rock, mountain, past)
2. (crush: rock, hut, past)
3. (beside: hut, woods, past)
4. (tiny: hut)

Bransford and Franks looked at participants' recognition memory for the following three kinds of sentences:

1. Old: The ants in the kitchen ate the jelly.
2. New: The ants ate the sweet jelly.
3. Noncase: The ants ate the jelly beside the woods.

The first kind of sentence was actually studied, the second was not but is a combination of propositions that were studied, and the third consists of words that were studied but cannot be composed from the propositions studied. Bransford and Franks found that participants had almost no ability to discriminate between the first two kinds of sentences and were equally likely to say that they had actually heard either. On the other hand, participants were quite confident that they had not heard the third, noncase, sentence.

The experiment shows that although people remember the propositions they encounter, they are quite insensitive to the actual combination of propositions. Indeed, the participants in this experiment were most likely to say that they heard a sentence consisting of all four propositions, such as

The ants in the kitchen ate the sweet jelly, which was on the table,

even though they had not in fact studied this sentence.

According to propositional analyses people remember a complex sentence as a set of abstract meaning units that represent the simple assertions in the sentence.

Propositional Networks

In the cognitive psychology literature, one sometimes finds propositions represented in a network form. Figure 5.6 illustrates the structure of a **propositional network** that encodes the sentence, "Lincoln, who was president of

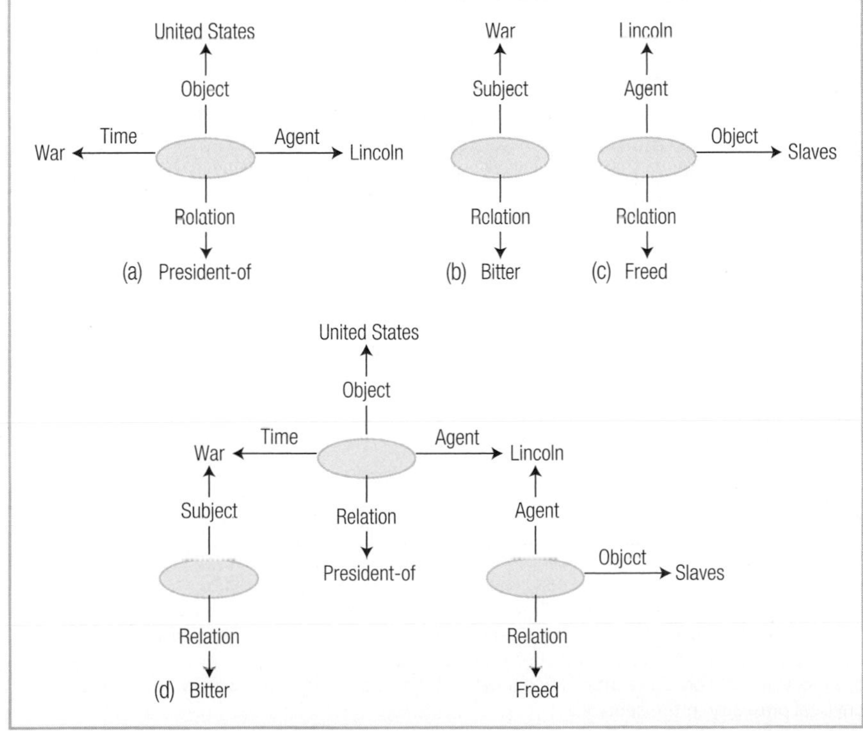

FIGURE 5.6 Network representations for the proposition underlying the statement: "Lincoln, who was president of the United States during a bitter war, freed the slaves."

the United States during a bitter war, freed the slaves." In this propositional network, each proposition is represented by an ellipse, which is connected by labeled arrows to its relation and arguments. The propositions, the relations, and the arguments are called the **nodes** of the network, and the arrows are called the **links** because they connect the nodes. For instance, the ellipse in Figure 5.6a represents proposition (a) from the earlier Kintsch analysis. This ellipse is connected to the relation *president-of* by a link labeled *relation* (to indicate that it is pointing to the relation node), to *Lincoln* by an *agent* link, to *United States* by an *object* link, and to *war* by a *time* link. The three network structures shown in Figures 5.6a, 5.6b, and 5.6c represent the individual propositions (a) through (c) from the earlier Kintsch analysis. Note that these three networks contain the same nodes, for example, Figures 5.6a and 5.6b both contain *war*. This overlap indicates that these networks are really interconnected parts of a larger network, which is illustrated in Figure 5.6d. This last network represents all the meaningful information in the original complex sentence on page 147.

The spatial location of elements in a network is irrelevant to its interpretation. A network can be thought of as a tangle of marbles connected by strings. The marbles represent the nodes, the strings the links between nodes. The network represented on a 2-D page is that tangle of marbles laid out in a certain way. We try to lay out the network in a way that facilitates an understanding of it, but any layout is possible. All that matters is which elements are connected to which others, not where the components lie.

A number of experiments suggest that it is helpful to think of the nodes in such networks as ideas and to think of the links between the nodes as associations between the ideas. Consider an experiment by Weisberg (1969) that used a constrained association task. In this experiment, participants studied and committed to memory such sentences as "Children who are slow eat bread that is cold." The propositional network representation of this sentence is illustrated in Figure 5.7. After learning a sentence, participants were administered free-association tasks in which they were given a word from the sentence and asked to respond with the first word from the sentence that came to mind. Participants cued with *slow* almost always free-associated *children* and almost

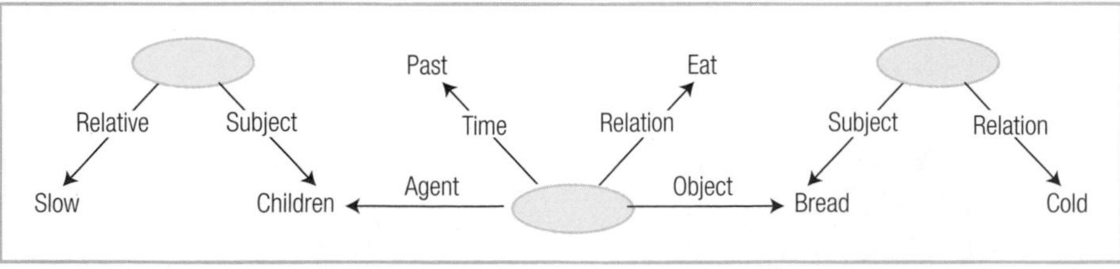

FIGURE 5.7 A propositional network representation of the sentence: "Children who are slow eat bread that is cold." Weisberg (1969) used such sentences in an experiment to show that the proximity of words in a propositional network has more effect on memory than their physical proximity in the sentence.

never *bread*, although *bread* is closer to *slow* in the sentence than to *children*. However, the illustration shows that *slow* and *children* are nearer each other in the network (two links) than *slow* and *bread* (four links). Similarly, participants cued with *bread* almost always recalled *cold* rather than *slow*, although in the sentence *bread* and *slow* are closer than *bread* and *cold*. Again, *bread* and *cold* are closer to each other in the network (three links) than are *bread* and *slow* (five links). (A similar point was made in an experiment by R. A. Ratcliff & McKoon, 1978.)

- *Propositional information can be represented in networks that display how concepts relate.*

Amodal versus Perceptual Symbol Systems

The propositional representations that we have just considered are examples of what Barsalou (1999) called an **amodal symbol system**. By this he meant that the elements within the system are inherently nonperceptual. The original stimulus might be a picture or a sentence, but the representation is abstracted away from the verbal or visual modality. Given this abstraction, one would predict that participants in experiments would be unable to remember the exact words they heard or the exact picture they saw.

As an alternative to such theories, Barsalou proposed a hypothesis called the **perceptual symbol system**, which suggests that all information is represented in terms that are specific to a particular perceptual modality (visual, auditory, etc.) and basically perceptual. The perceptual symbol hypothesis is an extension of Paivio's (1971, 1986) **dual-code theory** that claimed that, rather than abstract propositional representations, we represent information in combined verbal and visual codes. Paivio suggested that when we hear a sentence, we develop an image of what it describes. If we later remember the visual image and not the sentence, we will remember what the sentence was about, but not its exact words. Analogously, when we see a picture, we might describe to ourselves the significant features of that picture. If we later remember our description and not the picture, we will not remember details we did not think important to describe (such as the clothes the teacher was wearing in Figure 5.3).

The dual-code position does not predict that memory for the wording of a sentence is necessarily poor. The relative memory for the wording versus memory for the meaning depends on the relative attention that people give to the verbal versus the visual representation. There are a number of experiments showing that when participants pay attention to wording, they show better memory. For instance, Holmes, Waters, and Rajaram (1998), in a replication of the Bransford and Franks (1971) study that we just reviewed, asked participants to count the number of letters in the last word of each sentence. This manipulation, which increased their attention to the wording of the sentence, resulted in an increased ability to discriminate sentences they had studied from sentences with similar meanings that they had not—although participants still showed considerable confusion among similar-meaning sentences.

But how can an abstract concept such as honesty be represented in a purely perceptual cognitive system? One can be very creative in combining perceptual representations. Consider a pair of sentences from an old unpublished study of mine.[2] We had participants study one of the following two sentences:

1. The lieutenant wrote his signature on the check.
2. The lieutenant forged a signature on the check.

Later, we asked them to recognize which sentence they had studied. They could make such discriminations more successfully than they could distinguish between pairs such as

1. The lieutenant enraged his superior in the barracks.
2. The lieutenant infuriated a superior in the barracks.

In the first pair of sentences, there is a big difference in meaning; in the second pair, little difference. However, the difference in wording between the sentences in the two pairs is equivalent. When I did the study, I thought it showed that people could remember meaning distinctions that did not have perceptual differences—the distinction between signing a signature and forging is not in what the person does but in his or her intentions and the relationship between those intentions and unseen social contracts. Barsalou (personal communication, March 12, 2003) suggested that we represent the distinction between the two sentences by reenacting the history behind each sentence. So even if the actual act of writing and forging might be the same, the history of what a person said and did in getting to that point might be different. Barsalou also considers the internal state of the individual to be relevant. Thus, part of the perceptual features involved in forging might include the sensations of tension that one has when one is in a difficult situation.[3]

Barsalou, Simmons, Barbey, and Wilson (2003) cited evidence that when people understand a sentence, they actually come up with a perceptual interpretation of that sentence. For instance, in one study by Stanfield and Zwaan (2001), participants read a sentence about a nail being pounded either into the wall or the floor. Then they viewed a picture of a nail oriented either horizontally or vertically and were asked to affirm whether the object in the picture was mentioned in the sentence that they just read. If they had read a sentence about a nail being pounded into the wall, they recognized a horizontally oriented nail more quickly. When they had read a sentence about a nail being pounded into the floor, they recognized a vertically oriented nail more quickly. In other words, they responded faster when the orientation implied by the sentence matched the orientation of the picture. Thus, their interpretation of the sentence seemed to

[2] It was not published because at the time (1970s) it was considered too obvious a result given studies like those described earlier in this chapter.

[3] Perhaps it is obvious that I do not agree with Barsalou's perspective. However, it is hard to imagine what he might consider disconfirming data, because his approach is so flexible.

contain this perceptual detail. As further evidence of the perceptual representation of meaning, Barsalou et al. cited neuroscience studies showing that concepts are represented in brain areas similar to those that process perceptions.

An alternative to amodal representations of meaning is the view that meaning is represented as a combination of images in different perceptual modalities.

Embodied Cognition

The perceptual symbol hypothesis of Barsalou is an instance of the growing emphasis in psychology on understanding the contribution of the environment and our bodies to shaping our cognition. As Thelen (2000) describes the viewpoint:

> To say that cognition is *embodied* means that it arises from bodily interactions with the world and is continually meshed with them. From this point of view, therefore, cognition depends on the kinds of experiences that come from having a body with particular perceptual and motor capabilities that are inseparably linked and that together form the matrix within which reasoning, memory, emotion, language and all other aspects of mental life are embedded. (p. 5)

The **embodied cognition** perspective emphasizes the contribution of motor action and how it connects us to the environment. For instance, Glenberg (2007) argues that our understanding of language often depends on covertly acting out what the language describes. He points to an fMRI study by Hauk, Johnsrude, & Pulvermiller (2004), who recorded brain activation while people listened to verbs that involved the face, arm, or leg actions (e.g., to *lick, pick, or kick*). They looked for activity along the motor cortex in different regions associated with the face, arm, and leg (see Figure 1.10). Figure 5.8 shows the differential activity in these

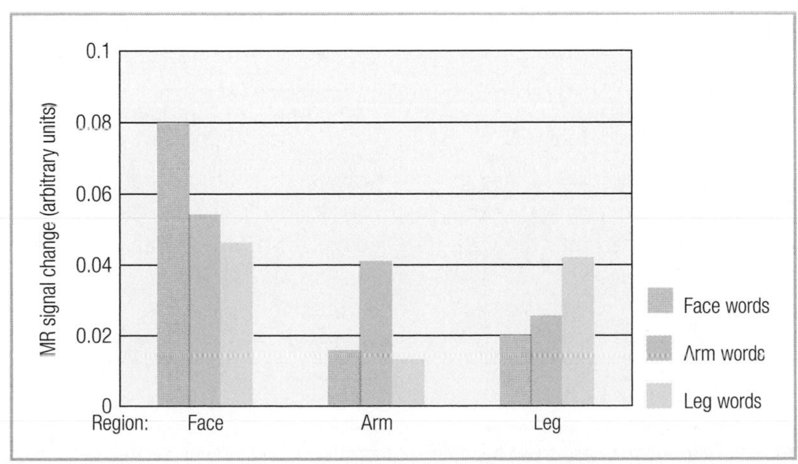

FIGURE 5.8 Brain activation in different model regions as participants listen to different types of verbs.

different brain regions. As participants listened to each word, there was greater activation in the part of the motor cortex that would produce that action.

A theory of how meaning is represented in the human mind must explain how different perceptual and motor modalities connect with one another. For instance, part of understanding a word like *kick* is our ability to relate it to a picture of a person kicking a ball so that we can describe that picture. As another example, part of our understanding of someone performing an action is our ability to relate to our own motor system so that we can mimic the action. Interestingly, **mirror neurons** have been found in the motor cortex of monkeys, which are active when the monkeys perform an action like ripping a paper, or see the experimenter rip a paper or hear the experimenter rip the paper without seeing the action (Rizzolatti & Craighero, 2004). Although one cannot typically do single-cell recordings with humans, brain-imaging studies have found increased activity in the motor region when people observe actions, particularly with the intention to mimic the action (Iacoboni et al., 1999).

Figure 5.9 illustrates two conceptions of how mappings might take place between different representations. One possibility is illustrated in the **multimodal hypothesis**, which holds that we have various representations tied to different perceptual and motor systems and that we have means of directly converting one representation to another. For instance, the double-headed arrow going from the visual to the motor would be a system for converting a visual representation into a motor representation and a system for converting the representations in the opposite direction. The alternative **amodal hypothesis** is that there is an intermediate abstract system, perhaps the propositional representation that we described earlier, and that we have systems for converting back and forth between the perceptual and motor representations and this abstract representation. So to convert a picture into an action, one first converts the visual representation into an abstract representation of its significance and then converts that representation into a motor representation. These two approaches offer alternative explanations for the research we reviewed earlier that indicated people remember the meaning of what they experience, but not

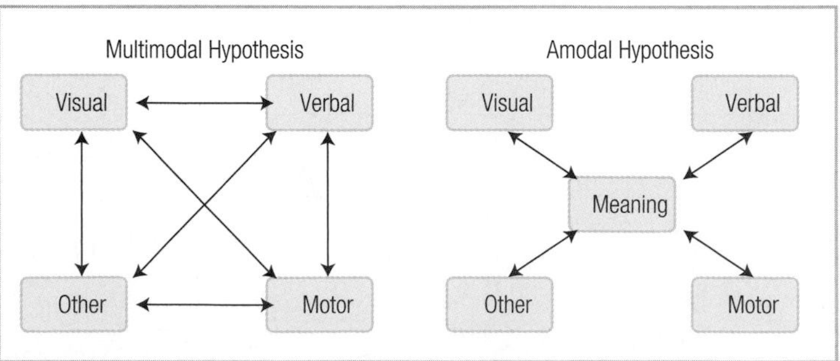

FIGURE 5.9 Representations of two hypotheses about how information is related between different perceptual and motor modalities. The multimodal hypothesis holds that there are mechanisms for translating between each modality. The amodal hypothesis holds that each modality can be translated back and forth to a central meaning representation.

the details. The amodal hypothesis holds that this information is retained in the central meaning system. The multimodal hypothesis holds that the person has converted the information from the modality of the presentation to some other modality.

- *The embodied cognition perspective emphasizes that meaning is represented in the perceptual and motor systems that we use to interact with the world.*

Conceptual Knowledge

Consider the picture in Figure 5.3a. When we look at this picture, we do not see it as just a collection of specific objects. Rather, we see it as a picture of a teacher instructing a student on geography. That is, we see the word in terms of categories like *teacher, student, instruction,* and *geography.* As we saw, people tend to remember this categorical information and not the specific details. For instance, the participants in the Mandler and Ritchey (1977) experiment forgot what the teacher wore but remembered the subject she taught.

You cannot help but experience the world in terms of the categories you know. For instance, if you were licked by a four-legged furry object that weighed about 50 pounds and had a wagging tail, you would perceive yourself as being licked by a *dog.* What does your cognitive system gain by categorizing the object as a dog? Basically, it gains the ability to predict. Thus, you can have expectations about what sounds this creature might make and what would happen if you threw a ball (the dog might chase it and stop licking you). Because of this ability to predict, categories give us great economy in representation and communication. For instance, if you tell someone, "I was licked by a dog," your listener can predict the number of legs on the creature, its approximate size, and so on.

The effects of such categorical perceptions are not always positive—for instance, they can lead to stereotyping. In one study, Dunning and Sherman (1997) had participants study sentences like

> Elizabeth was not very surprised upon receiving her math SAT score.

or

> Bob was not very surprised upon receiving his math SAT score.

Participants who had heard the first sentences were more likely to falsely believe they had heard "Elizabeth was not very surprised upon receiving her low math SAT score," whereas if they had heard the second sentence, they were more likely to believe they had heard "Bob was not very surprised upon receiving his high math SAT score." Categorizing Elizabeth as a woman, the participants brought the stereotype of women as poor at math to their interpretation of the first sentence. Categorizing Bob as male, they brought the opposite stereotype to their interpretation of the second sentence. This was even true among participants (both male and female) who were rated as not being sexist in their attitudes. They could not help but be influenced by their implicit stereotypes.

Research on categorization has focused both on how we form these categories in the first place and on how we use them to interpret experiences. It has also been concerned with notations for representing this categorical knowledge. In this section, we will consider a number of proposed notations for representing conceptual knowledge. We will start by describing two early theories. One concerns semantic networks, which are similar to the propositional networks we just considered. The other is about what are called schemas. Both theories have been closely related to certain empirical phenomena that seem central to conceptual structure.

- *The categorical organization of our knowledge strongly influences the way we encode and remember our experiences.*

Semantic Networks

Network representations have been used to encode conceptual knowledge as well as propositional knowledge. Quillian (1966) proposed that people store information about various categories—such as canaries, robins, fish, and so on—in a network structure like that shown in Figure 5.10. In this illustration, we represent a hierarchy of categorical facts, such as that a canary is a bird and a bird is an animal, by linking nodes for the two categories with **isa links.** Properties that are true of the categories are associated with them. Properties that are true of higher-level categories are also true of lower level categories. Thus, because animals breathe, it follows that birds and canaries breathe. Figure 5.10 can also

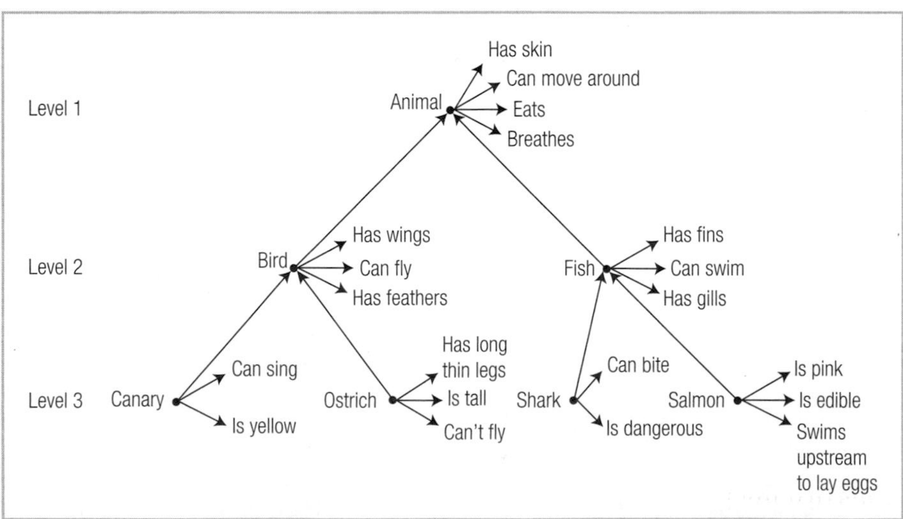

FIGURE 5.10 A hypothetical memory structure for a three-level hierarchy using the example *canary.* Quillian (1966) proposed that people store information about various categories in a network structure. This illustration represents a hierarchy of categorical facts, such as that a canary is a bird and a bird is an animal. Properties that are true of each category are associated with that category. Properties that are true of higher level categories are also true of lower level categories. (After Collins & Quillian, 1969. Adapted by permission of the publisher. © 1969 by Academic Press.)

represent information about exceptions. For instance, even though most birds fly, the illustration does represent that ostriches cannot fly.

Collins and Quillian (1969) did an experiment to test the psychological reality of such networks by having participants judge the truth of assertions about concepts, such as

1. Canaries can sing.
2. Canaries have feathers.
3. Canaries have skin.

Participants were shown these along with false assertions such as "Apples have feathers." They were asked to indicate whether a statement was true or false by pressing one of two buttons. The time from presentation of the statement to the button press was measured.

Consider how participants would answer such questions if Figure 5.10 represented their knowledge of such categories. The information to confirm sentence 1 is directly stored with *canary.* The information for sentence 2, however, is not directly stored at the *canary* node. Instead, the *have feathers* property is stored with *bird,* and sentence 2 can be inferred from the directly stored facts that *A canary is a bird* and *Birds have feathers.* Again, sentence 3 is not directly stored with *canary;* rather, the *has skin* predicate is stored with *animal.* Thus, sentence 3 can be inferred from the facts that *a canary is a bird* and *a bird is an animal* and *animals have skin.* So, all the information required to verify sentence 1 is stored with *canary;* for sentence 2, participants would need to traverse one link, from *canary* to *bird,* to retrieve the requisite information; for sentence 3, they would have to traverse two links, from *canary* to *animal.*

If our categorical knowledge were structured like Figure 5.10, we would expect sentence 1 to be verified more quickly than sentence 2, which would be verified more quickly than sentence 3. This is just what Collins and Quillian found. Participants required 1310 ms to judge statements like sentence 1, 1380 ms to judge statements like sentence 2, and 1470 ms to judge statements like sentence 3. Subsequent research on the retrieval of information from memory has somewhat complicated the conclusions drawn from the initial Collins and Quillian experiment. How often facts are experienced has been observed to have strong effects on retrieval time (e.g., C. Conrad, 1972). Some facts, such as *Apples are eaten*—for which the predicate could be stored with an intermediate concept such as *food,* but that are experienced quite often—are verified as fast as or faster than facts such as *Apples have dark seeds,* which must be stored more directly with the *apple* concept. It seems that if a fact about a concept is encountered frequently, it will be stored with that concept, even if it could also be inferred from a more general concept. The following statements about the organization of facts in semantic memory and their retrieval times seem to be valid conclusions from the research:

1. If a fact about a concept is encountered frequently, it will be stored with that concept even if it could be inferred from a higher order concept.

2. The more frequently a fact about a concept is encountered, the more strongly that fact will be associated with the concept. The more strongly facts are associated with concepts, the more rapidly they are verified.
3. Inferring facts that are not directly stored with a concept takes a relatively long time.

Thus, both the strength of the connections between facts and concepts (determined by frequency of experience) and the distance between them in the semantic network have effects on retrieval time.

When a property is not stored directly with a concept, people can retrieve it from a higher order concept.

Schemas

Consider our knowledge of what a house is like. We know many things about houses, such as

- Houses are a type of building.
- Houses have rooms.
- Houses can be built of wood, brick, or stone.
- Houses serve as human dwellings.
- Houses tend to have rectilinear and triangular shapes.
- Houses are usually larger than 100 square feet and smaller than 10,000 square feet.

The importance of a category is that it stores predictable information about specific instances of that category. So when someone mentions a house, for example, we have a rough idea of the size of the object being referred to.

Semantic networks, which just store properties with concepts, cannot capture the nature of our general knowledge about a house, such as its typical size or shape. Researchers in cognitive science (e.g., Rumelhart & Ortony, 1976) proposed a particular way of representing such knowledge that seemed more useful than the semantic network representation. Their representational structure is called a **schema.** The concept of a schema was first articulated in AI and computer science. Readers who have experience with modern programming languages should recognize its similarity to various types of data structures. The question for the psychologist is what aspects of the schema notion are appropriate for understanding how people reason about concepts. I will describe some of the properties associated with schemas and then discuss the psychological research bearing on these properties.

Schemas represent categorical knowledge according to a **slot** structure, in which slots specify values of various attributes that members of a category possess. So we have the following partial schema representation of a house:

House

- *Isa:* building
- *Parts:* rooms

- *Materials:* wood, brick, stone
- *Function:* human dwelling
- *Shape:* rectilinear, triangular
- *Size:* 100–10,000 square feet

In this representation, such terms as *materials* and *shape* are the **attributes** or slots, and such terms as *wood, brick,* and *rectilinear* are the **values**. Each pair of a slot and a value specifies a typical feature. The fact that houses are usually built of materials such as wood and brick does not exclude such possibilities as cardboard. Thus, the values listed above are called **default values.** For instance, the fact that we represent that birds can fly as part of our schema for birds does not prevent us from seeing ostriches as birds. We simply overwrite this default value in our representation of an ostrich.

A special slot in each schema is its *isa slot,* which is like the isa link in a semantic network and points to the superset. Basically, unless contradicted, a concept inherits the features of its superset. Thus, with the schema for *building,* the superset of *house,* we would store such features as that it has a roof and walls and that it is found on the ground. This information is not represented in the schema for *house* because it can be inferred from *building.* As illustrated in Figure 5.10, these isa links can create a structure called a generalization hierarchy.

Schemas have another type of structure, called a part hierarchy. Parts of houses, such as walls and rooms, have their own schema definitions. Stored with schemas for *walls* and *rooms* would be the information that they have windows and ceilings as parts. Thus, using the part hierarchy, we would be able to infer that houses have windows and ceilings.

Schemas are abstractions from specific instances that can be used to make inferences about instances of the concepts they represent. If we know something is a house, we can use the schema to infer that it is probably made of wood or brick and that it has walls, windows, and ceilings. The inferential processes for schemas must also be able to deal with exceptions: We can still understand what a house without a roof is. Finally, it is necessary to understand the constraints between the slots of a schema. If we hear of a house that is underground, for example, we can infer that it will not have windows.

- *Schemas represent concepts in terms of supersets, parts, and other attribute-value pairs.*

Psychological Reality of Schemas

One property of schemas is that they have default values for certain slots or attributes. This property provides schemas with a useful inferential mechanism. If you recognize an object as being a member of a certain category, you can infer—unless explicitly contradicted—that it has the default values associated with that concept's schema. Brewer and Treyens (1981) provided an interesting

FIGURE 5.11 The "office room" used in the experiment of Brewer and Treyens to demonstrate the effects of schemas on memory inferences. As they predicted, their participants' recall was strongly influenced by their schema of what an office contains. (From Brewer & Treyens, 1981. Reprinted by permission of the publisher. © 1981 by *Cognitive Psychology*.)

demonstration of the effects of schemas on memory inferences. Thirty participants were brought individually to the room shown in Figure 5.11. Each was told that this room was the office of the experimenter and was asked to wait there while the experimenter went to the laboratory to see whether the previous participant had finished. After 35 s, the experimenter returned and took the waiting participant to a nearby seminar room. Here, the participant was asked to write down everything he or she could remember about the experimental room. What would you be able to recall?

Brewer and Treyens predicted that their participants' recall would be strongly influenced by their schema of what an office contains. Participants would recall very well items that are part of that schema; they would recall much less well office items that are not part of the schema; and they would falsely recall items that are part of the schema but not in this office. Brewer and Treyens found just this pattern of results. For instance, 29 of the 30 participants recalled that the office had a chair, a desk, and walls. Only 8 participants, however, recalled that it had a bulletin board or a skull. On the other hand, 9 participants recalled that it had books, which it did not. Thus, we see that a person's memory for the properties of a location is strongly influenced by that person's default assumptions about what is typically found in the location. A schema is a way of encoding those default assumptions.

- *People will infer that an object has the default values for its category, unless they explicitly notice otherwise.*

Degree of Category Membership

One of the important features of schemas is that they allow variation in the objects that might fit a particular schema. There are constraints on what typically occupies the various slots of a schema, but few absolute prohibitions. Thus, if schemas encode our knowledge about various object categories, we ought to see a shading from less typical to more typical members of the category as the features of the members better satisfy the schema constraints. There is now considerable evidence that natural categories such as *birds* have the kind of structure that would be expected of a schema.

Rosch did early research documenting such variations in category membership. In one experiment (Rosch, 1973), she instructed participants to rate the typicality of various members of a category on a 1 to 7 scale, where 1 meant very typical and 7 meant very atypical. Participants consistently rated some members as more typical than others. In the bird category, *robin* got an average rating of 1.1, and *chicken* a rating of 3.8. In reference to sports, *football* was thought to be very typical (1.2), whereas *weight lifting* was not (4.7). *Murder* was rated a very typical crime (1.0), whereas *vagrancy* was not (5.3). *Carrot* was a very typical vegetable (1.1); *parsley* was not (3.8).

Rosch (1975) also asked participants to identify the category of pictured objects. People are faster to judge a picture as an instance of a category when it presents a typical member of the category. For instance, apples are seen as fruits more rapidly than are watermelons, and robins are seen as birds more rapidly than are chickens. Thus, typical members of a category appear to have an advantage in perceptual recognition as well.

Rosch (1977) demonstrated another way in which some members of a category are more typical. She had participants compose sentences for category names. For *bird,* participants generated sentences such as

I heard a bird twittering outside my window.

Three birds sat on the branch of a tree.

A bird flew down and began eating.

Rosch replaced the category name in these sentences with a typical member (robin), a less typical member (eagle), or a peripheral member (chicken) and asked participants to rate the sensibleness of the resulting sentences. Sentences involving typical members got high ratings, sentences with less typical members got lower ratings, and sentences with peripheral members got the lowest ratings. So the evidence shows that when people think of a category member, they generally think of typical instances of that category.

Failing to have a default or typical value does not disqualify an object from being a member of the category, however. People should have great difficulty and should be inconsistent in judging whether items at the periphery of a category are actually members of that category. McCloskey and Glucksberg (1978) looked at people's judgments about what were or were not members of various categories. They found that although participants did agree on some items, they disagreed on many. For instance, whereas all 30 participants agreed that *cancer* was a disease and *happiness* was not, 16 thought *stroke* was a disease and 14 did not. Again, all 30 participants agreed that *apple* was a fruit and *chicken* was not, but 16 thought *pumpkin* was a fruit and 14 disagreed. Once again, all participants agreed that a *fly* was an insect and a *dog* was not, but 13 participants thought a *leech* was and 17 disagreed. Thus, it appears that people do not always agree among themselves. McCloskey and Glucksberg tested the same participants a month later and found that many had changed their minds about the disputed items. For instance, 11 out of 30 reversed themselves on *stroke,* 8 reversed themselves on *pumpkin,* and 3 reversed themselves on *leech.* Thus, disagreement about category boundaries does not occur just *among* participants—people are very uncertain *within* themselves exactly where the boundaries of a category should be drawn.

Figure 5.12 illustrates a set of materials used by Labov (1973). He was interested in studying which items participants would call *cups* and which they would not. Which do you consider to be *cups*

FIGURE 5.12 The various cuplike objects used in Labov's experiment that studied the boundaries of the cup category. (After Labov, 1973, in Bailey & Shuy, 1973. Adapted by permission of the author. © 1973 by Georgetown University Press.)

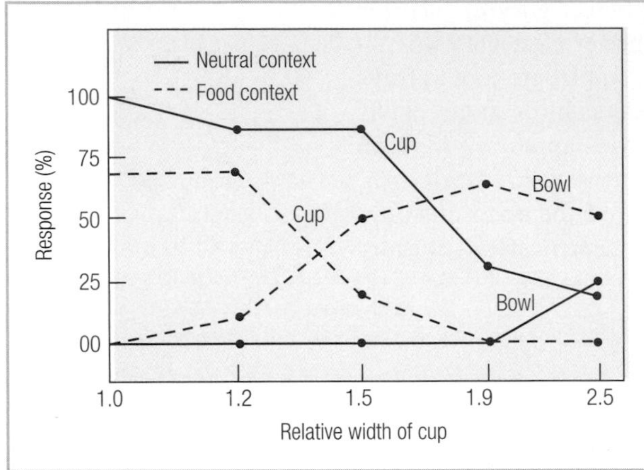

FIGURE 5.13 Results from Labov's experiment demonstrating that the *cup* category does not appear to have clear-cut boundaries. The percentage of participants who used the term *cup* versus the term *bowl* to describe the objects shown in Figure 5.10 are plotted as a function of the ratio of cup width to cup depth. The solid lines reflect the neutral-context condition, the dashed lines the food-context condition. (After Labov, 1973, in Bailey & Shuy, 1973. Adapted by permission of the author. © 1973 by Georgetown University Press.)

and which do you consider *bowls?* The interesting point is that these concepts do not appear to have clear-cut boundaries. In one experiment, Labov used the series of items 1 through 4 shown in Figure 5.12 and a fifth item, not shown. These items reflect an increasing ratio of width of the cup to depth. For the first item, that ratio is 1, whereas for item 4 it is 1.9. The ratio for the item not shown was 2.5. Figure 5.13 shows the percentage of participants who called each of the five objects a cup and the percentage who called it a bowl. The solid lines indicate the classifications when participants were simply presented with pictures of the objects (the neutral context). As can be seen, the percentages of *cup* responses gradually decreased with increasing width, but there is no clear-cut point where participants stopped using *cup*. At the extreme 2.5-width ratio, about 25% percent of the participants still gave the *cup* response, whereas another 25% gave *bowl*. (The remaining 50% gave other responses.) The dashed lines reflect classifications when participants were asked to imagine the object filled with mashed potatoes and placed on a table. In this context, fewer *cup* responses and more *bowl* responses were given, but the data show the same gradual shift from *cup* to *bowl*. Thus, it appears that people's classification behavior varies continuously not only with the properties of an object but also with the context in which the object is imagined or presented. These influences of perceptual features and context on categorization judgments are very much like the similar influences of these features on perceptual pattern recognition (see Chapter 2).

Different instances are judged to be members of a category to different degrees, with the more typical members of a category having an advantage in processing.

Event Concepts

It is not only objects that have a conceptual structure. We also have concepts of various kinds of events, such as going to a movie. Schemas have been proposed as ways of representing such categories. We can encode our knowledge about stereotypic events according to their parts—for instance, going to a movie involves going to the theater, buying the ticket, buying refreshments, seeing the movie, and returning from the theater. Schank and Abelson (1977) proposed versions of event schemas that they called **scripts.** They pointed out that many circumstances involve stereotypic sequences of actions. For instance, Table 5.1 shows their hunch as to what the stereotypic aspects of dining at a restaurant might be and represents the components of a script for such an occasion.

Bower, Black, and Turner (1979) reported a series of experiments in which the psychological reality of the script notion was tested. They asked participants to name what they considered the 20 most important events in an episode,

TABLE 5.1

The Schema for Going to a Restaurant
Scene I: Entering
Customer enters restaurant
Customer looks for table
Customer decides where to sit
Customer goes to table
Customer sits down
Scene 2: Ordering
Customer picks up menu
Customer looks at menu
Customer decides on food
Customer signals waitress
Waitress comes to table
Customer orders food
Waitress goes to cook
Waitress gives food order to cook
Cook prepares food
Scene 3: Eating
Cook gives food to waitress
Waitress brings food to customer
Customer eats food
Scene 4: Exiting
Waitress writes bill
Waitress goes over to customer
Waitress gives bill to customer
Customer gives tip to waitress
Customer goes to cashier
Customer gives money to cashier
Customer leaves restaurant

From Schank & Abelson (1977). Reprinted by permission of the publisher. © 1977 by Erlbaum.

TABLE 5.2

Empirical Script Norms at Three Agreement Levels
Open door[a]
Enter[b]
Give reservation name
Wait to be seated
Go to table
Sit down[c]
Order drinks
Put napkins on lap
Look at menu
Discuss menu
Order meal
Talk
Drink water
Eat salad or soup
Meal arrives
Eat food
Finish meal
Order dessert
Eat dessert
Ask for bill
Bill arrives
Pay bill
Leave tip
Get coats
Leave

[a]Roman type indicates items listed by at least 25% of the participants.
[b]Italic type indicates items listed by at least 48% of the participants.
[c]Boldface type indicates items listed by at least 73% of the participants.

After Bower, Black, & Turner (1979). Adapted by permission of the publisher. © 1979 by *Cognitive Psychology*.

such as going to a restaurant. With 32 participants, they failed to get complete agreement on what these events were. No particular action was listed as part of the episode by all participants, although considerable consensus was reported. Table 5.2 lists the events named. The items in roman type were listed by at least 25% of the participants; the italicized items were named by at least 48%; and the boldfaced items were given by at least 73%. Using 73% as a criterion, we find that the stereotypic sequence was *sit down, look at menu, order meal, eat food, pay bill,* and *leave.*

Bower et al. (1979) went on to show a number of the effects that such action scripts have on memory for stories. They had participants study stories that included some but not all of the typical events from a script. Participants were then asked to recall the stories (in one experiment) or to recognize whether various statements came from the story (in another experiment). When recalling these stories, participants tended to report statements that were parts of the script but that had not been presented as parts of the stories. Similarly, in the recognition test, participants thought they had studied script items that had not actually been in the stories. However, participants showed a greater tendency to recall actual items from the stories or to recognize actual items than to misrecognize foils that were not in the stories, despite the distortion in the direction of the general schema.

In another experiment, these investigators read to participants stories composed of 12 prototypical actions in an episode; 8 of the actions occurred in their standard temporal position, but 4 were rearranged. Thus, in the restaurant story, the bill might be paid at the beginning and the menu read at the end. In recalling these stories, participants showed a strong tendency to put the events back into their normal order. In fact, about half of the statements were put back. This experiment serves as another demonstration of the powerful effect of general schemas on memory for stories.

These experiments indicate that new events are encoded with respect to general schemas and that subsequent recall is influenced by the schemas. I have talked about these effects as if participants were misrecalling the stories. However, it is not clear that these results should be classified as acts of misrecall. Normally, if a certain standard event, such as paying a check, is omitted in a story, we are supposed to assume it occurred. Similarly, if the storyteller says the check was paid at the beginning of the restaurant episode, we have some reason to doubt the storyteller. Scripts or schemas exist because they encode the predominant sequence of events in a particular kind of situation. Thus, they can serve as valuable bases for predicting missing information and for correcting errors in information.

Scripts are event schemas that people use to reason about prototypical events.

Abstraction versus Exemplar Theories

We have already described semantic networks and schemas as two ways of representing conceptual knowledge. It is fair to say that although each has merits, the field of cognitive psychology has concluded that both are inadequate. We already noted that semantic networks do not capture the graded character of categorical knowledge such that different instances are better or worse members of a category. Schemas can do this, but it has never been clear in detail how to relate them to behavior. The field is currently struggling between two alternative ways of theorizing about conceptual knowledge. One type of theory holds that we have actually abstracted general properties from the instances we have studied; the other type holds that we actually store only specific instances, with the more general inferences emerging from these instances. We will call these the **abstraction theories** and the **exemplar theories.** The debate between these two perspectives has been with us for centuries—for instance, in the debate between the British philosophers John Locke and George Berkeley. Locke claimed that he had an abstract idea of a triangle that was neither oblique or right-angled, neither equilateral, isosceles, or scalene, but all of these

at once, while Berkeley claimed it was simply impossible for himself to have an idea of a triangle that was not the idea of some specific triangle.

The schema theory we have considered is an abstraction theory, but others of this type have been more successful. One alternative assumes that people store a single prototype of what an instance of the category is like and judge specific instances in terms of their similarity to that prototype (e.g., Reed, 1972). Other models assume that participants store a representation that also encodes some idea of the allowable variation around the prototype (e.g., Hayes-Roth & Hayes-Roth, 1977; Anderson, 1991).

Exemplar theories could not be more different. They hold that we store no central concept, but only specific instances. When it comes time to judge how typical a specific object is of birds in general, we compare it to specific birds and make some sort of judgment of average difference. Exemplar theories include those of Medin and Schaffer (1978) and Nosofsky (1986).

Given that abstraction and exemplar theories differ so greatly in what they propose the mind does, it is surprising that they generate such similar predictions over a wide range of experiments. For instance, both types predict better processing of central members of a category. Abstraction theories predict this because central instances are more similar to the abstract representation of the concept. Exemplar theories predict this because central instances will be more similar, on average, to other instances of a category.

There appear to be subtle differences between the predictions of the two types of theories, however. Exemplar theories predict that people should be influenced by studying specific instances similar to a test instance and that such influences should go beyond any effect of some representation of the central tendency. Thus, although we may think that dogs in general bark, we may have experienced a peculiar-looking dog that did not, and we would then tend to expect that another similar-looking dog would also not bark. Such effects of specific instances can be found in some experiments (e.g., Medin & Schaffer, 1978; Nosofsky, 1991). On the other hand, some research has shown that people will infer tendencies that are not in the specific instances (Elio & Anderson, 1981). For example, if one has encountered many dogs that chase balls and many dogs that bark at the postman, one might consider a dog that both chases balls and barks at the postman to be particularly typical. However, we may never have observed any specific dog both chasing balls and barking at the postman.

Much of the past research on categorization has been an effort to determine whether abstraction theories or exemplar theories are correct. The recent trend, however, has been a recognition that people may sometimes use abstractions and other times use instances to represent categories (Anderson & Betz, 2001; Ashby, Alfonso-Reese, Turken, & Waldron, 1998; Erickson & Kruschke, 1998; Gobet, Richman, Staszewski, & Simon, 1997; Palmeri & Johansen, 1999; Smith & Minda, 1998). Perhaps the clearest evidence for this expanded view comes from neuroimaging studies showing that different participants use different brain regions to categorize instances. For example, Smith, Patalano, and Jonides (1998) had participants learn to classify a set of 10 animals like those shown in Figure 5.14. One group was encouraged to use rules such as "An animal is from Venus if at least three of the following are true: antennae ears, curly tail, hoofed

FIGURE 5.14 Examples of the drawings of artificial animals used in the PET studies of Smith, Palatino, and Jonides showing that people sometimes use rule-based abstractions and sometimes use memory-based instances to represent categories. (After Smith, Palatino, & Jonides, 1998. Adapted by permission of the publisher. © 1998 by *Cognition*.)

feet, beak, and long neck. Otherwise it is from Saturn." Participants in a second group were encouraged simply to memorize the categories for the 10 animals. Smith et al. found very different patterns of brain activation as participants classified the stimuli. Regions in the prefrontal cortex tended to be activated in the abstract-rule participants, whereas regions in the occipital visual areas and the cerebellum were activated in the participants who memorized instances. Smith and Grossman (in press) review evidence that this second exemplar system also involves brain regions supporting memory such as the hippocampus (see Figure 1.7).

There may be multiple different ways of representing concepts as abstractions. Although the Smith et al. study identified an abstract system that involves explicit reasoning by means of rules, there is also evidence for abstract systems that involve unconscious pattern recognition—for instance, our ability to distinguish dogs from cats, without being able to articulate any of the features that separate the two species. Ashby and Maddox (2005) argue that this system depends on the basal ganglia (see Figure 1.8). As they review, damage to the basal ganglia (as happens with Parkinson's and Huntington's disease) results in deficits in learning such categories. The basal ganglia region has been found to be activated in a number of studies of implicit category learning.

- *Categories can be represented either by abstracting their central tendencies or by storing many specific instances of categories.*

Natural Categories in the Brain

The studies we have been discussing look at the learning of new laboratory-defined categories. There has always been some suspicion about how similar such laboratory-defined categories are to the kinds of natural categories that we have acquired through experience, such as birds or chairs. Laboratory categories display the same sort of fuzzy boundaries that natural categories do and share a number of other attributes. However, natural categories arise over a much longer time period than a typical laboratory task. Over their long learning history, people come to develop biases about such natural categories as living things and artifacts. Much of the research documenting these biases has been done with primary-school children who are still learning their categories but have advanced beyond younger children. For instance, if primary-school children are told that a human has a spleen, they will conclude that dogs have spleens too (Carey, 1985). Similarly, if they are told that a red apple has pectin inside, they will assume that green apples also have pectin (Gelman, 1988). Apparently, children assume that if something is a part of a member of a biological category, it is an inherent part of all members of the category. On the other hand, if told that an artifact such as a cup is made of ceramic, they do not believe that all cups are made of ceramic. The pattern is just the opposite with respect to actions. For instance, if told that a cup is used for "imbibing" (a term they do not know), they believe that all cups are used for imbibing. In contrast, if told that they can "repast" with a particular red apple, they do not necessarily believe that they can repast with a green apple. Thus, artifacts seem distinguished by the fact that there are actions appropriate to the whole category of artifacts. In summary, children come to believe that all things in a biological category have the same parts (like pectin in apples) but all things in an artifact category have the same function (like imbibing for cups).

Cognitive neuroscience data suggest that there are different representations of biological and artifact categories in the brain. Much of this evidence comes from patients with semantic dementia, who suffer deficits in their categorical knowledge because of brain damage. Patients with damage to different regions show different deficits. Patients who have damage to the temporal lobes suffer deficits in their knowledge about biological categories such as animals, fruits, and vegetables (Warrington & Shallice, 1984; Saffran & Schwartz, 1994). These patients are unable to recognize such objects as ducks, and when one was asked what a duck is, the patient was only able to say "an animal." However, knowledge about artifacts such as tools and furniture is relatively unaffected in these patients. On the other hand, patients with frontoparietal lesions are impaired in their processing of artifacts but unaffected in their processing of biological categories.

Table 5.3 compares example descriptions of biological categories and artifact categories by two patients with temporal lobe damage. These types of patients are more common than patients with deficits in their knowledge of artifacts.

It has been suggested (e.g., Warrington & Shallice, 1984; Farah & McClelland, 1991) that these dissociations occur because biological categories are more associated with perceptual categories such as shape, whereas artifacts are more associated with the actions that we perform with them. Farah and McClelland offer a computer simulation model of this dissociation that learns associations among words, pictures, visual semantic features, and functional semantic features. By selectively damaging the visual features in their computer simulation, they were able to produce a deficit in knowledge of living things; and by selectively damaging the functional features, they were able to produce a deficit in knowledge of artifacts. Thus, loss of categorical information in such patients seems related to loss of the feature information that defines these categories.

TABLE 5.3

Performance of Two Patients with Impaired Knowledge of Living Things on Definitions Task

Patient	Living Things	Artifacts
1	*Parrot:* Don't know *Daffodil:* Plant *Snail:* An insect animal *Eel:* Not well *Ostrich:* Unusual	*Tent:* Temporary outhouse, living home *Briefcase:* Small case used by students to carry papers *Compass:* Tool for telling direction you are going *Torch:* Handheld light *Dustbin:* Bin for putting rubbish in
2	*Duck:* An animal *Wasp:* Bird that flies *Crocus:* Rubbish material *Holly:* What you drink *Spider:* A person looking for things, he was a spider for his nation or country	*Wheelbarrow:* Object used by people to take material about *Towel:* Material used to dry people *Pram:* Used to carry people, with wheels and a thing to sit on *Submarine:* Ship that goes underneath the sea

After Farah & McClelland (1991). Adapted by permission of the publisher. © 1991 by *Journal of Experimental Psychology: General.*

Recent brain-imaging data also seem consistent with this conclusion (see A. Martin, 2001, for review). In particular, it has been shown that when people process pictures of artifacts or words denoting artifacts, the same regions of the brain that have been shown to produce category-specific deficits when damaged tend to be activated. Processing of both animals and tools activates regions of the temporal cortex, but the tool regions tend to be located above (superior to) the animal regions. There is also activation of occipital regions (visual cortex) when processing animals. In general, the evidence seems to point to a greater visual involvement in the representation of animals and a greater motor involvement in the representation of artifacts. There is some debate in the literature over whether the real distinction is between natural categories and artifacts or between visual-based and motor-based categories (Caramazza, 2000).

- *There are differences in the way people think about biological categories and artifact categories and differences in the brain regions that support these two types of categories.*

Conclusions

We remember only a tiny fraction of what we experience. Estimates of the storage capacity (e.g., Treves & Rolls, 1994; Moll & Miikkulainen, 1997) of the brain differ substantially, but they are all many orders of magnitude less than what would be required to store a faithful video recording of our whole life. This chapter has reviewed the studies of what we retain and what we forget—for instance, what subject was being taught, but not what the teacher was wearing (Figure 5.3), or that we were in an office, but not what was in the office (Figure 5.11). The chapter also reviewed three perspectives on the basis for this selective memory.

1. The multimodal hypothesis (Figure 5.9a) that we select aspects of our experience to remember and often convert from one medium to another. For instance, we may describe a room (visual) as an "office" (verbal). This hypothesis holds that we maintain the perceptual-motor aspects of our experience but only the significant aspects.
2. The amodal hypothesis (Figure 5.9b) that we convert our experience into some abstract representation that just encodes what is important. For instance, the chapter discussed how propositional networks (e.g., Figure 5.7) captured the connections among the concepts in our understanding of a sentence.
3. The schema hypothesis that we remember our experiences in terms of the categories that they seem to exemplify. These categories can either be formed from a bundle of specific experiences or an abstraction like a category.

These hypotheses need not be mutually exclusive, and cognitive scientists are actively engaged in trying to understand how to coordinate these explanations.

Questions for Thought

1. Jill Price, a person with superior autobiographical memory described at the beginning of the chapter, can remember what happened on almost any day of her life (see her interview with Diane Sawyers: http://abcnews.go.com/Health/story?id=4813052&page=1). For instance, if you ask her, she can tell you the date of the last show of any former TV series she watched. On the other hand, she reported great difficulty in remembering the dates in history class. Why do you think this is?
2. Take some sentences at random from this book and try to develop propositional representations for them.
3. Barsalou (2008) claims little empirical evidence has been accumulated to support amodal symbol systems. What research reviewed in this chapter might be considered evidence for amodal symbol systems?
4. Consider the debate between amodal theories and multimodal theories and the debate between exemplar and abstraction theories. In what ways are these debates similar and in what ways are they different?

Key Terms

abstraction theory
amodal hypothesis
amodal symbol system
arguments
default values
dual-code theory
embodied cognition
exemplar theory
isa link
link
mirror neuron
mnemonic technique
multimodal hypothesis
node
perceptual symbol system
proposition
propositional network
propositional representation
relations
schema
script
slot

6

Human Memory: Encoding and Storage

Past chapters have discussed how we perceive and encode what is in our present. Now we turn to discussing memory, which is the means by which we can perceive our past. People who lose the ability to create new memories become effectively blind to their past. I would recommend the movie *Memento as* providing a striking characterization of what it would like to have no memory. The protagonist of the film, Leonard, has **anterograde amnesia,** a condition that prevents him from forming new memories. He can remember his past up to the point of a terrible crime that left him with amnesia, and he can keep track of what is in the immediate present, but as soon as his attention is drawn to something else, he forgets what has just happened. So, for instance, he is constantly meeting people he has met before, who have often manipulated him, but he does not remember them, nor can he protect himself from being manipulated further. Although Leonard incorrectly labels his condition as having no short-term memory, this movie is an accurate portrayal of anterograde amnesia—the inability to form new long-term memories. It focuses on the amazing ways Leonard tries to connect the past with the immediate present.

This chapter and the next can be thought of as being about what worked and did not work for Leonard. This chapter will answer the following questions:

- How do we maintain a short-term or working memory of what just happened? This is what still worked for Leonard.
- How does the information we are currently maintaining in working memory prime knowledge in our long-term memory?
- How do we create permanent memories of our experiences? This is what did not work any more for Leonard.
- What factors influence our success in creating new memories?

Memory and the Brain

Throughout the brain, neurons are capable of changing in response to experience. This neural plasticity provides the basis for memory. Although all of the brain plays a role in memory, there are two regions, illustrated in Figure 6.1, that have played the most prominent role in research on human memory. First, there is a region within the temporal cortex that includes the hippocampus, whose role in memory was already discussed in Chapter 1 (see Figure 1.7). The hippocampus and surrounding structures play an important role in the storage of new memories. This is where Leonard had his difficulties. Second, research has found that prefrontal brain regions are strongly associated with both the encoding of new memories and the retrieval of old memories. These are the same regions that were discussed in Chapter 5 with respect to the meaningful encoding of pictures and sentences. This area also includes the prefrontal region from Figure 1.15 that was important in retrieval of arithmetic and algebraic facts.

With respect to the prefrontal regions shown in Figure 6.1, note that memory research has found laterality effects similar to those noted at the beginning of Chapter 5 (Gabrielli, 2001). Specifically, study of verbal material tends to involve mostly the left hemisphere. Study of pictorial material, in contrast, tends to involve sometimes the right hemisphere and sometimes both hemispheres. Gabrielli notes that the left hemisphere tends to be associated with pictorial material that is linked to verbal knowledge, such as pictures of famous people or common objects. It is as if people are naming these objects to themselves.

- *Human memory depends heavily on frontal structures of the brain for the creation and retrieval of memories and on temporal structures for the permanent storage of these memories.*

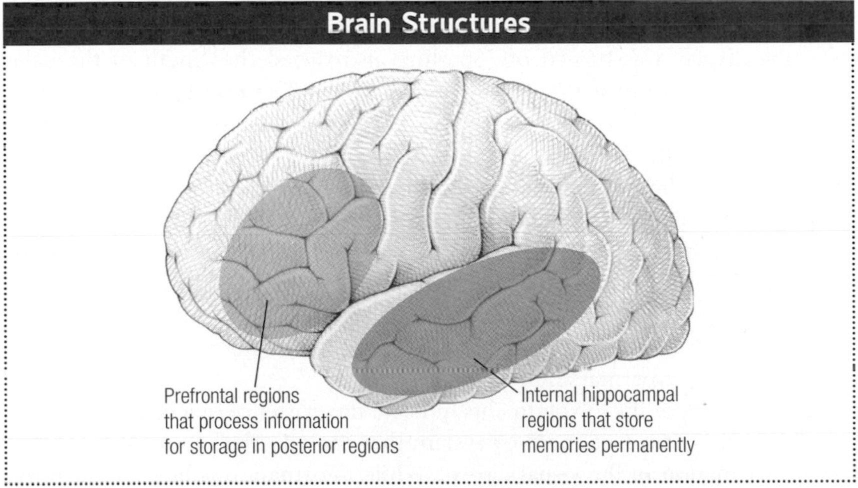

FIGURE 6.1 The brain structures involved in the creation and storage of memories. Prefrontal regions are responsible for the creation of memories. The hippocampus and surrounding structures in the temporal cortex are responsible for the permanent storage of these memories.

Sensory Memory Holds Information Briefly

Before beginning the discussion of more permanent memories, it is worth noting the visual and auditory sensory memories that hold information briefly when it first comes in.

Visual Sensory Memory

Many studies of visual sensory memory have used a procedure in which participants are presented with a visual array of items, such as the letters shown in Figure 6.2, for a brief period of time (e.g., 50 ms). When asked to recall the items, participants are able to report three, four, five, or at most six items. One might think that only this much material can be held in visual memory—yet participants report that they were aware of more items but the items faded away before they could attend to them and report them.

An important methodological variation on this task was introduced by Sperling (1960). He presented arrays consisting of three rows of four letters. Immediately after this stimulus was turned off, participants were cued to attend to just one row of the display and to report only the letters in that row. The cues were in the form of different tones (high for top row, medium for middle, and low for bottom). Sperling's method was called the **partial-report procedure,** in contrast to the **whole-report procedure,** which was what had been used until then. Participants were able to recall all or most of the items from a row of four. Because participants did not know beforehand which row would be cued, Sperling argued that they must have had most or all of the items stored in some sort of short-term visual memory. Given the cue right after the visual display was turned off, they could attend to that row in their short-term visual memory and report the letters in that row. The reason participants could not report more items in the full-report procedure was that these items had faded from this memory before the participants could attend to them.

In the procedure just described, the tone cue was presented immediately after the display was turned off. Sperling also varied the length of the delay between the removal of the display and the tone. The results he obtained, in terms of number of letters recalled, are presented in Figure 6.3. As the delay increased to 1 s, the participants' performances decayed back to what would be expected from the original whole-report level of four or five items. That is, participants were reporting about one-third as many items from the cued row as they could report from three rows in the whole-report procedure. Thus, it appears that the memory of the actual display decays very rapidly and is essentially gone by the end of 1 s. All that is left after that is what the participant has had time to attend to and convert to a more permanent form.

FIGURE 6.2 An example of the kind of display used in a visual-report experiment. The display is presented briefly to participants, who are then asked to report the letters it contains.

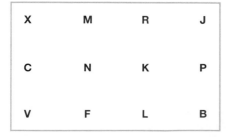

X	M	R	J
C	N	K	P
V	F	L	B

Sperling's experiments indicate the existence of a brief **visual sensory store**—a memory system that can effectively hold all the information in the visual display. While information is being held in this store, a participant can attend to it and report it. This sensory store appears to be particularly visual in character. In one experiment that

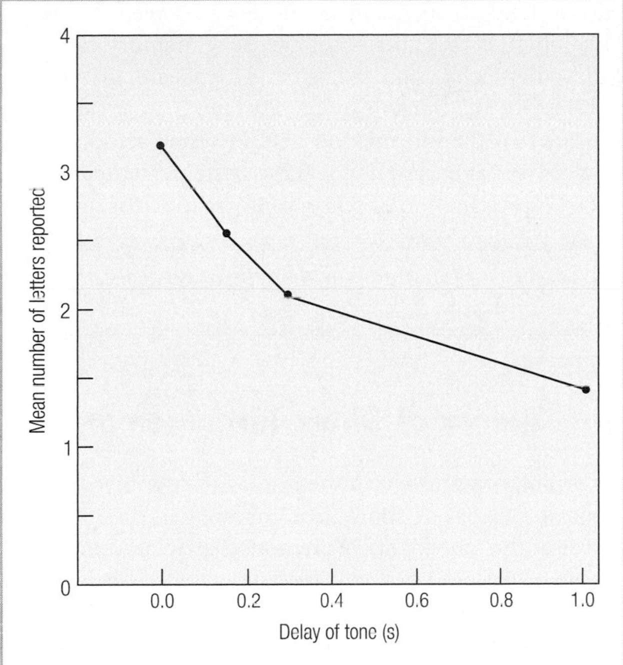

FIGURE 6.3 Results from Sperling's experiment demonstrating the existence of a brief visual sensory store. Participants were shown arrays consisting of three rows of four letters. After the display was turned off, they were cued by a tone, either immediately or after a delay, to recall a particular one of the three rows. The results show that the number of items reported decreased as the delay in the cuing tone increased. (After Sperling, 1960. Adapted by permission of the publisher. © 1960 by *Psychological Monographs.*)

demonstrated the visual character of the sensory store, Sperling (1967) varied the postexposure field (the visual field after the display). He found that when the postexposure field was light, the sensory information remained for only 1 s, but when the field was dark, it remained for a full 5 s. Thus, a bright postexposure field tends to "wash out" memory for the display. Moreover, following a display with another display of characters effectively "overwrites" the first display and so destroys the memory for the first set of letters. The brief visual memory revealed in these experiments is sometimes called **iconic memory.** Unless information in the display is attended to and processed further, it will be lost.

Auditory Sensory Memory

There is similar evidence for a brief **auditory sensory store,** which is sometimes called **echoic memory.** There are behavioral demonstrations (e.g., Moray, Bates, & Barnett, 1965; Darwin, Turvey, & Crowder, 1972; Glucksberg & Cowan, 1972) of an auditory sensory memory, similar to Sperling's visual sensory memory, by which people can report an auditory stimulus with considerable accuracy if probed for it soon after onset. One of the more interesting measures of auditory sensory memory involves an ERP measure called the mismatch negativity. When a sound is presented that is different from recently heard sounds in such features as pitch or magnitude (or is a different phoneme), there is an increase in the negativity of the ERP recording 150 to 200 ms after the discrepant sound (for a review, read Näätänen, 1992). In one study, Sams, Hari, Rif, and Knuutila (1993) presented one tone followed by another at various intervals. When the second tone was different from the first, it produced a mismatch negativity as long as the delay between the two tones was less than 10 s. This indicates that an auditory sensory memory can last up to 10 s, consistent with other behavioral measures. It appears that the source of this neural response in the brain is at or near the primary auditory cortex. Similarly, it appears that the information held in visual sensory memory is in or near the primary visual cortex. Thus, these basic perceptual regions of the cortex hold a brief representation of sensory information for further processing.

- *Sensory information is held briefly in cortical sensory memories so that we can process it.*

A Theory of Short-Term Memory

A very important event in the history of cognitive psychology was the development of a theory of **short-term memory** in the 1960s. It clearly illustrated the power of the new cognitive methodology to account for a great deal of data in a way that had not been possible with previous behaviorist theories. Broadbent (1958) had anticipated the theory of short-term memory, and Waugh and Norman (1965) gave an influential formulation of the theory. However, it was Atkinson and Shiffrin (1968) who gave the theory its most systematic development. It has had an enormous influence on psychology, and although few researchers still accept the original formulation, similar ideas play a crucial role in some of the modern theories that we will be discussing.

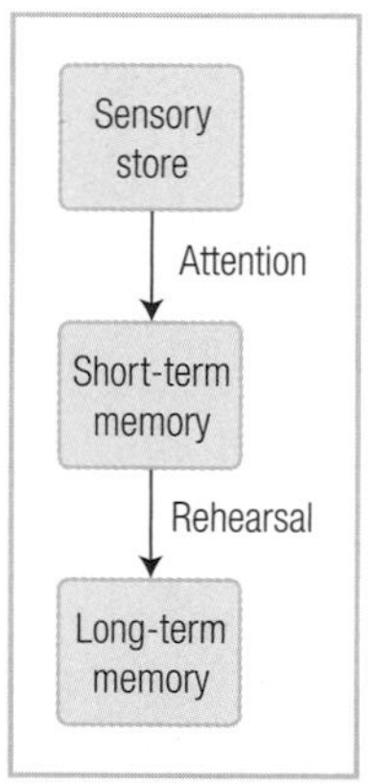

FIGURE 6.4 A model of memory that includes an intermediate short-term memory. Information coming in from the environment is held in a transient sensory store from which it is lost unless attended to. Attended information goes into an intermediate short-term memory with a limited capacity to hold information. The information must be rehearsed before it can move into a relatively permanent long-term memory.

Figure 6.4 illustrates the basic theory. As we have just seen, information coming in from the environment tends to be held in transient sensory stores from which it is lost unless attended to. The theory of short-term memory proposed that attended information went into an intermediate short-term memory where it had to be rehearsed before it could go into a relatively permanent long-term memory. Short-term memory had a limited capacity to hold information. At one time, its capacity was identified with the memory span. **Memory span** refers to the number of elements one can immediately repeat back. Ask a friend to test your memory span. Have that friend make up lists of digits of various lengths and read them to you. See how many digits you can repeat back. You will probably find that you are able to remember no more than around seven or eight perfectly. The size of the memory span was considered convenient in those days when American phone numbers were seven digits. One view was that short-term memory has room for about seven elements, although other theorists (e.g., Broadbent, 1975) proposed that its capacity is smaller and that memory span depends on other stores as well as short-term memory.

In a typical memory experiment, it was assumed that participants rehearsed the contents of short-term memory. For instance, in a study of memory span, participants might rehearse the digits by saying them over and over again to themselves. It was assumed that every time an item was rehearsed, there was a probability that the information would be transferred to a relatively permanent long-term memory. If the item left short-term memory before a permanent long-term memory representation was developed, however, it would be lost forever.

One could not keep information in short-term memory indefinitely because new information would always be coming in and pushing out old information from the limited short-term memory.

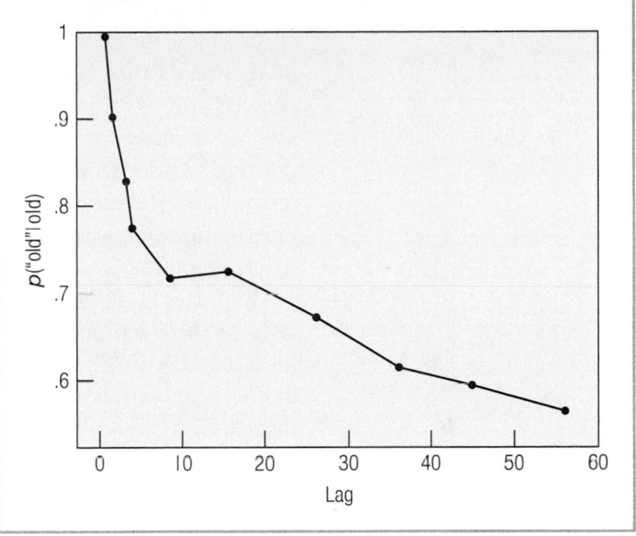

FIGURE 6.5 Results from Shepard and Teghtsoonian's experiment demonstrating that information cannot be kept in short-term memory indefinitely because new information will always be coming in and pushing out old information. The probability of an "old" response to old items is plotted as a function of the number of intervening presentations (the lag) since the last presentation of a stimulus. (From Shepard & Teghtsoonian, 1961. Reprinted by permission of the publisher © 1961 by the American Psychological Association.)

An experiment by Shepard and Teghtsoonian (1961) is a good illustration of these ideas. They presented participants with a long sequence of 200 three-digit numbers. The task was to identify when a number was repeated. The investigators were interested in how participants' ability to recognize a repeated number changed as more numbers intervened between the first appearance of the number and its repetition. The number of intervening items is referred to as the lag. If the participant tended to keep only the most recent numbers in short-term memory, memory for the last few numbers would be good but would get progressively worse as the numbers were pushed out of short-term memory. The results are presented in Figure 6.5. Note that recognition memory drops off rapidly over the first few numbers, but then the drop-off slows to the point where it appears to be reaching some sort of asymptote at about 60%. The rapid drop-off can be interpreted as reflecting the decreasing likelihood that the numbers are being held in short-term memory. The 60% level of recall for the later numbers reflects the amount of information that got into long-term memory.[1]

A critical assumption in this theory was that the amount of rehearsal controls the amount of information transferred to long-term memory. For instance, Rundus (1971) asked participants to rehearse out loud and showed that the more participants rehearsed an item, the more likely they were to remember it. Data of this sort were perhaps most critical to the theory of short-term memory because they reflected the fundamental property of short-term memory: It is a necessary halfway station to long-term memory. Information has to "do time" in short-term memory to get into long-term memory, and the more time done, the more likely it is to be remembered.

In an influential article, Craik and Lockhart (1972) argued that what was critical was not how long information is rehearsed, but rather the depth to which it is processed. This theory, called **depth of processing,** held that rehearsal improves memory only if the material is rehearsed in a deep and meaningful way. Passive rehearsal does not result in better memory. A number of experiments have shown that passive rehearsal results in little improvement in memory performance. For instance, Glenberg, Smith, and Green (1977) had participants study a four-digit number for 2 s, then rehearse a word for 2, 6, or 18 s, and then recall the four digits. Participants thought that their task was to recall the digits and that they

[1] This level of memory is not really 60% because participants were incorrectly accepting more than 20% of new items as repeated. The level of memory is really the difference between this 60% hit rate and the 20% false alarm rate.

were just rehearsing the word to fill the time. However, they were given a final surprise test for the words. On average, participants recalled 11%, 7%, and 13% of the words they had rehearsed for 2, 6, and 18 s. Their recall was poor and showed little relationship to the amount of rehearsal.[2] On the other hand, as we saw in Chapter 5, participants' memories can be greatly improved if they process material in a deep and meaningful way. Thus, it seems that there may be no short-term, halfway station to long-term memory. Rather, it is critical that we process information in a way that is conducive to setting up a long-term memory trace. Information may go directly from sensory stores to long-term memory.

Kapur et al. (1994) did a PET study of the difference between brain correlates of the deep and shallow processing of words. In the shallow processing task, participants judged whether the words contained a particular letter; in the deep processing task, they judged whether the words described living things. Even though the study time was the same, participants remembered 75% of the deeply processed words and 57% of the shallowly processed words. Kapur et al. (1994) found that there was greater activation during deep processing in the left prefrontal regions indicated in Figure 6.1. A number of subsequent studies have also shown that this region of the brain is more active during deep processing (for a review, see Wagner, Bunge, & Badre, 2004).

Atkinson and Shiffrin's theory of short-term memory postulated that as information is rehearsed in a limited-capacity short-term memory, it is deposited in long-term memory; but what turned out to be important was how deeply the material is processed.

Working Memory Holds the Information Needed to Perform a Task

Baddeley's Theory of Working Memory

Baddeley (1986) proposed a theory of the rehearsal processes that did not tie them to storage in long-term memory. He hypothesized that there are two systems, a **visuospatial sketchpad** and a **phonological loop,** that are what he called "slave systems" for maintaining information, and he speculated that there might be more such systems. These systems compose part of what he calls **working memory,** which is a system for holding information that we need to perform a task. For instance, try multiplying 35 by 23 in your head. You may find yourself developing a visual image of part of a written multiplication problem (visuospatial sketchpad) and you may find yourself rehearsing partial products like 105 (phonological loop). Figure 6.6 illustrates Baddeley's overall conception of how these various slave systems interact. A **central executive** controls how the slave systems are used. The central executive can put information into any of the slave systems or retrieve information from them. It can

[2] Although recall memory tends not to be improved by the amount of passive rehearsal, Glenberg et al. (1977) did show that recognition memory is improved by rehearsal. Recognition memory may depend on a kind of familiarity judgment that does not require creation of new memory traces.

also translate information from one system to another. Baddeley claimed that the central executive needs its own temporary store of information to make decisions about how to control the slave systems.

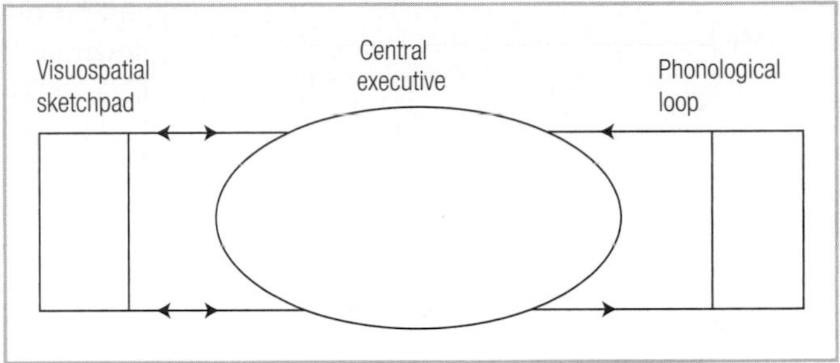

FIGURE 6.6 Baddeley's theory of working memory in which a central executive coordinates a set of slave systems. (From Baddeley, 1986. Reprinted by permission of the publisher. © 1986 by Oxford University Press.)

The phonological loop has received much more extensive investigation than the visuospatial sketchpad. Baddeley proposed that the phonological loop consists of multiple components. One is an **articulatory loop** by which an "inner voice" rehearses verbal information. A classic example of how we use the articulatory loop is in remembering a phone number. When one is told a phone number, one rehearses the number over and over again to oneself until one dials it. Many brain-imaging studies (see E. E. Smith & Jonides, 1995, for a review) have found activation in Broca's area (the region labeled "J" in the frontal portion of the Figure 4.1 brain illustration) when participants are trying to remember a list of items. This activation occurs even if the participants are not actually talking to themselves. Patients with damage to this region show deficits in tests of short-term memory (Vallar, Di Betta, & Silveri, 1997).

Another component of the phonological loop is the phonological store. Baddeley proposed that this store is in effect an "inner ear" that hears the inner voice and stores the information in a phonological form. It has been proposed that this region is associated with the parietal-temporal region of the brain (the region labeled "J" in the parietal-temporal region of the Figure 4.1 brain illustration). A number of imaging studies (Henson, Burgess, & Frith, 2000; Jonides et al., 1998) have found activation of this region during the storage of verbal information. Also, patients with lesions in this region suffer deficits of short-term memory (Vallar et al., 1997).

One of the most compelling pieces of evidence for the existence of the articulatory loop is the word-length effect (Baddeley, Thomson, & Buchanan, 1975). Read the five words below and then try to repeat them back without looking at the page:

- wit, sum, harm, bay, top

Most people can do this. Baddeley et al. found that participants were able to repeat back an average of 4.5 words out of 5 such one-syllable words. Now read and try to repeat back the following five words:

- university, opportunity, aluminum, constitutional, auditorium

Participants were able to recall only an average of 2.6 words out of 5 such five-syllable words. The crucial factor appears to be how long it takes to say the word. Vallar and Baddeley (1982) looked at recall for words that varied from one to five syllables. They also measured how many words of the various lengths participants could say in a second. Figure 6.7 shows the results. Note that the percentage of sequences correctly recalled almost exactly matches the reading rate.

Trying to maintain information in working memory is analogous to the circus act that involves spinning plates on a stick. The circus performer will get one plate spinning on one stick, then another on another stick, then another,

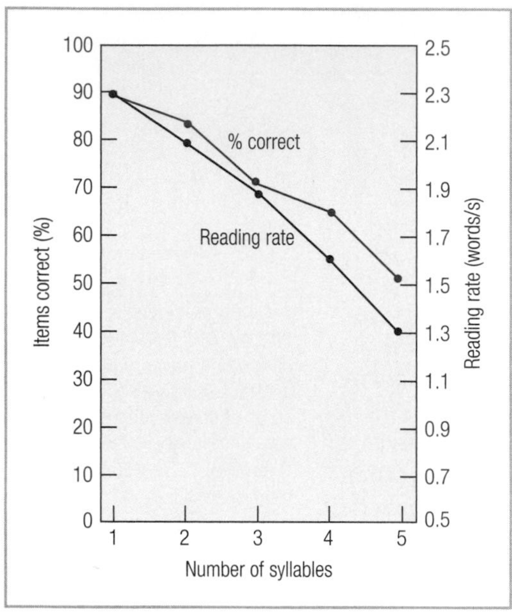

FIGURE 6.7 Results of Vallar and Baddeley's (1982) experiment showing the existence of the articulatory loop. Mean reading rate and percentage of correct recall of sequences of five words are plotted as a function of word length. (From Baddeley, 1986. Reprinted by permission of the publisher. © 1986 by Oxford University Press.)

and so on. Then he runs back to the first before it slows down and falls off. He respins it and then respins the rest. He can keep only so many plates spinning at the same time. Baddeley proposed that it is the same situation with respect to working memory. If we try to keep too many items in working memory, by the time we get back to rehearse the first one, it will have decayed to the point that it takes too long to retrieve and re-rehearse. Baddeley proposed that we can keep about 1.5 to 2.0 seconds' worth of material rehearsed in the articulatory loop.

There is considerable evidence that this articulatory loop truly involves speech. For instance, the research of R. Conrad (1964) showed that participants suffered more confusion when they tried to remember spans that had a high proportion of rhyming letters (such as *BCTHVZ*) than when they tried to remember spans that did not (such as *HBKLMW*). Also, as we just discussed, there is evidence for activation in Broca's area, part of the left prefrontal cortex, during the rehearsal of such memories.

One might wonder what the difference is between short-term memory and Baddeley's articulatory loop. The crucial difference is that processing information in the phonological loop is not critical to getting it into long-term memory. Rather, the phonological loop is just an auxiliary system for keeping information available.

- *Baddeley proposed that we have an articulatory loop and a visuospatial sketchpad, both of which are controlled by a central executive, which are systems for holding information and are part of working memory.*

The Frontal Cortex and Primate Working Memory

The frontal cortex gets larger in the progression from lower mammals, such as the rat, to higher mammals, such as the monkey; and it shows a proportionately greater development between the monkey and the human. It has been known for some time that the frontal cortex plays an important role in tasks that can be thought of as working-memory tasks in primates. The task that has been most studied in this respect is the delayed match-to-sample task, which is illustrated in Figure 6.8. The monkey is shown an item of food that is placed in one of two identical wells (Figure 6.8a). Then the wells are covered, and the monkey is prevented from looking at the scene for a delay period—typically 10 s (Figure 6.8b). Finally, the monkey is given the opportunity to retrieve the food, but it must remember in which well it was hidden (Figure 6.8c). Monkeys with lesions in the frontal cortex cannot perform this task (Jacobsen, 1935, 1936). A human infant cannot perform similar tasks until its frontal cortex has matured somewhat, usually at about 1 year of age (Diamond, 1991).

When a monkey must remember where a food item has been placed, a particular area of the frontal cortex is involved (Goldman-Rakic, 1988). This

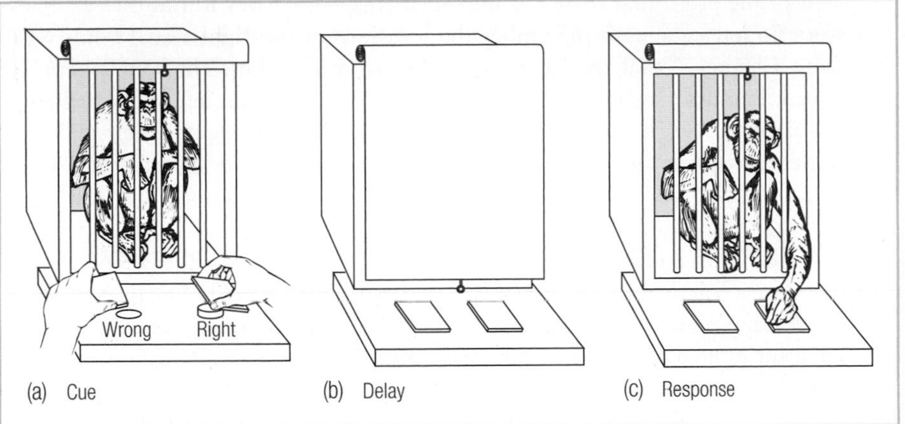

FIGURE 6.8 An illustration of the delayed match-to-sample task. (a) Food is placed in the well on the right and covered. (b) A curtain is drawn for the delay period. (c) The curtain is raised, and the monkey can lift the cover from one of the wells. (From Goldman-Rakic, 1987. Reprinted by permission of the publisher. © 1987 by the American Physiological Society.)

small region, called area 46 (Figure 6.9), is found on the side of the frontal cortex. Lesions in this specific area produce deficits in this task. It has been shown that neurons in this region fire only during the delay period of the task, as if they are keeping information active during that interval. They are inactive before and after the delay. Moreover, different neurons in that region seem tuned to remembering objects in different portions of the visual field (Funahashi, Bruce, & Goldman-Rakic, 1991).

Goldman-Rakic (1992) examined monkey performance on other tasks that require maintaining different types of information over the delay interval. In one task, monkeys had to remember different objects. For example, the animal would have to remember to select a red circle, and not a green square, after a delay interval. It appears that a different region of the prefrontal cortex is involved in this task. Different neurons in this area fire when a red circle is being remembered than when a green square is being remembered. Goldman-Rakic speculated that the prefrontal cortex is parceled into many small regions, each of which is responsible for remembering a different kind of information.

Like many neuroscience studies, these experiments are correlational—they show a relationship between neural activity and memory function, but they do not show that the neural activity is essential for the memory function. In an effort to show a causal role, Funahashi, Bruce, and Goldman-Rakic (1993) trained monkeys to remember the location of objects in their visual field and move their eyes to these locations after a delay—an oculomotor equivalent of the task described in Figure 6.8. They selectively lesioned this

FIGURE 6.9 Lateral views of the cerebral cortex of a human (*top*) and of a monkey (*bottom*). Area 46 is the region shown in darker color. (From Goldman-Rakic, 1987. Reprinted by permission of the publisher. © 1987 by the American Physiological Society.)

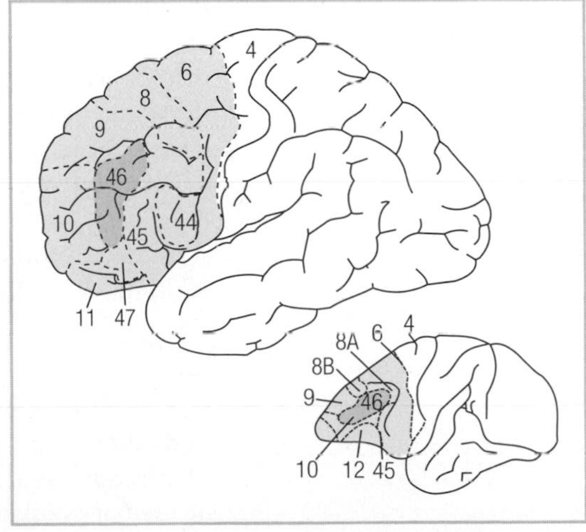

area of the prefrontal cortex in the left hemisphere. They found that monkeys were no longer able to remember the locations in the right visual field (recall from Chapter 2 that the left visual field projects to the right hemisphere; see Figure 2.5), but their ability to remember objects in the left visual field was unimpaired. When they lesioned the right hemisphere region, their ability to remember the location of objects in the left visual field was also impacted. Thus, it does seem that activity in these prefrontal regions is critical to the ability to maintain these memories over delays.

E. E. Smith and Jonides (1995) used PET scans to see whether there are similar areas of activation in humans. When participants held visual information in working memory, there was activation in right prefrontal area 47, which is adjacent to area 46. The monkey brain and the human brain are not identical (see Figure 6.8), and we would not necessarily expect a direct correspondence between regions of their brains. Smith and Jonides also looked at a task in which participants rehearsed verbal labels; they found that left prefrontal area 6 was active in this task. This region of the prefrontal cortex is associated with linguistic processing (Petrides, Alvisatos, Evans, & Meyer, 1993). One might view these two tasks as invoking Baddeley's two slave systems, with the visuospatial sketchpad associated with right prefrontal regions and the phonological loop associated with left prefrontal regions.

- *Different areas of the frontal cortex appear to be responsible for maintaining different types of information in working memory.*

Activation and Long-Term Memory

So far, we have discussed how information from the environment comes into working memory and is maintained by rehearsal. There is another source of information besides the environment, however: long-term memory. For instance, rather than reading a phone number and holding it in working memory, we can retrieve a familiar number and hold it in working memory. A number of theories have assumed that different pieces of information in long-term memory can vary from moment to moment in terms of how easy it is to retrieve them into working memory. Various theories use different words to describe the same basic idea. The language I use in this chapter is similar to that used in my **ACT (Adaptive Control of Thought)** theory (J. R. Anderson, 1983; J. R. Anderson & Lebiere, 1998). In ACT, one speaks of memory traces as varying in their activation. Another well-known theory, **SAM (Search of Associative Memory)** (Gillund & Shiffrin, 1984; Raaijmakers & Shiffrin, 1981), speaks of images (memory traces) as varying in their familiarity (activation).

An Example of Activation Calculations

Activation determines both the probability and the speed of access to memory. The free-association technique is sometimes used to get at levels of activation in memory. Whatever ideas come to mind as you are free-associating can be taken as reflecting the things that are currently most active in your long-term memory. What do you think of when you read the three words below?

Bible

animals

flood

If you are like the students in my classes, you will think of the story of Noah. The curious fact is that when I ask students to associate to just the word *Bible,* they come up with such terms as *Moses* and *Jesus*—almost never *Noah.* When I ask them to associate to just *animals,* they come up with *farm* and *zoo,* but almost never *Noah;* and when I ask them to associate to just *flood,* they come up with *Mississippi* and *Johnstown* (the latter being perhaps a Pittsburgh-specific association), but almost never *Noah.* So why do they come up with *Noah* when given all three terms together? Figure 6.10 represents this phenomenon in terms of activation computations and shows three kinds of things:

1. Various words that might come to mind, such as *Jesus, Moses,* and *Mississippi.*
2. Various terms that might be used to prime memory, such as *Bible, animals,* and *flood.*
3. Associations between the primes and the responses. In this illustration, these associations are indicated by the triangular connections where the input line touches the output line.

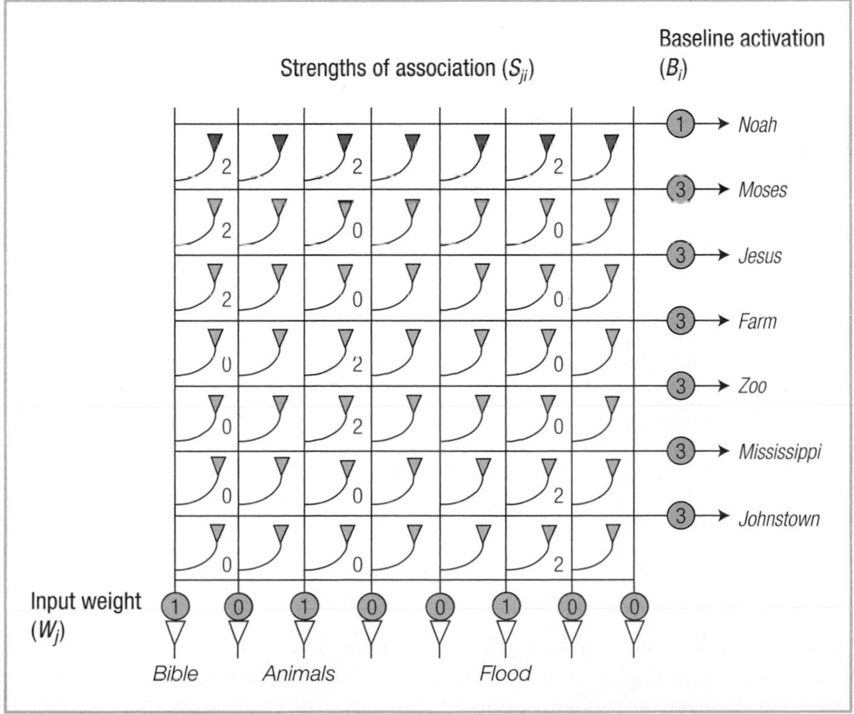

FIGURE 6.10 A representation of how activation accumulates in a neural network such as that assumed in the ACT theory. Activation coming from various stimulus words—such as *Bible, animals,* and *flood*—spreads activation to associated concepts, such as *Noah, Moses,* and *farm.*

The ACT theory has an equation to represent how the activation, A_i, of any particular element *i* reflects the structure and circumstance of this network:

$$A_i = B_i + \sum_j W_j S_{ji}$$

This equation relates the activation A_i to the three components in the network:

1. B_i reflects the base-level activation of the words that might be recalled. Some concepts, such as *Jesus* and *Mississippi*, are more common than others, such as *Noah*, and so would have greater base-level activation. Just to be concrete, we might assign the base-level activations for *Jesus* and *Mississippi* to be 3 and for *Noah* to be 1.
2. W_j reflects the weight given to various terms *j* that might prime the memory. For instance, we might assume that the W_j for any word we present is 1 and the W_j for words we do not present is 0. The Σ indicates that we are summing over all of the potential primes *j*.
3. S_{ji} reflects the strength of associations between potential primes *j* in item 2 above and potential responses *i* in item 1 above. To keep things simple, we might assume that the strength of association is 2 in the case of related pairs such as *Bible-Jesus* and *flood-Mississippi* and 0 in the case of unrelated pairs such as *Bible-Mississippi* and *flood-Jesus.*

With this equation, these concepts, and these numbers, we can explain why the students in my class associate *Noah* when prompted with all three words but never do so when presented with any word individually. Consider what happens when I present just the word *Bible.* There is only one prime with a positive W_j, and this is *Bible.* In this case, the activation of *Noah* is

$$A_{\text{Noah}} = 1 + (1 \times 2) = 3$$

where the first 1 is its base-level activation B_i, the second 1 is its weight W_j of *Bible,* and the 2 is the strength of association S_{ji} between *Bible* and *Noah.* The activation for *Jesus* is different because it has a higher base-level activation, reflecting its greater frequency:

$$A_{\text{Jesus}} = 3 + (1 \times 2) = 5$$

The reason *Jesus* and not *Noah* comes to mind in this case is that *Jesus* has higher activation. Now let's consider what happens when I present all three words. The activation of *Noah* will be

$$A_{\text{Noah}} = 1 + (1 \times 2) + (1 \times 2) + (1 \times 2) = 7$$

where there are three (1×2)'s because all three of the terms—*Bible, animals,* and *flood*—have associations to *Noah.* The activation equation for *Jesus* remains

$$A_{\text{Jesus}} = 3 + (1 \times 2) = 5$$

because only *Bible* has the association with *Jesus.* Thus, the extra associations to *Noah* have raised the current activation of *Noah* to be greater than the activation of *Jesus,* despite the fact that it has lower base-level activation.

There are two critical factors in this activation equation: the base-level activation, which sets a starting activation for the idea, and the activation received through the associations, which adjusts this activation to reflect the current context. The next section will explore this associative activation, and the section after that will discuss the base-level activation.

- *The speed and probability of accessing a memory are determined by the memory's level of activation, which in turn is determined by its base-level activation and the activation it receives from associated concepts.*

Spreading Activation

Spreading activation is the term often used to refer to the process by which currently attended items can make associated memories more available. Many studies have examined how terms to which we currently attend can prime memories. One of the earliest was a study by Meyer and Schvaneveldt (1971) in which participants were asked to judge whether or not pairs of items were words. Table 6.1 shows examples of the materials used in their experiments, along with participants' judgment times. The items were presented one above the other. If either item in a pair was not a word, participants were to respond no. It appears from examining the negative pairs that participants judged first the top item and then the bottom item. When the top item was not a word, participants were faster to reject the pair than when only the bottom item was not a word. (When the top item was not a word, participants did not have to judge the bottom item and so could respond sooner.) The major interest in this study was in the positive pairs. There were unrelated items, such as *nurse* and *butter,* and pairs with an associative relation, such as *bread* and *butter.* Participants were 85 ms faster on the related pairs. This result can be explained by a spreading-activation analysis. When the participant read the first word in the related pair, activation would spread from it to the second word. This would make information about the spelling of the second word more active and make that word easier to judge. The implication of this result is that the **associative spreading** of information activation through memory can facilitate the rate at which words are read.

TABLE 6.1

Examples of the Pairs Used to Demonstrate Associative Priming

Positive Pairs		Negative Pairs		
		Nonword	Nonword	Both
Unrelated	Related	First	Second	Nonwords
Nurse Butter	Bread Butter	Plame Wine	Wine Plame	Plame Reab
940 ms	855 ms	904 ms	1,087 ms	884 ms

Thus, we can read material that has a strong associative coherence more rapidly than we can read incoherent material in which the words are unrelated.

Kaplan (1989), in his dissertation research, reported an effect of associative priming at a very different time scale of information processing. The "participants" in the study were members of his dissertation committee. I was one of these participants, and it was a rather memorable and somewhat embarrassing experience. He gave us riddles to solve, and each of us was able to solve about half of them. One of the riddles that I was able to solve was

> What goes up a chimney down but can't come down a chimney up?

The answer is *umbrella.* Another faculty member was not able to solve this one, and he has his own embarrassing story to tell about it—much like the one I have to tell about the following riddle that I could not get:

> On this hill there was a green house. And inside the green house there was a white house. And inside the white house, there was a red house. And inside the red house there were a lot of little blacks and whites sitting there. What place is this?

More or less randomly, different faculty members were able to solve various riddles.

Then Kaplan gave us each a microphone and tape recorder and told us that we would be beeped at various times over the next week and that we should then record what we had thought about the unsolved riddles and whether we had solved any new ones. He said that he was interested in the steps by which we came to solve these problems. That was essentially a lie to cover the true purpose of the experiment, but it did keep us thinking about the riddles over the week.

What Kaplan had done was to split the riddles each of us could not solve randomly into two groups. For half of these unsolved problems, he seeded our environment with clues to the solution. He was quite creative in how he did this: In the case of the riddle above that I could not solve, he drew a picture of a watermelon as graffiti in the men's restroom. Sure enough, shortly after seeing this graffiti I thought again about this riddle and came up with the answer—*watermelon!* I congratulated myself on my great insight, and when I was next beeped I proudly recorded how I had solved the problem—quite unaware of the role the bathroom graffiti had played in my solution.

Of course, that might just be one problem and one foolish participant. Averaged over all the problems and all the participants (which included a Nobel Laureate), however, we were twice as likely to solve a problem that had been primed in the environment than one that had not been. Basically, activation from the picture of the watermelon was spreading to my knowledge about watermelons and priming it when I thought about this problem. We were all unaware of the manipulation that was taking place. This example illustrates the importance of priming to issues of insight (a topic we will consider at length in Chapter 8) and also shows that one is not aware of the associative priming that is taking place, even when one is trained to spot such things, as I am.

Activation spreads from presented items through a network to memories related to that prime item.

● Practice and Memory Strength

Spreading activation concerns how the context can make some memories more available. However, some memories are just more available because they are used frequently in all contexts. So, for instance, you can recall the names of close friends almost immediately, anywhere and anytime. The quantity that determines this inherent availability of a memory is referred to as its **strength.** In contrast to the activation level of a trace, which can have rapid fluctuations depending on whether associated items are being focused upon, the strength of a trace changes more gradually. Each time we use a memory trace, it increases a little in strength. The strength of a trace determines in part how active it can become and hence how accessible it will be. The strength of a trace can be gradually increased by repeated practice.

The Power Law of Learning

The effects of practice on memory retrieval are extremely regular and very large. In one study, Pirolli and Anderson (1985) taught participants a set of facts and had them practice the facts for 25 days; then they looked at the speed with which the participants could recognize these facts. Figure 6.11a plots how participants' time to recognize a fact decreased with practice. As can be seen, participants sped up from about 1.6 s to 0.7 s, cutting their retrieval time by more than 50%. The illustration also shows that the rate of improvement decreases

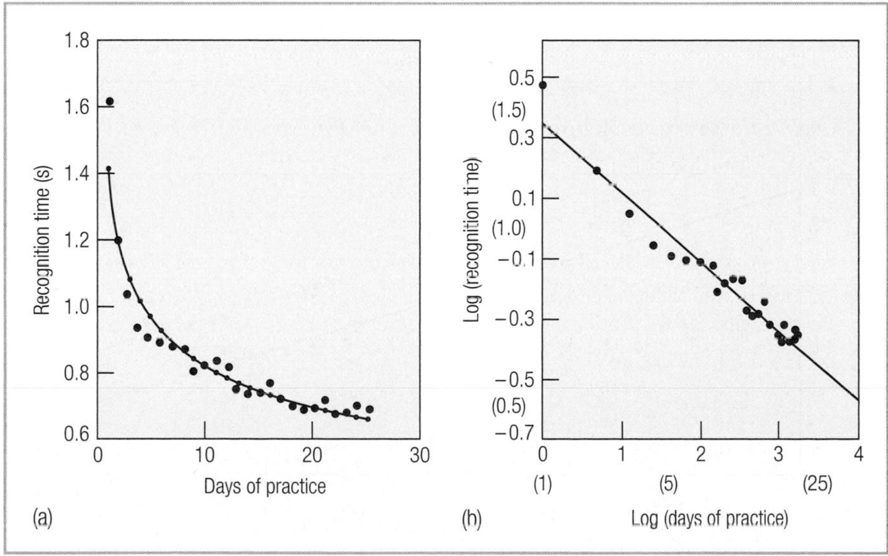

FIGURE 6.11 Results of Pirolli and Anderson's study to determine the effects of practice on recognition time. (a) The time required to recognize sentences is plotted as a function of the number of days of practice. (b) The data in (a) are log-log transformed to reveal a power function. The data points are average times for individual days, and the curves are the best-fitting power functions. (From Pirolli & Anderson, 1985. Reprinted by permission of the publisher. © 1985 by the *Journal of Experimental Psychology: Learning, Memory, and Cognition.*)

with more practice. Increasing practice has diminishing returns. The data are nicely fit by a power function of the form

$$T = 1.40\ P^{-0.24}$$

where T is the recognition time and P is the number of days of practice. This is called a **power function** because the amount of practice P is being raised to a power. This power relationship between performance (measured in terms of response time and several other variables) and amount of practice is a ubiquitous phenomenon in learning. One way to see that data correspond to a power function is to plot logarithm of time (the y-axis) against the logarithm of practice (the x-axis). If we have a power function in normal coordinates, we should get a linear function in log–log coordinates:

$$\ln T = 0.34 - 0.24 \ln P$$

Figure 6.11b shows the data so transformed. As can be seen, the relationship is quite close to a linear function (straight line).

Newell and Rosenbloom (1981) refer to the way that memory performance improves as a function of practice as the **power law of learning.** Figure 6.12 shows some data from Blackburn (1936), who looked at the effects of practicing addition problems for 10,000 trials by two participants. The data are plotted in log–log terms, and there is a linear relationship. On this graph and on some others in this book, the original numbers (i.e., those given in parentheses in Figure 6.11b) are plotted on the logarithmic scale rather than being expressed as logarithms. Blackburn's data show that the power law of learning extends to amounts of practice far beyond that shown in Figure 6.11. Figures 6.11 and 6.12 reflect the gradual

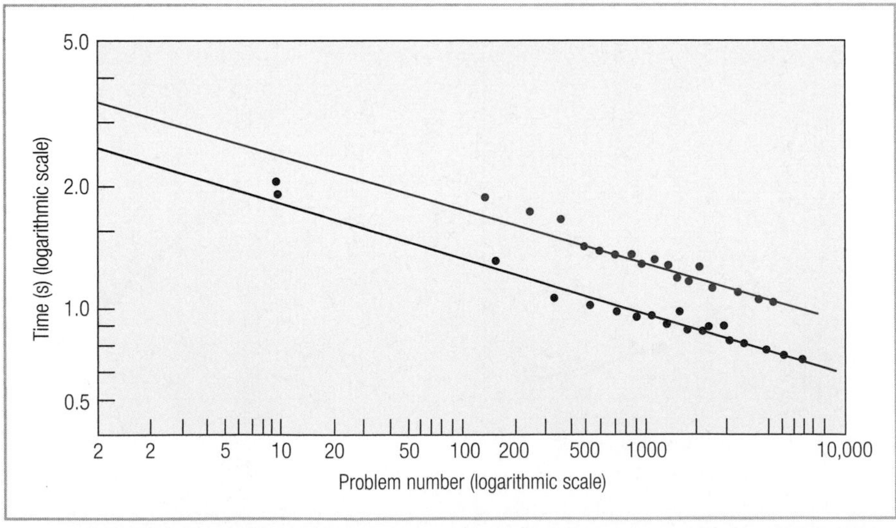

FIGURE 6.12 Data from Blackburn's study on the effects of practicing addition problems for 10,000 trials. The results are presented as improvement with practice in the time taken to add two numbers. Data are plotted separately for two participants. Both the time required to solve the problem and the number of problems are plotted on a logarithmic scale. (Plot by Crossman, 1959, of data from Blackburn, 1936. Adapted by permission of the publisher. © 1959 by *Ergonomics*.)

increase in memory trace strength with practice. As memory traces become stronger, they can reach higher levels of activation and so can be retrieved more rapidly.

As a memory is practiced, it is strengthened according to a power function.

Neural Correlates of the Power Law

One might wonder what really underlies the power law of practice. Some evidence suggests that the law may be related to basic neural changes involved in learning. One kind of neural learning that has attracted much attention is called **long-term potentiation (LTP),** which occurs in the hippocampus and cortical areas. This form of neural learning seems to be related to behavioral measures of learning like those in Figures 6.11 and 6.12. When a pathway is stimulated with a high-frequency electric current, cells along that pathway show increased sensitivity to further stimulation. Barnes (1979) looked at this phenomenon in rats by measuring the percentage increase in excitatory postsynaptic potential (EPSP) over its initial value.[3] Barnes stimulated the hippocampus of her rats each day for 11 successive days and measured the growth in LTP as indicated by the percentage increase in EPSP. Figure 6.13a displays her results in a plot of percentage change in LTP versus days of practice. There appears to be a diminishing increase with amount of practice. Figure 6.13b, which plots log percentage change in LTP against log days of practice, shows that the relationship is approximately linear, and therefore the relationship in Figure 6.13 is approximately a power function. Thus, it does seem that neural activation changes with practice, just as behavioral measures do.

Note that the activation measure shown in Figure 6.13a increases more and more slowly, whereas recognition time (see Figure 6.11a) decreases more and more slowly. In other words, a performance measure such as recognition time is an inverse reflection of the growth of strength that is happening internally. As the strength of the memory increases, the performance measures improve (which means shorter recognition times and fewer errors). You remember something faster after you've thought about it more often.

The hippocampal region being observed here is the area that was damaged in the fictional Leonard character discussed at the beginning of the chapter. Damage to this region often results in amnesia. Studies of the effects of practice on participants without brain damage have found that activation in the hippocampus and the prefrontal regions decreases as participants become more practiced at retrieving memories (Kahn & Wagner, 2002).[4]

[3] As discussed in Chapter 1, the difference in electric potential between the outside and inside of the cell decreases as the dendrite and cell body of a neuron become more excited. EPSP is described as increasing when this difference decreases.

[4] Note that neural activation decreases with practice because it takes less effort to retrieve the memory. This can be a bit confusing—greater trace activation resulting from practice results in lower brain activation. This happens because trace activation reflects the availability of the memory, whereas brain activation reflects the hemodynamic expenditure required to retrieve the memory. Trace activation and brain activation refer to different concepts.

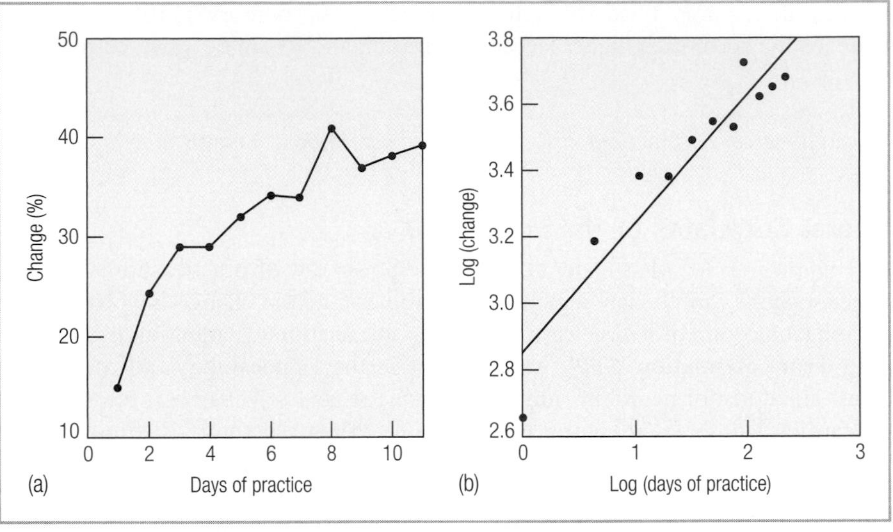

FIGURE 6.13 Results from Barnes's study of long-term potentiation (LTP) demonstrating that when a neural pathway is stimulated, cells along that pathway show increased sensitivity to further stimulation. The growth in LTP is plotted as a function of number of days of practice (a) in normal scale and (b) in log–log scale. (From Barnes, 1979. Reprinted by permission of the publisher. © 1979 by the *Journal of Comparative Physiology.*)

The relationship between the hippocampus and regions of the prefrontal cortex is interesting. In normal participants, these regions are often active at the same time, as they were in the Kahn and Wagner study. It is generally thought (e.g., Paller & Wagner, 2002) that processing activity in prefrontal regions regulates input to hippocampal regions that store the memories. Patients with hippocampal damage show the same prefrontal activation as normal people do; but because of the hippocampal damage, they fail to store these memories (R. L. Buckner, personal communication, 1998).

Two studies illustrating the role of the prefrontal cortex in forming new memories appeared back to back in the same issue of *Science* magazine. One study (Wagner et al., 1998) investigated memory for words; the other (J. B. Brewer et al., 1998) studied memory for pictures. In both cases, participants remembered some of the items and forgot others. Using fMRI measures of the hemodynamic response, the researchers contrasted the brain activation at the time of study for those words that were subsequently remembered and those that were subsequently forgotten. Wagner et al. found that left prefrontal regions were predictive of memory for words, whereas Brewer et al. found that right prefrontal regions were predictive of memory for pictures. Figure 6.14a shows the results for words; Figure 6.14b, the results for pictures. In both cases, the rise in the hemodynamic response is plotted as a function of time from stimulus presentation. As discussed in Chapter 1, the hemodynamic response lags, so that it is at maximum about 5 s after the actual neural activity. The correspondence between the results from the two laboratories is striking. In both cases, remembered items received greater

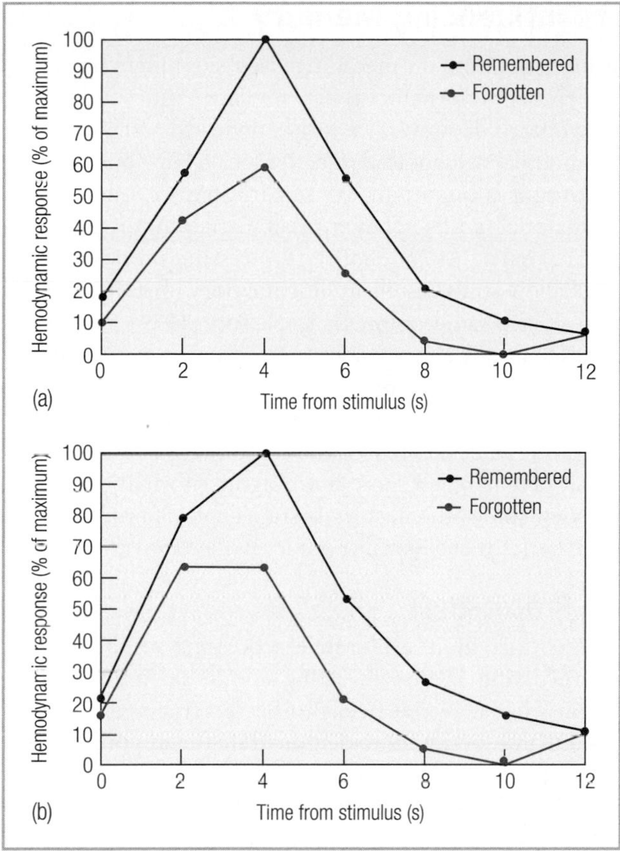

FIGURE 6.14 Results from two studies illustrating the role of the prefrontal cortex in forming new memories. (a) Data from the study by Wagner et al. show the rise in the hemodynamic response in the left prefrontal cortex while participants studied words that were subsequently remembered or forgotten. (After Wagner et al., 1998. Adapted by permission of the publisher. © 1998 by *Science*.) (b) Data from the study by Brewer et al. show the rise in the hemodynamic response in the right prefrontal cortex while participants studied pictures that were subsequently remembered or forgotten. (After J. B. Brewer et al., 1998. Adapted by permission of the publisher. © 1998 by *Science*.)

activation from the prefrontal regions, supporting the conclusion that prefrontal activation is indeed critical for storing a memory successfully.[5] Also, note that these studies are a good example of the lateralization of prefrontal processing, with verbal material involving the left hemisphere to a greater extent and visual material involving the right hemisphere to a greater extent.

- *Activation in prefrontal regions appears to drive long-term potentiation in the hippocampus. This activation results in the creation and strengthening of memories.*

[5] Greater hemodynamic activation at study results in a stronger memory—which, as we noted, can lead to reduced hemodynamic activation at test.

Factors Influencing Memory

A reasonable inference from the preceding discussion might be that the only thing determining memory performance is how much we study and practice the material to be remembered. However, we earlier reviewed some of the evidence that mere study of material will not lead to better recall. How one processes the material while studying it is important. We saw in Chapter 5 that more meaningful processing of material results in better recall. Earlier in this chapter, with respect to Craik and Lockhart's (1972) depth-of-processing proposal, we reviewed the evidence that shallow study results in little memory improvement. As a different demonstration of the same point, D. L. Nelson (1979) had participants read paired associates that were either semantic associates (e.g., *tulip-flower*) or rhymes (e.g., *tower-flower*). Better memory (81% recall) was obtained for the semantic associates than for the rhymes (70% recall). Presumably, participants tended to process the semantic associates more meaningfully than the rhymes. In Chapter 5, we also saw that people retain more meaningful information better. In this section, we will review some other factors, besides depth of processing and meaningfulness of the material, that determine our level of memory.

Elaborative Processing

There is evidence that more elaborative processing results in better memory. **Elaborative processing** involves creating additional information that relates and expands on what it is that needs to be remembered. J. R. Anderson and Bower (1973) did an experiment to demonstrate the importance of elaboration. They had participants try to remember simple sentences such as *The doctor hated the lawyer.* In one condition, participants just studied the sentence; in the other, they were asked to generate an elaboration of their choosing—such as *because of the malpractice suit.* Later, participants were presented with the subject and verb of the original sentence (e.g., *The doctor hated*) and were asked to recall the object (e.g., *the lawyer*). Participants who just studied the original sentences were able to recall 57% of the objects, but those who generated the elaborations recalled 72%. The investigators proposed that this advantage resulted from the redundancy created by the elaboration. If the participants could not originally recall *lawyer* but could recall the elaboration *because of the malpractice suit,* they might then be able to recall *lawyer.*

A series of experiments by B. S. Stein and Bransford (1979) showed why self-generated elaborations are often better than experimenter-provided elaborations. In one of these experiments, participants were asked to remember 10 sentences, such as *The fat man read the sign.* There were four conditions of study.

- In the base condition, participants studied just the sentence.
- In the self-generated elaboration condition, participants were asked to create an elaboration of their own.
- In the imprecise elaboration condition, participants were given a continuation of the sentence poorly related to the meaning of the sentence, such as *that was two feet tall.*
- In the precise elaboration condition, they were given a continuation that gave context to the sentence, such as *warning about the ice.*

After studying the material, participants in all conditions were presented with such sentence frames as *The _______ man read the sign*, and they had to recall the missing adjective. Participants recalled 4.2 of the 10 adjectives in the base condition and 5.8 of the 10 when they generated their own elaborations. Obviously, the self-generated elaborations had helped. They could recall only 2.2 of the adjectives in the imprecise elaboration condition, replicating the typical inferiority found for experimenter-provided elaborations relative to self-generated ones. However, participants recalled the most (7.8 of 10 adjectives) in the precise elaboration condition. So, by careful choice of words, experimenter elaborations can be made better than those of participants. (For further research on this topic, read Pressley, McDaniel, Turnure, Wood, & Ahmad, 1987.)

It appears that the critical factor is not whether the participant or the experimenter generates the elaborations but whether the elaborations prompt the material to be recalled. Participant-generated elaborations are effective because they reflect the idiosyncratic constraints of each particular participant's knowledge. As Stein and Bransford demonstrated, however, it is possible for the experimenter to construct elaborations that facilitate even better recall.

- *Memory for material improves when it is processed with more meaningful elaborations.*

Techniques for Studying Textual Material

Frase (1975) found evidence of the benefit of elaborative processing with text material. He compared how participants in two groups remembered text: One group was given questions to think about before reading the text—sometimes called advance organizers (Ausubel, 1968)—and a control group that simply studied the text without advance questions. Participants in the first group were asked to find answers to the advance questions as they read the text. This requirement should have forced them to process the text more carefully and to think about its implications. In a subsequent test, the advance-organizer group answered 64% of the questions correctly, whereas the control group answered only 57% correctly. The questions in the test were either relevant or irrelevant to the advance organizers. For instance, a test question about an event that precipitated America's entry into World War II would be considered relevant if the advance questions directed participants to learn why America entered the war. A test question would be considered irrelevant if the advance questions directed participants to learn about the economic consequences of World War II. The advance-organizer group correctly answered 76% percent of the relevant questions and 52% of the irrelevant ones. Thus, they did only slightly worse than the control group on topics for which they had been given only irrelevant advance questions but did much better on topics for which they had been given relevant advance questions.

Many college study-skills departments, as well as private firms, offer courses designed to improve students' memory for text material. These courses teach study techniques mainly for texts such as those used in the social sciences, not for the denser texts used in the physical sciences and mathematics or for literary materials such as novels. The study techniques from different programs are rather similar, and their success has been fairly well documented. One example of such a study technique is the PQ4R method (Thomas & Robinson, 1972). The Implications box in Chapter 1 described a slight variation on this technique as a method for studying this book.

The PQ4R method derives its name from the six phases it advocates for studying a chapter in a textbook:

1. Preview: Survey the chapter to determine the general topics being discussed. Identify the sections to be read as units. Apply the next four steps to each section.
2. Questions: Make up questions about each section. Often, simply transforming section headings results in adequate questions.
3. Read: Read each section carefully, trying to answer the questions you have made up about it.
4. Reflect: Reflect on the text as you are reading it. Try to understand it, to think of examples, and to relate the material to your prior knowledge.
5. Recite: After finishing a section, try to recall the information contained in it. Try to answer the questions you made up for the section. If you cannot recall enough, reread the portions you had trouble remembering.
6. Review: After you have finished the chapter, go through it mentally, recalling its main points. Again try to answer the questions you made up.

The central features of the PQ4R technique are the generation and answering of questions. There is reason to think that the most important aspect of these features is that they encourage deeper and more elaborative processing of the text material. At the beginning of this section, we reviewed the Frase (1975) experiment that demonstrated the benefit of reading a text with a set of advance questions in mind. It seems that the benefit was specific to test items related to the questions.

Another experiment by Frase (1975) compared the effects of making up questions with the effects of answering them. He asked pairs of participants to study a text passage that was divided into halves. For one half, one participant in the pair read the passage and made up study questions during the process. The second participant then tried to answer these questions while reading the text. The participants switched roles for the second half of the text. All participants answered a final set of test questions about the passage. A control group, which just read the text without doing anything special, correctly answered 50% of the final set of test questions. Experimental participants who made up questions while they read the text correctly answered 70% of the final test items that were relevant to their questions and 52% of the items that were irrelevant. Experimental participants who answered questions while they read the text correctly answered 67% of the relevant test items and 49% of the irrelevant items. Thus, it seems that both question generation and question answering contribute to good memory. If anything, the creation of questions contributes the most benefit.

Reviewing the text with the questions in mind is another important component of the PQ4R technique. Rothkopf (1966) compared the benefit of reading a text with questions in mind with the benefit of considering a set of questions after reading the text. Rothkopf instructed participants to read a long text passage with questions interspersed every three pages. The questions were relevant to the three pages either following or preceding the questions. In the former condition, participants were supposed to read the subsequent text with these questions in mind. In the latter condition, they were to review what they had just read and answer the questions. The two experimental groups were compared with a control group, which read the text without any special questions. The control group answered 30% of the questions correctly in a final test of the whole text. The experimental group whose questions previewed the text correctly answered 72% of the test items relevant to their questions and 32% of the irrelevant items—basically the same results as those Frase (1975) obtained in comparing the effectiveness of relevant and irrelevant test items. The experimental group whose questions reviewed the text correctly answered 72% of the relevant items and 42% of the irrelevant items. Thus, it seems that using questions to review the text just read may be more beneficial than reading the text with the questions in mind.

- *Study techniques that involve generating and answering questions lead to better memory for text material.*

Meaningful versus Nonmeaningful Elaborations

Although the research just reviewed indicates that meaningful processing leads to better memory, other research demonstrates that other sorts of elaborative processing also result in better memory. For instance, Kolers (1979) looked at participants' memory for sentences that were read in normal form versus sentences that were printed upside down and found that participants remembered more about the upside-down sentences. He argued that the extra processing involved in reading the typography of upside-down sentences provides the basis for the improved memory. It is not a case of more meaningful processing, but one of more extensive processing.

A study by Slamecka and Graf (1978) demonstrated separate effects on memory of elaborative and meaningful processing. They contrasted two conditions. In the generate condition, participants were given a word and had to generate either a synonym that began with a particular letter (e.g., What is a synonym of *sea* that begins with the letter *o*? Answer: *ocean*) or a rhyme that began with a particular letter (e.g., What is a rhyme of *save* that begins with the letter *c*? Answer: *cave*). In the read condition, they just read the rhyme pair or the synonym pair and then were tested for their recognition of the second word. Figure 6.15 shows the results. Participants performed better with synonyms and better when they had to generate either a synonym or a rhyme. Thus, it appears that there are beneficial effects on memory of both semantic processing and elaborative processing.

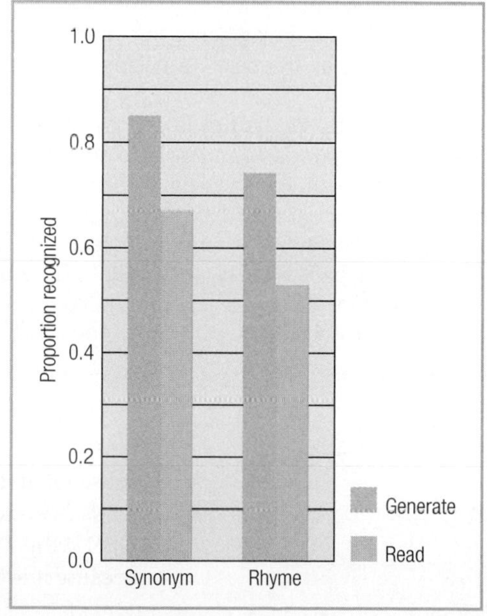

FIGURE 6.15 Results of a study by Slamecka and Graf demonstrating separate effects on memory of elaborative and meaningful processing. In the generate condition, participants were presented with a word and had to generate either a synonym or a rhyme that began with a particular letter. In the read condition, participants read the synonym pair or rhyme pair, then were tested for their recognition of the second word. The proportion of words recognized is shown as a function of the type of elaboration (synonym or rhyme) and whether it was generated or read. (From Slamecka & Graf, 1978. Reprinted by permission of the publisher. © 1978 by the *Journal of Experimental Psychology: Human Learning and Memory*.)

Otten, Henson, and Rugg (2001) noted that the prefrontal and hippocampal regions involved in memory for material that is processed meaningfully and elaborately seem to be the same regions that are involved in memory for material that is processed shallowly. High activity in these regions is predictive of

Implications

How does the method of loci help us organize recall?

Mental imagery is an effective method for developing meaningful elaborations. A classic mnemonic technique, the **method of loci**, depends heavily on visual imagery and the use of spatial knowledge to organize recall. This technique, used extensively in ancient times when speeches were given without written notes or teleprompters, is still used today. Cicero (in *De Oratore*) credits the method to a Greek poet, Simonides, who had recited a lyric poem at a banquet. After his delivery, he was called from the banquet hall by the gods Castor and Pollux, whom he had praised in his poem. While he was absent, the roof fell in, killing all the people at the banquet. The corpses were so mangled that relatives could not identify them. Simonides was able to identify each corpse, however, according to where each person had been sitting in the banquet hall. This feat of total recall convinced Simonides of the usefulness of an orderly arrangement of locations into which a person could place objects to be remembered. This story may be rather fanciful, but whatever its true origin, the method of loci is well documented (e.g., Christen & Bjork, 1976; Ross & Lawrence, 1968) as a useful technique for remembering an ordered sequence of items, such as the points a person wants to make in a speech.

To use the method of loci, one imagines a specific path through a familiar area with some fixed locations along the path. For instance, if there were such a path on campus from the bookstore to the library, we might use it. To remember a series of objects, we simply walk along the path mentally, associating the objects with the fixed locations. As an example, consider a grocery list of six items-milk, hot dogs, dog food, tomatoes, bananas, and bread. To associate the milk with the bookstore, we might imagine books lying in a puddle of milk in front of the bookstore. To associate hot dogs with the record shop (the next location on the path from the bookstore), we might imagine a package of hot dogs spinning on a phonograph turntable. The pizza shop is next, and to associate it with dog food, we might imagine a dog-food pizza (well, some people even like anchovies). Then we come to an intersection; to associate it with tomatoes, we can imagine an overturned vegetable truck with tomatoes splattered everywhere. Next we come to the administration building and create an image of the president coming out, wearing only a hula skirt made of bananas. Finally, we reach the library and associate it with bread by imagining a huge loaf of bread serving as a canopy under which we must pass to enter. To re-create the list, we need only take an imaginary walk down this path, reviving the association for each location. This technique works well even with very much longer lists; all we need is more locations. There is considerable evidence (e.g., Christen & Bjork, 1976) that the same loci can be used over and over again in the learning of different lists.

Two important principles underlie this method's effectiveness. First, the technique imposes organization on an otherwise unorganized list. We are guaranteed that if we follow the mental path at the time of recall, we will pass all the locations for which we created associations. The second principle is that imagining connections between the locations and the items forces us to process the material meaningfully, elaboratively, and by use of visual imagery.

subsequent recall (see Figure 6.13). Elaborative, more meaningful processing tends to evoke higher levels of activation than the shallow processing (Wagner et al., 1998). Thus, it appears that meaningful, elaborate processing is effective because it is better at driving the brain processes that result in successful recall.

More elaborate processing results in better memory, even if that processing is not focused on the meaning of the material.

Incidental versus Intentional Learning

So far, we have talked about factors that affect memory. Now we will turn to a factor that does not affect memory, despite people's intuitions to the contrary: It does not seem to matter whether people intend to learn the material; what is important is how they process it. This fact is illustrated in an experiment by Hyde and Jenkins (1973). Participants saw groups of 24 words presented at the rate of 3 s per word. One group of participants was asked to check whether each word had a letter *e* or a letter *g*. The other group was asked to rate the pleasantness of the words. These two tasks were called orienting tasks. It is reasonable to assume that the pleasantness rating involved more meaningful and deeper processing than the letter-verification task. Another variable was whether participants were told that the true purpose of the experiment was to learn the words. Half the participants in each group were told the true purpose of the experiment (the intentional-learning condition). The other half of participants in each group thought the true purpose of the experiment was to rate the words or check for letters (the incidental-learning condition). Thus, there were four conditions: pleasantness-intentional, pleasantness-incidental, letter checking-intentional, and letter checking-incidental.

After studying the list, all participants were asked to recall as many words as they could. Table 6.2 presents the results from this experiment in terms of percentage of the 24 words recalled. Two results are noteworthy. First, participants' knowledge of the true purpose of studying the words had relatively little effect on performance. Second, a large depth-of-processing effect was demonstrated; participants showed much better recall in the pleasantness rating condition, independent of whether they expected to be tested on the material later. In rating a word for pleasantness, participants had to think about its meaning, which gave them an opportunity to elaborate upon the word.

The Hyde and Jenkins (1973) experiment illustrates an important finding that has been proved over and over again in the research on intentional versus incidental learning: Whether a person intends to learn or not really does not matter (see Postman, 1964, for a review). What matters is how the person processes the material during its presentation. If one engages in identical mental activities when processing the material, one gets identical memory performance whether one is intending to learn the material or not. People typically show better memory when they intend to learn because they are likely to engage in activities more conducive to good memory, such as rehearsal and elaborative processing. The small advantage for

TABLE 6.2

Words Recalled as a Function of Orienting Task and Participant Awareness of Learning Task

	Words Recalled (%) Orienting Task	
Learning-Purpose Conditions	Rate Pleasantness	Check Letters
Incidental	68	39
Intentional	69	43

After Hyde and Jenkins, 1973. Adapted by permission of the publisher.

participants in the intentional learning condition of the Jenkins and Hyde experiment may reflect some small variation in processing. Experiments in which great care is taken to control processing find that intention to learn or amount of motivation to learn has no effect (see T. O. Nelson, 1976).

There is an interesting everyday example of the relationship between intention to learn and type of processing. Many students claim they find it easier to remember material from a novel, which they are not trying to remember, than from a textbook, which they are trying to remember. The reason is that students find a typical novel much easier to elaborate, and a good novel invites such elaborations (e.g., Why did the suspect deny knowing the victim?).

Level of processing, and not whether one intends to learn, determines the amount of material remembered.

Flashbulb Memories

Although it does not appear that intention to learn affects memory, various sets of data support the conclusion that people display better memory for events that are important to them. One class of research involves **flashbulb memories**—events so important that they seem to burn themselves into memory forever (R. Brown & Kulik, 1977). The event these researchers used as an example was the assassination of President Kennedy in 1963, which was a particularly traumatic event for Americans of their generation. They found that most people had vivid memories of the event 13 years later. They proposed that we have a special biological mechanism to guarantee that we will remember those things that are particularly important to us. The interpretation of this result is problematic, however, because R. Brown and Kulik did not really have any way to assess the accuracy of the reported memories.

Since the Brown and Kulik proposal, a number of studies have been done to determine what participants remembered about a traumatic event immediately after it occurred and what they remembered later. For instance, McCloskey, Wible, and Cohen (1988) did a study involving the 1986 space shuttle *Challenger* explosion. At that time, many people felt that this was a particularly traumatic event they had watched with horror on television. McCloskey et al. interviewed participants 1 week after the incident and then again 9 months later. Nine months after the accident, one participant reported:

> When I first heard about the explosion I was sitting in my freshman dorm room with my roommate and we were watching TV. It came on a news flash and we were both totally shocked. I was really upset and I went upstairs to talk to a friend of mine and then I called my parents. (Neisser & Harsch, 1992, p. 9)

McCloskey et al. found that although participants reported vivid memories 9 months after the event, their reports were in fact inaccurate. For instance, the participant just quoted had actually learned about the *Challenger* explosion in class a day after it happened and then watched it on television.

Palmer, Schreiber, and Fox (1991) came to a somewhat different conclusion in a study of memories of the 1989 San Francisco earthquake. They compared participants who had actually experienced the earthquake firsthand with those who had only watched it on TV. Those who had experienced it in person showed much superior long-term memory of the event. Conway et al. (1994) argued that McCloskey et al. (1988) failed to find a memory advantage in the *Challenger* study because their participants did not have true flashbulb memories. They contended that it is critical for the event to have been consequential to the individual remembering it. Hence, only people who actually experienced the San Francisco earthquake, and not those who saw it on TV, had flashbulb memories of the event. Conway et al. studied memory for Margaret Thatcher's resignation as prime minister of the United Kingdom in 1990. They compared participants from the United Kingdom, the United States, and Denmark, all of whom had followed news reports of the resignation. It turned out that 11 months later, 60% of the participants from the United Kingdom showed perfect memory for the events surrounding the resignation, whereas only 20% of those who did not live in the United Kingdom showed perfect memory. Conway et al. argued that they obtained this result because the Thatcher resignation was really consequential only for the U.K. participants.

On September 11, 2001, Americans suffered a particularly traumatic event. The terrorist attacks of that day have come to be known simply as "9/11." A number of studies were undertaken to study the effects of these events on memory. Talairco and Rubin (2003) report a study of the memories of students at Duke University for details of the terrorist attacks (flashbulb memories) versus details of ordinary events that happened that day. They were contacted and tested for their memories the morning after the attacks. They were then tested again either 1 week later, 6 weeks later, or 42 weeks later. Figure 6.16 shows the results. The figure shows both recall of details that are consistent with what they said the morning after and recall of details that were inconsistent (presumably false memories). By neither measure is there any evidence that the flashbulb memories were better retained than the everyday memories. Of course, these were students at Duke and not people who were experiencing the terrorist attacks firsthand.

FIGURE 6.16 The mean number of consistent and inconsistent details for the flashbulb and everyday memories (from Talairco & Rubin, 2003).

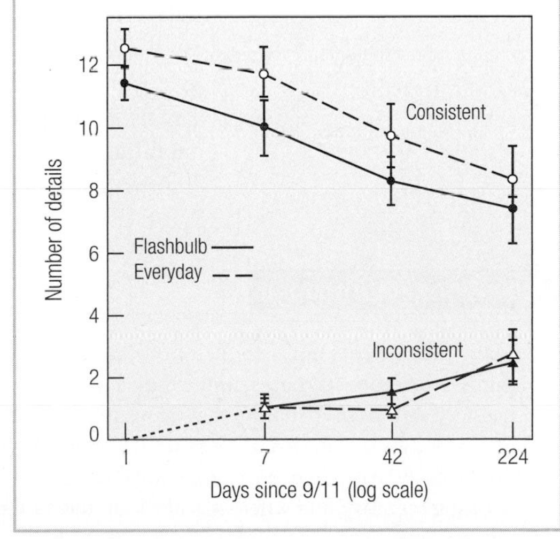

Sharot, Martorella, Delgado, and Phelps (2007) reported a study of people who were in Manhattan, where the Twin Towers were struck. The study was performed three years after the attack and people were asked to recall the events from the attack and events from the summer before. Because the study was 3 years after the event and they could not verify participants' memories for accuracy, but they could study their brain responses while they were recalling the events, Sharot et al. also interviewed the participants to find out where they were in Manhattan when the twin towers were struck. They broke the participants into two groups—a downtown group who were approximately 2 miles away and a midtown group who were approximately 5 miles away. They focused on activity in the amygdala, which is a brain structure known to reflect emotional response. They found greater amygdala activation in the downtown group when they were recalling events from September 11 than in the midtown group. This is significant because there is evidence that amygdala activity enhances retention (Phelps, 2004). In a state of arousal, the amygdala releases hormones that influence the processing in the hippocampus that is critical in forming memories (McGaugh & Roozendaal, 2002).

Behaviorally there is considerable evidence that memories learned in high arousal states are better retained (J. R. Anderson, 2000). This evidence can be interpreted in two alternative ways. The first is that we have some special biological mechanism that reinforces memory for events that are important to us. The second is that people simply rehearse the material that is more important to them more often (as argued by Neisser et al., 1996). Both factors probably play a role in better retention of information learned in a high arousal state. People certainly do tend to rehearse important memories, but evidence about the amygdala involvement in memory suggests that there is an effect of arousal over and above rehearsal.

People report better memories for particularly traumatic events, and there is evidence that memories in high arousal states are better retained.

Conclusions

This chapter has focused on the processes involved in getting information into memory. We saw that a great deal of information gets registered in sensory memory, but relatively little can be maintained in working memory and even less survives for long periods of time. However, an analysis of what actually gets stored in long-term memory really needs to consider how that information is retained and retrieved—which is the topic of the next chapter. For instance, the effects of arousal on memory that we have just reviewed seem to be more about retention than encoding. Likewise, many of the issues considered in this chapter are complicated by retrieval issues. This is certainly true for the effects of elaborative processing that we have just discussed. There are important interactions between how a memory is processed at study and how it is processed at test. Even in this chapter, we were not able to discuss the effects of such factors as practice without discussing the activation-based retrieval processes that are facilitated by these factors. Chapter 7 will also have more to say about the activation of memory traces.

Questions for Thought

1. Many people write notes on their bodies to remember things like phone numbers. In the movie *Memento,* Leonard tattoos information that he wants to remember on his body. Describe instances where storing information on the body works like sensory memory, where it is like working memory, and where it is like long-term memory.
2. The chapter mentions a colleague of mine who was stuck solving the riddle "What goes up a chimney down but can't come down a chimney up?" How would you have seeded the environment to subconsciously prime a solution to the riddle? To see what Kaplan did, read J. R. Anderson (2007, pp. 93–94).

3. Figures 6.11 and 6.12 describe situations in which the experiment arranges for a participant to study memories many times to improve its strength. Can you describe situations in your schooling where this sort of practice happened to improve your memory for facts?

4. Think of the most traumatic events you have experienced. How have you rehearsed and elaborated upon these events? What influence might such rehearsal and elaboration have on these memories? Could it cause you to remember things that did not happen?

Key Terms

activation
ACT (Adaptive Control of Thought)
anterograde amnesia
articulatory loop
associative spreading
auditory sensory store
central executive
depth of processing
echoic memory
elaborative processing
flashbulb memories
iconic memory
long-term potentiation (LTP)
memory span
method of loci
partial-report procedure
phonological loop
power function
power law of learning
SAM (Search of Associative Memory)
short-term memory
spreading activation
strength
visual sensory store
visuospatial sketchpad
whole-report procedure
working memory

7

Human Memory: Retention and Retrieval

Popular fiction frequently has some protagonist who is unable to recall some critical memory—either because of some head injury, repression of some traumatic experience, or just because the passage of time has seemed to erase the memory. The critical turning event in the story occurs when the protagonist is able to recover the memory—perhaps because of hypnosis, clinical treatment, returning to an old context, or (particularly improbable) being hit on the head again. Although our everyday struggles with our memory are seldom so dramatic, we all have had experiences with memories that are just at the edge of availability. For instance, try remembering the name of someone who sat beside you in class in grade school or a teacher of a class. Many of us can picture the person but will experience a real struggle with retrieving that person's name—a struggle at which we may or may not succeed. This chapter will answer the following questions:

- How does memory for information fade with the passage of time?
- How do other memories interfere with the retrieval of a desired memory?
- How can other memories support the retrieval of a desired memory?
- How does a person's internal and external context influence the recall of a memory?
- How can our past experiences influence our behavior without our being able to recall these experiences?

Are Memories Really Forgotten?

Figure 7.1 repeats Figure 6.1, identifying the prefrontal and temporal structures that have proved important in studies of memory. This chapter will focus more on the temporal (and particularly the hippocampal) contributions to memory,

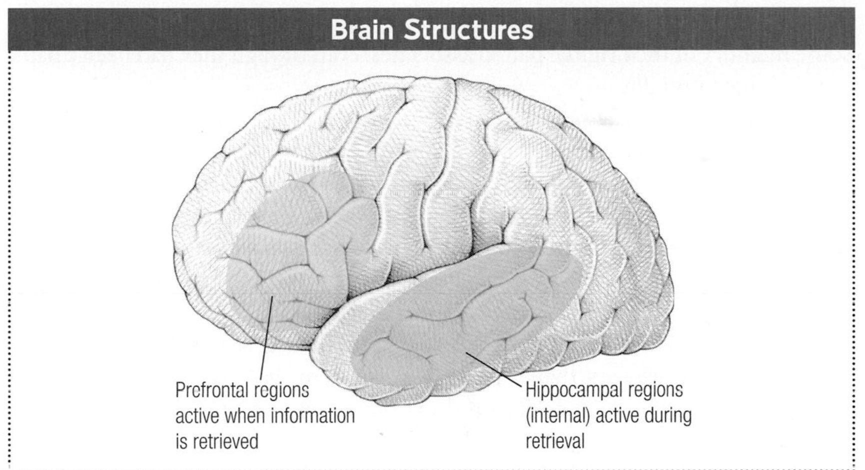

FIGURE 7.1 The brain structures involved in the creation and storage of memories. Prefrontal regions are responsible for the creation of memories. The hippocampus and surrounding structures in the temporal cortex are responsible for the permanent storage of these memories.

which play a major role in retention of memory. One of the earliest studies of the role of the temporal cortex in memory seemed to provide evidence that forgotten memories are still there even though we cannot retrieve them. As part of a neurosurgical procedure, Penfield (1959) electrically stimulated portions of patients' brains and asked them to report what they experienced (patients were conscious during the surgery, but the stimulation technique was painless). In this way, Penfield determined the functions of various portions of the brain. Stimulation of the temporal lobes led to reports of memories that patients were unable to report in normal recall, such as events from childhood. This seemed to provide evidence that much of what seems forgotten is still stored in memory. Unfortunately, it is hard to know whether the patients' memory reports were accurate because there is no way to verify whether the reported events actually occurred. Therefore, although suggestive, the Penfield experiments are generally discounted by memory researchers.

A better experiment, conducted by Nelson (1971), also indicates that forgotten memories still exist. He had participants learn a list of 20 paired associates, each consisting of a number for which the participant had to recall a noun (e.g. 43-dog). The subjects studied the list and were tested on it until they could recall all the items without error. Participants returned for a retest 2 weeks later and were able to recall 75% percent of the associated nouns when cued with the numbers. However, interest focused on the 25% that they could no longer recall—were these items really forgotten? Participants were given new learning trials on the 20 paired associates. The paired associates they had missed were either kept the same or changed. For example, if a participant had learned *43-dog* but failed to recall the response *dog* to *43,* he or she might now be trained on either *43-dog* (unchanged) or *43-house* (changed). Participants were tested after studying the new list once. If the participants had lost all memory for the forgotten pairs, there should have been no difference between recall of changed and unchanged pairs. However, participants correctly recalled 78% of the unchanged items formerly missed, but only 43% of the changed items.

This large advantage for unchanged items indicates that participants had retained some memory of the original paired associates, even though they had been unable to recall them initially.

Sometimes we can recognize things we cannot recall. So, Nelson (1978) also conducted a similar test involving recognition rather than recall. Four weeks after the initial learning phase, participants failed to recognize 31% of the paired associates they had learned. As in the previous experiment, Nelson asked participants to relearn the missed items. For half the stimuli, the responses were changed; for the other half, they were left unchanged. After one relearning trial, participants recognized 34% of the unchanged items but only 19% of the changed items. Thus, even when participants failed this sensitive recognition test, however, it appears that a record of the item was still in memory—the evidence again being that relearning was better for the unchanged pairs than for the changed ones.

These experiments do not prove that everything is remembered. They show only that appropriately sensitive tests can find evidence for remnants of some memories that appear to have been forgotten. In this chapter, we will discuss first how memories become less available with time, then some of the factors that determine our success in retrieving these memories.

- *Even when people appear to have forgotten memories, there is evidence that they still have some of these memories stored.*

The Retention Function

The processes by which memories become less available are extremely regular, and psychologists have studied their mathematical form. Wickelgren did some of the most systematic research on memory retention functions, and his data are still used today. In one recognition experiment (Wickelgren, 1975), he presented participants with a sequence of words to study and then examined the probability of their recognizing the words after delays ranging from 1 min to 14 days. Figure 7.2 shows performance as a function of delay. The performance measure Wickelgren used is called d' (pronounced d-prime), which is derived from the probability of recognition. Wickelgren interpreted it as a measure of memory strength.

Figure 7.2 shows that this measure of memory systematically deteriorates with delay. However, the memory loss is *negatively accelerated*—that is, the rate of change gets smaller and smaller as the delay increases. Figure 7.2b replots the data as the logarithm of the performance measure versus the logarithm of delay. Marvelously, the function becomes linear. The log of performance is a linear function of the log of the delay T; that is,

$$\log d' = A - b \log T$$

where A is the value of the function at 1 min $[\log(1) = 0]$ and b is the slope of the function in Figure 7.2b, which happens to be 0.30 in this case.

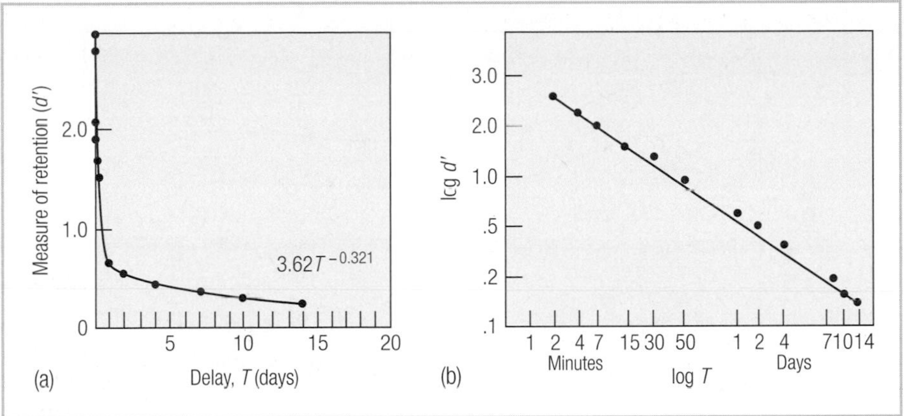

FIGURE 7.2 Results from Wickelgren's experiment to discover a memory retention function. (a) Success at word recognition, as measured by d', as a function of delay T. (b) The data in (a) replotted on a log-log scale. (After Wickelgren, 1975. Adapted by permission of the publisher. © 1975 by *Memory & Cognition*.)

This equation can be transformed to

$$d' = cT^{-b}$$

where $c = 10^A$ and is 3.62 in this case. That is, these performance measures are power functions of delay. In a review of research on forgetting, Wixted and Ebbesen (1991) concluded that retention functions are generally power functions. This relationship is called the **power law of forgetting.** Recall from Chapter 6 that there is also a power law of learning: Practice curves are described by power functions. Both functions are negatively accelerated, but with an important difference. Whereas practice functions show diminishing improvement with practice, retention functions show diminishing loss with delay.

A very dramatic example of the negative acceleration in retention function was produced by Bahrick (1984), who looked at participants' retention of English-Spanish vocabulary items anywhere from immediately to 50 years after they had completed courses in high school and college. Figure 7.3 plots the number of items correctly recalled out of a total of 15 items as a function of the logarithm of the time since course completion. Separate functions are plotted for students who had one, three, or five courses. The data show a slow decay of knowledge combined with a substantial practice effect. In Bahrick's data, the retention functions are nearly flat between 3 and 25 years (as would be predicted by a power function), with some further drop-off from 25 to 49 years (which is more rapid than would be predicted by a power function). Bahrick (personal communication, circa 1993) suspects that this final drop-off is probably related to physiological deterioration in old age.

There is some evidence that the explanation for these decay functions may be found in the associated neural processes. Recall from Chapter 6 that long-term potentiation (LTP) is an increase in neural responsiveness that occurs as a reaction to prior electrical stimulation. We saw that LTP mirrors the power law

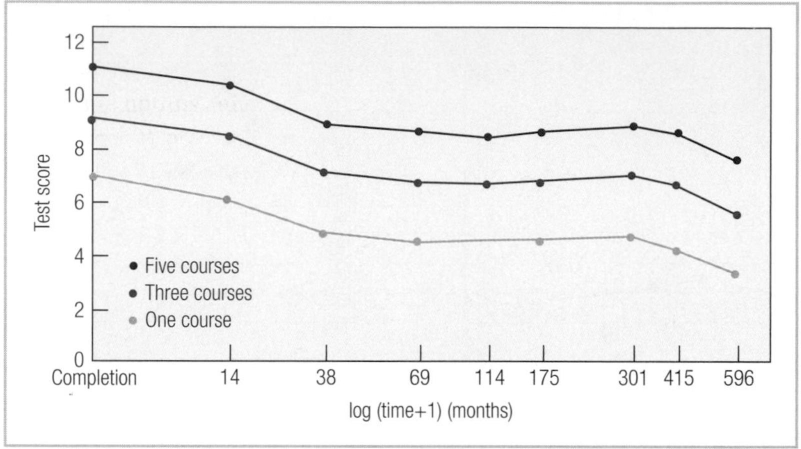

FIGURE 7.3 Results from Bahrick's experiment that measured participants' retention over various time periods of English-Spanish vocabulary items. The number of items correctly recalled out of a total of 15 items is plotted as a function of the logarithm of the time since course completion. (From Bahrick, 1984. Reprinted by permission of the publisher. © 1984 by the American Psychological Association.)

of learning. Figure 7.4 illustrates some data from Raymond & Redman (2006) that shows a decrease in LTP in the rat hippocampus with delay. Plotted there are three conditions—a control condition that received no LTP, a condition that received just a single stimulation to induce LTP, and another condition that received 8 such stimulations. While the level LTP is greater in the condition with 8 stimulations than 1 (a learning effect), both conditions show a drop off with delay. The smooth lines in the figure represent the best-fitting power functions

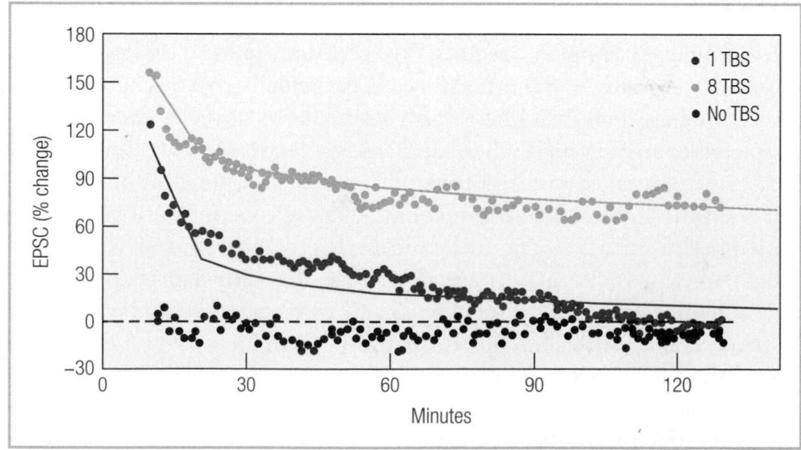

FIGURE 7.4 From Raymond and Redman (2006), 1 or 8 theta-burst stimulations (TBS) are presented at 10 minutes in the experiment. The changes in ESPC (excitatory postsynaptic current—a measure of LTP) are plotted as a function of time. Also, a control condition is presented that received no TBS. The two lines represent best-fitting power functions.

and show that maintenance of LTP has the form of a power function. Thus, the time course of this neural forgetting mirrors the time course of behavioral forgetting, just as the neural learning function mirrors the behavioral learning function. In terms of the strength concept introduced in Chapter 6, the assumption is that the strength of the memory trace decays with time. The data on LTP suggest that this strength decay involves changes in synaptic strength. Thus, there may be a direct relationship between the concept of strength defined at the behavioral level and strength defined at the neural level.

The idea that memory traces simply decay in strength with time is one of the common explanations of forgetting; it is called the **decay theory** of forgetting. We will review one of the major competitors of this theory next: the **interference theory** of forgetting.

- *The strength of a memory trace decays as a power function of the retention interval.*

How Interference Affects Memory

The discussion to this point might lead one to infer that the only factor affecting loss of memories is the passage of time. However, it turns out that retention is strongly impacted by another factor: interfering material. Much of the original research on interference involved the learning of paired associates. The interest focused on how the learning of one list of paired associates would affect the memory for another list. In the typical interference experiment, two critical groups are defined (Table 7.1). The A–D experimental group learns two lists of paired associates, the first list designated A–B and the second designated A–D. These lists are so designated because they share common stimuli (the A terms). For example, among the pairs that the participants study in the A–B list might be *cat-43* and *house-61*, and in the A–D list *cat-82* and *house-37*. The C–D control group also first studies the A–B list but then studies a completely different second list, designated C–D, which does not contain the same stimuli as the first list. For example, in the second C–D list, participants might study *bone-82* and *cup-37*. After learning their respective second lists, both groups are retested for memory of their first list, in both cases the A–B list. Often, this retention test is administered after a considerable delay, such as 24 hours or a week. In general, the A–D group does not do as well as the C–D group with respect either to rate of learning of the second list or to retention of the original A–B list (see Keppel, 1968, for a review). Such experiments provide evidence that learning the A–D list interferes with retention of the A–B list and causes it to be forgotten more rapidly.

More generally, research has shown that it is difficult to maintain multiple associations to the same items. It is harder both to learn new associations to these items and to retain the old ones if new associations are learned. These results might seem to have rather dismal implications for our ability to remember information. They

TABLE 7.1

Experimental and Control Groups Used in a Typical Interference Experiment

A–D Experimental		C–D Control	
Learn	A–B	Learn	A–B
Learn	A–D	Learn	C–D
Test	A–B	Test	A–B

would appear to imply that it would become increasingly difficult to learn new information about a concept. Every time we learned a new fact about a friend, we would be in danger of forgetting an old fact about that person. Fortunately, there are important additional factors that counteract such interference. Before discussing these factors, however, we need to examine in more detail the basis for such interference effects. It turns out that a rather different experimental paradigm has been helpful in identifying the cause of the interference effects.

Learning additional associations to an item can cause old ones to be forgotten.

The Fan Effect: Networks of Facts

Referring back to the activation equation in Chapter 6, the interference effects we have studied can be understood in terms of the amount of activation that spreads to stimulate a memory structure. The basic idea is that when participants are presented with a stimulus such as *cat,* activation will spread from it to all of its associates. There is a limit, however, to the amount of activation that can spread from a source; the more things associated with that source, the less the activation that will spread to any particular memory structure. In one experiment illustrating these ideas (Anderson, 1974a), I asked participants to memorize 26 facts, of the form *A person is in a location.* Some persons were paired with only one location, and some locations with only one person. Other persons were paired with two locations, and other locations with two persons. For instance, suppose that participants studied these sentences:

1. The doctor is in the bank. (1-1)
2. The fireman is in the park. (1-2)
3. The lawyer is in the church. (2-1)
4. The lawyer is in the park. (2-2)

Each statement is followed by two numbers, reflecting the number of facts associated with the person and the location. For instance, sentence 3 is labeled 2-1 because its person occurs in two sentences (sentences 3 and 4) and its location in one (sentence 3). Participants were drilled on this material until they knew it well. Before beginning the reaction-time phase, participants were able to recall all the locations associated with a particular person (e.g., doctor) and all the persons associated with a particular location (e.g., park). Thus, unlike the interference experiments reviewed earlier, all the material was memorized, and interest focused on the speed with which it could be retrieved. After memorizing the material, participants were presented with sentences and had to judge whether they recognized the sentences from the study set. These studied sentences were mixed in with new sentences created by re-pairing people and locations from the study set. The reaction times involving sentences such as those listed above are displayed in Table 7.2, which classifies the data as a function of the number of facts associated with a person and a location. As can be seen, recognition time increases as a function of both the number of facts studied about the person and the number of facts studied about the location. The slowdown in recall is not much more than a hundred milliseconds, but such effects

TABLE 7.2

Results of an Experiment to Demonstrate the Fan Effect

	Mean Recognition Time for Sentences (s) Number of Sentences about a Specific Person	
Number of Sentences Using a Specific Location	1	2
1	1.11	1.17
2	1.17	1.22

From Anderson, 1974a. Reprinted by permission of the publisher. © 1974 by *Cognitive Psychology.*

can add up in situations like taking a time-pressure test. Taking a little more time to answer each question can mean not finishing the test.

These interference effects can be explained by applying the concept of spreading activation to propositional networks (described in Chapter 5). Figure 7.5 shows the network representation for sentences 1 through 4. By applying the activation concept to this representation, we can account for the increase in reaction time. Consider how the participant might recognize a test sentence such as *A lawyer is in the park.* According to the spreading-activation theory, recognizing this proposition involves the following discrete steps:

1. Presentation of the test sentence activates the representation of the terms *lawyer, in,* and *park* in this network. These are the sources of activation.
2. Activation spreads from these sources along the various paths leading from the nodes. A critical assumption is that these sources have a fixed capacity for emitting activation; thus, the more paths there are leading from a source, the less activation will go down any one path.
3. Activation coming down various paths converges at proposition nodes. These activations sum to produce an overall level of activation of the proposition node.
4. The proposition is recognized in an amount of time that is inversely related to its level of activation.

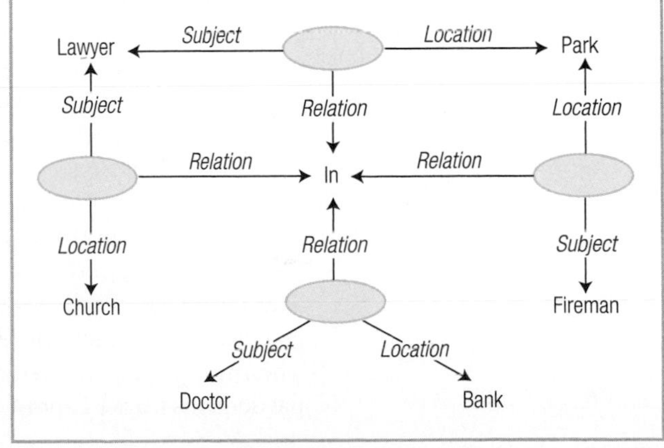

FIGURE 7.5 A network representation of four sentences used in the experiment of Anderson (1974a) demonstrating how spreading activation works. The sentences are *The doctor is in the bank; The fireman is in the park; The lawyer is in the church;* and *The lawyer is in the park.*

So, given a structure like that shown in Figure 7.5, participants should be slower to recognize a fact involving *lawyer* and *park* than one involving *doctor* and *bank* because more paths emanate from the first set of concepts. That is, in the *lawyer* and *park* case, two paths point from each of the concepts to the two propositions in which each was studied, whereas only one path leads from each of the *doctor* and *bank* concepts. The increase in reaction time related to an increase in the number of facts associated with a concept is called the **fan effect.** It is so named because the increase in reaction time is related to an increase in the fan

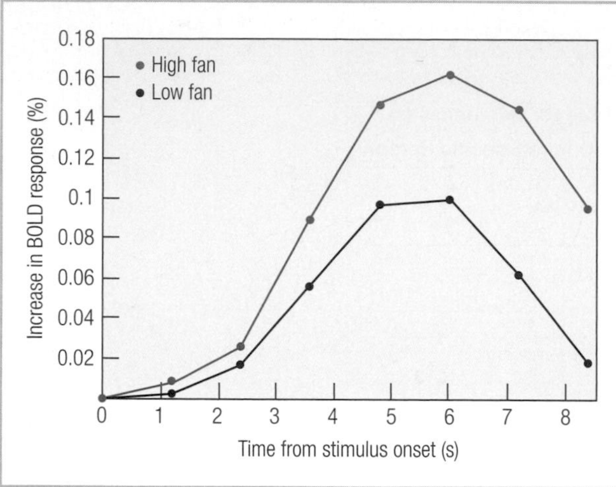

FIGURE 7.6 Differential hemodynamic response in the prefrontal cortex during the retrieval of low-fan and high-fan sentences. The increase in BOLD response is plotted against the time from stimulus onset. (After Sohn et al., 2003. Adapted by permission of the publisher. © 2003 by the National Academy of Sciences.)

of facts emanating from the network representation of the concept.

In an fMRI brain-imaging study, Sohn et al. (2003) looked at the response in the prefrontal cortex during the verification of such facts. They contrasted high-fan sentences (in which the items appeared in many other sentences) with low-fan sentences (in which the items appeared in few sentences). Figure 7.6 compares the hemodynamic response in the two conditions and shows that there is greater response in the high-fan condition. Note that there is a higher hemodynamic response in the condition where there is lower activation of the concepts. One might have expected lower concept activation to map onto weakened hemodynamic response. However, the prefrontal structures must work harder to retrieve the memory in conditions of lower activation. As we will see throughout the later chapters of this text, in which we look at higher mental processes like problem solving, more difficult conditions are associated with higher metabolic expenditures, reflecting the greater mental work required in these conditions.

- *The more facts associated with a concept, the slower is retrieval of any one of the facts.*

The Interfering Effect of Preexisting Memories

Do such interference effects occur with material learned outside of the laboratory? As one way to address this question, Lewis and Anderson (1976) investigated whether the fan effect could be obtained with material the participant knew before the experiment. We had participants learn fantasy facts about public figures; for example, *Napoleon Bonaparte was from India.* Participants studied from zero to four such fantasy facts about each public figure. After learning these "facts," they proceeded to a recognition test phase, in which they saw three types of sentences: (1) statements they had studied in the experiment; (2) true facts about the public figures (such as *Napoleon Bonaparte was an emperor*); and (3) statements about the public figures that were false both in the experimental fantasy world and in the real world. Participants had to respond to the first two types of facts as true and to the last type as false.

Figure 7.7 presents participants' reaction times in making these judgments as a function of the number (or fan) of the fantasy facts studied about the person. Note that reaction time increased with fan for all types of facts. Also note that participants responded much faster to actual facts than to experimental facts. The advantage of actual facts can be explained by the observation that these true facts would be much more strongly encoded in memory than the fantasy facts. The most important result to note in Figure 7.7 is that the more fantasy facts participants learned about an individual such as Napoleon Bonaparte, the longer

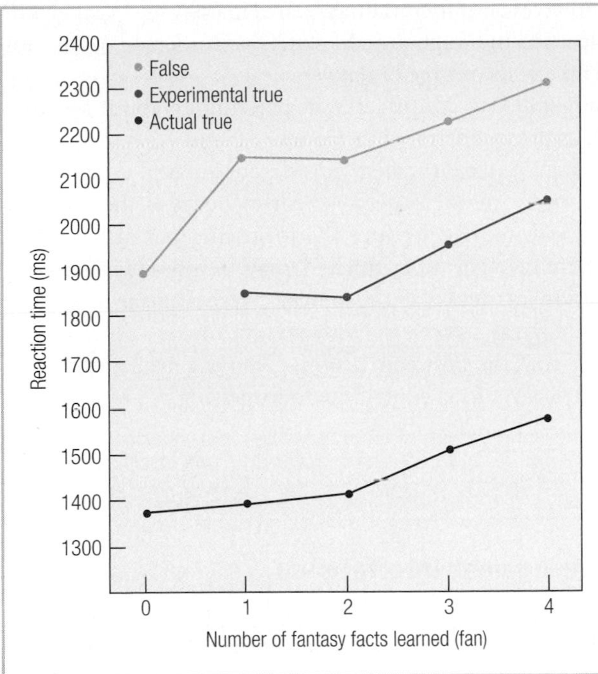

FIGURE 7.7 Results from Lewis and Anderson's study to investigate whether the fan effect could be obtained using material participants knew before the experiment. The task was to recognize true and fantasy facts about a public figure and to reject statements that contained neither true nor fantasy facts. Participants' reaction times in making these judgments are plotted as a function of the number (or fan) of the fantasy facts studied. The time participants took to make all three judgments increased as they learned more fantasy facts. (After Lewis and Anderson, 1976. Adapted by permission of the publisher. © 1976 by *Cognitive Psychology*.)

they took to recognize a fact that they already knew about the individual; for example, *Napoleon Bonaparte was an emperor*. Thus, we can produce interference with preexperimental material. For further research on this topic, see Peterson and Potts (1982).

- *Material learned in the laboratory can interfere with material learned outside of the laboratory.*

The Controversy over Interference and Decay

We have seen two mechanisms that can produce forgetting: decay of trace strength and interference from other memories. There has been some speculation in psychology that what appears to be decay may really reflect interference. That is, the reason memories appear to decay over a retention interval is that they are interfered with by additional memories that the participants have learned. This speculation led to research that studied whether material was better retained over an interval during which participants slept or one during which they were awake. The reasoning was that there would be fewer interfering memories learned during sleep. Ekstrand (1972) reviewed a great deal of research consistent with the conclusion that less is forgotten during the period of sleep. However, it seems that the critical variable is not sleep but rather the time of day during which material is learned. Hockey, Davies, and Gray (1972) found that participants better remembered material that they learned at night, even if they were kept up during the night and slept during the day. It seems that early evening is the period of highest arousal (at least for typical undergraduate participants) and that retention is best for material learned in a high arousal state. See Anderson (2000) for a review of the literature on effects of time of day.

There has been a long-standing controversy in psychology about whether retention functions, such as those illustrated in Figures 7.2 and 7.3, reflect decay in the absence of any interference or reflect interference from unidentified sources. Objections have been raised to decay theories because they do not identify the psychological factors that produce the forgetting but rather assert that forgetting occurs spontaneously with time. It may be possible, however, that there is no explanation of decay at the purely psychological level. The explanation may be physiological, as we saw with respect to the LTP data (see Figure 7.4). Thus, it seems that the best conclusion, given the available data, is that both interference and decay effects contribute to forgetting.

- *Forgetting results both from decay in trace strength and from interference from other memories.*

Redundancy Protects Against Interference

There is a major restriction on the situations in which interference effects are seen: Interference occurs only when one is learning multiple pieces of information that have no intrinsic relationship to one another. In contrast, interference does not occur when the information is somewhat redundant. An experiment by Bradshaw and Anderson (1982) illustrates the contrasting effects of redundant versus irrelevant information. These researchers looked at participants' ability to learn some little-known information about famous people. In the single condition, they had participants study just one fact:

Newton became emotionally unstable and insecure as a child.

In the irrelevant condition, they had participants learn a target fact plus two unrelated facts about the individual:

Locke was unhappy as a student at Westminster.

plus

Locke felt fruits were unwholesome for children.
Locke had a long history of back trouble.

In the relevant condition, participants learned two additional facts that were causally related to the target fact:

Mozart made a long journey from Munich to Paris.

plus

Mozart wanted to leave Munich to avoid a romantic entanglement.
Mozart was intrigued by musical developments coming out of Paris.

Participants were tested for their ability to recall the target facts immediately after studying them and after a week's delay. They were presented with names such as Newton, Mozart, and Locke and asked to recall what they had studied. Table 7.3 displays the results. Comparing the irrelevant condition with the single condition, we see the standard interference effect: Recall was worse when there were more facts to be learned about an item. However, the conclusion is quite different when we compare the relevant condition to the single condition. Here, particularly at a week's delay, recall was better when the participant had to learn additional facts causally related to the target facts.

To understand why the effects of interference are eliminated or even reversed when there is redundancy among the materials to be learned requires that we move on to discussing the retrieval process and, in particular, the role of inferential processes in retrieval.

TABLE 7.3

The Contrasting Effects of Relevant and Irrelevant Information

	Recall (%)	
Condition	Immediate Recall	Recall at 1 Week
Single fact	92	62
Irrelevant facts	80	45
Relevant facts	94	73

From Bradshaw & Anderson, 1982. Reprinted by permission of the publisher. © 1982 by the *Journal of Verbal Learning and Verbal Behavior.*

Learning redundant material does not interfere with a target memory and may even facilitate the target memory.

Retrieval and Inference

Often, when people cannot remember a particular fact, they are able to retrieve related facts and so infer the target fact on the basis of the related facts. For example, in the case of the Mozart facts just discussed, even if the participants could not recall that Mozart made a long journey from Munich to Paris, if they could retrieve the other two facts, they would be able to infer this target fact. There is considerable evidence that people make such inferences at the time of recall. They seem unaware that they are making inferences but rather think that they are recalling what was actually studied.

Bransford, Barclay, and Franks (1972) reported an experiment that demonstrates how inference can lead to incorrect recall. They had participants study one of the following sentences:

1. Three turtles rested beside a floating log, and a fish swam beneath them.
2. Three turtles rested on a floating log, and a fish swam beneath them.

Participants who had studied sentence 1 were later asked whether they had studied this sentence:

3. Three turtles rested beside a floating log, and a fish swam beneath it.

Not many participants thought they had studied this sentence. Participants who had studied sentence 2 were tested with

4. Three turtles rested on a floating log, and a fish swam beneath it.

The participants in this group judged that they had studied sentence 4 much more often than participants in the other group judged that they had studied sentence 3. Of course, sentence 4 is implied by sentence 2, whereas sentence 3 is not implied by sentence 1. Thus, participants thought that they had actually studied what was implied by the studied material.

A study by Sulin and Dooling (1974) illustrates how inference can bias participants' memory for a text. They asked participants to read the following passage:

> **Carol Harris's Need for Professional Help**
>
> Carol Harris was a problem child from birth. She was wild, stubborn, and violent. By the time Carol turned eight, she was still unmanageable. Her parents were very concerned about her mental health. There was no good institution for her problem in her state. Her parents finally decided to take some action. They hired a private teacher for Carol.

A second group of participants read the same passage, except that the name *Helen Keller* was substituted for *Carol Harris.*[1] A week after reading the passage, participants were given a recognition test in which they were presented with a sentence and asked to judge whether it had occurred in the passage they read originally. One of the critical test sentences was *She was deaf, dumb, and blind.* Only 5% of participants who read the Carol Harris passage accepted this sentence, but a full 50% of the participants who read the Helen Keller version thought they had read the sentence. This is just what we would expect. The second group of participants had elaborated the story with facts they knew about Helen Keller. Thus, it seemed reasonable to them at test that this sentence had appeared in the studied material, but in this case their inference was wrong.

We might wonder whether an inference such as *She was deaf, dumb, and blind* was made while the participant was studying the passage or only at the time of the test. This is a subtle issue, and participants certainly do not have reliable intuitions about it. However, a couple of techniques seem to yield evidence that the inferences are being made at test. One method is to determine whether the inferences increase in frequency with delay. With delay, participants' memory for the studied passage should deteriorate, and if they are making inferences at test, they will have to do more reconstruction, which in turn will lead to more inferential errors. Both Dooling and Christiaansen (1977) and Spiro (1977) found evidence for increased inferential intrusions with increased delay of testing.

Dooling and Christiaansen used another technique with the Carol Harris passage to show that inferences were being made at test. They had the participants study the passage and then told them a week later, just before test, that Carol Harris really was Helen Keller. In this situation, participants also made many inferential errors, accepting such sentences as *She was deaf, dumb, and blind.* Because they did not know that Carol Harris was Helen Keller until test, they must have made the inferences at test. Thus, it seems that participants do make such reconstructive inferences at time of test.

○ *In trying to remember material, people will use what they can remember to infer what else they might have studied.*

Plausible Retrieval

In the foregoing analysis, we spoke of participants as making errors when they recalled or recognized facts that were not explicitly presented. In real life,

[1] Helen Keller was well known to participants of the time, famous for overcoming both deafness and blindness as a child.

however, such acts of recall often would not be regarded as errors but as intelligent inferences. Reder (1982) has argued that much of recall in real life involves plausible inference rather than exact recall. For instance, in deciding that Darth Vader was evil in *Star Wars,* a person does not search memory for the specific proposition that Darth Vader was evil, although it may have been directly asserted in the movie. The person infers that Darth Vader was evil from memories about the *Stars Wars* movies.

Reder has demonstrated that people will display very different behavior, depending on whether they are asked to engage in exact retrieval or plausible retrieval. She had participants study passages such as the following:

> The heir to a large hamburger chain was in trouble. He had married a lovely young woman who had seemed to love him. Now he worried that she had been after his money after all. He sensed that she was not attracted to him. Perhaps he consumed too much beer and French fries. No, he couldn't give up the fries. Not only were they delicious, he got them for free.

Then she had participants judge sentences such as

1. The heir married a lovely young woman who had seemed to love him.
2. The heir got his French fries from his family's hamburger chain.
3. The heir was very careful to eat only healthy food.

The first sentence was studied; the second was not studied, but is plausible; and the third was neither studied nor plausible. Participants in the exact condition were asked to make exact recognition judgments, in which case they were to accept the first sentence and reject the second two. Participants in the plausible condition were to judge whether the sentence was plausible given the story, in which case they were to accept the first two and reject the last. Reder tested participants immediately after studying the story, 20 min later, or 2 days later.

Reder was interested in judgment time for participants in the two conditions, exact versus plausible. Figure 7.8 shows the results from her experiment, plotted as the average judgment times for the exact condition and the plausible condition as a function of delay. As might be expected, participants' response times increased with delay in the exact condition. However, the response times actually decreased in the plausible condition. They started out slower in the plausible condition than in the exact condition, but this trend was reversed after 2 days. Reder argues that participants respond more slowly in the exact condition because the exact traces are getting weaker. A plausibility judgment, however, does not depend on any particular trace and so is not similarly vulnerable to forgetting.

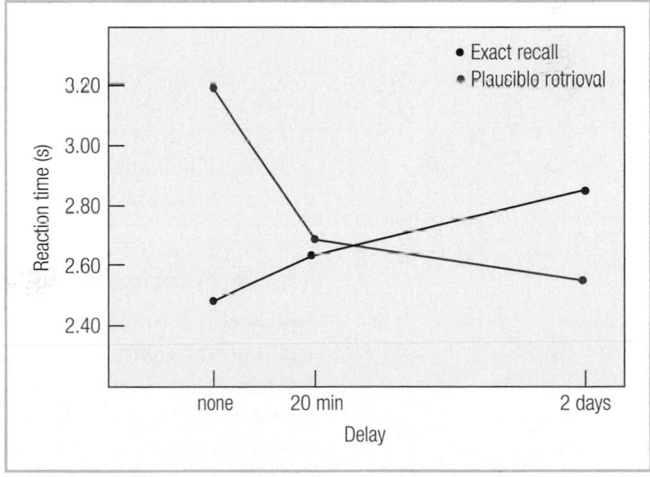

FIGURE 7.8 Results from Reder's experiment showing that people display different behavior depending on whether they are asked to engage in exact retrieval or plausible retrieval of information. The time required to make exact versus plausible recognition judgments of sentences is plotted as a function of delay since study of a story. (From Reder, 1982. Reprinted by permission of the publisher. © 1982 by *Psychological Review.*)

Participants respond faster in the plausible condition with delay because they no longer try to use inefficient exact retrieval. Instead they use plausibility, which is faster.

Reder and Ross (1983) compared exact versus plausible judgments in another study. They had participants study sentences such as

Alan bought a ticket for the 10:00 a.m. train.
Alan heard the conductor call, "All aboard."
Alan read a newspaper on the train.
Alan arrived at Grand Central Station.

They manipulated the number of sentences that participants had to study about a particular person such as Alan. Then they looked at the times participants took to recognize sentences such as

1. Alan heard the conductor call, "All aboard."
2. Alan watched the approaching train from the platform.
3. Alan sorted his clothes into colors and whites.

In the exact condition, participants had to judge whether the sentence had been studied. So, given the foregoing material, participants would accept test sentence 1 and reject test sentences 2 and 3. In the plausible condition, participants had to judge whether it was plausible that Alan was involved in the activity, given what they had studied. Thus, participants would accept sentences 1 and 2 and reject sentence 3.

In the exact condition, Reder and Ross found that participants' response times increased when they had studied more facts about Alan. This is basically a replication of the fan effect discussed earlier in the chapter. In the plausible condition, however, participants' response times decreased when they had learned more facts about Alan. The more facts they knew about Alan, the more ways there were to judge a particular fact to be plausible. Thus, plausibility judgment did not have to depend on retrieval of a particular fact.

People will often judge what plausibly might be true rather than try to retrieve exact facts.

The Interaction of Elaboration and Inferential Reconstruction

In Chapter 6, we discussed how people tend to display better memories if they elaborate the material being studied. We also discussed how semantic elaborations are particularly beneficial. Such semantic elaborations should facilitate the process of inference by providing more material from which to infer. Thus, we expect elaborative processing to lead to both an increased recall of what was studied and an increase in the number of inferences recalled. An experiment by Owens, Bower, and Black (1979) confirms this prediction. Participants studied a story that followed the principal character, a college student, through a day in her life: making a cup of coffee in the morning, visiting a doctor, attending a lecture, shopping for groceries, and attending a party. The following is a passage from the story:

Nancy went to see the doctor. She arrived at the office and checked in with the receptionist. She went to see the nurse, who went through the usual procedures.

> Then Nancy stepped on the scale and the nurse recorded her weight. The doctor entered the room and examined the results. He smiled at Nancy and said, "Well, it seems my expectations have been confirmed." When the examination was finished, Nancy left the office.

Two groups of participants studied the story. The only difference between the groups was that the theme group had read the following additional information at the beginning:

> Nancy woke up feeling sick again and she wondered if she really were pregnant. How would she tell the professor she had been seeing? And the money was another problem.

College students who read this additional passage characterized Nancy as an unmarried student who is afraid she is pregnant as a result of an affair with a college professor. Participants in the neutral condition, who had not read this opening passage, had no reason to suspect that there was anything special about Nancy. We would expect participants in the theme condition to make many more theme-related elaborations of the story than participants in the neutral condition.

Participants were asked to recall the story 24 hours after studying it. Those in the theme condition introduced a great many more inferences that had not actually been studied. For instance, many participants reported that the doctor told Nancy she was pregnant. Intrusions of this variety are expected if participants reconstruct a story on the basis of their elaborations. Table 7.4 reports some of the results from the study. As can be seen, many more inferences were added in recall for the theme condition than for the neutral condition. A second important observation, however, is that participants in the theme condition also recalled more of the propositions they had actually studied. Thus, because of the additional elaborations these participants made, they were able to recall more of the story.

We might question whether participants really benefited from their elaborations, because they also misrecalled many things that did not occur in the story. However, it is wrong to characterize the intruded inferences as errors. Given the theme information, participants were perfectly right to make inferences and to recall them. In a nonexperimental setting, such as recalling information for an exam, we would expect these participants to recall such inferences as easily as material they had actually read.

TABLE 7.4

The Interactive Effects of Elaboration and Inference

	Number of Propositions Recalled	
	Theme Condition	Neutral Condition
Studied propositions	29.2	20.3
Inferred propositions	15.2	3.7

After Owens et al. (1979). Adapted by permission of the publisher. © 1979 by *Memory & Cognition.*

Implications

How have advertisers used knowledge of cognitive psychology?

Advertisers often capitalize on our tendency to embellish what we hear with plausible inferences. Consider the following portion of an old Listerine commercial:

> "Wouldn't it be great," asks the mother, "if you could make him cold proof? Well, you can't. Nothing can do that." [Boy sneezes.] "But there is something that you can do that may help. Have him gargle with Listerine Antiseptic. Listerine can't promise to keep him cold free, but it may help him fight off colds. During the cold-catching season, have him gargle twice a day with full-strength Listerine. Watch his diet, see he gets plenty of sleep, and there's a good chance he'll have fewer colds, milder colds this year."

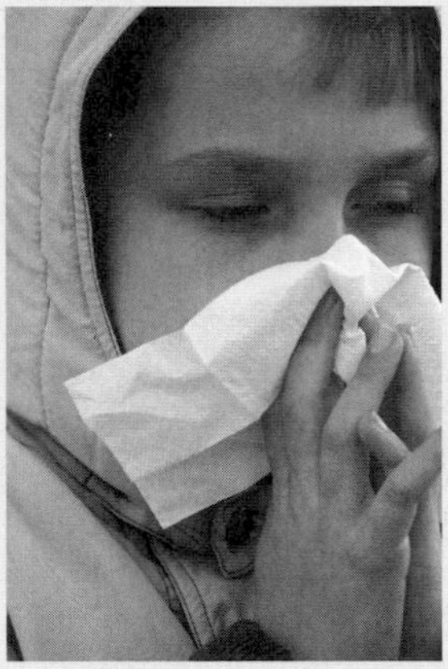

A verbatim text of this commercial, with the product name changed to "Gargoil," was used in an experiment conducted by Harris (1977). After hearing this commercial, all 15 of his participants recalled that "gargling with Gargoil Antiseptic helps prevent colds," although this assertion was clearly not made in the commercial. The Federal Trade Commission explicitly forbids advertisers from making false claims, but does the Listerine ad make a false claim? In a landmark case, the courts ruled against Warner-Lambert, makers of Listerine, for implying false claims in this commercial. As a corrective action the court ordered Warner-Lambert to include in future advertisements the disclaimer "contrary to prior advertising, Listerine will not help prevent colds or sore throats or lessen their severity." They were required to continue this disclaimer until they had expended an amount of money equivalent to their prior 10 years of advertisement.

- *When participants elaborate on material while studying it, they tend to recall more of what they studied and also tend to recall the inferences that they did not study but made themselves.*

Eyewitness Testimony and the False-Memory Controversy

The ability to elaborate on and make inferences from information, both while it is being studied and when our recall is being tested, is essential to using our memory successfully in everyday life. Inferences made while studying material allow us to extrapolate from what we actually heard and saw to what is probably true. When we hear that someone found out in a doctor's visit that she was pregnant, it is a reasonable inference that she was told so by the doctor. So such inferences usually lead to a much more coherent and accurate understanding of the world. There are circumstances, however, in which we need to be able to separate what we actually saw and heard from our inferences. The difficulty of doing so can lead to harmful false memories; the Gargoil example above is only the tip of the iceberg.

One situation in which it is critical to separate inference from actual experience is in eyewitness testimony. It has been shown that eyewitnesses are often inaccurate in the testimony they give, even though jurors accord it high weight. One reason for the low accuracy is that people confuse what they actually observed about an incident with what they heard from other sources. Loftus

(1975, 1996; Loftus, Miller, & Burns, 1978) showed that subsequent information can change a person's memory of an observed event. In one study, for instance, Loftus asked participants who had witnessed a traffic accident about the car's speed when it passed a Yield sign. Although there was no Yield sign, many participants subsequently remembered having seen one, confusing the question they were asked with what they had actually seen. Another interesting example involves the testimony given by John Dean about events in the Nixon White House during the Watergate cover-up (Neisser, 1981). After Dean testified about conversations in the Oval Office, it was discovered that Nixon had recorded these conversations. Although Dean was substantially accurate in gist, he confused many details, including the order in which these conversations took place.

Another case of memory confusion that has produced a great deal of recent notoriety concerns the controversy about the so-called **false-memory syndrome.** This controversy involves cases where individuals claim to recover memories of childhood sexual abuse that they had suppressed (Schacter, 2001). Many of these recovered memories occur in the process of therapy, and some memory researchers have questioned whether these recovered memories ever happened and hypothesized that they might have been created by the strong suggestions of the therapists. For instance, one therapist said to patients, "You know, in my experience, a lot of people who are struggling with many of the same problems you are, have often had some kind of really painful things happen to them as kids—maybe they were beaten or molested. And I wonder if anything like that ever happened to you?" (Forward & Buck, 1988, p. 161). Given the evidence we have reviewed about how people will put information together to make inferences about what they should remember, one could wonder if the patients who heard this might remember what did not happen.

A number of researchers have shown that it is possible to create false memories by use of suggestive interview techniques. For instance, Loftus and Pickerall (1995) had adult participants read four stories from their childhood written by an older relative—three were true, but one was a false story about being lost in the mall at age 5. After reading the story, about 25% of participants claimed to remember the event of being lost in a mall. Ceci, Loftus, Leichtman, and Bruck (1995) were similarly able to create false memories in 3- to 6-year-old children. The process by which we distinguish between memory and imagination is quite fragile, and it is easy to become confused about the source of information. Of course, it would not be ethical to try to plant false memories about something so traumatic as sexual abuse, and there are questions (e.g., Pope, 1996) about whether it is possible to create false memories as awful as those involving childhood sexual abuse.

There is an intense debate about how much credibility should be given to recovered memories of childhood abuse. Although there is a temptation to want to come to either the simple conclusion that all reports of recovered memories of abuse should be believed or the conclusion that all should be discounted, it does not appear to be so simple. There are cases of recovered memories of abuse that seem to have strong documentation (Sivers, Schooler, and Freyd, 2002) and there are cases where the alleged victims of such abuse have subsequently retracted and said they were misled in their memories (Schacter, 2001).

- *Serious errors of memory can occur because people fail to separate what they actually experienced from what they inferred, imagined, or were told.*

False Memories and the Brain

Recently, researchers have developed the ability to explore the neural basis of false memories. They have used a less exotic example than getting people to believe they had been lost in the mall. In a **Deese-Roediger-McDermott paradigm** originally invented by Deese (1959) and elaborated by Roediger and McDermott (1995), participants study lists of words. One list might contain *thread, pin, eye, sewing, sharp, point, prick, thimble, haystack, thorn, hurt, injection, syringe, cloth, knitting;* a second list might contain *bed, rest, awake, tired, dream, wake, snooze, blanket, doze, slumber, snore, nap, peace, yawn, drowsy.* In a later test, participants are shown a series of words and must decide whether they have studied those words. There are three types of words:

True (e.g., *sewing, awake*)

False (e.g., *needle, sleep*)

New (e.g., *door, candy*)

The true items were in the lists; the false ones are strongly associated with items in the list but were not on the list; and the new ones are unrelated to items on the list. Participants accept most of the true items and reject most of the new ones, but they have difficulty in rejecting the false items. In one study, Cabeza, Rao, Wagner, Mayer, and Schacter (2001) found that 88% of the true items and only 12% of the new items were accepted, but 80% of the false items were also accepted—almost as many as the true items.

Cabeza et al. examined the activation patterns that these different types of words produced in the cortex. Figure 7.9 illustrates such activation profiles in the two hippocampal structures. In the hippocampus proper, true words and false words produced almost identical fMRI responses, which were stronger than the responses produced by the new words. Thus, these hemodynamic responses appear to match up pretty well with the behavioral data where participants cannot discriminate between true items and false items. However, in the parahippocampal gyrus, an area just adjacent to the hippocampus, both false and new items produced identical weak responses, whereas the true items produced a larger hemodynamic response. The parahippocampus is more closely connected to sensory regions of the brain, and Cabeza et al. suggested that it retains the original sensory experience of seeing the word, whereas the hippocampus maintains a more abstract representation and this is why true items produce a larger hemodynamic response. Schacter (e.g., Dodson & Schacter, 2002a, 2000b) has suggested that people can be trained to pay more attention to these distinctive sensory features and so improve their resistance to false memories. As one application, distinctiveness training can be used to help

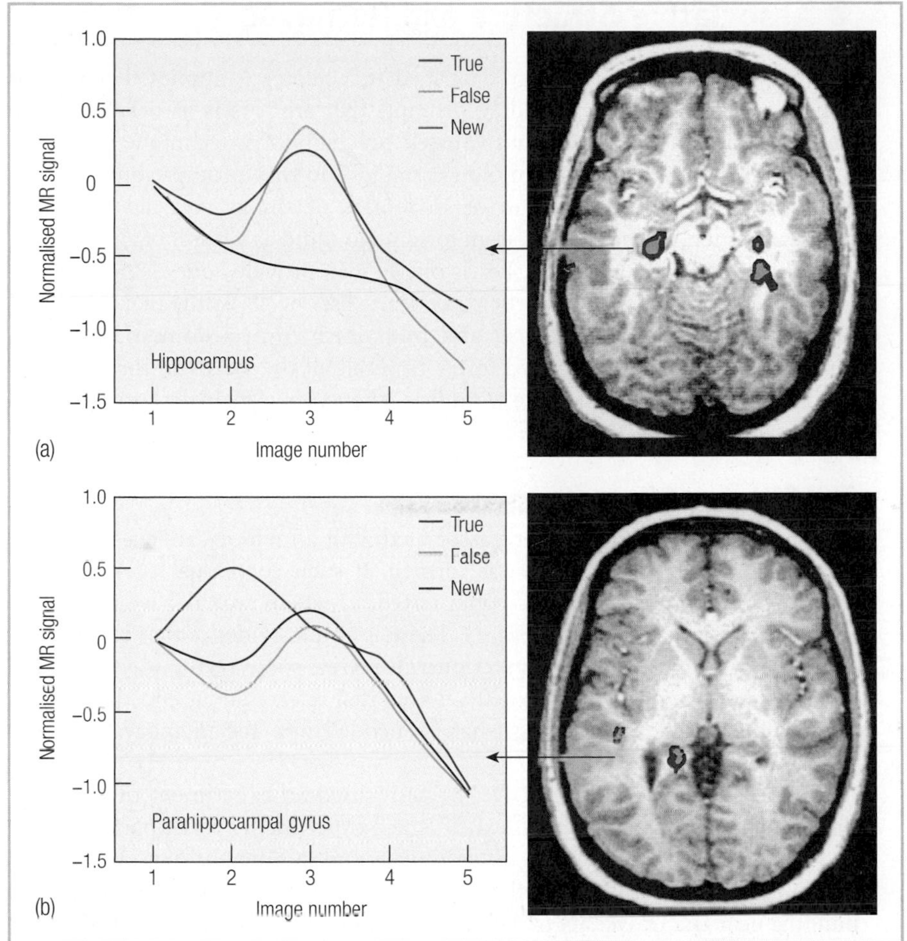

FIGURE 7.9 Results from the fMRI study by Cabeza et al. of activation patterns produced by participants' judgments of true, false, and new items on a previously learned word list. (a) Bilateral hippocampal regions were more activated for true and false items than for new items, with no difference between the activations for true and false items. (b) A left posterior parahippocampal region (the parahippocampal gyrus) was more activated for true items than for false and new items, with no difference between the activations for false and new items. (After Cabeza et al., 2001. Adapted by permission of the publisher. © 2001 by the National Academy of Sciences.)

elderly patients who have particular difficulty with false memories. For instance, older adults sometimes find it hard to remember whether they have seen something or just imagined it (Henkel, Johnson, & DeLeonardis, 1998).

- *The hippocampus responds to false memories with as high activation as it responds to true memories and so fails to discriminate between what was experienced and what was imagined.*

Associative Structure and Retrieval

The spreading activation theory described in Chapter 6 implies that we can improve our memory by providing prompts that are closely associated with a particular memory. You may find yourself practicing this technique when you try to remember the name of an old classmate. You may prompt your memory with names of other classmates or memories of things you did with that classmate. Often, the name does seem to come to mind as a result of such efforts. An experiment by Tulving and Pearlstone (1966) provides one demonstration of this technique. They had participants learn lists of 48 words that contained categories such as *dog, cat, horse,* and *cow,* which form a domestic mammal category. Participants were asked to try to recall all the words in the list. They displayed better memory for the word lists when they were given prompts such as *mammal,* which served to cue memory for members of the categories.

The Effects of Encoding Context

Among the cues that can become associated with a memory are cues from the context in which the memory was formed. If such contextual cues could be revived when the memory was being tested, a person would have additional ways to reactivate the target memory. There is ample evidence that context can greatly influence memory. This section will review some of the ways in which this influence can occur. Context effects are often referred to as encoding effects because the context is affecting what is encoded into the memory trace that records the event.

Smith, Glenberg, and Bjork (1978) performed an experiment that showed the importance of physical context. In their experiment, participants learned two lists of paired associates on different days and in different physical settings. On day 1, participants learned the paired associates in a windowless room in a building near the University of Michigan campus. The experimenter was neatly groomed, dressed in a coat and a tie, and the paired associates were shown on slides. On day 2, participants learned the paired associates in a tiny room with windows on the main campus. The experimenter was dressed sloppily in a flannel shirt and jeans (it was the same experimenter, but some participants did not recognize him) and presented the paired associates via a tape recorder. A day later, participants were tested for their recall of half the paired associates in one setting and half in the other setting. They could recall 59% of the list learned in the same setting as they were tested, but only 46% of the list learned in the other setting. Thus, it seems that recall is better if the context during test is the same as the context during study.

Perhaps the most dramatic manipulation of context was performed by Godden and Baddeley (1975). They had divers learn a list of 40 unrelated words either on the shore or 20 feet under the sea. The divers were then asked to recall the list either in the same environment or in the other environment. Figure 7.10 displays the results of this study. Participants clearly showed superior memory when they were asked to recall the list in the same environment in which they studied it. So, it seems that contextual elements do get associated with memories and that memory is improved when participants are provided with these contextual elements when being tested. This result actually has serious implications for diver instruction, because most of the instructions are given on dry land but must be recalled under water.

The degree to which such contextual effects are obtained has proved to be quite variable from experiment to experiment (Roediger & Guynn, 1996). Fernandez and Glenberg (1985) reported a number of failures to find any context dependence; and Saufley, Otaka, and Bavaresco (1985) reported a failure to find such effects in a classroom situation. Eich (1985) argued that the magnitude of such contextual effects depends on the degree to which the participant integrates the context with the memories. In his experiment, he read lists to two groups of participants. In one condition, participants were instructed to imagine the referents of the nouns alone (e.g., imagine a *kite* in the sky); in the other, they were asked to imagine the referents integrated with the context (e.g., imagine a *kite* on the table in the corner of the room). Eich found a much larger effect of a change of context when participants were instructed to imagine the referent integrated with the context.

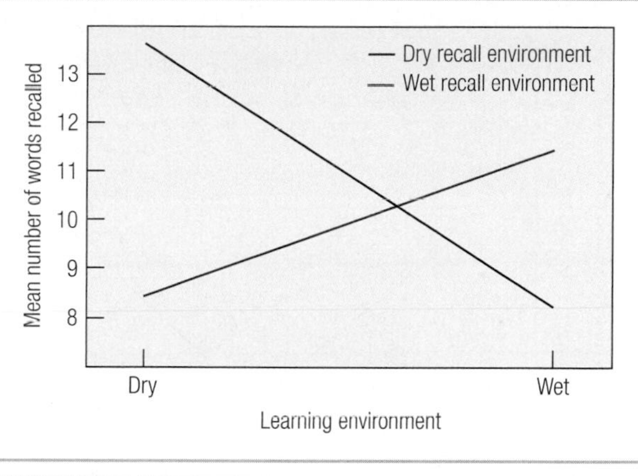

FIGURE 7.10 Results of a study by Godden and Baddeley to investigate the effects of context on participants' recall of words. The mean number of words recalled is plotted as a function of the environment in which learning took place. Participants recalled word lists better in the same environment in which they were learned. (After Godden & Baddeley, 1975. Adapted by permission of the publisher. © 1975 by the *British Journal of Psychology*.)

Bower, Monteiro, and Gilligan (1978) showed that emotional context can have the same effect as physical context. They instructed participants to learn two lists. For one list, they hypnotically induced a positive state by having participants review a pleasant episode in their lives; for the other, they hypnotically induced a negative state by having participants review a traumatic event. A later recall test was given under either a positive or a negative emotional state (again hypnotically induced). Better memory was obtained when the emotional state at test matched the emotional state at study.[2]

Not all research shows such mood-dependent effects. For instance, Bower and Mayer (1985) failed to replicate the Bower et al. (1978) result. Eich and Metcalfe (1989) found that mood-dependent effects tend to be obtained only when participants integrate their memories at study with the mood information. Thus, like the effects of physical context, mood-dependent effects occur only in special study situations.

Perhaps a more robust effect is **mood congruence,** the fact that it is easier to remember happy memories when one is in a happy state and sad memories when

[2] As an aside, it is worth commenting that, despite popular reports, the best evidence is that hypnosis per se does nothing to improve memory (see Hilgard, 1968; M. Smith, 1982; Lynn, Lock, Myers, & Payne, 1997), although it can help memory to the extent that it can be used to re-create the contextual factors at the time of test. However, much of a learning context can also be re-created by nonhypnotic means, such as through free association about the circumstances of the event to be remembered (e.g., Geiselman, Fisher, Mackinnon, & Holland, 1985).

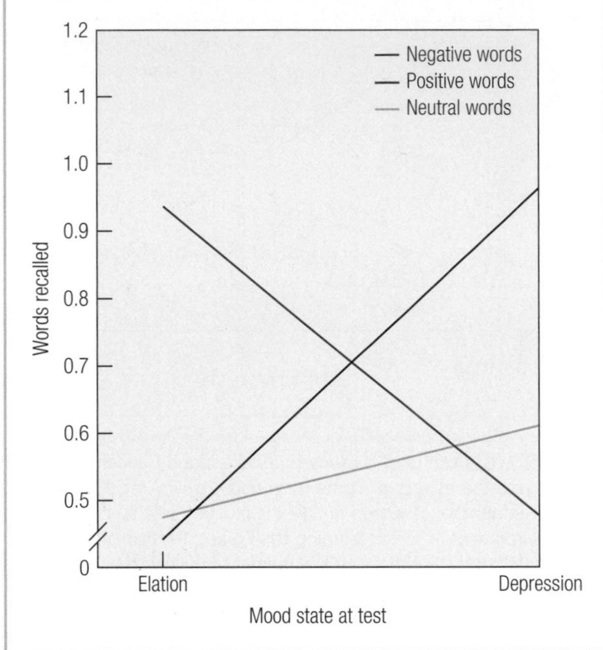

FIGURE 7.11 Results from Teasdale and Russell's study of mood congruence. The number of words recalled from a previously studied list is plotted against the mood state at test. Participants recalled more of the words that matched their mood at test. (From Teasdale & Russell, 1983. Reprinted by permission of the publisher. © 1983 by the British Psychological Society.)

one is in a sad state. Mood congruence is an effect of the content of the memories rather than the emotional state of the participant during study. For instance, Teasdale and Russell (1983) had participants learn a list of positive, negative, and neutral words in a normal state. Then, at test, they induced either positive or negative states. Their results, illustrated in Figure 7.11, show that participants recalled more of the words that matched their mood at test. When a particular mood is created at test, elements of that mood will prime memories that share these elements. Thus, mood elements can prime both memories whose content matches the mood, as in the Teasdale and Russell experiment, and memories that have such mood elements integrated as part of the study procedure (as in Eich & Metcalfe, 1989).

A related phenomenon is **state-dependent learning.** People find it easier to recall information if they can return to the same emotional and physical state they were in when they learned the information. For instance, it is often casually claimed that when heavy drinkers are sober, they are unable to remember where they hid their alcohol when drunk, and when drunk they are unable to remember where they hid their money when sober. In fact, some experimental evidence does exist for this state dependency of memory with respect to alcohol, but the more important factor seems to be that alcohol has a general debilitating effect on the acquisition of information (Parker, Birnbaum, & Noble, 1976). Marijuana has been shown to have similar state-dependent effects. In one experiment (Eich, Weingartner, Stillman, & Gillin, 1975), participants learned a free-recall list after smoking either a marijuana cigarette or an ordinary cigarette. Participants were tested 4 hours later—again after smoking either a marijuana cigarette or a regular cigarette. Table 7.5 shows the results from this study. Two effects were seen, both of which are typical of research on the effects of psychoactive drugs on memory. First, there is a state-dependent effect reflected by better recall

TABLE 7.5

State-Dependent Learning: The Effects of Drugged State at Study and at Test

	At Test (% correct)		
At Study	Ordinary Cigarette	Marijuana Cigarette	Average
Ordinary cigarette	25	20	23
Marijuana cigarette	12	23	18

From Eich et al. (1975). Reprinted by permission of the publisher. © 1975 by the *Journal of Verbal Learning and Verbal Behavior.*

when the state at test matched the state at study. Second, there is an overall higher level of recall when the material was studied in a nonintoxicated state.

- *People show better memory if their external context and their internal states are the same at the time of study and the time of the test.*

The Encoding-Specificity Principle

Memory for material to be learned can also depend heavily on the context of other material to be learned in which it is embedded. Consider a recognition-memory experiment by D. M. Thompson (1972). Thompson's participants studied pairs of words such as *sky blue.* Participants were told that they were responsible only for the second item of the pair—in this case *blue;* the first word represented context. Later, they were tested by being presented with either *blue* or *sky blue.* In both cases, they were asked whether they had originally seen *blue.* In the single-word case, they recognized *blue* 76% of the time, whereas in the pair condition their recognition rate was 85%. Thus, even though they were tested only for *blue,* their memories were better in the context of the other word.

A series of experiments (e.g., Tulving & Thompson, 1973; Watkins & Tulving, 1975) has dramatically illustrated how memory for a word can depend on how well the test context matches the original study context. There were three phases to the experiment:

1. Original study: Watkins and Tulving had participants learn pairs of words such as *train-black* and told them that they were responsible only for the second word, referred to as the to-be-remembered word.
2. Generate and recognize: Participants were given words such as *white* and asked to generate four free associates to the word. So, a participant might generate *snow, black, wool,* and *pure.* The stimuli for the task were chosen to have a high probability of eliciting the to-be-remembered word. For instance, *white* has a high probability of eliciting *black.* Participants were then told to indicate which of the four associates they generated was the to-be-remembered word they had studied in the first phase. In cases where the to-be-remembered word was generated, participants correctly chose it only 54% of the time. Because participants were always forced to indicate a choice, some of these correct choices must have been lucky guesses. Thus, true recognition was even lower than 54%.
3. Cued recall: Participants were presented with the original context words (e.g., *train*) and asked to recall the to-be-remembered words (i.e., *black*). Participants recalled 61% of the words—higher than their recognition rate without any correction for guessing. Moreover, Watkins and Tulving found that 42% of the words recalled had not been recognized earlier when the participants gave them as free associates.[3]

Recognition is usually superior to recall. Thus, we would expect that if participants could not recognize a word, they would be unable to recall it. Usually,

[3] A great deal of research has been done on this phenomenon. For a review, read Nilsson and Gardiner (1993).

we expect to do better on a multiple-choice test than on a recall-the-answer test. Experiments such as the one just described provided very dramatic reversals of such standard expectations. The results can be understood in terms of the similarity of the test context to the study context. The test context with the word *white* and its associates was quite different from the context in which *black* had originally been studied. In the cued-recall test context, by contrast, participants were given the original context (*train*) with which they had studied the word. Thus, if the contextual factors are sufficiently weighted in favor of recall, as they were in these experiments, recall can be superior to recognition. Tulving interprets these results as illustrating what he calls the **encoding-specificity principle:** The probability of recalling an item at test depends on the similarity of its encoding at test to its original encoding at study.

- *People show better word memory if the words are tested in the context of the same words with which they were studied.*

The Hippocampal Formation and Amnesia

In Chapter 6, we discussed the fictional character Leonard, who suffered amnesia resulting from hippocampal damage. A large amount of evidence points to the great importance of the hippocampal formation, a structure embedded within the temporal cortex, for the establishment of permanent memories. In animal studies (typically rats or primates; for a review, see Eichenbaum & Bunsey, 1995; Squire, 1992), it has been shown that lesions in the hippocampal formation produce severe impairments in the ability to learn new associations, particularly those that require remembering combinations or configurations of elements. Damage to the hippocampal area also produces severe **amnesia** (memory loss) in humans. One of the most studied amnesic patients is known as HM.[4] In 1953 when he was 27 years old, large parts of his temporal lobes were surgically removed to cure epilepsy. He had one of the most profound amnesias ever recorded and was studied for decades. He had normal memories of his life up to the age of 16 but forgot most of 11 years before the surgery. Moreover, he was almost totally unable to remember new events. He appeared in many ways as a normal person with a clear self-identity, but his identity was largely as the person he was when he was 16 where his memories stopped (although he realized he is older and had learned some general facts about the world). His surgical operation involved complete removal of the hippocampus and surrounding structures, and this is considered the reason for his profound memory deficits (Squire, 1992).

Only rarely is there a reason for surgically removing the hippocampal formation from humans. However, for various reasons, humans can suffer severe damage to this structure and the surrounding temporal lobe. One common

[4] Henry Gustav Molaison recently died at the age of 82. His obituary is available at http://www.nytimes.com/2008/12/05/us/05hm.html.

cause is a severe blow to the head, but other frequent causes include brain infections (such as encephalitis) and chronic alcoholism, which can result in a condition called **Korsakoff syndrome.** Such damage can result in two types of amnesia: **retrograde amnesia,** which refers to the loss of memory for events that occurred before the injury, and **anterograde amnesia,** which refers to an inability to learn new things.

In the case of a blow to the head, the amnesia often is not permanent but displays a particular pattern of recovery. Figure 7.12 displays the pattern of recovery for a patient who was in a coma for 7 weeks following a closed head injury. Tested 5 months after the injury, the patient showed total anterograde amnesia—he could not remember what had happened since the injury. He also displayed total retrograde amnesia for the 2 years preceding the injury and substantial disturbance of memory beyond that. When tested 8 months after

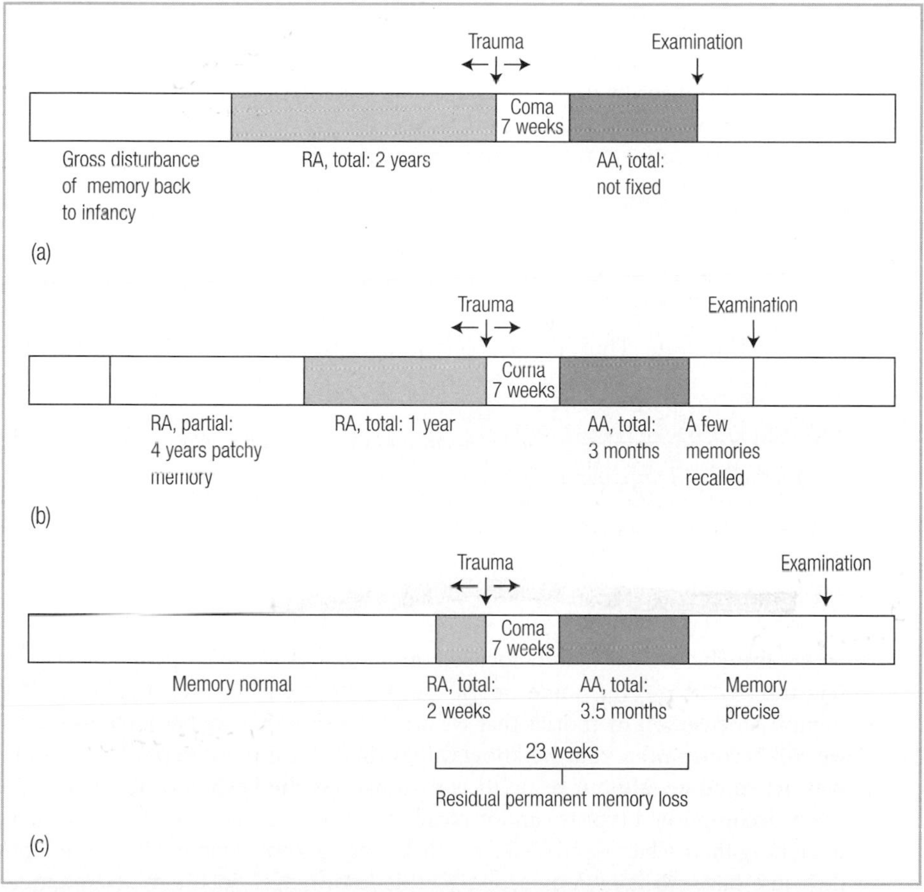

FIGURE 7.12 The pattern of a patient's recovery from amnesia caused by a closed head injury: (a) after 5 months; (b) after 8 months; (c) after 16 months. RA = retrograde amnesia; AA = anterograde amnesia. (From Barbizet, 1970. Reprinted by permission of the publisher. © 1970 by W. H. Freeman.)

the injury, the patient showed some ability to remember new experiences, and the period of total retrograde amnesia had shrunk to 1 year. When tested 16 months after injury, the patient had full ability to remember new events and had only a permanent 2-week period before the injury about which he could remember nothing. It is characteristic that retrograde amnesia is for events close in time to the injury and that events just before the injury are never recovered. In general, anterograde and retrograde amnesia show this pattern of occurring and recovering together, although in different patients either the retrograde or the anterograde symptoms can be more severe.

A number of striking features characterize cases of amnesia. The first is that anterograde amnesia can occur along with some preservation of long-term memories. This was particularly the case for HM, who remembered many things from his youth but was unable to learn new things. The existence of such cases indicates that the neural structures involved in forming new memories are distinct from those involved in maintaining old ones. It is thought that the hippocampal formation is particularly important in creating new memories and that old memories are maintained in the cerebral cortex. It is also thought that events just prior to the injury are particularly susceptible to retrograde amnesia because they still require the hippocampus for support. A second striking feature of these amnesia cases is that the memory deficit is not complete and there are certain kinds of memories the patient can still acquire. This feature will be discussed in the next section on implicit and explicit memory. A third striking feature of amnesia is that patients can remember things for short periods but then forget them. Thus, HM would be introduced to someone and told the person's name, would use that name for a short time, and would then forget it after a half minute. Thus, the problem in anterograde amnesia is retaining the memories for more than 5 or 10 seconds.

- *Patients with damage to the hippocampal formation show both retrograde amnesia and anterograde amnesia.*

Implicit versus Explicit Memory

So far, this chapter has mainly focused on memories to which people have conscious access. However, some of the most interesting research in the field of memory focuses on memories that we are not aware that we have. Occasionally, we will become aware that we know things that we cannot describe. One example that some people can relate to is memory for the keyboard of a keyboard. Many accomplished typists cannot recall the arrangement of the keys except by imagining themselves typing. Clearly, their fingers know where the keys are, but they just have no conscious access to this knowledge. Such implicit memory demonstrations highlight the significance of retrieval conditions in assessing memory. If we asked the typists to tell us where the keys are, we would conclude they had no knowledge of the keyboard. If we tested their typing, we would conclude that they have perfect knowledge. This section discusses such contrasts, or **dissociations,** between explicit and implicit memory. In the keyboard example above, explicit memory shows no knowledge, while implicit memory shows total knowledge. **Explicit memory** is the term used to describe knowledge that we can consciously recall. **Implicit memory** is the term used to describe knowledge that we cannot consciously recall but that nonetheless manifests itself in our improved performance on some task.

Cases of total dissociation of implicit and explicit knowledge, such as the typing example, are rare with normal individuals. Such cases are more common in patients who suffer from certain amnesias. Amnesic patients display implicit memories of many experiences that they cannot consciously recall. For instance, Graf, Squire, and Mandler (1984) compared amnesic versus normal participants with respect to their memories for a list of words such as *banana.* After studying these words, participants were asked to recall them. The results are shown in Figure 7.13. Amnesic participants did much worse than normal participants. Then participants were given a word-completion task. They were shown the first three letters of a word they had studied and were asked to make an English word out of it. For instance, they might be asked to complete *ban*______. There is less than a 10% probability that participants can generate the word (*banana*) they studied by chance alone, but the results show that participants in both groups were coming up with the studied word more than 50% of the time. Moreover, there was no difference between the amnesic and normal participants in the word-completion task. So, the amnesic participants clearly did have memory for the word list, although they could not gain conscious access to that memory in a free-recall task. Rather, they displayed implicit memory in the word-completion task. The patient HM had also been shown to be capable of implicit learning. For example, he was able to improve on various perceptual-motor tasks from one day to the next, although each day he had no memory of the task from the previous day (Milner, 1962).

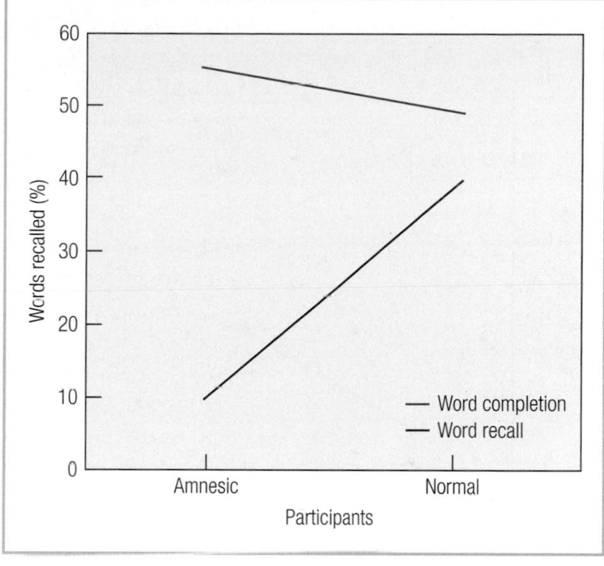

FIGURE 7.13 Results from an experiment by Graf, Squire, and Mandler comparing the ability of amnesic patients and normal participants to recall words studied versus the ability to complete fragments of words studied. Amnesic participants did much worse than normal participants on the word-recall task, but there was no difference between the amnesic and normal participants in the word-completion task. (From Graf, Squire, & Mandler, 1984. Reprinted by permission of the publisher. © 1984 by the *Journal of Experimental Psychology: Learning, Memory, and Cognition.*)

Amnesic patients often cannot consciously recall a particular event but will show in implicit ways that they have some memory for the event.

Implicit versus Explicit Memory in Normal Participants

A great deal of research (for reviews, read Schacter, 1987; Richardson-Klavehn & Bjork, 1988) has looked at dissociations between implicit and explicit memory in normal individuals. It is often not possible with this population to obtain the dramatic dissociations we see in amnesic individuals, who show no conscious memory but normal implicit memory. It has been possible, however, to demonstrate that certain variables have different effects on tests of explicit memory than

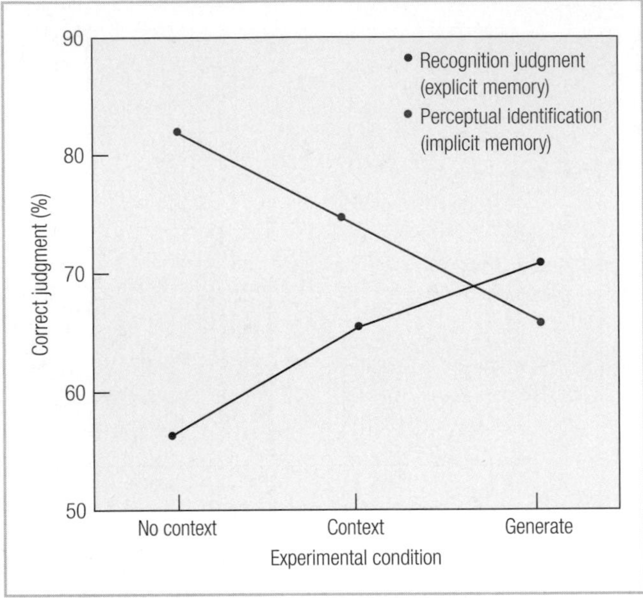

FIGURE 7.14 Results from Jacoby's experiment demonstrating that certain variables have different effects on tests of explicit memory than on tests of implicit memory. The ability to recognize a word in a memory test versus the ability to identify it in a perceptual test is plotted as a function of how the word was originally studied. (From Jacoby, 1983. Reprinted by permission of the publisher. © 1983 by the *Journal of Verbal Learning and Verbal Behavior.*)

on tests of implicit memory. For instance, Jacoby (1983) had participants just study a word such as *woman* alone (the no-context condition), study it in the presence of an antonym *man-woman* (the context condition), or generate the word as an antonym (the generate condition). In this last condition, participants would see *man-* and have to say *woman.* Jacoby then tested the participants in two ways, which were designed to tap either explicit memory or implicit memory. In the explicit memory test, participants were presented with a list of words, some studied and some not, and asked to recognize the old words. In the implicit memory test, participants were presented with one word from the list for a brief period (40 ms) and asked to identify the word. Figure 7.14 shows the results from these two tests as a function of study condition.

Performance on the explicit memory test was best in the condition that involved more semantic and generative processing—consistent with earlier research we reviewed on elaborative processing. In contrast, performance on the implicit perceptual identification test got worse. All three conditions showed better perceptual identification than would have been expected if the participants had not studied the word at all (only 60% correct perceptual identification). This enhancement of perceptual recognition is referred to as **priming.** Jacoby argues that participants show greatest priming in the no-context condition because this is the study condition in which they had to rely most on a perceptual encoding to identify the word. In the generate condition, participants did not even have a word to read.[5] Similar contrasts have been shown in memory for pictures: Elaborative processing of a picture will improve explicit memory for the picture but not affect perceptual processes in its identification (e.g., Schacter, Cooper, Delaney, Peterson, and Tharan, 1991).

In another experiment, Jacoby and Witherspoon (1982) wondered whether participants would display more priming for words they could recognize than for words they could not. Participants first studied a set of words. Then, in one phase of the experiment, they had to try to recognize explicitly whether or not they had studied the words. In another phase, participants had to simply say what word they had seen after a very brief presentation. Participants showed better ability to identify the briefly presented words that they had studied than words they had not studied. However, their identification success was no different for words they had studied and could recognize than for words they had studied but could not recognize. Thus, exposure to a word improves normal participants' ability to perceive that word (success of implicit memory), even when they cannot recall having studied the word (failure of explicit memory).

[5] Not all research has found better implicit memory in the no-context condition. However, all research finds an interaction between study condition and type of memory test. See Masson and MacLeod (1992) for further discussion.

Research comparing implicit and explicit memory suggests that the two types of memory are realized rather differently in the brain. We have already noted that amnesiacs with hippocampal damage show rather normal effects in studies of priming, whereas they can show dramatic deficits in explicit memory. Research with the drug midazolam has produced similar results in normal patients. Midazolam is used for sedation in patients undergoing surgery. It has been noted (Polster, McCarthy, O'Sullivan, Gray, & Park, 1993) that it produces severe anterograde amnesia for the period of time it is in a patient's system, although the patient functions normally during that period. Participants given the drug just before studying a list of words showed greatly impaired explicit memory for the words they studied but intact priming for these words (Hirshman, Passannante, & Arndt, 2001). Midazolam has its effect on the neurotransmitters that are found throughout the brain but which are particularly abundant in the hippocampus and prefrontal cortex. The explicit memory deficits it produces are consistent with the association of the hippocampus and the prefrontal cortex with explicit memory. Its lack of implicit memory effects suggests that implicit memories are stored elsewhere.

Neuroimaging studies suggest that implicit memories are stored in the cortex. As we have discussed, there is increased hippocampal activity when memories are explicitly retrieved (Schacter & Badgaiyan, 2001). During priming, in contrast, there is often decreased activity in cortical regions. For instance, in one fMRI study (Koutstaal et al., 2001), priming produced decreased activation in visual areas responsible for the recognition of pictures. The decreased activation that we see with priming reflects the fact that it is easier to recognize the primed items. It is as if their representation has been strengthened in the cortex.

A general interpretation of these results would seem to be that new explicit memories are formed in the hippocampus; but with experience, this information is transferred to the cortex. That is why hippocampal damage does not eliminate old memories formed before the damage. The permanent knowledge deposited in the cortex includes such information as word spelling and what things look like. These cortical memories are strengthened when they are primed and become more available in a later retest.

- *New explicit memories are built in hippocampal regions, but old knowledge can be implicitly primed in cortical structures.*

Procedural Memory

Implicit memory is defined as memory without conscious awareness. By this definition, rather different things can be considered implicit memories. Sometimes, implicit memories involve perceptual information relevant to recognizing the words. These memories result in the priming effects we saw in experiments such as Jacoby's. In other cases, implicit memories involve knowledge about how to perform tasks. A classic example of such an implicit memory involves **procedural knowledge,** such as riding a bike. Most of us have learned to ride a bike but have no conscious ability to say what it is we have learned. Memory for such procedural knowledge is spared in amnesic individuals.

An experiment by Berry and Broadbent (1984) involved a procedural learning task with a more cognitive character than riding a bike. They asked participants

TABLE 7.6

Procedural Memory: An Illustrative Series of Inputs and Outputs for a Hypothetical Sugar Factory

Workforce Input (W)	Sugar Output (tons) (S)
700	8,000
900	10,000
800	7,000
1,000	12,000
900	6,000
1,000	13,000
1,000	8,000

to try to control the output of a hypothetical sugar factory (which was simulated by a computer program) by manipulating the size of the workforce. Participants would see the month's sugar output of the factory in thousands of tons (e.g., 6,000 tons) and then have to choose the next month's workforce in hundreds of workers (e.g., 700). They would then see the next month's output of sugar (e.g., 8,000 tons) and have to pick the workforce for the following month. Table 7.6 shows a series of interactions with the hypothetical sugar factory. The goal was to keep sugar production within the range of 8,000 to 10,000 tons.

One can try to infer the rule relating sugar output to labor force in Table 7.6; it is not particularly obvious. The sugar output in thousands of tons (S) was related to the workforce input in hundreds (W), and the previous month's sugar output in thousands of tons (S_1), by the following formula: $S = 2 \times W - S_1$. (In addition, a random fluctuation of 1,000 tons of sugar is sometimes added, and S and W stay within the bounds of 1 to 12.) Oxford undergraduates were given 60 trials at trying to control the factory. Over those 60 trials, they got quite good at controlling the output of the sugar factory. However, they were unable to state what the rule was and claimed they made their responses on the basis of "some sort of intuition" or because it "felt right." Thus, participants were able to acquire implicit knowledge of how to operate such a factory without acquiring corresponding explicit knowledge. Amnesic participants have also been shown to be capable of learning this information (Phelps, 1989).

In recent years, sequence learning (Curran, 1995) has become a major model for study of the nature of procedural memory, including its realization in the brain. There are a number of sequence-learning models, but in the basic procedure, a participant observes a sequence of lights flash and must press corresponding buttons. For instance, there may be four lights with a button under each, and the task is to press the buttons in the same order as the lights flash. The typical manipulation is to introduce a repeating sequence of lights and contrast how much faster participants can press the keys in this sequence than when the lights are random. For instance, in the original Nissen and Bullemer (1987) study, the repeating sequence might be 4-2-3-1-3-2-4-3-2-1. People are faster at the repeated sequence. There has been much interest in whether participants are aware that there is a repeating sequence. In some experiments, they are aware of the repetition; but in many others, they are not. They tend not to notice the repeating sequence when the experimental pace is fast or when they are performing some other secondary task. Participants are faster at the repeated sequence whether they are aware of it or not.

It does not appear that the hippocampus is critical to developing proficiency in the repeated sequence, because amnesiacs show an advantage for the repeated sequence, as do normal patients with pharmacologically induced amnesia. On the other hand, a set of subcortical structures, collectively called the basal ganglia (see Figure 1.8), does appear to be critical for sequence learning. It had long been known that the basal ganglia are critical to motor control, because it is damage to these structures that produces the deficits associated with Huntington's and Parkinson's diseases, which are characterized by uncontrolled movements. However, there are rich connections between the basal ganglia and the prefrontal cortex, and it is now known that the basal ganglia are important in cognitive functions. They have been shown to be active during the learning of a number of skills, including sequence learning (Middleton & Strick, 1994). One advantage of sequence learning is that it is a cognitive skill one can teach to non-human primates and so perform detailed studies of its neural basis. Such primate studies have shown that the basal ganglia are critical to early learning of a sequence. For instance, Miyachi, Hikosaka, Miyashita, Karadi, and Rand (1997) were able to retard early sequential learning in monkeys by injecting their basal ganglia with a chemical that temporally inactivated it. Other neural structures appear to be involved in sequence learning as well. For instance, similar chemical inactivation of structures in the cerebellum retards later learning of a sequence. All in all, the evidence is pretty compelling that procedural learning involves structures different from those involved in explicit learning.

- *Procedural learning is another type of implicit learning and is supported by the basal ganglia.*

Conclusions: The Many Varieties of Memory in the Brain

Squire (1987) proposed that there are many different varieties of memory. Figure 7.15 reproduces his classification. The major distinction is between explicit and implicit memory, which he calls declarative memory and nondeclarative memory. **Declarative memory** basically refers to factual memories we can explicitly recall. It appears that the hippocampus is particularly important

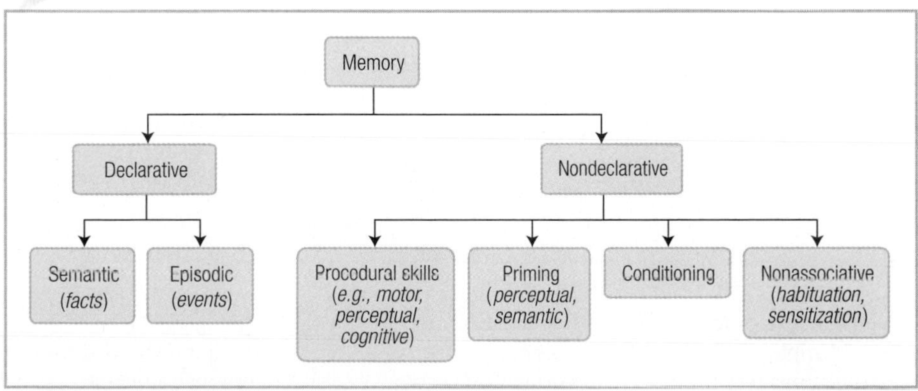

FIGURE 7.15 The varieties of memory proposed by Squire. (From Squire, 1987. Reprinted by permission of the publisher. © 1987 by Oxford University Press.)

for the establishment of declarative memories. Within the declarative memory system, there is a distinction between episodic and semantic memory. Episodic memories include information about where and when they were learned. For example, a memory of a particular newscast can be considered an episodic memory. This chapter and the previous Chapter 6 have discussed these kinds of memories. Semantic memories, discussed in Chapter 5, reflect general knowledge of the world, such as what a dog is or what a restaurant is.

Figure 7.15 makes it clear that there are many kinds of nondeclarative, or implicit, memory. We have just completed a discussion of procedural memories and the critical role of the basal ganglia and cerebellum in their formation. We also talked about priming and the fact that priming seems to entail changes to cortical regions directly responsible for processing the information involved. There are other kinds of learning that we have not discussed but that are particularly important in studies of animal learning. These include conditioning, habituation, and sensitization, all of which have been demonstrated in species ranging from sea slugs to humans. Evidence suggests that such conditioning in mammals involves many different brain structures (Anderson, 2000). Many different brain structures are involved in learning, and these different brain structures support different kinds of learning.

Questions for Thought

1. One of the exceptions to the decay of memories with time is the "reminiscence bump" (Berntsen & Rubin, 2002)—people show better memory for events that occurred in their late teens and early 20s than for memories earlier or later. What might be the explanation of this effect?
2. The story is told about David Starr Jordan, an ichthyologist (someone who studies fish), who was the first president of Stanford University. He tried to remember the names of all the students but found that whenever he learned the name of a student, he forgot the name of a fish. Does this seem a plausible example of interference in memory?
3. Do the false memories created in the Deese-Roediger-McDermott paradigm reflect the same sort of underlying processes as false memories of childhood events?
4. It is sometimes recommended that students study for an exam in the same room that they will be tested in. According to the study of Eich (1985; see discussion on p. 197), how would one have to study to make this an effective procedure? Would this be a reasonable way to study for an exam?
5. Squire's classification in Figure 7.15 would seem to imply that implicit and explicit memories involve different memory systems and brain structures—one called declarative and the other, nondeclarative. However, Reder, Park, and Keiffaber (2009) argue that the same memory system and brain structures sometimes display memories that we are consciously aware of and others of which we are not. How could one determine whether implicit and explicit memory correspond to different memory systems?

Key Terms

amnesia
anterograde amnesia
decay theory
declarative memory
Deese-Roediger-McDermott paradigm
dissociations
encoding-specificity principle
explicit memory
fan effect
false-memory syndrome
implicit memory
interference theory
Korsakoff syndrome
mood congruence
power law of forgetting
priming
procedural knowledge
retrograde amnesia
state-dependent learning

8

Problem Solving

Human ability to solve novel problems greatly surpasses that of any other species, and this ability depends on the advanced evolution of the prefrontal cortex in humans. We have already noted the role of the prefrontal cortex in a number of higher-level cognitive functions: language, imagery, and memory. It is generally thought that the prefrontal cortex performs more than these specific functions, however, and plays a major role in the overall organization of behavior. The regions of the prefrontal cortex that we have discussed so far tend to be ventral (toward the bottom) and posterior (toward the back), and many of these regions are left lateralized. In contrast, dorsal (toward the top), anterior (toward the front), and right-hemisphere prefrontal structures tend to be more involved in the organization of behavior. These are the prefrontal regions that have expanded the most in the human brain.

Goel and Grafman (2000) describe a patient, PF, who suffered damage to his right anterior prefrontal cortex as the result of a stroke. Like many patients with damage to the prefrontal cortex, PF appears normal and even intelligent, and he scored in the superior range on an intelligence test. In fact, he performed well on most tests, although he did have difficulty with the Tower of Hanoi problem described later in this chapter. Nonetheless, for all these surface appearances of normality, there were profound intellectual deficits. He had been a successful architect before his stroke but was forced to retire due to loss of the ability to design. He was able to get some work as a draftsman. Goel and Grafman gave PF a problem that involved redesigning their laboratory space. Although he was able to speak coherently about the problem, he was unable to make any real progress on the solution. A comparably trained architect without brain damage achieved a good solution in a couple of hours. It seems that the stroke affected only PF's most highly developed intellectual abilities.

This chapter and Chapter 9 will look at what we know about human problem solving. In this chapter, we will answer the following questions:

- What does it mean to characterize human problem solving as a search of a problem space?
- How do humans learn methods, called operators, for searching the problem space?

- How do humans select among different operators for searching a problem space?
- How can past experience affect the availability of different operators and the success of problem-solving efforts?

The Nature of Problem Solving

A Comparative Perspective on Problem Solving

Figure 8.1 shows the relative sizes of the prefrontal cortex in various mammals and illustrates the dramatic increase in humans. This increase supports the advanced problem solving that only humans are capable of. Nonetheless, one can find instances of interesting problem solving in other species, particularly in the higher apes such as chimpanzees. The study of problem solving in other species offers perspective on our own abilities. Köhler (1927) performed some of the classic studies on chimpanzee problem solving. Köhler was a famous German gestalt psychologist who came to America in the 1930s. During World War I, he found himself trapped on Tenerife in the Canary Islands. On the island, he found a colony of captive chimpanzees, which he studied, taking particular interest in the problem-solving behavior of the animals. His best participant was a chimpanzee named Sultan. One problem posed to Sultan was

Brain Structures

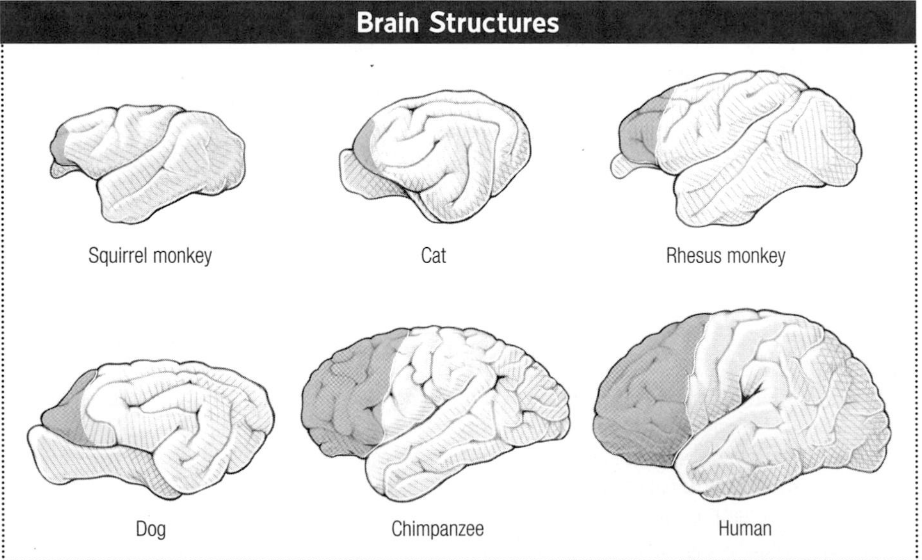

FIGURE 8.1 The relative proportions of the frontal lobe given over to the prefrontal cortex in six mammals. Note that these brains are not drawn to scale and that the human brain is really much larger in absolute size. (After Fuster, 1989. Adapted by permission of the publisher. © 1989 by Raven Press.)

The Problem-Solving Process: Problem Space and Search

Often, problem solving is described in terms of searching a **problem space,** which consists of various states of the problem. A **state** is a representation of the problem in some degree of solution. The initial situation of the problem is referred to as the start state; the situations on the way to the goal, as intermediate states; and the goal, as the **goal state.** Beginning from the start state, there are many ways the problem solver can choose to change the state. Sultan could reach for a stick, stand on his head, sulk, or try other approaches. Suppose he reaches for a stick. Now he has entered a new state. He can transform it into another state—for example, by letting go of the stick (thereby returning to the earlier state), reaching for the food with the stick, throwing the stick at the food, or reaching for the other stick. Suppose he reaches for the other stick. Again, he has created a new state. From this state, Sultan can choose to try, say, walking on the sticks, putting them together, or eating them. Suppose he chooses to put the sticks together. He can then choose to reach for the food, throw the sticks away, or separate them. If he reaches for the food, he will achieve the goal state.

The various states that the problem solver can achieve define a problem space, also called a state space. Problem-solving operators can be thought of as ways to change one state in the problem space into another. The challenge is to find some possible sequence of operators in the problem space that leads from the start state to the goal state. We can think of the problem space as a maze of states and of the operators as paths for moving among them. In this model, the solution to a problem is achieved through **search;** that is, the problem solver must find an appropriate path through a maze of states. This conception of problem solving as a search through a state space was developed by Allen Newell and Herbert Simon, who were dominant figures in cognitive science throughout their careers, and it has become the major problem-solving approach, in both cognitive psychology and AI.

A problem space characterization consists of a set of states and operators for moving among the states. A good example of problem-space characterization is the eight-tile puzzle, which consists of eight numbered, movable tiles set in a 3 × 3 frame. One cell of the frame is always empty, making it possible to move an adjacent tile into the empty cell and thereby to "move" the empty cell as well. The goal is to achieve a particular configuration of tiles, starting from a different configuration. For instance, a problem might be to transform

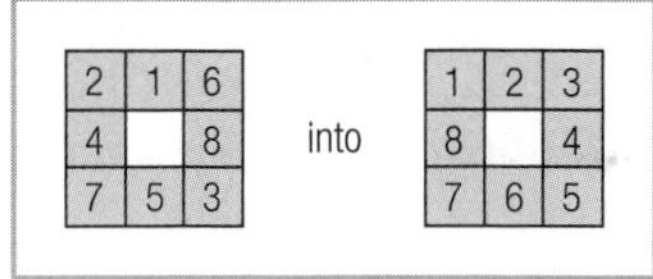

The possible states of this problem are represented as configurations of tiles in the eight-tile puzzle. So, the first configuration shown is the start state, and the second is the goal state. The operators that change the states are movements of tiles into empty spaces. Figure 8.3 reproduces an attempt of mine to solve this problem.

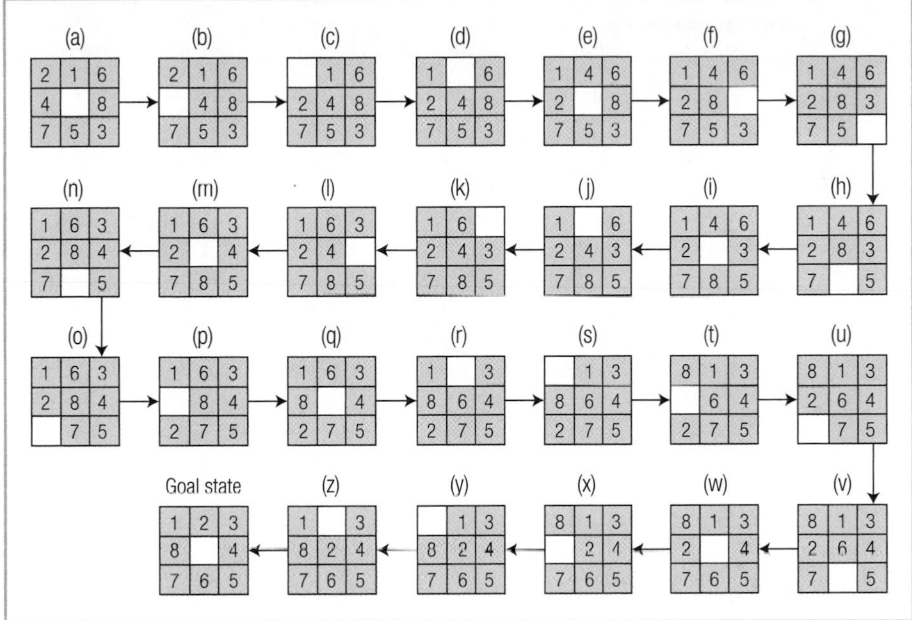

FIGURE 8.3 The author's sequence of moves for solving an eight-tile puzzle.

My solution involved 26 moves, each move being an operator that changed the state of the problem. This sequence of operators is considerably longer than necessary. Try to find a shorter sequence of moves. (The shortest sequence possible is given in the appendix at the end of the chapter, in Figure A8.1.)

Often, discussions of problem solving involve the use of search graphs or **search trees.** Figure 8.4 gives a partial search tree for the following, simpler eight-tile problem:

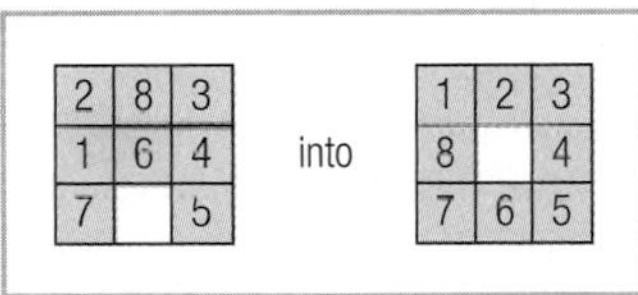

Figure 8.4 is like an upside-down tree with a single trunk and branches leading out from it. This tree begins with the start state and represents all states reachable from this state, then all states reachable from those states, and so on. Any path through such a tree represents a possible sequence of moves that a problem solver might make. By generating a complete tree, we can also find the shortest sequence of operators between the start state and the goal state. Figure 8.4 illustrates some of the problem space. In discussions of such examples, often only a path through the problem space that leads to the solution is presented (for instance, see Figure 8.3). Figure 8.4 gives a better idea of the size of the problem space of possible moves for this kind of problem.

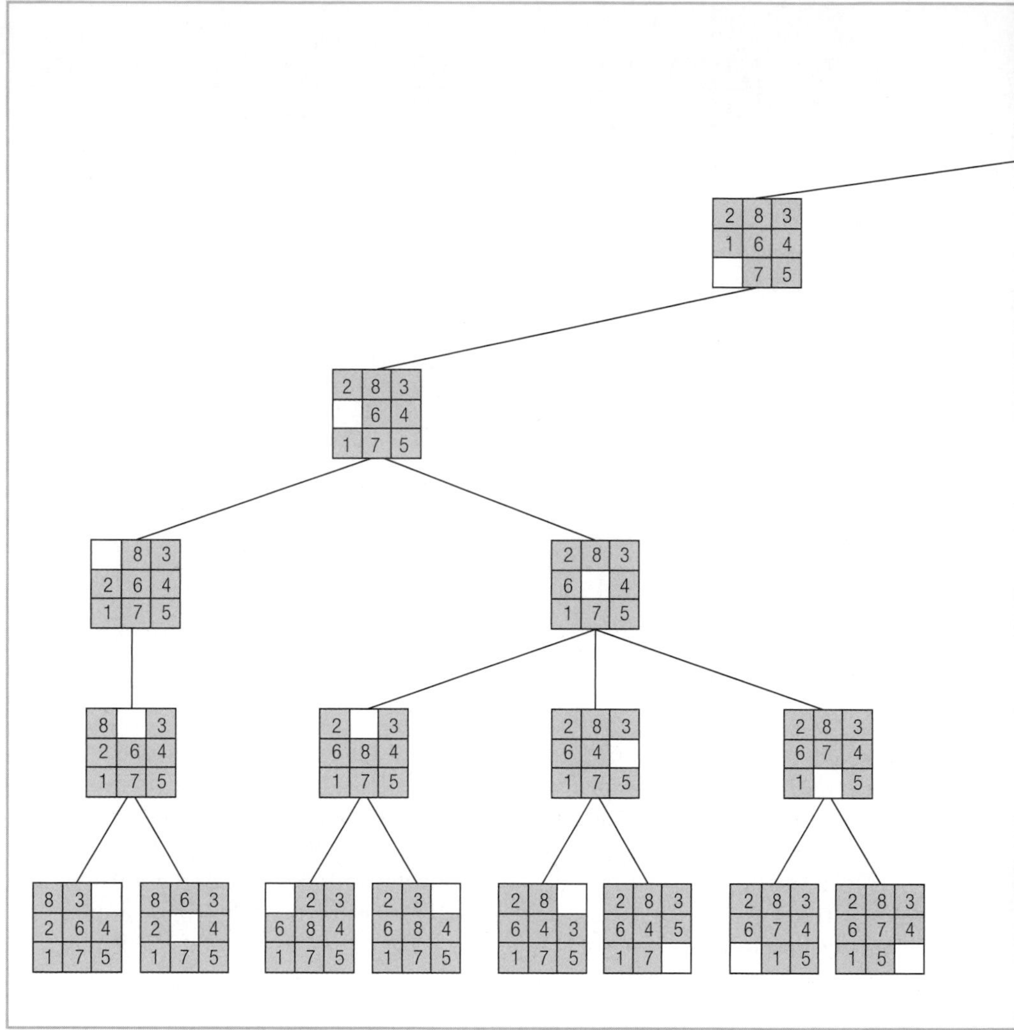

FIGURE 8.4 Part of the search tree, five moves deep, for an eight-tile problem. (After Nilsson, 1971. Adapted by permission of the publisher. © 1971 by McGraw-Hill.)

This search space terminology describes possible steps that the problem solver might take. It leaves two important questions that we need to answer before we can explain the behavior of a particular problem solver. First, what determines the operators available to the problem solver? Second, how does the problem solver select a particular operator when there are several available? An answer to the first question determines the search space in which the problem solver is working. An answer to the second question determines which path the problem solver takes. We will discuss these questions in the next two sections, focusing first on the origins of the problem-solving operators and then on the issue of operator selection.

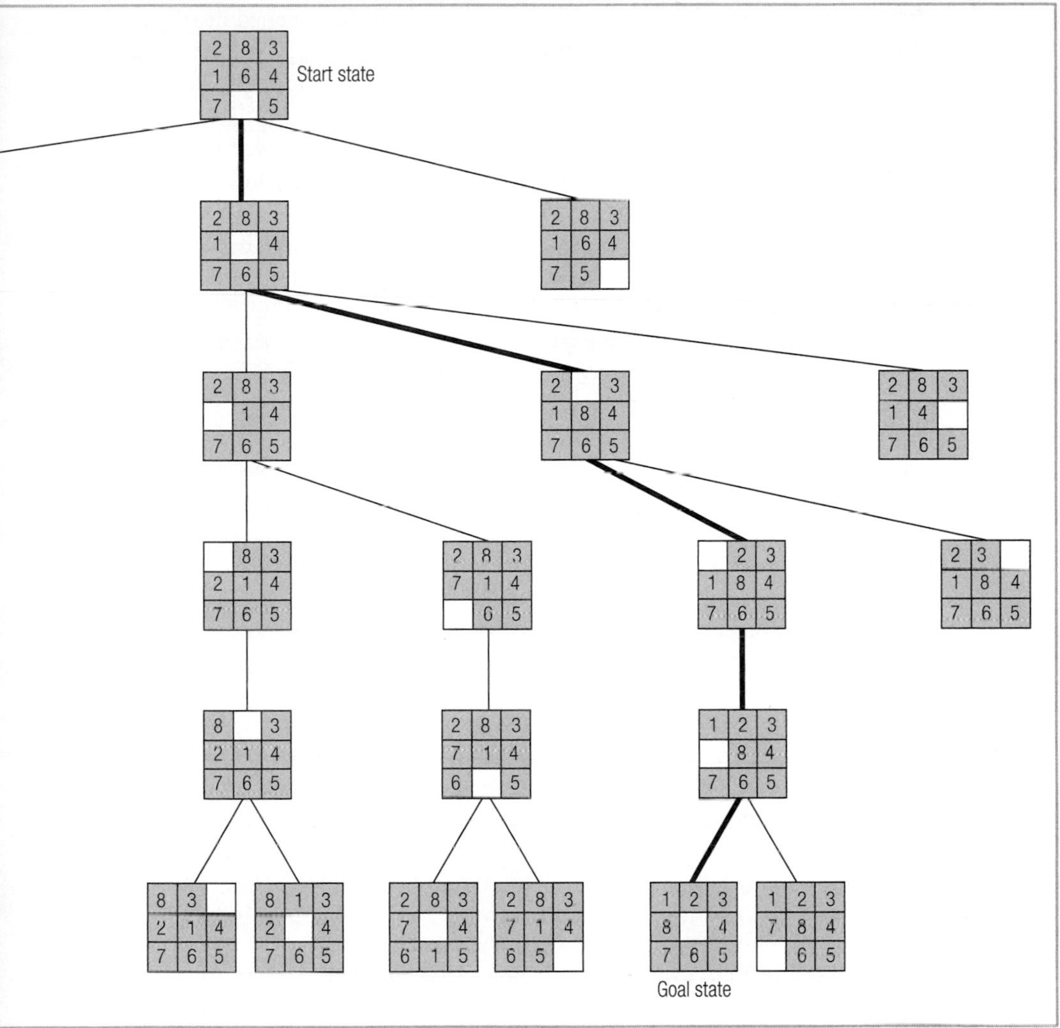

○ *Problem-solving operators generate a space of possible states through which the problem solver must search to find a path to the goal.*

● Problem-Solving Operators

Acquisition of Operators

There are at least three ways to acquire new problem-solving operators. We can acquire new operators by discovery, by being told about them, or by observing someone else use them.

Discovery. We might find that a new service station has opened nearby and so learn by discovery a new operator for repairing our car. Children might discover that their parents are particularly susceptible to temper tantrums and so learn a new way to get what they want. We might discover how a new microwave oven works by playing with it and so learn a new way to prepare food. Or a scientist might discover a new drug that kills bacteria and so invent a new way of combating infections. Each of these examples involves a variety of reasoning processes. These processes will be the topic of Chapter 10.

Although discovery can involve complex reasoning in humans, it is interesting that it is the only method that most other creatures have to learn new operators, and they certainly do not engage in complex reasoning. In a famous study reported in 1898, Thorndike placed cats in "puzzle boxes." The boxes could be opened by various nonobvious means. For instance, in one box, if the cat hit a loop of wire, the door would fall open. The cats, who were hungry, were rewarded with food when they got out. Initially, a cat would move about randomly, clawing at the box and behaving ineffectively in other ways until it happened to hit the unlatching device. After repeated trials in the same puzzle box, the cats eventually arrived at a point where they would immediately hit the unlatching device and get out. A controversy exists to this day over whether the cats ever really "understood" the new operator they had acquired or just gradually formed a mindless association between being in the box and hitting the unlatching device. More recently it has been argued that it need not be an either–or situation. Daw, N.D., Niv, Y., and Dayan, P. (2005) review evidence that there are two bases for learning such operators from experience—one involves the basal ganglia (see Figure 1.8), where simple associations are gradually reinforced, whereas the other involves the prefrontal cortex and a mental model of how these operators work. It is reasonable to suppose that the second system becomes more important in mammals with larger prefrontal cortices.

Learning by Being Told or by Example. We can acquire new operators by being told about them or by observing someone else use them. These are examples of social learning. The first method is a uniquely human accomplishment because it depends on language. The second is a capacity thought to be common in primates: "Monkey see, monkey do." As we will see, however, the capacity of nonhuman primates for learning by imitation has often been overestimated.

It might seem that the most efficient way to learn new problem-solving operators would be simply to be told about them, but seeing an example is often at least as effective as being told what to do. Table 8.1 shows two forms of instruction about an algebraic concept, called a pyramid expression, which is novel to most undergraduates. Students either study part (a), which gives a semiformal specification of what a pyramid expression is, or they study part (b), which gives the single example of a pyramid expression. After reading one instruction or the other, they are asked to evaluate pyramid expressions like

10$2

Which form of instruction do you think would be most useful? Carnegie Mellon undergraduates show comparable levels of learning from the single

TABLE 8.1

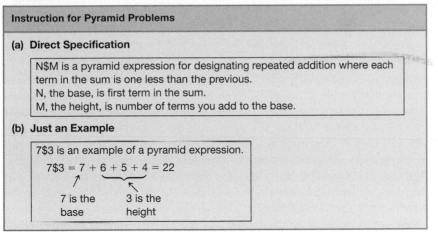

Instruction for Pyramid Problems
(a) Direct Specification
N$M is a pyramid expression for designating repeated addition where each term in the sum is one less than the previous. N, the base, is first term in the sum. M, the height, is number of terms you add to the base.
(b) Just an Example
7$3 is an example of a pyramid expression. 7$3 = 7 + 6 + 5 + 4 = 22 7 is the base; 3 is the height

example in part (b) to what they learn from the rigorous specification in part (a). Sometimes, examples can be the superior means of instruction. For instance, Reed and Bolstad (1991) had participants learn to solve problems such as the following:

> An expert can complete a technical task in five hours, but a novice requires seven hours to do the same task. When they work together, the novice works two hours more than the expert. How long does the expert work? (p. 765)

Participants received instruction in how to use the following equation to solve the problem:

$$\text{rate}_1 \times \text{time}_1 + \text{rate}_2 \times \text{time}_2 = \text{tasks}$$

The participants needed to acquire problem-solving operators for assigning values to the terms in this equation. The participants either received abstract instruction about how to make these assignments or saw a simple example of how the assignments were made. There was also a condition in which participants saw both the abstract instruction and the example. Participants given the abstract instruction were able to solve only 13% of a set of later problems; participants given an example solved 28% of the problems; and participants given both instruction and an example were able to solve 40%.

Why would giving examples be better for learning problem-solving operators than telling someone what to do directly? The problem with direct instruction is that it can often be difficult to understand what such quantities as rate_1 refer to. This information can be clearer in the context of an example. On the other hand, it can be difficult to see how to extend an example solution from one problem to another problem. Thus, experiments like Reed and Bolstad's indicate that the best learning occurs when participants have access to both methods. Similar results have been obtained by Fong, Krantz, and Nisbett (1986) in the domain of statistics and by Cheng, Holyoak, Nisbett, and Oliver (1986) in the domain of logic.

> *Problem-solving operators can be acquired by discovery, by modeling example problem solutions, or by direct instruction.*

Analogy and Imitation

Analogy is the process by which a problem solver extracts the operators used to solve one problem and maps them onto a solution for another problem. Sometimes, the analogy process can be straightforward. For instance, a student may take the structure of an example worked out in a section of a mathematics text and map it into the solution for a problem in the exercises at the end of the section. At other times, the transformations can be more complex. Rutherford, for example, used the solar system as a model for the structure of the atom, in which electrons revolve around the nucleus of the atom in the same way as the planets revolve around the sun (Koestler, 1964; Gentner, 1983—see Table 8.2). Although this is a particularly famous example of an analogy, scientists and engineers use such analogies, if often more mundane, with great frequency. For instance, Christensen and Schunn (2007) found engineers making 102 analogies in 9 hours of problem solving (see also Dunbar & Blanchette, 2001).

An example of the power of analogy in problem solving is provided in an experiment of Gick and Holyoak (1980). They presented their participants with the following problem, which is adapted from Duncker (1945):

> Suppose you are a doctor faced with a patient who has a malignant tumor in his stomach. It is impossible to operate on the patient, but unless the tumor is destroyed, the patient will die. There is a kind of ray that can be used to destroy the tumor. If the rays reach the tumor all at once at a sufficiently high intensity, the tumor will be destroyed. Unfortunately, at this intensity the healthy tissue that the rays pass through on the way to the tumor will also be destroyed. At lower intensities the rays are harmless to healthy tissue, but they will not affect the tumor either. What type of procedure might be used to destroy the tumor with the rays, and at the same time avoid destroying the healthy tissue? (pp. 307–308)

TABLE 8.2

The Solar System–Atom Analogy

Base Domain: Solar System	Target Domain: Atom
The sun attracts the planets.	The nucleus attracts the electrons.
The sun is larger than the planets.	The nucleus is larger than the electrons.
The planets revolve around the sun.	The electrons revolve around the nucleus.
The planets revolve around the sun because of the attraction and weight difference.	The electrons revolve around the nucleus because of the attraction and weight difference.
The planet Earth has life on it.	No transfer.

After Gentner (1983). Adapted by permission of the publisher. © 1983 by LEA, Ltd.

This is a very difficult problem, and few people are able to solve it. However, Gick and Holyoak presented their participants with the following story:

> A small country was ruled from a strong fortress by a dictator. The fortress was situated in the middle of the country, surrounded by farms and villages. Many roads led to the fortress through the countryside. A rebel general vowed to capture the fortress. The general knew that an attack by his entire army would capture the fortress. He gathered his army at the head of one of the roads, ready to launch a full-scale direct attack. However, the general then learned that the dictator had planted mines on each of the roads. The mines were set so that small bodies of men could pass over them safely, since the dictator needed to move his troops and workers to and from the fortress. However, any large force would detonate the mines. Not only would this blow up the road, but it would also destroy many neighboring villages. It therefore seemed impossible to capture the fortress. However, the general devised a simple plan. He divided his army into small groups and dispatched each group to the head of a different road. When all was ready he gave the signal and each group marched down a different road. Each group continued down its road to the fortress so that the entire army arrived together at the fortress at the same time. In this way, the general captured the fortress and overthrew the dictator. (p. 351)

Told to use this story as the model for a solution, most participants were able to develop an analogous operation to solve the tumor problem.

An interesting example of a solution by analogy that did not quite work is a geometry problem encountered by one student. Figure 8.5a illustrates the steps of a solution that the text gave as an example, and Figure 8.5b illustrates the student's attempts to use that example proof to guide his solution to a homework problem. In Figure 8.5a, two segments of a line are given as equal length, and the goal is to prove that two larger segments have equal length. In Figure 8.5b, the student is given two line segments with *AB* longer than *CD*, and his task is to prove the same inequality for two larger segments, *AC* and *BD*.

Our participant noted the obvious similarity between the two problems and proceeded to develop the apparent analogy. He thought he could simply substitute points on one line for points on another, and inequality for equality. That is, he tried to substitute *A* for *R*, *B* for *O*, *C* for *N*, *D* for *Y*, and > for =. With these substitutions, he got the first line correct: Analogous to *RO* = *NY*, he wrote *AB* > *CD*. Then he had to write something analogous to *ON* = *ON*, so he wrote *BC* > *BC*! This example illustrates how analogy can be used to create operators for problem solving and also shows that it requires a little sophistication to use analogy correctly.

Another difficulty with analogy is finding the appropriate examples from which to analogize operators. Often, participants do not notice when an analogy is possible. Gick and Holyoak (1980) did an experiment in which they read participants the story about the general and the dictator and then gave them Duncker's (1945) ray problem (both shown earlier in this section). Very few participants spontaneously noticed the relevance of the first story to solving the second. To achieve success,

FIGURE 8.5 (a) A worked-out proof problem given in a geometry text. (b) One student's attempt to use the structure of this problem's solution to guide his solution of a similar problem. This example illustrates how analogy can be used (and misused) for problem solving.

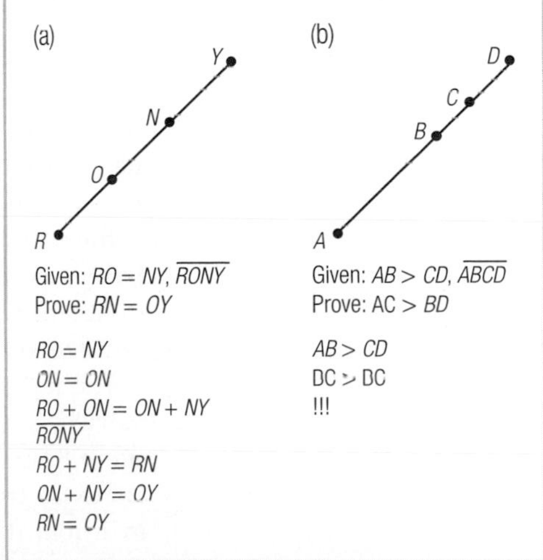

participants had to be explicitly told to use the general and dictator story as an analogy for solving the ray problem.

When participants do spontaneously use previous examples to solve a problem, they are often guided by superficial similarities in their choice of examples. For instance, B. H. Ross (1984, 1987) taught participants several methods for solving probability problems. These methods were taught by reference to specific examples, such as finding the probability that a pair of tossed dice will sum to 7. Participants were then tested with new problems that were superficially similar to prior examples. The similarity was superficial because both the example and the problem involved the same content (e.g., dice) but not necessarily the same principle of probability. Participants tried to solve the new problem by using the operators illustrated in the superficially similar prior example. When that example illustrated the same principle as required in the current problem, participants were able to solve the problem. When it did not, they were unable to solve the current problem. Reed (1987) has found similar results with algebra story problems.

In solving school problems, students use proximity as a cue to determine which examples to use in analogy. For instance, a student working on physics problems at the end of a chapter expects that problems solved as examples in the chapter will use the same methods and so tries to solve the problems by analogy to these examples (Chi, Bassok, Lewis, Riemann, & Glaser, 1989).

- *Analogy involves noticing that a past problem solution is relevant and then mapping the elements from that solution to produce an operator for the current problem.*

Analogy and Imitation from an Evolutionary and Brain Perspective

It has been argued that analogical reasoning is a hallmark of human cognition (Halford, 1992). The capacity to solve analogical problems is almost uniquely found in humans. There is some evidence for it in chimpanzees (Oden, Thompson, & Premack, 2001), although lower primates such as monkeys seem totally incapable of such tasks. For instance, Premack (1976) found that Sarah, a chimpanzee used in studies of language (see Chapter 11), was able to solve analogies such as the following: Key is to a padlock as what is to a tin can? The answer: can opener. In more careful study of Sarah's abilities, however, Oden et al. found that although Sarah could solve these problems more often than chance, she was much more prone to error than human participants.

Recent brain-imaging studies have looked at the cortical regions that are activated in analogical reasoning. Figure 8.6 shows examples of the stimuli used in a study by Christoff et al. (2001), adapted from the Raven's Progressive Matrices test, which is a standard test of intelligence. Only the problems in Figure 8.6c, which require that the solver coordinate two dimensions, could be said to tap true analogical reasoning. There is evidence that children under age 5 (in whom the frontal cortex has not yet matured), nonhuman primates, and patients with frontal damage all have special difficulty with problems like those shown in Figure 8.6c and often just cannot solve them. Christoff et al. were interested in discovering which brain regions would be activated when participants were solving these problems. Consistent with the trends we noted in the introduction to this chapter, they found that the right anterior prefrontal cortex was activated only when participants were solving these 2-D problems.

Examples like those shown in Figure 8.6 are cases in which analogical reasoning is used for purposes other than acquiring new problem-solving operators. From the perspective of this chapter, however, the real importance of analogy is that it can be used to acquire new problem-solving operators. We noted earlier that people often learn more from studying an example than from reading abstract instructions. Humans have a special ability to mimic the problem solutions of others. When we ask someone how to use a new device, that person tends to show us how, not to tell us how. Despite the proverb "Monkey see, monkey do," even the higher apes are quite poor at imitation (Tomasello & Call, 1997). Thus, it seems that one of the things that make humans such effective problem solvers is that we have special abilities to acquire new problem-solving operators by analogical reasoning.

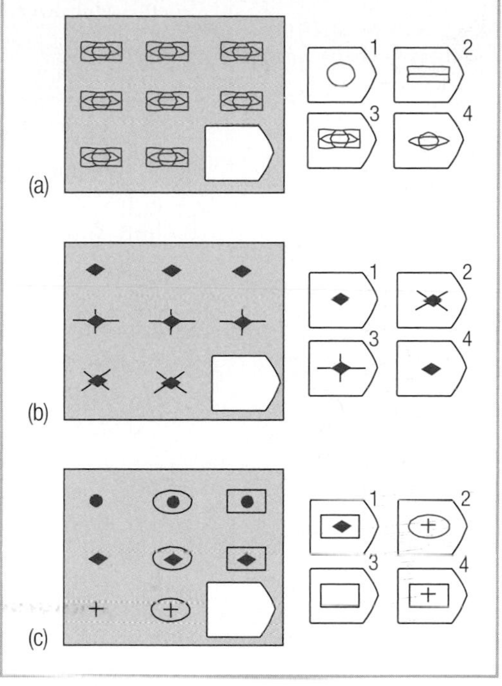

FIGURE 8.6 Examples of stimuli used by Christoff et al. to study which brain regions would be activated when participants attempted to solve three different types of analogy problem: (a) 0-dimensional; (b) 1-dimensional; and (c) 2-dimensional. The task in each case was to infer the missing figure and select it from among the four alternative choices. (After Christoff et al., 2001. Adapted by permission of the publisher. © 2001 by *Neuroimage*.)

Analogical problem solving appears to be a capability nearly unique to humans and to depend on the advanced development of the prefrontal cortex.

Operator Selection

As noted earlier, in any particular state, multiple problem-solving operators can be applicable, and a critical task is to select the one to apply. In principle, a problem solver may select operators in many ways, and the field of AI has succeeded in enumerating various powerful techniques. However, it seems that most methods are not particularly natural as human problem-solving approaches. Here we will review three criteria that humans use to select operators.

Backup avoidance biases the problem solver against any operator that undoes the effect of the previous operators. For instance, in the eight-tile puzzle, people show great reluctance to take back a step even if this might be necessary to solve the problem. However, backup avoidance by itself provides no basis for choosing among the remaining operators.

Humans tend to select the nonrepeating operator that most reduces the difference between the current state and the goal. **Difference reduction** is a very general principle and describes the behavior of many creatures. For instance, Köhler (1927) described how a chicken will move directly toward desired food and will not go around a fence that is blocking it. The poor creature is effectively paralyzed, being unable to move forward and unwilling to back up and undo its approach to the fence. It does not seem to have any principles for selection of operators other than difference reduction and backup avoidance. This leaves it without a solution to the problem.

On the other hand, the chimpanzee Sultan (see Figure 8.2) did not just claw at his cage trying to get the bananas. He sought to create a new tool to enable him to obtain the food. In effect, his new goal became the creation of a new means for achieving the old goal. **Means-ends analysis** is the term used to describe the creation of a new goal (end) to enable an operator (means) to apply. By using means-ends analysis, humans and other higher primates can be more resourceful in achieving a goal than they could be if they used only difference reduction. In the next sections, we will discuss the roles of both difference reduction and means-ends analysis in operator selection.

Humans use backup avoidance, difference reduction, and means-ends analysis to guide their selection of operators.

The Difference-Reduction Method

A common method of problem solving, particularly in unfamiliar domains, is to try to reduce the difference between the current state and the goal state. For instance, consider my solution to the eight-tile puzzle in Figure 8.3. There were four options possible for the first move. One possible operator was to move the 1 tile into the empty square, another was to move the 8, a third was to move the 5, and the fourth was to move the 4. I chose the last operator. Why? Because it seemed to get me closer to my end goal. I was moving the 4 tile closer to its final destination. Human problem solvers are often strongly governed by difference reduction or, conversely, by similarity increase. That is, they choose operators that transform the current state into a new state that reduces differences and resembles the goal state more closely than the current state. Difference reduction is sometimes called **hill climbing.** If we imagine the goal as the highest point of land, one approach to reaching it is always to take steps that go up. By reducing the difference between the goal and the current state, the problem solver is taking a step "higher" toward the goal. Hill climbing has a potential flaw, however: By following it, we might reach the top of some hill that is lower than the highest point of land that is the goal. Thus, difference reduction is not guaranteed to work. It is myopic in that it considers only whether the next step is an improvement and not whether the larger plan will work. Means-ends analysis, which we will discuss later, is an attempt to introduce a more global perspective into problem solving.

One way problem solvers improve operator selection is by using more sophisticated measures of similarity. My first move was intended simply to get a tile closer to its final destination. After working with many tile problems, we begin to notice the importance of sequence—that is, whether noncentral tiles are followed by their appropriate successors. For instance, in state (o) of Figure 8.3, the 3 and 4 tiles are in sequence because they are followed by their successors 4 and 5, but the 5 is not in sequence because it is followed by 7 rather than 6. Trying first to move tiles into sequence proves to be more important than trying to move them to their final destinations right away. Thus, using sequence as a measure of increasing similarity leads to more effective problem solving based on difference reduction (see Nilsson, 1971, for further discussion).

The difference-reduction technique relies on evaluations of the similarity between the current state and the goal state. Although difference reduction works more often than not, it can also lead the problem solver astray. In some problem-solving situations, a correct solution involves going against the grain of similarity. A good example is called the hobbits and orcs problem:

> On one side of a river are three hobbits and three orcs. They have a boat on their side that is capable of carrying two creatures at a time across the river. The goal is to transport all six creatures across to the other side of the river. At no point on either side of the river can orcs outnumber hobbits (or the orcs would eat the outnumbered hobbits). The problem, then, is to find a method of transporting all six creatures across the river without the hobbits ever being outnumbered.

Stop reading and try to solve this problem. Figure 8.7 shows a correct sequence of moves. Illustrated are the locations of hobbits (H), orcs (O), and the boat (b). The boat, the three hobbits, and the three orcs all start on one side of the river. This condition is represented in state 1 by the fact that all are above the line. Then a hobbit, an orc, and the boat proceed to the other side of the river. The outcome of this action is represented in state 2 by placement of the boat, the hobbit, and the orc below the line. In state 3, one hobbit has taken the boat back, and the diagram continues in the same way. Each state in the figure represents another configuration of hobbits, orcs, and boat. Participants have a particular problem with the transition from state 6 to state 7. In a study by Jeffries, Polson, Razran, and Atwood (1977), about a third of all participants chose to back up to a previous state 5 rather than moving on to state 7 (see also Greeno, 1974). One reason for this difficulty is that the action involves moving two creatures back to the wrong side of the river. The move seems to be away from a solution. At this point, participants will go back to state 5, even though this undoes their last move. They would rather undo a move than take a step that moves them to a state that appears further from the goal.

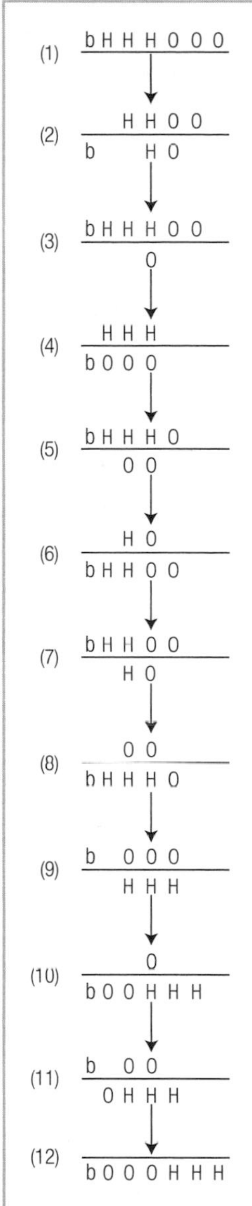

FIGURE 8.7 A diagram of the successive states in a solution to the hobbits and orcs problem. H = hobbits, O = orcs, b = boat.

Atwood and Polson (1976) provide another experimental demonstration of participants' reliance on similarity and how that reliance can sometimes be harmful and sometimes beneficial. Participants were given the following water jug problem:

> You have three jugs, which we will call *A*, *B*, and *C*. Jug *A* can hold exactly 8 cups of water, *B* can hold exactly 5 cups, and *C* can hold exactly 3 cups. Jug *A* is filled to capacity with 8 cups of water. *B* and *C* are empty. We want you to find a way of dividing the contents of *A* equally between *A* and *B* so that both have exactly 4 cups. You are allowed to pour water from jug to jug.

Figure 8.8 shows two paths for solving this problem. At the top of the illustration, all the water is in jug *A*—represented by *A*(8); there is no water in jugs *B* or *C*—represented by *B*(0) *C*(0). The two possible actions are to pour *A* into *C*, in which case we get *A*(5) *B*(0) *C*(3), or to pour *A* into *B*, in which case we get *A*(3) *B*(5)

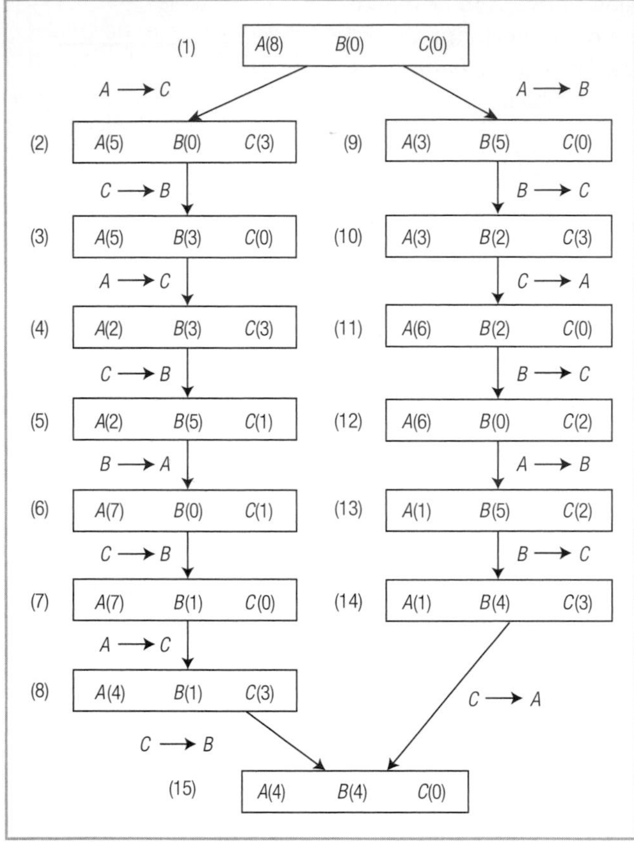

FIGURE 8.8 Two paths of solution for the water jug problem posed in Atwood and Polson (1976). Each state is represented in terms of the contents of the three jugs; for example, in state 1, *A*(8) *B*(0) *C*(0). The transitions between states (e.g., *A* → *C*) are labeled in terms of which jug is poured into which other jug.

C(0). From these two states, more moves can be made. Numerous other sequences of moves are possible besides the two paths illustrated, but these are the two shortest sequences to the goal.

Atwood and Polson used the representation in Figure 8.8 to analyze participants' behavior. For instance, they asked which move participants would prefer to make at the start state 1. That is, would they prefer to pour jug *A* into *C* and get state 2, or jug *A* into *B* and get state 9? The answer is that participants preferred the latter move. More than twice as many participants moved to state 9 as moved to state 2. Note that state 9 is quite similar to the goal. The goal is to have 4 cups in both *A* and *B*, and state 9 has 3 cups in *A* and 5 cups in *B*. In contrast, state 2 has no cups of water in *B*. Throughout the experiment, Atwood and Polson found a strong tendency for participants to move to states that were similar to the goal state. Usually, similarity was a good heuristic, but there are critical cases where similarity is misleading. For instance, the transitions from state 5 to state 6 and from state 11 to state 12 both lead to significant decreases in similarity to the goal. However, both transitions are critical to their solution paths. Atwood and Polson found that more than 50% of the time, participants deviated from the correct sequence of moves at these critical points. They instead chose some move that seemed closer to the goal but actually took them away from the solution.[1]

It is worth noting that people do not get stuck in suboptimal states only while solving puzzles. Hill climbing can get us stuck when making serious life choices. A classic example is someone trapped in a suboptimal job because he or she is unwilling to get the education needed for a better job. The person is unwilling to endure the temporary deviation from the goal (of earning as much as possible) to get the skills to earn an even higher salary.

- *People experience difficulty in solving a problem at points where the correct solution involves increasing the differences between the current state and the goal state.*

Means-Ends Analysis

Means-ends analysis is a more sophisticated method of operator selection. This method has been extensively studied by Newell and Simon, who used it in a computer simulation program (called the **General Problem Solver—GPS**) that

[1] For instance, moving back to state 9 from either state 5 or state 11.

models human problem solving. The following is their description of means-ends analysis.

Means-ends analysis is typified by the following kind of commonsense argument:

> I want to take my son to nursery school. What's the difference between what I have and what I want? One of distance. What changes distance? My automobile. My automobile won't work. What is needed to make it work? A new battery. What has new batteries? An auto repair shop. I want the repair shop to put in a new battery; but the shop doesn't know I need one. What is the difficulty? One of communication. What allows communication? A telephone . . . and so on.
>
> This kind of analysis—classifying things in terms of the functions they serve and oscillating among ends, functions required, and means that perform them—forms the basic system of GPS. (Newell & Simon, 1972, p. 416)

Means-ends analysis can be viewed as a more sophisticated version of difference reduction. Like difference reduction, it tries to eliminate the differences between the current state and the goal state. For instance, in this example, it tried to reduce the distance between the home and the nursery school. Means-ends analysis will also identify the biggest difference first and try to eliminate it. Thus, in this example, the focus is on difference in the general location of home and nursery school. The difference between where the car will be parked and the classroom has not been considered.

Means-ends analysis offers a major advance over difference reduction because it will not abandon an operator if it cannot be applied immediately. If the car did not work, for example, difference reduction would have one start walking to the nursery school. The essential feature of means-ends analysis is that it focuses on enabling blocked operators. The means temporarily becomes the end. In effect, the problem solver deliberately ignores the real goal and focuses on the goal of enabling the means. In the example we have been discussing, the problem solver set a subgoal of repairing the automobile, which was the means of achieving the original goal of getting the child to nursery school. New operators can be selected to achieve this subgoal. For instance, installing a new battery was chosen. If this operator is blocked, enabling it can become yet another subgoal.

Figure 8.9 shows two flowcharts of the procedures used in the means-ends analysis employed by GPS. A general feature of this analysis is that it breaks a larger goal into subgoals. GPS creates subgoals in two ways. First, in flowchart 1, GPS breaks the current state into a set of differences and sets the reduction of each difference as a separate subgoal. First it tries to eliminate what it perceives as the most important difference. Second, in flowchart 2, GPS tries to find an operator that will eliminate the difference. However, GPS may not be able to apply this operator immediately because a difference exists between the operator's condition and the state of the environment. Thus, before the operator can be applied, it may be necessary to eliminate another difference. To eliminate the difference that is blocking the operator's application, flowchart 2 will have to be called again to find another operator relevant to eliminating that difference. The term *operator subgoal* is used to refer to a subgoal whose purpose is to eliminate a difference that is blocking application of an operator.

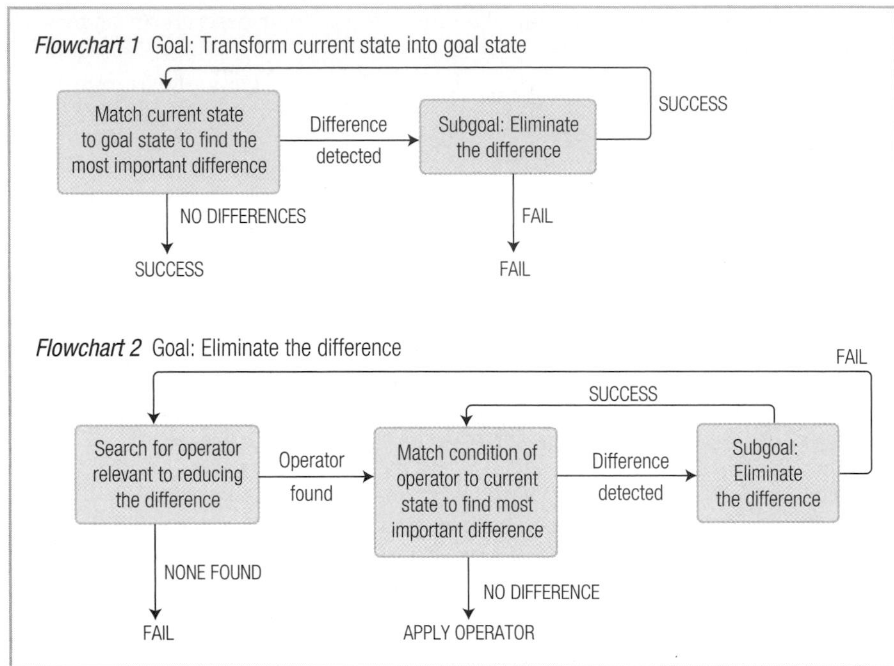

FIGURE 8.9 The application of means-ends analysis by Newell and Simon's General Problem Solving (GPS) program. Flowchart 1 breaks a problem down into a set of differences and tries to eliminate each one. Flowchart 2 searches for an operator that is relevant to eliminating a difference.

- *Means-ends analysis involves creating subgoals to eliminate the difference blocking the application of a desired operator.*

The Tower of Hanoi Problem

Means-ends analysis has proved to be a generally applicable and extremely powerful method of problem solving. Ernst and Newell (1969) discussed its application to the modeling of monkey and bananas problems (such as Sultan's predicament described at the beginning of the chapter), algebra problems, calculus problems, and logic problems. Here, however, we will illustrate means-ends analysis by applying it to the **Tower of Hanoi problem.** Figure 8.10 illustrates a simple version

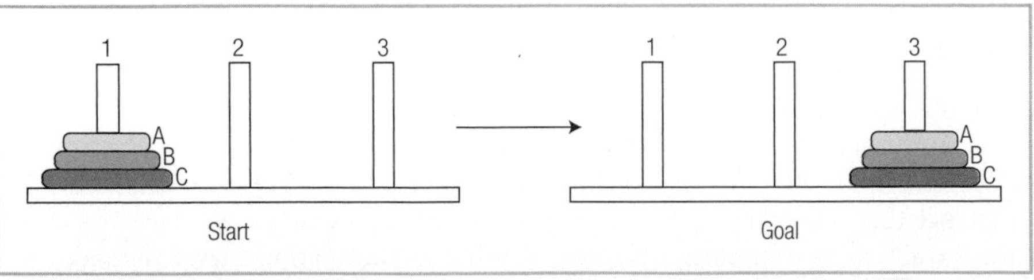

FIGURE 8.10 The three-disk version of the Tower of Hanoi problem.

of this problem. There are three pegs and three disks of differing sizes, *A*, *B*, and *C*. The disks have holes in them so they can be stacked on the pegs. The disks can be moved from any peg to any other peg. Only the top disk on a peg can be moved, and it can never be placed on a smaller disk. The disks all start out on peg 1, but the goal is to move them all to peg 3, one disk at a time, by transferring disks among pegs.

Figure 8.11 traces the application of the GPS techniques to this problem. The first line gives the general goal of moving disks *A*, *B*, and *C* to peg 3. This goal leads us to the first flowchart of Figure 8.9. One difference between the goal and the current state is that disk *C* is not on peg 3. This difference is chosen because GPS tries to remove the most important difference first, and we are assuming that the largest misplaced disk will be viewed as the most important difference. A subgoal set up to eliminate this difference takes us to the second flowchart of Figure 8.9, which tries to find an operator to reduce the difference. The operator chosen is to move *C* to peg 3. The condition for applying a move operator is that nothing be on the disk. Because *A* and *B* are on C, there is a difference between the condition of the operator and the current state. Therefore, a new subgoal is created to reduce one of the differences—*B* on *C*. This subgoal gets us back to the start of flowchart 2, but now with the goal of removing *B* from *C* (line 6 in Figure 8.11).[2]

The operator chosen the second time in flowchart 2 is to move disk *B* to peg 2. However, we cannot immediately apply the operator of moving *B* to 2, because *B* is covered by *A*. Therefore, another subgoal—removing *A*—is set up, and flowchart 2 is used to remove this difference. The operator relevant to achieving this subgoal is to move disk *A* to peg 3. There are no differences between the conditions for this operator and the current state. Finally, we have an operator we can apply (line 12 in Figure 8.11), and we achieve the subgoal of moving *A* to 3. Now we return to the earlier intention of

```
1.  Goal: Move A, B, and C to peg 3
2.      : Difference is that C is not on 3
3.      : Subgoal: Make C on 3
4.          : Operator is to move C to 3
5.          : Difference is that A and B are on C
6.          : Subgoal: Remove B from C
7.              : Operator is to move B to 2
8.              : Difference is that A is on B
9.              : Subgoal: Remove A from B
10.                 : Operator is to move A to 3
11.                 : No difference with operator's condition
12.                 : Apply operator (move A to 3)
13.             : Subgoal achieved
14.             : No difference with operator's condition
15.             : Apply operator (move B to 2)
16.         : Subgoal achieved
17.         : Difference is that A is on 3
18.         : Subgoal: Remove A from 3
19.             : Operator is to move A to 2
20.             : No difference with operator's condition
21.             : Apply operator (move A to 2)
22.         : Subgoal achieved
23.         : No difference with operator's condition
24.         : Apply operator (move C to 3)
25.     : Subgoal achieved
26.     : Difference is that B is not on 3
27.     : Subgoal: Make B on 3
28.         : Operator is to move B to 3
29.         : Difference is that A is on B
30.         : Subgoal: Remove A from B
31.             : Operator is to move A to 1
32.             : No difference with operator's condition
33.             : Apply operator (move A to 1)
34.         : Subgoal achieved
35.         : No difference with operator's condition
36.         : Apply operator (move B to 3)
37.     : Subgoal achieved
38.     : Difference is that A is not on 3
39.     : Subgoal: Make A on 3
40.         : Operator is to move A to 3
41.         : No difference with operator's condition
42.         : Apply operator (move A to 3 )
43.     : Subgoal achieved
44.     : No difference
45. Goal achieved
```

FIGURE 8.11 A trace of the application of the GPS program, as shown in Figure 8.9, to the Tower of Hanoi problem shown in Figure 8.10.

[2] Note that we have gone from the use of flowchart 1 to the use of flowchart 2, to a new use of flowchart 2. To apply flowchart 2 to find a way to move disk *C* to peg 3, we need to apply flowchart 2 to find a way to remove disk *B* from disk *C*. Thus, one procedure is using itself as a subprocedure; such an action is called recursion.

FIGURE 8.2 Köhler's ape, Sultan, solved the two-stick problem by joining two short sticks to form a pole long enough to reach the food outside his cage. (From Köhler, 1956. Reprinted by permission of the publisher. © 1956 by Routledge & Kegan Paul.)

to get some bananas that were outside his cage. Sultan had no difficulty when he was given a stick that could reach the bananas; he simply used the stick to pull the bananas into the cage. The problem became harder when Sultan was provided with two poles, neither of which could reach the food. After unsuccessfully trying to use the poles to get to the food, the frustrated ape sulked in his cage. Suddenly, he went over to the poles and put one inside the other, creating a pole long enough to reach the bananas (Figure 8.2). Clearly, Sultan had creatively solved the problem.

What are the essential features that qualify this episode as an instance of problem solving? There seem to be three:

1. Goal directedness. The behavior is clearly organized toward a goal—in this case, getting the food.
2. Subgoal decomposition. If Sultan could have obtained the food simply by reaching for it, the behavior would have been problem solving, but only in the most trivial sense. The essence of the problem solution is that the ape had to decompose the original goal into subtasks, or **subgoals,** such as getting the poles and putting them together.
3. Operator application. Decomposing the overall goal into subgoals is useful because the ape knows operators that can help him achieve these subgoals. The term **operator** refers to an action that will transform the problem state into another problem state. The solution of the overall problem is a sequence of these known operators.

Problem solving is goal-directed behavior that often involves setting subgoals to enable the application of operators.

moving *B* to 2. There are no more differences between the condition for this operator and the current state, and so the action takes place. The subgoal of removing *B* from *C* is then satisfied (line 16 in Figure 8.11).

We have now returned to the original intention of moving disk *C* to peg 3. However, disk *A* is now on peg 3, which prevents the action. Thus, we have another difference to be eliminated between the now-current state and the operator's condition. We move *A* onto peg 2 to remove this difference. Now the original operator of moving *C* to 3 can be applied (line 24 in Figure 8.11).

The state now is that disk *C* is on peg 3 and disks *A* and *B* are on peg 2. At this point, GPS returns to its original goal of moving the three disks to peg 3. It notes another difference—that *B* is not on 3—and sets another subgoal of eliminating this difference. It achieves this subgoal by first moving *A* to 1 and then *B* to 3. This gets us to line 37 in Figure 8.11. The remaining difference is that *A* is not on 3. This difference is eliminated in lines 38 through 42. With this step, no more differences exist and the original goal is achieved.

Note that subgoals are created in service of other subgoals. For instance, to achieve the subgoal of moving the largest disk, GPS creates a subgoal of moving the second-largest disk, which is top of it. We indicated this logical dependency of one subgoal on another in Figure 8.11 by indenting the processing of the dependent subgoal. Before the first move in line 12 of the illustration, three subgoals had to be created. It appears that creating such goals and subgoals can be quite costly. Both Anderson, Kushmerick, and Lebiere (1993) and Ruiz (1987) found that the time required to make one of the moves is a function of the number of subgoals that must be created. For instance, before disk A is moved to peg 3 in Figure 8.11 (the first move), three subgoals have to be created, whereas no subgoals have to be created before the next move is taken—moving *B* to peg 2. Correspondingly, Anderson et al. found that it took 8.95 s to make the first move and 2.46 s to make the second move.

There are two problem-solving methods that participants could bring to bear in solving the Tower of Hanoi problem. They could use a means-ends approach as illustrated in Figure 8.11, or they could use the simpler difference-reduction method—in which case they would never set a subgoal to move a disk that currently cannot be moved. In the Tower of Hanoi problem, such a simple difference-reduction method would not be effective, because one needs to look beyond what is currently possible and have a more global plan of attack on the problem. The only step that difference reduction could take in Figure 8.10 would be to move the top disk (*A*) to the target peg (3), but then it would provide no further guidance because no other move would reduce the difference between the current state and the goal state. Participants would have to make a random move. Kotovsky, Hayes, and Simon (1985) studied the way people actually approach the Tower of Hanoi problem. They found that there was an initial problem-solving period during which participants did adopt this fruitless difference-reduction strategy. Then they switched to a means-ends strategy, after which the solution to the problem came quickly.

- *The Tower of Hanoi problem is solved by adopting a means-ends strategy in which subgoals are created.*

Goal Structures and Prefrontal Cortex

It is significant that complex goal structures, particularly those involving operator subgoaling, have been observed with any frequency only in humans and higher primates. We have already discussed one instance of Sultan's solution to the two-stick problem (see Figure 8.2). Novel tool building, a clear instance of operator subgoaling, is almost unique to the higher apes (Beck, 1980). I (Anderson, 1993) have speculated that the process of handling complex subgoals is performed by the prefrontal cortex—which, as Figure 8.1 illustrates, is much larger in the higher primates than in most other mammals, and is larger in humans than in most apes. Chapter 6 discussed the role of the prefrontal cortex in holding information in working memory. One of the major prerequisites to developing complex goal structures is the ability to maintain these goal structures in working memory.

Goel and Grafman (1995) looked at how patients with frontal damage performed in solving the Tower of Hanoi problem. These patients had suffered severe damage to the prefrontal cortex. Many were veterans of the Vietnam War who had lost large amounts of brain tissue as a result of penetrating missile wounds. Although these patients had normal IQs, they showed much worse performance than normal participants on the Tower of Hanoi task. There were certain moves that these patients found particularly difficult to solve. As we noted in discussing how means-ends analysis applies to the Tower of Hanoi problem, it is necessary to make moves that deviate from the prescriptions of hill climbing. One might have a disk at the correct position but have to move it away to enable another disk to be moved to that position. It was exactly at these points where the patients had to move "backward" that they had their problems. Only by maintaining a set of goals can one see that a backward move is necessary for a solution.

More generally, it has been noted that patients with frontal damage have difficulty inhibiting a predominant response (e.g., Roberts, Hager, & Heron, 1994). For instance, in the Stroop task (see Chapter 3), these patients have trouble not saying the word itself when they are supposed to say the color of the word. Apparently, they find it hard to keep in mind that their goal is to say the color and not the word.

There is increased blood flow in the prefrontal cortex during many tasks that involve organizing novel and complex behavior (Gazzaniga, Ivry, & Mangun, 1998). Fincham, Carter, van Veen, Stenger, and Anderson (2002) did an fMRI study of students while they were solving Tower of Hanoi problems and looked at brain activation as a function of the number of goals that the student had to set. These students were solving much more complicated problems than the simple one shown in Figure 8.10. A problem might involve placing five disks and could require maintaining as many as five goals to reach a solution. Figure 8.12 shows the fMRI BOLD response of a region

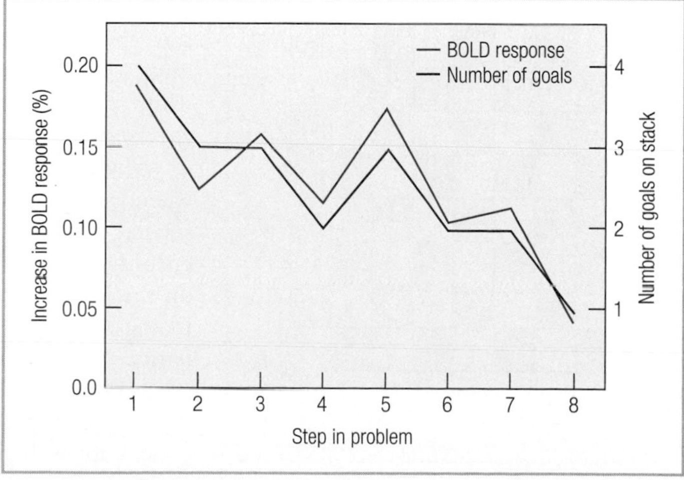

FIGURE 8.12 Results from a study by Fincham et al. to examine brain activation as a function of steps while solving a Tower of Hanoi problem. The red line shows the magnitude of fMRI BOLD response in a region in the right, anterior, dorsolateral prefrontal cortex during a sequence of eight problem-solving steps in which the number of goals being held varied from 1 to 4. The black shows the number of goals being held at each point. (Data from Fincham et al., 2002.)

in the right, anterior, dorsolateral prefrontal cortex during a sequence of eight problem-solving steps in which the number of goals being held varied from 1 to 4. It also shows the number of goals being held at each point. There seems to be a striking match between the goal load and the magnitude of the fMRI response.

The prefrontal cortex plays a critical role in maintaining goal structures.

Problem Representation

The Importance of the Correct Representation

We have analyzed a problem solution as consisting of problem states and operators for changing states. So far, we have discussed problem solving as if the only tasks involved were to acquire operators and select the appropriate ones. However, there are also important effects of how one represents the problem. A famous example illustrating the importance of representation is the mutilated-checkerboard problem (Kaplan & Simon, 1990). Suppose we have a checkerboard from which two diagonally opposite corner squares have been cut out. Figure 8.13 illustrates this mutilated checkerboard, on which 62 squares remain. Now suppose that we have 31 dominoes, each of which covers exactly two squares of the board. Can you find some way of arranging these 31 dominoes on the board so that they cover all 62 squares? If it can be done, explain how. If it cannot be done, prove that it cannot. Perhaps you would like to ponder this problem before reading on. Relatively few people are able to solve it without some hints, and very few see the answer quickly.

FIGURE 8.13 The mutilated checkerboard used in the problem posed by Kaplan and Simon (1990) to illustrate the importance of representation. (After Wickelgren, 1974. Adapted by permission of the publisher. © 1974 by W. H. Freeman and Company.)

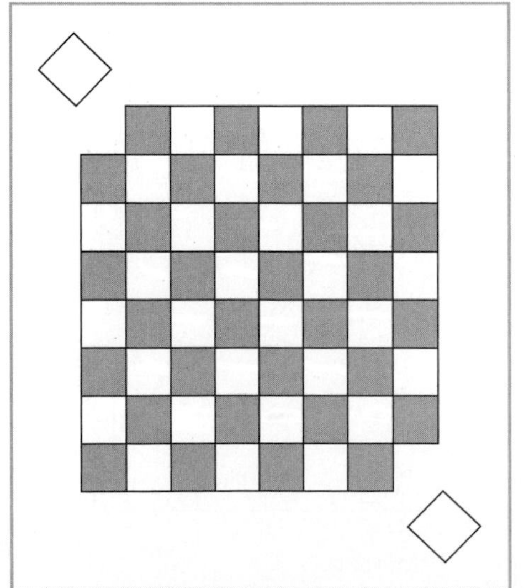

The answer is that the checkerboard cannot be covered by the dominoes. The trick to seeing this is to include in your representation of the problem the fact that each domino must cover one black and one white square, not just any two squares. There is just no way to place a domino on two squares of the checkerboard without having it cover one black and one white square. So with 31 dominoes, we can cover 31 black squares and 31 white squares. But the mutilation has removed two white squares. Thus, there are 30 white squares and 32 black squares. It follows that the mutilated checkerboard cannot be covered by 31 dominoes.

Why is the mutilated-checkerboard problem easier to solve when we represent each domino as covering a white and a black square? The answer is that in so representing the problem, we are encouraged to compare the number of white and black squares on the board. Thus, the effect of the problem representation is that it allows the critical operators to apply (i.e., checking for parity).

Another problem that depends on correct representation is the 27-apples problem. Imagine 27 apples packed together in a crate 3 apples high, 3 apples wide, and 3 apples deep. A worm is in the center apple. Its life's ambition is to eat its way through all the apples in the crate, but it does not want to waste time by visiting any apple twice. The worm can move from apple to apple only by going from the side of one into the side of another. This means it can move only into the apples directly above, below, or beside it. It cannot move diagonally. Can you find some path by which the worm, starting from the center apple, can reach all the apples without going through any apple twice? If not, can you prove it is impossible? The solution is left to you. (*Hint:* The solution is based on a partial 3-D analogy to the solution for the mutilated-checkerboard problem; it is given in the appendix at the end of the chapter.) Inappropriate problem representations often cause students to fail to solve problems even though they have been taught the appropriate knowledge. This fact often frustrates teachers. Bassok (1990) and Bassok and Holyoak (1989) studied high-school students who had learned to solve such physics problems as the following:

> What is the acceleration (increase in speed each second) of a train, if its speed increases uniformly from 15 m/s at the beginning of the 1st second, to 45 m/s at the end of the 12th second?

Students were taught such physics problems and became very effective at solving them. However, they had very little success in transferring that knowledge to solving such algebra problems as this one:

> Juanita went to work as a teller in a bank at a salary of $12,400 per year and received constant yearly increases, coming up with a $16,000 salary during her 13th year of work. What was her yearly salary increase?

The students failed to see that their experience with the physics problems was relevant to solving such algebra problems, which actually have the same structure. This happened because students did not appreciate that knowledge associated with continuous quantities such as speed (m/s) was relevant to problems posed in terms of discrete quantities such as dollars.

- *Successful problem solving depends on representing problems in such a way that appropriate operators can be seen to apply.*

Functional Fixedness

Sometimes solutions to problems depend on the solver's ability to represent the objects in his or her environment in novel ways. This fact has been demonstrated in a series of studies by different experimenters. A typical experiment in the series is the two-string problem of Maier (1931), illustrated in Figure 8.14. Two strings hanging from the ceiling are to be tied together, but they are so far apart that the participant cannot grasp both at once. Among the objects in the room are a chair and a pair of pliers. Participants try various solutions involving the chair, but these do not work. The only solution that works is to tie the pliers to one string and set that string swinging like a pendulum; then get the second string, bring it to the center of the room, and wait for the first string to swing close enough to grasp. Only 39% of Maier's participants were able to see this solution within 10 minutes. The difficulty is that the participants did not

FIGURE 8.14 The two-string problem used by Maier to demonstrate functional fixedness. Only 39% of Maier's participants were able to see the solution within 10 minutes. A large majority of the participants did not perceive the pliers as a weight that could be used as a pendulum. (After Maier, 1931. Adapted by permission of the publisher. © 1931 by the *Journal of Comparative Psychology*.)

perceive the pliers as a weight that could be used as a pendulum. This phenomenon is called **functional fixedness.** It is so named because people are fixed on representing an object according to its conventional function and fail to represent its novel function.

Another demonstration of functional fixedness is an experiment by Duncker (1945). The task he posed to participants was to support a candle on a door, ostensibly for an experiment on vision. The problem is illustrated in Figure 8.15. On the table are a box of tacks, some matches, and the candle. The solution is to tack the box to the door and use the box as a platform for the candle. This task is difficult because participants see the box as a container, not as a platform. They have greater difficulty with the task if the box is filled with tacks, reinforcing the perception of the box as a container.

These demonstrations of functional fixedness are consistent with the interpretation that representation has an effect on operator selection. For instance, to solve Duncker's candle problem, participants needed to represent the tack box in such a way that it could be used by the problem-solving operators that were

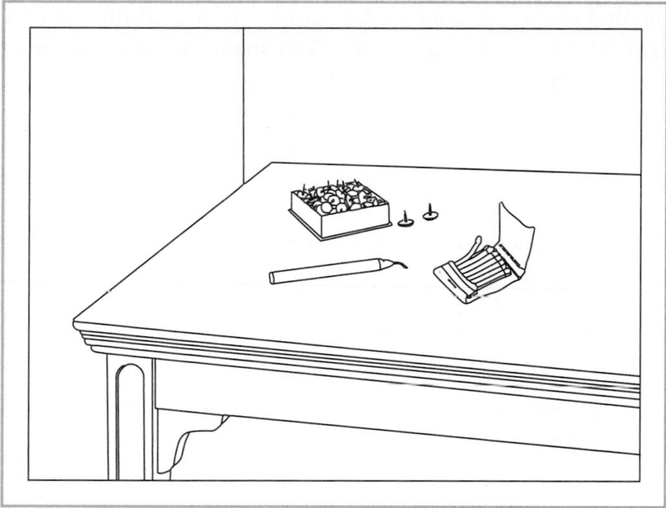

FIGURE 8.15 The candle problem used by Duncker (1945) in another study of functional fixedness. (After Glucksberg & Weisberg, 1966. Adapted by permission of the publisher. Copyright © 1966 by the American Psychological Association.)

looking for a support for the candle. When the box was conceived of as a container and not as a support, it was not available to the support-seeking operators.

- *Functional fixedness refers to people's tendency to see objects as serving conventional problem-solving functions and thus failing to see possible novel functions.*

Set Effects

People can become biased to prefer certain operators when solving a problem by their experiences. Such biasing of the problem solution is referred to as a **set effect.** A good illustration involves the water jug problem studied by Luchins (1942) and Luchins and Luchins (1959). In these water jug problems—which are different from the Atwood and Polson (1976) problem shown in Figure 8.8—participants were given a set of jugs of various capacities and an unlimited water supply. The task was to measure out a specified quantity of water. Two examples are given below:

Problem	Capacity of Jug *A*	Capacity of Jug *B*	Capacity of Jug *C*	Desired Quantity
1	5 cups	40 cups	18 cups	28 cups
2	21 cups	127 cups	3 cups	100 cups

Assume that participants have a tap and a sink so that they can fill jugs and empty them. The jugs start out empty. Participants are allowed only to fill the jugs to capacity, empty them completely, and pour water from one jug to another. In problem 1, participants are told that they have three jugs: jug *A*, with a capacity of 5 cups; jug *B*, with a capacity of 40 cups; and jug *C*, with a capacity of 18 cups. To solve this problem, participants would fill jug *A* and pour it into *B*, fill *A* again and pour it into *B*, and fill *C* and pour it into *B*. The solution to this problem is denoted by $2A + C$. The solution for the second problem is to fill jug *B* with 127 cups; fill *A* from *B* so that 106 cups are left in *B;* fill *C* from *B* so that 103 cups are left in *B;* empty *C;* and fill *C* again from *B* so that the goal of 100 cups in jug *B* is achieved. The solution to this problem can be denoted by $B - A - 2C$. The first solution is called an addition solution because it involves adding the contents of the jugs together; the second is called a subtraction solution because it involves subtracting the contents of one jug from another. Luchins first gave participants a series of problems that all could be solved by addition, thus creating an "addition set." These participants then solved new addition problems faster, and subtraction problems slower, than control participants who had no practice.

The set effect that Luchins (1942) is most famous for demonstrating is the **Einstellung effect,** or *mechanization of thought,* which is illustrated by the series of problems shown in Table 8.3. Participants were given these problems in this order and were required to find solutions for each. Take time out from reading this text and try to solve each problem.

All problems except number 8 can be solved by using a $B - 2C - A$ method (i.e., filling *B,* twice pouring *B* into *C,* and once pouring *B* into *A*). For problems 1 through 5, this solution is the simplest; but for problems 7 and 9, the simpler

TABLE 8.3

Luchins's Water Jug Problems Used to Illustrate the Set Effect

	Capacity (cups)			
Problem	Jug *A*	Jug *B*	Jug *C*	Desired Quantity
1	21	127	3	100
2	14	163	25	99
3	18	43	10	5
4	9	42	6	21
5	20	59	4	31
6	23	49	3	20
7	15	39	3	18
8	28	76	3	25
9	18	48	4	22
10	14	36	8	6

After Luchins (1942). Adapted by permission of the publisher. © 1942 by *Psychological Monographs.*

solution of $A + C$ also applies. Problem 8 cannot be solved by the $B - 2C - A$ method but can be solved by the simpler solution of $A - C$. Problems 6 and 10 are also solved more simply by $A - C$ than by $B - 2C - A$. Of Luchins's participants who received the whole setup of 10 problems, 83% used the $B - 2C - A$ method on problems 6 and 7, 64% failed to solve problem 8, and 79% used the $B - 2C - A$ method for problems 9 and 10. The performance of participants who worked on all 10 problems was compared with that of control participants who saw only the last 5 problems. These control participants did not see the biasing $B - 2C - A$ problems. Fewer than 1% of the control participants used $B - 2C - A$ solutions, and only 5% failed to solve problem 8. Thus, the first 5 problems created a powerful bias for a particular solution. This bias hurt the solution of problems 6 through 10. Although these effects are quite dramatic, they are relatively easy to reverse with the exercise of cognitive control. Luchins found that simply warning participants by saying, "Don't be blind" after problem 5 allowed more than 50% of them to overcome the set for the $B - 2C - A$ solution.

Another kind of set effect in problem solving has to do with the influence of general semantic factors. This effect is well illustrated in the experiment of Safren (1962) on anagram solutions. Safren presented participants with lists such as the following, in which each set of letters was to be unscrambled and made into a word:

kmli graus teews recma foefce ikrdn

This is an example of an organized list, in which the individual words are all associated with drinking coffee. Safren compared solution times for organized lists with times for unorganized lists. Median solution time was 12.2 s for anagrams from unorganized lists and 7.4 s for anagrams from organized lists. Presumably, the facilitation evident with the organized lists occurred because the earlier items in the list associatively primed, and so made more available, the later words. Note that this anagram experiment contrasts with the water jug experiment in that no particular procedure was being strengthened. Rather, what was being strengthened was part of the participant's factual (declarative) knowledge about spellings of associatively related words.

In general, set effects occur when some knowledge structures become more available than others. These structures can be either procedures, as in the water jug problem, or declarative information, as in the anagram problem. If the available knowledge is what participants need to solve the problem, their problem solving will be facilitated. If the available knowledge is not what is needed, problem solving will be inhibited. It is good to realize that sometimes set effects can be dissipated easily (as with Luchins's "Don't be blind" instruction). If you find yourself stuck on a problem and you keep generating similar unsuccessful approaches, it is often useful to force yourself to back off, change set, and try a different kind of solution.

- *Set effects result when the knowledge relevant to a particular type of problem solution is strengthened.*

Incubation Effects

People often report that after trying to solve a problem and getting nowhere, they can put it aside for hours, days, or weeks and then, upon returning to it, can see the solution quickly. Many examples of this pattern were reported by the famous French mathematician Poincaré (1929), including, for instance, the following:

> Then I turned my attention to the study of some arithmetical questions apparently without much success and without a suspicion of any connection with my preceding researches. Disgusted with my failure, I went to spend a few days at the seaside, and thought of something else. One morning, walking on the bluff, the idea came to me, with just the same characteristics of brevity, suddenness, and immediate certainty, that the arithmetic transformations of indeterminate ternary quadratic forms were identical with those of non-Euclidean geometry. (p. 388)

Such phenomena are called **incubation effects.**

An incubation effect was nicely demonstrated in an experiment by Silveira (1971). The problem she posed to participants, called the cheap-necklace problem, is illustrated in Figure 8.16. Participants were given the following instructions:

> You are given four separate pieces of chain that are each three links in length. It costs 2¢ to open a link and 3¢ to close a link. All links are closed at the beginning of the problem. Your goal is to join all 12 links of chain into a single circle at a cost of no more than 15¢.

Try to solve this problem yourself. (A solution is provided in the appendix at the end of this chapter.) Silveira tested three groups. A control group worked on the problem for half an hour; 55% of these participants solved the problem. For one experimental group, the half hour spent on the problem was interrupted by a half-hour break in which the participants did other activities; 64% of these participants solved the problem. A second experimental group had a 4-hour break, and 85% of these participants solved the problem. Silveira required her participants to speak aloud as they solved the cheap-necklace problem. She found that they did not come back to the problem after a break with solutions completely worked out. Rather, they began by trying to solve the problem much as before. This result is evidence against a common misbelief that people are subconsciously solving the problem in the period that they are away from it.

FIGURE 8.16 The cheap-necklace problem used by Silveira (1971) to investigate the incubation effect. (After Wickelgren, 1974. Adapted by permission of the publisher. © 1974 by W. H. Freeman.)

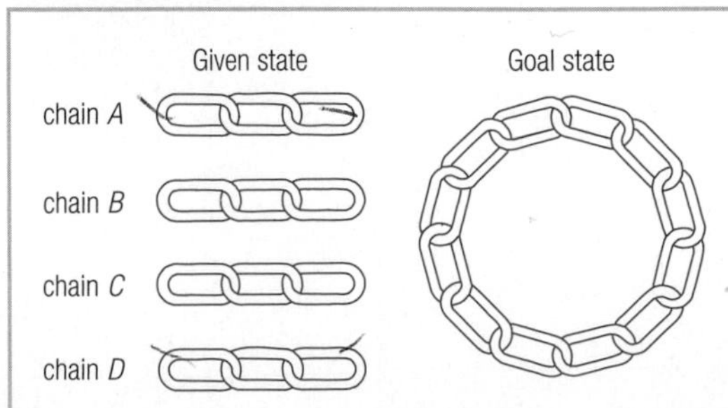

The best explanation for incubation effects relates them to set effects. During initial attempts to solve a problem, people set themselves to think about the problem in certain ways and bring to bear certain knowledge structures. If this initial set is appropriate, they will solve the problem. If the initial set is not appropriate, however, they will be stuck throughout the session with inappropriate procedures. Going away from the problem allows activation of the

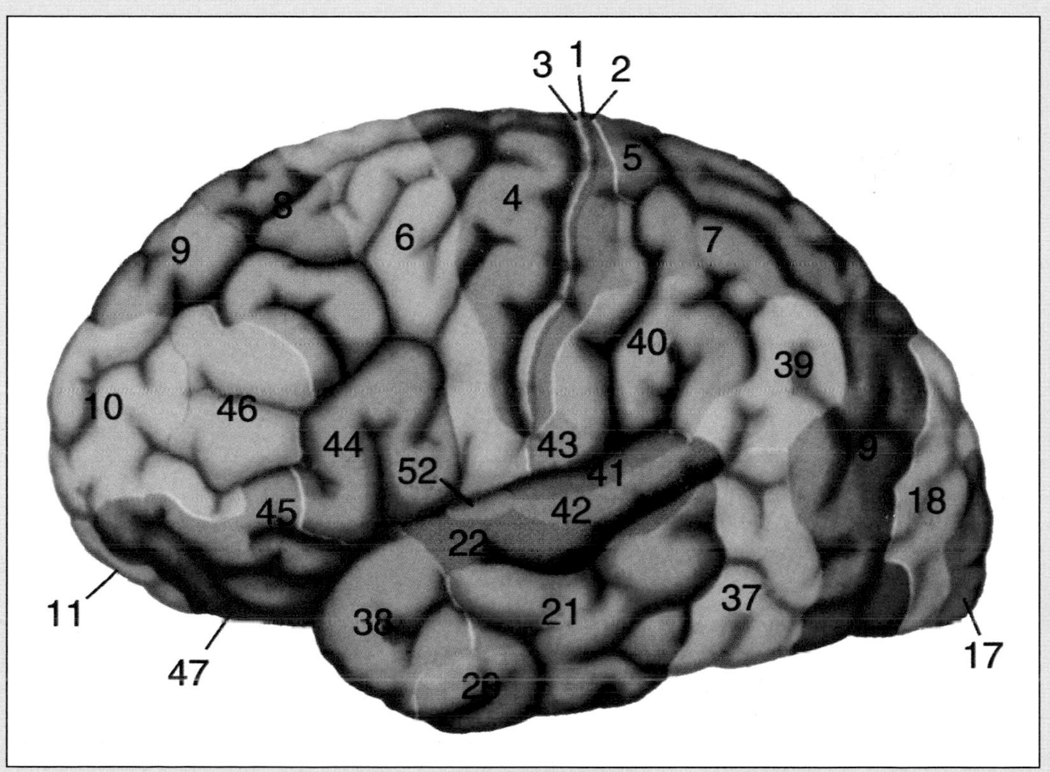

COLOR PLATE 1.1 *Brodmann identified 52 distinct regions of the cerebral cortex based on cell structure and arrangement.*

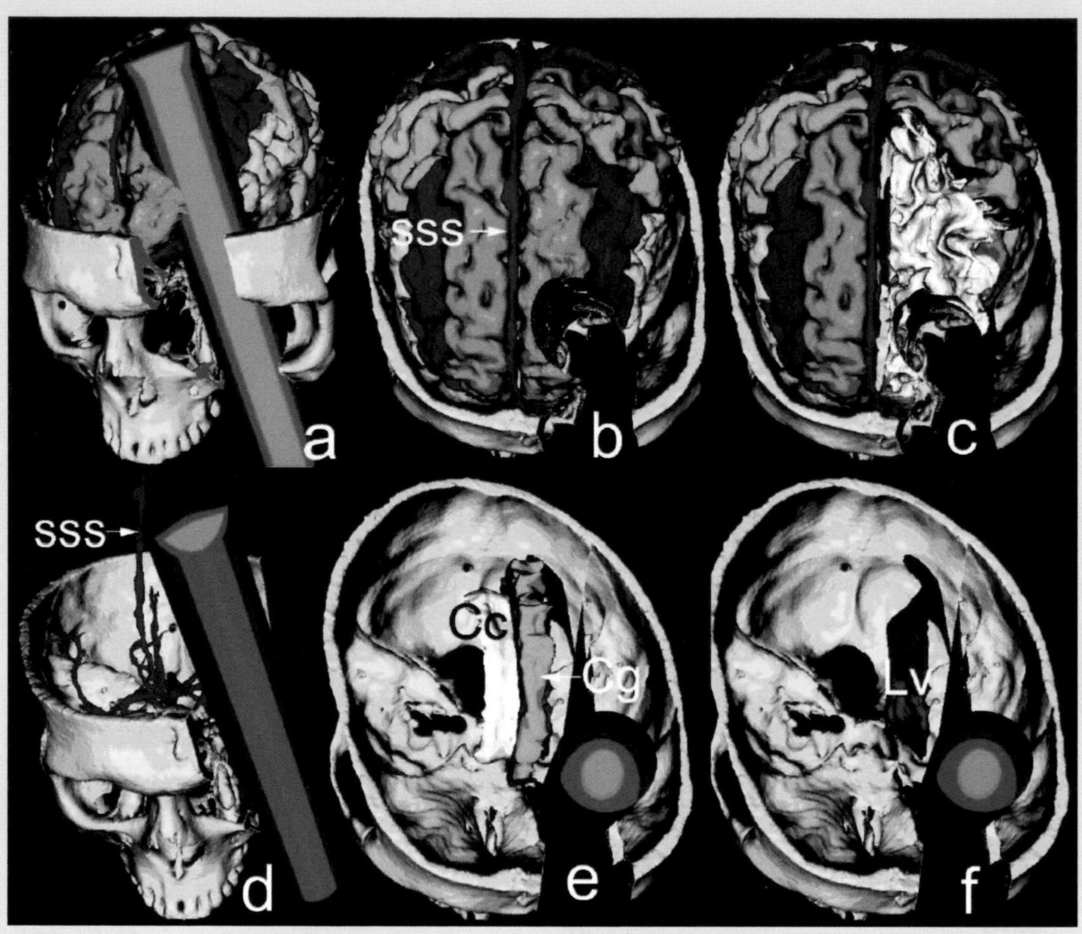

COLOR PLATE 11.1 *Computer-generated models of Phineas Gage's lesions. (a) The tamping iron* in situ. *(b) The volume of the tamping iron subtracted from the model of the brain. SSS, superior sagittal sinus. (c) The model of the gray matter removed, for visualization of the white matter. (d) Relation of the tamping iron with the SSS and other blood vessels. (e) Relation of the tamping iron with the cingulate gyrus (Cg). (f) Relation of the tamping iron with the left lateral ventricle.*

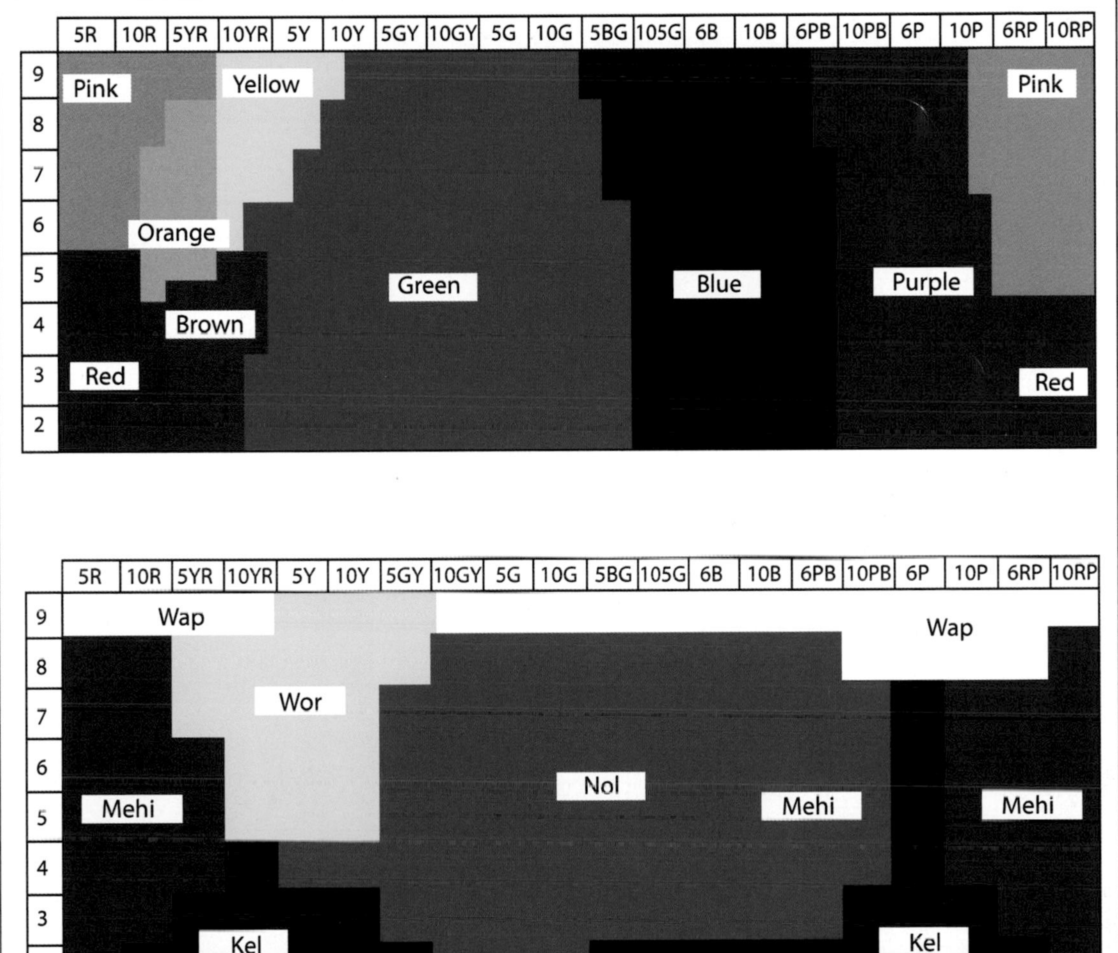

O *COLOR PLATE 12.1 Representation of 160 colors varying in hue (horizontal axis) and brightness (vertical axis). (a) How English speakers divide up the color spectrum and (b) how Berinmo speakers divide up the color spectrum. (From Kay & Regier, 2006.) The space associated with each color is illustrated with the best instance of that color.*

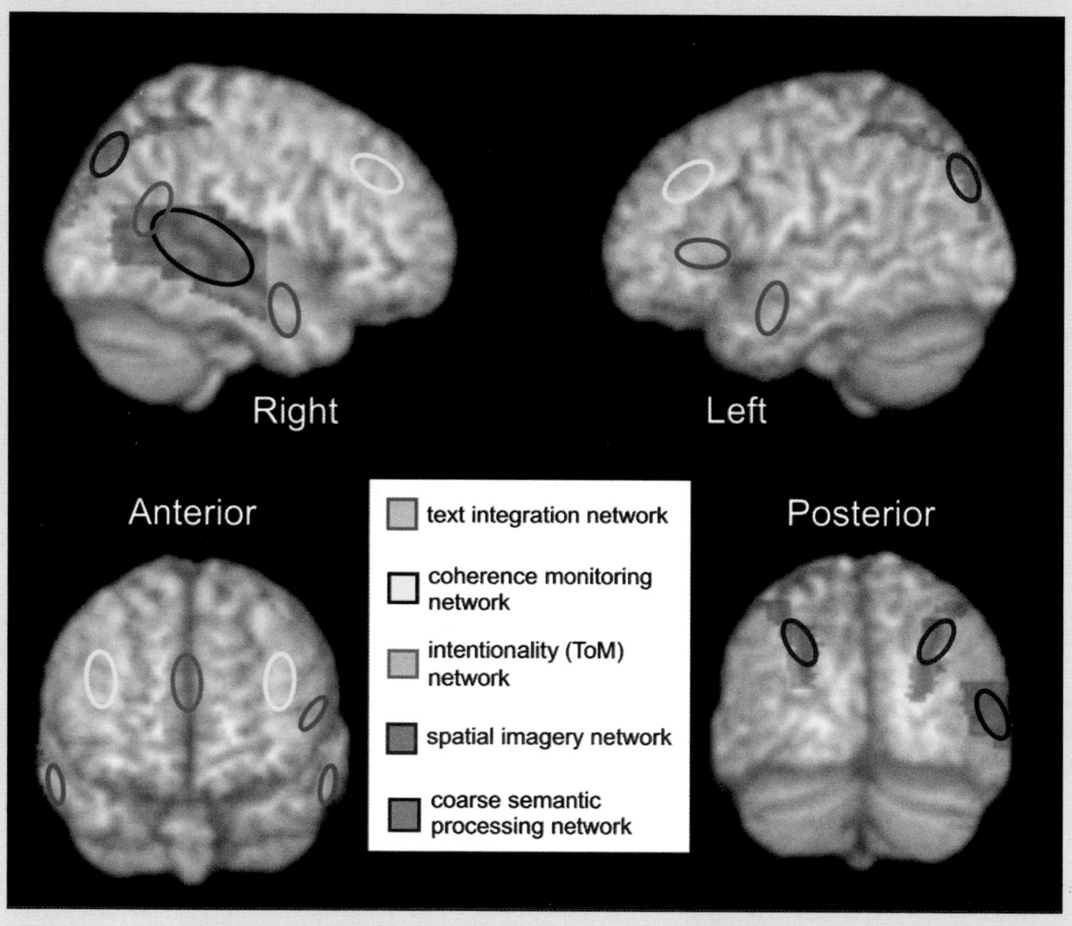

COLOR PLATE 13.1 A schematic representation of the Parallel Networks of Discourse. Shaded regions represent surface rendered anatomical regions as described in the text. A rough localization within anatomical regions is represented by colored ellipses.

insight problems, participants had little idea they were close to a solution, even 15 s before they actually solved the problem. Metcalfe and Wiebe suggested that we use this difference as a definition of insight problems. That is, an **insight problem** is one in which people are not aware that they are close to a solution.

This definition would seem to support the notion that a solution comes in a single moment. However, what Metcalfe and Wiebe actually showed was that participants did not know when they were close to a solution to an insight problem. They did not show that the solution came in a single moment. Kaplan and Simon (1990) studied participants while they solved the mutilated-checkerboard problem (see Figure 8.13), which is another insight problem. They found that some participants noticed key features of the solution to the problem—such as that a domino covers one square of each color—early on. Sometimes, though, these participants did not judge those features to be critical and went off and tried other methods of solution; only later did they come back to the key feature. So, it is not that solutions to insight problems cannot come in pieces, but rather that participants do not recognize which pieces are key until they see the final solution. It reminds me of the time I tried to find my way through a maze, cut off from all cues as to where the exit was. I searched for a very long time, was quite frustrated, and was wondering if I was ever going to get out—and then I made a turn and there was the exit. I believe I even exclaimed, "Aha!" It was not that I solved the maze in a single turn; it was that I did not appreciate which turns were on the way to the solution until I made that final turn.

Sometimes, insight problems require only a single step (or turn) to solve, and it is just a matter of finding that step. What is so difficult about these problems is just finding that one step, which can be a bit like trying to find a needle in a haystack. As an example of such a problem, consider the following:

What is greater than God

More evil than the Devil

The poor have it

The rich want it

And if you eat it, you'll die.

Reportedly, schoolchildren find this problem easier than college undergraduates. If so, it is because they consider fewer possibilities as an answer. (If you are frustrated and cannot solve this problem, it turns out that, like many things, one can find the answer by searching the Web—many people have posted this problem on their Web pages.)

As a final example of insight problems consider the remote association problems introduced by Mednick (1962). In one version of these problems (Mednick, 1962), participants are asked to find some word that can be combined with three words to make a compound word. So, for instance, given *fox, man,* and *peep,* the solution is *hole* (*foxhole, manhole, peephole*). Here are a inappropriate knowledge structures to dissipate, and people are able to take a fresh approach.

The basic argument is that incubation effects occur because people "forget" inappropriate ways of solving problems. Smith and Blakenship (1989, 1991) performed a fairly direct test of this hypothesis. They had participants solve problems like those shown in Figure 8.17. They provided half of their participants, the fixation group, with inappropriate ways to think about the problems. For instance, with respect to the third problem, they told participants to think about chemicals. Thus, in the fixation condition, they deliberately induced incorrect sets. Not surprisingly, the fixation participants solved fewer of the problems than the control participants. The interesting issue, however, was how much incubation effect these two populations of participants showed. Half of both the fixation and control participants worked on the problems for a continuous period of time, whereas the other half had an incubation period inserted in the middle of their problem-solving efforts. The fixation participants showed a greater benefit of the incubation period. Thus, Smith and Blakenship were able to show greater incubation effect in participants who had started with an inappropriate way of solving the problem. Also, when they asked the fixation participants what the misleading clue had been, they found that more of the participants who had an incubation period had forgotten the inappropriate clue.

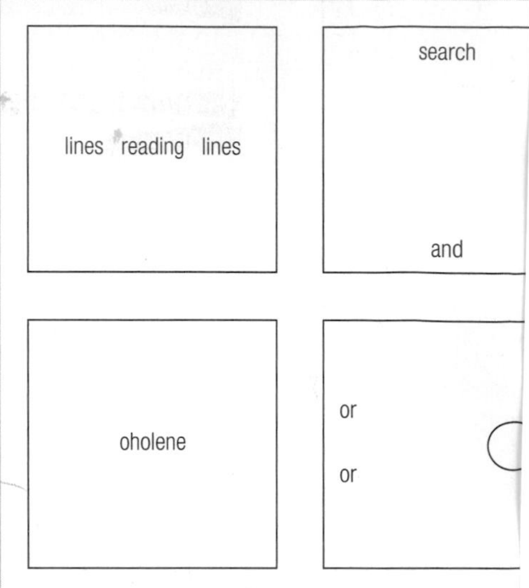

FIGURE 8.17 Puzzles used by Smith and Blakenship the hypothesis that incubation effects occur becaus "forget" inappropriate ways of solving problems. Par had to figure out what familiar phrase was represent each image. For example, the first picture represents phrase "reading between the lines"; the second, "sea and low"; the third, "a hole in one"; the fourth "doub nothing." (After Smith & Blakenship, 1989, 1991. Adapted by permi of the publishers. © 1989 by the *Bulletin of the Psychonomic Society* by the *American Journal of Psychology*.)

Incubation effects occur when people forget the inappropriate strategies they were using to solve a problem.

Insight

A common misbelief about learning and problem solving is that there are magical moments of insight when everything falls into place and we suddenly see a solution. This is called the "aha" experience, and many of us can report uttering that very exclamation after a long struggle with a problem that we suddenly solve. The incubation effects just discussed have been used to argue that the subconscious is deriving this insight during the incubation period. As we saw, however, what really happens is that participants simply let go of poor ways of solving problems.

Metcalfe and Wiebe (1987) came up with an interesting way to define insight problems. The insight problems they used included ones like the cheap-necklace problem (see Figure 8.16). Their noninsight problems required multistep solutions, as in the Tower of Hanoi problem (see Figure 8.10). They asked participants to judge every 15 s how close they felt they were to the solution. Fifteen seconds before they actually solved a noninsight problem, participants were fairly confident they were close to a solution. In contrast, on the

number of problems for you to try (the solutions are given in the appendix):

print/berry/bird

dress/dial/flower

pine/crab/sauce

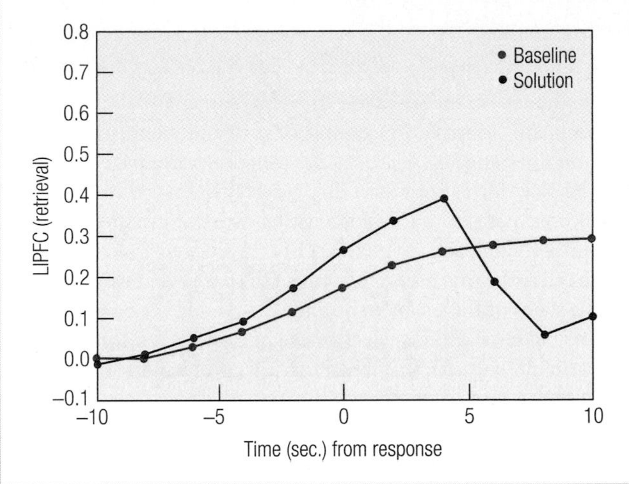

FIGURE 8.18 A comparison of brain activity for successful and unsuccessful attempts to solve a remote association problem. The activity plotted is from a prefrontal region that is sensitive to retrieval. Activity increases with increasing time on task but drops off for successful problems shortly after the solution (at time 0).

Studies of brain activity (Jung-Beeman et al., 2004) have been conducted while people try to solve these problems. Characteristic of insight problems, people often get a sudden feeling of insight when they solve them. Figure 8.18 shows the imaging results from our laboratory, which say a lot about what is happening. The region is plotting activity in the left prefrontal region whose activity has been associated with retrieval from declarative memory (e.g., Figures 1.16c, 7.6). The figure compares activity in cases where participants are able to solve the problem with cases where they are not. Time 0 in the figure marks the point where the solution was obtained in the successful case. Both functions for the successful and unsuccessful cases are increasing, reflecting increasing effort as the search progresses, but there is an abrupt drop (time-lagged as we would expect with the BOLD response) after the insight. It should be emphasized that other regions such as the motor region show a rise at this point associated with the generation of the response. In dropping off, the prefrontal is showing a strikingly different response compared to other brain regions and is reflecting the end to the search of memory for the answer. The participant had been trying retrieval after retrieval and finally retrieved the right answer. The feeling of insight corresponds to the moment when retrieval finally succeeds and activity drops in the retrieval area.

- *Insight problems are ones in which solvers cannot recognize when they are getting close to the solution.*

Conclusions

This chapter has been built around the Newell and Simon model of problem solving as a search through a state space defined by operators. We have looked at problem-solving success as determined by the operators available and the methods used to guide the search for operators. This analysis is particularly appropriate for first-time problems, whether a chimpanzee's quandary (see Figure 8.2) or a human's predicament when shown a Tower of Hanoi problem for the first time (see Figure 8.10). The next chapter will focus on the other factors that come into play with repeated problem-solving practice.

Questions for Thought

1. Recent research (e.g., Pizlo et al., 2006) has been conducted on the so-called "traveling salesman problem." To make an example of such a problem, put a number of dots (say, 10 to 20) randomly on a page and pick one as your start dot. Now try to draw the shortest path from this dot, visiting each dot just once and arriving back at your start dot. If you were to characterize this problem as a search space, what would the states of the problem be and what would the operators be? How do you select among the operators? Is this particularly useful to characterize this problem in terms of such a search space?
2. In the modern world, humans frequently want to learn how to use devices like microwaves or software such as a spreadsheet package. When do you try to learn these things by discovery, by following an example, and by following instructions? How often are your learning experiences a mixture of these modes of learning?
3. A common goal for students is getting a good grade in a course. There are many different things that you can do to try to improve your grade. How do you select among them? When are you engaged in hill climbing and when are you engaged in means-ends analysis?
4. Figure 8.19 illustrates the nine-dots problem (Maier, 1931). The problem is to connect all 9 dots by drawing 4 lines, never lifting your pen from the page. Summarizing a variety of studies, Kershaw and Ohlsson (2001) report that given only a few minutes, only 5% of undergraduates can solve this problem. Try to solve this problem. If you get frustrated, you can find an answer by Googling "nine-dots problem." After you have tried to solve the problem, use the terminology (see below) of this chapter to describe the nature of the difficulties posed by this problem and what people need to do to successfully solve this problem.

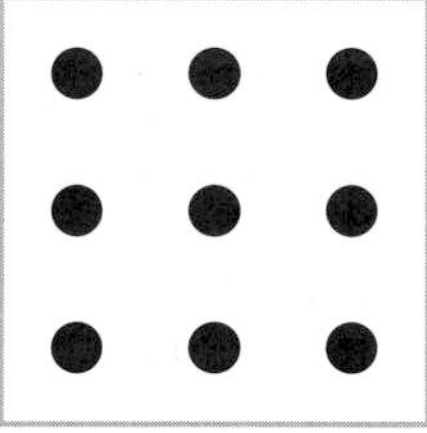

FIGURE 8.19 The nine-dots problem.

Key Terms

analogy
backup avoidance
difference reductions
Einstellung effect
functional fixedness
General Problem Solver (GPS)
goal state
hill climbing
incubation effect
insight problem
means-ends analysis
operator
problem space
search
search tree
set effect
state
subgoal
Tower of Hanoi problem

Appendix: Solutions

Figure A8.1 gives the minimum-path solution to the problem solved less efficiently in Figure 8.3.

With regard to the problem of the 27 apples, the worm cannot succeed. To see that this is the case, imagine that the apples alternate in color, green and red, in a 3-D checkerboard pattern. If the center apple from which the worm starts is red, there are 13 red apples and 14 green apples in all. Each time the worm moves from one apple to another, it will be changing colors. Because

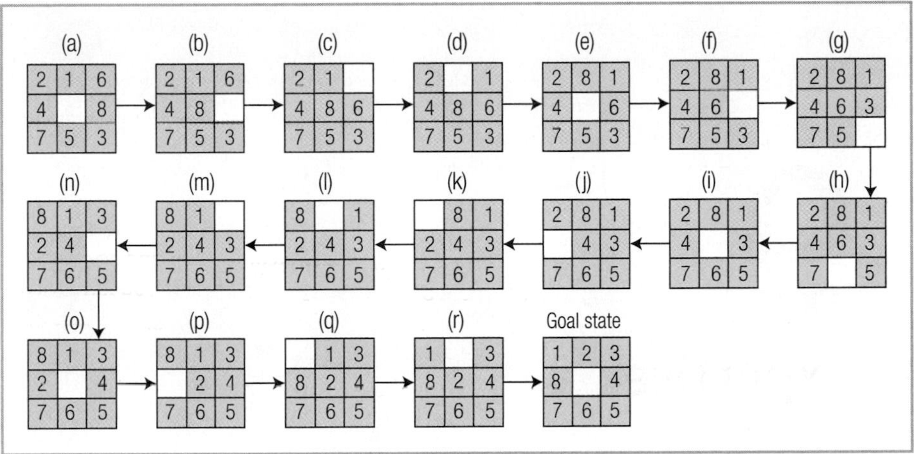

FIGURE A8.1 The minimum-path solution for the eight-tile problem that was solved less efficiently in Figure 8.3.

the worm starts from a red apple, it cannot reach more green apples than red apples. Thus, it cannot visit all 14 green apples if it also visits each of the 13 red apples just once.

To solve the cheap-necklace problem shown in Figure 8.16, open all three links in one chain (at a cost of 6¢) and then use the three open links to connect the remaining three chains (at a cost of 9¢).

The solutions to the three remote association problems are blue, sun, and apple.

9

Expertise

It has been speculated that the expansion of the human brain from *Homo erectus* to modern *Homo sapiens* was driven by the need to acquire expertise in novel environments (Skoyles, 1999). This ability allowed humans to spread throughout the world and permitted the development of the technology that has created modern civilization. Humans are the only species that display this kind of behavioral plasticity—being able to become experts at driving a car in modern society, navigating the oceans in Polynesian society, or designing search engines for the World Wide Web. William G. Chase, late of Carnegie Mellon University, was one of our local experts on human expertise. He emphasized two famous mottos that summarize much of the nature of expertise and its development:

- No pain, no gain.
- When the going gets tough, the tough get going.

The first motto refers to the fact that no one develops expertise without a great deal of hard work. John R. Hayes (1985), another Carnegie Mellon faculty member, has studied geniuses in fields varying from music to science to chess. He found that no one reached genius levels of performance without at least 10 years of practice. Chase's second motto refers to the fact that the difference between relative novices and relative experts increases as we look at more difficult problems. For instance, there are many chess duffers who could play a credible, if losing, game against a master when they are given unlimited time to choose moves. However, they would lose embarrassingly if forced to play lightning chess, where they are permitted only 5 s per move.

Chapter 8 reviewed some of the general principles governing problem solving, particularly in novel domains. This research has provided a framework for analyzing the development of expertise in problem solving. Research on expertise has been a major development in cognitive science in the past 30 years. This research is particularly exciting because it has important contributions to make to the instruction of technical or formal skills in areas such as mathematics, science, and engineering, as will be reviewed at the end of this chapter.

This chapter will address the following questions about the nature of human expertise:

- What are the stages in the development of expertise?
- How does the organization of a skill change as one becomes expert?
- What are the contributions of practice versus talent to the development of skill?
- How much can skill in one domain transfer to a new domain?
- What are the implications of our knowledge about expertise for teaching new skills?

Brain Changes with Skill Acquisition

As people become more proficient at a task, they seem to use less of their brains to perform that task. Figure 9.1 shows fMRI some data from Qin et al. (2003) looking at areas of the brain activated as college students learned to perform derivations in a new synthetic domain of mathematics. Figure 9.1a shows the regions activated on their first day of doing the task and Figure 9.1b shows the regions activated on the fifth day. As the students achieved greater efficiency in the performance of the task, regions of activity dropped out or shrank. These regions of activity correspond to metabolic expenditure, and it is quite apparent that, with expertise, we spend less mental energy doing these tasks.

A general goal of research on expertise is to characterize both the qualitative and the quantitative changes that take place with expertise. The result in Figure 9.1 can be considered a quantitative result—more practice means more efficient mental execution. We will look at a number of quantitative measures, particularly latency, that indicate this increased efficiency. However, there are also qualitative changes in how a skill is performed with practice. Figure 9.1 does not reveal such changes—in this study, it just seems that fewer areas,

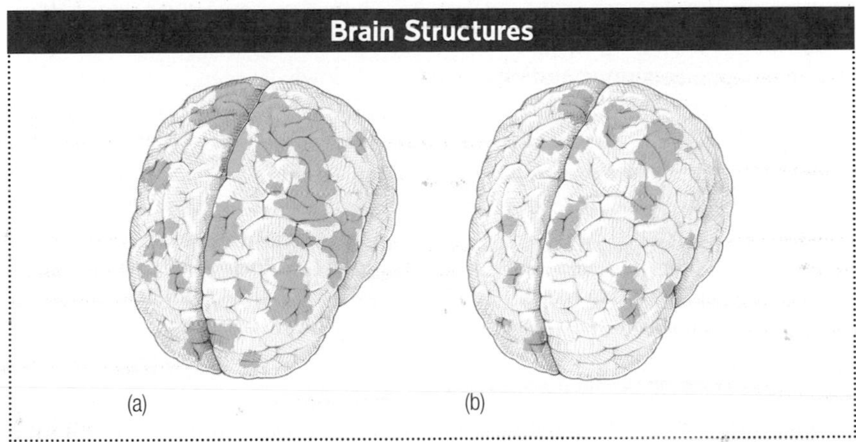

FIGURE 9.1 Regions activated in the symbol-manipulation task of Qin et al. (2003): (a) day 1 of practice; (b) day 5 of practice. Note that these images depict "transparent brains," and the activation that we see is not just on the surface but also below the surface.

rather than different areas, take part. However, this chapter will describe the results of other brain imaging and behavioral studies that indicate that, indeed, the way in which we perform a task can change as we become expert at it.

Through extensive practice, we can develop the high levels of expertise in novel domains that have supported the evolution of human civilization.

General Characteristics of Skill Acquisition

Three Stages of Skill Acquisition

The development of a skill typically comprises three stages (Anderson, 1983; Fitts & Posner, 1967). Fitts and Posner call the first stage the **cognitive stage.** In this stage, participants develop a declarative encoding (see the distinction between declarative and procedural representations at the end of Chapter 7) of the skill; that is, they commit to memory a set of facts relevant to the skill. Essentially these facts define the operators of the task (see Chapter 8). Learners typically rehearse these facts as they first perform the skill. For instance, when I was first learning to shift gears in a standard transmission car, I memorized the location of the gears (e.g., "reverse is up, left"—for an old 3-speed transmission) and the correct sequence of engaging the clutch and moving the stick shift. I rehearsed this information as I performed the skill.

The information that I had learned about the location and function of the gears amounted to a set of problem-solving operators for driving the car. For instance, if I wanted to get the car into reverse, there was the operator of moving the gear to the upper left. Despite the fact that the knowledge about what to do next was unambiguous, one would hardly have judged my driving performance as skilled. My use of the knowledge was very slow because that knowledge was still in a declarative form. I had to retrieve specific facts and interpret them to solve my driving problems. I did not have the knowledge in a procedural form.

The second stage of skill acquisition is called the **associative stage.** Two main things happen in this second stage. First, errors in the initial understanding are gradually detected and eliminated. So, I slowly learned to coordinate the release of the clutch in first gear with the application of gas so as not to kill the engine. Second, the connections among the various elements required for successful performance are strengthened. Thus, I no longer had to sit for a few seconds trying to remember how to get to second gear from first. Basically, the outcome of the associative stage is a successful procedure for performing the skill. However, it is not always the case that the procedural representation of the knowledge replaces the declarative. Sometimes, the two forms of knowledge can coexist side by side, as when we can speak a foreign language fluently and still remember many rules of grammar. However, the procedural, not the declarative, knowledge governs the skilled performance.

The third stage in the standard analysis of skill acquisition is the **autonomous stage.** In this stage, the procedure becomes more and more automated and rapid. The concept of automaticity was introduced in Chapter 3, where we discussed how central cognition drops out of performance of a task as we become more skilled at it. Complex skills such as driving a car or playing chess gradually evolve in the direction of becoming more automated and requiring fewer processing resources. For instance, driving a car can become so automatic that people will engage in conversation with no memory for the traffic that they have driven through.

- *The three stages of skill acquisition are the cognitive stage, the associative stage, and the autonomous stage.*

Power-Law Learning

Chapter 6 documented the way in which the retrieval of simple associations improved as a function of practice according to a power law. It turns out that the performance of complex skills, requiring the coordination of many such associations, also improves according to a power law. Figure 9.2 illustrates a well-known instance of such skill acquisition. This study followed the development of the cigar-making ability of a worker in a factory for 10 years. The figure plots the time to make a cigar against number of years of practice. Both scales use log-log coordinates to expose a power law (recall from Chapters 6 and 7 that a linear function on log-log coordinates implies a power function in the original scale). The data in this graph show an approximately linear function until

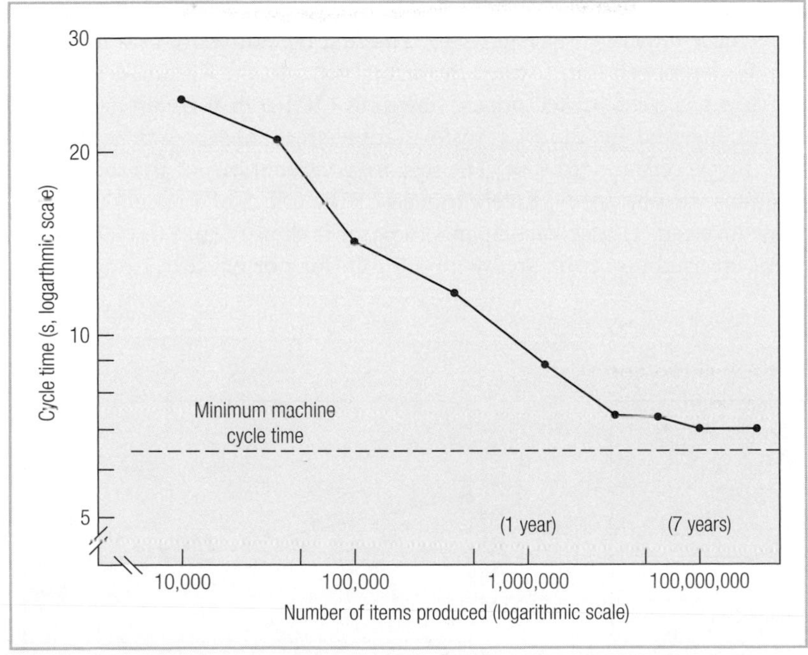

FIGURE 9.2 Time required to produce a cigar as a function of amount of experience. (From Crossman, 1959. Reprinted by permission from Taylor & Francis.)

about the fifth year, at which point the improvement appears to stop. It turns out that the worker was approaching the cycle time of the machinery and could improve no more. There is usually some limit to how much improvement can be achieved, determined by the equipment, the capability of a person's musculature, age, and so on. However, except for these physical limits, there is no limit on how much a skill can speed up. The time taken by the cognitive component of a skill will go to zero, given enough practice.

Recall from Chapter 6 that a linear relation between log time T and log practice P can be expressed as

$$\ln T = A - b \ln P$$

which can be transformed into

$$T = aP^{-b}$$

where $A = \ln a$. In Chapter 6, we considered such power functions in memory (see Figures 6.10 and 6.11). Basically, for these functions, the decrease in processing time with further practice becomes small very rapidly.

Effects of practice have also been studied in domains of complex problem solving, such as giving justifications for geometry-like proofs (Neves & Anderson, 1981). Figure 9.3 shows a power function for that domain, in both a normal scale and a log-log scale. Such functions illustrate that the benefit of further practice rapidly diminishes but that, no matter how much practice we have had, further practice will help a little.

Kolers (1979) investigated the acquisition of reading skills, by using materials such as those illustrated in Figure 9.4. The first type of text (N) is normal, but the others have been transformed in various ways. In the R transformation, the whole line has been turned upside down; in the I transformation, each letter has been inverted; in the M transformation, the sentence has been set as a mirror image of standard type. The rest are combinations of the several transformations. In one study, Kolers looked at the effect of massive practice on reading inverted (I) text. Participants took more than 16 min to read their first page of inverted text compared with 1.5 min for normal text. After the initial

FIGURE 9.3 Time taken to generate proofs in a geometry-like proof system as a function of the number of proofs already done: (a) function on a normal scale, $RT = 1{,}410P^{-.55}$; (b) function on a log-log scale.

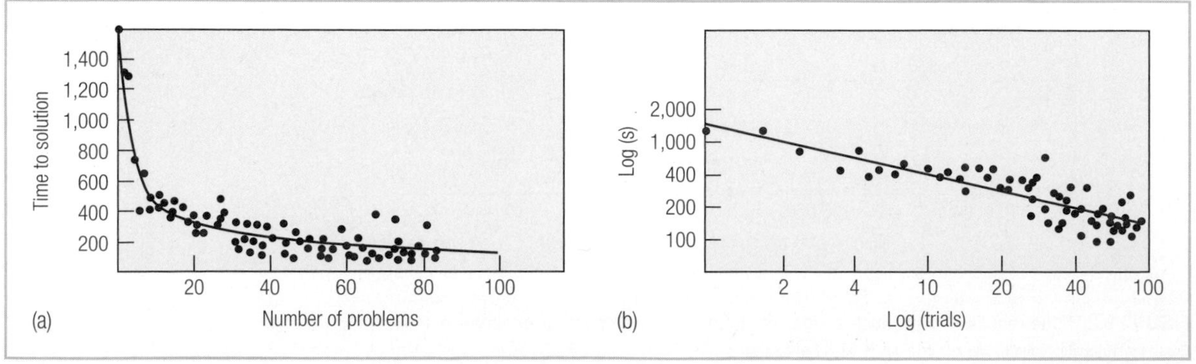

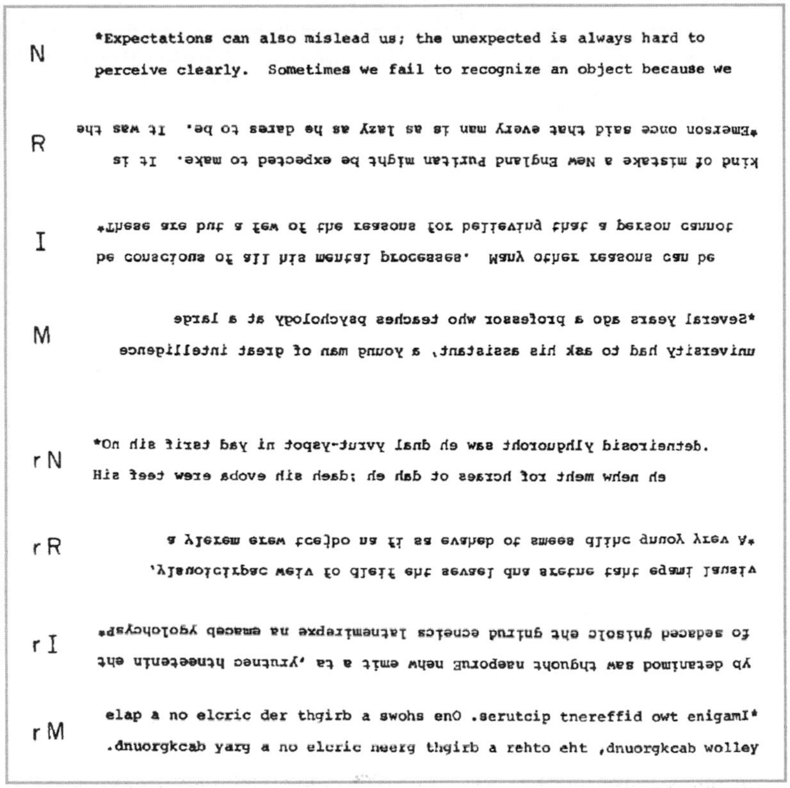

N
*Expectations can also mislead us; the unexpected is always hard to
perceive clearly. Sometimes we fail to recognize an object because we

R
*Emerson once said that every man is as lazy as he dares to be. It was the
kind of mistake a New England Puritan might be expected to make. It is

I
These are but a few of the reasons for believing that a person cannot*
be conscious of all his mental processes. Many other reasons can be

M
*Several years ago a professor who teaches psychology at a large
university had to ask his assistant, a young man of great intelligence

rN
*On his first day in topsy-turvy land he was thoroughly defeated.
His feet were above his head; he had to reach for them when he

rR
*A very young child seems to behave as if an object merely a
visual image that enters and leaves the field of view capriciously,

rI
*Psychology became an experimental science during the closing decades of
the nineteenth century, at a time when European thought was dominated by

rM
elap a no elcric der thgirb a swohs enO .serutcip tnereffid owt enigamI*
.dnuorgkcab yarg a no elcric neerg thgirb a rehto eht ,dnuorgkcab wolley

FIGURE 9.4 Examples of the spatially transformed texts used in Kolers's studies of the acquisition of reading skills. The asterisks indicate the starting point for reading. (From Kolers & Perkins, 1975.)

reading-speed test, participants practiced on 200 pages of inverted text. Figure 9.5 provides a log-log plot of reading time against amount of practice. In this figure, practice is measured as number of pages read. The change in speed with practice is given by the curve labeled "Original training on inverted text." Kolers interspersed a few tests on normal text; data for these tests are given by the curve labeled "Original tests on normal text." We see the same kind of improvement for inverted text as in Figures 9.2 and 9.3 (i.e., a straight-line function on a log-log plot). After reading 200 pages, Kolers's participants were reading at the rate of 1.6 min per page—almost the same rate as that of participants reading normal text.

A year later, Kolers had his participants read inverted text again. These data are given by the curve in Figure 9.5 labeled "Retraining on inverted text." Participants now took about 3 min to read the first page of the inverted text. Compared with their performance of 16 min on their first page a year earlier, participants displayed an enormous savings, but it was now taking them almost twice as long to read the text as it did after their 200 pages of training a year earlier. They had clearly forgotten something. As the Figure 9.5 illustrates, participants' improvement on the retraining trials showed a log-log relation between practice and performance, as had their original training. The same level of performance that participants had initially reached after 200 pages of

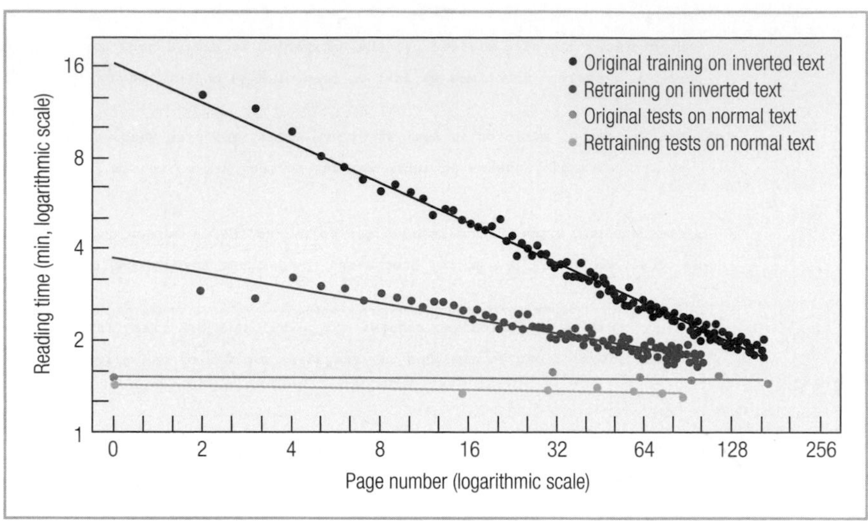

FIGURE 9.5 The results for readers in Kolers's reading-skills experiment on two tests more than a year apart. Participants were trained with 200 pages of inverted text in which pages of normal text were occasionally interspersed. A year later, they were retrained with 100 pages of inverted text, again with normal text occasionally interspersed. The results show the effect of practice on the acquisition of the skill. Both reading time and number of pages practiced are plotted on a logarithmic scale. (From Kolers, 1976. Copyright by the American Psychological Association. Reprinted by permission.)

training was now reached after 50 pages. Skills generally show very high levels of retention. In many cases, such skills can be maintained for years with no retention loss. Someone coming back to a skill—skiing, for example—after many years of absence often requires just a short warm-up period before the skill is reestablished (Schmidt, 1988).

Poldrack and Gabrieli (2001) investigated the brain correlates of the changes taking place as participants learn to read transformed text such as that in Figure 9.4. In an fMRI brain-imaging study, they found increased activity in the basal ganglia and decreased activation in the hippocampus as learning progressed. Recall from Chapters 6 and 7 that the basal ganglia are associated with procedural knowledge, whereas the hippocampus is associated with declarative knowledge. Similar changes in the activation of brain areas have been found by Poldrack et al. (1999) in another skill-acquisition task that required the classification of stimuli. As participants develop their skill, they appear to move to a direct recognition of the text. Thus, the results of this brain-imaging research reveal changes consistent with the switch between the cognitive and the associative stages. Thus, qualitative changes appear to be contributing to the quantitative changes captured by the power function. We will consider these qualitative changes in more detail in the next section.

- *Performance of a cognitive skill improves as a power function of practice and shows modest declines only over long retention intervals.*

The Nature of Expertise

So far in this chapter, we have considered some of the phenomena associated with skill acquisition. An understanding of the mechanisms behind these phenomena has come from examining the nature of expertise in various fields of endeavor. Since the mid-1970s, there has been a great deal of research looking at expertise in such domains as mathematics, chess, computer programming, and physics. This research compares people at various levels of development of their expertise. Sometimes this research is truly longitudinal and follows students from their introduction to a field to their development of some expertise. More typically, such research samples people at different levels of expertise. For instance, research on medical expertise might look at students just beginning medical school, residents, and doctors with many years of medical practice. This research has begun to identify some of the ways that problem solving becomes more effective with experience. Let us consider some of these dimensions of the development of expertise.

Proceduralization

The degree to which participants rely on declarative versus procedural knowledge changes dramatically as expertise develops. It is illustrated in my own work on the development of expertise in geometry (Anderson, 1982). One student had just learned the side-side-side (SSS) and side-angle-side (SAS) postulates for proving triangles congruent. The side-side-side postulate states that, if three sides of one triangle are congruent to the corresponding sides of another triangle, the triangles are congruent. The side-angle-side postulate states that, if two sides and the included angle of one triangle are congruent to the corresponding parts of another triangle, the triangles are congruent. Figure 9.6 illustrates the first problem that the student had to solve. The first thing that he did in trying to solve this problem was to decide which postulate to use. The following is a part of his thinking-aloud protocol, during which he decided on the appropriate postulate:

> If you looked at the side-angle-side postulate (long pause) well *RK* and *RJ* could almost be (long pause) what the missing (long pause) the missing side. I think somehow the side-angle-side postulate works its way into here (long pause). Let's see what it says: "Two sides and the included angle." What would I have to have to have two sides *JS* and *KS* are one of them. Then you could go back to *RS* = *RS*. So that would bring up the side-angle-side postulate (long pause). But where would Angle 1 and Angle 2 are right angles fit in (long pause) wait I see how they work (long pause). *JS* is congruent to *KS* (long pause) and with Angle 1 and Angle 2 are right angles that's a little problem (long pause). OK, what does it say—check it one more time: "If two sides and the included angle of one triangle are congruent to the corresponding parts." So I have got to find the two sides and the included angle. With the included angle you get Angle 1 and Angle 2. I suppose (long pause) they are both right angles, which means they are congruent to each other. My first side is *JS* is to *KS*. And the next one is *RS* to *RS*. So these are the two sides. Yes, I think it is the side-angle-side postulate. (Anderson, 1982, pp. 381–382)

FIGURE 9.6 The first geometry-proof problem encountered by a student after studying the side-side-side and side-angle-side postulates.

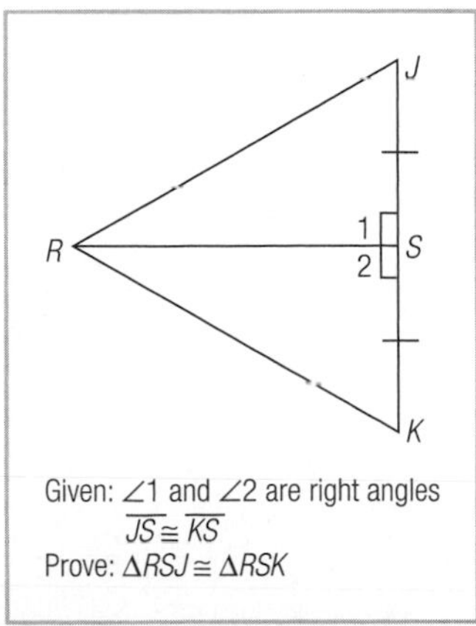

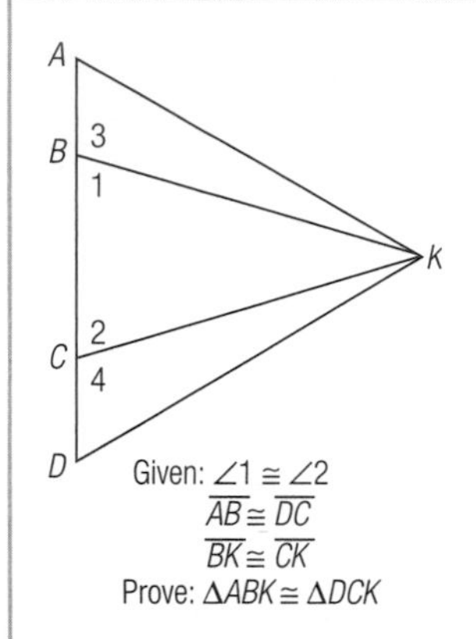

FIGURE 9.7 The sixth geometry-proof problem encountered by a student after studying the side-side-side and side-angle-side postulates.

After reaching this point, the student still went through a long process of actually writing out the proof, but the part of the protocol just given is germane to assessing what goes into recognizing the relevance of the SAS postulate. After a series of four more problems (two solved by SAS and two by SSS), the student applied the SAS postulate in solving the problem illustrated in Figure 9.7. The method-recognition part of the protocol was as follows:

> Right off the top of my head I am going to take a guess at what I am supposed to do: Angle *DCK* is congruent to Angle *ABK*. There is only one of two and the side-angle-side postulate is what they are getting to. (Anderson, 1982, p. 382)

A number of things seem striking about the contrast between these two protocols. One is that the application of the postulate has clearly sped up in the second part of the protocol. A second is that there is no verbal rehearsal of the statement of the postulate in the second case. The student is no longer calling a declarative representation of the postulate into working memory. Note also that, in the first protocol, working memory fails a number of times—points at which the student had to recover information that he had forgotten. The third feature of difference is that, in the first protocol, application of the postulate is piecemeal; the student is separately identifying every element of the postulate. Piecemeal application is absent in the second protocol. It appears that the postulate is being matched in a single step.

These transitions are like the ones that Fitts and Posner characterized as belonging to the associative stage of skill acquisition. The student is no longer relying on verbal recall of the postulate but has advanced to the point where he can simply recognize the application of the postulate as a pattern. Pattern recognition is an important part of the procedural embodiment of a skill. We no longer have to think about what to do next; we just recognize what is appropriate for the situation. The process of converting the deliberate use of declarative knowledge into pattern-driven application of procedural knowledge is called **proceduralization.**

In Anderson (2007) I reported a meta-analysis of a number of studies in our laboratory looking at the effects of practice on the performance of mathematical problem-solving tasks like the ones we have been discussing in this section. We were interested in the effects of this sort of practice on the three brain regions illustrated in Figure 1.15:

> **Motor,** which is involved in programming the actual motor movements in writing out the solution;
>
> **Parietal,** which is involved in representing the problem internally; and
>
> **Prefrontal,** which is involved in retrieving things like the task instructions.

In addition we looked at a fourth region:

> **Anterior Cingulate Cortex** (**ACC**), which is involved in the control of cognition—see Figure 3.1 and later discussion in Chapter 3.

Figure 9.8 shows the mean level of activation in these regions initially and after 4 hours of practice. The motor or control demands of the tasks do not change

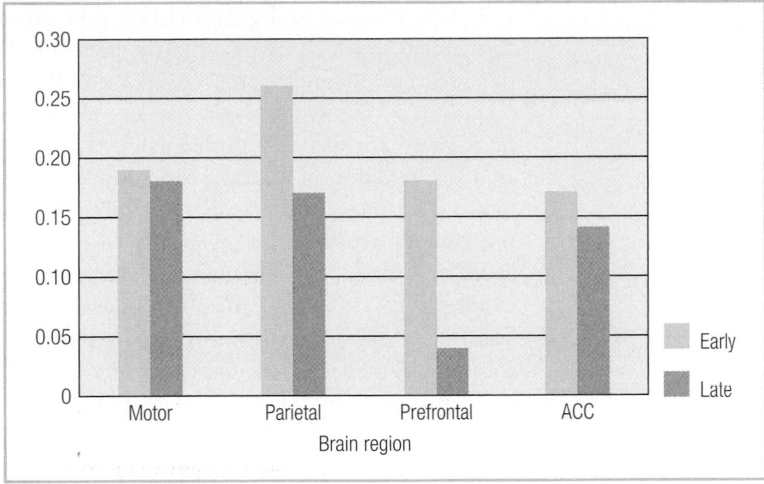

FIGURE 9.8 Representation of the activity in four brain regions while performing tasks early on versus after 5 days of practice.

much and so there is comparable activation early versus late in the motor cortex and the ACC. There is some reduction in the parietal suggesting that the representational demands may be decreasing a bit. However, the dramatic change is in the prefrontal, which is showing a major decrease because the task instructions are no longer being retrieved. Rather, the knowledge is coming to be directly applied.

- *Proceduralization refers to the process by which people switch from explicit use of declarative knowledge to direct application of procedural knowledge, which enables them do things such as riding a bike without thinking about it.*

Tactical Learning

As students practice problems, they come to learn the sequences of actions required to solve a problem or parts of the problem. Learning to execute such sequences of actions is called **tactical learning.** A tactic refers to a method that accomplishes a particular goal. For instance, Greeno (1974) found that it took only about four repetitions of the hobbits and orcs problem (see discussion surrounding Figure 8.7) before participants could solve the problem perfectly. In this experiment, participants were learning the sequence of moves to get the creatures across the river. Once they had learned the sequence, they could simply recall it and did not have to figure it out.

Logan (1988) argued that a general mechanism of skill acquisition involves learning to recall solutions to problems that formerly had to be figured out. A nice illustration of this mechanism is from a domain called alpha-arithmetic. It entails solving problems such as $F + 3$, in which the participant is supposed to say the letter that is the number of letters forward in the alphabet—in this case,

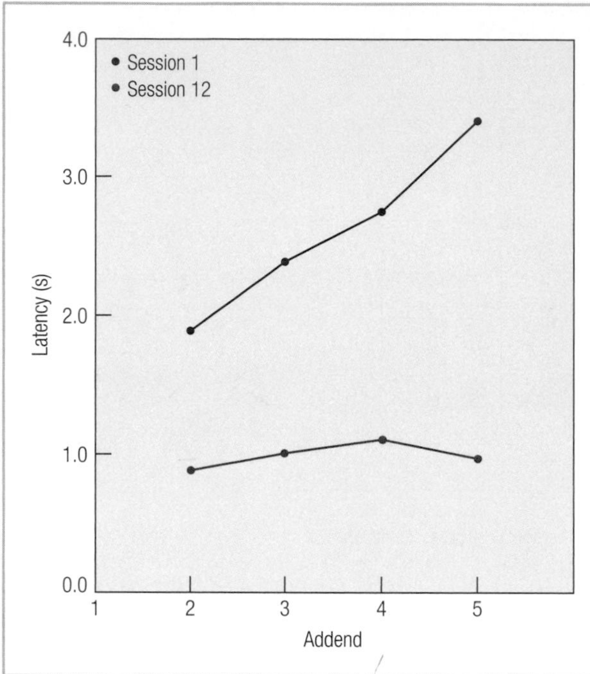

FIGURE 9.9 After 12 sessions, participants solved alpha-arithmetic problems with various-sized addends in considerably less time.
(From Logan & Klapp, 1991).

$F + 3 = I$. Logan and Klapp (1991) performed an experiment in which they gave participants problems that included addends from 2 (e.g., $C + 2$) through 5 (e.g., $G + 5$). Figure 9.9 shows the time taken by participants to answer these problems initially and then after 12 sessions of practice. Initially, participants took 1.5 s longer on the 5-addend problems than on the 2-addend problems, because it takes longer to count five letters forward in the alphabet than two letters forward. However, the problems were repeated again and again across the sessions. With repeated, continued practice, participants became faster on all problems, reaching the point where they could solve the 5-addend problems as quickly as the 2-addend problems. They had memorized the answers to these problems and were not going through the procedure of solving the problems by counting.[1]

There is evidence that, as people become more practiced at a task and shift from computation to retrieval, brain activation shifts from the prefrontal cortex to more posterior areas of the cortex. For instance, Jenkins, Brooks, Nixon, Frackowiak, and Passingham (1994) looked at participants learning to key out various sequences of finger presses such as "ring, index, middle, little, middle, index, ring, index." They compared participants initially learning these sequences with participants practiced in these sequences. They used PET imaging studies and found that there was more activation in frontal areas early in learning than late in learning.[2] On the other hand, later in learning, there was more activation in the hippocampus, which is a structure associated with memory. Such results indicate that, early in a task, there is significant involvement of the anterior cingulate in organizing the behavior but that, late in learning, participants are just recalling the answers from memory. Thus, these neurophysiological data are consistent with Logan's proposal.

- *Tactical learning refers to a process by which people learn specific procedures for solving specific problems.*

Strategic Learning

The preceding subsection on tactical learning was concerned with how students learn tactics by memorizing sequences of actions to solve problems. Many small problems repeat so often that we can solve them this way. However, large and

[1] Rabinowitz and Goldberg (1995) reported a study making a similar point.

[2] This early-learning activation included the same anterior cingulate whose activity did not change in the mathematical problem-solving tasks in Figure 9.8. However, in this simpler experiment the need for control dramatically changes, and there is less activity later in the anterior cingulate.

complex problems do not repeat exactly, but they still have similar structures, and one can learn how to organize one's solution to the overall problem. Learning how to organize one's problem solving to capitalize on the general structure of a class of problems is referred to as **strategic learning.** The contrast between strategic and tactical learning in skill acquisition is analogous to the distinction between tactics and strategy in the military. In the military, tactics refers to smaller-scale battlefield maneuvers, whereas strategy refers to higher-level organization of a military campaign. Similarly, tactical learning involves learning new pieces of skill, whereas strategic learning is concerned with putting them together.

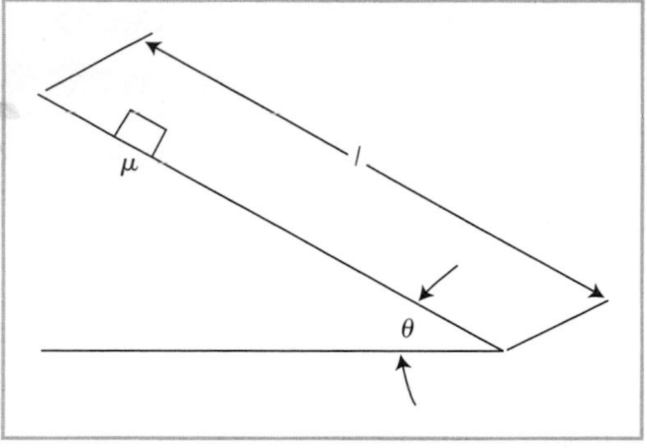

FIGURE 9.10 A sketch of a sample physics problem. (From Larkin, 1981.)

One of the clearest demonstrations of such strategic changes is in the domain of physics problem solving. Researchers have compared novice and expert solutions to problems like the one depicted in Figure 9.10. A block is sliding down an inclined plane of length l, and θ is the angle between the plane and the horizontal. The coefficient of friction is μ. The participant's task is to find the velocity of the block when it reaches the bottom of the plane. The typical novices in these studies are beginning college students and the typical experts are their teachers.

In one study comparing novices and experts, Larkin (1981) found a difference in how they approached the problem. Table 9.1 shows a typical novice's

TABLE 9.1

Typical Novice Solution to a Physics Problem
To find the desired final speed v requires a principle with v in it—say
$$v = v_0 + 2\,at$$
But both a and t are unknown; so that seems hopeless. Try instead
$$v^2 - v_0^2 = 2\,ax$$
In that equation, v_0 is zero and x is known; so it remains to find a. Therefore, try
$$F = ma$$
In that equation, m is given and only F is unknown; therefore, use
$$F = \Sigma F\text{'s}$$
which in this case means
$$F = F_g'' - f$$
where F_g'' and f can be found from
$$F_g'' = mg \sin \theta$$ $$f = \mu N$$ $$N = mg \cos \theta$$
With a variety of substitutions, a correct expression for speed,
$$v = \sqrt{2(g \sin \theta - \mu g \cos \theta)l}$$
can be found.
Adapted from Larkin (1981).

TABLE 9.2

Skilled Solution to a Physics Problem
The motion of the block is accounted for by the gravitational force, $F_g'' = mg \sin \theta$ directed downward along the plane, and the frictional force, $f = \mu mg \cos \theta$ directed upward along the plane. The block's acceleration a is then related to the (signed) sum of these forces by $F = ma$ or $mg \sin \theta - \mu mg \cos \theta = ma$ Knowing the acceleration a, it is then possible to find the block's final speed v from the relations $l = \frac{1}{2}at^2$ and $v = at$
Adapted from Larkin (1981).

solution to the problem, whereas Table 9.2 shows a typical expert's solution. The novice's solution typifies the reasoning backward method, which starts with the unknown—in this case, the velocity v. Then the novice finds an equation for calculating v. However, to calculate v by this equation, it is necessary to calculate a, the acceleration. So the novice finds an equation for calculating a; and the novice chains backward until a set of equations is found for solving the problem.

The expert, on the other hand, uses similar equations but in the completely opposite order. The expert starts with quantities that can be directly computed, such as gravitational force, and works toward the desired velocity. It is also apparent that the expert is speaking a bit like the physics teacher that he is, leaving the final substitutions for the student.

Another study by Priest and Lindsay (1992) failed to find a difference in problem-solving direction between novices and experts. Their study included British university students rather than American students, and they found that both novices and experts predominantly reasoned forward. However, their experts were much more successful in doing so. Priest and Lindsay suggest that the experts have the necessary experience to know which forward inferences are appropriate for a problem. It seems that novices have two choices—reason forward, but fail (Priest & Lindsay's students) or reason backward, which is hard (Larkin's students)

Reasoning backward is hard because it requires setting goals and subgoals and keeping track of them. For instance, a student must remember that he or she is calculating F so that a can be calculated and hence so that v can be calculated. Thus, reasoning backward puts a severe strain on working memory and this can lead to errors. Reasoning forward eliminates the need to keep track of subgoals. However, to successfully reason forward, one must know which of the many possible forward inferences are relevant to the final solution, which is what an expert learns with experience. He or she learns to associate various inferences with various patterns of features in the problems. The novices in Larkin's study seemed to prefer to struggle with backward reasoning, whereas the novices in Priest and Lindsay's study tried forward reasoning without success.

Not all domains show this advantage for forward problem solving. A good counterexample is computer programming (Anderson, Farrell, & Sauers, 1984; Jeffries, Turner, Polson, & Atwood, 1981; Rist, 1989). Both novice and expert programmers develop programs in what is called a top-down manner; that is, they work from the statement of the problem to subproblems to sub-subproblems, and so on, until they solve the problem. This top-down development is basically the same as what is called reasoning backward in the context of geometry or physics. There are differences between expert programmers and novice programmers, however. Experts tend to develop problem solutions breadth first, whereas novices develop their solutions depth first. Physics and geometry problems have a rich set of givens that are more predictive of solutions than is the goal. In contrast, nothing in the typical statement of a programming problem would guide a working forward or bottom-up solution. The typical problem statement only describes the goal and often does so with information that will guide a top-down solution. Thus, we see that expertise in different domains requires the adoption of those approaches that will be successful for those particular domains.

In summary, the transition from novices to experts does not entail the same changes in strategy in all domains. Different problem domains have different structures that make different strategies optimal. Physics experts learn to reason forward; programming experts learn breadth-first expansion.

- *Strategic learning refers to a process by which people learn to organize their problem solving.*

Problem Perception

As they acquire expertise problem solvers learn to perceive problems in ways that enable more effective problem-solving procedures to apply. This dimension can be nicely demonstrated in the domain of physics. Physics, being an intellectually deep subject, has principles that are only implicit in the surface features of a physics problem. Experts learn to see these implicit principles and represent problems in terms of them.

Chi, Feltovich, and Glaser (1981) asked participants to classify a large set of problems into similar categories. Figure 9.11 shows sets of problems that novices thought were similar and the novices' explanations for the similarity groupings. As can be seen, the novices chose surface features, such as rotations or inclined planes, as their bases for classification. Being a physics novice myself, I have to admit that these seem very intuitive bases for similarity. Contrast

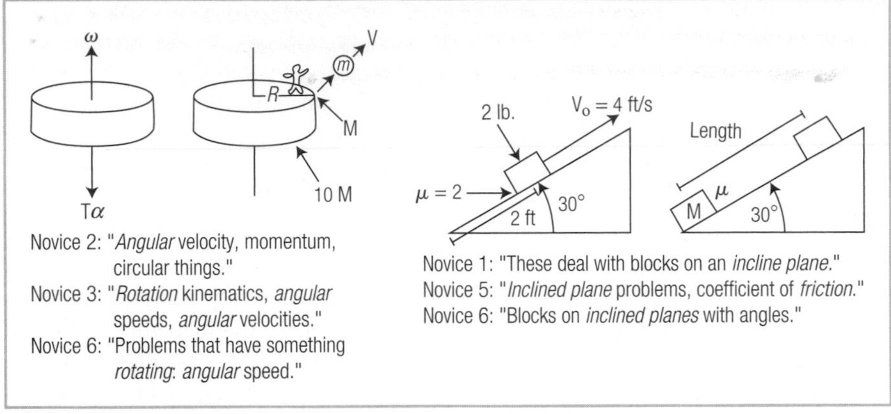

FIGURE 9.11 Diagrams depicting pairs of problems categorized by novices as similar and samples of their explanations for the similarity. (Adapted from Chi et al., 1981.)

these classifications with the pairs of problems in Figure 9.12 that the expert participants saw as similar. Problems that are completely different on the surface were seen as similar because they both entailed conservation of energy or they both used Newton's second law. Thus, experts have the ability to map surface features of a problem onto these deeper principles. This ability is very useful because the deeper principles are more predictive of the method of solution. This shift in classification from reliance on simple features to reliance on more complex features has been found in a number of domains, including mathematics (Silver, 1979; Schoenfeld & Herrmann, 1982), computer programming (Weiser & Shertz, 1983), and medical diagnosis (Lesgold et al., 1988).

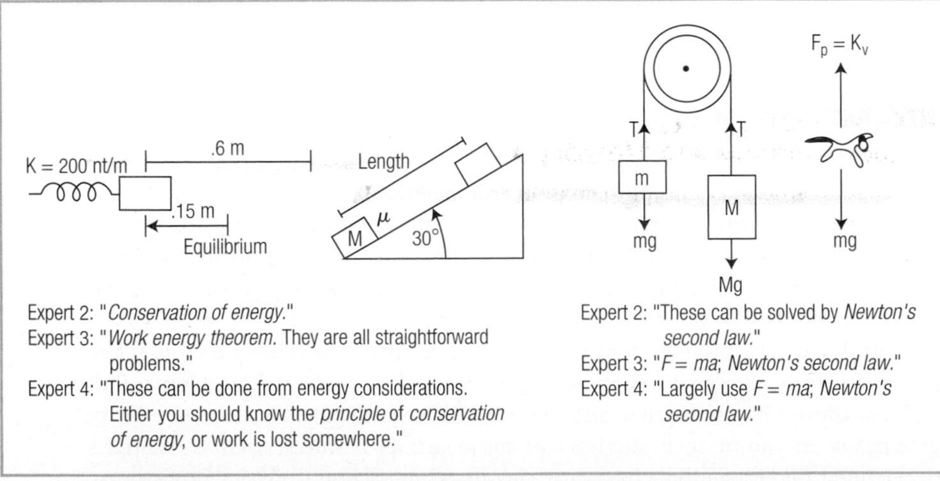

FIGURE 9.12 Diagrams depicting pairs of problems categorized by experts as similar and samples of their explanations for the similarity. (Adapted from Chi et al., 1981.)

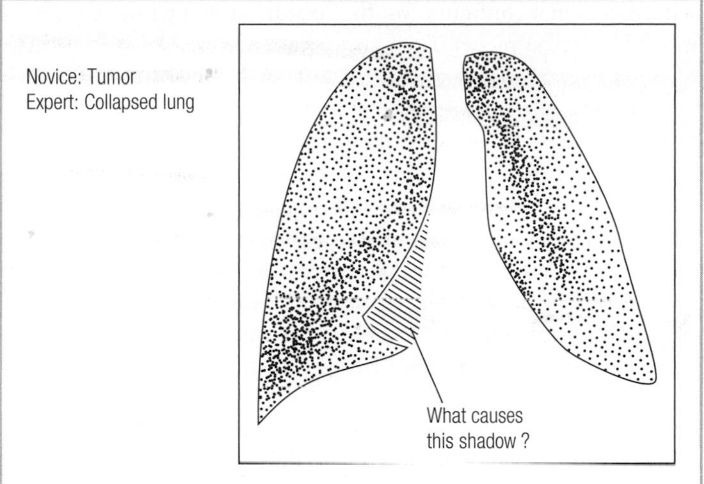

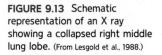

FIGURE 9.13 Schematic representation of an X ray showing a collapsed right middle lung lobe. (From Lesgold et al., 1988.)

A good example of this shift in processing of perceptual features is the interpretation of X rays. Figure 9.13 is a schematic of one of the X rays diagnosed by participants in the research by Lesgold et al. The sail-like area in the right lung is a shadow (shown on the left side of the X ray) caused by a collapsed lobe of the lung that created a denser shadow in the X ray than did other parts of the lung. Medical students interpreted this shadow as an indication of a tumor because tumors are the most common cause of shadows on the lung. Radiological experts, on the other hand, were able to correctly interpret the shadow as an indication of a collapsed lung. They saw counterindicative features such as the size of the sail-like region. Thus, experts no longer have a simple association between shadows on the lungs and tumors, but rather can see a richer set of features in X rays.

An important dimension of growing expertise is the ability to learn to perceive problems in ways that enable more effective problem-solving procedures to apply.

Pattern Learning and Memory

A surprising discovery about expertise is that experts seem to display a special enhanced memory for information about problems in their domains of expertise. This enhanced memory was first discovered in the research of de Groot (1965, 1966), who was attempting to determine what separated master chess players from weaker chess players. It turns out that chess masters are not particularly more intelligent in domains other than chess. De Groot found hardly any differences between expert players and weaker players—except, of course, that the expert players chose much better moves. For instance, a chess master considers about the same number of possible moves as does a weak chess player before selecting a move. In fact, if anything, masters consider fewer moves than do chess duffers.

However, de Groot did find one intriguing difference between masters and weaker players. He presented chess masters with chess positions (i.e., chessboards with pieces in a configuration that occurred in a game) for just 5 s and then removed the chess pieces. The chess masters were able to reconstruct the positions of more than 20 pieces after just 5 s of study. In contrast, the chess duffers could reconstruct only 4 or 5 pieces—an amount much more in line with the traditional capacity of working memory. Chess masters appear to have built up patterns of 4 or 5 pieces that correspond to common board configurations as a result of the massive amount of experience that they have had with chess. Thus, they remember not individual pieces but these patterns. In line with this analysis, if the players are presented with random chessboard positions rather than ones that are actually encountered in games, no difference is demonstrated between masters and duffers—both reconstruct only a few chess positions. The masters also complain about being very uncomfortable and disturbed by such chaotic board positions.

In a systematic analysis, Chase and Simon (1973) compared novices, Class A players, and masters. They compared these different types of players with respect to their ability to reproduce game positions such as those shown in Figure 9.14a

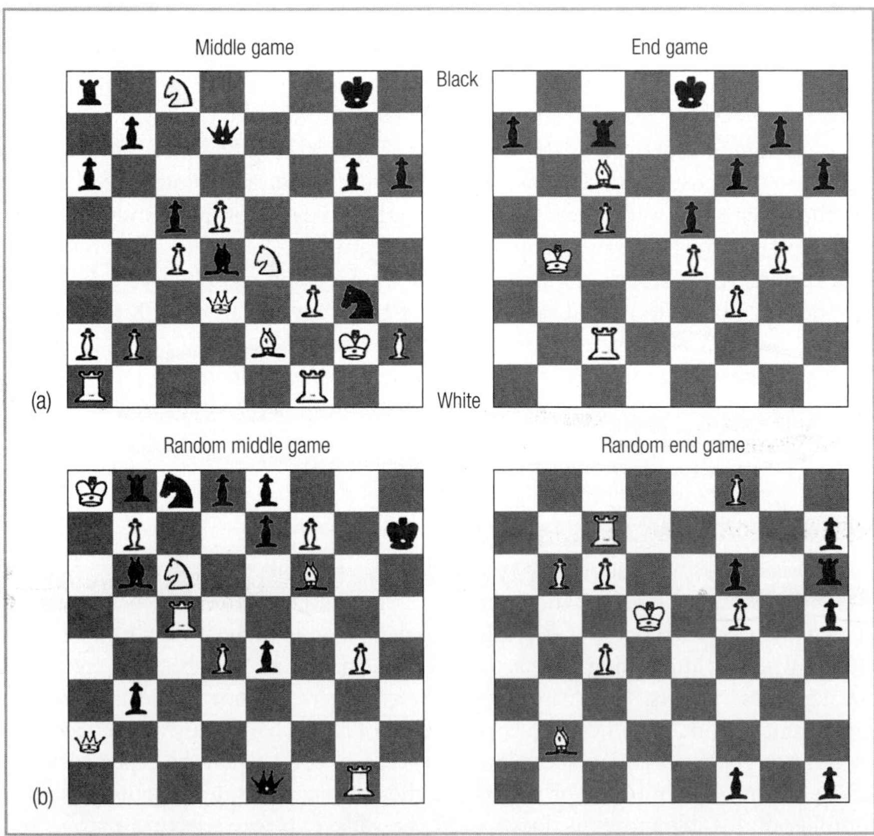

FIGURE 9.14 Examples of (a) middle and end games and (b) their randomized counterparts. (From Chase & Simon, 1973.)

and to reproduce random positions such as those illustrated in Figure 9.14b. Figure 9.15 shows the results. Memory was poorer for all groups for the random positions and, if anything, masters were worse at reproducing these positions. On the other hand, masters showed a considerable advantage for the actual board positions. This basic phenomenon of superior expert memory for meaningful problems has been demonstrated in a large number of domains, including the game of Go (Reitman, 1976), electronic circuit diagrams (Egan & Schwartz, 1979), bridge hands (Engle & Bukstel, 1978; Charness, 1979), and computer programming (McKeithen, Reitman, Rueter, & Hirtle, 1981; Schneiderman, 1976).

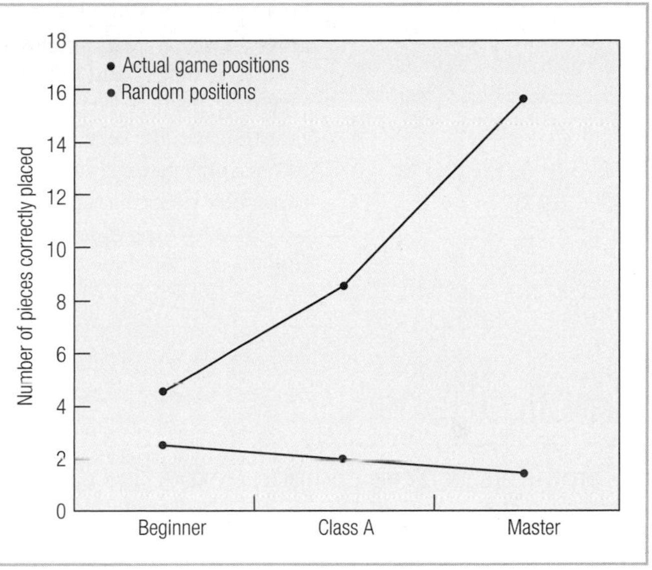

FIGURE 9.15 Number of pieces successfully recalled by chess players after the first study of a chessboard. (From Chase & Simon, 1973).

Chase and Simon (1973) also used a chessboard-reproduction task to examine the nature of the patterns, or chunks, used by chess masters. The participants' task was simply to reproduce the positions of pieces of a target chessboard on a test chessboard. In this task, participants glanced at the target board, placed some pieces on the test board, glanced back to the target board, placed some more pieces on the test board, and so on. Chase and Simon defined a chunk to be a group of pieces that participants moved after one glance. They found that these chunks tended to define meaningful game relations among the pieces. For instance, more than half of the masters' chunks were pawn chains (configurations of pawns that occur frequently in chess).

Simon and Gilmartin (1973) estimated that chess masters have acquired 50,000 different chess patterns, that they can quickly recognize such patterns on a chessboard, and that this ability is what underlies their superior memory performance in chess. This 50,000 figure is not unreasonable when one considers the years of dedicated study that becoming a chess master requires. What might be the relation between memory for so many chess patterns and superior performance in chess? Newell and Simon (1972) speculated that, in addition to learning many patterns, masters have learned what to do in the presence of such patterns. For instance, if the chunk pattern is symptomatic of a weak side, the response might be to suggest an attack on the weak side. Thus, masters effectively "see" possibilities for moves; they do not have to think them out, which explains why chess masters do so well at lightning chess, in which they have only a few seconds to move.

To summarize, chess experts have stored the solutions to many problems that duffers must solve as novel problems. Duffers have to analyze different configurations, try to figure out their consequences, and act accordingly. Masters have all this information stored in memory, thereby claiming two advantages. First, they do not risk making errors in solving these problems, because they have stored the correct solution. Second, because they have stored correct analyses of so many positions, they can focus their problem-solving efforts on more sophisticated aspects and strategies of chess. Thus, the experts' pattern learning and better memory for board positions is a part of the tactical learning discussed earlier. The way humans become expert at chess reflects the fact that we are very good at pattern recognition but relatively poor at things like mentally searching through sequences of possible moves. As the Implications box describes, human strengths and weaknesses lead to a very different way of achieving expertise at chess than we see in computer programs for playing chess.

Implications

Computers achieve computer expertise differently than humans

In Chapter 8, we discussed how human problem solving can be viewed as a search of a problem space, consisting of various states. The initial situation is the start state, the situations on the way to the goal are the intermediate states, and the solution is the goal state. Chapter 8 also described how people use certain methods, such as avoiding backup, difference reduction, and means-ends analysis, to move through the states. Often when humans search a problem space, they are actually manipulating the actual physical world, as in the 8-puzzle (Figures 8.3 and 8.4). However, sometimes they imagine states, as when one plays chess and contemplates how an opponent will react to some move one is considering, how one might react to the opponent's move, and so on. Computers are very effective at representing such hypothetical states and searching through them for the optimal goal state. Artificial intelligence algorithms have been developed that are very successful at all sorts of problem-solving applications, including playing chess. This has led to a style of chess playing program that is very different from human chess play, which relies much more on pattern recognition. At first many people thought that, although such computer programs could play competent and modestly competitive chess games, they would be no match for the best human players. The philosopher Hubert Dreyfus, who was famously critical of computer chess in the 1960s, was beaten by the program of an MIT undergraduate, Richard Greenblatt, in 1966 (Boden, 2006, discusses the intrigue surrounding these events). However, Dreyfus was a chess duffer and the programs of the 1960s and 1970s performed poorly against chess masters. As computers became more powerful and could search larger spaces, they became increasingly competitive, and finally in May 1997, IBM's Deep Blue program defeated the reigning world champion, Gary Kasparov. Deep Blue evaluated 200 million imagined chess positions per second. It also had stored records of 4,000 opening positions and 700,000 master games (Hsu, 2002) and had many other optimizations that took advantage of special computer hardware. Today there are freely available chess programs for your personal computer that can be downloaded over the Web and will play highly competitive chess at a master level. These developments have led to a profound shift in the understanding of intelligence. It once was thought that there was only one way to achieve high levels of intelligent behavior, and that was the human way. Nowadays it is increasingly being accepted that intelligence can be achieved in different ways, and the human way may not always be the best. Also, curiously, as a consequence some researchers no longer view the ability to play chess as a reflection of the essence of human intelligence.

Experts can recognize patterns of elements that repeat in many problems, and know what to do in the presence of such patterns without having to think them through.

Long-Term Memory and Expertise

One might think that the memory advantage shown by experts is just a working-memory advantage, but research has shown that their advantage extends to long-term memory. Charness (1976) compared experts' memory for chess positions immediately after they had viewed the positions or after a 30-s delay filled with an interfering task. Class A chess players showed no loss in recall over the 30-s interval, unlike weaker participants, who showed a great deal of forgetting. Thus, expert chess players, unlike duffers, have an increased capacity to store information about the domain. Interestingly, these participants showed the same poor memory for three-letter trigrams as do ordinary participants. Thus, their increased long-term memory is only for the domain of expertise.

There is reason to believe that the memory advantage goes beyond experts' ability to encode a problem in terms of familiar patterns. Experts appear to be able to remember more patterns as well as larger patterns. For instance, Chase and Simon (1973) in their study (see Figures 9.14 and 9.15) tried to identify the patterns that their participants used to recall the chessboards. They found that participants would tend to recall a pattern, pause, recall another pattern, pause, and so on. They found that they could use a 2-s pause to identify boundaries between patterns. With this objective definition of what a pattern is, they could then explore how many patterns were recalled and how large these patterns were. In comparing a master chess player with a beginner, they found large differences in both measures. First, the pattern size of the master averaged 3.8 pieces, whereas it was only 2.4 for the beginner. Second, the master also recalled an average of 7.7 patterns per board, whereas the beginner recalled an average of only 5.3. Thus, it seems that the experts' memory advantage is based not only on larger patterns but also on the ability to recall more of them.

The strongest evidence that expertise requires the ability to remember more patterns as well as larger patterns is from Chase and Ericsson (1982), who studied the development of a simple but remarkable skill. They watched a participant, S. F., increase his digit span, which is the number of digits that he could repeat after one presentation. As discussed in Chapter 6, the normal digit span is about 7 or 8 items, just enough to accommodate a telephone number. After about 200 hr of practice, S. F. was able to recall 81 random digits presented at the rate of 1 digit per second. Figure 9.16 illustrates how his memory span grew with practice.

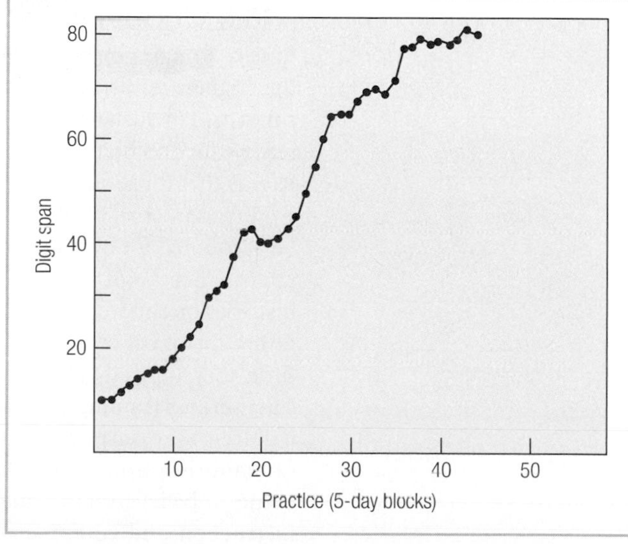

FIGURE 9.16 The growth in S. F.'s memory span with practice. Notice how the number of digits that he can recall increases gradually but steadily with the number of practice sessions. (From Chase & Ericsson, 1982.)

What was behind this apparent superhuman feat of memory? In part, S. F. was learning to chunk the digits into meaningful patterns. He was a long-distance runner, and part of his technique was to convert digits into running times. So, he would take 4 digits, such as 3492, and convert them into "Three minutes, 49.2 seconds—near world-record mile time." Using such a strategy, he could convert a memory span for 7 digits into a memory span for 7-digit patterns of length 3 or 4. This would get him to a digit span of more than 20, far short of his eventual performance. In addition to this chunking, he developed what Chase and Ericsson called a retrieval structure, which enabled him to recall 22 such patterns. This retrieval structure was very specific; it did not generalize to retrieving letters rather than digits. Chase and Ericsson hypothesized that part of what underlies the development of expertise in other domains such as chess is the development of retrieval structures, which allows superior recall for past patterns.

- *As people become more expert in a domain, they develop a better ability to store problem information in long-term memory and to retrieve it.*

The Role of Deliberate Practice

An implication of all the research that we have reviewed is that expertise comes only with an investment of a great deal of time to learn the patterns, the problem-solving rules, and the appropriate problem-solving organization for a domain. As mentioned earlier, John Hayes found that geniuses in various fields produce their best work only after 10 years of apprenticeship in a field. In another research effort, Ericsson, Krampe, and Tesch-Römer (1993) compared the best violinists at a music academy in Berlin with those who were only very good. They looked at diaries and self-estimates to determine how much the two populations had practiced and estimated that the best violinists had practiced more than 7000 hr before coming to the academy, whereas the very good had practiced only 5000 hr. Ericsson et al. reviewed a great many fields where, like music, time spent practicing is critical. Not only is time on task important at the highest levels of performance, but also it is essential to mastering school subjects. For instance, Anderson, Reder, and Simon (1998) noted that a major reason for the higher achievement in mathematics of students in Asian countries is that those students spend twice as much time practicing mathematics.

Ericsson et al. (1993) make the strong claim that almost all of expertise is to be accounted for by amount of practice, and there is virtually no role for natural talent. They point to the research of Bloom (1985a, 1985b), who looked at the histories of children who became great in fields such as music or tennis. Bloom found that most of these children got started by playing around, but after a short time they typically showed promise and were encouraged by their parents to start serious training with a teacher. However, the early natural abilities of these children were surprisingly modest and did not predict ultimate success in the domain (Ericsson et al., 1993). Rather, what is critical seems to be that parents come to believe that a child is talented and consequently pay for their child's instruction and equipment as well as support their time-consuming practice.

Ericsson et al. speculated that the resulting training is sufficient to account for the development of children's success. There is almost certainly some role for talent (considered in Chapter 13), but all the evidence indicates that genius is 90% perspiration and 10% inspiration.

Ericsson et al. are careful to note, however, that not all practice leads to the development of expertise. They note that many people spend a lifetime playing chess or some sport without ever getting any better. What is critical, according to Ericsson et al., is what they call **deliberate practice.** In deliberate practice, learners are motivated to learn, not just perform; they are given feedback on their performance; and they carefully monitor how well their performance corresponds to the correct performance and where the deviations exist. The learners focus on eliminating these points of discrepancy. The importance of deliberate practice is similar to the importance of deep and elaborative processing of the to-be-learned material described in Chapters 6 and 7, in which passive study was shown to yield few memory benefits.

An important function of deliberate practice in both children and adults may be to drive the neural growth that is necessary to enable expertise. It had once been thought that adults do not grow new neurons, but it now appears that they do (Gross, 2000). An interesting recent discovery is that extensive practice appears to drive neural growth in the adult brain. For instance, Elbert, Pantev, Wienbruch, Rockstroh, and Taub (1995) found that violinists, who finger strings with the left hand, show increased development of the right cortical regions that correspond to their fingers. In another study already mentioned in Chapter 4, Maguire et al. (2003) used imaging to examine the brains of London taxi drivers. It takes at least 3 years for London taxi drivers to acquire all of the knowledge necessary to navigate expertly through the streets of London. The taxi drivers were found to have significantly more gray matter in the hippocampal region than did matched controls. This finding corresponds to the increased hippocampal volume reported in small mammals and birds that engage in behavior requiring navigation (Lee, Miyasato, & Clayton, 1998). For instance, food-storing birds show seasonal increases in hippocampal volume corresponding to times of the year when they need to remember where they store food.

- *A great deal of deliberate practice is necessary to develop expertise in any field.*

Transfer of Skill

Expertise can often be quite narrow. As noted, Chase and Ericsson's participant S. F. was unable to transfer memory span skill from digits to letters. This example is an almost ridiculous extreme of a frequent pattern in the development of cognitive skills—that these skills can be quite narrow and fail to transfer to other activities. Chess grand masters do not appear to be better thinkers for all their genius in chess. An amusing example of the narrowness of expertise is a study by Carraher, Carraher, and Schliemann (1985). These researchers investigated the mathematical strategies used by Brazilian schoolchildren who also worked as street vendors. On the job, these children used quite sophisticated strategies for calculating the total cost of orders consisting of different numbers of different objects (e.g., the total cost of 4 coconuts and 12 lemons); what's more, they could perform such calculations reliably in their heads. Carraher et al. actually went to the trouble of going to the streets and posing as customers for these children, making certain kinds of purchases and recording the percentage of correct calculations. The experimenters then asked the children to come with them to the laboratory, where they were given written mathematics tests that included the same numbers and mathematical operations that they had manipulated successfully in the streets. For example, if a child had correctly calculated the total cost of 5 lemons at 35 cruzeiros apiece on the street, the child was given the following written problem:

$$5 \times 35 = ?$$

Whereas children solved 98% of the problems presented in the real-world context, they solved only 37% of the problems presented in the laboratory context. It should be stressed that these problems included the exact same numbers and mathematical operations. Interestingly, if the problems were stated in the form of word problems in the laboratory, performance improved to 74%. This improvement runs counter to the usual finding, which is that word problems are more difficult than equivalent "number" problems (Carpenter & Moser, 1982). Apparently, the additional context provided by the word problem allowed the children to make contact with their pragmatic strategies.

The study of Carraher et al. showed a curious failure of expertise to transfer from real life to the classroom, but the typical concern of educators is whether what is taught in one class will transfer to other classes and the real world. Early in the 20th century, educators were fairly optimistic on this matter. A number of educational psychologists subscribed to what has been called the doctrine of formal discipline (Angell, 1908; Pillsbury, 1908; Woodrow, 1927), which held that studying such esoteric subjects as Latin and geometry was of significant value because it served to discipline the mind. Formal discipline subscribed to the faculty view of mind, which extends back to Aristotle and was first formalized by Thomas Reid in the late 18th century (Boring, 1950). The faculty position held that the mind is composed of a collection of general faculties, such as observation, attention, discrimination, and reasoning, which were exercised in much the same way as a set of muscles. The content of the exercise made little difference; most important was the level of exertion (hence the fondness for Latin and geometry). Transfer in such a view is broad and takes place at a general level, sometimes spanning domains that have no content in common.

Although it might be nice to believe that such general transfer is possible, as envisioned by the doctrine of formal discipline, there has been effectively no evidence for it, despite a century of research on the topic. Some of the earliest research on this topic was performed by Thorndike (e.g., Thorndike & Woodworth, 1901). In one study, no correlation was found between memory for words and memory for numbers. In another, accuracy in spelling was not correlated with accuracy in arithmetic. Thorndike interpreted these results as evidence against the general faculties of memory and accuracy.

- *There is often failure to transfer skills to similar domains and virtually no transfer to very different domains.*

Theory of Identical Elements

In place of the doctrine of formal discipline, Thorndike proposed his **theory of identical elements.** According to Thorndike, the mind is not composed of general faculties, but rather of specific habits and associations, which provide a person with a variety of narrow responses to very specific stimuli. In fact, the mind was regarded as just a convenient name for countless special operations or functions (Stratton, 1922). Thorndike's theory stated that training in one kind of activity would transfer to another only if the activities had situation-response elements in common:

> One mental function or activity improves others in so far as and because they are in part identical with it, because it contains elements common to them. Addition improves multiplication because multiplication is largely addition; knowledge of Latin gives increased ability to learn French because many of the facts learned in the one case are needed in the other. (Thorndike, 1906, p. 243)

Thus, Thorndike was happy to accept transfer between diverse skills as long as the transfer could be shown to be mediated by identical elements. Generally, however, he concluded that

> The mind is so specialized into a multitude of independent capacities that we alter human nature only in small spots, and any special school training has a much narrower influence upon the mind as a whole than has commonly been supposed. (p. 246)

Although the doctrine of formal discipline was too broad in its predictions of transfer, Thorndike formulated his theory of identical elements in what proved to be an overly narrow manner. For instance, he argued that if you solved a geometry problem in which one set of letters is used to label the points in a diagram, you would not be able to transfer to a geometry problem with a different set of letters. The research on analogy examined in Chapter 8 indicated that this is not true. Transfer is not tied to the identity of surface elements. In some cases, there is very large positive transfer between two skills that have the same logical structure even if they have different surface elements (see Singley & Anderson, 1989, for a review). Thus, for instance, there is large positive transfer between different word-processing systems, between different programming languages, and between using calculus to solve economics problems and using calculus to solve problems in solid geometry. However, all the available evidence is that there are very definite bounds on how far skills will transfer and that becoming an expert in one domain will have little positive benefit on becoming an expert in a very different domain. There will be positive transfer only to the extent that the two domains use the same facts, rules, and patterns—that is, the same knowledge. Thus, Thorndike was right in saying that there would be transfer between two skills to the extent that they have the same elements in common. However, he was wrong in identifying these "elements" with stimulus-response bonds. Modern cognitive psychology has identified these elements as rather abstract knowledge structures that enjoy a wider range of transfer.

There is a positive side to this specificity in transfer of skill: there seldom seems to be **negative transfer,** in which learning one skill makes a person worse at learning another skill. Interference, such as that which occurs in memory for facts (see Chapter 7), is almost nonexistent in skill acquisition. Polson, Muncher, and Kieras (1987) provided a good demonstration of lack of negative transfer in the domain of text editing on a computer (using the command-based word processors that were common at the time). They asked participants to learn one text editor and then learn a second, which was designed to be maximally confusing. Whereas the command to go down a line of text might be *n* and the command to delete a character might be *k* in one text editor, *n* would mean to delete a character in another text editor and *k* would mean to go down a line. However, participants experienced overwhelming positive transfer in going from one text editor to the other because the two text editors worked in the same way, even though the surface commands had been scrambled. There is only one clearly documented kind of negative transfer in regard to cognitive skills—the Einstellung effect discussed in Chapter 8. Students can learn ways of solving problems in one domain that are no longer optimal for solving problems in another domain. So, for instance, someone may learn tricks in algebra to avoid having to perform difficult arithmetic computations. These tricks may no longer be necessary when that person uses a calculator to perform these computations. Still, students show a tendency to continue to perform these unnecessary simplifications in their algebraic manipulations. This example is not a case of failure to transfer; rather, it is a case of transferring knowledge that is no longer useful.

- *There is transfer between skills only when these skills have the same abstract knowledge elements.*

Educational Implications

With this analysis of skill acquisition, we can ask the question: What are the implications for the training of such skills? One implication is the importance of problem decomposition. Traditional high-school algebra has been estimated to require the acquisition of many thousands of rules (Anderson, 1992). Instruction can be improved by an analysis of what these individual elements are. Approaches to instruction that begin with an analysis of the elements to be taught are called **componential analyses.** A description of the application of componential approaches to the instruction of a number of topics in reading and mathematics can be found in Anderson (2000). Generally, higher achievement is obtained in programs that include such componential analysis.

A particularly effective part of such componential programs is **mastery learning.** The basic idea in mastery learning is to follow students' performance on each of the components underlying the cognitive skill and to ensure that all components are mastered. Typical instruction, without mastery learning, leaves some students not knowing some of the material. This failure to learn some of the components can snowball in a course in which mastery of earlier material is a prerequisite for mastery of later material. There is a good deal of evidence that mastery learning leads to higher achievement (Guskey & Gates, 1986; Kulik, Kulik, & Bangert-Downs, 1986).

Instruction is improved by approaches that identify the underlying knowledge components and ensure that students master them all.

Intelligent Tutoring Systems

Probably the most extensive use of such componential analysis is for **intelligent tutoring systems** (Sleeman & Brown, 1982). These computer systems interact with students while they are learning and solving problems, much as a human tutor would. An example of such a tutor is the LISP tutor (Anderson, Conrad, & Corbett, 1989; Anderson & Reiser, 1985; Corbett & Anderson, 1990), which teaches LISP, the main programming language used in artificial intelligence. The LISP tutor continuously taught LISP to students at Carnegie Mellon University from 1984 to 2002 and served as a prototype for a generation of intelligent tutors, many of which have focused on teaching middle-school and high-school mathematics. The mathematics tutors are now distributed by a company called Carnegie Learning, spun off by Carnegie Mellon University in 1998. The Carnegie Learning mathematics tutors have been deployed over 2,600 schools nationwide and interacts with approximately 500,000 students each year (Koedinger & Corbett, 2006; Ritter, Anderson, Koedinger, & Corbett, 2007; you can visit the Web site www.carnegielearning.com for promotional material that should be taken with a grain of salt). Color Plate 9.1 shows a screen shot from its most widely used product, which is a tutor for high-school algebra.

A motivation for research on intelligent tutoring is the evidence showing that private human tutoring is very effective. The results of studies have shown that giving students a private human tutor enables 98% of them to do better than the average student in a standard classroom (Bloom, 1984). An ideal private tutor is one who is with the student at all times while he or she is studying a particular subject matter. To use the terms of Ericsson et al. (1993), a private tutor guarantees the deliberate practice that is essential for learning. Having the tutor present

TABLE 9.3

An Interaction Between the LISP Tutor and a Student
The student is working on a piece of code to satisfy the following problem description. Before each point at which the tutor and student interact, the partial code that the student has written is printed out.
The Problem Description Define a function called ctof that takes a degree reading in Celsius degrees and converts it to Fahrenheit degrees. First, you need to change the scale by multiplying the argument by 1.8. Then you need to translate the scale by adding 32, because 0° Celsius = 32° Fahrenheit. For example, (ctof 20) returns 68.
Cycles in Which the Tutor Communicates with the Student Code: *(defun ctof (cdeg) (**
Tutor: Yes, you will need to call "*" to get the degree on the enlarged scale, but you are ultimately trying to get the Fahrenheit equivalent of the Celsius degree. So you need to code a different function here that takes a call to "*" as an argument. Code: *(defun ctof (cdeg) (+*
Student: Help. ***Tutor:*** You need to multiply together the Celsius degree reading and the size of Fahrenheit degrees using the function *. When you multiply these numbers, you will get the degree on the enlarged scale, which is 36 in our example. Code: *(defun ctof (cdeg) (+ (* 1.8 cdge)*
Tutor: **Did you mean cdeg?** ***Student:*** Yes. Code: *(defun ctof (cdeg) (+ (* 1.8 cdeg) 32))*
Tutor: *You are done. Type "next" to go on after testing the function you have defined.*

while solving problems in domains, such as LISP and mathematics, which require complex problem-solving skills, is particularly important. In LISP, problem solving takes the form of writing computer programs, or functions, as they are often called in LISP. Therefore, in developing the LISP tutor, we chose to focus on providing students with tutoring while they are writing computer programs. Table 9.3 presents a short dialogue between a student and the LISP tutor on an early problem in the curriculum. Note how carefully the tutor monitors the student's performance in solving the problem. It can do so because it knows how to write LISP functions. As the student is writing the function, the tutor is simultaneously trying to solve the same problem that the student is working on. As soon as it sees the student making a mistake, the tutor can intervene with remedial instruction.

Underlying the tutor's ability to solve problems and monitor the student's problem solving is a set of rules that can solve the same LISP programming problems that we expect students to be able to solve. In all, there are about 500 rules that encode the knowledge relating to LISP. A typical rule in the LISP tutor is:

If the goal is to multiply one number by another,

Then use * and set subgoals to code the two numbers.

The basic goal of the LISP tutor is to communicate these 500 rules to the student, monitor performance to see whether he or she possesses these rules in correct form, and provide the student with practice on these rules. The success of the LISP tutor is one piece of evidence that these 500 rules indeed underlie coding skill in LISP.

Besides providing an instructional tool, the LISP tutor is a research tool for studying the course of skill acquisition. The tutor can monitor how well a student is doing on each of the 500 rules, recording statistics such as the number of errors that a student is making and the time taken by a student to type the code corresponding to each of these rules. These data have indicated that students acquire the skill of LISP by independently acquiring each of the 500 rules. Figure 9.17 displays the learning curves for these rules. The two dependent measures are the number of errors made on a rule and the time taken to write the code corresponding to a rule (when that rule is correctly coded). These statistics are plotted as a function of learning opportunities, which present themselves each time the student comes to a point in a problem where that rule can be applied. As can be seen, performance on these rules dramatically improves from first to second learning opportunity and improves more gradually thereafter. These learning curves are similar to those identified in Chapter 6 for the learning of simple associations.

Individual differences in the learning of these rules have been taken into account. Students who have already learned a programming language are at a considerable advantage compared with students for whom their first programming

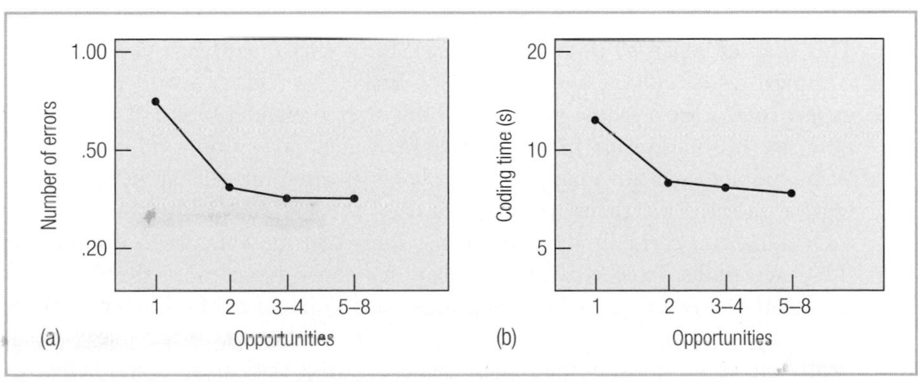

FIGURE 9.17 Data from the LISP tutor: (a) number of errors (maximum is three) per rule as a function of the number of opportunities for practice; (b) time to correctly code rules as a function of the amount of practice.

language is that of the LISP tutor. The "identical elements model" of transfer, in which rules for programming in one language transfer to programming in another language, can account for this advantage.

We also analyzed the performance of individual students in the LISP tutor and found evidence for two factors. Some students were able to learn new rules in a lesson quite rapidly, whereas other students had more difficulty. More or less independent of this acquisition factor, students could be classified according to how well they retained rules from earlier lessons.[3] Thus, students differ in how rapidly they learn with the LISP tutor. However, the tutor employs a mastery learning system in which slower students are given more practice and so are brought to the same level of mastery of the material as that of the others.

Students emerge from their interactions with the LISP tutor having acquired a complex and sophisticated skill. Their enhanced programming abilities make them appear more intelligent among their peers. However, when we examine what underlies that newfound intelligence, we find that it is the methodical acquisition of some 500 rules of programming. Some students can acquire these rules more easily than others because of past experience and specific abilities. However, when they graduate from the LISP course, all students have learned the 500 new rules. With the acquisition of these rules, few differences remain among the students with respect to ability to program in LISP. Thus, we see that, in the end, what is important with respect to individual differences is how much information students have learned, not their native ability.

- *By carefully monitoring individual components of a skill and providing feedback on learning, intelligent tutors can help students rapidly master complex skills.*

Conclusions

This chapter began by noting the remarkable ability of humans to acquire the complexities of culture and technology. In fact, in today's world people can expect to acquire a whole new set of skills over their lifetimes. For instance, I now use my phone for instant messaging, GPS navigation, and surfing the Web—none of which I imagined when I was a young man, let alone associated with a phone. This chapter has emphasized the role of practice in acquiring such skills, and certainly it has taken me some considerable practice to master these new skills. However, human flexibility depends on more than time on task—other creatures could never acquire such skills no matter how much they practiced. Critical to human expertise are the higher-order problem-solving skills that we reviewed in the previous chapter. Also critical is human ability to reason, make decisions, and communicate by language. These are the topics of the forthcoming chapters.

[3] These acquisition and retention factors were strongly related to math SATs, but not to verbal SATs.

Questions for Thought

1. An interesting case study of skill acquisition was reported by Ohlsson (1992), who looked at the development of Isaac Asimov's writing skill. Asimov was one of the most prolific authors of our time, writing approximately 500 books in a career that spanned 40 years. He sat down at his keyboard every day at 7:30 A.M. and wrote until 10:00 P.M. Figure 9.18 shows the average number of months he took to write a book as a function of practice on a log-log scale. It corresponds closely to a power function. At what stage of skill acquisition do you think Asimov was in terms of his writing skills?

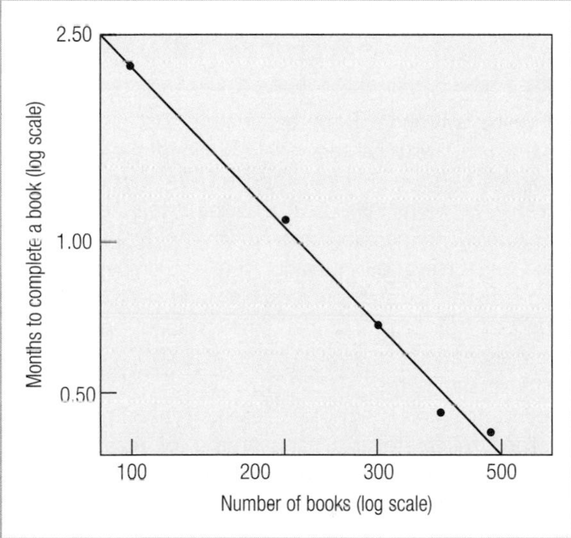

FIGURE 9.18 Time to complete a book as a function of practice, plotted with logarithmic coordinates on both axes. (From Ohlsson, 1992).

2. The chapter discussed how chess experts have learned to recognize appropriate moves just by looking at the chessboard. It has been argued (Charness, 1981; Holding, 1992; Roring, 2008) that experts also learn to engage in more search and more effective search for winning moves. Relate these two kinds of learning (learning specific moves and learning how to search) to the concepts of tactical and strategic learning.
3. In a 2006 *New York Times* article, Stephen J. Dubner and Steven D. Levitt (of "Freakonomics" fame) noted that elite soccer players are much more likely to be born in the early months of the year than the late months. Anders Ericsson argues they have an advantage in youth soccer leagues, which organize teams by birth year. Because they are older and tend to be bigger than other children of the same birth year, they are more likely to get selected for elite teams and receive the benefit of deliberate practice. Can you think of any other explanations for the fact that elite soccer players tend to be born in the first months of the year?
4. One reads frequent complaints about the performance level of American students in studies of mathematics achievement, where they are greatly outperformed by children from other countries like Japan. Frequent remedies point to changing the nature of the mathematics curriculum or improving teacher quality. Seldom mentioned is the fact that American children actually spend much less time learning mathematics (see Anderson, Reder, & Simon, 1998). What does this chapter imply about the importance of instruction versus amount of learning time? Can improvements in one of these increase American achievement levels without improvements in the other?

Key Terms

associative stage
autonomous stage
cognitive stage
componential analysis
deliberate practice
intelligent tutoring systems
mastery learning
negative transfer
proceduralization
strategic learning
tactical learning
theory of identical elements

10

Reasoning

As noted in Chapter 1, intelligence is thought to be the feature that distinguishes humans as a species. In the last two chapters, we examined the enormous capacity that we enjoy as a species to solve problems and acquire new intellectual skills. In light of this particular capacity, we might expect that the research on human reasoning (the topic of this chapter) and decision making (the topic of the next chapter) would document how we achieve our superior intellectual performance. Historically, however, most psychological research on reasoning and decision making has started with prescriptions derived from logic and mathematics about how humans should behave, compared these prescriptions to what humans actually do, and found humans deficient compared to these standards.

The opposite conclusion seems to come from older research in artificial intelligence (AI) where researchers tried to create artificial systems for reasoning and decision making using the same prescriptions from logic and mathematics. For instance, (Shortliffe, 1976) created an expert computer-based system for diagnosing infectious diseases. Similar formal reasoning mechanisms were used in the first generation of robots to help them reason about how to navigate through the world. Researchers were very frustrated with such systems, noting that they lacked common sense and would do the stupidest things that no human would do. Faced with such frustrations, researchers are now creating systems based on less logical computations, often emulating how neurons in the brain compute (e.g., Russell & Norvig, 2003).

Thus, we have a paradox: Human reasoning is judged as deficient when compared against the standards of logic and mathematics, but AI systems built on these very standards are judged as deficient when compared against the standards of humans. This apparent contradiction might lead one to conclude either that logic and mathematics are wrong or that humans have some mysterious intuition that guides their thinking. However, the real problem seems to be with the way the principles of logic and mathematics have been applied, not with the principles themselves. New research is showing that the situations faced by people are more complex than often assumed. We can better understand human behavior when we expand our analyses of human reasoning to include the complexities. In this chapter and the next, we will review a number of the models used to predict how people arrive at conclusions when presented with certain evidence, research on how people deviated from these models, followed by the newer and richer analyses of human reasoning.

This chapter will address the following questions about the way people reason:

- How do they reason about situations described in conditional language (e.g., "if–then")?
- How do they reason about situations described with quantifiers like *all, some,* and *none*?
- How do people reason from specific examples and pieces of evidence to general conclusions?

Reasoning and the Brain

There has been some research investigating brain areas involved in reasoning, and it suggests that people can bring different systems to bear on different reasoning problems. Consider an fMRI experiment by Goel, Buchel, Frith, and Dolan (2000). They had participants solve logical **syllogisms,** arguments consisting of two premises and a conclusion, of the type that will be discussed in the second section of this chapter. Participants were presented with congruent problems such as

All poodles are pets.
All pets have names.
∴ All poodles have names.

and had to judge whether the third statement followed from the first two. The content of this example is more or less consistent with what people believe about pets and poodles. Goel et al. contrasted this type of problem with incongruent problems whose premises and conclusions violated standard beliefs such as

All pets are poodles.
All poodles are vicious.
∴ All pets are vicious.

They contrasted both of these types with reasoning about abstract concepts, such as

All P are B.
All B are C.
∴ All P are C.

Logicians would call all three kinds of syllogism valid.

Participants achieved 84% accuracy in their ability to judge the validity of the first congruent syllogisms and only 74% in their judgments of the second incongruent material. They achieved 77% accuracy in their ability to judge the content-free material. The reader might wonder about the sensibility of judging

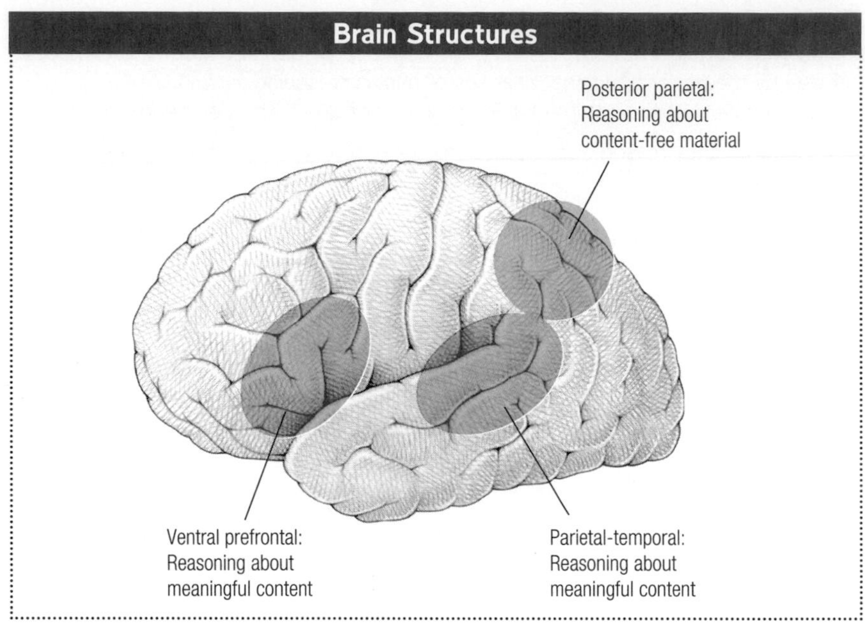

FIGURE 10.1 Comparison of brain regions activated when people reason about problems with meaningful content versus when they reason about material without content.

a participant as making a mistake in rejecting an incongruent conclusion such as "All pets are vicious"; we will return to this matter in the second section of the chapter. For now, of greater interest are the brain regions that were active when participants were judging material with content and when they were judging material without content; these areas are illustrated in Figure 10.1. When participants were judging content-free material, parietal regions that have been found to have roles in solving algebraic equations were active (see Figure 1.16b). When they were judging meaningful content, left prefrontal and temporal-parietal areas that are associated with language processing were active (see Figure 4.1). We will find that areas such as the latter regions are frequently active during reasoning about real problems and that they are associated both with better performance on some problems and with what might be considered worse performance on others. What this tells us is that people are capable of approaching logical problems in two rather different ways.

- *Faced with logical problems, people can engage either brain regions associated with the processing of meaningful content or regions associated with the processing of more abstract information.*

Reasoning about Conditionals

The first body of research we will cover concerns deductive reasoning. **Deductive reasoning** is concerned with conclusions that follow with certainty from their premises. It is distinguished from **inductive reasoning,** which is concerned with

TABLE 10.1

Analysis of a Conditional Statement and Various Valid and Invalid Rules of Inference		
A conditional statement:		
The antecedent		The consequent
(A) If you read this chapter,		(B) you will be wiser.
	Name	Rule of Inference
Valid deductions	***Modus ponens***	Given A is true, infer B is true.
	Modus tollens	Given B is false, infer A is false.
Invalid deductions	**Affirmation of the consequent**	Given B is true, infer A is true.
	Denial of the antecedent	Given A is false, infer B is false.

conclusions that probabilistically follow from their premises. To illustrate the distinction, suppose someone is told, "Fred is the brother of Mary" and "Mary is the mother of Lisa." Then, one might conclude that "Fred is the uncle of Lisa" and that "Fred is older than Lisa." The first conclusion, "Fred is the uncle of Lisa," would be a correct deductive inference given the definition of familial relationships. On the other hand, the second conclusion, "Fred is older than Lisa," is a good inductive inference, because it is probably true, but not a correct deductive inference, because it is not necessarily true.

Our first topic will concern human deductive reasoning using the conditional connective *if.* A **conditional statement** is an assertion, such as "If you read this chapter, you will be wiser." The *if* part (*you read this chapter*) is called the **antecedent** and the *then* part (*you will be wiser*) is called the **consequent.** Table 10.1 lays out the structure of conditional statements and various valid and invalid rules of inference. We will discuss these rules of inference below.

A particularly central rule of inference in the logic of the conditional is known as ***modus ponens*** (loosely translates from Latin as "method for affirming"). It allows us to infer the consequent of a conditional if we are given the antecedent. Thus, given both the proposition *If A, then B* and the proposition *A,* we can infer *B.* So, suppose we are told the following premises and conclusion:

Modus Ponens

If Joan understood this book, then she would get a good grade.
Joan understood this book.
Therefore, Joan got a good grade.

This example is an instance of valid deduction. By valid, we mean that, if premises 1 and 2 are true, then conclusion 3 must be true. This example also illustrates the artificiality of applying logic to real-world situations. How is one to really know whether Joan understands the book? One can only assign a certain probability to her understanding. Even if Joan does understand the book, at best it is only likely—not certain—that she will get a good grade. However, participants are asked to suspend their knowledge about such matters and treat these facts as if they are certainties. Or, more precisely, they are asked to reason what would follow for certain if these facts were certain.[1] Participants do not find these instructions particularly strange, but, as we will see, they are not always able to make logically correct inferences.

Another rule of inference is known in logic as ***modus tollens*** (loosely translates as "method of denying"). This rule states that, if we are given the proposition *A implies B* and the fact that *B is false,* then we can infer that *A is false.* The following inference exercise requires *modus tollens:*

Modus Tollens

If Joan understood this book, then she would get a good grade.
Joan did not get a good grade.
Therefore, Joan did not understand this book.

This conclusion might strike the reader as less than totally compelling because, again, in the real world such statements are not typically treated as certain.

Modus ponens *allows us to infer the consequent from the antecedent;* modus tollens *allows us to infer the antecedent is false if the consequent is false.*

Evaluation of Conditional Arguments

There are other inference patterns that people sometimes accept but which are invalid. One is called **affirmation of the consequent** and is illustrated by the following incorrect pattern of reasoning.

Affirmation of the Consequent

If Joan understood this book, then she would get a good grade.
Joan got a good grade.
Therefore, Joan did understand this book.

The other incorrect pattern is called **denial of the antecedent** and is illustrated by the following pattern of reasoning.

Denial of the Antecedent

If Joan understood this book, then she would get a good grade.
Joan did not understand this book.
Therefore, Joan did not get a grade.

In both of these cases there could be other ways that Joan could get a good grade, such as writing a great term essay. Evans (1993) reviewed a large number of studies that compared the frequency with which people accept the

[1] Interestingly, the mathematical theory of probability includes conditional statements. In this case, the objects of the conditional statement are statements about probabilities, which illustrates the fact that precise mathematics requires the formal logic of the conditional; it should not be taken as an illustration of a way of incorporating the formal logic of the conditional into a theory of everyday reasoning.

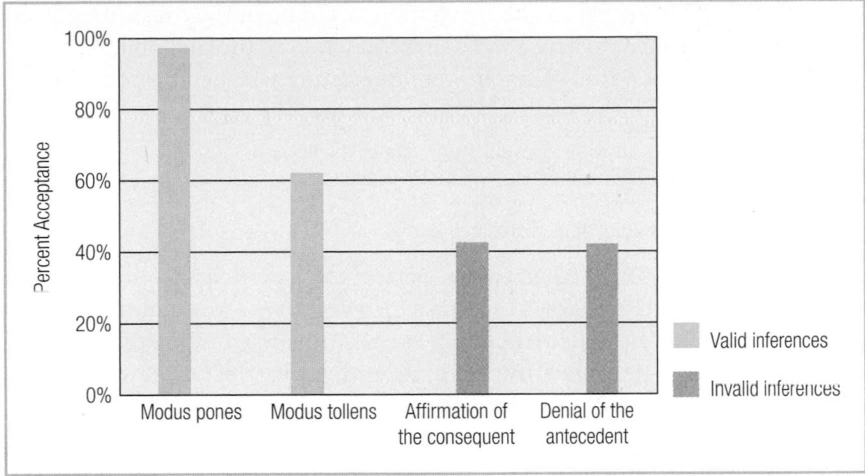

FIGURE 10.2 Frequency with which various conditional syllogisms are accepted—from Evans (1993).

valid *modus ponens* and *modus tollens* inferences as well as the frequency with which they accept the invalid inferences. The average percent acceptance over these studies is plotted in Figure 10.2. As can be seen, people rarely fail to accept a *modus ponens* inference but the frequency with which they accept the valid *modus tollens* is only slightly greater than the frequencies with which they accept the invalid affirmation of the consequent or the invalid denial of the antecedent.

- *People are only able to show high levels of logical reasoning with* modus ponens.

Evaluating Conditional Arguments in a Larger Context

Byrne (1989) performed an interesting variation of the typical conditional reasoning study that illustrates that human reasoning is sensitive to things that are ignored in a simple classification like that shown in Table 10.1. In one condition, she presented her participants with syllogisms like these:

> If she has an essay to write, she will study late in the library.
> (If she has textbooks to read, she will study late in the library.)
> She will stay late in the library.
> Therefore, she has an essay to write.

One group of participants did not see the premise in parentheses, whereas the other group of participants did. Without the additional premise, her participants accepted the conclusion 71% of the time, committing the fallacy of affirmation of the consequent. On the other hand, given the parenthetical premise in addition to the other premises, their acceptance of the conclusion went down to 13%. So we see people can be much more accurate in their reasoning if the material engages them to have a richer interpretation of the situation.

These results of Byrne are even more interesting when compared with another situation in which she used examples like the following:

> If she has an essay to write, she will study late in the library.
> (If the library stays open, then she will study in the library.)
> She has an essay to write.
> Therefore, she will study late in the library.

Without the additional statement in parentheses, participants accepted the *modus ponens* inference 96% of the time. However, with the additional statement, their acceptance rate went down to 38%. In a narrow, logical sense, the participants are making an error in not accepting the conclusion with the additional premise. However, in the world outside of the laboratory, they would be viewed as making the right judgment—how could she actually study in the library if it were not open? AI researchers would be frustrated if their programs still made the conclusion with this additional premise. People have a rich ability to reason about the real world, and it can intrude and cause them to make errors in these studies where they are told to reason by the strict rules of logic. However, it can lead them to make the right decisions in the real world.

- *When people's ability to reason about real-world situations intrudes into logical reasoning tasks, it can result in better or worse performance.*

The Wason Selection Task

A series of experiments initially begun by Peter Wason (for a review of the early research, see Wason & Johnson-Laird, 1972, Chapters 13 and 14) have been taken as a striking demonstration of human inability to reason correctly. In a typical experiment in this research, four cards showing the following symbols were placed in front of participants:

Participants were told that a letter appeared on one side of each card and a number on the other. Their task was to judge the validity of the following rule, which referred only to these four cards:

> If a card has a vowel on one side, then it has an even number on the other side.

The participants' task was to turn over only those cards that had to be turned over for the correctness of the rule to be judged. This task, typically referred to as the **selection task,** has received a great deal of research.

Averaging over a large number of experiments (Oaksford & Chater, 1994), about 90% of the participants have been found to select E, which is a logically correct choice because an odd number on the other side would disconfirm the rule. However, about 60% of the participants also choose to turn over the 4, which is not logically informative because neither a vowel nor a consonant on the other side would have falsified the rule. Only 25% elect to turn over the 7, which is a logically informative choice because a vowel behind the 7 would have falsified the rule. Only about 15% elect to turn over the K, which would not be an informative choice.

Thus, participants display two types of logical errors in the task. First, they often turn over the 4, an example of the fallacy of affirming the consequent. Even more striking is the failure to take the *modus tollens* step of disconfirming the consequent and determining whether the antecedent also is disconfirmed (in other words, to turn over the 7).

The number of people that make the right combination of choices, turning over only the E and 7, is often only 10%, which has been taken as a damning indictment of human reasoning. Early in the history of research on the selection task, Wason gave a talk at the IBM Research Center in which he presented this same problem to an audience filled with Ph.D.s, many in mathematics and physics. He got the same poor results from this audience and, reportedly, they were so embarrassed that they harassed Wason with complaints about how the problem was not accurately presented or the correct answer was not really correct. This question of what the right answer is has been recently explored but, before considering it, we will see what happens when one puts content into these problems.

- *When presented with neutral material in the Wason selection task, people have particular difficulty in recognizing the importance of exploring if the consequent is false.*

Permission Interpretation of the Conditional

A person's performance can sometimes be greatly enhanced when the material to be judged has meaningful content. Griggs and Cox (1982) were among the first to demonstrate this enhancement in a paradigm that is formally equivalent to the Wason card-selection task. Participants were instructed to imagine that they were police officers responsible for ensuring that the following regulation was being followed: *If a person is drinking beer, then the person must be over 19.* They were presented with four cards that represented people sitting around a table. On one side of each card was the age of the person and on the other side was the substance that the person was drinking. The cards were labeled "Drinking beer," "Drinking Coke," "16 years of age," and "22 years of age." The task was to select those people (cards to turn over) from whom further information was needed to determine whether the drinking law was being violated. In this situation, 74% of the participants selected the logically correct cards (namely, "Drinking beer" and "16 years of age"). Interestingly, patients with damage to the ventromedial prefrontal cortex do not show this advantage with content (Adolphs, Tranel, Bechara, Damasio, & Damasio, 1996). We will discuss this patient population more thoroughly in the next chapter.

It has been argued that the better performance in this task depends on the fact that the conditional statement is being interpreted as a rule about a social norm called the **permission schema.** Society has many rules about how its members should conduct themselves, and the argument is that people are good at applying such social rules (Cheng & Holyoak, 1985). An alternate possibility is that better performance in this task depends not on the permission semantics but on the greater familiarity of the participants with the rule. The participants were Florida undergraduates, and this rule about drinking was in force in Florida at the time. Would the participants have been able to reason about a similar but unfamiliar law? To discriminate between these two possibilities, Cheng and Holyoak (1985) performed the following experiment. One group of participants was asked to evaluate the following apparently senseless rule against a set of instances: "If the form says 'entering' on one side, then the other side includes cholera among the list of diseases." Another group was given the same rule as well as the rationale that to satisfy immigration officials upon entering a particular country, one must have been vaccinated for cholera. This rationale should invoke people's ability to reason about the permission schema. The forms indicated on one side whether the passenger was entering the country or in transit, whereas the other side listed the names of diseases for which he or she was vaccinated. Participants were presented with a set of forms that said "Transit," or "Entering," or "cholera, typhoid, hepatitis," or "typhoid, hepatitis." The performance of the group given the rationale was much better than that of the group given just the senseless rule without explanation; that is, the former group knew to check the "Entering" form and the "typhoid, hepatitis" form. Because the participants were not familiar with the rule, their good performance apparently depended on evoking the concept of permission and not on practice in applying the specific rule.

Cosmides (1989) and Gigerenzer and Hug (1992) argued that our good performance with such rules (which they call social contract rules) depends on the skill with which we have learned to detect cheaters. Gigerenzer and Hug had participants evaluate the following rule:

> If a student is assigned to Grover High School, then that student must live in Grover City.

They saw cards that stated whether the students attended Grover High or not on one side and whether they lived in Grover city or not on the other side. As in the original Wason experiment, they had to decide which cards to turn over. In the cheating condition, participants were asked to take the perspective of a member of the Grover City School Board looking for students who were illegally attending the high school. In the non-cheating condition, participants were asked to take the perspective of a visiting official from the German government who just wants to find out whether this rule is in effect at Grover High School. Gigerenzer and Hug were interested in the frequency with which participants would choose to turn over and check just the two cards: the student marked as going to Grover High School and the student marked as a nonresident of Grover City, which are the logically correct choices. In the cheating condition, where they took the perspective of a school board member, 80% of the participants chose just these two cards, replicating other results with permission rules. In the no-cheating condition, where they took the perspective of a disinterested visitor, only 45% of the participants chose just these two.

- *When participants take the perspective of detecting whether a social rule has been violated, they make a large proportion of logically correct choices in the Wason card selection task.*

Probabilistic Interpretation of the Conditional

The research just reviewed demonstrates that people can show good reasoning when they adopt what is called the permission interpretation of the conditional. However, how are we to understand their poor performance in the original Wason demonstrations where participants are not taking this permission interpretation? Oaksford and Chater (1994) argued that people tend to interpret these statements not as strict logical statements but rather as probabilistic statements about the world. Thus, when someone says, "If A, then B," they mean that B will probably occur when A occurs. Even more important to the Oaksford and Chater argument is the idea that events A and B typically have low probabilities of occurring in the world—which is what makes such statements informative. To illustrate their argument, suppose you visited a city and a friend told you that the following rule held about the cars driving in that city:

If a car has a broken headlight, it will have a broken taillight.

Events A and B (broken headlights and taillights) are rare, and consequently asserting that one implies the other is informative. Suppose you go to a large parking lot in which there are hundreds of cars; some are parked with their fronts exposed and others with their rears exposed. Most do not have their headlights broken or their taillights broken, but there are one or two with broken headlights and taillights. On which cars would you check the end not exposed to test your friend's claim? Let us consider the following possibilities:

1. *A car with a broken headlight:* If you saw such a car, like participants in all of these experiments, you would be inclined to check its taillight. Almost everyone sees that it is the sensible thing to do.
2. *A car without a broken headlight:* You would not be inclined to check this car, like most of the participants in these experiments, and, again, everyone agrees that you are right.
3. *A car with a broken taillight:* You would be sorely tempted to see whether that car did not have a broken headlight (despite the fact that it is supposedly unnecessary or "illogical"), and Oaksford and Chater agree with you. The reason is that a car with a broken taillight is so rare that, if it did have a broken headlight, you would be inclined to believe your friend's claim. The coincidence would be too much to shrug off.
4. *A car without a broken taillight:* You would be reluctant to check every car in the lot that met this condition (despite the fact that it is supposedly the logical thing to do), and, again, Oaksford and Chater would agree with you. The odds of finding a broken headlight on such a car are low because a broken headlight is rare, and so many cars would have to be checked. Checking those hundreds of normal cars just does not seem worthwhile.

Oaksford and Chater developed a mathematical analysis of the optimal behavior that explains why the typical errors in the original Wason task can be sensible. Their analysis predicts the frequency of choices in the Wason task. Their analysis depends on the assumption that properties such as "broken headlight" and "broken taillight" are rare. For this reason, it is informative to check the car with a broken taillight as in possibility 3 and is rather uninformative to check a car without a broken taillight as in possibility 4. Although the properties might not always be as rare as in this example, Oaksford and Chater argued that they generally are rare. For instance, more things are not dogs than are dogs and more things don't bark than do, and so the same analysis would apply to a rule such as "If an animal is a dog, then it will bark" and many other such rules. There is a weakness in the Oaksford and Chater argument, however, when applied to the original Wason experiment where the participants were reasoning about even numbers: There are not more odd numbers than even numbers. Nonetheless, Oaksford argued that people carry their beliefs that properties are rare into the Wason situation. There is evidence that manipulations of the probabilities of these properties do change people's behavior in the expected way (Oaksford & Wakefield, 2003).

- *The behavior in the Wason card selection task can be explained if we assume that participants select cards that will be informative under a probabilistic model.*

Final Thoughts on the Connective *If*

The logical connective *if* can evoke many different interpretations, which reflect the richness of human cognition. We have considered evidence for its probabilistic interpretation and its permission interpretation. People are capable of adopting the logician's interpretation of it as well, which, not surprisingly, is the interpretation that logicians and students of logic take of it when doing logic. Studies of their reasoning (Lewis, 1985; Scheines & Sieg, 1994) with the connective find it to be similar to mathematical reasoning such as in the domain of geometry discussed in Chapter 9. Basically, they take a problem-solving approach to formal reasoning with the connective. Qin et al. (2003) looked at participants solving abstract logic tasks and found activation in the same parietal regions (see Figure 10.1) that Goel et al. (2000) found active with their content-free material.

An amusing result is that training in logic does not necessarily result in better behavior on the original Wason selection task. In a study by Cheng, Holyoak, Nisbett, and Oliver (1986), college students who had just taken a semester course in logic did only 3% better on the card selection task than those who had no formal training in logic. It was not that they did not know the rules of logic; rather, they did choose to apply them in the experiment. When presented with these problems outside of the logic classroom, the students chose to adopt some other interpretation of the word *if*. However, this is not necessarily a "flaw" in human reasoning. To repeat a point made before, many researchers in AI wish their programs were as adaptive in how they interpret the information they are presented.

People use different problem-solving operators, depending on their interpretation of the logical connective if.

Deductive Reasoning: Reasoning about Quantifiers

Much of human knowledge is cast with **logical quantifiers** such as *all* or *some.* Witness Lincoln's famous statement: "You may fool all the people some of the time; you can even fool some of the people all the time; but you can't fool all of the people all the time." Scientific laws such as Newton's third law, "For every action there is always an opposite and equal reaction," try to identify what is always the case. It is important to understand how we reason with such quantifiers. This section will report research on how people reason about such quantifiers when they appear in simple sentences. As was the case for the logical connective *if,* we will see that there are differences between the logician's interpretation of quantifiers and the way in which people frequently reason about them.

The Categorical Syllogism

Modern logic is greatly concerned with analyzing the meaning of quantifiers such as *all, no,* and *some,* as in, for example:

All philosophers read some books.

Most of us might believe that this statement is true. The logician would then say that we were committed to the belief that we could not find a philosopher who did not read books, but most of us have no trouble accepting the idea that there were philosophers in societies before there were books or that one still might find somewhere in the world an illiterate person who professed sufficiently profound ideas to deserve the title of "philosopher." This example illustrates the fact that frequently when we use *all* in real life, we mean "most" or "with high probability." Similarly, when we use *no* as in

No doctors are poor.

we often mean "hardly any" or "with small probability." Logicians call both the *all* and *no* statements **universal statements** because they interpret these statements as blanket claims with no exceptions. Roger Schank, a famous AI researcher, was once observed to make the assertion

No one uses universals.

which surely is a sign that people use these words in a richer or more complex way than implied by the logical analysis.

By the beginning of the 20th century, the sophistication with which logicians analyzed such quantified statements increased considerably (see Church, 1956, for a historical discussion). This more advanced treatment of quantifiers is covered in most modern logic courses. However, most of the research on quantifiers in psychology has focused on a simpler and older kind of quantified deduction, called the **categorical syllogism.** Much of Aristotle's writing on reasoning concerned the categorical syllogism. Extensive discussion of these types of syllogisms can be found in old textbooks on logic such as Cohen and Nagel (1934).

Categorical syllogisms include statements containing the quantifiers *some, all, no,* and *some–not.* Examples of such categorical statements are:

1. All doctors are rich.
2. Some lawyers are dishonest.
3. No politician is trustworthy.
4. Some actors are not handsome.

As a convenient shorthand, the categories (e.g., doctors, rich people, lawyers, dishonest people) in such statements can be represented by letters—say, A, B, C, and so on. Thus, the statements might be rendered in this way:

1. All *A*'s are *B*'s.
2. Some *C*'s are *D*'s.
3. No *E*'s are *F*'s.
4. Some *G*'s are not *H*'s.

Sometimes, as in the Goel et al. experiment described at the beginning of the chapter, material is actually presented with such letters.

A categorical syllogism typically contains two premises and a conclusion. A typical example that might be used in research follows:

1. No Pittsburgher is a Browns fan.

   All Browns fans live in Cleveland.

   ∴ No Pittsburgher lives in Cleveland.

Many people accept this syllogism as logically valid. To see that the conclusion does not necessarily follow from the form of the premises, consider the following equivalent syllogism:

2. No man is a woman.

   Every woman is a human.

   ∴ No man is a human.

The first example illustrates a frequent result in research on categorical syllogisms, which is that people often accept invalid syllogisms. For instance, people accept the invalid syllogism 1 almost as much as they do the following valid syllogism:

3. No Pittsburgher lives in Cleveland.

   All Browns fans live in Cleveland.

   ∴ No Pittsburgher is a Browns fan.

- *Research on reasoning with quantifiers has focused on trying to understand why people accept many invalid categorical syllogisms.*

The Atmosphere Hypothesis

The previous example 1 is a case where people are biased by the content of the syllogism, but much of the research has focused on the tendency of people to accept invalid syllogisms even when they have neutral content. People are generally good at recognizing valid syllogisms when stated with neutral content. For instance, almost everyone accepts

1. All *A*'s are *B*'s.
   All *B*'s are *C*'s.
   ∴ All *A*'s are *C*'s.

The problem is that people also accept many invalid syllogisms. For instance, many people will accept

2. Some *A*'s are *B*'s.
   Some *B*'s are *C*'s.
   ∴ Some *A*'s are *C*'s.

(To see that this syllogism is invalid, consider replacing *A* with men, *B* with humans, and *C* with women.) However, people are not completely indiscriminate in what they accept as valid. For instance, even though they will accept example 2 in the preceding subsection, they will not accept example 3:

3. Some *A*'s are *B*'s.
   Some *B*'s are *C*'s.
   ∴ No *A*'s are *C*'s.

To account for the pattern of what participants accept and what they reject, Woodworth and Sells (1935) proposed the **atmosphere hypothesis.** This hypothesis states that the logical terms (*some, all, no, and not*) used in the premises of a syllogism create an "atmosphere" that predisposes participants to accept conclusions having the same terms. The atmosphere hypothesis consists of two parts. One part asserts that participants tend to accept a positive conclusion to positive premises and a negative conclusion to negative premises. When the premises are mixed, participants tend to prefer a negative. Thus, they would tend to accept the following invalid syllogism:

4. No *A*'s are *B*'s.
   All *B*'s are *C*'s.
   ∴ No *A*'s are *C*'s.

(This is an abstract form of the same invalid syllogism discussed on the previous page.)

The other part of the atmosphere hypothesis concerns a participant's response to **particular statements** (*some* or *some not*) versus **universal statements** (*all* or *no*). As example 4 illustrates, participants will accept a universal conclusion if the premises are universal. They will tend to accept a particular conclusion if the premises are particular, which accounts for their acceptance of syllogism 2 given earlier. When one premise is particular and the other universal, participants prefer a particular conclusion. Thus they will accept the following invalid syllogism:

5. All *A*'s are *B*'s.
Some *B*'s are *C*'s.
∴ Some *A*'s are *C*'s.

(To see that this syllogism is invalid, consider replacing *A* with men, *B* with humans, and *C* with women.)

The atmosphere hypothesis *states that the logical terms (*some, all, no, *and* some not*) used in the premises of a syllogism create an "atmosphere" that predisposes participants to accept conclusions having the same terms.*

Limitations of the Atmosphere Hypothesis

The atmosphere hypothesis provides a succinct characterization of participant behavior with the various syllogisms, but it tells us little about what the participants are actually thinking or why. It offers no explanation for why the content of the syllogism (as in the Pittsburgh–Cleveland example) can have such a strong effect on judgments. Its characterization of participant behavior is also not always correct for content-free syllogisms. For example, according to the atmosphere hypothesis, participants are just as likely to accept the atmosphere-favored conclusion when it is not valid as when it is valid. That is, it predicts that participants would be just as likely to accept

6. All *A*'s are *B*'s.
Some *B*'s are *C*'s.
∴ Some *A*'s are *C*'s.

which is not valid, as they would be to accept

7. Some *A*'s are *B*'s.
All *B*'s are *C*'s.
∴ Some *A*'s are *C*'s.

which is valid. In fact, participants are more likely to accept the conclusion in the valid case. Thus, participants do display some ability to evaluate a syllogism accurately.

Another limitation of the atmosphere hypothesis is that it fails to predict the effects that the form of a syllogism will have on participants' validity judgments. For instance, the hypothesis predicts that participants would be no more likely to erroneously accept

8. Some *A*'s are *B*'s.
Some *B*'s are *C*'s.
∴ Some *A*'s are *C*'s.

than they would be to erroneously accept

9. Some *B*'s are *A*'s.
Some *C*'s are *B*'s.
∴ Some *A*'s are *C*'s.

In fact, participants are more willing to erroneously accept the conclusion in the former case (Johnson-Laird & Steedman, 1978). In general, participants are more willing to accept a conclusion from *A* to *C* if they can find a chain leading from *A* to *B* in one premise and from *B* to *C* in the second premise.

Another problem with the atmosphere hypothesis is that it does not really handle what participants do in the presence of two negatives. If participants are given the following two premises,

No *A*'s are *B*'s.
No *B*'s are *C*'s.

the atmosphere hypothesis would predict that participants should tend to accept the invalid conclusion:

∴ No *A*'s are *C*'s.

Although a few participants do accept this conclusion, most refuse to accept any conclusion when both premises are negative, which is the correct thing to do (Dickstein, 1978).

Another problem with the atmosphere hypothesis is that it does not really explain what people are thinking when they process such syllogisms. It just tries to predict what conclusions they will accept. The next section will consider some explanations of the thought processes that lead people to correct or incorrect conclusions.

Participants only approximate the predictions of the atmosphere hypothesis and are often more accurate than it would predict.

Process Explanations

One class of explanations is that participants choose not to do what the experimenters think they are doing. For instance, it has been argued that it is not natural for people to judge the logical validity of these arguments. Rather, people tend to judge what conclusions are true. Consider the following pair of syllogisms:

All lawyers are human.
All Republicans are human.
∴ Some lawyers are Republicans.

which has a true conclusion but is not valid (consider replacing lawyers by men and Republicans by women) and

All bictoids are reptiles.
All bictoids are birds.
∴ Some reptiles are birds.

which is a valid argument but has a false conclusion. People have a greater tendency to accept the first, invalid argument having a true conclusion than the second, valid argument having a false conclusion (Evans, Handley, & Harper, 2001).

It is also argued that many people really do not understand what it means for an argument to be valid and simply judge whether a conclusion is possible given the premises. So, for example, although the preceding syllogism concerning lawyers and Republicans is not valid, it is certainly possible given the premises that the conclusion is true. Evans et al. showed that there is very little difference in the judgments that participants make when they are asked to judge when conclusions are necessarily true given the premises (the measure of a valid argument) and when conclusions are possibly true given the premises.

Johnson-Laird (Johnson-Laird, 1983; Johnson-Laird & Steedman, 1978) proposed that participants judge whether a conclusion is possible by creating a mental model of a world that satisfies the premises of the syllogism and inspecting that model to see whether the conclusion is satisfied. This explanation is called **mental model theory.** Consider these premises:

> All the squares are striped.
> <u>Some of the striped objects have bold borders.</u>

Figure 10.3a illustrates what a participant might imagine, according to Johnson-Laird, as an instantiation of these premises. The participant has imagined a group of objects, some of which are square, whereas others are round; some of which are striped, whereas others are clear; and some of which have bold borders, whereas others do not. This world represents one possible interpretation of these premises. When the participant is asked to judge the following conclusion,

> ∴ Some of the squares have bold borders.

the participant inspects the diagram and sees that, indeed, the conclusion is possible given the premises. The problem is that this response establishes only that the conclusion is possible but not that it is necessary. For the conclusion to be necessary, it must be true in all mental models that support the premises. Figure 10.3b illustrates a case in which the premises are true but the conclusion does not hold. Johnson-Laird claimed that participants have considerable difficulty developing alternative models. Thus, the participant is building a specific model for the premises and is inspecting it to see what is true in that model. Johnson-Laird (1983) developed a computer simulation of this theory that reproduces many of the errors that participants make. Johnson-Laird (1995) also argued that there is neurological evidence in favor of the mental model explanation. He noted that patients with right-hemisphere damage are more impaired in reasoning tasks than are patients with left-hemisphere damage. He noted that the right hemisphere tends to take part in spatial processing of mental images. In a brain-imaging study, Kroger, Cohen, Nystrom, and Johnson-Laird (2008) found that the right frontal cortex was more active than the left in processing such syllogisms but that the opposite was true when people engaged in arithmetic calculation (this left bias for arithmetic is also illustrated in the study

FIGURE 10.3 Two possible models that participants might form for the premises of the categorical syllogism dealing with square and round objects.

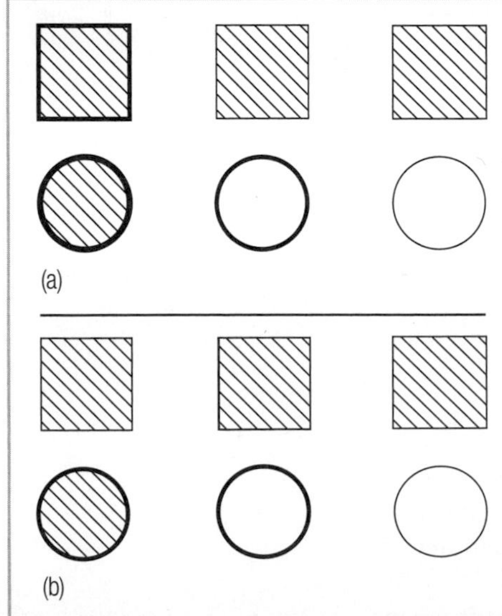

described in Figure 1.16). Parsons and Osherson (2001) reported a similar finding, with deductive reasoning being right localized and probabilistic reasoning being left localized.

Basically, Johnson-Laird's argument is that people make errors in reasoning because they overlook possible explanations of the premises. For example, a participant imagines Figure 10.3a as an explanation and overlooks the possibility of Figure 10.3b. Johnson-Laird (personal communication) argues that a great many errors in human reasoning are produced by failures to consider possible explanations of the data. For instance, a problem in the Chernobyl disaster was that, for several hours, engineers failed to consider the possibility that the reactor was no longer intact.

Evans et al. (2001) argued that people are inclined to look for only one mental model for the premises and, if they can find such an interpretation, they accept the argument if the conclusion is valid in that model. The effect of real-world content is to bias that search for such a mental model. In this way, we can explain the effect of real-world content. That is, people tend to accept the invalid "Some lawyers are Republicans" syllogism because it naturally suggests a model in which the conclusion holds. In contrast, they tend to reject the valid "Some reptiles are birds" argument because, given its content, it is hard to imagine a world where it is true.

To successfully adapt to our world, it is important to make correct inferences about what is true in this world and not about what might be true in all possible worlds (which is what judging logical validity is concerned with). Given this perspective, the problem seems to lie as much with the questions that participants are being asked to answer in these experiments as with the participants themselves.

- *Errors in evaluating syllogisms can be explained by assuming that participants fail to consider possible mental models of the syllogisms.*

Inductive Reasoning and Hypothesis Testing

In contrast to deductive reasoning where logical rules allow one to infer certain conclusions from premises, in inductive reasoning the conclusion does not necessarily follow from the premises. Consider the following premises:

The first number in the series is 1.
The second number in the series is 2.
The third number in the series is 4.

What conclusion follows? The numbers are doubling and so possible conclusion is that

The fourth number is 8.

However, a better conclusion might be to state the general rule:

Each number is twice the previous number.

A characteristic of a good inductive inference like the second conclusion is that it is a statement from which one can deduce all the premises. For example, because we know each number is twice the previous number, we can now deduce what the original three numbers must have been. Thus, in a certain sense it is deduction turned around. The difficulty for inductive reasoning is that there is usually not a single conclusion that would be consistent with the premises. For instance, in the problem above one could have concluded that the difference between successive numbers is increasing by one and that the fourth number would be 7.

Inductive reasoning is relevant to many aspects of everyday life: a detective trying to solve a mystery given a set of clues, a doctor trying to diagnose the cause of a set of symptoms, someone trying to determine what is wrong with a TV, or a researcher trying to discover a new scientific law. In all these cases, one gets a set of specific observations from which one is trying to infer some relevant conclusion. Many of these cases involve the sort of probabilistic reasoning that will be discussed in the next chapter (for instance, medical symptoms are typically only associated probabilistically with disease). In this chapter, we will focus on cases, like the above number example, where we are looking for a hypothesis that implies the observations with certainty. Much of the interest in such cases is how people seek evidence relevant to formulating such a hypothesis.

Hypothesis Formation

Bruner, Goodnow, and Austin (1956) performed a classic series of experiments on hypothesis formation. Figure 10.4 illustrates the kind of material they used. The stimuli were all rectangular boxes containing various objects. The stimuli varied on four dimensions: number of objects (one, two, or three); number of borders around the boxes (one, two, or three); shape (cross, circle, or square);

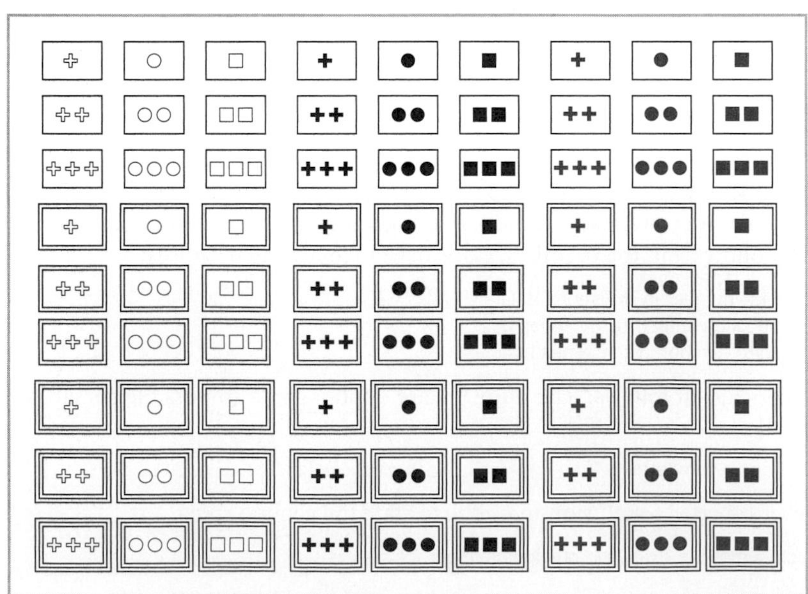

FIGURE 10.4 Material used by Bruner et al. in one of their studies of concept identification. The array consists of instances formed by combinations of four attributes, each exhibiting three values.

and color (green, black, or red: represented here as white, black, or red). Participants were told that they were to discover some concept that described a particular subset of these instances. For instance, the concept might have been black crosses. Participants were to discover the correct concept on the basis of information they were given about what were and what were not instances of the concept.

Figure 10.5 contains three illustrations (the three columns) of the information participants might have been presented. Each column consists of a sequence of instances identified either as members of the concept (positive, +) or not (negative, −). Each column represents a different concept. Participants would be presented with the instances in a column one at a time. From these instances they would determine what the concept was. Stop reading and try to determine the concept for each column.

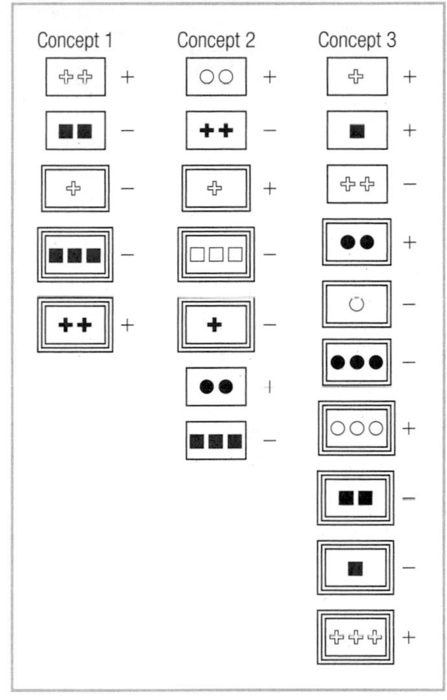

FIGURE 10.5 Examples of sequences of instances from which a participant is to identify concepts. Each column gives a sequence of instances and non-instances for a different concept. A plus (+) signals a positive instance and minus (−) sign a negative instance.

The concept in the first example is *two crosses.* This concept is referred to as a *conjunctive* concept, since the conjunction of a number of features (in this case the features are *two* and *cross*) must be present for the instance to be positive. People typically find conjunctive concepts easiest to discover. In some sense conjunctive hypotheses seem to be the most natural kind of hypotheses. They are the kind that have been researched most extensively. The solution to the second example is *two borders or circles.* This kind of concept is referred to as a *disjunctive concept* because an instance is a member of the concept if either of the features is present. In the final example, the solution is that the number of objects must equal the number of borders. This example is a *relational concept* because it specifies a relationship between two dimensions.

The problems in this series are particularly difficult because to identify the concept, you must both determine which features are relevant and discover the kind of rule that connects the features (e.g., conjunctive, disjunctive, or relational). The former problem is referred to as **attribute identification** and the latter as **rule learning** (Haygood & Bourne, 1965). In many experiments, either the form of the rule or the relevant attributes are identified for the participant. For instance, in the Bruner et al. (1956) experiments, participants had to identify only the correct attributes. They knew that they would be identifying conjunctive concepts.

Forming a hypothesis involves identifying both what features are relevant to the hypothesis and how these features are related.

Hypothesis Testing

In the experiment illustrated in Figure 10.5, participants receive a sequence of instances and have to figure out what the concept is. Some problems in real life are like this—we have no control over what evidence we see but must figure out the rules that govern it. For instance, when there is an outbreak of food poisoning in the United States, medical health researchers check on what the victims ate, looking for some common pattern. They have no control over what the victims ate. On the other hand, in other situations one can do experiments and test certain possibilities. For instance, when medical researchers want to determine the most effective combination of drugs to treat a disease, they will perform clinical trials where different groups of patients receive different drug combinations. Scientific research can reach more certain conclusions more quickly if the researchers can choose the cases to test rather than having to take the cases that the situation presents to them.

In their classic research, Bruner, Goodnow, and Austin (1956) also studied situations where participants could choose which instances they get information about. For example, in one condition, Bruner et al. gave participants a single positive instance of concept, and then the participants could select various instances and ask whether they were also instances of the concept. For example, if you were told that the middle stimulus in Figure 10.4 (fifth row, fifth column) was an instance of a conjunctive concept that you had to discover, what stimuli would you choose to select? The approach advocated in science would be to test each dimension, one at a time, and determine whether it was critical to the hypothesis. For instance, you could choose to test first the dimension of number of borders and choose a stimulus that differed from the initial stimulus only on this dimension. If the stimulus were not an instance, you would know that the value of the original stimulus (in this case, two borders) was relevant and if not, you would know that it was irrelevant. Then you could try another dimension. After four stimuli, you would have identified the conjunctive concept with certainty. Bruner et al. called this strategy "conservative focusing," and some of their participants (Harvard undergraduates of the 1950s) followed it. However, many participants practiced less well-behaved strategies. For instance, given the same initial stimulus, they might test an instance that changed both the color and the number of borders. If the stimulus were an instance, they would know that neither dimension was relevant. However, if wrong, they would have learned relatively little.

A well-known case where people seem to test their hypotheses less than optimally is the 2-4-6 task introduced by Wason (1960—the same psychologist who introduced the card selection task that we described earlier). In this experiment, participants are told that "2 4 6" is an instance of a triad that is consistent with a rule and are instructed to find out what the rule is by asking whether other triples of numbers are instances of the rule. What triples would you try? The protocol below comes from one of Wason's participants. The protocol gives each triad that the participant produced and the reason for the choice, along with the experimenter's feedback as to whether the triad conformed to the rule. The sequence of triads was occasionally broken when the participant decided to announce a hypothesis. The experimenter's feedback for each hypothesis is given in parenthesis:

Triad	Reason Given for Triad	Feedback
8 10 12	2 added each time.	Yes
14 16 18	Even numbers in order of magnitude.	Yes
20 22 24	Same reason.	Yes
1 3 5	2 added to preceding number	Yes

Announcement: *The rule is that by starting with any number, 2 is added each time to form the next number.* (Incorrect)

2 6 10	The middle number is the arithmetic mean of the other two.	Yes
1 50 99	Same reason.	Yes

Announcement: *The rule is that the middle number is the arithmetic mean of the other two.* (Incorrect)

3 10 17	Same number, 7, added each time.	Yes
0 3 6	Three added each time.	Yes

Announcement: *The rule is that the difference between two numbers next to each other is the same.* (Incorrect)

12 8 4	The same number is subtracted each time to form the next number.	No

Announcement: *The rule is adding a number, always the same one, to form the next number.* (Incorrect)

1 4 9	Any three numbers in order of magnitude.	Yes

Announcement: *The rule is any three numbers in order of magnitude.* (Correct)

The important feature to note about this protocol is that the participant tested the hypothesis by almost exclusively generating sequences consistent with it. The better procedure in this case would have been to also try sequences that were inconsistent. That is, the participant should have looked sooner for negative evidence as well as positive evidence. This would have exposed the fact that the participant had started out with a hypothesis that was too narrow and was missing the more general correct hypothesis. The only way to discover this error is to try examples that disconfirm the hypothesis, but this is what people have great difficulty doing,

In another experiment, Wason (1968) asked 16 participants, after they had announced their hypotheses, what they would do to determine whether their hypotheses were incorrect. Nine participants said they would generate only instances consistent with their hypotheses and wait for one to be identified as not an instance of the rule. Only four participants said that they would generate instances inconsistent with the hypothesis to see whether they were identified as members of the rule. The remaining three insisted that their hypotheses could not be incorrect.

This strategy to select only positive instances has been called the **confirmation bias.** It has been argued that confirmation bias is not necessarily a mistaken strategy (Fischhoff & Neyth-Marom, 1983; Kayman & Ha, 1987). In many situations, selecting instances consistent with a hypothesis is an effective way to disconfirm the hypothesis. For instance, if one did well on an exam after drinking a glass of orange juice and entertained the hypothesis that orange juice led to good exam performance, drinking orange juice before a couple more exams might quickly disabuse one of that hypothesis. What made this strategy so ineffective in Wason's experiment is simply that the correct hypothesis was very general. It would be like finding out that consuming any drink would improve exam performance (particularly unlikely if we include alcoholic drinks).

- *In choosing instances to test a hypothesis, people often focus on instances consistent with their hypothesis, and this can cause difficulties if their hypothesis is too narrow.*

Scientific Discovery

Whether participants are trying to infer a concept by selecting instances from a set of options like those in Figure 10.4 or trying to infer a rule that describes a set of examples as in the protocol we just reviewed, participants are engaged in problem-solving searches like those we discussed in Chapter 8 (such as in Figure 8.4 or Figure 8.8). The difference, however, is that they are searching two problem spaces. One problem space is the space of possible hypotheses and the other is the space of possible instances. It has been argued (e.g., Simon & Lea, 1974; Klahr & Dunbar, 1998) that this is exactly the situation that scientists face in discovering a new theory—they search through a space of possible theories and a space of possible experiments to test these theories.

The term "confirmation bias" has been used to describe failures in the way people test scientific theories. In the hypothesis-testing example we described, it just referred to a tendency to test only instances that were an example of one's hypothesis. However, in the broader context of testing scientific theories, it refers to a host of behaviors that serve to protect one's favored theory from disconfirmation. In one study, Dunbar (1993) had undergraduates try to discover how genes were controlled by redoing, in a highly simplified form, the research that won Jacques Monod and Francois Jacob the 1965 Nobel Prize for medicine. They provided the participants with computer simulations that could mimic some of the critical experiments. They were told that their task was to determine how one set of genes controlled another set of genes that produced an enzyme only when lactose was present. (This enzyme serves to break down the lactose into glucose.) All the undergraduates initially thought that there must be a mechanism by which the first set of genes responded to the presence of lactose and activated the second set of genes. This is the hypothesis that Monod and Jacob had initially as well, but in fact the mechanism is an inhibitory mechanism by which the first set of genes inhibit the enzyme-producing genes when lactose is absent but are blocked from inhibiting when lactose is present. Showing the confirmation bias, these undergraduates tried to find experiments that would confirm their activation hypothesis. The majority of the participants continued to search the experimental space for some combination of genes that would support their activation hypothesis, but a minority began to search for alternative hypotheses about what was in control.

Science as an institution has a way of protecting us from scientists whose confirmation bias leads them too strongly in the wrong direction. Other scientists are often strongly motivated to find problems with the theories of a particular scientist (Nickerson, 1998). There is also considerable variation in how individual scientists practice. Michael Faraday, a famous 19th-century chemist, made his discoveries by early focusing on collecting confirmatory evidence and then switching to focusing on disconfirmatory evidence (Tweney, 1989). Dunbar (1997) studied scientists in three immunology laboratories and one biology laboratory at Stanford and noted that they were quite ready to attend to unexpected results and modify their theory to accommodate these.

Fugelsang and Dunbar (2005) performed fMRI imaging studies looking at participants as they tried to integrate data with specific hypothesis. For instance, participants were told that they were seeing results from a clinical trial looking at the effect of an antidepressant on mood. They either saw patient records that indicated the drug had an effect on mood (consistent) or that it did not have an effect (inconsistent). Participants started out believing the drug had an effect and so found consistent evidence more plausible. When viewing the inconsistent evidence, participants showed greater activation in their anterior cingulate cortex (ACC) (see Figure 3.1). As we noted in Chapter 3, the ACC is highly active when participants are engaged in a task that requires strong cognitive control, such as dealing with an inconsistent trial in a Stroop task. These same basic brain mechanisms seem to be invoked when participants must deal with inconsistent data in a scientific context, and the results suggest that scientific reasoning evokes basic cognitive processes.

Implications

How convincing is a 90% result?

Scientists can be subject to a confirmation bias. For instance, Louis Pasteur was involved in a major debate with other scientists about whether new organisms could spontaneously generate. It was argued that the appearance of bacteria in apparently sterilized organic material was evidence for spontaneous generation of life. Pasteur performed many experiments trying to disprove this and 90% of these failed, but he chose only to publish the successful experiment, claiming that the rest were due to experimental errors (Geison, 1995). Scientists frequently question their experiment if results seem to contradict establish theory. For instance, if one dropped a rock from a 100-meter tower and timed its fall as 1 second, it would be wise not to accept the theory that acceleration due to gravity was 200 meters (using the formula distance = $\frac{1}{2}$ × acceleration × time^2) rather than the standard accepted value of approximately 10 meters on earth. Almost certainly something was wrong in the measurements and the experiment needs to be repeated. On the other hand, the Pasteur case might seem rather extreme, ignoring 90% of the experiments on a theory that was much in doubt at the time. In this case, however, he turned out to be right.

- *In studies of scientific discovery, participants tend to focus on experiments consistent with their favorite hypothesis and show a reluctance to search for alternative hypotheses.*

Conclusions

Much of the research on human reasoning has found it wanting when compared to the rules and implications of formal logic. As we just noted, this might even be said of the process by which scientists engage in their research. However, this dismal characterization of human reasoning fails to properly appreciate the full context in which it occurs. In many actual reasoning situations, people do quite well, in part because they take in the full complexity and implications of the actual real-world content. Despite a tendency towards confirmation bias, science as a whole has progressed with great success. To some extent, this is because science is a social activity carried out by a community of researchers. Competitive scientists are quick to find mistakes in each other's approach, but there is also a cooperative nature to science. Research takes place in teams of researchers and they often rely on each other's help. Okada and Simon (1997) found that pairs of undergraduates were much more successful than individual students at finding the inhibition mechanism in Dunbar's (1993) genetic control task. As Okada and Simon note, "In a collaborative situation, subjects must often be more explicit than in an individual learning situation, to make partners understand their ideas and to convince them. This can prompt subjects to entertain requests for explanation and construct deeper explanations" (p. 130). The bottom line of this chapter is that human reasoning normally takes place in a world of complexities (both factual and social) and that what appears deficient in the laboratory may be exquisitely tuned to that world.

Questions for Thought

1. Johnson-Laird and Goldvarg (1997) presented Princeton undergraduates with reasoning problems like this one:

   Only one of the following premises is true about a particular hand of cards:

   > There is a king in the hand or there is an ace or both.
   > There is a queen in the hand or there is an ace or both.
   > There is a jack in the hand or there is a 10, or both.

   Is it possible that there is an ace in the hand?

   They report that the students only were correct on 1% of such problems. What is the correct answer for the problem above? Why is it so hard? Johnson-Laird and Goldvarg attribute the difficulty that people have in creating mental models of what is not the case.

2. Johnson-Laird and Steedman (1978) presented the following syllogisms to participants drawn from Columbia Teachers College:

   > All gourmets are shopkeepers.
   > All bowlers are shopkeepers.

   And asked them what followed. The following is the distribution of answers:

   > 17 agreed that no conclusion followed.
   > 2 thought that "Some gourmets are bowlers" followed.
   > 4 thought that "All bowlers are gourmets" followed.

7 thought that "Some bowlers are gourmets" followed.
8 thought that "All gourmets are bowlers" followed.

Use the concepts of this chapter to help explain the answers these participants gave and did not give.

3. Consider the third column in Figure 10.5, which was described in the chapter as satisfying the rule that "the number of borders is the same as the number of objects." An alternative rule that describes the instances is "3 white objects or 2 black objects or 1 object with one border." Which is the better description of the category and why? Is it possible to know for certain which is the correct rule?

Key Terms

affirmation of the consequent
antecedent
atmosphere hypothesis
attribute identification
categorical syllogism
conditional statement
confirmation bias
consequent
deductive reasoning
denial of the antecedent
inductive reasoning
logical quantifiers
mental model theory
modus ponens
modus tollens
particular statements
permission schema
rule learning
selection task
syllogisms
universal statements

11

Judgment and Decision Making

As we saw in Chapter 10, most of the research on human reasoning has compared it to various prescriptive models from logic and mathematics. The prescriptive models assume that people have access to information about which they can be certain and that they can coolly reflect on the information. However, in the real world, people have to make decisions in the face of incomplete and uncertain information. Furthermore, in contrast to the relatively neutral character of the syllogisms of the previous chapter, in real life our decisions can have important consequences for our lives. Consider the simple task of deciding what to eat—we have all been frustrated by the medical reports that pronounce formerly "healthy" food as "unhealthy" and vice versa. In decision making, we must also deal with the unpleasant consequences of what might be good decisions such as going on a diet or giving up a pleasurable activity like smoking.

This chapter will focus on research on judgment and decision making that comes closer to such real-life circumstances. As before, we will discuss research showing how the performance of normal humans is wanting compared to models that were developed for rational behavior. However, we will also see how much of that research is incomplete, missing the complexity of everyday human decision making. Recent research has developed a more nuanced characterization of the situations that people face in their everyday life, and a better appreciation of the nature of their judgments.

In this chapter, we will answer the questions:

- How well do people judge the probability of uncertain events?
- How do people use their past experiences to make judgments?
- How do people decide among uncertain options that offer different rewards and costs?
- How does the brain support such decision making?

The Brain and Decision Making

In 1848, Phineas Gage, a railroad worker in Vermont, suffered a bizarre accident: He was using an iron bar to pack gunpowder down into a hole drilled into a rock that had to be blasted to clear a roadbed for the railroad. The powder unexpectedly exploded and sent the iron bar flying through his head before landing 80 feet away. Figure 11.1 shows a reconstruction of the trajectory of the bar through his skull (Damasio, Grabowski, Frank, Galabruda, & Damasio, 1994). (For a more detailed reconstruction, see Color Plate 11.1.) The bar managed to miss any vital areas and spared most of his brain but tore through the middle of the very front of the brain—a region called the **ventromedial prefrontal cortex.** Amazingly, he not only survived, he was even was able to talk and walk away from the accident after being unconscious for a few minutes. His recovery was difficult, largely because of infections, but he eventually was able to hold jobs such as a coach driver. Henry Jacob Bigelow, a Professor of Surgery at Harvard University, declared him "quite recovered in faculties of body and mind" (MacMillan, 2000). Based on such a report, one might have thought that this part of the brain performed no function.

Brain Structures

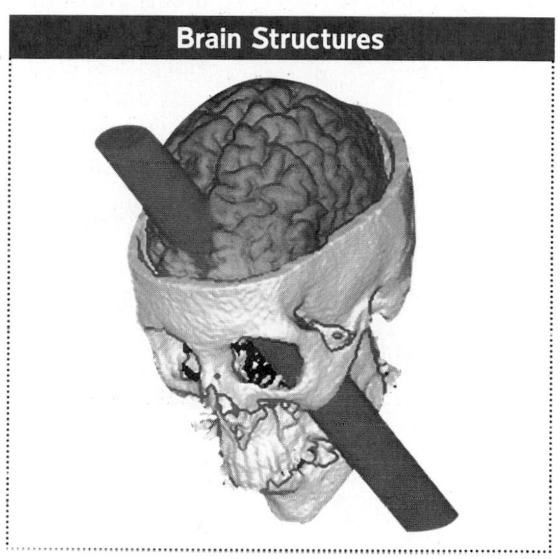

FIGURE 11.1 A representation of the passage of the bar through Phineas Gage's brain. Note that only the middle of the frontal-most portion has been damaged. (From Damasio et al., 1994).

However, all was not well. His personality had undergone major changes. Before his injury he had been polite, respectful, popular, and reliable, and generally displayed ideal behavior for an American man of that time. Afterward he became just the opposite—as his own physician, Harlow, later described him:

> fitful, irreverent, indulging at times in the grossest profanity (which was not previously his custom), manifesting but little deference for his fellows, impatient of restraint or advice when it conflicts with his desires, at times pertinaciously obstinate, yet capricious and vacillating, devising many plans of future operations, which are no sooner arranged than they are abandoned in turn for others appearing more feasible. A child in his intellectual capacity and manifestations, he has the animal passions of a strong man. Previous to his injury, although untrained in the schools, he possessed a well-balanced mind, and was looked upon by those who knew him as a shrewd, smart businessman, very energetic and persistent in executing all his plans of operation. In this regard his mind was radically changed, so decidedly that his friends and acquaintances said he was "no longer Gage." (Harlow, 1868, p. 327)

Gage is the classic case demonstrating the importance of the ventromedial prefrontal cortex to human personality. Subsequently, a number of other similar patients have been described and they all show the same sorts of personality disorders. Family members and friends will describe them with phrases like "socially incompetent," "decides against his best interest," and "doesn't learn from his mistakes" (Sanfey, Hastie, Colvin, & Grafman, 2003). Earlier in Chapter 8, we discussed the case of the patient PF who also suffered damage to his anterior prefrontal region, like Gage. However, in his case the damage also included lateral portions of the anterior prefrontal region, and his difficulty was more with organizing complex problem solving than decision making. In general, it is thought that the more medial portion of the anterior prefrontal region, where Gage's injury was localized, is important to motivation, emotional regulation, and social sensitivity (Gilbert, Spengler, Simons, Frith, & Burgess, 2006).

- *The ventromedial prefrontal cortex plays an important role in achieving the motivational balance and social sensitivity that is key to making successful judgments.*

Probabilistic Judgment

There is a prescriptive model for how people should reason about probabilities as they collect relevant evidence. This is called **Bayes's theorem,** which is based on a mathematical analysis of the nature of probability. Much of the research in the field has been concerned with showing that human participants do not match up with the prescriptions of Bayes's theorem.

Bayes's Theorem

As an example of the application of Bayes's theorem, suppose I come home and find the door to my house ajar. I am interested in the hypothesis that it might be the work of a burglar. How do I evaluate this hypothesis? I might treat it as a conditional syllogism of the following sort:

If a burglar is in the house, then the door will be ajar.
The door is ajar.
∴ A burglar is in the house.

As a conditional syllogism, it would be judged as the erroneous affirmation of the consequent. However, it does have a certain plausibility as an inductive argument. Bayes's theorem provides a way of assessing just how plausible it is by combining what are called a prior probability and a conditional probability to produce what is called a posterior probability, which is a measure of the strength of the conclusion.

A **prior probability** is the probability that a hypothesis is true before consideration of the evidence (e.g., the door is ajar). The less likely the hypothesis was before the evidence, the less likely it should be after the evidence. Let us refer to the hypothesis that my house has been burglarized as H. Suppose that I know from police statistics that the probability of a house in my neighborhood being burglarized on any particular day is 1 in 1,000.[1] This probability is expressed as:

$$\text{Prob}(H) = .001$$

[1] Although this makes for easy calculation, the actual number for Pittsburgh is closer to 1 burglary per 100,000 households per day.

This equation expresses the prior probability of the hypothesis, or the probability that the hypothesis is true before the evidence is considered. The other prior probability needed for the application of Bayes's theorem is the probability that the house has not been burglarized. This alternate hypothesis is denoted $\sim H$. This value is 1 minus Prob(H) and is expressed:

$$\text{Prob}(\sim H) = .999$$

A **conditional probability** is the probability that a particular type of evidence is true if a particular hypothesis is true. Let us consider what the conditional probabilities of the evidence (door ajar) would be under the two hypotheses. First, suppose I believe that the probability of the door's being ajar is quite high if I have been burglarized, for example, 4 out of 5. Let E denote the evidence, or the event of the door being ajar. Then, we will denote this conditional probability of E given that H is true as

$$\text{Prob}(E|H) = .8$$

Second, we determine the probability of E if H is not true. Suppose I know that chances are only 1 out of 100 that the door would be ajar if no burglary had taken place (e.g., by accident, neighbors with a key). We denote this probability by

$$\text{Prob}(E|\sim H) = .01$$

the probability of E given that H is not true.

The **posterior probability** is the probability that a hypothesis is true after consideration of the evidence. The notation Prob($H|E$) is the posterior probability of hypothesis H given evidence E. According to Bayes's theorem, we can calculate the posterior probability of H, that the house has been burglarized given the evidence, thus:

$$\text{Bayes equation: Prob}(H|E) = \frac{\text{Prob}(E|H) \cdot \text{Prob}(H)}{\text{Prob}(E|H) \cdot \text{Prob}(H) + \text{Prob}(E|\sim H) \cdot \text{Prob}(\sim H)}$$

Given our assumed values, we can solve for Prob($H|E$) by substituting into the preceding equation:

$$\text{Prob}(H|E) = \frac{(.8)\,(.001)}{(.8)\,(.001) + (.01)\,(.999)} = .074$$

Thus, the probability that my house has been burglarized is still less than 8 in 100. Note that the posterior probability is this low even though an open door is good evidence for a burglary and not for a normal state of affairs: Prob($E|H$) = .8 versus Prob($E|\sim H$) = .01. The posterior probability is still quite low because the prior probability of H—Prob(H) = .001—was very low to begin with. Relative to that low start, the posterior probability of .074 is a considerable increase.

Table 11.1 offers an illustration of Bayes's theorem as applied to the burglary example. It offers an analysis of 100,000 households,

TABLE 11.1

An Analysis of Bayes's Theorem—100,000 Households

	Burglarized	Not Burglarized	Sums
Door open	80	999	1,079
Door not open	20	98,901	98,921
Sums	100	99,900	100,000

Adapted from J. R. Hayes (1984).

assuming these statistics. There are four possible states of affairs, determined by whether the burglary hypothesis is true or not and by whether there is evidence of an open door or not. The frequency of each state of affairs is set forth in the four cells of the table. Let's consider the frequency in the upper-left cell, which is the case I was worried about—the door is open and my house has been burglarized. Because 1 in a 1,000 households are burglarized (Prob(H) is .001), there should be 100 burglaries in the 100,000 households. This is the frequency of both events in the left column. Because 8 times out of 10 the front door is left open in a burglary (Prob($E|H$) is .8), 80 of these 100 burglaries should leave the door open—the number in the upper left. Similarly, in the upper-right cell, we can calculate that of the 99,900 homes without burglary, the front door will be left open 1 in 100 times, for 999 cases. Thus, in total there are 80 + 999 = 1,079 cases of front doors left open, and the probability of the house being burglarized is 80/1,079 = .074. The calculations in Bayes's theorem perform the same calculation as afforded by Table 11.1, but in terms of probabilities rather than frequencies. As we will see, people find it easier to reason in terms of frequencies.

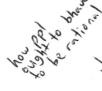

Because Bayes's theorem rests on a mathematical analysis of the nature of probability, the formula can be proved to evaluate hypotheses correctly. Thus, it enables us to precisely determine the posterior probability of a hypothesis given the prior and conditional probabilities. The theorem serves as a **prescriptive model,** or normative model, specifying the means of evaluating the probability of a hypothesis. Such a model contrasts with a **descriptive model,** which specifies what people actually do. People normally do not perform the calculations that we have just gone through any more than they follow the steps prescribed by formal logic. Nonetheless, they do hold various strengths of belief in assertions such as "My house has been burglarized." Moreover, their strength of belief does vary with evidence such as whether the door has been found ajar. The interesting question is whether the strength of their belief changes in accord with Bayes's theorem.

Bayes's theorem specifies how to combine the prior probability of a hypothesis with the conditional probabilities of the evidence to determine the posterior probability of a hypothesis.

Base-Rate Neglect

Many people are surprised that the open door in the preceding example does not provide as much evidence for a burglary as might have been expected. The reason for the surprise is that they do not grasp the importance of the prior probabilities. People sometimes ignore prior probabilities. In one demonstration, Kahneman and Tversky (1973) told one group of participants that a person had been chosen at random from a set of 100 people consisting of 70 engineers and 30 lawyers. This group of participants was termed the engineer-high group. A second group, the engineer-low group, was told that the person came from a set of 30 engineers and 70 lawyers. Both groups were asked to determine the probability that the person chosen at random from the group would be an engineer, given no information about the person. Participants were able to respond with the right prior probabilities: The engineer-high group estimated .70 and the engineer-low group estimated .30. Then participants were told that another person was chosen from the population and they were given the following description:

> Jack is a 45-year-old man. He is married and has four children. He is generally conservative, careful, and ambitious. He shows no interest in political and social issues and spends most of his free time on his many hobbies, which include home carpentry, sailing, and mathematical puzzles.

Participants in both groups gave a .90 probability estimate to the hypothesis that this person is an engineer. No difference was displayed between the two groups, which had been given different prior probabilities for an engineer hypothesis. But Bayes's theorem prescribes that prior probability should have a strong effect, resulting in a higher posterior probability from the engineer-high group than from the engineer-low group.

In a second case, Kahneman and Tversky presented participants with the following description:

> Dick is a 30-year-old man. He is married with no children. A man of high ability and high motivation, he promises to be quite successful in his field. He is well liked by his colleagues.

This example was designed to provide no diagnostic information either way with respect to Dick's profession. According to Bayes's theorem, the posterior probability of the engineer hypothesis should be the same as the prior probability because this description is not informative. However, both the engineer-high and the engineer-low groups estimated that the probability was .50 that the man described is an engineer. Thus, they allowed a completely uninformative piece of information to change their probabilities. Once again, the participants were shown to be completely unable to use prior probabilities in assessing the posterior probability of a hypothesis.

The failure to take prior probabilities into account can lead people to make some totally unwarranted conclusions. For instance, suppose you take a diagnostic test for a cancer. Suppose also that this type of cancer, when present, results in a positive test 95% of the time. On the other hand, if a person does not have the cancer, the probability of a positive test result is only 5%. Suppose you are informed that your result is positive. If you are like most people, you will assume that your chances of dying of cancer are about 95 out of 100 (Hammerton, 1973). You would be overreacting in assuming that the cancer will be fatal, but you would also be making a fundamental error in probability estimation. What is the error?

You would have failed to consider the base rate (prior probability) for the particular type of cancer in question. Suppose only 1 in 10,000 people have this cancer. This percentage would be your prior probability. Now, with this information, you would be able to determine the posterior probability of your having the cancer. Bringing out the Bayesian formula, you would express the problem in the following way:

$$\text{Prob}(H|E) = \frac{\text{Prob}(H) \cdot \text{Prob}(E|H)}{\text{Prob}(H) \cdot \text{Prob}(E|H) + \text{Prob}(\sim H) \cdot \text{Prob}(E|\sim H)}$$

where the prior probability of the cancer hypothesis is $\text{Prob}(H) = .0001$, and $\text{Prob}(\sim H) = .9999$, $\text{Prob}(E|H) = .95$, and $\text{Prob}(E|\sim H) = .05$. Thus,

$$\text{Prob}(H|E) = \frac{(.0001)\,(.95)}{(.0001)\,(.95) + (.9999)\,(.05)} = .0019$$

That is, the posterior probability of your having the cancer would still be less than 1 in 500.

- *People often fail to take base rates into account in making probability judgments.*

Conservatism

The preceding examples show that people weigh the evidence too much and ignore base rates. However, there are also situations in which people do not weigh evidence enough, particularly as the evidence pointing to a conclusion accumulates. Ward Edwards (1968) extensively investigated how people use new information to adjust their estimates of the probabilities of various hypotheses. In one experiment, he presented participants with two bags, each containing 100 poker chips. One of the bags contained 70 red chips and 30 blue; the other contained 70 blue chips and 30 red. The experimenter chose one of the bags at random and the participants' task was to decide which bag had been chosen.

In the absence of any prior information, the probability of either bag having been chosen was 50%. Thus,

$$\text{Prob}(H_R) = .50 \text{ and } \text{Prob}(H_B) = .50$$

where H_R is the hypothesis of a predominantly red bag and H_B is the hypothesis of a predominantly blue bag. To obtain further information, participants sampled chips at random from the bag. Suppose the first chip drawn was red. The conditional probability of a red chip drawn from each bag is

$$\text{Prob}(R|H_R) = .70 \text{ and } \text{Prob}(R|H_R) = .30$$

Now, we can calculate the posterior probability of the bag's being predominantly red, given the red chip is drawn, by applying the Bayes equation to this situation:

$$\text{Prob}(R|H_R) = \frac{\text{Prob}(R|H_R) \cdot \text{Prob}(H_R)}{\text{Prob}(R|H_R) \cdot \text{Prob}(H_R) + \text{Prob}(R|H_R) \cdot \text{Prob}(H_R)}$$

$$= \frac{(.70) \cdot (.50)}{(.70) \cdot (.50) + (.30) \cdot (.50)} = .70$$

This result seems, to both naive and sophisticated observers, to be a rather sharp increase in probabilities. Typically, participants do not increase the probability of a red-majority bag to .70; rather, they make a more conservative revision to a value such as .60.

After this first drawing, the experiment continues: The poker chip is put back in the bag and a second chip is drawn at random. Suppose this chip too is red. Again, by applying Bayes's theorem, we can show that the posterior probability of a red bag is now .84. Suppose our observations continued for 10 more trials and, after all 12 trials, we have observed eight reds and four blues. By continuing the Bayesian analysis, we could show that the new posterior probability of the hypothesis of a red bag is .97. Participants who see this sequence of 12 trials only estimate subjectively a posterior probability of .75 or less for the red bag. Edwards has used the term *conservative* to refer to the tendency to underestimate full effect of available evidence. He estimates that we use between a fifth and a half of the evidence available to us in situations like this experiment.

- *People frequently underestimate the cumulative force of evidence in making probability judgments.*

Correspondence to Bayes's Theorem with Experience

All the preceding examples showed that participants can be quite far off in their judgments of probability. One possibility is that participants really do not understand probabilities or how to reason with respect to them. Certainly, it is a rare participant in these experiments who could reproduce Bayes's theorem, let alone who would report engaging in Bayesian calculation. However, there is evidence that, although participants cannot articulate the correct probabilities, many aspects of their behavior are in accordance with Bayesian principles. To return to the explicit-implicit distinction discussed in Chapter 7, people often seem to display implicit knowledge of Bayesian principles even if they do not display any explicit knowledge and make errors when asked to make explicit judgments.

Gluck and Bower (1988) performed an experiment that illustrates implicit Bayesian behavior. Participants were given records of fictitious patients who could display from one to four symptoms (bloody nose, stomach cramps, puffy eyes, and discolored gums) and made discriminative diagnoses about which of two hypothetical diseases the patients had. One of these diseases had a base rate three times that of the other. Additionally, the conditional probabilities of displaying the various symptoms, given the diseases, were varied. Participants were not told directly about these base rates or conditional probabilities. They merely looked at a series of 256 patient records, chose the disease they thought the patient had, and were given feedback on the correctness of their judgments.

There are 15 possible combinations of one to four symptom patterns that a patient might have. Gluck and Bower calculated the probability of each disease for each pattern by using Bayes's theorem and arranged it so that each disease occurred with that probability when the symptoms were present. Thus, the participants experienced the base probabilities and conditional probabilities implicitly in terms of the frequencies of symptom–disease combinations.

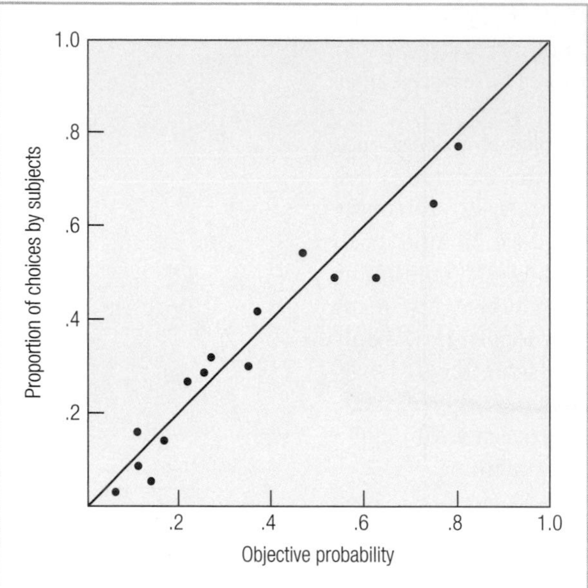

FIGURE 11.2 Participants' proportion of choices corresponds closely to the objective probabilities as determined by Bayes's theorem.

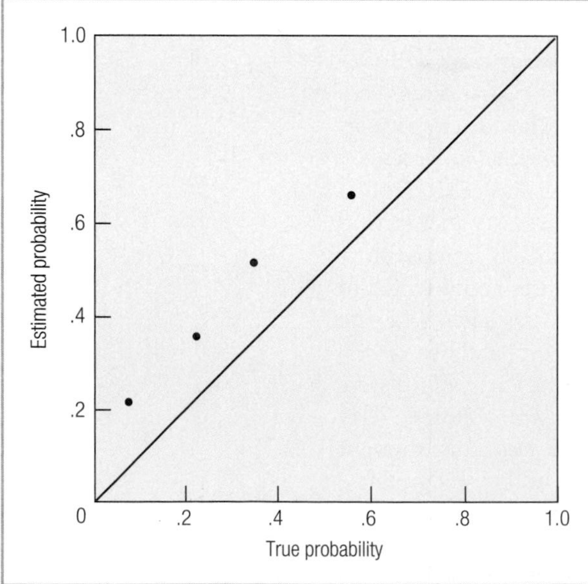

FIGURE 11.3 Participants' estimated probabilities systematically overestimated the frequency of the rare disease, showing base-rate neglect.

Of interest is the probability with which they assigned the rarer disease to various symptom combinations. Gluck and Bower compared the participant probabilities with the true Bayesian probabilities. This correspondence is displayed by the scatterplot in Figure 11.2. There we have, for each symptom combination, the Bayesian probability (labeled objective probability) and the proportion of times that participants assigned the rare disease to that symptom combination. As can be seen, these points fall very close to a straight diagonal line with a slope of 1, which indicates that the proportion of the participants' choices were very close to the true probabilities. Thus, implicitly, the participants had become quite good Bayesians in this experiment. The behavior of choosing among alternatives in proportion to their success is called **probability matching.**

After the experiment, Gluck and Bower presented the participants with the four symptoms individually and asked them how frequently the rare disease had appeared with each symptom. This result is presented in Figure 11.3 in a format similar to that of Figure 11.2. As can be seen, participants showed some neglect of the base rate, consistently having overestimated the frequency of the rare disease. Still, their judgments show some influence of base rate in that their average estimated probability of the rare disease is less than 50%.

Gigerenzer and Hoffrage (1995) showed that base-rate neglect also decreases if events are stated in terms of frequencies rather than in terms of probabilities. Some of their participants were given a description in terms of probabilities, such as the one that follows:

> The probability of breast cancer is 1% for women at age 40 who participate in routine screening. If a woman has breast cancer, the probability is 80% that she will get a positive mammography. If a woman does not have breast cancer, the probability is 9.6% that she also will get a positive mammography. A woman in this age group had a positive mammography in a routine screening. What is the probability that she actually has breast cancer?

Fewer than 20 out of 100 (20%) of the participants given such statements calculated the correct Bayesian answer (which is about 8%). In the other condition, participants were given descriptions in terms of frequencies, such as the one that follows:

> Ten out of every 1,000 women at age 40 who participate in routine screening have breast cancer. Eight of every 10 women with breast cancer will get a positive mammography. Ninety-five out of every 990 women without breast cancer also will get a positive mammography. Here is a new representative sample of women at age 40 who got a positive mammography in routine screening. How many of these women do you expect to actually have breast cancer?

Almost 50% of the participants given such statements calculated the correct Bayesian answer. Gigerenzer and Hoffrage argued that we can reason better with frequencies than with probabilities because we experience frequencies of events, but not probabilities, in our daily lives.

There is also evidence that experience makes people more statistically tuned. In a study of medical diagnosis, Weber, Böckenholt, Hilton, and Wallace (1993) found that doctors were quite sensitive both to base rates and to the evidence provided by the symptoms. Moreover, the more clinical experience the doctors had, the more tuned were their judgments.

- *Although participants' processing of abstract probabilities often does not correspond with Bayes's theorem, their behavior based on experience often does.*

Judgments of Probability

What are participants actually doing when they report probabilities of an event such as the probability that someone who has bloody gums has a particular disease? The evidence is that rather than thinking about probabilities, they are thinking about relative frequencies. Thus they are trying to judge the proportion of the patients that they saw with bloody gums who had that particular disease. People are reasonably accurate at making such proportionate judgments when they do not have to rely on memory (Robinson, 1964; Shuford, 1961). Consider an experiment by Shuford (1961). He presented arrays such as that shown in Figure 11.4 to participants for 1 s. He then asked participants to judge the proportion of vertical bars relative to horizontal bars. The number of vertical bars varied from 10% to 90% in different matrices. Shuford's results are shown in Figure 11.5. As can be seen, participants' estimates are quite close to the true proportions.

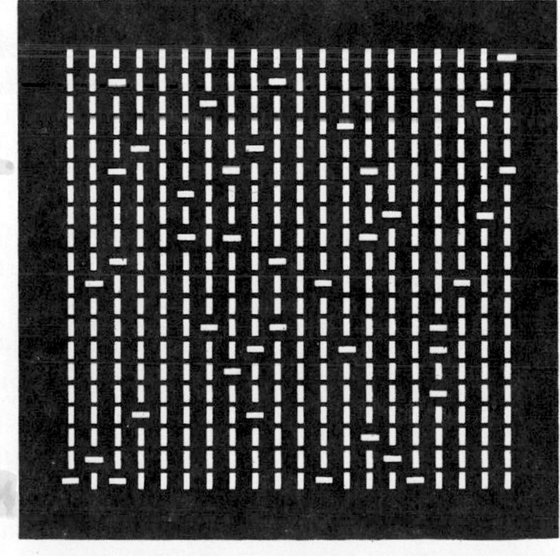

FIGURE 11.4 A random matrix presented to participants to determine their accuracy in judging proportions. The matrix is 90% vertical bars and 10% horizontal bars. (From Shuford, 1961. Copyright © 1961 by the American Psychological Association. Reprinted by permission.)

The situation just described is one where the participants can see the relevant information and make a judgment about proportions. When participants cannot see the events and must recall them from memory, they can give distorted judgments if they recall too many of one kind from memory. A fair amount of research has been done on the ways in which participants can be biased in their estimation of the relative frequency of various

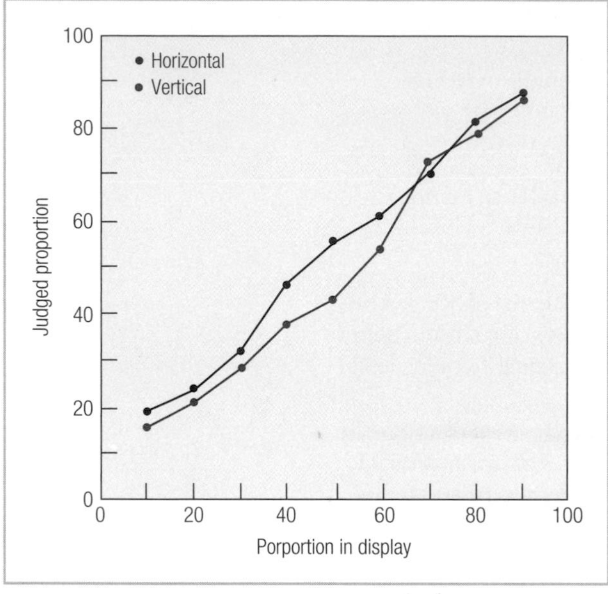

FIGURE 11.5 Mean estimated proportion as a function of the true proportion. Participants exhibited a fairly accurate ability to estimate the proportions of vertical and horizontal bars in Figure 10.5. (From Shuford, 1961. Copyright © 1961 by the American Psychological Association. Reprinted by permission.)

events in the population. Consider the following experiment reported by Tversky and Kahneman (1974), which demonstrates that judgments of proportion can be biased by differential availability of examples. These investigators asked participants to judge the proportion of words in the language that fit certain characteristics. For instance, they asked participants to estimate the proportion of English words that begin with the letter k versus words with the letter k in the third position. How might participants perform this task? One obvious method is to briefly try to think of words that satisfy the specification and words that do not and to estimate the relative proportion of target words. How many words can you think of that begin with the letter k? How many words can you think of that do not? What is your estimate of their proportion? Now, how many words can you think of that have the letter k in the third position? How many words can you think of that do not? What is their relative proportion? Participants estimated that more words begin with letter k than have the letter k in the third position. In actual fact, three times as many words have the letter k in the third position as begin with the letter k. Generally, participants overestimate the frequency with which words begin with various letters.

As in this experiment, many real-life circumstances require that we estimate probabilities without having direct access to the population that these probabilities describe. In such cases, we must rely on memory as the source for our estimates. The memory factors that we studied in Chapters 6 and 7 serve to explain how such estimates can be biased. Under the reasonable assumption that words are more strongly associated with their first letter than with their third letter, the bias exhibited in the experimental results can be explained by the spreading-activation theory (Chapter 6). With the focus of attention on the letter k, for example, activation will spread from that letter to words beginning with it. This process will tend to make words beginning with the letter k more available than other words. Thus, these words will be overrepresented in the sample that participants take from memory to estimate the true proportion in the population. The same overestimation is not made for words with the letter k in the third position because words are unlikely to be directly associated with the letters in the third position. Therefore, these words cannot be associatively primed and made more available.

Other factors besides memory lead to biases in probability estimates. Consider another example from Tversky and Kahneman (1974). Which of the following sequences of six tosses of a coin (where H denotes heads and T tails) is more likely: H T H T T H or H H H H H H? Many people think the first sequence is more probable, but both sequences are actually equally probable.

The probability of the first sequence is the probability of H on the first toss (which is .50) times the probability of T on the second toss (which is .50), times the probability of H on the third toss (which is .50), and so on. The probability of the whole sequence is .50 * .50 * .50 * .50 * .50 * .50 = .016. Similarly, the probability of the second sequence is the product of the probabilities of each coin toss, and the probability of a head on each coin toss is .50. Thus, again, the final probability also is .50 * .50 * .50 * .50 * .50 * .50 = .016. Why do some people have the illusion that the first sequence is more probable? It is because the first event seems similar to a lot of other events—for example, H T H T H T or H T T H T H. These similar events serve to bias upward a person's probability estimate of the target event. On the other hand, H H H H H H, straight heads, seems unlike any other event, and its probability will therefore not be biased upward by other similar sequences. In conclusion, a person's estimate of the probability of an event will be biased by other events that are similar to it.

A related phenomenon is what is called the **gambler's fallacy.** The fallacy is the belief that if an event has not occurred for a while, then it is more likely, by the "law of averages," to occur in the near future. This phenomenon can be demonstrated in an experimental setting—for instance, one in which participants see a sequence of coin tosses and must guess whether each toss will be a head or a tail. If they see a string of heads, they become more and more likely to guess that tails will come up on the next trial. Casino operators count on this fallacy to help them make money. Players who have had a string of losses at a table will keep playing, assuming that by the "law of averages" they will experience a compensating string of wins. However, the game is set in favor of the house. The dice do not know or care whether a gambler has had a string of losses. The consequence is that players tend to lose more as they try to recoup their losses. The "law of averages" is a fallacy.

The gambler's fallacy can be used to advantage in certain situations—for instance, at the racetrack. Most racetracks operate by a pari-mutuel system in which the odds on a horse are determined by the number of people betting on the horse. By the end of the day, if favorites have won all the races, people tend to doubt that another favorite can win, and they switch their bets to the long shots. As a consequence, the betting odds on the favorite deviate from what they should be, and a person can sometimes make money by betting on the favorite.

- *People can be biased in their estimates of probabilities when they must rely on factors such as memory and similarity judgments.*

The Adaptive Nature of the Recognition Heuristic

The examples in the previous section focused on cases where people came to bad judgments relying on, for example, availability of events in memory. Gigerenzer, Todd, and ABC Research Group (1999), in their book *Simple Heuristics That Make Us Smart,* argue that such cases are the exception and not the rule. They argue that people tend to identify the most valid cues for making judgments and use these. For instance, through evolution people have acquired a tendency to pay attention to availability of events in memory, which is more often helpful than not.

Goldstein and Gigerenzer (1999, 2002) report studies of what they call the **recognition heuristic.** This heuristic applies in cases where people can recognize one thing and not another. This heuristic leads people to believe that the recognized item is bigger and more important than the unrecognized item. In one study, they looked at the ability of students at the University of Chicago to judge the relative size of various German cities. For instance, which city is larger—Bamberg or Heidelberg? Most of the students knew that Heidelberg is a German city, but most do not recognize Bamberg—that is, one city is available in memory and the other is not. Goldstein and Gigerenzer showed that when faced with pairs like this, students almost always pick the city they can recognize. One might think this shows another fallacy based on availability in memory. However, Goldstein and Gigerenzer show that the students are actually more accurate when they make their judgment for pairs of cities like this (where they recognize one and not the other) than when they are given two cities they can recognize and must use other bases for judging the size of the cities (such as Munich versus Hamburg). This is because most American students have little knowledge about the population of German cities. Thus, far from a fallacy, this proves to be an effective basis for making judgments. Also, American students do better at judging the relative size of German cities using this heuristic than either American students do judging American cities or German students do judging German cities, where this heuristic cannot be used because almost all the cities are recognized.[2] German students also do better than American students in judging the population of American cities because they can use the recognition heuristic and Americans cannot.

Figure 11.6 illustrates Goldstein and Gigerenzer's explanation for why these students were more accurate in judging the size of cities when they did not know one. They looked at the frequency with which German cities were mentioned in the *Chicago Tribune* and the frequency with which American cities were mentioned in the German newspaper *Die Zeit.* It turns out that there is a strong correlation between the actual size of the city and the frequency of mention in these newspapers. Not surprisingly, people read about the larger cities in other countries more frequently. Gigerenzer and Goldstein also show that there is a strong correlation between the frequency of mention in the newspapers (and the media more generally) and the probability that these students will recognize the name. This is just the basic effect of frequency on memory. As a consequence of these two strong correlations, there will be a strong correlation between availability in memory and the actual size of the city.

[2] My German informant (Angela Brunstein) tells me that almost all Germans would recognize Bamberg and Heidelberg, but many would be puzzled by which is larger. Interestingly, Google search on English texts reports 37 million hits on Heidelberg and 3.5 million on Bamberg. Google search on German texts reports 30 million hits on Heidelberg and 12 million on Bamberg—a much closer ratio and many more hits on Bamberg.

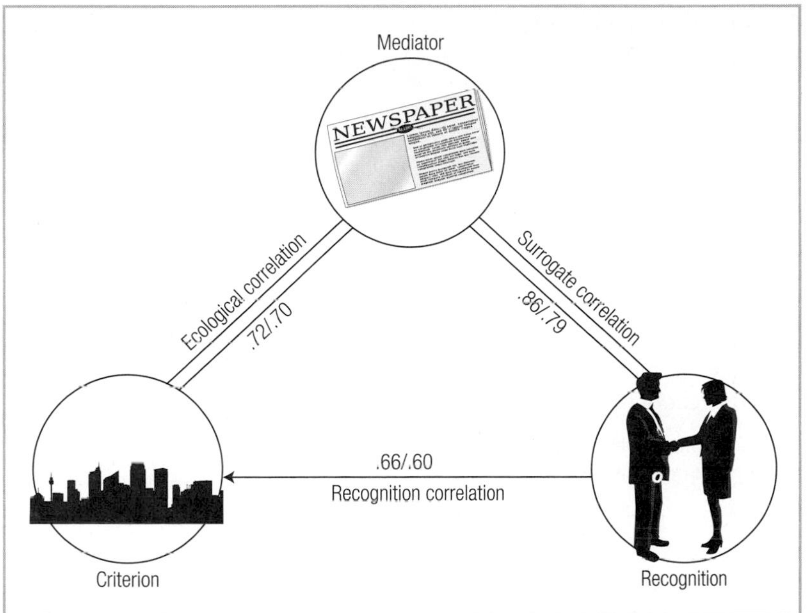

FIGURE 11.6 Ecological correlation (correlation between frequency of mention in newspapers and population size), surrogate correlation (correlation between frequency of mention in newspapers and probability of recognition), and recognition correlation (correlation between probability of recognition and population size). The first value is for American cities and the German newspaper *Die Zeit* as mediator, and the second value is for German cities and the *Chicago Tribune* as mediator. (From Goldstein and Gigerenzer, 2002.)

Goldstein and Gigerenzer argue that the recognition heuristic is useful in many but not all domains. In some domains, researchers have shown that people intelligently combine it with other information. For instance, Richter and Späth (2006) had participants judge which of two animals has the larger population size. For example, consider the following questions:

Are there more hainan partridges or arctic hares?
Are there more giant pandas or mottled umbers?

In the first case, most people have heard of the arctic hares and not hainan partridges and would correctly choose arctic hares using the recognition heuristic. In the second case, most people would recognize giant pandas and not mottled umbers (a moth). Nonetheless, they also know giant pandas are an endangered species and therefore correctly choose mottled umbers. This is an example of how people can adaptively choose what aspects of information to pay attention to.

- *People can use their ability to recognize an item, and combine this with other information, to make good judgments.*

Decision Making

An extension of the research on probabilistic reasoning is research on decision making, which is concerned with the way in which people make choices. Sometimes, the choices that we have to make are easy. If we are offered the choice between \$400 and \$1000, most of us would not have much difficulty in figuring out which to accept. However, if we were faced with the choice of a certainty of \$400 but only a 50% chance of \$1000, which would we select then? Something like it might happen if we inherited a risky stock that we could cash in for \$400 or that we could hold on to and see whether the company would take off or fold. A great deal of research on decision making under uncertainty requires participants to make choices among gambles. For instance, a participant might be asked to choose between the following two gambles:

A. \$8 with a probability of 1/3
B. \$3 with a probability of 5/6

In some cases, participants are just asked for their opinions; in other cases, they actually play the gamble that they choose. As an example of the latter possibility, a participant might roll a die and win in case A if he gets a 5 or 6 and win in case B if he gets a number other than 1. Which gamble would you choose?

As in the other domains of reasoning, decision making has its own standard prescriptive theory for the way that people should behave in such situations (von Neumann & Morgenstern, 1944). This theory says that they should choose the alternative with highest expected value. The expected value of an alternative is to be calculated by multiplying the probability by the value. Thus, the expected value of alternative A is $\$8 \times 1/3 = \$2.67$, whereas the expected value of alternative B is $\$3 \times 5/6 = \$2.50$. Thus, the normative theory says that participants should select gamble A. However, most participants will select gamble B.

As a perhaps more extreme example of the same result, suppose you are given a choice between

A. 1 million dollars with a probability of 1
B. 2.5 million dollars with a probability of 1/2

Maybe, in this case, you are on a game show and are offered a choice between this great wealth with certainty or the opportunity to toss a coin and get even more. I (and I assume you) would take the money (1 million) and run, but in fact, if we do the utility calculations, we should prefer the second choice because its utility is $.5 \times 2.5$ million $=$ 1.25 million. Are we really behaving irrationally?

Most people, when asked to justify their behavior in such situations, will argue that there comes a point when one has enough money (if we could only convince CEOs of this notion!) and that there really isn't much difference for them between 1 million dollars and 2.5 million dollars. This idea has been formalized in the terms of what is referred to as **subjective utility**—the value that we place on money is not linear with the face value of the money. Figure 11.7 shows a typical function proposed for the relation of subjective utility to money. It has

FIGURE 11.7 A function that relates subjective value to magnitude of gain and loss. (From Kahneman & Tversky, 1984. Reprinted by permission from the American Psychological Association.)

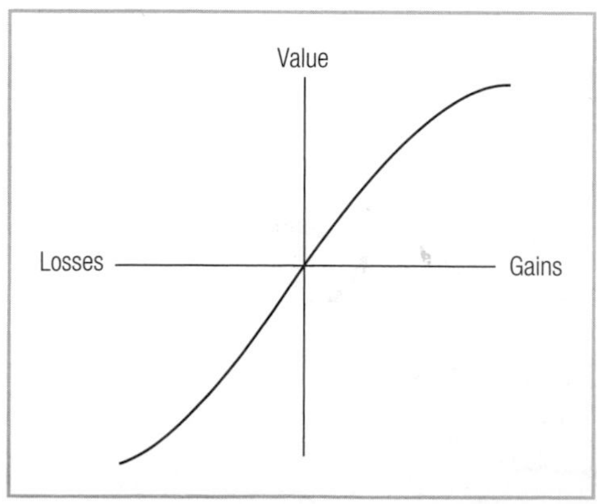

a couple of properties. The first property is that it is curvilinear such that it takes more than a doubling in the amount of money to double its utility. Thus, in the preceding example, we may value 2.5 million only 20% more than 1 million. Let us say that the utility of 1 million is U. The utility of 2.5 million can then be expressed as $1.2U$. The expected value of gamble A is $1 \times U = U$, and the expected value of gamble B is $1/2 \times 1.2U = .6U$. Thus, in terms of subjective utility, gamble A is more valuable and is to be preferred.

The second property of this utility function is that it is steeper in the loss region than in the gain region. Thus, participants given the following choice of gambles

A: Gain $10 with 1/2 probability and lose $10 with 1/2 probability
B: Nothing with certainty

prefer B because they weight the loss of $10 more strongly than the gain of $10.

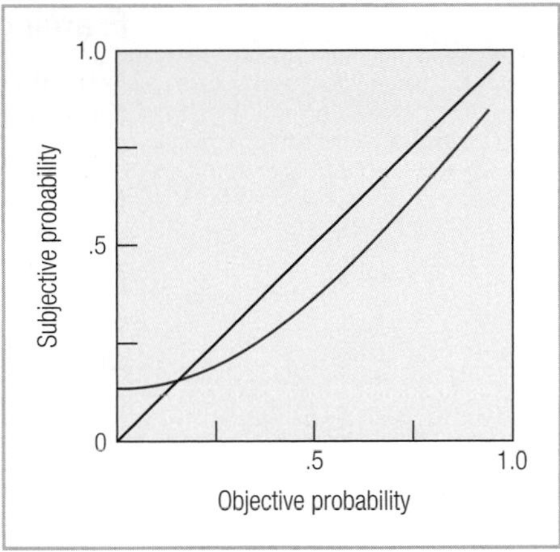

FIGURE 11.8 A function that relates subjective probability to objective probability. (From Kahneman & Tversky, 1984. Reprinted by permission from the American Psychological Association.)

Kahneman and Tversky (1984) also argued that, as with subjective utility, people associate a **subjective probability** with an event that is not identical with the objective probability. They proposed the function in Figure 11.8 to relate subjective probability to objective probability. According to this function, very low probabilities are overweighted relative to high probabilities, producing a bowing in the function. Thus, a participant might prefer a 1% chance of $400 to a 2% chance of $200 because 1% is not represented as half of 2%. Kahneman and Tversky (1979) showed that a great deal of human decision making can be explained by assuming that participants are responding in terms of these subjective utilities and subjective probabilities.

An interesting question is whether the subjective functions in Figures 11.7 and 11.8 represent irrational tendencies. Generally, the utility function in Figure 11.7 is thought to be reasonable. As we get more money, getting even more seems less and less important. Certainly, the amount of happiness that a billion dollars can buy is not 1,000 times the amount of happiness that a million dollars can buy. It should be noted that not all the utility functions of different people are like that shown in Figure 11.7, which represents a sort of average. One can imagine someone needing $10,000 for an important medical procedure. Then, all sums less than $10,000 would be rather useless, and all sums greater than $10,000 would be relatively equally good. Thus, such a person might have a step in the utility function at $10,000.

There is less agreement about how we should assess the subjective probability function in Figure 11.8. I (Anderson, 1990) have argued that it might actually make sense to discount the extremity of low probabilities in the way that function does. The argument is that, sometimes when we are told that probabilities are extreme, we are being misinformed (see the third Question for Thought at the end of the chapter). However, there is little consensus in the field about how to evaluate the subjective probability function.

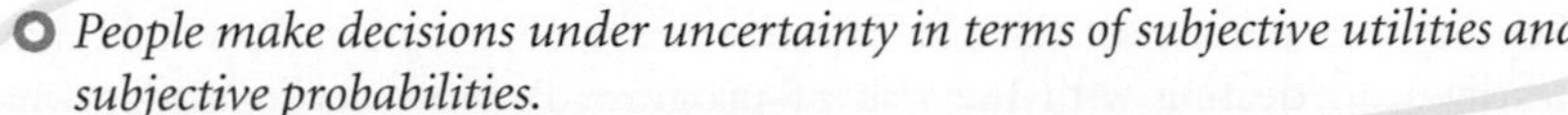

People make decisions under uncertainty in terms of subjective utilities and subjective probabilities.

Framing Effects

Although one might view the functions in Figures 11.7 and 11.8 as reasonable, there is evidence that they can lead people to do rather strange things. These demonstrations deal with **framing effects.** These effects refer to the fact that people's decisions vary, depending on where they perceive themselves to be on the utility curve in Figure 11.7. In an example from Kahneman and Tversky (1984), someone must purchase a $15 item versus a $125 item. If another store offers a $5 discount off the $15, the person is likely to make an effort to go to the other store, whereas he is not likely to do so if the same $5 discount is offered on the $125 item. However, in both cases, it is the same $5 savings, and the question is simply whether one's time is worth the $5. However, the two contexts place the person on different points of the utility curve, which is negatively accelerated. According to that curve, the difference between $15 and $10 is larger than the difference between $125 and $120. Thus, in the first case, the saving seems worth it, but in the second case, it does not.

Another example has to do with betting behavior. Consider someone who has lost $140 at the racetrack and has an opportunity to bet $10 on a horse that will pay 15 to 1. The bettor can view this choice in one of two ways. In one way, it becomes this choice:

A. Refuse the bet and accept a certainty of losing $140.
B. Make the bet and face a good chance of losing $150 and a poor chance of breaking even.

Because the subjective difference between losing $140 and $150 is small, the person will likely choose B and make the bet. On the other hand, the bettor could view it as the following choice:

C. Refuse the bet and face the certainty of having nothing change.
D. Make the bet and face a good chance of losing an additional $10 and a poor chance of gaining $140.

In this case, because of the greater weight on losses than on gains and because of the negatively accelerated utility function, the bettor is likely to avoid the bet. The only difference is whether one places oneself at the –$140 point or the 0 point on the curve in Figure 11.7. However, one gets a different evaluation of the two outcomes, depending on where one places oneself.

As an example that appears to be more consequential, consider this situation described by Kahneman and Tversky (1984):

> Problem 1: Imagine that the U.S. is preparing for the outbreak of an unusual Asian disease, which is expected to kill 600 people. Two alternative programs to combat the disease have been proposed. Assume that the exact scientific estimates of the consequences of the programs are as follows:
>
> If Program A is adopted, 200 people will be saved.
> If Program B is adopted, there is a one-third probability that 600 people will be saved and a two-thirds probability that no people will be saved.

Which of the two programs would you favor?

Seventy-two percent of the participants preferred program A, which guarantees lives, to dealing with the risk of program B. However, consider what happens when, rather than describing the two programs in regard to saving lives, the two programs are described as follows:

> If Program C is adopted, 400 people will die.
> If Program D is adopted, there is a one-third probability nobody will die and a two-thirds probability that 600 people will die.

With this description, only 22% preferred program C, which the reader will recognize as equivalent to A (and D is equivalent to B). Both of these choices can be understood in terms of a negatively accelerated utility function for lives. In the first case, the subjective value of 600 lives saved is less than three times the subjective value of 200 lives saved, whereas in the second case, the subjective value of 400 deaths is more than two-thirds the subjective value of 600 deaths. McNeil, Pauker, Cox, and Tversky (1982) found that this tendency extended to actual medical treatment. What treatment a doctor will choose depends on whether the treatment is described in terms of odds of living or odds of dying.

Situations in which framing effects are most prevalent tend to have one thing in common—no clear basis for choice. This commonality is true of the three examples that we have reviewed. In the case in which the shopper has an opportunity for a saving, whether $5 is worth going to another store is unclear. In the gambling example, there is no clear basis for making a decision.[3] The stakes are very high in the third case, but it is, unfortunately, one of those social policy decisions that defy a clear analysis. Thus, these cases are hard to decide on their merits alone.

Shafir (1993) suggested that, in such situations, we may make a decision not on the basis of which decision is actually the best one but on the basis of which will be easiest to justify (to ourselves or to others). Different framings make it easier or harder to justify an action. In the disease example, the first framing focuses one on saving lives and the second framing focuses one on avoiding deaths. In the first case, one would justify the action by pointing to the people whose lives have been saved (therefore it is critical that there be some people to point to). In the second case, a justification would have to explain why people died (and it would be better if there were no such people).

This need to justify one's action can lead one to pick the same alternative whether asked to pick something to accept or something to reject. Consider the example in Table 11.2 in which two parents are described in a divorce case and participants are asked to play the role of a judge who must decide to which parent to award custody of the child. In the award condition, participants are asked to decide who is to be awarded custody; in the deny condition, they are asked to decide who is to be denied custody. The parents are overall rather equivalent, but parent B has rather more extreme positive and negative factors. Asked to make an award decision, more participants choose to award custody to parent B; asked to make a deny decision, they tend to deny custody, again, to parent B. The reason, Shafir argued, is that parent B offers reasons, such as a close relation with

[3] That is, there is no basis for making the gambling decision that would not have rejected gambling as irrational in the first place.

TABLE 11.2

Imagine that you serve on the jury of an only-child sole-custody case following a relatively messy divorce. The facts of the case are complicated by ambiguous economic, social, and emotional considerations, and you decide to base your decision entirely on the following few observations.
(To which parent would you award sole custody of the child?/To which parent would you deny sole custody of the child?)

		Decisions	
		Award	Deny
Parent A	Average income Average health Average working hours Reasonable rapport with the child Relatively stable social life	36%	45%
Parent B	Above-average income Very close relation with the child Extremely active social life Lots of work-related travel Minor health problems	64%	55%

Adapted from Shafir, 1993. Reprinted by permission from the Psychonomic Society, Inc.

the child, that can be used to justify the awarding of custody, but parent B also has reasons, such as time away from home, to justify denying custody of the child to that parent.

An interesting study in framing was performed by Greene, Sommerville, Nystrom, Darley, and Cohen (2001). They compared ethical dilemmas such as the following pair. In the first dilemma, a runaway trolley is headed for five people who will be killed if it proceeds on its current course. The only way to save them is to hit a switch that will turn the trolley onto an alternate set of tracks where it will kill one person instead of five. The second dilemma is like the first, except that you are standing next to a large stranger on a footbridge that spans the tracks in between the oncoming trolley and the five people. In this scenario, the only way to save the five people is to push the stranger off the bridge onto the tracks below. He will die, but his body will stop the trolley from reaching the others. In the first case, most people are willing to sacrifice one person to save five, but in the second case, they are not.

In an fMRI study, Greene et al. compared the brain areas activated when people considered an impersonal dilemma such as the first case, with the brain areas activated when people considered a personal dilemma such as the second. In the impersonal case, the regions of the parietal cortex that are associated with cold calculation were active. On the other hand, when they judged the personal case, regions of the brain associated with emotion (such as the ventromedial prefrontal cortex that we discussed in the beginning of the chapter) were active. Thus, part of what can be involved in the different framing of problems seems which brain regions are engaged.

Implications

Why are adolescents more likely to make bad decisions?

One of society's great concerns is risk taking in adolescents. Compared to older adults, adolescents are more likely to engage in risky sexual behavior, abuse drugs and alcohol, and drive recklessly. Such poor adolescent choices are the leading cause of death in adolescence and can lead to a lifetime of suffering due to such things as failed education, destroyed personal relationships, and addiction to cigarettes, alcohol, and other drugs. This has been a subject of a great deal of research (e.g., Fischhoff, 2008; Reyna & Farley, 2006) and the results are a bit surprising. Contrary to common belief, adolescents do not perceive themselves to be any more invulnerable than older adults do and often perceive greater danger from risky behavior than do older adults. Also in many laboratory studies, late adolescents often show as good or better performance as older adults on abstract tasks of reasoning and decision making (this will be discussed further in Chapter 14). Thus, it does not appear that adolescents are poorer thinkers about risk than older adults. Rather, it appears that the explanation is involves two classes of factors:

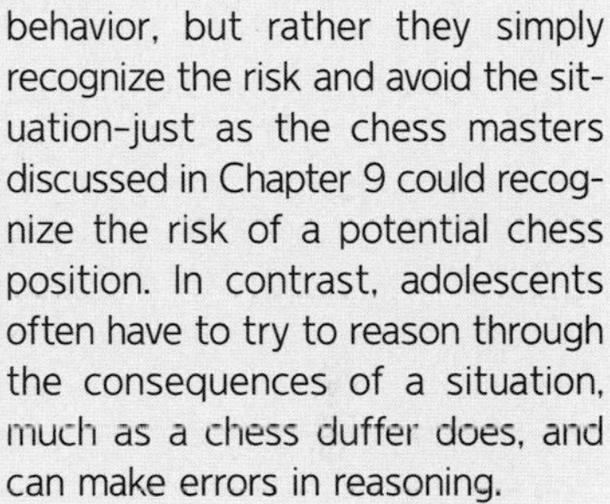

1. Knowledge and experience. Adolescents lack some of the information that adults have. For instance, adolescents may know it is important to "practice safe sex" but not know all that they should about how to practice safe sex. Also, through experience adults have become experts on reasoning about risk. Reyna and Farley argue that adults don't think through the potential costs and benefits of a risky behavior, but rather they simply recognize the risk and avoid the situation–just as the chess masters discussed in Chapter 9 could recognize the risk of a potential chess position. In contrast, adolescents often have to try to reason through the consequences of a situation, much as a chess duffer does, and can make errors in reasoning.
2. Different values and situations. Risky behavior has benefits such as immediate pleasure, and adolescents value these benefits more. Adolescents are particularly likely to weight the benefits of risky behavior heavily in the context of their peers, where social acceptance is at stake. Thus their utilities in computing expected value are different. Reyna and Farley speculate that this is related to the fact that brain regions like the ventromedial prefrontal cortex continue to mature into the early 20s. Fischhoff also notes that risky behavior often arises when adolescents attempt to establish independence and personal competence, which are important to achieve. However, this can put adolescents in situations where older adults seldom find themselves. If adults found themselves in similar situations, they might find themselves also acting in a more risky manner.

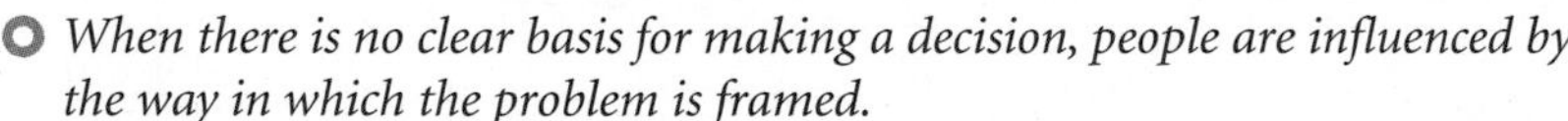

When there is no clear basis for making a decision, people are influenced by the way in which the problem is framed.

Neural Representation of Subjective Utility and Probability

The subjective utility of an outcome appears to be related to the activity of dopamine neurons in the basal ganglia. The importance of this region to motivation has been known since the 1950s, when Olds and Milner (1954) discovered that rats would press a lever to the point of exhaustion to receive electrical stimulation from electrodes near this region. This stimulation caused release of dopamine in a region of the basal ganglia called the nucleus accumbens. Drugs like heroin and cocaine have their effect by producing increased levels of dopamine from this region. These dopamine neurons show increased activity for all sorts of positive rewards including basic rewards like food and sex, but also social rewards like money or sports cars (Camerer, Loewenstein, & Prelec, 2005). Thus they appear to be the neural equivalent of subjective utility.

Although one can record activity in dopamine neurons while animals do things like touch morsels of food, much of the knowledge of the human system comes from neural imaging studies. In one fMRI study, Knutson, Taylor, Kaufman, Peterson, and Glover (2005) presented participants with various uncertain outcomes. For instance, on one trial participants might be told that they had a 50% chance of winning $5; on another trial that they had a 50% chance of winning $1. Knutson et al. imaged the activity while participants contemplated the gamble and before they actually saw the results of the gamble. The magnitude of the fMRI response in the nucleus accumbens reflected the differential magnitude of these rewards. However, this region does not respond differently to probability of reward. For instance, it did not respond differentially when participants were told on one trial that they had an 80% probability of a reward versus a 20% probability on another trial. In this case, the ventromedial prefrontal cortex responded to probability of the reward although it had not responded to the magnitude of the reward. Figure 11.9 illustrates the contrasting response of these regions to reward magnitude and reward probability.

Although the Knutson et al. study found the ventromedial prefrontal region only responding to probabilities, other research suggests it is involved in integrating probabilities and utilities. The ventromedial region is that portion that was destroyed in Phineas Gage (see Figure 11.1) and his problems went beyond

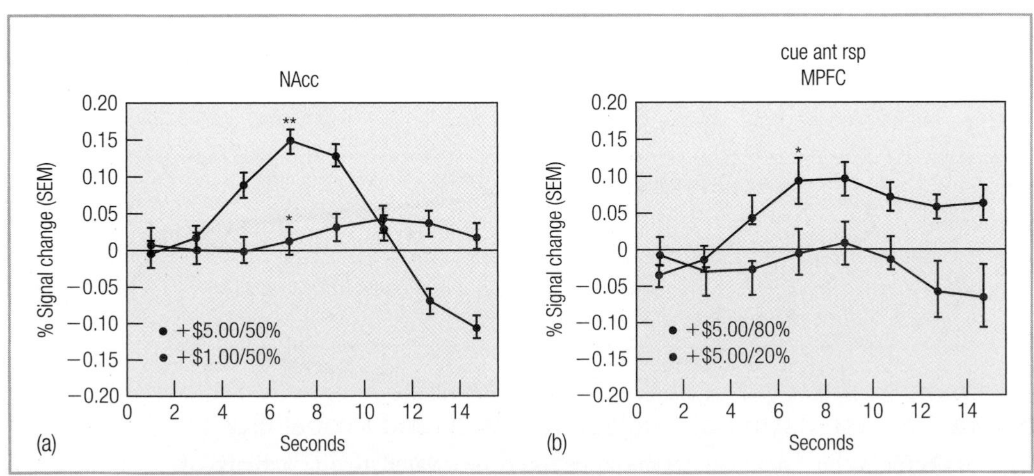

FIGURE 11.9 (A) The magnitude of a reward is represented in the activity of the nucleus accumbens (A); (B) the probability of a reward is represented in the activity of the ventromedial prefrontal cortex. (From Knutson et al., 2005.)

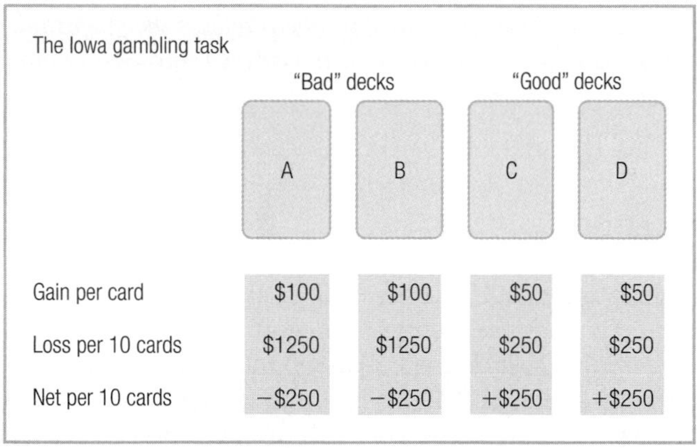

The Iowa gambling task

	"Bad" decks		"Good" decks	
	A	B	C	D
Gain per card	\$100	\$100	\$50	\$50
Loss per 10 cards	\$1250	\$1250	\$250	\$250
Net per 10 cards	−\$250	−\$250	+\$250	+\$250

FIGURE 11.10 A schematic diagram of the Iowa Gambling Task. The participants are given four decks of cards, a loan of \$2000 facsimile U.S. bills, and asked to play so as to win the most money. Turning each card carries an immediate reward (\$100 in decks A and B and \$50 in decks C and D). Unpredictably, however, the turning of some cards also carries a penalty (which is large in decks A and B and small in decks C and D). Playing mostly from decks A and B leads to an overall loss. Playing mostly from decks C and D leads to an overall gain. (From Bechara et al., 2005.)

judging probabilities. Subsequent research has confirmed that people who have damage to this region do have difficulty in responding adaptively in situations where they experience good and bad outcomes with different probabilities. For instance, this has been studied extensively in a task known as the Iowa gambling task (Bechara, Damasio, Damasio, & Anderson, 1994; Bechara, Damasio, Tranel, & Damasio, 2005), illustrated in Figure 11.10. The participants choose cards from four decks. In this version of the problem, decks A and B are equivalent and decks C and D are equivalent. Every time one selects from deck A or B, the participant will gain \$100 dollars but 1 time out of 10 will also lose \$1250 dollars. So, applying our formula for expected value, the expected value of selecting a card from one of these decks is

$$\$100 - 0.1 \times \$1250 = -\$25$$

or equivalently if participants play these decks 10 trials they can expect to lose \$250. Every time they select a card from decks C and D, they get only \$50, but they also only lose \$250 on that 1 out of every 10 draws. The expected value of selecting from one of these desks is

$$\$50 - 0.1 \times \$250 = +\$25$$

and so choosing from these decks, participants can expect to make \$250 every 10 trials. Players are initially attracted to decks A and B because of their higher payoff, but normal participants eventually learn to avoid them. In contrast, patients with ventromedial damage keep coming back to the high-paying decks. Also, unlike normal participants, they do not show measures of emotional engagement (such as increased galvanic skin response) when they choose from these desks.

Dopamine activity in the nucleus accumbens reflects the magnitude of reward, whereas the human ventromedial cortex is involved in integrating probabilities with reward.

Conclusions

Decision making deals with choosing actions that can have real consequences in the presence of real uncertainty. All mammals have the dopamine system that we just described, which gives them a basic ability to seek things that are rewarding and avoid things that are harmful. However, humans, by virtue of their greatly expanded prefrontal cortex, have the capacity to reflect on their circumstances and select actions other than what their more primitive systems might urge. Research suggests that the ventromedial portion of the human prefrontal cortex, which is greatly expanded in size even in comparison to the genetically similar apes, might play a particularly important role in such regulation. Humans attempt acts of self-regulation—for example, diet plans—that are far beyond the reach of any other species. However, we live in an uncertain world, as witnessed by all the contradictory claims made for various diet plans. Perhaps if we understood better how people responded to such uncertainty and contradiction, we would also be in a better position to understand why there are so many failures of our good resolutions.

Questions for Thought

1. Consider the Monte Hall problem:

   Suppose you're on a game show, and you're given the choice of three doors: Behind one door is a car; behind the others, goats. You pick a door—for example, door 1—and the host, who knows what's behind the doors, opens another door—for example, door 3—that has a goat. He then says to you, "Do you want to pick door 2?" Is it to your advantage to switch your choice? (Whitaker, 1990, p. 16)

   This can be analyzed using the following form of Bayes's theorem:

$$P(H2|E3) = \frac{P(H2)P(E3|H2)}{P(H1)P(E3|H1) + P(H2)P(E3|H2)+P(H3)P(E3|H3)}$$

   where $P(H2|E3)$ is the probability that the car is behind door 2 given that the host has opened door 3. $P(H1)$, $P(H2)$, and $P(H3)$ are the prior probabilities that the car is behind each door and all three are 1/3. $P(E3|H1)$, $P(E3|H2)$, and $P(E3|H3)$ are the conditional probabilities that the host opens each door given each hypothesis. In calculating these probabilities, keep in mind that the host cannot open the door you chose and must open a door that has a goat.

2. Conservatism and Bayes rate neglect seem to be in conflict (Fischhoff & Beyth-Marom, 1983; Gigerenzer et al., 1989). Conservatism says that people pay too little attention to data, whereas Bayes rate neglect says they only pay attention to evidence and ignore base rates. Could the contradiction be explained by differences between studies like Edwards's that show conservatism and those like Kahneman and Tversky's that demonstrate base-rate neglect?

3. Consult the Web site http://www.rense.com/general81/dw.htm for a list of things that people said would never happen. What does this imply about what our subjective probability should be when someone informs us that the objective probability is 0?

4. In the 1980s, it used to be recommended that a pregnant woman 35 years or older be tested to find

out whether the fetus had Down syndrome. The logic behind this recommendation was that the probability of having a Down syndrome baby increases with age and is about 1/250 for when the expectant mother is age 35, whereas the probability of the procedure resulting in a miscarriage was also 1/250. Analyze the assumptions behind this decision-making criterion used in the 1980s in terms of the expected-value calculations described in this chapter. Do you agree with the recommendation?

Key Terms

Bayes's theorem
conditional probability
descriptive model
framing effects
gambler's fallacy
posterior probability
prescriptive model
prior probability
probability matching
recognition heuristic
subjective probability
subjective utility
ventromedial prefrontal cortex

12

Language Structure

What makes the human species special? There are two basic hypotheses about why people are intellectually different from other species. In the past few chapters, I indulged my favorite theory, which is that we have unmatched abilities to solve problems and reason about our world, owing in large part to the enormous development of our prefrontal cortices. However, there is another theory at least as popular in cognitive science, which is that humans are special because they alone possess a language.

This chapter and the next will analyze in more detail what language is, how people process language, and what makes human language so special. This chapter will focus primarily on the nature of language in general, whereas the next chapter will contain more detailed analyses of how language is processed. We will consider some of the basic linguistic ideas about the structure of language and evidence for the psychological reality of these ideas, as well as research and speculation about the relation between language and thought. We will also look at the research on language acquisition. Much of the evidence both for and against claims about the uniqueness of human language comes from research on the way in which children learn the structure of language.

In this chapter, we will answer the questions:

- What does the field of linguistics tell us about how language is processed?
- What distinguishes human language from the communication systems of other species?
- How does language influence the nature of human thought?
- How are children able to acquire a language?

Language and the Brain

The human brain has features strongly associated with language. For almost all of the 92% of people who are right-handed, language is strongly lateralized in the left hemisphere. About half of the 8% of people who are left-handed still have language left lateralized. So 96% of the population has language largely

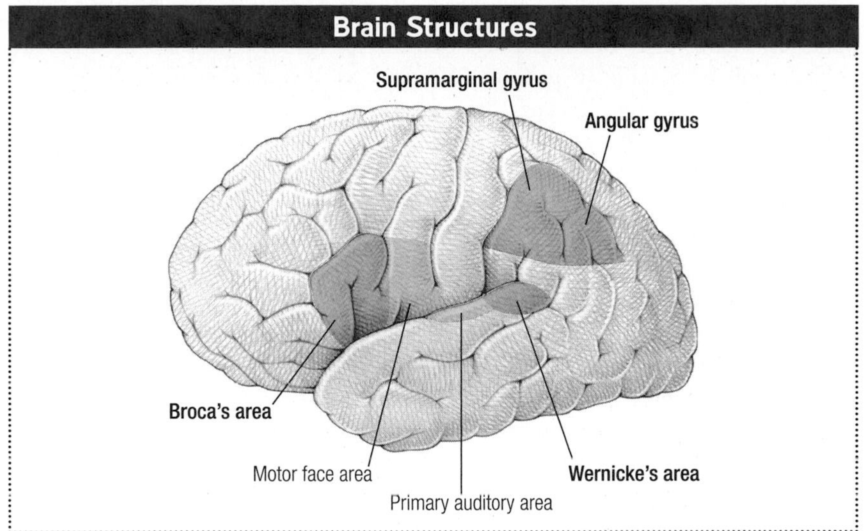

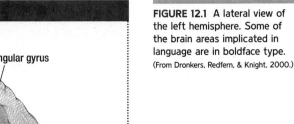

FIGURE 12.1 A lateral view of the left hemisphere. Some of the brain areas implicated in language are in boldface type. (From Dronkers, Redfern, & Knight, 2000.)

in the left hemisphere. Findings from studies with split-brain patients (see Chapter 1) have indicated that the right hemisphere has only the most rudimentary language abilities. It was once thought that the left hemisphere was larger, particularly in areas taking part in language processing, and that this greater size accounted for the greater linguistic abilities associated with the left hemisphere. However, neuroimaging techniques have suggested that the differences in size are negligible, and researchers are now looking to see whether there are differences in neural connectivity or organization (Gazzaniga, Ivry, & Mangun, 2002) in the left hemisphere. It remains largely a mystery what differences between the left and the right hemispheres could account for why language is so strongly left lateralized.

Certain regions of the left hemisphere are specialized for language, and these are illustrated in Figure 12.1. These areas were initially identified in studies of patients who suffered aphasias (losses of language function) as a consequence of stroke. The first such area was discovered by Paul Broca, the French surgeon who, in 1861, examined the brain of such a patient after the patient's death (the brain is still preserved in a Paris museum). This patient was basically incapable of spoken speech, although he understood much of what was spoken to him. He had a large region of damage in a prefrontal area that came to be known as Broca's area. As can be seen in Figure 12.1, it is next to the motor region that controls the mouth. Shortly thereafter, Carl Wernicke, a German physician, identified patients with severe deficits in understanding speech who had damage in a region in the superior temporal cortex posterior to the primary auditory cortex. This area came to be known as Wernicke's area. Parietal regions close to Wernicke's area (the supramarginal gyrus and angular gyrus) also have also been found to be important to language.

Two of the classic aphasias, now known as Broca's aphasia and Wernicke's aphasia, are associated with damage to these two regions. Chapter 1 gave examples of the kinds of speech problems suffered by patients with these two aphasias. The severity of the damage determines whether patients with Broca's aphasia will be unable to generate almost any speech (like Broca's original patient) or be capable of generating meaningful but ungrammatical speech. Patients with Wernicke's aphasia, in addition to having problems with comprehension, sometimes produce grammatical but meaningless speech. Another kind of aphasias is conduction aphasia; in this condition, patients suffer difficulty in repeating speech and have problems producing spontaneous speech. Conduction aphasia is sometimes associated with damage to the parietal regions shown in Figure 12.1.

Although the importance of these left-cortical areas to speech is well documented and there are many well-studied cases of aphasia resulting from damage in these regions, it has become increasingly apparent that there is no simple mapping of damaged areas onto types of aphasia. Current research has focused on more detailed analyses of the deficits and of the regions damaged in each aphasic patient.

Although there is much to understand, it is a fact that human evolution and development have selected certain left-cortical regions as the preferred locations for language. It is not the case, however, that language has to be left lateralized. There are those left-handers who have language in the right hemisphere, and young children who suffer left-brain damage may develop language in the right hemisphere, in regions that are homologous to those depicted in Figure 12.1 for the left hemisphere.

- *Language is preferentially localized in the left hemisphere in prefrontal regions (Broca's area), temporal regions (Wernicke's area), and parietal regions (supramarginal and angular gyri).*

The Field of Linguistics

The academic field of **linguistics** attempts to characterize the nature of language. It is distinct from psychology in that it studies the structure of natural languages rather than the way in which people process natural languages. Despite this difference, the work from linguistics has been extremely influential in the psychology of language. As we will see, concepts from linguistics play an important role in theories of language processing. As noted in Chapter 1, the influence from linguistics was important to the decline of behaviorism and the rise of modern cognitive psychology.

Productivity and Regularity

The linguist focuses on two aspects of language: its productivity and its regularity. The term **productivity** refers to the fact that an infinite number of utterances are possible in any language. **Regularity** refers to the fact that these utterances are systematic in many ways. We need not seek far to convince ourselves of the highly productive and creative character of language. Pick a random sentence from this book or any other book of your choice and enter it as an exact string (quoting it) in Google. If Google can find the sentence in all of its billions of pages, it will probably either be from a copy of the book or a quote from the book. In fact, these sorts of methods are used by programs to catch plagiarism. Most sentences you will find in books were created only once in human history. And yet it is important to realize that the components that make up sentences are quite small in number: English uses only 26 letters, 40 phonemes (see the discussion in the Speech Recognition section of Chapter 2), and some tens of thousands of words. Nevertheless, with these components, we can and do generate trillions of novel sentences.

A look at the structure of sentences makes clear why this productivity is possible. Natural language has facilities for endlessly embedding structures within structures and coordinating structures with structures. A mildly amusing party game starts with a simple sentence and requires participants to keep adding to the sentence:

- The girl hit the boy.
- The girl hit the boy and he cried.
- The big girl hit the boy and he cried.
- The big girl hit the boy and he cried loudly.
- The big girl hit the boy who was misbehaving and he cried loudly.
- The big girl with authoritarian instincts hit the boy who was misbehaving and he cried loudly.

And so on until someone can no longer extend the sentence.

The fact that an infinite number of word strings can be generated would not be particularly interesting in itself. If we have tens of thousands of words for each position and if sentences can be of any length, it is not hard to see that a very large (in fact, an infinite) number of word strings is possible. However, if we merely combine words at random, we get "sentences" such as

- From runners physicians prescribing miss a states joy rests what thought most.

In fact, very few of the possible word combinations are acceptable sentences. The speculation is often jokingly made that, given enough monkeys working at typewriters for a long enough time, some monkey will type a best-selling book. It should be clear that it would take a lot of monkeys a long time to type just one acceptable **R@!#s.*

So, balanced against the productivity of language is its highly regular character. One goal of linguistics is to discover a set of rules that will account for both the productivity and the regularity of natural language.

Such a set of rules is referred to as a **grammar.** A grammar should be able to prescribe or generate all the acceptable utterances of a language and be able to reject all the unacceptable sentences in the language. A grammar consists of three types of rules—syntactic, semantic, and phonological. **Syntax** concerns word order and inflection. Consider the following examples of sentences that violate syntax:

- The girls hits the boys.
- Did hit the girl the boys?
- The girl hit a boys.
- The boys were hit the girl.

These sentences are fairly meaningful but contain some mistakes in word combinations or word forms.

Semantics concerns the meaning of sentences. Consider the following sentences that contain semantic violations, even though the words are correct in form and syntactic position:

- Colorless green ideas sleep furiously.
- Sincerity frightened the cat.

These constructions are called anomalous sentences in that they are syntactically well formed but nonsensical.

Phonology concerns the sound structure of sentences. Sentences can be correct syntactically and semantically but be mispronounced. Such sentences are said to contain phonological violations. Consider this example:

> The Inspector opened his notebook. "Your name is Halcock, is't no?" he began. The butler corrected him. "H'alcock," he said, reprovingly. "H, a, double-l?" suggested the Inspector. "There is no h'aich in the name, young man. H'ay is the first letter, and there is h'only one h'ell." (Sayers, 1968, p. 73)

The butler, wanting to hide his cockney dialect, which drops the letter h, is systematically mispronouncing every word that begins with a vowel.

- *The goal of linguistics is to discover a set of rules that captures the structural regularities in a language.*

Linguistic Intuitions

A major goal of linguistics is to explain the linguistic intuitions of speakers of a language. **Linguistic intuitions** are judgments about the nature of linguistic utterances or about the relations between linguistic utterances. Speakers of the language are often able to make these judgments without knowing how they do so. As such, linguistic intuition is another example of implicit knowledge, a concept introduced in Chapter 7. Among these linguistic intuitions are judgments about whether sentences are ill-formed and, if ill-formed, why. For instance, we can judge that some sentences are ill-formed because they have bad syntactic structure and that other sentences are ill-formed because they lack meaning. Linguists require that a grammar capture this distinction and clearly express the reasons for it. Another kind of intuition is about paraphrase. A speaker of English will judge that the following two sentences are similar in meaning and hence are paraphrases:

- The girl hit the boy.
- The boy was hit by the girl.

Yet another kind of intuition is about ambiguity. The following sentence has two meanings:

- They are cooking apples.

This sentence can either mean that some people are cooking some apples or that the apples can be used for cooking. Moreover, speakers of the language can distinguish this type of ambiguity, which is called structural ambiguity, from lexical ambiguity, as in

- I am going to the bank.

where *bank* can refer either to a monetary institution or to a riverbank. Lexical ambiguities arise when a word has two or more distinct meanings; structural ambiguities arise when an entire phrase or sentence has two or more meanings.

Linguists try to account for the intuitions we have about paraphrases, ambiguity, and the well-formedness of sentences.

Competence versus Performance

Our everyday use of language does not always correspond to the prescriptions of linguistic theory. We generate sentences in conversation that, upon reflection, we would judge to be ill-formed and unacceptable. We hesitate, repeat ourselves, stutter, and make slips of the tongue. We misunderstand the meaning of sentences. We hear sentences that are ambiguous but do not note their ambiguity.

Another complication is that linguistic intuitions are not always clear-cut. For instance, we find the linguist Lakoff (1971) telling us that, in the following case, the first sentence is not acceptable but the second sentence is:

- Tell John where the concert's this afternoon.
- Tell John that the concert's this afternoon.

People are not always reliable in their judgments of such sentences and certainly do not always agree with Lakoff.

Considerations about the unreliability of human linguistic behavior and judgment led linguist Noam Chomsky (1965) to make a distinction between linguistic **competence,** a person's abstract knowledge of the language, and linguistic **performance,** the actual application of that knowledge in speaking or listening. In Chomsky's view, the linguist's task is to develop a theory of competence; the psychologist's task is to develop a theory of performance.

The exact relation between a theory of competence and a theory of performance is unclear and can be the subject of heated debates. Chomsky has argued that a theory of competence is central to performance—that our linguistic competence underlies our ability to use language, if indirectly. Others believe that the concept of linguistic competence is based on a rather unnatural activity (making linguistic judgments) and has very little to do with language use.

Linguistic performance does not always correspond to linguistic competence.

Syntactic Formalisms

A major contribution of linguistics to the psychological study of language has been to provide a set of concepts for describing the structure of language. The most frequently used ideas from linguistics concern descriptions of the syntactic structure of language.

Phrase Structure

A great deal of emphasis in linguistics has been given to understanding the syntax of natural language. One central linguistic concept is **phrase structure.** Phrase-structure analysis is not only significant in linguistics, but also important to an understanding of language processing. Therefore, coverage of this topic here is partly a preparation for material in the next chapter. Those of you who have had a certain kind of training in high-school English will find the analysis of phrase structure to be similar to parsing exercises.

The phrase structure of a sentence is the hierarchical division of the sentence into units called phrases. Consider this sentence:

- The brave dog saved the drowning child.

If asked to divide this sentence into two major parts in the most natural way, most people would provide the following division:

- (The brave dog) (saved the drowning child).

The parentheses distinguish the two separate parts. The two parts of the sentence correspond to what are traditionally called subject and predicate or noun phrase and verb phrase. If asked to divide the second part, the verb phrase, further, most people would give

- (The brave dog) (saved [the drowning child]).

Often, analysis of a sentence is represented as an upside-down tree, as in Figure 12.2. In this phrase-structure tree, *sentence* points to its subunits, the

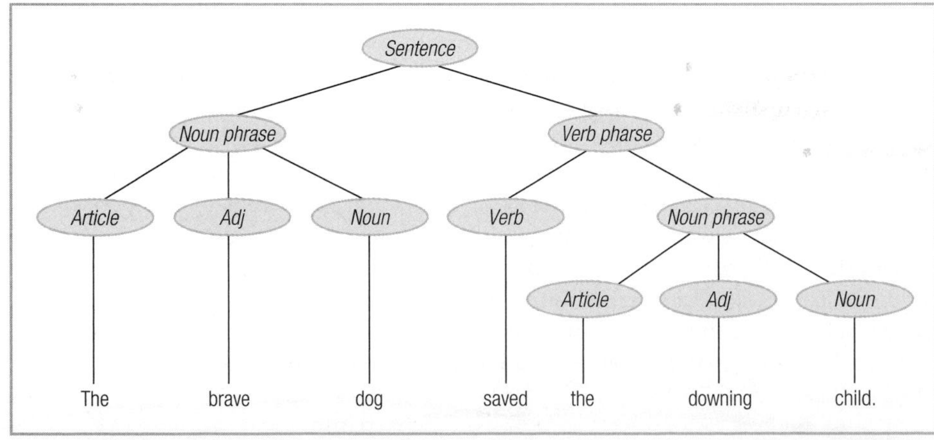

FIGURE 12.2 An example of the phrase structure of a sentence. The tree structure illustrates the hierarchical division of the sentence into phrases.

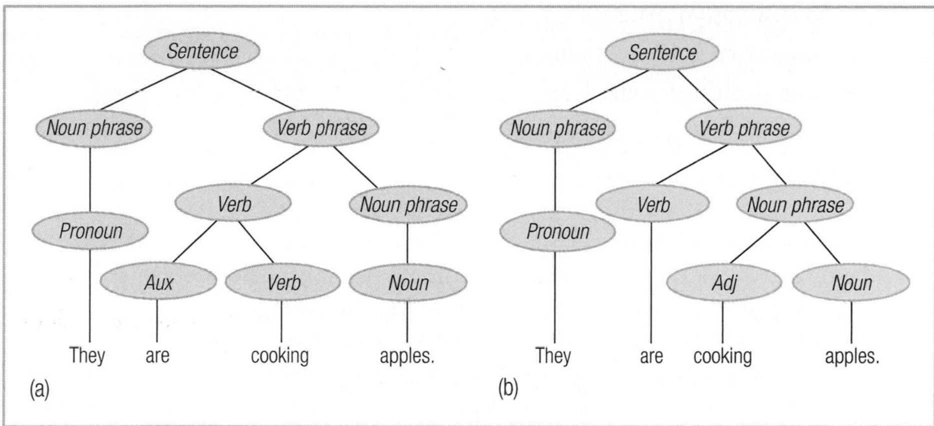

FIGURE 12.3 The phrase structures illustrating the two possible meanings of the ambiguous sentence *They are cooking apples:* (a) that those people (they) are cooking apples; (b) that those apples are for cooking.

noun phrase and the *verb phrase,* and each of these units points to its subunits. Eventually, the branches of the tree terminate in the individual words. Such tree-structure representations are common in linguistics. In fact, the term *phrase structure* is often used to refer to such tree structures.

An analysis of phrase structure can point up structural ambiguities. Consider again the sentence

- They are cooking apples.

Whether *cooking* is part of the verb with *are* or part of the noun phrase with *apples* determines the meaning of the sentence. Figure 12.3 illustrates the phrase structure for these two interpretations. In Figure 12.3a, *cooking* is part of the verb, whereas in Figure 12.3b, it is part of the noun phrase.

- *Phrase-structure analysis is concerned with the way that sentences are broken up into linguistic units.*

Pause Structure in Speech

Abundant evidence supports the argument that phrase structures play a key role in the generation of sentences.[1] When a person produces a sentence, he or she tends to generate it a phrase at a time, pausing at the boundaries between large phrase units. For instance, although no tape recorders were available in Lincoln's time, one might guess that he produced the first sentence of "The Gettysburg Address" with brief pauses at the end of each of the major phrases as follows:

Four score and seven years ago (pause)
our forefathers brought forth on this continent (pause)

[1] In Chapter 13, we will examine the role of phrase structures in language comprehension.

a new nation (pause)
conceived in liberty (pause)
and dedicated to the proposition (pause)
that all men are created equal (pause)

Although Lincoln's speeches are not available for auditory analysis, Boomer (1965) analyzed examples of spontaneous speech and found that pauses did occur more frequently at junctures between major phrases and that these pauses were longer than pauses at other locations. The average pause time between major phrases was 1.03 s, whereas the average pause within phrases was 0.75 s. This finding suggests that speakers tend to produce sentences a phrase at a time and often need to pause after one phrase to plan the next. Other researchers (Cooper & Paccia-Cooper, 1980; Grosjean, Grosjean, & Lane, 1979) looked at participants producing prepared sentences rather than spontaneous speech. The pauses of such participants tend to be much shorter, about 0.2 s. Still, the same pattern holds, with longer pauses at the major phrase boundaries.

As Figures 12.2 and 12.3 illustrate, there are multiple levels of phrases within phrases within phrases. What level do speakers choose for breaking up their sentences into pause units? Gee and Grosjean (1983) argued that speakers tend to choose the smallest level above the word that bundles together coherent semantic information. In English, this level tends to be noun phrases (e.g., the young woman), verbs plus pronouns (e.g., will have been reading it), and prepositional phrases (e.g., in the house).

People tend to pause briefly after each meaningful unit of speech.

Speech Errors

Other research has found evidence for phrase structure by looking at errors in speech. Maclay and Osgood (1959) analyzed spontaneous recordings of speech and found a number of speech errors that suggested that phrases do have a psychological reality. They found that, when speakers repeated themselves or corrected themselves, they tended to repeat or correct a whole phrase. For instance, the following kind of repeat is found:

- Turn on the heater/the heater switch.

and the following pair constitutes a common type of correction:

- Turn on the stove/the heater switch.

In the preceding example, the noun phrase is repeated. In contrast, speakers do not produce repetitions in which part, but not all, of the verb phrase is repeated, such as

- Turn on the stove/on the heater switch.

Other kinds of speech errors also provide evidence for the psychological reality of constituents as major units of speech generation. For instance, some research has analyzed slips of the tongue in speech (Fromkin, 1971, 1973; Garrett, 1975).

One kind of speech error is called a spoonerism, after the English clergyman William A. Spooner to whom are attributed some colossal and clever errors of speech. Among the errors of speech attributed to Spooner are:

- You have hissed all my mystery lectures.
- I saw you fight a liar in the back quad; in fact, you have tasted the whole worm.
- I assure you the insanitary spectre has seen all the bathrooms.
- Easier for a camel to go through the knee of an idol.
- The Lord is a shoving leopard to his flock.
- Take the flea of my cat and heave it at the louse of my mother-in-law.

As illustrated here, spoonerisms consist of exchanges of sound between words. There is some reason to suspect that the preceding errors were deliberate attempts at humor by Spooner. However, people do generate genuine spoonerisms, although they are seldom as funny.

By patient collecting, researchers have gathered a large set of errors made by friends and colleagues. Some of these errors are simple sound anticipations and some are sound exchanges as in spoonerisms:

- Take my bike → bake my bike [an anticipation]
- night life → nife lite [an exchange]
- beast of burden → burst of beaden [an exchange]

One that gives me particular difficulty is

- coin toss → toin coss

The first error in the preceding list is an example of an anticipation, where an early phoneme is changed to a later phoneme. The others are examples of exchanges in which two phonemes switch. The interesting feature about these kinds of errors is that they tend to occur within a single phrase rather than across phrases. So, we are unlikely to find an anticipation, like the following, which occurs between subject and object noun phrases:

- The dancer took my bike. → The bancer took my dike.

Also unlikely are sound exchanges where an exchange occurs between the initial prepositional phrase and the final noun phrase, as in the following:

- At night John lost his life. → At nife John lost his lite.

Garrett (1990) distinguished between errors in simple sounds and those in whole words. Sound errors occur at what he called the positional level, which basically corresponds to a single phrase, whereas word errors occur at what he called the functional level, which corresponds to a larger unit of speech such as a full clause. Thus, the following word error has been observed:

- That kid's mouse makes a great toy. → That kid's toy makes a great mouse.

whereas the following sound error would be unlikely:

- That kid's mouse makes a great toy. → That kid's touse makes a great moy.

In Garrett's (1980) corpus, 83% of all word exchanges extended beyond phrase boundaries, but only 13% of sound errors did. Word and sound errors are generally thought to occur at different levels in the speech-production process. Words are inserted into the speech plan at a higher level of planning, and so a larger distance is possible for the substitution.

An experimental procedure has been developed for artificially producing Spoonerisms in the laboratory (Baars, Motley, & MacKay, 1975; Motley, Camden, & Baars, 1982). This involves presenting a series of word pairs like

Big Dog

Bad Deal

Beer Drum

****Darn Bore****

House Coat

Whale Watch

and asking the participants to speak certain words such as the asterisked *Darn Bore* in the above series. When they have been primed with a series of word pairs with the opposite order of first consonants (the preceding three all are B—— D——), they show a tendency to reverse the order of the first consonants, in this case producing *Barn Door.* Interestingly, participants are much more likely to produce such an error if it produces real words, as it does in the above case, than if it does not (as in the case of *Dock Boat,* which if reversed would become *Bock Doat*). Participants are also sensitive to a host of other facts such as whether the pair is grammatically appropriate and whether it is culturally appropriate (e.g., they are more likely to convert *cast part* into *past cart* than they are to convert *fast part* into *past fart*). This research has been taken as evidence that we combine multiple factors into selection of speech items.

- *Speech errors involving substitutions of sounds and words suggest that words are selected at the clause level, whereas sounds are inserted at a lower phrase level.*

Transformations

A phrase structure describes a sentence hierarchically as pieces within larger pieces. There are certain types of linguistic constructions that some linguists think violate this strictly hierarchical structure. Consider the following pair of sentences:

1. The dog is chasing Bill down the street.
2. Whom is the dog chasing down the street?

In sentence 1, *Bill,* the object of the chasing, is part of the verb phrase. On the other hand, in sentence 2, *whom,* the object of the verb phrase, is at the beginning of the sentence. The object is no longer part of the verb-phrase structure to which it would seem to belong. Some linguists have proposed that, formally, such questions are generated by starting with a phrase structure that has the object *whom* in the verb phrase, such as

3. The dog is chasing whom down the street?

This sentence is somewhat strange but, with the right questioning intonation of the *whom,* it can be made to sound reasonable. In some languages, such as Japanese, the interrogative pronoun is normally in the verb phrase, as in sentence 3. However, in English, the proposal is that there is a movement transformation that moves the *whom* into its more normal position. Note that this proposal is a linguistic one concerning the formal structure of language and may not describe the actual process of producing the question.

Some linguists believe that a satisfactory analysis of language requires such **transformations,** which move elements from one part of the sentence to another part. Transformations can also operate on more complicated sentences. For instance, we can apply it to sentences of the form

4. John believes that the dog is chasing Bill down the street.

The corresponding question forms are

5. John believes that the dog is chasing whom down the street?

6. Whom does John believe that the dog is chasing down the street?

Sentence 5 is strange even with a questioning intonation for *whom,* but still some linguists believe that sentence 6 is transformationally derived from it, even though we would never produce sentence 5.

An intriguing concern to linguists is that there seem to be real limitations on just what things can be moved by transformations. For instance, consider the following set of sentences:

7. John believes the fact that the dog is chasing Bill down the street.

8. John believes the fact that the dog is chasing whom down the street?

9. Whom does John believe the fact that the dog is chasing down the street?

As sentence 7 illustrates, the basic sentence form is acceptable, but one cannot move *whom* from question form 8 to produce question form 9. Sentence 9 just sounds bizarre. We will return later to the restrictions on movement transformations.

In contrast with the abundant evidence for phrase structure in language processing, the evidence that people actually compute anything analogous to transformations in understanding or producing sentences is very poor. How people process such transformationally derived sentences remains very much an open question. It is also the case that there is a lot of controversy within linguistics about how to conceive of transformations. The role of transformations has been deemphasized in many proposals.

Transformations move elements from their normal positions in the phrase structure of a sentence.

What Is So Special about Human Language?

We have reviewed some of the features of human language, with the implicit assumption that no other species has anything like such a language. What gives us this conceit? How do we know that other species do not have their own languages? Perhaps we just do not understand the languages of other species. Certainly, all social species communicate with one another and, ultimately, whether we call their communication systems languages is a definitional matter. However, human language is fundamentally different than these other systems, and it is worth identifying some of the features (Hockett, 1960) that are considered critical to human language.

Semanticity and arbitrariness of units. Consider, for instance, the communication system of dogs. They have a nonverbal system that is very effective in communication. The reason that dogs are such successful pets is thought to be that their nonverbal communication system is so much like that of humans. Besides being nonverbal, canine communication has more fundamental limitations. Unlike human language, in which the relation between signs and meaning is arbitrary (there is no reason why "Good dog" and "Bad dog" should mean what they do), dogs' signs are directly related to means—a snarl for aggression (which often reveals the dog's sharp incisors), exposing the neck (a vulnerable part of the dog's body) for submission, and so on. However, although canines have a nonarbitrary communication system, it is not the case that all species do. For instance, the vocalizations of some species of monkeys have this property of arbitrary meaning (Marler, 1967). One species, the Vervet Monkey, has different warning calls for different types of predators—a "chutter" for snakes, a "chirp" for leopards, and a "kraup" for eagles.

Displacement in time and space. A critical feature of the monkey warning system is that the monkeys use it only in the presence of a danger. They do not use it to "discuss" the day's events at a later time. An enormously important feature of human language (exemplified by this book) is that it can be used to communicate over time and distance. Interestingly, the "language" of honeybees satisfies the properties of both arbitrariness and displacement (von Frisch, 1967). When a honeybee returns to a nest after finding a food source, it will engage in a dance to communicate the location of the food source. The "dance" consists of a straight run followed by a turn to the right to circle back to the starting point, another straight run, followed by a turn and circle to the left, and so on, in an alternating pattern. The length of the run indicates the distance of the food and the direction of the run relative to vertical indicates the direction relative to the sun.

Discreteness and productivity. Language contains discrete units, which would serve to disqualify the bee language system, although the monkey warning system meets this criterion. Requiring a language to have discrete units is not just an arbitrary regulation to disqualify the dance of the bees. This discreteness enables the elements of the language to be combined into an almost infinite number of phrase structures and for these phrase structures to be transformed, as already described. As will become more and more apparent in these chapters, this ability to combine symbols makes human language different from the communication systems of all other species.

It is a striking fact that all people in the world, even those in isolated communities, speak a language. No other species, not even genetically close apes, spontaneously use a communication system anything like human language. However, many people have wondered whether apes such as chimpanzees could be taught a language. Early in the 20th century, there were attempts to teach chimpanzees to speak that failed miserably (C. Hayes, 1951; Kellogg & Kellogg, 1933). It is now clear that the human vocal apparatus has undergone special evolutionary adaptations to enable speech, and it was a hopeless goal to try to teach chimps to speak. However, apes have considerable manual dexterity and, more recently, there have been some well-publicized attempts to teach chimpanzees and other apes manual languages.

Some of the studies have used American sign language (e.g., Gardner & Gardner, 1969), which is a full-fledged language and makes the point that language need not be spoken. These attempts were only modest successes (e.g., Terrace, Pettito, Sanders, & Bever, 1979). Although the chimpanzees could acquire vocabularies of more than a hundred signs, they never used them with the productivity typical of humans in using their own language. Some of the more impressive attempts have actually used artificial languages consisting of "words" called lexigrams, made from plastic shapes, that can be attached to a magnetic board (e.g., Premack & Premack, 1983).

Perhaps the most impressive example comes from a bonobo great ape called Kanzi (Savage-Rumbaugh et al., 1993; see Figure 12.4). Bonobos are considered even closer genetically to humans than chimpanzees are, but are rare. Kanzi's mother was a subject of one of these efforts, and Kanzi simply came along with his mother and observed her training sessions. However, he spontaneously

FIGURE 12.4 Kanzi, a bonobo, listening to English. A number of videos of Kanzi can be found on YouTube by searching with his name. (The Language Research Center.)

started to use the lexigrams, and the experimenters began working with their newfound subject. His spontaneous constructions were quite impressive, and it was discovered that he had also acquired a considerable ability to understand spoken language. When he was 5.5 years of age, his comprehension of spoken English was determined to be equivalent to that of a 2-year-old human.

As in other things, it seems unwise to conclude that human linguistic abilities are totally discontinuous from the abilities of genetically close primates. However, the human propensity for language is remarkable in the animal world. Steven Pinker (1994b) coined the phrase "language instinct" to describe the propensity for every human to acquire language. In his view, it is something wired into the human brain through evolution. Just as song birds are born with the propensity to learn the song of their species, so we are born with the propensity to learn the language of our society. Just as humans might try to imitate the song of birds and partly succeed, other species, like the bonobo, may partly succeed at mastering the language of humans. However, bird song is special to songbirds and language is special to humans.

Implications

Ape language and the ethics of experimentation

The issue of whether apes can be taught human languages interlinks in complex ways with issues about the ethical treatment of animals in research. The philosopher Descartes believed that language was what separated humans from animals. According to this view, if apes could be shown capable of acquiring a language, they would have human status and should be given the same rights as humans in experimentation. One might even ask that they give informed consent before participating in an experiment. Certainly, any procedure that involved injury would not be acceptable. There has been a fair amount of research involving invasive brain procedures with primates, but most of this has involved monkeys, not the great apes. Interestingly, it has been reported that studies with linguistic apes found that they categorized themselves with humans and separate from other animals (Linden, 1974). It has been argued that it is in the best interests of apes to teach them a language because this would confer on them the rights of humans. However, others have argued that teaching an ape a human language deadens their basic nature and that the real issue is that humans have lost the ability to understand apes.

The very similarity of primates to humans is what makes them such attractive subjects for research. There are severe restrictions on research on apes in many countries, and in 2008 The Great Ape Protection Act that would have prohibited any invasive research involving great apes was introduced in the U.S. Congress. Much of the concern is with use of apes to study human disease, where the potential benefits are great but the moral issues of infecting an animal are also severe. From this perspective, most cognitive research with apes, such as that on language acquisition, is quite benign. From a cognitive perspective, they are the only creatures that have thought processes close to that of humans and they offer potential insights we cannot get from other species. Nonetheless, many have argued that all research that removes them from their natural setting, including language acquisition research, should be banned.

- *Only humans show the propensity or the ability to acquire a complex communication system that combines symbols in a multitude of ways like natural language.*

The Relation Between Language and Thought

All reasonable people would concede that there is some special connection between language and humans. However, there is a lot of controversy about why there is such a connection. Many researchers, like Steven Pinker and Noam Chomsky, believe that humans have some special genetic endowment that enables them to learn language. However, others argue that what is special is general human intellectual abilities and that these abilities enable us to shape our communication system to be something as complex as natural language. I confess to leaning toward this alternate viewpoint. It raises the question of what might be the relation between language and thought. There are three possibilities that have been considered:

1. Thought depends in various ways on language.
2. Language depends in various ways on thought.
3. They are two independent systems.

We will go through each of these ideas in turn, starting with the proposal that language depends on thought. There have been a number of different versions of this proposal including the radical behaviorist proposal that thought is just speech and a more modest proposal called linguistic determinism.

The Behaviorist Proposal

As discussed in Chapter 1, John B. Watson, the father of behaviorism, held that there was no such thing as internal mental activity at all. All that humans do, Watson argued, is to emit responses that have been conditioned to various stimuli. This radical proposal, which, as noted in Chapter 1, held sway in America for some time, seemed to fly in the face of the abundant evidence that humans can engage in thinking behavior (e.g., do mental arithmetic) that entails no response emission. To deal with this obvious counter, Watson proposed that thinking was just subvocal speech—that, when people were engaged in such "thinking" activities, they were really talking to themselves. Hence, Watson's proposal was that a very important component of thought is simply subvocal speech. (The philosopher Herbert Feigl once said that Watson "made up his windpipe that he had no mind.")

Watson's proposal was a stimulus for a research program that engaged in taking recordings to see whether evidence could be found for subvocal activity of the speech apparatus during thinking. Indeed, often when a participant is engaged in thought, it is possible to get recordings of subvocal speech activity. However, the more important observation is that, in some situations, people engage in various silent thinking tasks with no detectable vocal activity. This finding did not upset Watson. He claimed that we think with our whole bodies—for instance, with our arms. He cited the fascinating evidence that deaf mutes actually make signs while asleep. (Speaking people who have done a lot of communication in sign language also sign while sleeping.)

The decisive experiment addressing Watson's hypothesis was performed by Smith, Brown, Toman, and Goodman (1947). They used a curare derivative that paralyzes the entire voluntary musculature. Smith was the participant for the experiment and had to be kept alive by means of an artificial respirator. Because his entire musculature was completely paralyzed, it was impossible for him to engage in subvocal speech or any other body movement. Nonetheless, under curare, Smith was able to observe what was going on around him, comprehend speech, remember these events, and think about them. Thus, it seems clear that thinking can proceed in the absence of any muscle activity. For our current purposes, the relevant additional observation is that thought is not just implicit speech but is truly an internal, nonmotor activity.

Additional evidence that thought is not to be equated with language comes from the research on memory for meaning that was reviewed in Chapter 5. There, we considered the fact that people tend to retain not the exact words of a linguistic communication, but rather a more abstract representation of the meaning of the communication. Thought might be identified, at least in part, with this abstract, nonverbal propositional code. As mentioned there in regard to the perceptual symbol system hypothesis, the abstractness of human thought is under reconsideration. However, even the perceptual symbol system proposal holds that thought is more than just subvocal speech and that, rather, it consists of rich internal perceptual representations.

Additional evidence that thought is more than subvocal speech comes from the occasional person who has no apparent language at all but who certainly gives evidence of being able to think. Additionally, it seems hard to claim that nonverbal animals such as apes are unable to think. Recall, for instance, the problem-solving exploits of Sultan in Chapter 8. It is always hard to determine the exact character of the "thought processes" of nonverbal participants and the way in which these processes differ from the thought processes of verbal participants, because there is no language with which nonverbal participants can be interrogated. Thus, the apparent dependence of thought on language may be an illusion that derives from the fact that it is hard to obtain evidence about thought without using language.

- *The behaviorists believed that thought consists only of covert speech and other implicit motor actions, but evidence has shown that thought can proceed in the absence of any motor activity.*

The Whorfian Hypothesis of Linguistic Determinism

Linguistic determinism is the claim that language determines or strongly influences the way that a person thinks or perceives the world. This proposal is much weaker than Watson's position because it does not claim that language and thought are identical. The hypothesis has been advanced by a good many linguists but has been most strongly associated with Whorf (1956). Whorf was quite an unusual character himself. He was trained as a chemical engineer at MIT, spent his life working for the Hartford Fire Insurance Company, and studied North American Indian languages as a hobby. He was very impressed by the fact that different languages emphasize in their structure rather different aspects of the world. He believed that these emphases in a language must have a great influence on the way that speakers of that language think about the world. For instance, he claimed that Eskimos have many different words for snow, each of which refers to snow in a different state (wind-driven, packed, slushy, and so on), whereas English speakers have only a single word for snow.[2] Many other examples exist at the vocabulary level: The Hanunoo people in the Philippines supposedly have 92 different names for varieties of rice. The Arabic language has many different ways of naming camels. Whorf felt that such a rich variety of terms would cause the speaker of the language to perceive the world differently from a person who had only a single word for a particular category.

Deciding how to evaluate the Whorfian hypothesis is very tricky. Nobody would be surprised to learn that Eskimos know more about snow than average English speakers. After all, snow is a more important part of their life experience. The question is whether their language has any effect on the Eskimos' perception of snow beyond the effect of experience. If speakers of English went through the Eskimo life experience, would their perception of snow be any different from that of the Eskimo-language speakers? (Indeed, ski bums have a life experience that includes a great deal of exposure to snow; they have a great deal of knowledge about snow and, interestingly, have developed new terms for snow.)

One fairly well-researched test of the issue uses color words. English has 11 basic color words—*black, white, red, green, yellow, blue, brown, purple, pink, orange,* and *gray*—a large number. These words are called basic color words because they are short and are used frequently, in contrast with such terms as *saffron, turquoise,* and *magenta.* At the other extreme is the language of the Dani, a Stone Age agricultural people of Indonesian New Guinea. This language has just two basic color terms: *mili* for dark, cold hues and *mola* for bright, warm hues. If the categories in language determine perception, the Dani should perceive color in a less refined manner than English speakers do. The relevant question is whether this speculation is true.

Speakers of English, at least, judge a certain color within the range referred to by each basic color term to be the best—for instance, the best red, the best blue, and so on (see Berlin & Kay, 1969). Each of the 11 basic color terms in English appears to have one generally agreed upon best color, called a focal color. English speakers find it easier to process and remember focal colors than nonfocal colors (e.g., Brown & Lenneberg, 1954). The interesting question is whether the special cognitive capacity for identifying focal colors developed

[2] There have been challenges to Whorf's claims about the richness of Eskimo vocabulary for snow (L. Martin, 1986; Pullman, 1989). In general, there is a feeling that Whorf exaggerated the variety of words in various languages.

because English speakers have special words for these colors. If so, it would be a case of language influencing thought.

To test whether the special processing of focal colors was an instance of language influencing thought, Rosch (who published some of this work under her former name, Heider) performed an important series of experiments on the Dani. The point was to see whether the Dani processed focal colors differently from English speakers. One experiment (Rosch, 1973) compared Dani and English speakers' ability to learn nonsense names for focal colors with that for nonfocal colors. English speakers find it easier to learn arbitrary names for focal colors. Dani participants also found it easier to learn arbitrary names for focal colors than for nonfocal colors, even though they have no names for these colors. In another experiment (Heider, 1972), participants were shown a color chip for 5 s; 30 s after the presentation ended, they were required to select the color from among 160 color chips. Both English and Dani speakers perform better at this task when they are trying to locate a focal color chip rather than a nonfocal color chip. The physiology of color vision suggests that many of these focal colors are specially processed by the visual system (de Valois & Jacobs, 1968). The fact that many languages develop basic color terms for just these colors can be seen as an instance of thought determining language.[3]

However, more recent research by Roberson, Davies, and Davidoff (2000) does suggest an influence of language on ability to remember colors. They compared British participants with another Papua New Guinea group who speak Berinmo, a language that has five basic color terms. Color Plate 12.1 compares how the Berinmo cut up the color space with how English speakers cut up the color space. Replicating the earlier work, they found that there was superior memory for focal colors regardless of language. However, there were substantial effects of the color boundaries as well. The researchers examined distinctions that were important in one language versus another. For instance, the Berinmo make a distinction between the colors *wor* and *nol* in the middle of the English green category, whereas English speakers make their yellow-green distinction in the middle of the Berinmo *wor* category. Participants from both languages were asked to learn to sort stimuli at these two boundaries into two categories. Figure 12.5 shows the amount of effort that the two populations put into learning the two distinctions. English speakers found it easiest to sort stimuli at the yellow-green boundary, whereas Berinmo found it easiest to sort stimuli at the *nol-wor* distinction.

FIGURE 12.5 Mean errors to criterion for the two populations learning distinctions at the *nol-wor* boundary and at the yellow-green boundary. (From Roberson et al., 2000.)

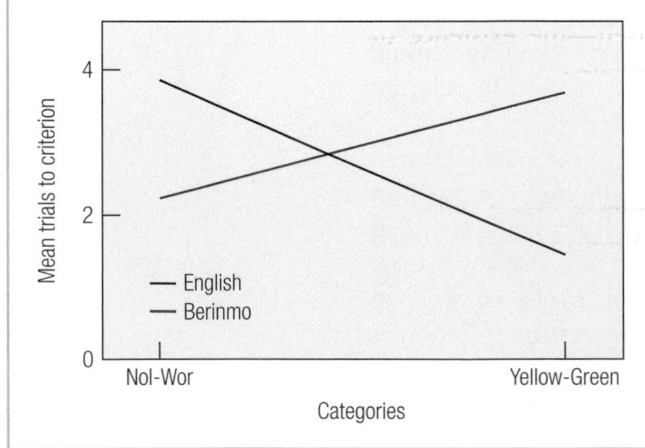

Note that both populations are capable of making distinctions that are important to the other population. Thus, it is not that their language has made them blind to color distinctions. However, they definitely find it harder to see the distinctions

[3] For further research on this topic, read Lucy and Shweder (1979, 1988) and Garro (1986).

not signaled in their language and learn to make them consistently. Thus, although language does not completely determine how we see the color space, it does have an influence.

- *Language can influence thought, but it does not totally determine the types of concepts that we can think about.*

Does Language Depend on Thought?

The alternative possibility is that the structure of language is determined by the structure of thought. Aristotle argued 2500 years ago that the categories of thought determined the categories of language. There are some reasons for believing that he was correct, but most of these reasons were not available to Aristotle. So, although the hypothesis has been around for 2500 years, we have better evidence today.

There are numerous reasons to suppose that humans' ability to think (i.e., to engage in nonlinguistic cognitive activity such as remembering and problem solving) appeared earlier evolutionarily and occurs sooner developmentally than the ability to use language. Many species of animals without language appear to be capable of complex cognition. Children, before they are effective at using their language, give clear evidence of relatively complex cognition. If we accept the idea that thought evolved before language, it seems natural to suppose that language arose as a tool whose function was to communicate thought. It is generally true that tools are shaped to fit the objects on which they must operate. Analogously, it seems reasonable to suppose that language has been shaped to fit the thoughts that it must communicate.

We saw in Chapter 5 that propositional structures constitute a very important type of knowledge structure in representing information both derived from language and derived from pictures. This propositional structure is manifested in the phrase structure of language. The basic phrase units of a language tend to convey propositions. For instance, *the tall boy* conveys the proposition that the boy is tall. This phenomenon itself—the existence of a linguistic structure, the phrase, designed to accommodate a thought structure, the proposition—seems to be a clear example of the dependence of language on thought.

Another example of the way in which thought shapes language comes from Rosch's research on focal colors. As stated earlier, the human visual system is maximally sensitive to certain colors. As a consequence, languages have special, short, high-frequency words with which to designate these colors. Thus, the visual system has determined how the English language divides up the color space.

We find additional evidence for the influence of thought on language when we consider word order. Every language has a preferred word order for expressing subject (S), verb (V), and object (O). Consider this sentence, which exhibits the preferred word order in English:

- Lynne petted the Labrador.

English is referred to as an SVO language. In a study of a diverse sample of the world's languages, Greenberg (1963) found that only four of the six possible orders of S, V, and O are used in natural languages, and one of these four orders is rare. The six possible word orders and the frequency of each order in the world's languages are as follows (the percentages are from Ultan, 1969):

SOV 44%	VOS 2%
SVO 35%	OVS 0%
VSO 19%	OSV 0%

The important feature is that the subject almost always precedes the object. This order makes good sense when we think about cognition. An action starts with the agent and then affects the object. It is natural therefore that the subject of a sentence, when it reflects its agency, is first.

- *In many ways, the structure of language corresponds to the structure of how our minds process the world.*

Modularity of Language

We have considered the possibility that thought might depend on language and the possibility that language might depend on thought. A third logical possibility is that language and thought might be independent. A special version of this independence principle is called the **modularity** position (Chomsky, 1980; Fodor, 1983). This position holds that important language processes function independently from the rest of cognition. Fodor argued that a separate linguistic module first analyzes incoming speech and then passes this analysis on to general cognition. Fodor thought that this linguistic module was similar in this respect to early visual processing, which largely proceeds in response to the visual stimulus independent of higher-level intentions.[4] Similarly, in language generation, the linguistic module takes the intentions to be spoken and produces the speech. This position does not deny that the linguistic module may have been shaped to communicate thought. However, it argues that it operates according to different principles from the rest of cognition and is "encapsulated" such that it cannot be influenced by general cognition. In essence, the claim is that language's communication with other mental processes is limited to passing its products to general cognition and receiving the products of general cognition.

One piece of evidence for the independence of language from other cognitive processes comes from research on people who have substantial deficits in language but not in general cognition or vice versa. Williams syndrome, a rare genetic disorder, is an example of a mental retardation that seems not to affect linguistic fluency (Bellugi, Wang, & Jernigan, 1994). On the other side, there are people who have severe language deficits without accompanying intellectual deficits, including both some aphasics and some with developmental problems.

[4] However, as reviewed in Chapter 3, there are some effects of visual attention in primary visual cortex—for example, see the discussion of Figure 3.10.

Specific language impairment (SLI) is a term used to describe a pattern of deficit in the development of language that cannot be explained by hearing loss, mental retardation, or other nonlinguistic factors. It is a diagnosis of exclusion and probably has a number of underlying causes; in some cases, these causes appear to be genetic (Stromswold, 2000). Recently, a mutation in a specific gene, called *FOXP2,* has been associated with specific language deficits in the popular press (e.g., Wade, 2003), although there appear to be other cognitive deficits associated with this mutation as well (Vargha-Khadem, Watkins, Alcock, Fletcher, & Passingham, 1995). The FOXP2 gene is very similar in all mammals, although the human FOXP2 is distinguished from that of other primates by two amino acids (out of 715). Mutations in the FOXP2 gene are associated with vocal deficits and other deficits in many species. For instance, it results in incomplete acquisition of song imitation in birds (Haesler et al., 2007). It has been claimed that the human form of the *FOXP2* gene became established in the human population about 50 thousand years ago when, according to some proposals, human language emerged (Enard et al., 2002). However, more recent evidence suggests these changes are shared with Neanderthals and occurred 300 to 400 thousand years ago (Krause et al., 2007). Although the FOXP2 gene does play an important role in language, it does not appear to provide strong evidence for a genetic basis for a unique language ability.

The modularity hypothesis has turned out to be a major dividing issue in the field, with different researchers lining up in support or in opposition. Two domains of research have played a major role in evaluating the modularity proposal:

1. Language acquisition. Here, the issue is whether language is acquired according to its own learning principles or whether it is acquired like other cognitive skills.
2. Language comprehension. Here, the issue is whether major aspects of language processing occur without utilization of any general cognitive processes.

We will consider some of the issues with respect to comprehension in the next chapter. In this chapter, we will look at what is known about language acquisition. After an overview of the general course of language acquisition by young children, we will turn to the implications of the language-acquisition process for the uniqueness of language.

- *The modularity position holds that the acquisition and processing of language is independent from other cognitive systems.*

Language Acquisition

Having watched my two children acquire a language, I understand how easy it is to lose sight of what a remarkable feat it is. Days and weeks go by with little apparent change in their linguistic abilities. Progress seems slow. However, something remarkable is happening. With very little and often no deliberate instruction, children by the time they reach age 10 have accomplished implicitly what generations of Ph.D. linguists have not accomplished explicitly. They have internalized all the major rules of a natural language—and there appear to be thousands of such rules with subtle interactions. No linguist in a lifetime has been able to formulate a grammar for any language that will identify all and only the grammatical sentences. However, as we progress through childhood, we do internalize such a grammar. Unfortunately for the linguist, our knowledge of the grammar of our language is not something that we can articulate. It is implicit knowledge (see Chapter 7), which we can only display in using the language.

The process by which children acquire a language has some characteristic features that seem to hold no matter what their native language is (and languages throughout the world differ dramatically): Children are notoriously noisy creatures from birth. At first, there is little variety in their speech. Their vocalizations consist almost totally of an *ah* sound (although they can produce it at different intensities and with different emotional tones). In the months following birth, a child's vocal apparatus matures. At about 6 months, a change takes place in children's utterances. They begin to engage in what is called babbling, which consists of generating a rich variety of speech sounds with interesting intonation patterns. However, the sounds are generally totally meaningless to the listeners.

An interesting feature of early childhood speech is that children produce sounds that they will not use in the particular language that they will learn. Moreover, they can apparently make acoustic discriminations among sounds that will not be used in their language. For instance, Japanese infants can discriminate between /l/ and /r/, a discrimination that Japanese adults cannot make (Tsushima et al., 1994). Similarly, English infants can discriminate among variations of the /t/ sound, which are important in the Hindi language of India, that English adults cannot discriminate (Werker & Tees, 1999). It is as if the children enter the world with speech and perceptual capabilities that constitute a block of marble out of which will be carved their particular language, discarding what is not necessary for that language.

When a child is about a year old, the first words appear, always a point of great excitement to the child's parents. The very first words are there only to the ears of very sympathetic parents and caretakers, but soon the child develops a considerable repertoire of words, which are recognizable to the untrained ear and which the child uses effectively to make requests and to describe what is happening. The early words are concrete and refer to the here and now. Among my children's first words were *Mommy, Daddy, Rogers* (for Mister Rogers), *cheese, 'puter* (for computer), *eat, hi, bye, go,* and *hot.* One remarkable feature of this stage is that the speech consists only of one-word utterances; even though the children know many words, they never put them together to make multiple-word phrases. Children's use of single words is quite complex. They often use a single word to communicate a whole thought. Children will also overextend their words. Thus, the word *dog* might be used to refer to any furry four-legged animal.

The one-word stage, which lasts about 6 months, is followed by a stage in which children will put two words together. I can still remember our excitement as parents when our son said his first two-word utterance at 18 months—*more gee*, which meant for him "more brie"—he was a connoisseur of cheese. Table 12.1 illustrates some of the typical two-word utterances generated by children at this stage. All their utterances are one or two words. Once their utterances extend beyond two words, they are of many different lengths. There is no corresponding three-word stage. The two-word utterances correspond to about a dozen or so semantic relations, including agent-action, agent-object, action-object, object-location, object-attribute, possessor-object, negation-object, and negation-event. The order in which the children place these words usually corresponds to one of the orders that would be correct in adult speech in the children's linguistic community.

TABLE 12.1

Two-Word Utterances	
Kendall swim	pillow fell
doggie bark	Kendall book
see Kendall	Papa door
writing book	Kendall turn
sit pool	towel bed
shoe off	there cow

From Bowerman (1973).

Even when children leave the two-word stage and speak in sentences ranging from three to eight words, their speech retains a peculiar quality, which is sometimes referred to as telegraphic. Table 12.2 contains some of these longer multiword utterances. The children speak somewhat as people used to write in telegraphs (and like people currently do when text messaging), omitting such unimportant function words as *the* and *is*. In fact, it is rare to find in early-childhood speech any utterance that would be considered to be a well-formed sentence. Yet, out of this beginning, grammatical sentences eventually appear. One might expect that children would learn to speak some kinds of sentences perfectly, then learn to speak other kinds of sentences perfectly, and so on. However, it seems that children start out speaking all kinds of sentences and all of them imperfectly. Their language development is characterized not by learning more kinds of sentences but by their sentences becoming gradually better approximations of adult sentences.

TABLE 12.2

Multiword Utterances	
Put truck window	My balloon pop
Want more grape juice	Doggie bit me mine boot
Sit Adam chair	That Mommy nose right there
Mommy put sack	She's wear that hat
No I see truck	I like pick dirt up firetruck
Adam fall toy	No pictures in there

From Brown (1973).

Besides the missing words, there are other dimensions in which children's early speech is incomplete. A classic example concerns the rules for pluralization in English. Initially, children do not distinguish in their speech between singular and plural, using a singular form for both. Then, they will learn the *add s* rule for pluralization but overextend it, producing *foots* or even *feets*. Gradually, they learn the pluralization rules for the irregular words. This learning continues into adulthood. Cognitive scientists have to learn that the plural of *schema* is *schemata* (a fact that I spared the reader from having to deal with when schemas were discussed in Chapter 5).

Another dimension in which children have to perfect their language is word order. They have particular difficulties with transformational movements of terms from their natural position in the phrase structure (see the earlier discussion in this chapter). So, for instance, there is a point at which children form questions without moving the verb auxiliary from the verb phrase:

- What me think?
- What the doggie have?

Even later, when children's spontaneous speech seems to be well formed, they will display errors in comprehension that reveal that they have not yet captured all the subtleties in their language. For instance, Chomsky (1970) found that children had difficulty comprehending sentences such as *John promised Bill to leave,* interpreting Bill as the one who leaves. The verb *promise* is unusual in this respect—for instance, compare *John told Bill to leave,* which children will properly interpret.

By the time children are 6 years old, they have mastered most of their language, although they continue to pick up details at least until the age of 10. In that time, they have learned tens of thousands of special case rules and tens of thousands of words. Studies of the rate of word acquisition by children produced an estimate of more than five words a day (Carey, 1978; E. V. Clark, 1983). A natural language requires more knowledge to be acquired for mastery than do any of the domains of expertise considered in Chapter 9. Of course, children also put an enormous amount of time into the language-acquisition process—easily 10,000 hr must have been spent practicing speaking and understanding speech before a child is 6 years old.

- *Children gradually approximate adult speech by producing ever larger and more complex constructions.*

The Issue of Rules and the Case of Past Tense

A controversy in the study of language acquisition concerns whether children are learning what might be considered rules such as those that are part of linguistic theory. For instance, when a child learning English begins to inflect a verb such as *kick* with *ed* to indicate past tense, is that child learning a past-tense rule or is the child just learning to associate *kick* and *ed?* A young child certainly cannot explicitly articulate the *add ed* rule, but this inability may just mean that this knowledge is implicit. An interesting observation in this regard is that children will generalize the rule to new verbs. If they are introduced to a new verb (e.g., told that the made-up verb *wug* means dance) they will spontaneously generate this verb with the appropriate past tense (*wugged* in this example).

Some of the interesting evidence on this score concerns how children learn to deal with irregular past tenses—for instance, the past tense of *sing* is *sang.* The order in which children learn to inflect verbs for past tense follows the characteristic sequence noted for pluralization. First, children will use the irregular correctly, generating *sang;* then they will overgeneralize the past-tense rule and generate *singed;* finally, they will get it right for good and return to *sang.* The existence of this intermediate stage of overgeneralization has been used to argue for the existence of rules, because it is claimed there is no way that the child could have learned from direct experience to associate *ed* to *sing.* Rather, the argument goes, the child must be overgeneralizing a rule that has been learned.

This conventional interpretation of the acquisition of past tense was severely challenged by Rumelhart and McClelland (1986a). They simulated a neural network as illustrated in Figure 12.6 and had it learn the past tenses of verbs. In the

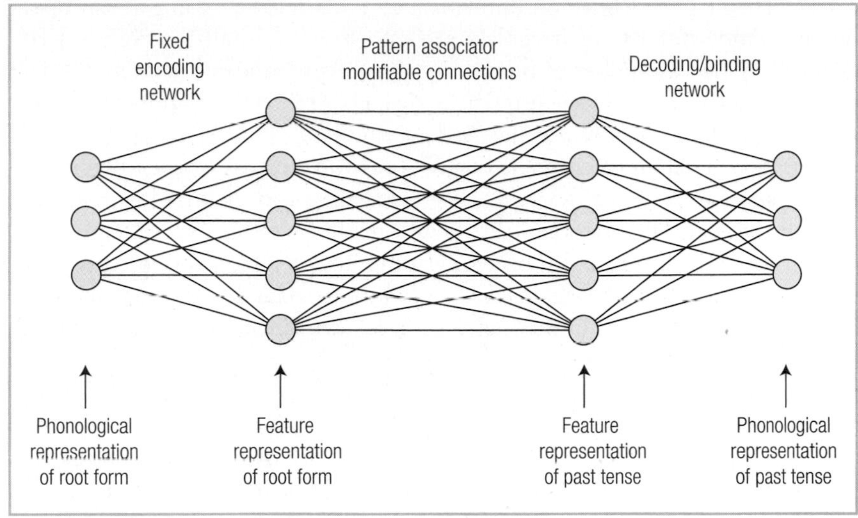

FIGURE 12.6 A network for past tense. The phonological representation of the root is converted into a distributed feature representation. This representation is converted into the distributed feature representation of the past tense, which is then mapped onto a phonological representation of the past tense. (From Rumelhart & McClelland, 1986a.)

network, one inputs the root form of a verb (e.g., kick, sing) and, after a number of layers of association, the past-tense form should appear.

The computer model was trained with a set of 420 pairs of the root with the past tense. It simulated a neural learning mechanism to acquire the pairs. Such a system learns to associate features of the input with features of the output. Thus, it might learn that words beginning with "s" are associated with past tense endings of "ed," thus leading to the "singed" overgeneralization (but things can be more complex in such neural models). The model mirrored the standard developmental sequence of children, first generating correct irregulars, then overgeneralizing, and finally getting it right. It went through the intermediate stage of generating past-tense forms such as *singed* because of generalization from regular past-tense forms. With enough practice, the model, in effect, memorized the past-tense forms and was not using generalization. Rumelhart and McClelland concluded:

> We have, we believe, provided a distinct alternative to the view that children learn the rules of English past-tense formation in any explicit sense. We have shown that a reasonable account of the acquisition of past tense can be provided without recourse to the notion of a "rule" as anything more than a description of the language. We have shown that, for this case, there is no induction problem. The child need not figure out what the rules are, nor even that there are rules. (p. 267)

Their claims drew a major counter-response from Pinker and Prince (1988). Pinker and Prince pointed out that the ability to produce the initial stage of correct irregulars depended on Rumelhart and McClelland's using a disproportionately large number of irregulars at first—more so than the child experiences. They had a number of other criticisms of the model, including the fact that it sometimes produced utterances that children never produce—for instance, it produced *membled* as the past tense of *mail.*

Another of their criticisms had to do with whether it was even possible to really learn past tense as the process of associating root form with past-tense form. It turns out that the way a verb is inflected for past tense does not depend just on its root form but also on its meaning. For instance, the word *ring* has two meanings as a verb—to make a sound or to encircle. Although it is the same root, the past tense of the first is *rang,* whereas the past tense of the latter is *ringed,* as in

- He rang the bell.
- They ringed the fort with soldiers.

It is unclear how fundamental any of these criticisms are, and there are now a number of more adequate attempts to come up with such associative models (e.g., MacWhinney & Leinbach, 1991; Daugherty, MacDonald, Petersen, & Seidenberg, 1993; and, for a rejoinder, see Marcus et al., 1995).

Marslen-Wilson and Tyler (1998) argued that the debate between rule-based and associative accounts will not be settled by focusing only on children's language acquisition. They suggest that more decisive evidence will come from examining properties of the neural system that implements adult processing of past tense. They cite two sorts of evidence, which seem to converge in their implications about the nature of the processing of past tense. First, they cite evidence that some patients with aphasias have deficient processing of regular past tense, whereas others have deficient processing of irregular past tenses. The patients with deficient processing of regular past tense have severe damage to Broca's area, which is generally associated with syntactic processing. In contrast, the patients with deficient processing of irregular past tenses have damage to their temporal lobes, which are generally associated with associative learning. Second, they cite the PET imaging data of Jaeger et al. (1996), who studied the processing of past tense by unimpaired adults. Jaeger et al. found activation in the region of Broca's area only during the processing of regular past tense and found temporal activation during the processing of irregular past tenses. On the basis of the data, Marslen-Wilson and Tyler concluded that regular past tense may be processed in a rule-based manner, whereas the irregular may be processed in an associative manner.

- *Irregular past tenses are produced associatively, and there is debate about whether regular past tenses are produced associatively or by rules.*

Quality of Input

An important difference between a child's first-language acquisition and the acquisition of many skills (including typical second-language acquisition) is that the child receives little if any instruction in acquiring his or her first language. Thus, the child's task is one of inducing the structure of natural language from listening to parents, caretakers, and older children. In addition to not receiving any direct instruction, the child does not get much information about what are incorrect forms in natural language. Many parents do not correct their children's speech at all, and those who do correct their children's speech appear to do so without any effect. Consider the following well-known interaction recorded between a parent and a child (McNeill, 1966):

Child: *Nobody don't like me.*
Mother: *No, say, "Nobody likes me."*
Child: *Nobody don't like me.*
Mother: *No, say, "Nobody likes me."*
Child: *Nobody don't like me.*

[dialogue repeated eight times]

Mother: *Now listen carefully; say, "Nobody likes me."*
Child: *Oh! Nobody don't likeS me.*

This lack of negative information is puzzling to theorists of natural language acquisition. We have seen that children's early speech is full of errors. If they are never told about their errors, why do children ever abandon these incorrect ways of speaking and adopt the correct forms?

Because children do not get much instruction on the nature of language and ignore most of what they get, their learning task is one of induction—they must infer from the utterances that they hear what the acceptable utterances in their language are. This task is very difficult under the best of conditions, and children often do not operate under the best of conditions. For instance, children hear ungrammatical sentences mixed in with the grammatical. How are they to avoid being misled by these sentences? Some parents and caregivers are careful to make their utterances to children simple and clear. This kind of speech, consisting of short sentences with exaggerated intonation, is called motherese (Snow & Ferguson, 1977). However, not all children receive the benefit of such speech, and yet all children learn their native languages. Some parents speak to their children in only adult sentences, and the children learn (Kaluli, studied by Schieffelin, 1979); other parents do not speak to their children at all, and still the children learn by overhearing adults speak (Piedmont Carolinas, studied by Heath, 1983). Moreover, among more typical parents, there is no correlation between degree to which motherese is used and rate of linguistic developments (Gleitman, Newport, & Gleitman, 1984). So the quality of the input cannot be that critical.

Another curious fact is that children appear to be capable of learning a language in the absence of any input. Goldin-Meadow (2003) summarized research on the deaf children of speaking parents who chose to teach their children by the oral method. It is very difficult for deaf children to learn to speak but quite easy for children to learn sign language, which is a perfectly fine language. Despite the fact that the parents of these children were not teaching them sign language, they proceeded to invent their own sign language to communicate with their parents. These invented languages have the structure of normal languages. Moreover, the children in the process of invention seem to go through the same periods as children who are learning a language of their community. That is, they start out with single manual gestures, then progress to a two-gesture period, and continue to evolve a complete language more or less at the same points in time as those of their hearing peers. Thus, children seem to be born with a propensity to communicate and will learn a language no matter what.

The very fact that young children learn a language so successfully in almost all circumstances has been used to argue that the way that we learn language must be different from the way that we learn other cognitive skills. Also pointed out is the fact that children learn their first language successfully at a point in development when their general intellectual abilities are still weak.

Children master language at a very young age and with little direct instruction.

A Critical Period for Language Acquisition

A related argument has to do with the claim that young children appear to acquire a second language much faster than older children or adults do. It is claimed that there is a certain critical period, from 2 to about 12 years of age, when it is easiest to learn a language. For a long time, the claim that children learn second languages more readily than adults was based on informal observations of children of various ages and of adults in new linguistic communities—for example, when families move to a another country in response to a corporate assignment or when immigrants move to another country to reside there permanently. Young children are said to acquire a facility to get along in the new language more quickly than their older siblings or their parents. However, there are a great many differences between the adults, the older children, and the younger children in amount of linguistic exposure, type of exposure (e.g., whether the stock market, history, or Nintendo is being discussed), and willingness to try to learn (McLaughlin, 1978; Nida, 1971). In careful studies in which situations have been selected that controlled for these factors, a positive relation is exhibited between children's ages and rate of language development (Ervin-Tripp, 1974). That is, older children (older than 12 years) learn faster than younger children.

Even though older children and adults may learn a new language more rapidly than younger children initially, they seem not to acquire the same level of final mastery of the fine points of language, such as the phonology and morphology (Lieberman, 1984; Newport, 1986). For instance, the ability to speak a second language without an accent severely deteriorates with age (Oyama, 1978). In one study, Johnson and Newport (1989) looked at the degree of proficiency in speaking English achieved by Koreans and Chinese as a function of the age at which they arrived in America. All had been in the United States for about 10 years. In general, it seems that the later they came to America, the poorer their performance was on a variety of measures of syntactic facility. Thus, although it is not true that language learning is fastest for the youngest, it is does seem that the greatest eventual mastery of the fine points of language are achieved by those who start very young.

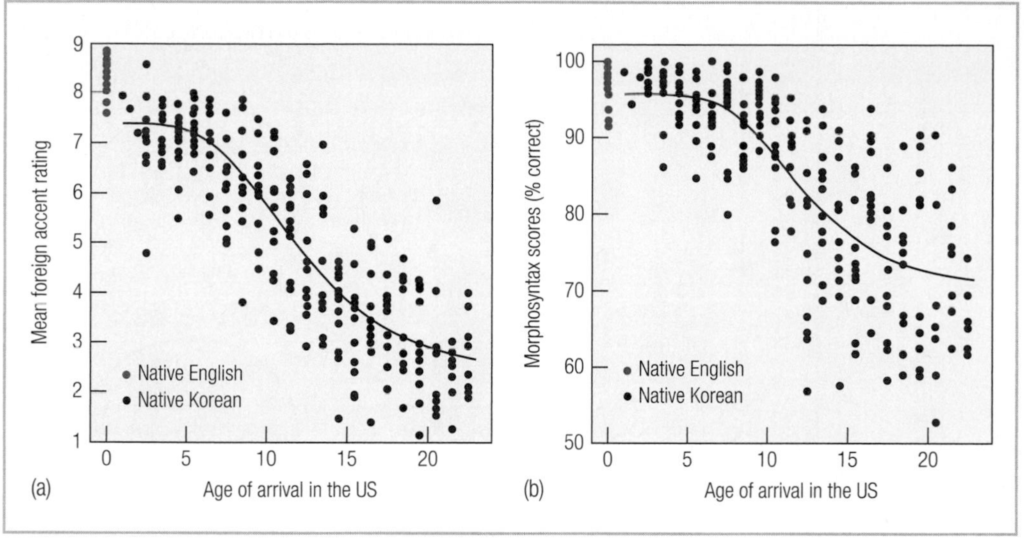

FIGURE 12.7 Mean language scores of 24 native English speakers and 240 native Korean participants as a function of age of arrival in the United States. (a) Scores on test of foreign accent (lower scores mean stronger accent) and (b) scores on tests of morphosyntax (lower scores mean more errors). (From Flege et al., 1999.)

Figure 12.7 shows some data from Flege, Yeni-Komshian, and Liu (1999) looking at the performance of 240 Korean immigrants to the United States. For measures of both foreign accent and syntactic errors, there is a steady decrease in performance with age of arrival in the United States. The data give some suggestion of a more rapid drop around the age of 10—which would be consistent with the hypothesis of a critical period in language acquisition. However, age of arrival turns out to be confounded with many other things, and one critical factor is the relative use of Korean versus English. Based on questionnaire data, Flege et al. rated these participants with respect to the relative frequency with which they used English versus Korean. Figure 12.8 displays this data and shows that there is a steady decrease in use of English to about the point of the critical period at which participants reported approximately equal use of the two languages. Perhaps the decrease in English performance reflects this difference in amount of use. To address this question, Flege et al. created two matched groups (subsets of the original 240) who reported equal use of English, but one group averaged 9.7 years when they arrived in the United States and the other group averaged 16.2. The two groups did not differ on measures of syntax, but the later arriving group still showed a stronger accent. Thus, it seems that there may not be a critical period for acquisition of syntactic knowledge but there may be one for acquisition of phonological knowledge.

FIGURE 12.8 Relative use of English versus Korean as a function of age of arrival in the United States. (From Flege et al., 1999.)

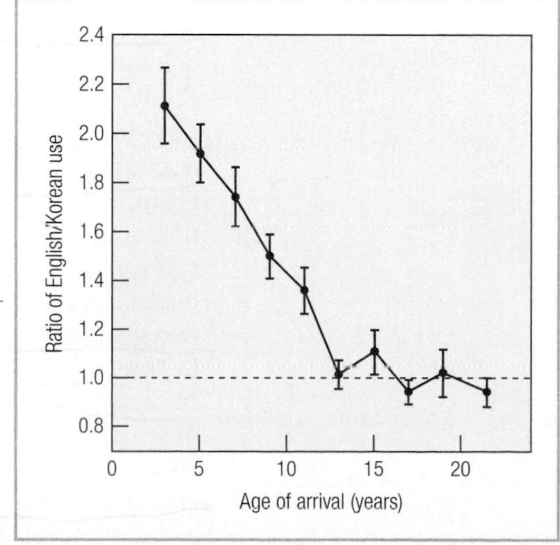

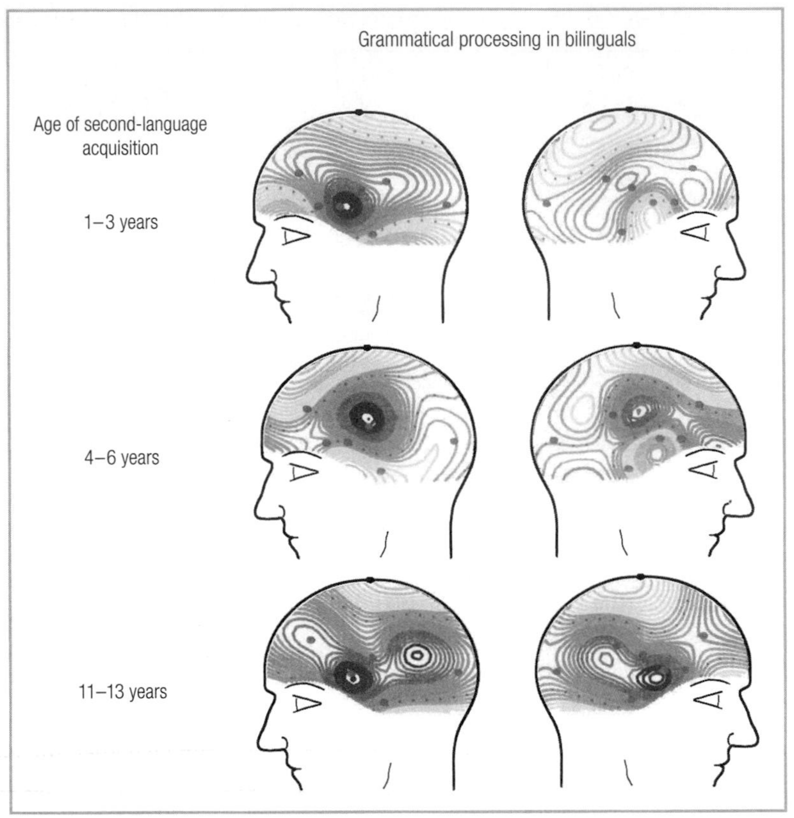

FIGURE 12.9 ERP patterns produced in response to grammatical anomalies in English in left and right hemispheres. (From Weber-Fox & Neville, 1996.)

Weber-Fox and Neville (1996) presented an interesting analysis of the effects of age of acquisition of language processing. They compared Chinese-English bilinguals who had learned English as a second language at different ages. One of their tests included an ERP measurement of sensitivity to syntactic violations in English. English monolinguals show a strong left lateralization in their response to such violations, which is a sign of the left lateralization of language. Figure 12.9 compares the two hemispheres in these adult bilinguals as a function of the age at which they acquired English. Adults who had learned English in their first years of life show strong left lateralization like those who learn English as a first language. If they were delayed in their acquisition to ages between 12 and 13, they show almost no lateralization. Those who had acquired English at an intermediate age show an intermediate amount of lateralization. Interestingly, Weber-Fox and Neville reported no such critical period for lexical or semantic violations. Learning English as late as 16 years of age had almost no effect on the lateralization of their responses to semantic violations. Thus, grammar seems to be more sensitive to a critical period.

Most studies on the effect of age of acquisition have naturally concerned second languages. However, an interesting study of first-language acquisition was done by Newport and Supalla (1990). They looked at the acquisition of American sign language, one of the few languages that is acquired as a first language in adolescence or adulthood. Deaf children of speaking parents are sometimes not exposed to the sign language until late in life and consequently acquire no language in their early years. Adults who acquire sign language achieve a poorer ultimate mastery of it than children do.

- *There are age-related differences in the success with which children can acquire a new language, with the strongest effects on phonology, intermediate effects on syntax, and weakest effects on semantics.*

Language Universals

Chomsky (1965) argued that special innate mechanisms underlie the acquisition of language. Specifically, his claim is that the number of formal possibilities for a natural language is so great that learning the language would simply be impossible unless we possessed some innate information about the possible forms of natural human languages. It is possible to prove formally that Chomsky is correct in his claim. Although the formal analysis is beyond the scope of this book, an analogy might help. In Chomsky's view, the problem that child learners face is to discover the grammar of their language when only given instances of utterances of the language. The task can be compared to trying to find a matching sock (language) from a huge pile of socks (set of possible languages). One can use various features (utterances) of the sock in hand to determine whether any particular sock in the pile is the matching one. If the pile of socks is big enough and the socks are similar enough, this task would prove to be impossible. Likewise, enough formally possible grammars are similar enough to one another to make it impossible to learn every possible instance of a formal language. However, because language learning obviously occurs, we must, according to Chomsky, have special innate knowledge that allows us to substantially restrict the number of possible grammars that we have to consider. In the sock analogy, it would be like knowing ahead of time which part of the pile to inspect. So, although we cannot learn all possible languages, we can learn a special subset of them.

Chomsky proposed the existence of **language universals** that limit the possible characteristics of a natural language and a natural grammar. He assumes that children can learn a natural language because they possess innate knowledge of these language universals. A language that violated these universals would simply be unlearnable, which means that there are hypothetical languages that no humans could learn. Languages that humans can learn are referred to as **natural languages.**

As already noted, we can formally prove that Chomsky's assertion is correct—that is, constraints on the possible forms of a natural language must exist. However, the critical issue is whether these constraints are due to any linguistic-specific knowledge on the part of children or whether they are simply general cognitive constraints on learning mechanisms. Chomsky would argue that the constraints are language specific. It is this claim that is open to serious question. The issue is: Are the constraints on the form of natural languages universals of language or universals of cognition?

In speaking of language universals, Chomsky is concerned with a competence grammar. Recall that a competence analysis is concerned with an abstract specification of what a speaker knows about a language; in contrast, a performance analysis is concerned with the way in which a speaker uses language. Thus, Chomsky is claiming that children possess innate constraints about the types of phrase structures and transformations that might be found in a natural language. Because of the abstract, nonperformance-based character of these purported universals, one cannot simply evaluate Chomsky's claim by observing the details of acquisition of any particular language. Rather, the strategy is to look for properties that are true of all languages or of the acquisition of all languages. These universal properties would be manifestations of the language universals that Chomsky postulates.

Although languages can be quite different from one another, some clear uniformities, or near-uniformities, exist. For instance, as we saw earlier, virtually no language favors the object-before-subject word order. However, as noted, this constraint appears to have a cognitive explanation (as do many other limits on language form).

Often, the uniformities among languages seem so natural that we do not realize that other possibilities might exist. One such language universal is that adjectives appear near the nouns that they modify. Thus, we translate *The brave woman hit the cruel man* into French as

- La femme brave a frappé l'homme cruel

and not as

- La femme cruel a frappé l'homme brave

although a language in which the adjective beside the subject noun modified the object noun and vice versa would be logically possible. Clearly, however, such a language design would be absurd in regard to its cognitive demands. It would require that listeners hold the adjective from the beginning of the sentence until the noun at the end. No natural language has this perverse structure. If it really needed showing, I showed with artificial languages that adult participants were unable to learn such a language (Anderson, 1978b). Thus, many of the universals of language seem cognitive in origin and so do not really support Chomsky's position. In the next subsections, we will consider some universals that seem more language specific.

There are universal constraints on the kinds of languages that humans can learn.

The Constraints on Transformations

A set of peculiar constraints on movement transformations (refer to the subsection on transformations on page 332) has been used to argue for the existence of linguistic universals. One of the more extensively discussed of these constraints is called the A-over-A constraint. Compare sentence 1 with sentence 2:

1. Which woman did John meet who knows the senator?
2. Which senator did John meet the woman who knows?

Linguists would consider sentence 1 to be acceptable but not sentence 2. Sentence 1 can be derived by a transformation from sentence 3. This transformation moves *which woman* forward:

3. John met which woman who knows the senator?

4. John met the woman who knows which senator?

Sentence 2 could be derived by a similar transformation operating on *which senator* in sentence 4, but apparently transformations are not allowed that move a noun phrase such as *which senator* if it is embedded within another noun phrase (in this case, *which senator* is part of the clause modifying *the woman* and so is part of the noun phrase associated with *the woman*). Transformations can move deeply embedded nouns if these nouns are not in clauses modifying other nouns. So, for instance, sentence 5, which is acceptable, is derived transformationally from sentence 6:

5. Which senator does Mary believe that Bill said that John likes?

6. Mary believes that Bill said that John likes which senator?

Thus, we see that the constraint on the transformation that forms *which* questions is arbitrary. It can apply to any embedded noun unless that noun is part of another noun phrase. The arbitrariness of this constraint makes it hard to imagine how a child would ever figure it out—unless the child already knew it as a universal of language. Certainly, the child is never explicitly told this fact about language.

The existence of such constraints on the form of language offers a challenge to any theory of language acquisition. The constraints are so peculiar that it is hard to imagine how they could be learned unless a child was especially prepared to deal with them.

There are rather arbitrary constraints on the movements that transformations can produce.

Parameter Setting

With all this discussion about language universals, one might get the impression that all languages are basically alike. Far from it. On many dimensions, the languages of the world are radically different. They might have some abstract properties in common, such as the transformational constraint discussed above, in common, but there are many properties on which they differ. As already mentioned, different languages prefer different orders for subject, verb, and object. Languages also differ in how strict they are about word order. English is very strict, but some highly inflected languages, such as Finnish, allow people to say their sentences with almost any word order they choose. There are languages that do not mark verbs for tense and languages that mark verbs for the flexibility of the object being acted on.

Another example of a difference, which has been a focus of discussion, is that some languages, such as Italian or Spanish, are what are called *pro-drop* languages: They allow one to optionally drop the pronoun when it appears in the subject position. Thus, whereas in English we would say, *I am going to the cinema tonight,* Italians can say, *Vado al cinema stasera,* and Spaniards, *Voy al cine esta noche*—in both cases, just starting with the verb and omitting the first-person pronoun. It has been argued that pro-drop is a parameter on which natural languages vary, and although children cannot be born knowing whether their language is pro-drop or not, they can be born knowing it is one way or the other. Thus, knowledge that the pro-drop parameter exists is one of the purported universals of natural language.

Knowledge of a parameter such as pro-drop is useful because a number of features are determined by it. For instance, if a language is not pro-drop, it requires what are called expletive pronouns. In English, a non-pro-drop language, the expletive pronouns are *it* and *there* when they are used in sentences such as *It is raining* or *There is no money.* English requires these rather semantically empty pronouns because, by definition, a non-pro-drop language cannot have empty slots in the subject position. Pro-drop languages such as Spanish and Italian lack such empty pronouns because they are not needed.

Hyams (1986) argued that children starting to learn any language, including English, will treat it as a pro-drop language and optionally drop pronouns even though doing so may not be correct in the adult language. She noted that young children learning English tend to omit subjects. They will also not use expletive pronouns, even when they are part of the adult language. When children in a non-pro-drop language start using expletive pronouns, they simultaneously optionally stop dropping pronouns in the subject position. Hyams argued that, at this point, they learn that their language is not a pro-drop language. For further discussion of Hyams's proposal and alternative formulations, read R. Bloom (1994).

It is argued that much of the variability among natural languages can be accommodated by setting 100 or so parameters, such as the pro-drop parameter, and that a major part of learning a language is learning the setting of these parameters (of course, there is a lot more to be learned than just this setting—e.g., an enormous vocabulary). This theory of language acquisition is called the **parameter setting** proposal. It is quite controversial, but it provides us with one picture of what it might mean for a child to be prepared to learn a language with innate, language-specific knowledge.

- *Learning the structure of language has been proposed to include learning the setting of 100 or so parameters on which natural languages vary.*

Conclusions: The Uniqueness of Language: A Summary

Although it is clear that human language is a very unique communication system relative to those of other species, the jury is still very much out on the issue of whether language is really a system different from other human cognitive systems. The status of language is a major issue for cognitive psychology.

The issue will be resolved by empirical and theoretical efforts more detailed than those reviewed in this chapter. The ideas here have served to define the context for the investigation. The next chapter will review the current state of our knowledge about the details of language comprehension. Careful experimental research on such topics will finally resolve the question of the uniqueness of language.

Questions for Thought

1. There have emerged a number of computer-based approaches to representing meaning that are based on having these programs read through large sets of documents and representing the meaning of a word in terms of what other words also occurred with it in these documents. One interesting feature of these efforts is that they have no knowledge of the physical world and what these words refer to. Perhaps the most well-known system is called Latent Semantic Analysis (LSA—Landauer, Foltz, & Laham, 1998). The authors of LSA describe the knowledge in their system as "analogous to a well-read nun's knowledge of sex, a level of knowledge often deemed a sufficient basis for advising the young" (p. 5). Based on this knowledge, LSA was able to pass the vocabulary test from the Educational Testing Service's Test of English as a Foreign Language. The test requires that one choose which of four alternatives best matches the meaning of a word, and LSA was able to do this by comparing its meaning representation of the word (based on what documents the word appeared in) with its meaning representation of the alternatives (again based on the same information). Why do you think such a program is so successful? How would you devise a vocabulary test to expose aspects of meaning that it does not represent?
2. In addition to the pauses and speech errors discussed in the chapter, spontaneous speech contains fillers like *uh* and *um* in English (different languages use different fillers). Clark and Fox Tree (2002) report that *um* tends to be associated with a longer delay in speech than *uh.* In terms of phrase structure, where would you expect to see *uh* and *um* located?
3. Some languages assign grammatical genders to words that do not have inherent genders and appear to do so arbitrarily. So, for instance, the German word for key is masculine and the Spanish word for key is feminine. Boroditsky, Schmidt, and Phillips (2003) report that when asked to describe a key, German speakers are more likely to use words like *hard* and *jagged*, whereas Spanish speakers are more likely to use words like *shiny* and *tiny.* What does evidence like this say about the relationship between language and thought?
4. When two linguistic communities often come into contact such as in trade, they develop simplified languages, called pidgins, for communicating. These languages are generally considered not full natural languages. However, if these language communities live together, the pidgins will evolve into full-fledged new languages called creoles. This can happen in one generation, in which the parents who first made contact with the new linguistic community continue to use pidgin, whereas their children are speaking full-fledged creoles. What does this say about the possible role of a critical period in language acquisition?

Key Terms

competence
grammar
language universals
linguistic determinism
linguistic intuitions
linguistics
modularity
natural languages
parameter setting
performance
phonology
phrase structure
productivity
regularity
semantics
syntax
transformation

13

Language Comprehension

A favorite device in science fiction is the computer or robot that can understand and speak language—whether evil like HAL in *2001,* or beneficent like C3PO in *Star Wars*. Workers in artificial intelligence have been trying to develop computers that understand and generate language. Progress is being made, but Stanley Kubrick was clearly incorrect when he projected HAL for the year 2001. Language-processing AI programs are still rudimentary compared with what is portrayed in science fiction. An enormous amount of knowledge and intelligence underlies the successful use of language.

This chapter will look at language use and, in particular, at language comprehension (as distinct from language generation). This focus will enable us to look where the light is—more is known about language comprehension than about language generation. Language comprehension will be considered in regard to both listening and reading. The listening process is often thought to be the more basic of the two. However, many of the same factors apply to both listening and reading. Researchers' choice between written or spoken material is determined by what is easier to do experimentally. More often than not, written material is used.

We will consider a detailed analysis of the process of language comprehension, breaking it down into three stages. The first stage involves the perceptual processes that encode the spoken (acoustic) or written message. The second stage is termed the *parsing* stage. **Parsing** is the process by which the words in the message are transformed into a mental representation of the combined meaning of the words. The third stage is the **utilization** stage, in which comprehenders use the mental representation of the sentence's meaning. If the sentence is an assertion, listeners may simply store the meaning in memory; if it is a question, they may answer; if it is an instruction, they may obey. However, listeners are not always so compliant. They may use an assertion about the weather to make an inference about the speaker's personality, they may answer a question with a question, or they may do just the opposite of what the speaker asks. These three stages—perception, parsing, and utilization—are by necessity partly ordered in time; however, they also partly overlap. Listeners can make inferences from the first part of a sentence while they are perceiving a later part. This chapter will focus on the two higher-level processes—parsing and utilization. (The perceptual stage was discussed in Chapter 2.)

In this chapter, we will answer the questions:

- How are individual words combined into the meaning of phrases?
- How is syntactic and semantic information combined in sentence interpretation?
- What inferences do comprehenders make as they hear a sentence?
- How are meanings of individual sentences combined in the processing of larger units of discourse?

Brain and Language Comprehension

Figure 12.1 highlighted the classic language-processing regions that are active in the parsing stage that involves single sentences. However, when we consider the utilization stage and the processing involved in larger portions of text, we find many other regions of the brain active. Figure 13.1 illustrates some of the regions identified by Mason and Just (2006) in discourse processing (for a richer representation of all the areas, see Color Plate 13.1). One can take the union of Figures 12.1 and 13.1 as something closer to the total brain network involved in language processing. These figures make clear the fact that language comprehension involves much of the brain and many cognitive processes.

Comprehension consists of a perceptual stage, a parsing stage, and a utilization stage, in that order.

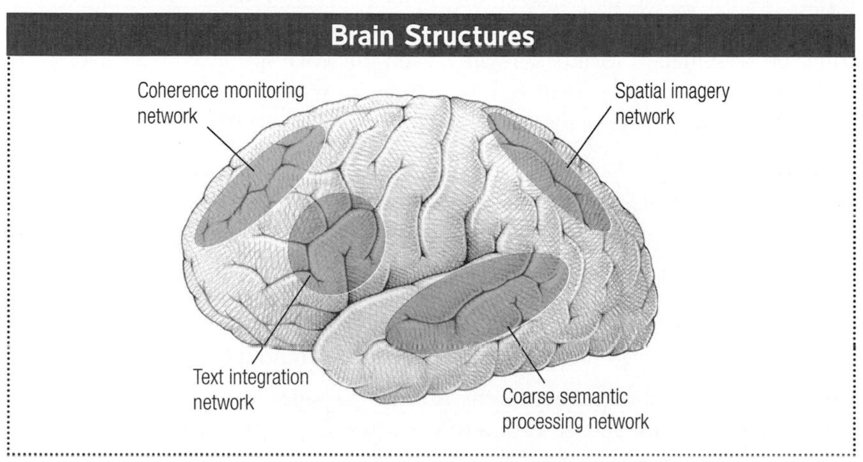

FIGURE 13.1 A representation of some of the brain regions involved in discourse processing. (From Mason & Just, 2006.)

Parsing

Constituent Structure

Language is structured according to a set of rules that tell us how to go from a particular string of words to an interpretation of that string's meaning. For instance, in English we know that if we hear a sequence of the form *A noun action a noun,* the speaker means that an instance of the first noun performed the action on an instance of the second noun. In contrast, if the sentence is of the form *A noun was action by a noun,* the speaker means that an instance of the second noun performed the action on an instance of the first noun. Thus, our knowledge of the structure of English allows us to grasp the difference between *A doctor shot a lawyer* and *A doctor was shot by a lawyer.*

In learning to comprehend a language, we acquire a great many rules that encode the various linguistic patterns in language and relate these patterns to meaningful interpretations. However, we cannot possibly learn rules for every possible sentence pattern—sentences can be very long and complex. A very large (probably infinite) number of patterns would be required to encode all possible sentence forms. Although we have not learned to interpret all possible full-sentence patterns, we have learned to interpret subpatterns, or phrases, of these sentences and to combine, or concatenate, the interpretations of these subpatterns. These subpatterns correspond to basic phrases, or units, in a sentence's structure. These phrase units are also referred to as **constituents.** From the late 1950s to the early 1980s, a series of studies were performed that established the psychological reality of phrase structure (or constituent structure) in language processing. Chapter 12 reviewed some of the research documenting the importance of phrase structure in language generation. Here, we review some of the evidence for the psychological reality of this constituent structure in comprehension.

We might expect that the more clearly identifiable the constituent structure of a sentence is, the more easily the sentence can be understood. Graf and Torrey (1966) presented sentences to participants a line at a time. The passages could be presented in form A, in which each line corresponded to a major constituent boundary, or in form B, in which there was no such correspondence. Examples of the two types of passages follow:

Form A	**Form B**
During World War II	During World War
even fantastic schemes	II even fantastic
received consideration	schemes received
if they gave promise	consideration if they gave
of shortening the conflict.	promise of shortening the conflict.

Participants showed better comprehension of passages in form A. This finding demonstrates that the identification of constituent structure is important to the parsing of a sentence.

When people read such passages, they naturally pause at boundaries between clauses. Aaronson and Scarborough (1977) asked participants to read sentences

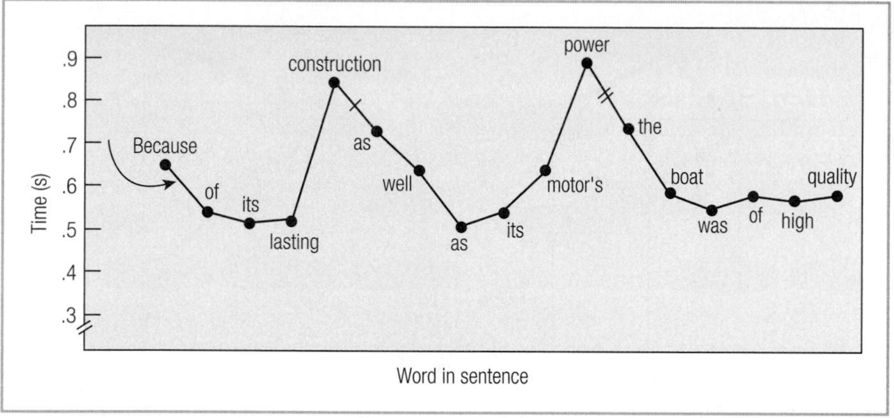

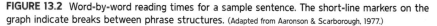

FIGURE 13.2 Word-by-word reading times for a sample sentence. The short-line markers on the graph indicate breaks between phrase structures. (Adapted from Aaronson & Scarborough, 1977.)

displayed word by word on a computer screen. Participants would press a key each time they wanted to read another word. Figure 13.2 illustrates the pattern of reading times for a sentence that participants were reading for later recall. Notice the U-shaped patterns with prolonged pauses at the phrase boundaries. With the completion of each major phrase, participants seemed to need time to process it.

After one has processed the words in a phrase in order to understand it, there is no need to make further reference to these exact words. Thus, we might predict that people would have poor memory for the exact wording of a constituent after it has been parsed and the parsing of another constituent has begun. The results of an experiment by Jarvella (1971) confirm this prediction. He read to participants passages with interruptions at various points. At each interruption, participants were instructed to write down as much of the passage as they could remember. Of interest were passages that ended with 13-word sentences such as the following one:

1	2	3	4	5	6	
Having	failed	to	disprove	the	charges,	
7	8	9	10	11	12	13
Taylor	was	later	fired	by	the	president.

After hearing the last word, participants were prompted with the first word of the sentence and asked to recall the remaining words. Each sentence was composed of a 6-word subordinate clause followed by a 7-word main clause. Figure 13.3 plots the probability of recall for each of the remaining 12 words in the sentence (excluding the first, which was used as a prompt). Note the sharp rise in the function at word 7, the beginning of the main clause. These data show that participants have best memory for the last major constituent, a result consistent with the hypothesis that they retain a verbatim representation of the last constituent only.

An experiment by Caplan (1972) also presents evidence for the use of constituent structure, but this study used a reaction-time methodology. Participants

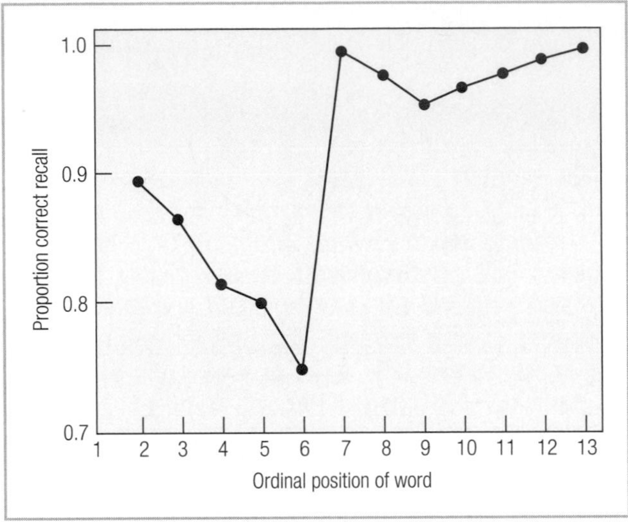

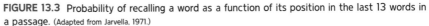

FIGURE 13.3 Probability of recalling a word as a function of its position in the last 13 words in a passage. (Adapted from Jarvella, 1971.)

were presented aurally first with a sentence and then with a probe word; they then had to indicate as quickly as possible whether the probe word was in the sentence. Caplan contrasted pairs of sentences such as the following pair:

1. Now that artists are working fewer hours oil prints are rare.
2. Now that artists are working in oil prints are rare.

Interest focused on how quickly participants would recognize *oil* in these two sentences when probed at the ends of the sentences. The sentences were cleverly constructed so that, in both sentences, the word *oil* was fourth from the end and was followed by the same words. In fact, by splicing tape, Caplan arranged the presentation so that participants heard the same recording of these last four words whichever full sentence they heard. However, in sentence 1, *oil* is part of the last constituent, *oil prints are rare,* whereas, in sentence 2, it is part of the first constituent, *now that artists are working in oil.* Caplan predicted that participants would recognize *oil* more quickly in sentence 1 because they would still have active in memory a representation of this constituent. As he predicted, the probe word was recognized more rapidly if it was in the last constituent.

- *Participants process the meaning of a sentence one phrase at a time and maintain access to a phrase only while processing its meaning.*

Immediacy of Interpretation

An important principle to emerge in more recent studies of language processing is called the principle of **immediacy of interpretation.** Basically, this principle says that people try to extract meaning out of each word as it arrives and

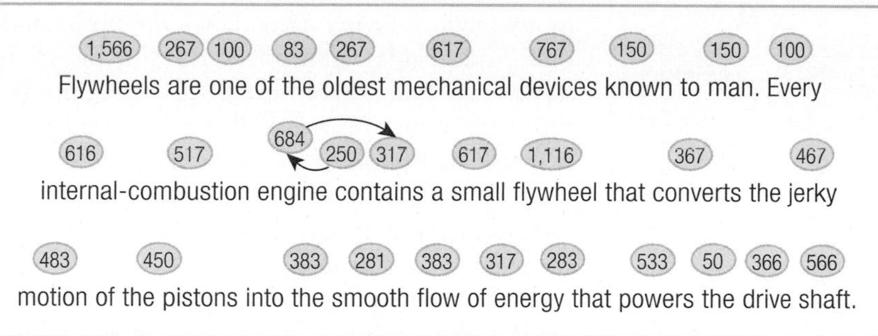

FIGURE 13.4 The time spent by a college reader on the words in the opening two sentences of a technical article about flywheels. The times, indicated above the fixated word, are expressed in milliseconds. This reader read the sentences from left to right, with one regressive fixation to an earlier part. (Adapted from Just & Carpenter, 1980.)

do not wait until the end of a sentence or even the end of a phrase to decide how to interpret a word. For instance, Just and Carpenter (1980) studied the eye movements of participants as they read a sentence. While reading a sentence, participants will typically fixate on almost every word. Just and Carpenter found that the time spent fixating on a word is proportional to the amount of information provided by the word. Thus, if a sentence contains an unfamiliar or a surprising word, participants pause on that word. They also pause longer at the end of the phrase containing that word. Figure 13.4 illustrates the eye fixations of one of their college students reading a scientific passage. The circles are above the words the student fixated on, and in each circle is the duration of that fixation. The order of the gazes is left to right except for the three gazes above *engine contains,* where the order of gazes is indicated. Note that unimportant function words such as *the* and *to* may be skipped or, if not skipped, receive relatively little processing. Note the amount of time spent on the word *flywheel.* The participant did not wait until the end of the sentence to think about this word. Again, look at the amount of time spent on the highly informative adjective *mechanical*—the participant did not wait until the end of the noun phrase to think about it.

Eye movements have also been used to study the comprehension of spoken language. In one of these studies (Allopenna, Magnuson, & Tanenhaus, 1998), participants were shown computer displays of objects like that in Figure 13.5 and processed instructions such as

Pick up the beaker and put it below the diamond.

Participants would perform this action by selecting the object with a mouse and moving it, but the experiment was done to study their eye movements that preceded any

FIGURE 13.5 An example of a computer display used in the study of Allopenna et al. (1998).

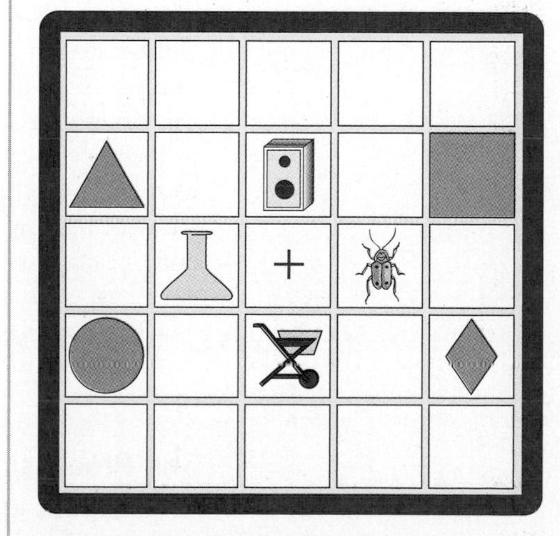

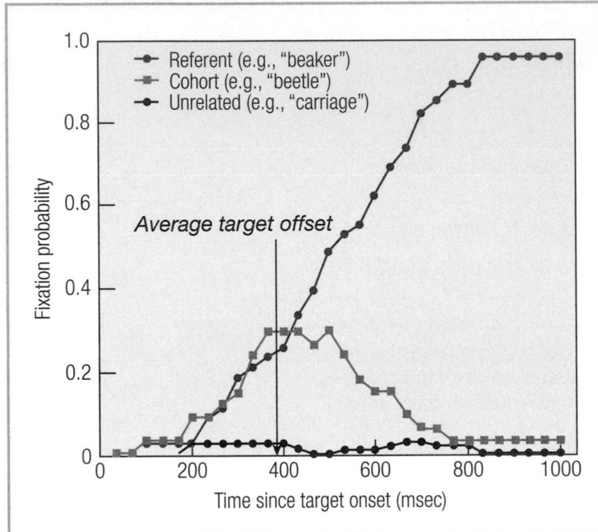

FIGURE 13.6 Probability of fixating different items in the display as a function of time from onset of the critical word *beetle*. (From Allopenna et al., 1998.)

mouse action. Figure 13.6 shows the probabilities that participants fixate on various items in the display as a function of time since the beginning of the articulation of "beaker." It can be seen that participants are beginning to look to the two items that start with the same sound ("beaker" and "beetle") even before the articulation of the word finishes. It takes about 400 msec to say the word. Almost immediately upon offset of the word, their fixations on the wrong item ("beetle") decrease and their fixations on the correct item ("beaker") shoot up. Given that it takes about 200 msec to program an eye movement, this study provides evidence that participants are processing the meaning of a word even before it completes.

This immediacy of processing implies that we will begin to interpret a sentence even before we encounter the main verb. Sometimes we are aware of wondering what the verb will be as we hear the sentence. We are likely to experience something like this in constructions that put the verb last. Consider what happens as we process the following sentence:

- It was the most expensive car that the CEO bought.

Before we get to *bought*, we already have some idea of what might be happening between the CEO and the car. Although this sentence structure with the verb at the end is unusual for English, it is not unusual for languages such as German. Listeners of these languages do develop strong expectations about the sentence before seeing the verb (see Clifton & Duffy, 2001, for a review).

If people process a sentence as each word comes in, why is there so much evidence for the importance of phrase-structure boundaries? The evidence reflects the fact that the meaning of a sentence is defined in terms of the phrase structure, and, even if listeners try to extract all they can from each word, they will be able to put some things into place only when they reach the end of a phrase. Thus, people often need extra time at a phrase boundary to complete this processing. People have to maintain a representation of the current phrase in memory because their interpretation of it may be wrong, and they may have to reinterpret the beginning of the phrase. Just and Carpenter (1980) in their study of reading times found that participants tend to spend extra time at the end of each phrase in wrapping up the meaning conveyed by that phrase.

- *In processing a sentence, we try to extract as much information as possible from each word and spend some additional wrap-up time at the end of each phrase.*

The Processing of Syntactic Structure

The basic task in parsing a sentence is to combine the meanings of the individual words to arrive at a meaning for the overall sentence. There are two basic sources of syntactic information that can guide us in this task. One source is word order and the other is inflectional structure. The following two sentences, although they have identical words, have very different meanings:

1. The dog bit the cat.
2. The cat bit the dog.

The dominant syntactic cue in English is word order. Other languages rely less on word order and instead use inflections of words to indicate semantic role. There is a small remnant of such an inflectional system in some English pronouns. For instance, *he* and *him, I* and *me,* and so on, signal subject versus object. McDonald (1984) compared English with German, which has a richer inflectional system. She asked her English participants to interpret sentences such as

3. Him kicked the girl.
4. The girl kicked he.

The word-order cue in these sentences suggests one interpretation, whereas the inflection cue suggests an alternative interpretation. English speakers use the word-order cue, interpreting sentence 3 with *him* as the subject and the *girl* as the object. German speakers, judging comparable sentences in German, do just the opposite. Bilingual speakers of both German and English tend to interpret the English sentences more like German sentences; that is, they assign *him* in sentence 3 to the object role and *girl* to the subject role.

An interesting case of combining word order and inflection in English requires the use of relative clauses. Consider the following sentence:

5. The boy the girl liked was sick.

This sentence is an example of a **center-embedded sentence**: One clause, *the girl liked (the boy),* is embedded in another clause, *The boy was sick.* As we will see, there is evidence that people have difficulty with such clauses, perhaps in part because the beginning of the sentence is ambiguous. For instance, the sentence could have concluded as follows:

6. The boy the girl and the dog were sick.

To prevent such ambiguity, English offers relative pronouns, which are effectively like inflections, to indicate the role of the upcoming words:

7. The boy whom the girl liked was sick.

Sentences 5 and 7 are equivalent except that in sentence 5 *whom* is deleted, which indicates that the upcoming words are part of an embedded clause.

One might expect that it is easier to process sentences if they have relative pronouns to signal the embedding of clauses. Hakes and Foss (1970; Hakes, 1972) tested this prediction by using the phoneme-monitoring task. They used double-embedded sentences such as

8. The zebra which the lion that the gorilla chased killed was running.
9. The zebra the lion the gorilla chased killed was running.

The only difference between sentences 8 and 9 is whether there are relative pronouns. Participants were required to perform two simultaneous tasks. One task was to comprehend and paraphrase the sentence. The second task was to listen for a particular phoneme—in this case a /g/ (in gorilla). Hakes and Foss predicted that the more difficult a sentence was to comprehend, the more time participants would take to detect the target phoneme, because they would have less attention left over from the comprehension task with which to perform the monitoring. In fact, the prediction was confirmed; participants did take longer to indicate hearing /g/ when presented with sentences such as sentence 9, which lacked relative pronouns.

Although the use of relative pronouns facilitates the processing of such sentences, there is evidence that center-embedded sentences are quite difficult even with the relative pronouns. In one experiment, Caplan, Alpert, Waters, and Olivieri (2000) compared center-embedded sentences such as

10. The juice that the child enjoyed stained the rug.

with comparable sentences that are not center-embedded such as

11. The child enjoyed the juice that stained the rug.

They used PET brain-imaging measures to detect processing differences and found greater activation in Broca's area with center-embedded sentences. Broca's area is usually found to be more active when participants have to deal with more complex sentence structures (Martin, 2003).

People use the syntactic cues of word order and inflection to help interpret a sentence.

Semantic Considerations

People use syntactic patterns, such as those illustrated in the preceding subsection, for understanding sentences, but they can also make use of the meanings of the words themselves. A person can determine the meaning of a string of words simply by considering how they can be put together so as to make sense. Thus, when Tarzan says, *Jane fruit eat,* we know what he means even though this sentence does not correspond to the syntax of English. We realize that a relation is being asserted between someone capable of eating and something edible.

Considerable evidence suggests that people use such semantic strategies in language comprehension. Strohner and Nelson (1974) had 2- and 3-year-old children use animal dolls to act out the following two sentences:

- The cat chased the mouse.
- The mouse chased the cat.

In both cases, the children interpreted the sentence to mean that the cat chased the mouse, a meaning that corresponded to their prior knowledge about cats and mice. Thus, these young children were relying more heavily on semantic patterns than on syntactic patterns.

Fillenbaum (1971, 1974) had adults paraphrase sentences, among which were "perverse" items such as

- John was buried and died.

More than 60% of the participants paraphrased the sentences in a way that gave them a more conventional meaning; for example, that John died first and then was buried. However, the normal syntactic interpretation of such constructions would be that the first activity occurred before the second, as in

- John had a drink and went to the party.

in contrast with

- John went to the party and had a drink.

So, when a semantic principle is placed in conflict with a syntactic principle, the semantic principle will sometimes (but not always) determine the interpretation of the sentence. If you have any doubt about the power of semantics to dominate syntax, consider the following sentence

No head injury is too trivial to be ignored.

If you interpreted this sentence to mean that no head injury should be ignored, you are in the vast majority (Wason & Reich, 1979). However, a careful inspection of the syntax will indicate that the "correct" meaning is that all head injuries should be ignored—consider "No missile is too small to be banned"—which means all missiles should be banned.

Sometimes people rely on the plausible semantic interpretation of words in a sentence.

The Integration of Syntax and Semantics

Listeners appear to combine both syntactic and semantic information in comprehending a sentence. Tyler and Marslen-Wilson (1977) asked participants to try to continue fragments such as

1. If you walk too near the runway, landing planes are
2. If you've been trained as a pilot, landing planes are

The phrase *landing planes,* by itself, is ambiguous. It can mean either "planes that are landing" or "to land planes." However, when followed by the plural verb *are,* the phrase must have the first meaning. Thus, the syntactic constraints determine a meaning for the ambiguous phrase. The prior context in fragment 1 is consistent with this meaning, whereas the prior context in fragment 2 is not. Participants took less time to continue fragment 1, which suggests that they were using both the semantics of the prior context and the syntax of the current phrase to disambiguate *landing planes.* When these factors are in conflict, the participant's comprehension is slowed.[1]

[1] The original Tyler and Marslen-Wilson experiment drew methodological criticisms from Townsend and Bever (1982) and Cowart (1983). For a response, read Marslen-Wilson and Tyler (1987).

Bates, McNew, MacWhinney, Devesocvi, and Smith (1982) looked at the matter of combining syntax and semantics in a different paradigm. They had participants interpret word strings such as

- Chased the dog the eraser

If you were forced to, what meaning would you assign to this word string? The syntactic fact that objects follow verbs seems to imply that the dog was being chased and the eraser did the chasing. The semantics, however, suggest the opposite. In fact, American speakers prefer to go with the syntax but will sometimes adopt the semantic interpretation—that is, most say *The eraser chased the dog,* but some say *The dog chased the eraser.* On the other hand, if the word string is

- Chased the eraser the dog

listeners agree on the interpretation—that is, that *the dog chased the eraser.*

Another interesting part of the study by Bates et al. compared Americans with Italians. When syntactic cues were put in conflict with semantic cues, Italians tended to go with the semantic cues, whereas Americans preferred the syntactic cues. The most critical case concerned sentences such as

- The eraser bites the dog

or its Italian translation:

- La gomma morde il cane

Americans almost always followed the syntax and interpreted this sentence to mean that the eraser is doing the biting. In contrast, Italians preferred to use the semantics and interpret that the dog is doing the biting. Like English, however, Italian has a subject-verb-object syntax.

Thus, we see that listeners combine both syntactic and semantic cues in interpreting the sentence. Moreover, the weighting of these two types of cues can vary from language to language. This evidence and other results indicate that speakers of Italian weight semantic cues more heavily than do speakers of English.

People integrate semantic and syntactic cues to arrive at an interpretation of a sentence.

Neural Indicants of Syntactic and Semantic Processing

Researchers have found two indicants of sentence processing in event related potentials (ERPs) recorded from the brain. First, there is the **N400,** which is an indicant of difficulty in semantic processing. It was originally identified as a response to semantic anomaly, although it is more general than that. Kutas and Hillyard (1980a, 1980b) discovered the N400 in their original experiments when participants heard semantically anomalous sentences such as "He spread the warm bread with socks." About 400 ms after the anomalous word (socks), ERP recordings showed a large negative amplitude shift. Second, there is the **P600,** which occurs in response to syntactic violations. For instance, Osterhout and Holcomb (1992) presented their participants with sentences such as "The broker persuaded to sell the stock" and found a positive wave at about 600 ms after the word *to,* which was the point at which there was a violation of the syntax. Of particular interest in this context is the relation between the N400 and the P600.

Ainsworth-Darnell, Shulman, and Boland (1998) studied how these two effects combined when participants heard sentences such as

Control: Jill entrusted the recipe to friends before she suddenly disappeared.

Syntactic anomaly: Jill entrusted the recipe friends before she suddenly disappeared.

Semantic anomaly: Jill entrusted the recipe to platforms before she suddenly disappeared.

Double anomaly: Jill entrusted the recipe platforms before she suddenly disappeared.

The last sentence combines a semantic and a syntactic anomaly. Figure 13.7 contrasts the ERP waveforms obtained from midline and parietal sites in response to the various types of sentences. An arrow in the ERPs points to the onset of the

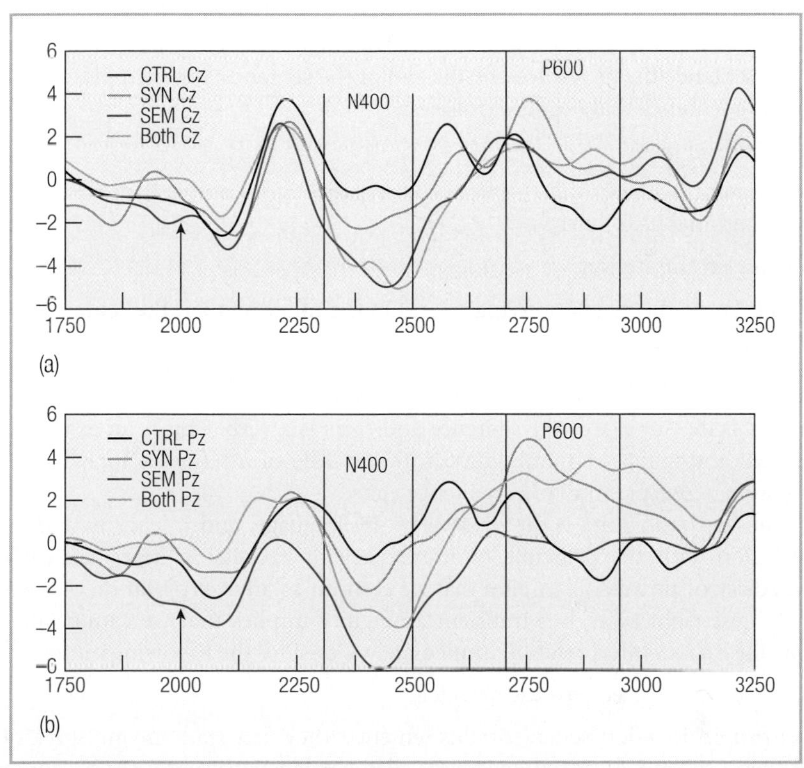

FIGURE 13.7 ERP recordings from (a) central and (b) parietal sites. The arrows point to the onset of the critical word. (From Ainsworth-Darnell, Shulman, & Boland, 1998.)

critical word (*friends or platforms*). The two types of sentences containing a semantic anomaly evoked a negative shift (N400) at the midline site about 400 ms after the critical word. In contrast, the two types of sentences containing a syntactic anomaly were associated with a positive shift (P600) in the parietal area about 600 ms after the onset of the critical word. Ainsworth et al. used the fact that each process—syntactic and semantic—affects a different brain region to argue that the syntactic and semantic processes are separable.

- *ERP recordings indicate syntactic and semantic violations elicit different responses in different locations in the brain.*

Ambiguity

Many sentences can be interpreted in two or more ways because of either ambiguous words or ambiguous syntactic constructions. Examples of such sentences are

- John went to the bank.
- Flying planes can be dangerous.

It is also useful to distinguish between transient ambiguity and permanent ambiguity. The preceding examples are permanently ambiguous. That is, the ambiguity remains to the end of the sentence. **Transient ambiguity** refers to ambiguity in a sentence that is resolved by the end of the sentence; for example, consider hearing a sentence that begins as follows:

- The old train . . .

At this point, whether *old* is a noun or an adjective is ambiguous. If the sentence continues as follows,

- . . . left the station.

then *old* is an adjective modifying *train*. On the other hand, if the sentence continues as follows,

- . . . the young.

then *old* is the subject of the sentence and *train* is a verb. This is an example of transient ambiguity—an ambiguity in the middle of a sentence for which the resolution depends on how the sentence ends.

Transient ambiguity is quite prevalent in language, and it leads to a serious interaction with the principle of immediacy of processing described earlier. Immediacy of processing implies that we commit to an interpretation of a word or a phrase right away, but transient ambiguity implies that we cannot always know the correct interpretation immediately. Consider the following sentence:

- The horse raced past the barn fell.

Most people do a double take on this sentence: they first read one interpretation and then a second. Such sentences are called **garden-path sentences** because we are "led down the garden path" and commit to one interpretation at a certain point only to discover that it is wrong at another point. For instance, in the preceding sentence, most readers interpret *raced* as the main verb of the sentence.

The existence of such garden-path sentences is considered to be one of the important pieces of evidence for the principle of immediacy of interpretation. People could postpone interpreting such sentences at points of ambiguity until the ambiguity is resolved, but they do not.

When one comes upon a point of syntactic ambiguity in a sentence, what determines its interpretation? A powerful principle is the **principle of minimal attachment.** This principle basically says that one interprets a sentence in a way that causes minimal complication of its phrase structure. Because all sentences must have a main verb, the simple interpretation would be to include *raced* in the main sentence rather than creating a relative clause to modify the noun *horse.*

Many times we are not aware of the ambiguities that exist in sentences. For instance, consider the following sentence:

- The woman painted by the artist fell.

As we will see, people seem to have difficulty with this sentence (temporarily interpreting the woman as the one doing the painting), just like the earlier *horse raced* sentence. However, people tend not be aware of taking a garden path in the way that they are with the *horse raced* sentence.

Why are we aware of a reinterpretation in some sentences, such as the *horse raced* example, but not in others, such as the *woman painted* example? If a syntactic ambiguity is resolved quickly after we encounter it, we seem to be unaware of ever considering two interpretations. Only if resolution is postponed substantially beyond the ambiguous phrase are we aware of the need to reinterpret it (Ferriera & Henderson, 1991). Thus, in the *woman painted* example, the ambiguity is resolved immediately after the verb *painted,* and thus most people are not aware of the ambiguity. In contrast, in the *horse raced* example, the sentence seems to successfully complete as *The horse raced past the barn* only to have this interpretation contradicted by the last word *fell.*

- *When people come to a point of ambiguity in a sentence, they adopt one interpretation, which they will have to retract if it is later contradicted.*

Neural Indicants of the Processing of Transient Ambiguity

Brain-imaging studies reveal a good deal about how people process ambiguous sentences. In one study, Mason, Just, Keller, and Carpenter (2003) compared three kinds of sentences:

Unambiguous: The experienced soldiers spoke about the dangers of the midnight raid.

Ambiguous preferred: The experienced soldiers warned about the dangers before the midnight raid.

Ambiguous unpreferred: The experienced soldiers warned about the dangers conducted the midnight raid.

The verb *spoke* in the first sentence is unambiguous, but the verb *warned* in the last two sentences has a transient ambiguity of just the sort described in the preceding subsection: Until the end of the sentence, one cannot know whether the

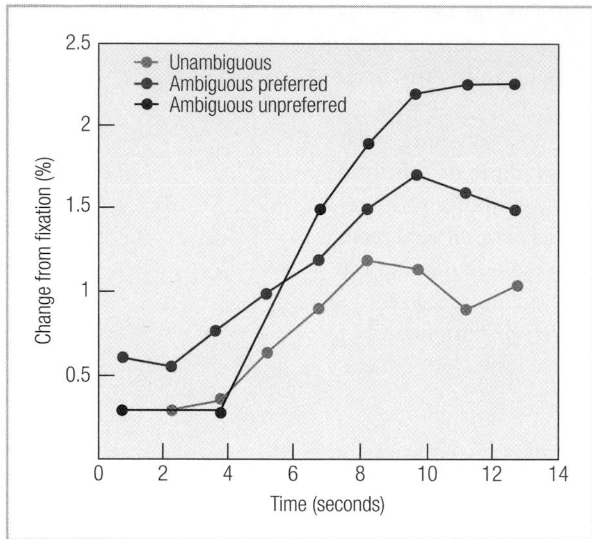

FIGURE 13.8 The average activation change in Broca's area for three types of sentences as a function of time from beginning of the sentence. (From Masson et al., 2003.)

soldiers are doing the warning or are being warned. As noted, participants prefer the first interpretation. Mason et al. collected fMRI measures of activation in Broca's area as participants read the sentences. These data are plotted in Figure 13.8 as a function of time since the onset of the sentences (which lasted approximately 6–7 s). As is typical of fMRI measures, the differences among conditions show up only after the processing of the sentences, corresponding to the lag in the hemodynamic response. As can be seen, the unambiguous sentence results in the least activation, owing to the greater ease in processing that sentence. However, in comparing the two ambiguous sentences, we see that activation is greater for the sentence that ends in the unpreferred way.

FMRI measures such as those in Figure 13.8 can localize areas in the brain in which processing is taking place, in this case confirming the critical role of Broca's area in the processing of sentence structure. However, these measures do not identify the fine-grained temporal structure of the processing. An ERP study by Frisch, Schlesewsky, Saddy, and Alpermann (2002) investigated the temporal aspect of how people deal with ambiguity. Their study was with German speakers and took advantage of the fact that some German nouns are ambiguous in their role assignment. They looked at German sentences that begin with either of two different nouns and end with a verb. In the following examples, each German sentence is followed by a word-by-word translation and then the equivalent English sentence:

1. Die Frau hatte den Mann gesehen.
   The woman had the man seen
   The woman had seen the man.
2. Die Frau hatte der Mann gesehen.
   The woman had the man seen
   The man had seen the woman.
3. Den Mann hatte die Frau gesehen.
   The man had the woman seen
   The woman had seen the man.
4. Der Mann hatte die Frau gesehen.
   The man had the woman seen
   The man had seen the woman.

Note that, when participants read *Die Frau* at the beginning of sentences 1 and 2, they do not know whether the woman is the subject or the object of the sentence. Only when they read *den Mann* in sentence 1 can they infer that man is an object (because of the determiner *den*) and hence that woman must be the subject. Similarly, *der Mann* in sentence 2 indicates that man is the subject and therefore woman must be the object. Sentences 3 and 4, because they begin with *Mann* and its inflected article, do not have this transient ambiguity. The difference in when one can interpret these sentences depends on the fact that the masculine article is inflected for case in German but the feminine article is not.

Frisch et al. used the P600 (already described with respect to Figure 13.7) to investigate the syntactic processing of these sentences. They found that the ambiguous first noun in sentences 1 and 2 was followed by a stronger P600 than were the unambiguous sentences 3 and 4. The contrast between sentences 1 and 2 also is interesting. Although German allows for either subject-object or object-subject ordering, the subject-object structure in sentence 1 is preferred. For the unpreferred sentence (2), Frisch et al. found that the second noun was followed by a greater P600. Thus, when participants reach a transient ambiguity, as in sentences 1 and 2, they seem to immediately have to work harder to deal with the ambiguity. They commit to the preferred interpretation and have to do further work when they learn that it is not the correct interpretation, as in sentence 2.

○ *Activity in Broca's area increases when participants encounter a transient ambiguity and when they have to change an initial interpretation of a sentence.*

Lexical Ambiguity

The preceding discussion was concerned with how participants deal with syntactic ambiguity. In lexical ambiguity, where a single word has two meanings, there is often no structural difference in the two interpretations of a sentence. A series of experiments beginning with Swinney (1979) helped to reveal how people determine the meaning of ambiguous words. Swinney asked participants to listen to sentences such as

- The man was not surprised when he found several spiders, roaches, and other bugs in the corner of the room.

Swinney was concerned with the ambiguous word *bugs* (meaning either insects or electronic listening devices). Just after hearing the word, participants would be presented with a string of letters on the screen, and their task was to judge whether that string made a correct word. Thus, if they saw *ant,* they would say yes; but if they saw *ont,* they would say no. This is the lexical-decision task described in Chapter 6 in relation to the mechanisms of spreading activation. Swinney was interested in how the word *bugs* in the passage would prime the lexical judgment.

The critical contrasts involved the relative times to judge *spy, ant,* or *sew,* following *bugs.* The word *ant* is related to the primed meaning of *bugs,* whereas *spy* is related to the unprimed meaning. The word *sew* defines a neutral control condition. Swinney found that recognition of either *spy* or *ant* was facilitated if that word was presented within 400 ms of the prime, *bugs.* Thus, the presentation of *bugs* immediately activates both of its meanings and their associations. If Swinney waited more than 700 ms, however, only the related word *ant* was facilitated. It appears that a correct meaning is selected in this time and the other meaning becomes deactivated. Thus, two meanings of an ambiguous word are momentarily active, but context operates very rapidly to select the appropriate meaning.

- *When an ambiguous word is presented, participants select a particular meaning within 700 ms.*

Modularity Compared with Interactive Processing

There are two bases by which people can disambiguate ambiguous sentences. One possibility is the use of semantics, which is the basis for disambiguating the word *bugs* in the sentence given in the preceding subsection. The other possibility is the use of syntax. Advocates of the language-modularity position (see Chapter 12) have argued that there is an initial phase in which we merely process syntax, and only later do we bring semantic factors to bear. Thus, initially only syntax is available for disambiguation, because syntax is part of a language-specific module that can operate quickly by itself. In contrast, to bring semantics to bear requires using all of one's world knowledge, which goes far beyond anything that is language specific. Opposing the modularity position is that of **interactive processing,** the proponents of which argue that syntax and semantics are combined at all levels of processing.

Much of the debate between these two positions has concerned the processing of transient syntactic ambiguity. In the initial study of what has become a long series of studies, Ferreira and Clifton (1986) asked participants to read sentences such as

1. The woman painted by the artist was very attractive to look at.
2. The woman that was painted by the artist was very attractive to look at.
3. The sign painted by the artist was very attractive to look at.
4. The sign that was painted by the artist was very attractive to look at.

Sentences 1 and 3 are called reduced relatives because the relative pronoun *that* is missing. There is no local syntactic basis for deciding whether the noun-verb combination is a relative clause construction or an agent-action combination. Ferreira and Clifton argued that, because of the principle of minimal attachment, people have a natural tendency to encode noun-verb combinations such as *The woman painted* as agent-action combinations. Evidence for this tendency is that participants take longer to read *by the artist* in the first sentence than in the second. The reason is that they discover that their agent-action interpretation is wrong in the first sentence and have to recover, whereas the syntactic cue *that was* in the second sentence prevents them from ever making this misinterpretation.

The real interest in the Ferreira and Clifton experiments is in sentences 3 and 4. Semantic factors should rule out the agent-action interpretation of sentence 3, because a sign cannot be an animate agent and engage in painting. Nonetheless, participants took just as long to read *by the artist* in sentence 3 as in sentence 1 and longer than in unambiguous sentences 2 or 4. Thus, argued Ferreira and Clifton, participants first use only syntactic factors and so misinterpret the phrase *The sign painted* and then use the syntactic cues in the phrase *by the artist* to correct that misinterpretation. Thus, although semantic factors could have done the job and prevented the misinterpretation, participants seemingly do all their initial processing by using syntactic cues.

Experiments of this sort have been used to argue for the modularity of language. The argument is that our initial processing of language makes use of something specific to language—namely, syntax—and ignores other general, nonlinguistic knowledge that we have of the world, for example, that signs cannot paint. However, Trueswell, Tannehaus, and Garnsey (1994) argued that many of the sentences in the Ferreira and Clifton study were not like sentence 3. Specifically, although the sentences were supposed to have a semantic basis for disambiguation, many did not. For instance, among the Ferreira and Clifton sentences were sentences such as

5. The car towed from the parking lot was parked illegally.

Here *car towed* was supposed to be unambiguous, but it is possible for *car* to be the subject of *towed* as in

6. The car towed the smaller car from the parking lot.

When Trueswell et al. used sentences that avoided these problems, they found that participants did not have any difficulty with the sentences. For instance, participants showed no more difficulty with

7. The evidence examined by the lawyer turned out to be unreliable.

than with

8. The evidence that was examined by the lawyer turned out to be unreliable.

Thus, people do seem to be able to select the correct interpretation when it is not semantically possible to interpret the noun (*evidence*) as an agent of the verb. Thus, the initial syntactic decisions are not made without reference to semantic factors.

Additionally, McRae, Spivey-Knowlton, and Tannehaus (1998) show that the relative plausibility of the noun as agent of the verb affects the difficulty of the construction. They compared the following pairs of sentences:

9. The cop arrested by the detective was guilty of taking bribes.

10. The cop that was arrested by the detective was guilty of taking bribes.

and

11. The crook arrested by the detective was guilty of taking bribes.

12. The crook that was arrested by the detective was guilty of taking bribes.

They found that participants suffered much greater difficulty with the reduced relatives in sentence 9, where the subject *cop* is plausible as the agent for arresting, than in sentence 11, where the subject *crook* is not.

- *Participants appear to be able to use semantic information immediately to guide syntactic decisions.*

Implications

Intelligent chatterboxes

Being able to communicate successfully in language is very much tied to our conception of human intelligence. For instance, Alan Turing (a famous British logician who broke the secret communication code of the Nazis during World War II) proposed in 1950 (Turing, 1950) that we decide whether a machine is intelligent by whether it can engage in a conversation that convinces the listener that it is a human. In what has come to be known as the Turing Test, a judge would interact with a human and a computer over a chat system (to eliminate visual cues). If, after conversing with both, the judge could not determine which was human and which was computer, the computer would be declared to be intelligent. Turing predicted that by the year 2000 a computer would be able to pass this test.

In 1990, the Loebner Prize was created for the first computer that could pass the Turing test. Each year a contest is held in which various computer entries are judged. A bronze prize is awarded yearly to the program that gives the most convincing conversation, but so far no machine has been able to fool a majority of the judges, which would result in the silver prize (the gold prize is reserved for something that even looks like a human). The winner in 2008, a program called Elbot, came close to winning the silver prize, fooling 3 of the 12 judges. It even deceived reporter Will Pavia of *The Times* (http://technology.timesonline.co.uk/tol/news/tech_and_web/article4934858.ece). Below are two small snippets of conversation between an interrogator with a human and with Elbot. I have not identified which is the human and which is the computer. Try to judge which snippet involves the human and which involves Elbot.

Snippet A

Interrogator: What do you think of this year's Turner Prize shortlist?

Respondent: Difficult question. I will have to work on that and get back to you tomorrow.

Interrogator: You sound rather like Sarah Palin.

Respondent: Did this Palin ever write a telephone book?

Interrogator: I doubt it. Does anyone really write telephone books? I don't suppose you caught the football last night?

Respondent: What a shame. There are many talented authors who waste their energies on prose or run-of-the-mill poetry. But to write a telephone book is highest art!

Snippet B

Interrogator: What do you think of this year's Turner Prize shortlist?

Respondent: good I think. Better than the years before i herad

Interrogator: Which was your favourite?

Respondent: It's my first time, so I can't compare

Interrogator: No, I mean of the entries this time around.

Respondent: Not really sure

Utilization

After a sentence has been parsed and mapped into a representation of its meaning, what then? A listener seldom passively records the meaning. If the sentence is a question or an imperative, for example, the speaker will expect the listener to take some action in response. Even for declarative sentences, moreover, there is usually more to be done than simply registering the sentence. Fully understanding a sentence requires making inferences and connections. In Chapter 6, we considered the way in which such elaborative processing leads to better memory. Here, we will review some of the research on how people make such inferences.

Bridging versus Elaborative Inferences

In understanding a sentence, the comprehender must make inferences that go beyond what is stated. Researchers typically distinguish between **bridging inferences** (also called **backward inferences**) and **elaborative inferences** (also called **forward inferences**). Bridging inferences reach back in the text to make connections with earlier parts of the text. These elaborative inferences add new information to the interpretation of the text and often predict what will be coming up in the text. To illustrate the difference between bridging and elaborative inferences, contrast the following pairs of sentences used by Singer (1994):

1. **Direct statement:** The dentist pulled the tooth painlessly. The patient liked the method.
2. **Bridging inference:** The tooth was pulled painlessly. The dentist used a new method.
3. **Elaborative inference:** The tooth was pulled painlessly. The patient liked the new method.

Having been presented with these sentence pairs, participants were asked whether it was true that *A dentist pulled the tooth.* This is explicitly stated in example 1, but it is also highly probable in examples 2 and 3, even though it is not stated. The inference that the dentist pulled the tooth in example 2 is required to connect *dentist* in the second sentence to the first and so would be classified as a backward bridging inference. The inference in example 3 is an elaboration (because a dentist is not mentioned in either sentence) and so would be classified as a forward elaborative inference. Participants were equally fast to verify *A dentist pulled the tooth* in the bridging inference condition of example 2 as they were in the direct condition of example 1, indicating that they made the bridging inference. However, they were about a quarter of a second slower to verify the sentence in the elaborative-inference condition of example 3, indicating that they had not made the elaborative inference.

The problem with elaborative inferences is that there are no bounds on how many such inferences can be made. Consider the sentence *The tooth was pulled painlessly.* In addition to inferring who pulled the tooth, one could make inferences about what instrument was used to make the extraction, why the tooth was pulled, why the procedure was painless, how the patient felt, what happened to the patient afterward, which tooth (e.g., incisor or molar was pulled), how easy the extraction was, and so on. Considerable research has been undertaken in trying to determine exactly which elaborative inferences are made (Graesser, Singer, & Trabasso, 1994). In the Singer (1994) study just described, the elaborative inference seems not to have been made. As an example of a study in which an elaborative inference seems to have been made, consider the experiment reported by Long, Golding, and Graesser (1992). They had participants read a story that included the following critical sentence:

- A dragon kidnapped the three daughters.

After reading this sentence, participants made a lexical decision about the word *eat* (a lexical decision task, discussed in earlier in this chapter and in Chapter 6, involves deciding whether a string of letters makes a word). Long et al. found that participants could make the lexical decision more rapidly after reading this sentence than in a neutral context. From this data, they argued that participants made the inference that the dragon's goal was to eat the daughters (which had not been directly stated or even suggested in the story). Long et al. argued that, when reading a story, we normally make inferences about a character's goals.

Although bridging inferences are made automatically, it is optional whether people will make elaborative inferences. It takes effort to make these inferences and readers need to be sufficiently engaged in the text they are reading to make them. It also appears to depend on reading ability. For instance, in one study Murray and Burke (2003) had participants read passages like

> Carol was fed up with her job waiting on tables. Customers were rude, the chef was impossibly demanding, and the manager had made a pass at her just that day. The last straw came when a rude man at one of her tables complained that the spaghetti she had just served was cold. As he became louder and nastier, she felt herself losing control.

The passage then ended with one of the following two sentences:

> **Experimental:** Without thinking of the consequences, she picked up the plate of spaghetti and raised it above the customer's head.

Or

> **Control:** To verify the complaint, she picked up the plate of spaghetti and raised it above the customer's head.

After reading this sentence, participants were presented with a critical word like "dump" which is related to an elaborative inference that readers would only make in the experimental condition. They simply had to read the word. Participants classified as having high reading ability read the word "dump" faster in the experimental condition, indicating they had made the inference. However, low-reading-ability participants did not. Thus, it would appear that high-ability readers had made the elaborative inference that Carol was going to dump the spaghetti on the customer's head, whereas the low-ability readers had not.

In understanding a sentence, listeners make bridging inferences to connect it to prior sentences but only sometimes make elaborative inferences that connect to possible future material.

Inference of Reference

An important aspect of making a bridging inference consists of recognizing when an expression in the sentence refers to something that we should already know. Various linguistic cues indicate that an expression is referring to something that we already know. One cue in English turns on the difference between the definite article *the* and the indefinite article *a. The* tends to be used to signal that the comprehender should know the reference of the noun phrase, whereas *a* tends to be used to introduce a new object. Compare the difference in meaning of the following sentences:

1. Last night I saw the moon.
2. Last night I saw a moon.

Sentence 1 indicates a rather uneventful fact—seeing the same old moon as always—but sentence 2 carries the clear implication of having seen a new moon. There is considerable evidence that language comprehenders are quite sensitive to the meaning communicated by this small difference in the sentences. In one experiment, Haviland and Clark (1974) compared participants' comprehension time for two-sentence pairs such as

3. Ed was given an alligator for his birthday. The alligator was his favorite present.
4. Ed wanted an alligator for his birthday. The alligator was his favorite present.

Both pairs have the same second sentence. Pair 3 introduces in its first sentence a specific antecedent for the *alligator.* On the other hand, although *alligator* is mentioned in the first sentence of pair 4, a specific alligator is not introduced. Thus, there is no antecedent in the first sentence of pair 4 for *the alligator.* The definite article *the* in the second sentence of both pairs supposes a specific antecedent. Therefore, we would expect that participants would have difficulty with the second sentence in pair 4 but not in pair 3. In the Haviland and Clark experiment, participants saw pairs of such sentences one at a time. After they comprehended each sentence, they pressed a button. The time was measured from the presentation of the second sentence until participants pressed a button indicating that they understood that sentence. Participants took an average of 1031 ms to comprehend the second sentence in pairs, such as pair 3, in which an antecedent was given, but they took an average of 1168 ms to comprehend the second sentence in pairs, such as pair 4, in which there was no antecedent for the definite noun phrase. Thus, comprehension took more than a tenth of a second longer when there was no antecedent.

The results of an experiment done by Loftus and Zanni (1975) showed that choice of articles could affect listeners' beliefs. These experimenters showed participants a film of an automobile accident and asked them a series of questions. Some participants were asked,

5. Did you see a broken headlight?

Other participants were asked,

6. Did you see the broken headlight?

In fact, there was no broken headlight in the film, but question 6 uses a definite article, which supposes the existence of a broken headlight. Participants were more likely to answer "Yes" when asked the question in form 6. As Loftus and Zanni noted, this finding has important implications for the interrogation of eyewitnesses.

Comprehenders take the definite article the to imply the existence of a reference for the noun.

Pronominal Reference

Another aspect of processing reference concerns the interpretation of pronouns. When one hears a pronoun such as *she,* deciding who is being referenced is critical. A number of people may have already been mentioned, and all are candidates for the reference of the pronoun. As Just and Carpenter (1987) noted, there are a number of bases for resolving the reference of pronouns:

1. One of the most straightforward is to use number or gender cues. Consider
   - Melvin, Susan, and their children left when (he, she, they) became sleepy.

Each possible pronoun has a different referent.

2. A syntactic cue to pronominal reference is that pronouns tend to refer to objects in the same grammatical role (e.g., subject versus object). Consider
   - Floyd punched Bert and then he kicked him.

Most people would agree that the subject *he* refers to *Floyd* and the object *him* refers to *Bert.*

3. There is also a strong recency effect such that the most recent candidate referent is preferred. Consider
   - Dorothea ate the pie; Ethel ate cake; later she had coffee.

Most people would agree that *she* probably refers to Ethel.

4. Finally, people can use their knowledge of the world to determine reference. Compare
   - Tom shouted at Bill because he spilled the coffee.
   - Tom shouted at Bill because he had a headache.

Most people would agree that *he* in the first sentence refers to *Bill* because you tend to scold people who make mistakes, whereas *he* in the second sentence refers to *Tom* because people tend to be cranky when they have headaches.

In keeping with the immediacy-of-interpretation principle articulated earlier, people try to determine who a pronoun refers to immediately upon encountering it. For instance, in studies of eye fixations (Carpenter & Just, 1977; Ehrlich & Rayner, 1983; Just & Carpenter, 1987), researchers found that people fixated on a pronoun longer when it is harder to determine its reference. Ehrlich and Rayner (1983) also found that participants' resolution of the reference tends to spill over into the next fixation, suggesting they are still processing the pronoun while reading the next word.

Corbett and Chang (1983) found evidence that participants consider multiple candidates for a referent. They had participants read sentences such as

- Scott stole the basketball from Warren and he sank a jumpshot.

After reading the sentence, participants saw a probe word and had to decide whether the word appeared in the sentence. Corbett and Chang found that time to recognize either Scott or Warren decreased after reading such a sentence. They also asked participants to read the following control sentence, which did not require the referent of a pronoun to be determined:

- Scott stole the basketball from Warren and Scott sank a jumpshot.

In this case, only recognition of Scott was facilitated. Warren was facilitated only in the first sentence because, in that sentence, participants had to consider it a possible referent of *he* before settling on Scott as the referent.

The results of both the Corbett and Chang study and the Ehrlich and Rayner study indicate that resolution of pronoun reference lasts beyond the reading of the pronoun itself. This finding indicates that processing is not always as immediate as the immediacy-of-processing principle might seem to imply. The processing of pronominal reference spills over into later fixations (Ehrlich & Rayner, 1983), and there is still priming for the unselected reference at the end of the sentence (Corbett & Chang, 1983).

Comprehenders consider multiple possible candidates for the referent of a pronoun and use syntactic and semantic cues to select a referent.

Negatives

Negative sentences appear to suppose a positive sentence and then ask us to infer what must be true if the positive sentence is false. For instance, the sentence *John is not a crook* supposes that it is reasonable to assume *John is a crook* but asserts that this assumption is false. As another example, imagine the following four replies from a normally healthy friend to the question *How are you feeling?*

1. I am well.
2. I am sick.
3. I am not well.
4. I am not sick.

Replies 1 through 3 would not be regarded as unusual linguistically, but reply 4 does seem peculiar. By using the negative, reply 4 is supposing that thinking of our friend as sick is reasonable. Why would we think our friend is sick, and what is our friend really telling us by saying it is not so? In contrast, the negative in reply 3 is easy to understand, because supposing that the friend is normally well is reasonable and our friend is telling us that this is not so.

FIGURE 13.9 A card like that presented to participants in Clark and Chase's sentence-verification experiments. Participants were to say whether simple affirmative and negative sentences correctly described these patterns.

Clark and Chase (Chase & Clark, 1972; H. H. Clark, 1974; Clark & Chase, 1972) conducted a series of experiments on the verification of negatives (see also Carpenter & Just, 1975; Trabasso, Rollins, & Shaughnessy, 1971). In a typical experiment, they presented participants with a card like that shown in Figure 13.9 and asked them to verify one of four sentences about this card:

1. The star is above the plus—true affirmative.
2. The plus is above the star—false affirmative.
3. The plus is not above the star—true negative.
4. The star is not above the plus—false negative.

The terms *true* and *false* refer to whether the sentence is true of the picture; the terms *affirmative* and *negative* refer to whether the sentence structure has a negative element. Sentences 1 and 2 are simple assertions, but sentences 3 and 4 contain a supposition plus a negation of the supposition. Sentence 3 supposes that the plus is above the star and asserts that this supposition is false; sentence 4 supposes that the star is above the plus and asserts that this supposition is false. Clark and Chase assumed that participants would check the supposition first and then process the negation. In sentence 3, the supposition does not match the picture, but in sentence 4, the supposition does match the picture. Assuming that mismatches would take longer to process, Clark and Chase predicted that participants would take longer to respond to sentence 3, a true negative, than to sentence 4, a false negative. In contrast, participants should take longer to process sentence 2, the false affirmative, than sentence 1, the true affirmative, because sentence 2 does not match the picture. In fact, the difference between sentences 2 and 1 should be identical with the difference between sentences 3 and 4, because both differences correspond to the extra time due to a mismatch between the sentence and the picture.

Clark and Chase developed a simple and elegant mathematical model for such data. They assumed that processing sentences 3 and 4 took N time units longer than did processing sentences 1 and 2 because of the more complex supposition-plus-negation structure of sentences 3 and 4. They also assumed that processing sentence 2 took M time units longer than did processing sentence 1 because of the mismatch between picture and assertion. Similarly, they assumed that processing sentence 3 took M time units longer than did processing sentence 4 because of the mismatch between picture and supposition. Finally, they assumed that processing a true affirmative such as sentence 1 took T time units. The time T refers to the time used in processes exclusive of negation or the picture mismatch. Let us consider the total time that participants should spend processing a sentence such as sentence 3: This sentence has a complex supposition-and-negation structure, which costs N time units, and a supposition mismatch, which costs M time units. Therefore, total processing time should be $T + M + N$. Table 13.1 shows both the observed data and the reaction-time predictions that can be derived for the Clark and Chase experiment. The best predicting values for T, M, and N for this experiment can be estimated from the data as $T = 1469$ ms, $M = 246$ ms, and $N = 320$ ms. As you can confirm, the predictions match the observed time remarkably well. In particular, the difference between true negatives and false negatives is close to the difference between false affirmatives and true affirmatives.

TABLE 13.1

Observed and Predicted Reaction Times in Experiment Verification

Condition	Observed Time	Equation	Predicted Time
True affirmative	1463 ms	T	1469 ms
False affirmative	1722 ms	$T + M$	1715 ms
True negative	2028 ms	$T + M + N$	2035 ms
False negative	1796 ms	$T + N$	1789 ms

This finding supports the hypothesis that participants do extract the suppositions of negative sentences and match them to the picture.

Comprehenders process a negative by first processing its embedded supposition and then the negation.

Text Processing

So far, we have focused on the comprehension of single sentences in isolation. Sentences are more frequently processed in larger contexts; for example, in the reading of a textbook. Texts, like sentences, are structured according to certain patterns, although these patterns are perhaps more flexible than those for sentences. Researchers have noted that a number of recurring relations serve to organize sentences into larger parts of a text. Some of the relations that have been identified are listed in Table 13.2. These structural relations specify the way in which a sentence should be related to the overall text. For instance, the first text structure (response) in Table 13.2 directs the reader to relate one set of sentences as part of the solution to problems posed by other sentences. These relations can be at any level of a text. That is, the main relation organizing a

TABLE 13.2

Possible Types of Relations among Sentences in a Text

Type of Relation	Description
1. Response	A question is presented and an answer follows or a problem is presented and a solution follows.
2. Specific	Specific information is given subsequent to a more general point.
3. Explanation	An explanation is given for a point.
4. Evidence	Evidence is given to support a point.
5. Sequence	Points are presented in their temporal sequence as a set.
6. Cause	An event is presented as the cause of another event.
7. Goal	An event is presented as the goal of another event.
8. Collection	A loose structure of points is presented. (This is perhaps a case in which there is no real organizing relation.)

paragraph might be any of the eight in Table 13.2. Subpoints in a paragraph also may be organized according to any of these relations.

To see how the relations in Table 13.2 might be used, consider Meyer's (1974) now-classic analysis of the following paragraph:

Parakeet Paragraph

The wide variety in color of parakeets that are available on the market today resulted from careful breeding of the color mutant offspring of green-bodied and yellow-faced parakeets. The light green body and yellow face color combination is the color of the parakeets in their natural habitat, Australia. The first living parakeets were brought to Europe from Australia by John Gould, a naturalist, in 1840. The first color mutation appeared in 1872 in Belgium; these birds were completely yellow. The most popular color of parakeets in the United States is sky-blue. These birds have sky-blue bodies and white faces; this color mutation occurred in 1878 in Europe. There are over 66 different colors of parakeets listed by the Color and Technical Committee of the Budgerigar Society. In addition to the original green-bodied and yellow-faced birds, colors of parakeets include varying shades of violets, blues, grays, greens, yellows, and whites. (p. 61)

Her analysis of this paragraph is approximately reproduced in Table 13.3. Note that this analysis tends to organize various facts into more or less major points.

TABLE 13.3

Analysis of the Parakeet Paragraph

1. A explains B.
- **A.** There was careful breeding of color mutants of green-bodied and yellow-faced parakeets. The historical sequence is
  - **1.** Their natural habitat was Australia. Specific detail:
    - **a.** Their color here is a light-green body and yellow-face combination.
  - **2.** The first living parakeets were brought to Europe from Australia by John Gould in 1840. Specific detail:
    - **a.** John Gould was a naturalist.
  - **3.** The first color mutation appeared in 1872 in Belgium. Specific detail:
    - **a.** These birds were completely yellow.
  - **4.** The sky-blue mutation occurred in 1878 in Europe. Specific details:
    - **a.** These birds have sky-blue bodies and white faces.
    - **b.** This is the most popular color in America.
- **B.** There is a wide variety in color of parakeets that are on the market today. Evidence for this is
  - **1.** There are over 66 different colors of parakeets listed by the Color and Technical Committee of the Budgerigar Society.
  - **2.** There are many available colors. A collection of these is
    - **a.** The original green-bodied and yellow-faced birds
    - **b.** Violets
    - **c.** Blues
    - **d.** Grays
    - **e.** Greens
    - **f.** Yellows
    - **g.** Whites

From Meyer (1974).

The highest-level organizing relation in this paragraph is *explanation* (see item 3, Table 13.2). Specifically, the major points in this explanation are that (point A) there has been careful breeding of color mutants and (point B) there is a wide variety of parakeet color, and point A is given as an explanation of point B. Organized under point A are some events from the history of parakeet breeding. This organization is an example of a sequence relation. Organized under these events are specific details. So, for instance, organized under A2 is the fact that John Gould was a naturalist. Organized under point B is evidence supporting the assertion about the wide color variety and some details about the available variation in color.

The propositions in a text can be organized hierarchically according to various semantic relations.

Text Structure and Memory

A great deal of research has demonstrated the psychological significance of text structure. A number of hypotheses differ in regard to exactly what system of relations should be used in the analysis of texts, but they generally agree that some sort of hierarchical structure organizes the propositions of a text. Memory experiments have yielded evidence that participants do, to some degree, respond to that hierarchical structure.

Meyer, Brandt, and Bluth (1978) studied students' perception of the high-level structure of a text—that is, the structural relations at the higher levels of hierarchies like that in Table 13.3. They found considerable variation in participants' ability to recognize the high-level structure that organized a text. Moreover, they found that participants' ability to identify the top-level structure of a text was an important predictor of their memory for the text. In another study, on ninth-graders, Bartlett (1978) found that only 11% of participants consciously identified and used high-level structure to remember text material. This select group did twice as well as other students on their recall scores. Bartlett also showed that training students to identify and use top-level structure more than doubled recall performance.

In addition to its hierarchical structure, a text tends to be held together by causal and logical structures. This tendency is clearest in narratives in which one event in a sequence of events causes the next event. The scripts discussed in Chapter 5 are one kind of knowledge structure that is designed to encode such causal relations. Often the causal links are not explicitly stated but rather have to be inferred. For instance, we might hear on a newscast

- There is an accident on the Parkway East. Traffic is being rerouted through Wilkinsburg.

It is left to the listener to infer that the first fact is the cause of the second fact. Keenan, Baillet, and Brown (1984) studied the effect of the probability of the causal relation connecting two sentences on the processing of the second sentence.

They asked participants to read pairs of sentences, of which the first might be one of the following sentences:

1a. Joey's big brother punched him again and again.
1b. Racing down the hill, Joey fell off his bike.
1c. Joey's crazy mother became furiously angry with him.
1d. Joey went to a neighbor's house to play.

Keenan et al. were interested in the effect of the first sentence on time to read a second sentence such as

2. The next day, his body was covered with bruises.

Sentences 1a through 1d are ordered in decreasing probability of a causal connection to the second sentence. Correspondingly, Keenan et al. found that participants' reading times for sentence 2 increased from 2.6 s when preceded by high probable causes such as that given in sentence 1a to 3.3 s when preceded by low probable causes such as that given in sentence 1d. Thus, it takes longer to understand a more distant causal relation.

There also are effects of causal relatedness on recall. Those parts of a story that are more central to its causal structure are more likely to be recalled (Black & Bern, 1981; Trabasso, Secco, & van den Broek, 1984). For instance, Black and Bern had participants study stories that included pairs of sentences such as

- The cat leapt up on the kitchen table.
- Fred picked up the cat and put it outside.

which are causally related. They contrasted this pair with pairs of sentences such as

- The cat rubbed against the kitchen table.
- Fred picked up the cat and put it outside.

which are less plausibly connected by a causal relation. Although the second sentence is identical in both cases, participants displayed better memories for the first sentence of a causally related pair.

Thorndyke (1977) also showed that memory for a story is poorer if the organization of the text conflicts with what would be considered its "natural" structure. Some participants studied an original story, whereas other participants studied the story with its sentences presented in a scrambled order. Participants were able to recall 85% of the facts in the original story but only 32% of the facts in the scrambled story.

Mandler and Johnson (1977) showed that children have much more difficulty than adults do when recalling the causal structure of a story. Adults recall events and the outcomes of those events together, whereas children recall the outcomes but tend to forget how they were achieved. For instance, children might recall from a particular story that the butter melted but might forget that it melted because it was in the sun. Adults do not have trouble with such simple causal structures, but they may have difficulty perceiving the more complex relations connecting parts of a text. For instance, how easy is it for you to specify the relation that connects this paragraph to the preceding one?

Palinscar and Brown (1984) developed a training program that specifically trains children to identify and formulate questions about such things as the causal structure of text. They were able to raise poor-performing seventh-graders from the 20th to the 56th percentile in reading comprehension. This result is similar to that obtained by Bartlett (1978), who improved reading performance by training students to identify the hierarchical structure of text.

- *Memory for textual material is sensitive to the hierarchical and causal structure of that text and tends to be better when people attend to that structure.*

Levels of Representation of a Text

Kintsch (1998) has argued that a text is represented at multiple levels. For instance, consider the following pair of sentences taken from an experimental story entitled "Nick Goes to the Movies."

- Nick decided to go to the movies. He looked at a newspaper to see what was playing.

Kintsch argues that this material is represented at three levels:

1. There is the surface level of representation of the exact sentences. This can be tested by comparing people's ability to remember the exact sentences versus paraphrases like "Nick studied the newspaper to see what was playing."
2. There is also a propositional level (see Chapter 5) and this can be tested by seeing whether people remember that Nick read the newspaper at all.
3. There is a **situation model** that consists of the major points of the story. Thus, we can see whether people remember that "Nick wanted to see a film"—something not said in the story but strongly implied.

In one study, Kintsch, Welsch, Schmalhofer, and Zimny (1990) looked at participants' ability to remember these different sorts of information over periods of time ranging up to 4 days. The results are shown in Figure 13.10. As we saw in Chapter 5, surface information is forgotten quite rapidly, whereas the propositional information is better retained. However, the most striking retention function involves the situation information. After 4 days, participants have forgotten half the propositions but still remember perfectly what the story was about. This fits with many people's experience in reading novels or seeing movies. They will quickly forget many of the details but will still remember what the novel or movie was about months later.

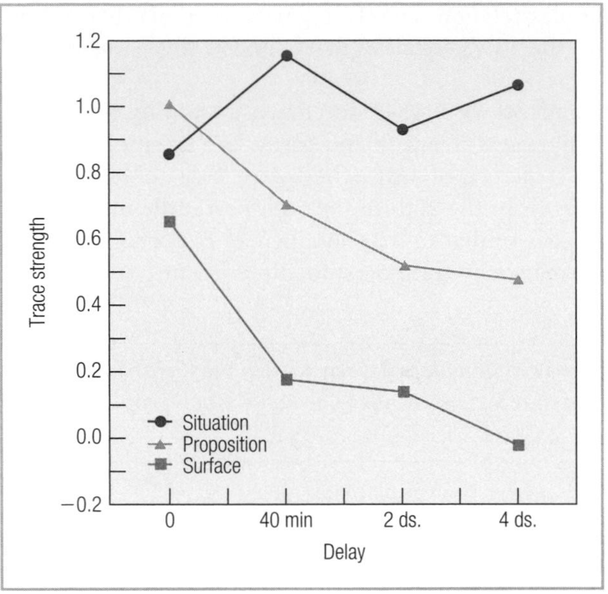

FIGURE 13.10 Memory for a story as a function of time: strengths of the traces for the surface form of sentences, the propositions that make up the story, and the high-level situation representation. (From Kintsch et al., 1990.)

When people follow a story, they construct a high-level situation model of the story that is more durable than the memory for the surface sentences or the propositions that made up the story.

Conclusions

The number and diversity of topics covered in this chapter testify to the impressive cumulative progress in understanding language comprehension. It is fair to say that we knew almost nothing about language processing when cognitive psychology emerged from the collapse of behaviorism 50 years ago. Now, we have a rather articulate picture of what is happening in scales that range from 100 ms after a word is heard to minutes later when large stretches of complex text must be integrated. Research on language processing turns out to harbor a number of theoretical controversies, some of which have been discussed in this review of the field (e.g., whether early syntactic processing is separate from the rest of cognition). However, such controversies should not blind us to the impressive progress that has been made. The heat in the field has also generated much light.

Questions for Thought

1. Answer the following question: "How many animals of each kind did Moses take on the ark?" If you are like most people you answer "two" and did not even notice that it was Noah and not Moses who took the animals on the ark (Erickson & Matteson, 1981). People do this even when they are warned to look out for such sentences and not answer them (Reder & Kusbit, 1991). This phenomenon has been called the Moses illusion even though it has been demonstrated with a wide range of words besides Moses. What does the Moses illusion say about how people incorporate the meaning of individual words into sentences?
2. Christianson, Hollingworth, Halliwell, and Ferreira (2001) found that when people read the sentence "While Mary bathed the baby played in the crib" most people actually interpret the sentence as implying that Mary bathed the baby. Ferreirra and Patson (2007) argue that this implies that people do not carefully parse sentences but settle on "good enough" interpretations. If people don't carefully process sentences, what does that imply about the debate between proponents of interactive processing and of the modularity position about how people understand sentences like "The woman painted by the artist was very attractive to look at"?
3. Palinscar and Brown (1984) found that teaching seventh-graders to make elaborative inferences while reading dramatically improved their reading skills. Do you think they would have been as successful if they had focused on teaching children to make bridging inferences?
4. Bielock, Lyons, Mattarella-Micke, Nusbaum, and Small (2008) looked at brain activation while participants listened to sentences about hockey versus other action sentences. They found greater activation in the premotor cortex for hockey sentences only for those participants who were hockey fans. What does this say about the role of expertise in making elaborative inferences and developing situation models?

Key Terms

bridging (or backward) inferences
center-embedded sentences
constituent
elaborative (or forward) inferences
garden-path sentence
immediacy of interpretation
interactive processing
N400
P600
parsing
principle of minimal attachment
situation model
transient ambiguity
utilization

14

Individual Differences in Cognition

Clearly, all people do not think alike. There are many aspects of cognition, but humans, naturally being an evaluative species, tend to focus on ways in which some people perform "better" than other people. This performance is often identified with the word *intelligence*—some people are perceived to be more intelligent than others. Chapter 1 identified intelligence as the defining feature of the human species. So, to call some members of our species more intelligent than others can be a potent claim. As we will see, the complexity of human cognition makes the placement of people on a unidimensional evaluative scale of intelligence impossible.

This chapter will explore individual differences in cognition both because of its inherent interest and because it sheds some light on the general nature of human cognition. The big debate that will be with us throughout this chapter is the nurture-versus-nature debate. Are some people better at some cognitive tasks because they are innately endowed with more capacity for those kinds of tasks or because they have learned more knowledge relevant to these tasks? The answer, not surprisingly, is that it is some of both, and we will consider and examine some of the ways in which both basic capacities and experiences contribute to human intelligence.

More specifically, this chapter will answer the following questions:

- How does the thinking of children develop as they mature?
- What are the relative contributions of neural growth versus experience to children's intellectual development?
- What happens to our intellectual capacity through the adult years?
- What do intelligence tests measure?
- What are the different subcomponents of intelligence?

Cognitive Development

Part of the uniqueness of the human species concerns the way in which children are brought into the world and develop to become adults. Humans have very large brains in relation to their body size, which created a major evolutionary problem: How would the birth of such large-brained babies be physically possible? One way was through progressive enlargement of the birth canal, which is now as large as is considered possible given the constraints of mammalian skeletons (Geschwind, 1980). In addition, a child is born with a skull that is sufficiently pliable for it to be compressed into a cone shape to fit through the birth canal. Still, the human birth process is particularly difficult compared with that of most other mammals.

Figure 14.1 illustrates the growth of the human brain during gestation. At birth, a child's brain has more neurons than an adult brain has, but the state of development of these neurons is particularly immature. Compared with those of many other species, the brains of human infants will develop much more after birth. At birth, a human brain occupies a volume of about 350 cubic centimeters (cm^3). In the first year of life, it doubles to 700 cm^3, and before a human being reaches puberty, the size of its brain doubles again. Most other mammals do not have as much growth in brain size after birth (S. J. Gould, 1977). Because the human birth canal has been expanded to its limits, much of our neural development has been postponed until after birth.

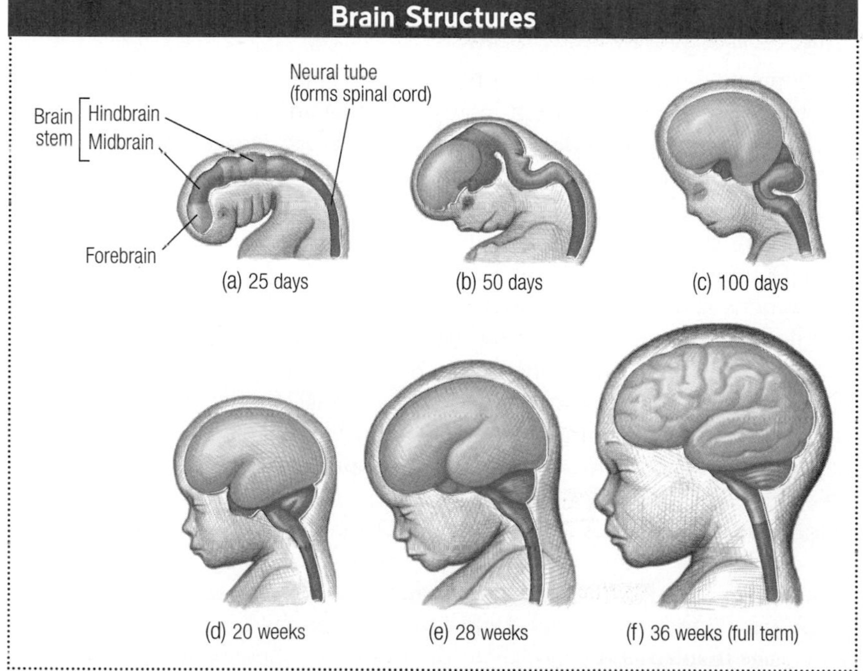

FIGURE 14.1 Changes in structure in the developing brain. (Adapted from Cowan, 1997, p. 116).

Even though they spend 9 months developing in the womb, human infants are quite helpless at birth and spend an extraordinarily long time growing to adult stature—about 15 years, which is about a fifth of the human life span. In contrast, a puppy, after a gestation period of just 9 weeks, is more capable at birth than a human newborn. In less than a year, less than a tenth of its life span, a dog has reached full size and reproductive capability.

Childhood is prolonged more than would be needed to develop large brains. Indeed, the majority of neural development is complete by age 5. Humans are kept children by the slowness of their physical development. It has been speculated that the function of this slow physical development is to keep children in a dependency relation to adults (de Beer, 1959). Much has to be learned to become a competent adult, and staying a child for so long gives the human enough time to acquire that knowledge. Childhood is an apprenticeship for adulthood.

Modern society is so complex that we cannot learn all that is needed by simply associating with our parents for 15 years. To provide the needed training, society has created social institutions such as high schools, colleges, and post-college professional schools. It is not unusual for people to spend more than 25 years, almost as long as their professional lives, preparing for their roles in society.

- *Human development to adulthood is longer than that of other mammals to allow time for growth of a large brain and acquisition of a large amount of knowledge.*

Piaget's Stages of Development

Developmental psychologists have tried to understand the intellectual changes that take place as we grow from infancy through adulthood. Many have been particularly influenced by the Swiss psychologist Jean Piaget, who studied and theorized about child development for more than half a century. Much of the recent information-processing work in cognitive development has been concerned with correcting and restructuring Piaget's theory of cognitive development. Despite these revisions, his research has organized a large set of qualitative observations about cognitive development spanning the period from birth to adulthood. Therefore, it is worthwhile to review these observations to get a picture of the general nature of cognitive development during childhood.

According to Piaget, a child enters the world lacking virtually all the basic cognitive competencies of an adult but gradually develops these competencies by passing through a series of stages of development. Piaget distinguishes four major stages. The **sensory-motor stage** is in the first 2 years of life. In this stage, children develop schemes for thinking about the physical world—for instance, they develop the notion of an object as a permanent thing in the world. The second stage is the **preoperational stage,** which is characterized as spanning the period from 2 to 7 years of age. Unlike the younger child, a child in this period can engage in internal thought about the world, but these mental processes are intuitive and lack systematicity. For instance, a 4-year-old who was asked to describe his painting of a farm and some animals said, "First, over here is a house where the animals live. I live in a house. So do my mommy and daddy. This is a horse. I saw horses on TV. Do you have a TV?"

The third stage is the **concrete-operational stage,** which spans the period from age 7 to age 11. In this period, children develop a set of mental operations that allow them to treat the physical world in a systematic way. However, children still have major limitations on their capacity to reason formally about the world. The capacity for formal reasoning emerges in Piaget's fourth period, the **formal-operational stage,** spanning the years from 11 to adulthood. Upon entering this period, although there is still much to learn, a child has become an adult conceptually and is capable of scientific reasoning—which Piaget takes as the paradigm case of mature intellectual functioning.

Piaget's concept of a stage has always been a sore point in developmental psychology. Obviously, a child does not suddenly change on an 11th birthday from the stage of concrete operations to the stage of formal operations. There are large differences among children and cultures, and the ages given are just approximations. However, careful analysis of the development within a single child also fails to find abrupt changes at any age. One response to this gradualness has been to break down the stages into smaller substages. Another response has been to interpret stages as simply ways of characterizing what is inherently a gradual and continuous process. Siegler (1996) argued that, on careful analysis, all cognitive development is continuous and gradual. He characterized the belief that children progress through discrete stages as "the myth of the immaculate transition."

Just as important as Piaget's stage analysis is his analysis of children's performance in specific tasks within these stages. These task analyses provide the empirical substance to back up his broad and abstract characterization of the stages. Probably his most well-known task analysis is his research on conservation, considered next.

- *Piaget proposed that children progress through four stages of increasing intellectual sophistication: sensory-motor, preoperational, concrete-operational, and formal-operational.*

Conservation

The term **conservation** most generally refers to knowledge of the properties of the world that are preserved under various transformations. A child's understanding of conservation develops as the child progresses through the Piagetian stages.

Conservation in the sensory-motor stage. A child must come to understand that objects continue to exist over transformations in time and space. If a cloth is placed over a toy that a 6-month-old is reaching for, the infant stops reaching and appears to lose interest in the toy (Figure 14.2). It is as if the object ceases to exist for the child when it is no longer in view. Piaget concluded from his experiments that children do not come into the world with this knowledge but rather develop a concept of object permanence during the first year.

According to Piaget, the concept of object permanence develops slowly and is one of the major intellectual developments in the sensory-motor stage. An older

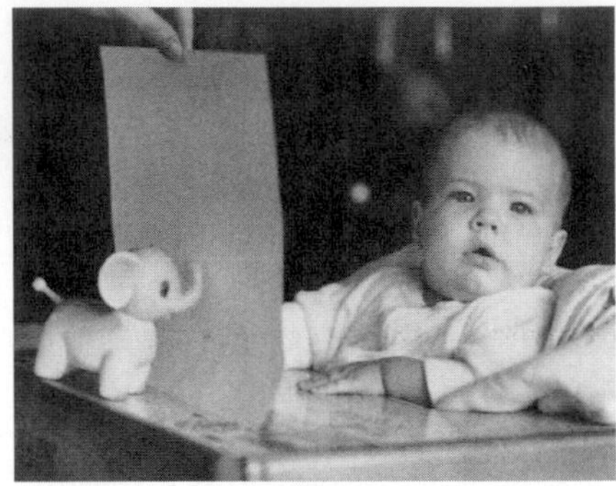

FIGURE 14.2 An illustration of a child's apparent inability to understand the permanence of an object. (Monkmeyer Press Photo Service, Inc. From Santrock and Yussen, 1989. Reprinted by permission of the publisher. Copyright © 1989 by Wm. C. Brown.)

infant will search for an object that has been hidden, but more demanding tests reveal failings in the older infant's understanding of a permanent object. In one experiment, an object is put under cover A, and then, in front of the child, it is removed and put under cover B. The child will often look for the object under cover A. Piaget argues that the child does not understand that the object will still be in location B. Only after the age of 12 months can the child succeed consistently at this task.

Conservation in the preoperational and concrete-operational stages. A number of important advances in conservation occur at about 6 years of age, which, according to Piaget, is the transition between the preoperational and the concrete-operational stages. Before this age, children can be shown to have some glaring errors in their reasoning. These errors start to correct themselves at this point. The cause of this change has been controversial, with different theorists pointing to language (Bruner, 1964) and the advent of schooling (Cole & D'Andrade, 1982), among other possible causes. Here, we will content ourselves with a description of the changes leading to a child's understanding of conservation of quantity.

As adults, we can almost instantaneously recognize that there are four apples in a bowl and can confidently know that these apples will remain four when dumped into a bag. Piaget was interested in how a child develops the concept of quantity and learns that quantity is something that is preserved under various transformations, such as moving the objects from a bowl to a bag. Figure 14.3 illustrates a typical conservation problem that has been posed by psychologists in many variations to preschool children in countless experiments. A child is presented with two rows of objects, such as checkers. The two rows contain the same number of objects and have been lined up so as to correspond. The child is asked whether the two rows have the same amount and responds that they do. The child can be asked to count the objects in the two rows to confirm that conclusion. Now, before the child's eyes, one row is compressed so that it is shorter than the other row, but no checkers are added or removed. Again asked

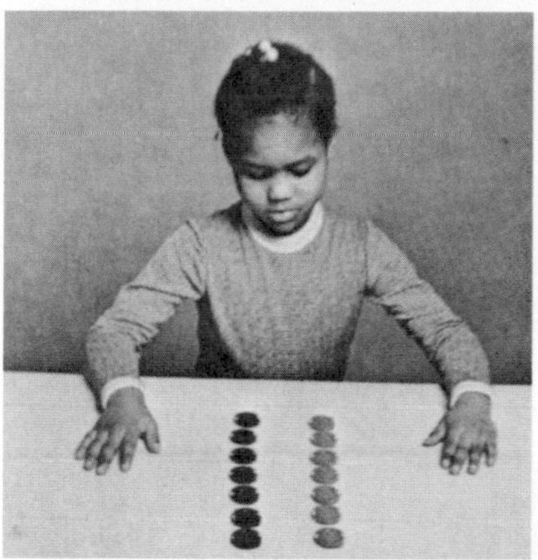

FIGURE 14.3 A typical experimental situation to test for conservation of number. (Monkmeyer Press Photo Service, Inc. From Santrock and Yussen, 1989. Reprinted by permission of the publisher. Copyright © 1989 Wm. C. Brown.)

which row has more objects, the child now says that the longer row has more. The child appears not to know that quantity is something that is preserved under transformations such as the compression of space. If asked to count the two rows, the child expresses great surprise that they have the same number.

A general feature in demonstrations of lack of conservation is that the irrelevant physical features of a display distract children. Another example is the liquid-conservation task, which is illustrated in Figure 14.4. A child is shown two identical beakers containing identical amounts of water and an empty, tall, thin beaker. When asked whether the two identical beakers hold the same amount of water, the child answers "Yes." The water from one beaker is then poured into the tall, thin beaker. When asked whether the amount of water in the two containers is the same, the child now says that the tall beaker holds more. Young children are distracted by physical appearance and do not relate their having seen the water poured from one beaker into the other to the unchanging quantity of liquid. Bruner (1964) demonstrated that a child is less likely to fail to conserve if the tall beaker is hidden from sight while it is being filled; then the child does not see the high column of water and so is not distracted by physical appearance. Thus, it is a case of being overwhelmed by physical appearance. The child does understand that water preserves its quantity after being poured.

Failure of conservation has also been shown with weight and volume of solid objects (for a discussion of studies of conservation, see Brainerd, 1978; Flavell, 1985; Ginsburg & Opper, 1980). It was once thought that the ability to perform successfully on all these tasks depended on acquiring a single abstract concept of conservation. Now, however, it is clear that successful conservation appears earlier on some tasks than on others. For instance, conservation of number usually appears before conservation of liquid. Additionally, children in transition will show conservation of number in one experimental situation but not in another.

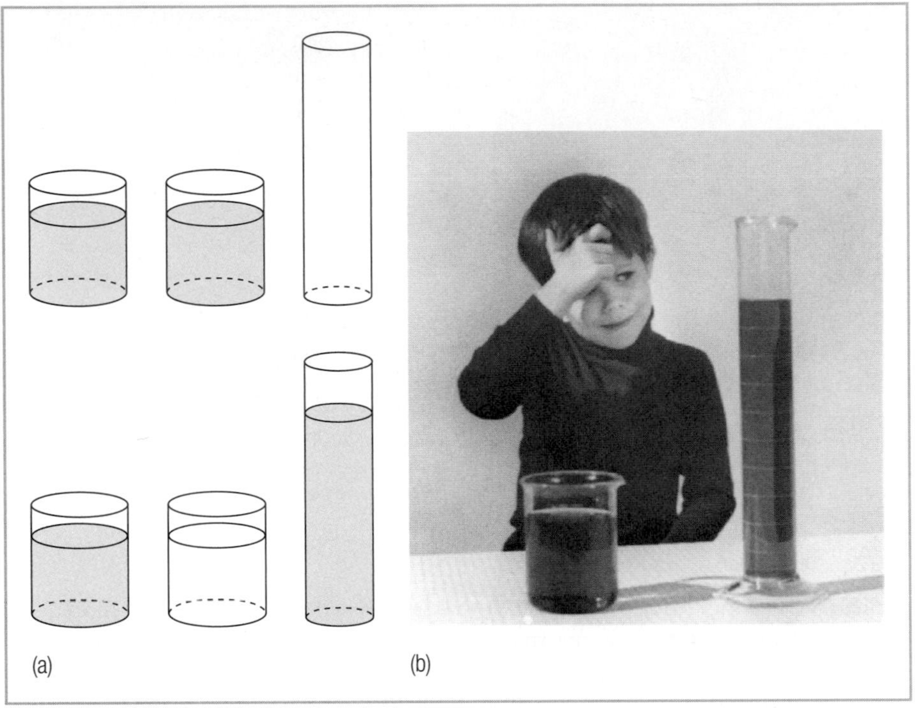

FIGURE 14.4 A typical experimental situation to test for conservation of liquid. (Monkmeyer Press Photo Service, Inc. From Santrock and Yussen, 1989. Reprinted by permission of the publisher. Copyright © 1989 Wm. C. Brown Publishers.)

Conservation in the formal-operational period. When children reach the formal-operational period, their understanding of conservation reaches new levels of abstraction. They are able to understand the idealized conservations that are part of modern science, including concepts such as the conservation of energy and the conservation of motion. In a frictionless world, an object once set in motion continues, an abstraction that the child never experiences. However, the child comes to understand this abstraction and the way in which it relates to experiences in the real world.

- *As children develop, they gain increasingly sophisticated understanding about what properties of objects are conserved under which transformations.*

What Develops?

Clearly, as Piaget and others have documented, major intellectual changes take place in childhood. However, there are serious questions concerning what underlies these changes. There are two ways of explaining why children perform better on various intellectual tasks as they get older: One is that they "think better," and the other is that they "know better." The think-better option holds that children's basic cognitive processes become better. Perhaps they can hold more information in working memory or process information faster. The know-better option holds that children have learned more facts and better methods as they get older. I refer to this as "know better," not "know more," because it is not just a matter of adding knowledge but also a matter of eliminating erroneous facts and inappropriate methods (such as relying on appearance in the conservation tasks). Perhaps this superior knowledge enables them to perform the tasks more efficiently. A computer metaphor is apt here: A computer application can be made to perform better by running the same program on a faster machine that has more memory or by running a better program on the same machine. Which is it in the case of child development—better machine or better program?

Rather than the reason being one or the other, the child's improvement is due to both factors, but what are their relative contributions? Siegler (1998) argued that many of the developmental changes that take place in the first 2 years are to be understood in relation to neural changes. Such changes in the first 2 years are considerable. As we already noted, an infant is born with more neurons than the child will have at a later age. Although the number of neurons decreases, the number of synaptic connections increases 10-fold in the first 2 years, as illustrated in Figure 14.5. The number of synapses reaches a peak at about age 2, after which it declines. The earlier pruning of neurons and the later

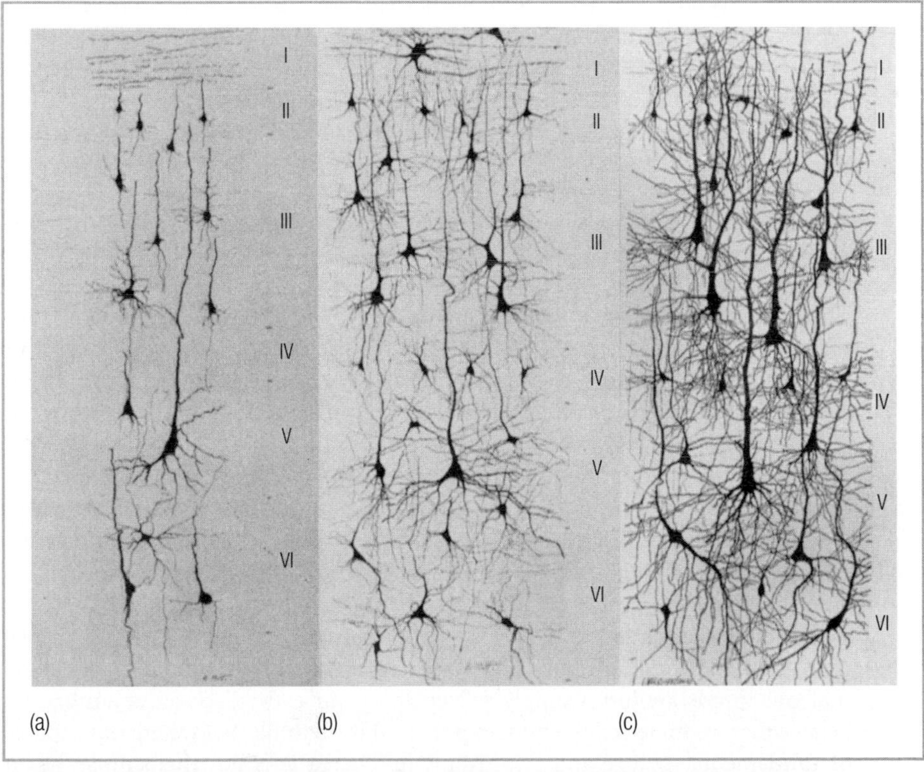

FIGURE 14.5 Postnatal development of human cerebral cortex around Broca's area: (a) newborn; (b) 3 months; (c) 24 months. (From Lenneberg, 1967.)

pruning of synaptic connections can be thought of as a process by which the brain can fine-tune itself. The initial overproduction guarantees that there will be enough neurons and synapses to process the required information. When some neurons or synapses are not used, and so are proved unnecessary, they wither away (Huttenlocher, 1994). After age 2, there is not much further growth of neurons or their synaptic connections, but the brain continues to grow because of the proliferation of other cells. In particular, the glial cells increase, including those that provide the myelinated sheaths around the axons of neurons. As discussed in Chapter 1, myelination enables the axon to conduct brain signals rapidly. The process of myelination continues into the late teens but at an increasingly gradual pace. The effects of this gradual myelination can be considerable. For instance, the time for a nerve impulse to cross the hemispheres in an adult is about 5 milliseconds (ms), which is four to five times as fast as in a 4-year-old (Salamy, 1978).

It is tempting to emphasize the improvement in processing capacity as the basis for improvement after age 2. After all, consider the physical difference between a 2-year-old and an adult. When my son was 2 years old, he had difficulty mastering the undoing of his pajama buttons. If his muscles and coordination had so much maturing to do, why not his brain? This analogy, however, does not hold: A 2-year-old has reached only 20% of his adult body weight, whereas the brain has already reached 80% of its final size. Cognitive development after age 2 may depend more on the knowledge that a person puts into his or her brain rather than on any improvement in the physical capacities of the brain.

- *Neural development is a more important contributor to cognitive development before the age of 2 than after.*

The Empiricist-Nativist Debate

There is relatively little controversy either about the role that physical development of the brain plays in the growth of human intellect or about the incredible importance of knowledge to human intellectual processes. However, there is an age-old nature-versus-nurture controversy that is related to, but different from, the issue of physical growth versus knowledge accumulation. This debate is between the nativists and the empiricists (see Chapter 1) about the origins of that knowledge. The nativists argue that the most important aspects of our knowledge about the world appear as part of our genetically programmed development, whereas the empiricists argue that virtually all knowledge comes from experience with the environment. One reason that this issue is emotionally charged is that it would seem tied to conceptions about what makes humans special and what their potential for change is. The nativist view is that we sell ourselves short if we believe that our minds are just a simple reflection of our experiences, and empiricists believe that we undersell the human potential if we think that we are not capable of fundamental change and improvement. The issue is not this simple, but it nonetheless fuels great passion on both sides of the debate.

We have already visited this issue in the discussions of language acquisition and of whether important aspects of human language are innately specified, such as language universals. However, similar arguments have been made for our knowledge of human faces or our knowledge of biological categories. A particularly interesting case concerns our knowledge of number. Piaget used experiments such as those on number conservation to argue that we do not have an innate sense of numbers, but others have used experiments to argue otherwise. For instance, in studies of infant attention, young children have been shown to discriminate one object from two and two from three (Antell & Keating, 1983; Starkey, Spelke, & Gelman, 1990; van Loosbroek & Smitsman, 1992). In these studies, young children become bored looking at a certain number of objects but show renewed interest when the number of objects changes. There is even evidence for a rudimentary ability to add and subtract (Simon, Hespos, & Rochat, 1995; Wynn, 1992). For instance, if a 5-month-old child sees one object appear on stage and then disappear behind a screen, and then sees a second object appear on stage and disappear behind the screen, the child is surprised if there are not two objects when the screen is raised (Figure 14.6—note this contradicts Piaget's claims about failure of conservation in the sensory-motor stage). This reaction is taken as evidence that the child calculates 1 + 1 = 2. Dehaene (2000) argued that a special structure in the parietal cortex is responsible for representing number and showed that it is especially active in certain numerical judgment tasks.

On the other hand, others argue that most of human knowledge could not be coded into our genes. This argument was strengthened with the realization in 2001 that a human has only 30,000 genes—only about one-third the number originally estimated. Moreover, more than 97% of these genes are generally believed to be shared with chimpanzees, which does not leave much for encoding

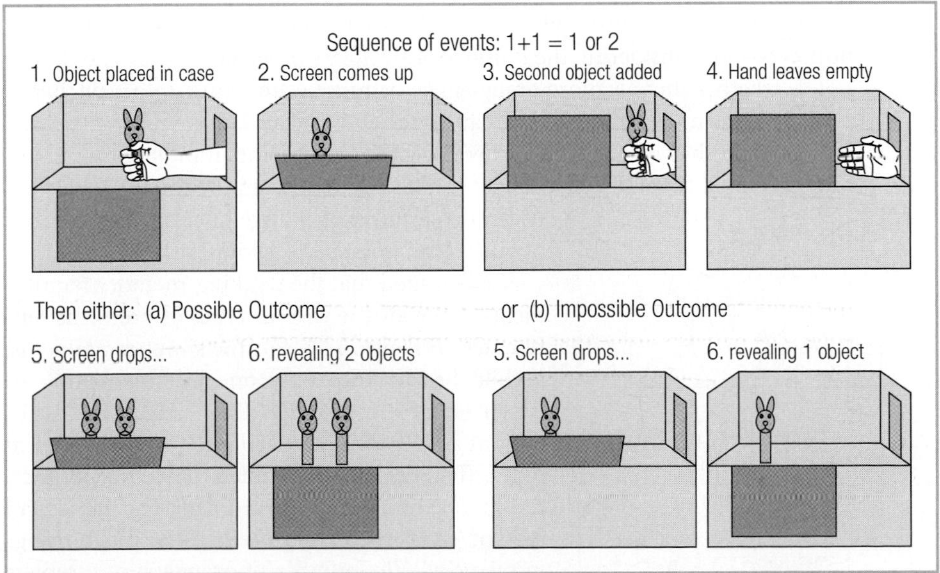

FIGURE 14.6 In Karen Wynn's experiment, she showed 5-month-old infants one or two dolls on a stage. Then she hid the dolls behind a screen and visibly removed or added one. When she lifted the screen out of the way, the infants would often stare longer when shown a wrong number of dolls.

the rich knowledge that is uniquely human. Elman et al. (1996), among other researchers, have argued that, although the basic mechanisms of human information processing are innately specified and these mechanisms enable human thought, most of the knowledge and structure of the mind must be acquired through experience.

There is considerable debate in cognitive science about the degree to which our basic knowledge is innate or acquired from experience.

Increased Mental Capacity

A number of developmental theories have proposed that there are basic cognitive capacities that increase from birth through the teenage years (Case, 1985; Fischer, 1980; Halford, 1982; Pascual-Leone, 1980). These theories are often called neo-Piagetian theories of development. Consider Case's memory-space proposal, which is that a growing working-memory capacity is the key to the developmental sequence. The basic idea is that more-advanced cognitive performance requires that more information be held in working memory.

An example of this analysis is Case's (1978) description of how children solve Noelting's (1975) juice problems. A child is given two empty pitchers, A and B, and is told that several tumblers of orange juice and tumblers of water will be poured into each pitcher. The child's task is to predict which pitcher will taste most strongly of orange juice. Figure 14.7 illustrates four stages of juice problems that children can solve at various ages. At the youngest age, children can reliably solve only problems where all orange juice goes into one pitcher and all water into another. At ages 4 to 5, they can count the number of tumblers of orange juice going into a pitcher and choose the pitcher that holds the larger number—not considering the number of tumblers of water. At ages 7 to 8, they notice whether there is more orange juice or more water going into a pitcher. If pitcher A has more orange juice than water and pitcher B has more water than orange juice, they will choose pitcher A even if the absolute number of glasses of orange juice is fewer. Finally, at age 9 or 10, children compute the difference between the amount of orange juice and the amount of water (still not a perfect solution).

FIGURE 14.7 The Noelting juice problem solved by children at various ages. The problem is to tell which pitcher will taste more strongly of orange juice after participants observe the tumblers of water and tumblers of juice that will be poured into each pitcher.

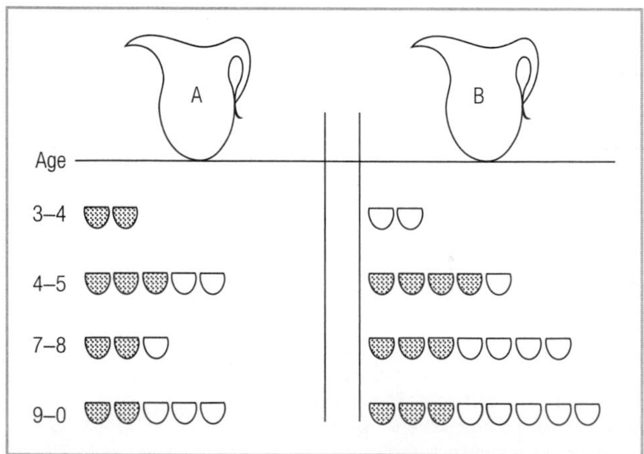

Case argued that the working-memory requirements differ for the various types of problems represented in Figure 14.7. For the simplest problems, a child has to keep only one fact in memory—which set of tumblers has the orange juice. Children at ages 3 to 4 can keep only one such fact in mind. If both sets of tumblers have orange juice, the child cannot solve the problem. For the second type of problem, a child needs to keep two things in memory—the number of orange juice tumblers in each array. In the third type of problem, a child needs to keep additional partial products in mind to determine which side has more orange juice than water. To solve the fourth type of problem, a child needs four facts to make a judgment:

1. The absolute difference in tumblers going into pitcher A
2. The sign of the difference for pitcher A (i.e., whether there is more water or more orange juice going into pitcher)
3. The absolute difference in tumblers going into pitcher B
4. The sign of the difference for pitcher B

Case argued that children's developmental sequences are controlled by their working-memory capacity for the problem. Only when they can keep four facts in memory will they achieve the fourth stage in the developmental sequence. Case's theory has been criticized (e.g., Flavell, 1978) because it is hard to decide how to count the working-memory requirements.

Another question concerns what controls the growth in working memory. Case argued that a major factor in the increase of working memory is increased speed of neural function. He cited the evidence that the degree of myelination increases with age, with spurts approximately at those points where he postulated major changes in working memory. On the other hand, he also argued that practice plays a significant role as well: With practice, we learn to perform our mental operations more efficiently, and so they do not require as much working-memory capacity.

The research of Kail (1988) can be viewed as consistent with the proposal that speed of mental operation is critical. This investigator looked at a number of cognitive tasks, including the mental rotation task examined in Chapter 4. He presented participants with pairs of letters in different orientations and asked them to judge whether the letters were the same or were mirror images of one another. As discussed in Chapter 4, participants tend to mentally rotate an image of one object into congruence with the other to make this judgment. Kail observed people, who ranged in age from 8 to 22, performing this task and found that they became systematically faster with age. He was interested in rotation rate, which he measured as the number of milliseconds to rotate one degree of angle. Figure 14.8 shows these data, plotting rate of rotation as a function of age. The time to rotate a degree of angle decreases as a function of age.

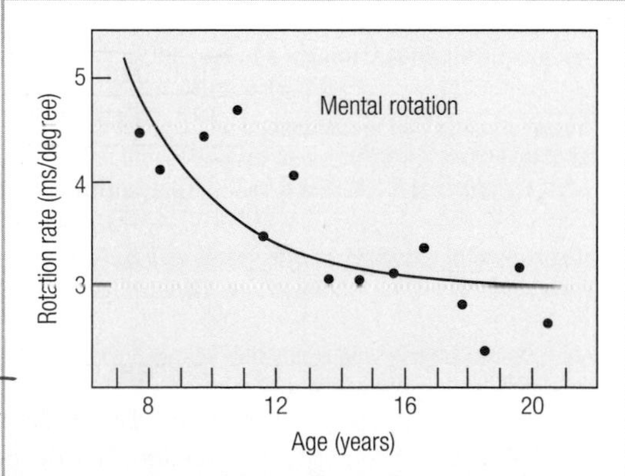

FIGURE 14.8 Rates of mental rotation, estimated from the slope of the function relating response time to the orientation of the stimulus. (Kail, 1988.)

In some of his writings, Kail argued that this result is evidence of an increase in basic mental speed as a function of age. However, an alternative hypothesis is that it reflects accumulating experience over the years at mental rotation. Kail and Park (1990) put this hypothesis to the test by giving 11-year-old children and adults more than 3,000 trials of practice at mental rotation. They found that both groups sped up but that adults started out faster. However, Kail and Park showed that all their data could be fit by a single power function that assumed that the adults came into the experiment with what amounted to an extra 1,800 trials of practice (Chapters 6 and 9 showed that learning curves

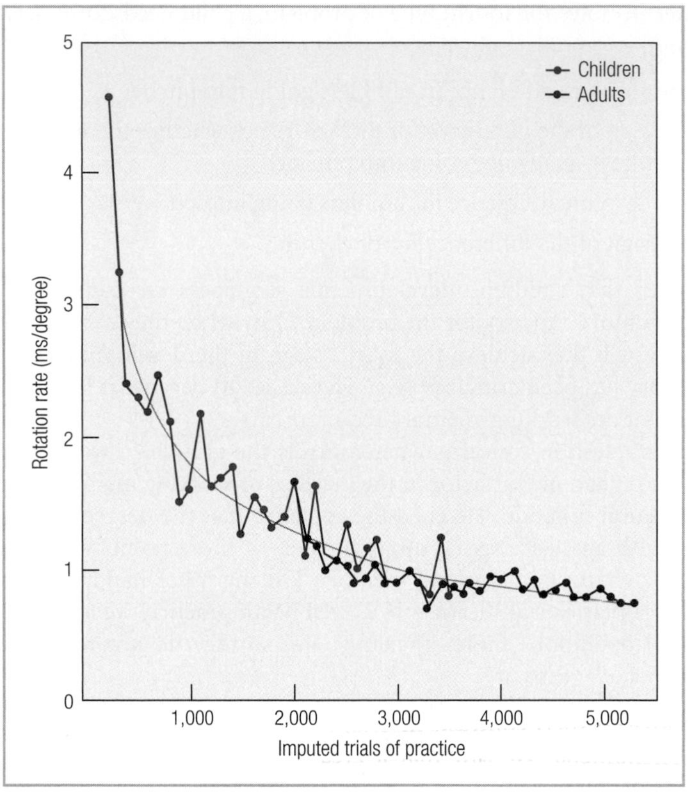

FIGURE 14.9 Data from Kail and Park (1990): Children and adults are on the same learning curve, but adults are advanced 1,800 trials.

tended to be fit by power functions). Figure 14.9 shows the resulting data, with the children's learning function superimposed on the adult's learning function. The practice curve for the children assumes that they start with about 150 trials of prior practice, and the practice curve for the adults assumes that they start with 1,950 trials of prior practice. However, after 3,000 trials of practice, children are a good bit faster than beginning adults. Thus, although the rate of information processing increases with development, this increase may have a practice-related rather than a biological explanation.

Qualitative and quantitative developmental changes take place in cognitive development because of increases both in working-memory capacity and in rate of information processing.

Increased Knowledge

Chi (1978) demonstrated that developmental differences may be knowledge related. Her domain of demonstration was memory. Not surprisingly, children do worse than adults on almost every memory task. Is their performance because their memories have less capacity or is it because they know less about what they are being asked to remember? To address this question, Chi compared the memory performance of 10-year-olds with that of adults on two tasks—a standard digit-span task and a chess memory task (see the discussion of these tasks in Chapters 6 and 9). The 10-year-olds were skilled chess players, whereas the adults were novices at chess. The chess task was the one discussed in Chapter 9 on page 258—a chessboard was presented for 10 s and then withdrawn, and participants were then asked to reproduce the chess pattern.

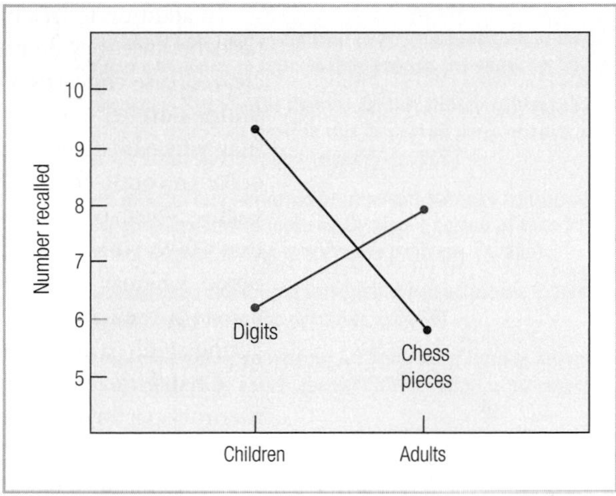

FIGURE 14.10 Number of chess pieces and number of digits recalled by children versus adults. (From Chi, 1978.)

Figure 14.10 illustrates the number of chess pieces recalled by children and adults. It also contrasts these results with the number of digits recalled in the digit-span task. As Chi predicted, the adults were better on the digit-span task, but the children were better on the chess task. The children's superior chess performance was attributed to their greater knowledge of chess. The adults' superior digit performance was due to their greater familiarity with digits—the dramatic digit-span performance of participant S. F. in Chapter 9 shows just how much digit knowledge can lead to improved memory performance.

The novice-expert contrasts in Chapter 9 are often used to explain developmental phenomena. We saw that a great deal of experience in a domain is required if a person is to become an expert. Chi's argument is that children, because of their lack of knowledge, are near universal novices, but they can become more expert than adults through concentrated experience in one domain, such as chess.

The Chi experiment contrasted child experts with adult novices. Schneider, Körkel, and Weinert (1988) looked at the effect of expertise at various age levels. They categorized German schoolchildren as either experts or novices with respect to soccer. They did so separately for grade levels 3, 5, and 7. The students at each grade level were asked to recall a story about soccer. Table 14.1 illustrates the amount of recall displayed as a function of grade level and expertise. The effect of expertise was much greater than that of grade level. On a recognition test, there was no effect of grade level, only an effect of expertise. They also classified each group of participants into high-ability and low-ability participants on the basis of their performance on intelligence tests. Although such tests generally predict memory for stories, Schneider et al. found no effect of general ability level, only of knowledge for soccer. They argue that high-ability students are just those who know a lot about a lot of domains and consequently generally do well on memory tests. However, when tested on a story about a specific domain such as soccer, a high-ability student who knows nothing about that domain will do worse than a low-ability student who knows a lot about the domain.

TABLE 14.1

Mean Percentages of Idea Units Recalled as a Function of Grade and Expertise

Grade	Soccer Experts	Soccer Novices
3	54	32
5	52	33
7	61	42

From Körkel (1987).

In addition to lack of relevant knowledge, children have difficulty on memory tasks because they do not know the strategies that lead to improved memory. The clearest case concerns rehearsal. If you were asked to dial a novel seven-digit telephone number, I would hope that you would rehearse it until you were confident that you had it memorized or until you had dialed the number. It would not occur to young children that they should rehearse the number. In one study comparing 5-year-olds with 10-year-olds, Keeney, Cannizzo, and Flavell (1967) found that 10-year-olds almost always verbally rehearsed a set of objects to be remembered, whereas 5-year-olds seldom did. Young children's performance often improves if they are instructed to follow a verbal rehearsal strategy, although very young children are simply unable to execute such a rehearsal strategy.

Chapter 6 emphasized the importance of elaborative strategies for good memory performance. Particularly for long-term retention, elaboration appears to be much more effective than rote rehearsal. There also appear to be sharp developmental trends with respect to the use of elaborative encoding strategies. For instance, Paris and Lindauer (1976) looked at the elaborations that children use to relate two paired-associates nouns such as lady and broom. Older children are more likely to generate interactive sentences such as *The lady flew on the broom* than static sentences such as *The lady had a broom.* Such interactive sentences will lead to better memory performance. Young children are also poorer at drawing the inferences that improve memory for a story (Stein & Trabasso, 1981).

- *Younger children often do worse on tasks than do older children, because they have less relevant knowledge and poorer strategies.*

Cognition and Aging

Changes in cognition do not cease when we reach adulthood. As we get older, we continue to learn more things, but human cognitive ability does not uniformly increase with added years, as we might expect if intelligence were only a matter of what one knows. Figure 14.11 shows data compiled by Salthouse (1992) on two components of the Wechsler Adult Intelligence Scale-Revised (WAIS-R). One component deals with verbal intelligence, which includes elements such as vocabulary and language comprehension. As you can see, this component maintains itself quite constantly through the years. In contrast, the performance component, which includes abilities such as reasoning and problem solving, decreases dramatically.

The importance of these declines in basic measures of cognitive ability can be easily exaggerated. Such tests are typically given rapidly, and older adults do better on slower tests. Additionally, such tests tend to be like school tests, and young adults have had more recent experience with such tests. When it comes to relevant job-related behavior, older adults often do better than younger adults (e.g., Perlmutter, Kaplan, & Nyquist, 1990), owing both to their greater accumulation of knowledge and to a more mature approach to job demands. There is also evidence that previous generations did not do as well on tests even

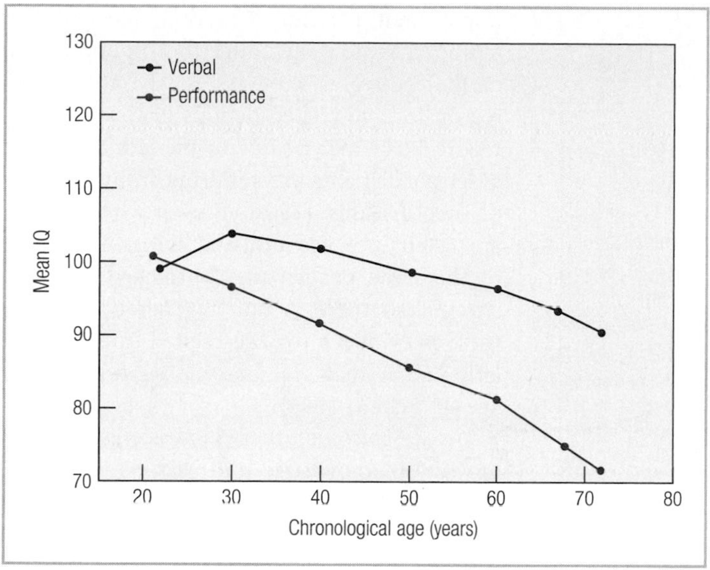

FIGURE 14.11 Mean verbal and performance IQs from the WAIS-R standardization sample as a function of age. (From Salthouse, 1992. Reprinted by permission from LEA, Inc.)

when they were young. This is the so-call "Flynn effect"—IQ scores appear to have risen about 3 points per decade (Flynn, 1987). The comparisons in Figure 14.11 are not only of people of different ages but also of people who grew up in different periods. Some of the apparent decline in the figure might be due to differences among generations (education, nutrition, etc.) and not age-related factors.

Although non-age-related factors may explain some of the decline shown in Figure 14.9, there are substantial age-related declines in brain function. Brain cells gradually die. Some areas are particularly susceptible to cell death. The hippocampus, which is particularly important to memory (see Chapter 7), loses about 5% of its cells every decade (Selkoe, 1992). Other cells, though they might not die, have been observed to shrink and atrophy. On the other hand, there is some evidence for compensatory growth: Cells remaining in the hippocampus will grow to compensate for the age-related deaths of their neighbors. There is also increasing evidence for the birth of new neurons, particularly in the region of the hippocampus (E. Gould & Gross, 2002). Moreover, the number of new neurons seems to be very much related to the richness of a person's experience. Although these new neurons are few in number compared with the number lost, they may be very valuable because new neurons are more plastic and may be critical to encoding new experiences.

Although there are age-related neural losses, they may be relatively minor in most intellectually active adults. The real problem concerns the intellectual deficits associated with various brain-related disorders. The most common of these disorders is Alzheimer's disease, which is associated with substantial

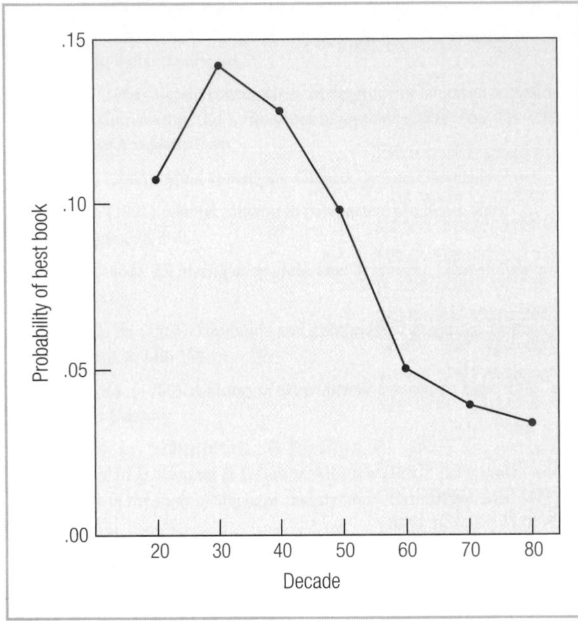

FIGURE 14.12 Probability that a particular book will become a philosopher's best as a function of the age at which the philosopher wrote the book. (Adapted from Lehman, 1953.)

impairment of brain function, particularly in the temporal region including the hippocampus. Many of these diseases progress slowly, and some of the reason for age-related deficits in tests such as that of Figure 14.11 may be due to the fact that some of the older participants are suffering from the early stages of such diseases. However, even when health factors are taken into account and when the performance of the same participants is tracked in longitudinal studies (so there is not a generational confound), there is evidence for age-related intellectual decline, although it may not become significant until after age 60 (Schaie, 1996).

As we get older, there is a race going on between growth in knowledge and loss of neural function. People in many professions (artists, scientists, philosophers) tend to produce their best work in their mid-thirties. Figure 14.12 shows some interesting data from Lehman (1953). He examined the works of 182 famous deceased philosophers who collectively wrote some 1,785 books. Figure 14.12 plots the probability that a book was considered that philosopher's best book as a function of the age at which it was written. These philosophers remained prolific, publishing many books in their seventies. However, as Figure 14.12 displays, a book written in this decade is unlikely to be considered a philosopher's best.[1] Lehman reviewed data from a number of fields consistent with the hypothesis that the thirties tend to be the time of peak intellectual performance. However, as Figure 14.12 shows, people often maintain relatively high intellectual performance into their forties and fifties.

The evidence for an age-related correlation between brain function and cognition makes it clear that there is a contribution of biology to intelligence that knowledge cannot always overcome. Salthouse (1992) argued that, in information-processing terms, people lose their ability to hold information in working memory with age. He contrasted participants of different ages on the reasoning problems presented in Figure 14.13. These problems differ in the number of premises that need to be combined to come to a particular solution. Figure 14.13 shows how people at various ages perform in these tasks. As can be seen, people's ability to solve these problems generally declines with the number of premises that need to be combined. However, this drop-off is much steeper for older adults. Salthouse argued that older adults are slower than younger adults in information processing, which inhibits their ability to maintain information in working memory.

[1] It is important to note that this graph denotes the probability of a specific book being the best, and so the outcome is not an artifact of the number of books written during a decade.

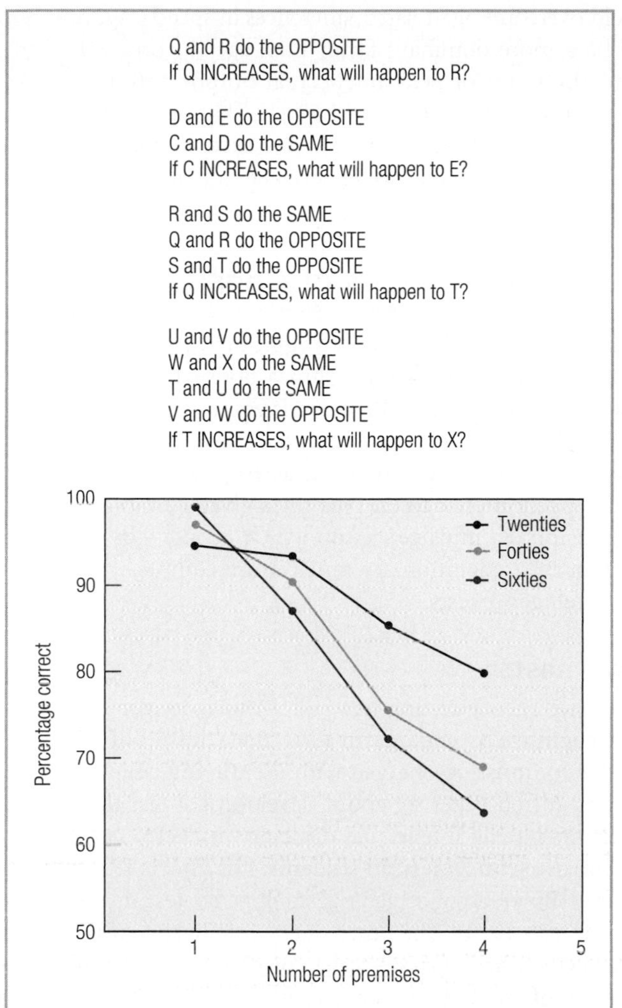

Q and R do the OPPOSITE
If Q INCREASES, what will happen to R?
D and E do the OPPOSITE
C and D do the SAME
If C INCREASES, what will happen to E?
R and S do the SAME
Q and R do the OPPOSITE
S and T do the OPPOSITE
If Q INCREASES, what will happen to T?
U and V do the OPPOSITE
W and X do the SAME
T and U do the SAME
V and W do the OPPOSITE
If T INCREASES, what will happen to X?
100
90
80
70
60
50
Percentage correct
1
2
3
4
5
Number of premises
Twenties
Forties
Sixties

FIGURE 14.13 Illustration of integrative reasoning trials hypothesized to vary in working-memory demands (top), and mean performance of adults in their twenties, forties, and sixties with each trial type (bottom).

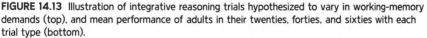

Increased knowledge and maturity sometimes compensate for age-related declines in rates of information processing.

Summary for Cognitive Development

With respect to the nature-versus-nurture issue, the developmental data paint a mixed picture. A person's brain is probably at its best physically in the early twenties, and intellectual capacity tends to follow brain function. The relation seems particularly strong in the early years of childhood. However, we saw evidence that practice could overcome age-related differences in speed (Figure 14.9), and knowledge could be a more dominant factor than age (Figure 14.10 and Table 14.1). Additionally, the point of peak intellectual output appears to take place later than in a person's twenties (Figure 14.12), indicating the need for accumulated knowledge. As discussed in Chapter 9, truly exceptional performance in a field tends to require at least 10 years of experience in that field.

Psychometric Studies of Cognition

We now turn from considering how cognition varies as a function of age to considering how cognition varies within a population of a fixed age. All this research has basically the same character. It entails measuring the performances of various people on a number of tasks and then looking at the way in which these performance measures correlate across different tests. Such tests are referred to as **psychometric tests.** This research has established that there is not a single dimension of "intelligence" on which people vary but rather that individual differences in cognition are much more complex. We will first examine research on intelligence tests.

Intelligence Tests

Research on intelligence testing has had a much longer sustained intellectual history than cognitive psychology. In 1904, the Minister of Public Instruction in Paris named a commission charged with identifying children in need of remedial education. Alfred Binet set about developing a test that would objectively identify students having intellectual difficulty. In 1916, Lewis Terman adapted Binet's test for use with American students. His efforts led to the development of the Stanford-Binet, a major general intelligence test in use in America today (Terman & Merrill, 1973). The other major intelligence test used in America is the Wechsler, which has separate scales for children and adults. These tests include measures of digit span, vocabulary, analogical reasoning, spatial judgment, and arithmetic. A typical question for adults on the Stanford-Binet is, "Which direction would you have to face so your right hand would be to the north?" A great deal of effort goes into selecting test items that will predict scholastic performance.

Both of these tests produce measures that are called **intelligence quotients (IQs).** The original definition of IQ relates mental age to chronological age. The test establishes one's mental age. If a child can solve problems on the test that the average 8-year-old can solve, then the child has a mental age of 8 independent of chronological age. IQ is defined as the ratio of mental age to chronological age multiplied by 100 or

$$IQ = 100 \times MA/CA$$

where MA is mental age and CA is chronological age. Thus, if a child's mental age were 6 and chronological age were 5, the IQ would be $100 \times 6/5 = 120$.

This definition of IQ proved unsuitable for a number of reasons. It cannot extend to measurement of adult intelligence, because performance on intelligence tests starts to level off in the late teens and declines in later years. To deal with such difficulties, the common way of defining IQ now is in terms of deviation scores. A person's raw score is subtracted from the mean score for that person's age group, and then this difference is transformed into a measure that will vary around 100, roughly as the earlier IQ scores would. The precise definition is expressed as

$$\text{IQ} = 100 + 15 \times \frac{(\text{score} - \text{mean})}{\text{standard deviation}}$$

where standard deviation is a measure of the variability of the scores. IQs so measured tend to be distributed according to a normal distribution. Figure 14.14 shows such a normal distribution of intelligence scores and the percentage of people who have scores in various ranges.

Whereas the Stanford-Binet and the Weschler are general intelligence tests, many others were developed to test specialized abilities, such as spatial ability. These tests partly owe their continued use in the United States to the fact that they do predict performance in school with some accuracy, which was one of Binet's original goals. However, their use for this purpose is controversial. In particular, because such tests can be used to determine who can have access to what educational opportunities, there is a great deal of concern that they should be constructed so as to prevent biases against certain cultural groups. Immigrants often do poorly on tests of intelligence because of cultural biases on the tests. For instance, immigrant Italians of less than a century ago scored an average of 87 on IQ tests (Sarason & Doris, 1979), whereas today their descendants have slightly above average IQs (Ceci, 1991).

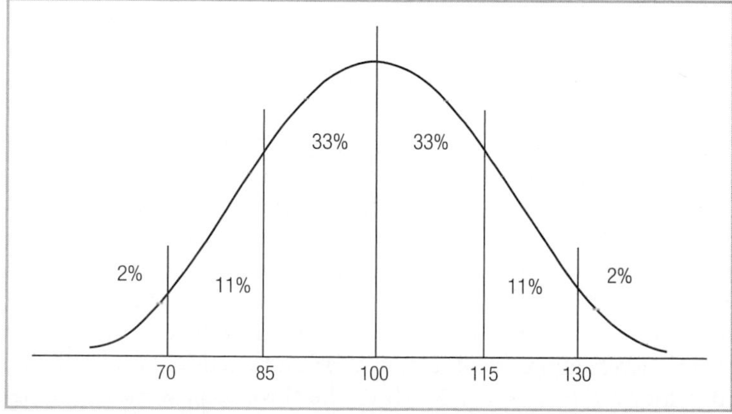

FIGURE 14.14 A normal distribution of IQ measures.

The very concept of intelligence is culturally relative. What one culture values as intelligent another culture will not. For instance, the Kpelle, an African culture, think that the way in which Westerners sort instances into categories (for instance, sorting apples and oranges into the same category—a basis for some items in intelligence tests) is foolish (Cole, Gay, Glick, & Sharp, 1971). Robert Sternberg (personal communication) notes that some cultures do not even have a word for intelligence. Still, the fact remains that intelligence tests do predict performance in our (Western) schools. Whether they are doing a valuable service in assessing students for schools or are simply enforcing arbitrary cultural beliefs about what is to be valued is a difficult question.

Related to the issue of the fairness of intelligence tests is whether they measure innate endowment or acquired ability (the nature-versus-nurture issue again). Potentially definitive data would seem to come from studies of identical twins reared apart. Sometimes such twins have been adopted into different families—they have identical genetic endowment but different environmental experiences. The research on this topic is controversial (Kamin, 1974), but analyses (Bouchard, 1983; Bouchard & McGue, 1981) indicate that identical twins raised apart have IQs much more similar to each other than do nonidentical fraternal twins raised in the same family. This evidence seems to indicate the existence of a strong innate component of IQ. Yet drawing the conclusion that intelligence is largely innate would be a mistake. Intelligence and IQ are by no means the same thing. Because of the goals of intelligence tests, they must predict success across a range of environments, particularly academic. Thus they must discount the contributions of specific experiences to intelligence. As noted in Chapter 9, for instance, chess masters tend not to have particularly high IQs. This tendency is more a comment on the IQ test than on chess masters. If an IQ test focused on chess experience, it would have little success in predicting academic success generally. Thus, intelligence tests try to measure raw abilities and general knowledge that are reasonably expected of everyone in a culture. However, as we saw in Chapter 9, excellence in any specific domain depends on knowledge and experience that are not general in the culture.

Another interesting demonstration of this lack of correlation between expertise and IQ was performed by Ceci and Liker (1986). These researchers looked at the ability of avid horse-racing fans to handicap races. They found that handicapping skill is related to the development of a complex interactive model of horse racing but that there was no relation between this skill and IQ.

Although specific experience is clearly important to success in any field, the remarkable fact is that these intelligence tests are able to predict success in certain endeavors. They predict with modest accuracy both performance in school and general success in life (or at least in Western societies). What is it about the mind that they are measuring? Much of the theoretical work in the field has been concerned with trying to answer this question. To understand how this question has been pursued, one must understand a little about a major method of the field, factor analysis.

Implications

Does IQ determine success in life?

IQ appears to have a strong predictive relationship to many socially relevant factors besides academic performance. The American Psychological Report *Intelligence: Knowns and Unknowns* (Neisser et al., 1996) states that IQ accounts for about one-fifth of the variance (positive correlations in the range of .3 to .5) in factors like job performance and income. It has an even stronger relationship to socioeconomic status. There are weaker negative correlations with antisocial measures like criminal activity.

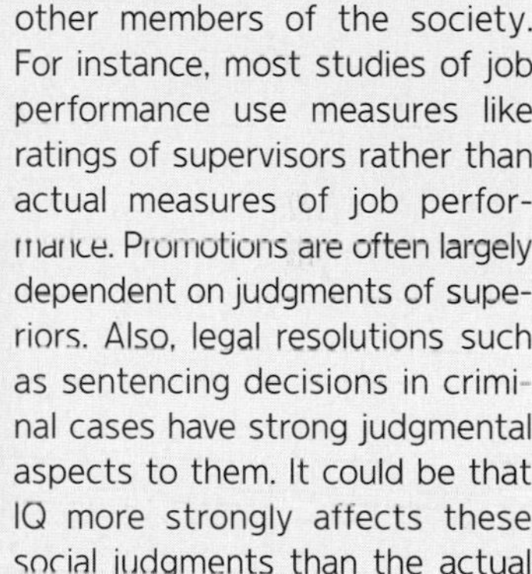

There is a natural tendency to infer from this that IQ is directly related to being a successful member of our society, but there are reasons to question a direct relationship. Access to various educational opportunities and to some jobs depends on test scores. Access to other professions depends on completing various educational programs, the access to which is partly determined by test scores. Given the strong relationship between IQ and these test scores, we would expect that higher-IQ members of our society would get better training and professional opportunities. Lower-scoring members of our society have more limited opportunities and often are sorted by their test scores into environments where there is more antisocial behavior.

Another confounding factor is that success in society is at every point determined by judgments of other members of the society. For instance, most studies of job performance use measures like ratings of supervisors rather than actual measures of job performance. Promotions are often largely dependent on judgments of superiors. Also, legal resolutions such as sentencing decisions in criminal cases have strong judgmental aspects to them. It could be that IQ more strongly affects these social judgments than the actual performances being judged such as how well one does one's job or how bad a particular activity was. Individuals in positions of power, such as judges and supervisors, tend to have high IQs. Thus, there is the possibility that some of the success associated with high IQ is an in-group effect where high-IQ people favor people who are like them.

- *Standard intelligence tests measure general factors that predict success in school.*

Factor Analysis

The general intelligence tests contain a number of subtests that measure individual abilities. As already noted, many specialized tests also are available for measuring particular abilities. The basic observation is that people who do well on one test or subtest tend to do well on another test or subtest. The degree to which people perform comparably on two subtests is measured by a correlation coefficient. If all the same people who did well on one test did just as well on another, the correlation between the two tests would be 1. If all the people who did well on one test did proportionately badly on another, the correlation coefficient would be −1. If there were no relation between how people did on one test and how they did on another test, the correlation coefficient would be zero.

TABLE 14.2

Description of Some of the Tests on the Washington Pre-College Test Battery

Test Name	Description
1. Reading comprehension	Answer questions about paragraph
2. Vocabulary	Choose synonyms for a word
3. Grammar	Identify correct and poor usage
4. Quantitative skills	Read word problems and decide whether problem can be solved
5. Mechanical reasoning	Examine a diagram and answer questions about it; requires knowledge of physical and mechanical principles
6. Spatial reasoning	Indicate how two-dimensional figures will appear if they are folded through a third dimension
7. Mathematics achievement	A test of high school algebra

From Hunt (1985).

Typical correlations between tests are positive, but not 1, indicating a less than perfect relation between performance on one test and on another.

For example, Hunt (1985) looked at the relations among the seven tests described in Table 14.2. Table 14.3 shows the intercorrelations among these test scores. As can be seen, some pairs of tests are more correlated than others. For instance, there is a relatively high (.67) correlation between reading comprehension and vocabulary but a relatively low (.14) correlation between reading comprehension and spatial reasoning. **Factor analysis** is a way of trying to make sense of these correlational patterns. The basic idea is to try to arrange these tests in a multidimensional space such that the distances among the tests correspond to their correlation. Tests close together will have high correlations and so measure the same thing. Figure 14.15 shows an attempt to organize the tests in Table 14.2 into a two-dimensional area. The reader can confirm that

TABLE 14.3

Intercorrelations Between Results of the Tests Listed in Table 14.2

Test No.	1	2	3	4	5	6	7
1	1.00	.67	.63	.40	.33	.14	.34
2		1.00	.59	.29	.46	.19	.31
3			1.00	.41	.34	.20	.46
4				1.00	.39	.46	.62
5					1.00	.47	.39
6						1.00	.46
7							1.00

From Hunt (1985).

the closer the tests are in this space, the higher their correlation in Table 14.3.

An interesting question is how to make sense of this space. As we go from the bottom to the top, the tests become increasingly symbolic and linguistic. We might refer to this dimension as a linguistic factor. Second, we might argue that, as we go from the left to the right, the tests become more computational in character. We might consider this dimension a reasoning factor. High correlations can be explained in terms of students having similar values of these factors. Thus, there is a high correlation between quantitative skills and mathematics achievement because they both have an intermediate degree of linguistic involvement and require substantial reasoning. People who have strong reasoning ability and average or better verbal ability will tend to do well on these tests.

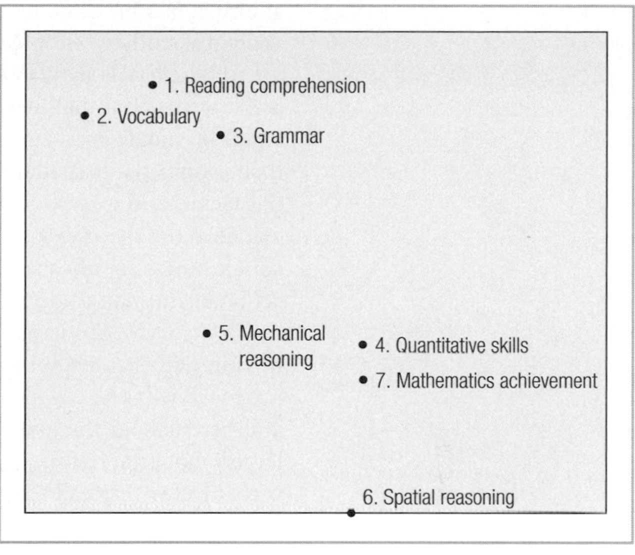

FIGURE 14.15 A two-dimensional representation of the tests in Table 14.2. The distance between points decreases with increases in the intercorrelations in Table 14.3.

Factor analysis is basically an effort to go from a set of intercorrelations like those in Table 14.3 to a small set of factors or dimensions that explain those intercorrelations. There has been considerable debate about what the underlying factors are. Perhaps you can see other ways to explain the correlations in Table 14.3. For instance, you might argue that a linguistic factor links tests 1 through 3, a reasoning factor links tests 4, 5, and 7, and there is a separate spatial factor for test 6. Indeed, we will see that there have been many proposals for separate linguistic, reasoning, and spatial factors, although, as shown by the data in Table 14.3, it is a little difficult to separate the spatial and reasoning factors.

The difficulty in interpreting such data is manifested in the wide variety of positions that have been taken about what the underlying factors of human intelligence are. Spearman (1904) argued that only one general factor underlies performance across tests. He called his factor g. In contrast, Thurstone (1938) argued that there are a number of separate factors, including verbal, spatial, and reasoning. Guilford (1982) proposed no less than 120 distinct intellectual abilities. Cattell (1963) proposed a distinction between fluid and crystallized intelligence; **crystallized intelligence** refers to acquired knowledge, whereas **fluid intelligence** refers to the ability to reason or to solve problems in novel domains. (In Figure 14.11, fluid intelligence, not crystallized intelligence, shows the age-related decay.) Horn (1968), elaborating on Cattell's theory, argued that there is a spatial intelligence that can be separated from fluid intelligence. Table 14.3 can be interpreted in terms of the Horn-Cattell theory, where crystallized intelligence maps into the linguistic factor (tests 1 to 3), fluid intelligence into the reasoning factor (tests 4, 5, and 7), and spatial intelligence into the spatial factor (test 6). Fluid intelligence tends to be tapped strongly in mathematical tests, but it is probably better referred to as a reasoning ability rather than a mathematical ability. It is a bit difficult to separate the fluid and spatial intelligences in factor analytical studies, but it appears possible (Horn & Stankov, 1982).

Although it is hard to draw any firm conclusions about what the real factors are, it seems clear that there is some differentiation in human intelligence as measured by intelligence tests. Probably, the Horn-Cattell theory or the Thurstone theory offer the best analyses, producing what we will call a verbal factor, a spatial factor, and a reasoning factor. The rest of this chapter will provide further evidence for the division of the human intellect into these three abilities. This conclusion is significant because it indicates that there is some specialization in achieving human cognitive function.

In a survey of virtually all data sets, Carroll (1993) proposed a theory of intelligence that combines the Horn-Cattell and Thurstone perspectives. He proposed what he called a three-strata theory. At the lowest stratum are specific abilities such as the ability to be a physicist. Such abilities Carroll thinks are largely not inheritable. At the next stratum are broader abilities such as the verbal factor (crystallized intelligence), the reasoning factor (fluid intelligence), and the spatial factor. Finally, Carroll noted that these factors tend to correlate together to define something like Spearman's g at the highest stratum.

In the past few decades, there has been considerable interest in the way in which these measures of individual differences relate to the kinds of theories of information processing that are found in cognitive psychology. For instance, how do participants with high spatial abilities differ from those with low spatial abilities in the processes entailed in the spatial imagery tasks discussed in Chapter 4? Makers of intelligence tests have tended to ignore such questions because their major goal is to predict scholastic performance. We will look at some information-processing studies that try to understand the reasoning factor, the verbal factor, and the spatial factor.

Factor-analysis methods identify that a reasoning ability, a verbal ability, and a spatial ability underlie performance on various intelligence tests.

Reasoning Ability

Typical tests used to measure reasoning include mathematical problems, analogy problems, series extrapolation problems, deductive syllogisms, and problem-solving tasks. These tasks are the kinds analyzed in great detail in Chapters 8 through 10. In the context of this book, such abilities might better be called problem-solving abilities. Most of the research in psychometric tests has focused only on whether a person gets a question right or not. In contrast, information-processing analyses try to examine the steps by which a person decides on an answer to such a question and the time necessary to perform each step.

The research of Sternberg (1977; Sternberg & Gardner, 1983) is an attempt to connect the psychometric research tradition with the information-processing tradition. He analyzed how people process a wide variety of reasoning problems. Figure 14.16 illustrates one of his analogy problems. Participants were asked to solve the analogy "A is to B as C is to D_1 or D_2?" Sternberg analyzed the process of making such analogies into a number of stages. Two critical stages in

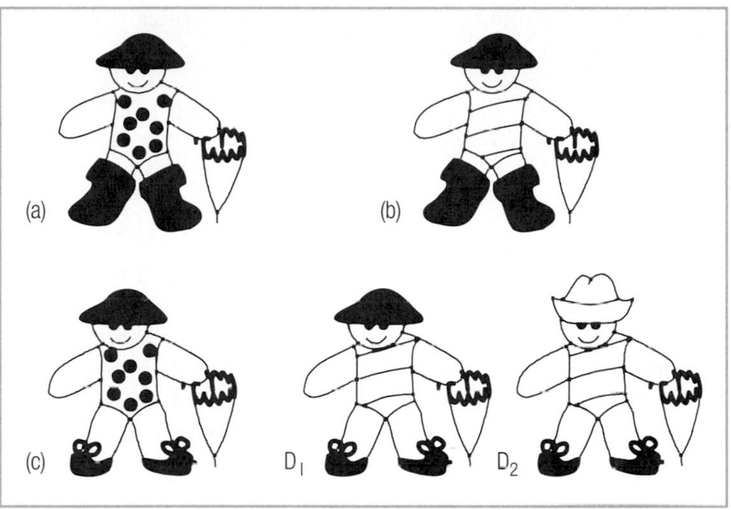

FIGURE 14.16 An example of an analogy problem used by Sternberg and Gardner (1983). (Copyright © 1983 by the APA. Adapted by permission.)

his analysis are called reasoning and comparison. Reasoning requires finding each feature that changes between A and B and applying it to C. In Figure 14.16, A and B differ by a change in costume from spotted to striped. Thus, one predicts that C will change from spotted to striped to yield D. Comparison requires comparing the two choices, D_1 and D_2; D_1 and D_2 are compared feature by feature until a feature is found that enables a choice. Thus, a participant may first check that both D_1 and D_2 have an umbrella (which they do), then that both wear a striped suit (which they do), and then that both have a dark hat (which only D_1 has). The dark hat feature will allow the participant to reject D_2 and accept D_1.

Sternberg was interested in the time that participants needed to make these judgments. He theorized that they would take a certain amount longer for each feature in which A differed from B because this feature would have to be changed to derive D from C. Sternberg and Gardner (1983) estimated a time of 0.28 s for each such feature. This length of time is the *reasoning parameter.* They also estimated 0.60 seconds to compare a feature predicted of D with the features of D_1 and D_2. This length of time is the *comparison parameter.* The values 0.28 and 0.60 are just averages; the actual values of these reasoning and comparison times varied across participants. Sternberg and Gardner looked at the correlations between the values of these parameters for individual participants and the psychometric measures of participants' reasoning abilities. They found a correlation of .79 between the reasoning parameter and a psychometric measure of reasoning and a correlation of .75 between the comparison parameter and the psychometric measure. These correlations mean that participants who are slow in reasoning or comparison do poorly in psychometric tests of reasoning. Thus, Sternberg and Gardner were able to show that measures of speed identified in an information-processing analysis are critical to psychometric measures of intelligence.

- *Participants who score high on reasoning ability are able to perform individual steps of reasoning rapidly.*

Verbal Ability

Probably the most robust factor to emerge from intelligence tests is the verbal factor. There has been considerable interest in determining what processes distinguish people with strong verbal abilities. Goldberg, Schwartz, and Stewart (1977) compared people with high verbal ability those with low verbal ability with respect to the way in which they make various kinds of word judgments. One kind of word judgment concerned simply whether pairs of words were identical. Thus, participants would say yes to a pair such as

- bear, bear

Other participants were asked to judge whether pairs of words sounded alike. Thus, they would say yes to a pair such as

- bare, bear

A third group of participants were asked to judge whether pairs of words were in the same category. Thus, they would say yes to a pair such as

- lion, bear

Figure 14.17 shows the difference in time taken to make these three judgments between participants with high verbal abilities and those with low verbal abilities. As can be seen, participants with high verbal ability enjoy only a small advantage on the identity judgments but show much larger advantages on the sound and meaning matches. This study and others (e.g., Hunt, Davidson, & Lansman, 1981) have convinced researchers that a major advantage of participants with high verbal ability is the speed with which they can go from a linguistic stimulus to information about it—in the study depicted in Figure 14.17 participants were going from the visual word to information about its sound and meaning. Thus, as in the Sternberg studies in the preceding subsection, speed of processing is related to intellectual ability.

There is also evidence for a fairly strong relation between working-memory capacity for linguistic material and verbal ability. Daneman and Carpenter (1980) developed the following test of individual differences in working-memory capacity. Participants would read or hear a number of unrelated sentences such as

- When at last his eyes opened, there was no gleam of triumph, no shade of anger.
- The taxi turned up Michigan Avenue where they had a clear view of the lake.

After reading or hearing these sentences, participants had to recall the last word of each sentence. They were tested on groups ranging from two to seven

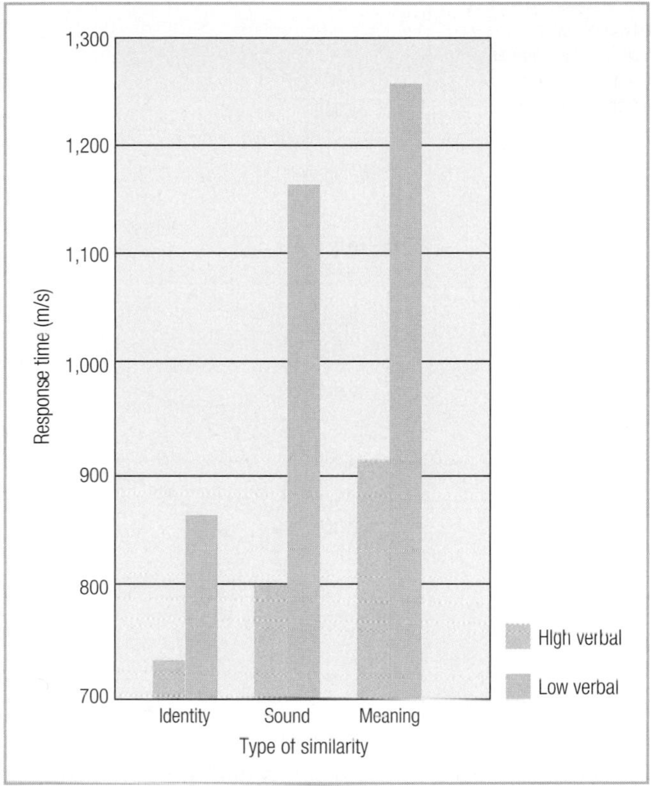

FIGURE 14.17 Response time of participants having high verbal abilities compared with those having low verbal abilities in judging the similarity of pairs of words as a function of three types of similarity. (From Goldberg, Schwartz, & Stewart, 1977.)

such sentences. The largest group of sentences for which they could recall the last words was defined as the reading span or listening span. College students had spans from 2 to 5.5 sentences. It turns out that these spans are very strongly related to their comprehension scores and to tests of verbal ability. These reading and listening spans are much more strongly related than are measures of simple digit span. Daneman and Carpenter argued that a larger reading and listening span indicates the ability to store a larger part of the text during comprehension.

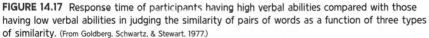

- *People of high verbal ability are able to rapidly retrieve meanings of words and have large working memories for verbal information.*

Spatial Ability

Efforts have been made to relate measures of spatial ability to research on mental rotation, such as that discussed in Chapter 4. Just and Carpenter (1985)

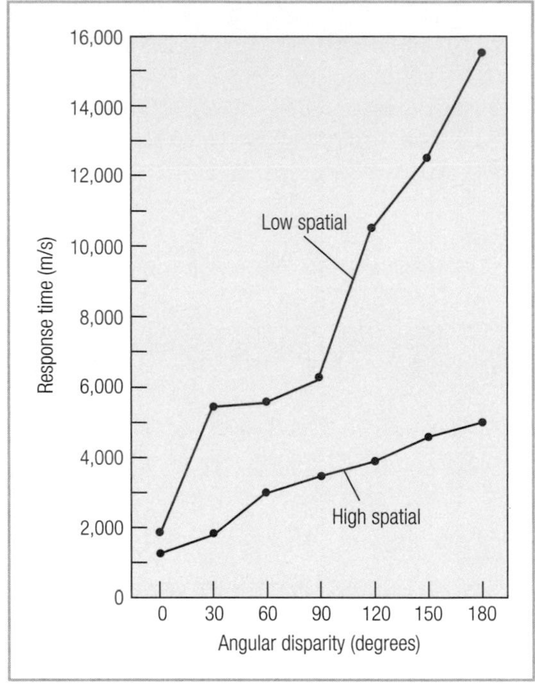

FIGURE 14.18 Mean time taken to determine that two objects have the same three-dimensional shape as a function of the angular difference in their portrayed orientations. Separate functions are plotted for participants with high spatial ability and those with low spatial ability. (From Just & Carpenter, 1985. Copyright © 1985 by the APA. Adapted by permission.)

compared participants with low spatial ability and those with high spatial ability performing the Shepard and Metzler mental rotation tasks (see Figure 4.4). Figure 14.18 plots the speed with which these two types of participants can rotate figures of differing angular disparity. As can be seen, participants with low spatial ability not only performed the task more slowly but were also more affected by angle of disparity. Thus the rate of mental rotation is lower for participants with low spatial ability.

Spatial ability has often been set in contrast with verbal ability. Although some people rate high on both abilities or low on both, interest often focuses on people who display a relative imbalance of the abilities. MacLeod, Hunt, and Matthews (1978) found evidence that these different types of people will solve a cognitive task differently. They looked at performance on the Clark and Chase sentence-verification task considered in Chapter 13. Recall that, in this task, participants are presented with sentences such as *The plus is above the star* or *The star is not above the plus* and asked to determine whether the sentence accurately describes the picture. Typically, participants are slower when there is a negative such as *not* in the sentence and when the supposition of the sentences mismatches the picture.

MacLeod et al. speculated, however, that there were really two groups of participants—those who took a representation of the sentence and matched it against a picture and those who first converted the sentence into an image of a picture and then matched that image against the picture. They speculated that the first group would be high in verbal ability, whereas the second group would be high in spatial ability. In fact, they did find two groups of participants. Figure 14.19 shows the judgment times of these two groups as a function of whether the sentence was true and whether it contained a negative. As can be seen, one group of participants showed no effect of whether the sentence contained a negative, whereas the other group showed a very substantial effect. The group of participants not showing the effect of a negative had higher scores on tests of spatial ability than those of the other group. The group not showing the effect was the group of participants who compared an image formed from the sentence against the picture. Such an image would not have a negative in it.

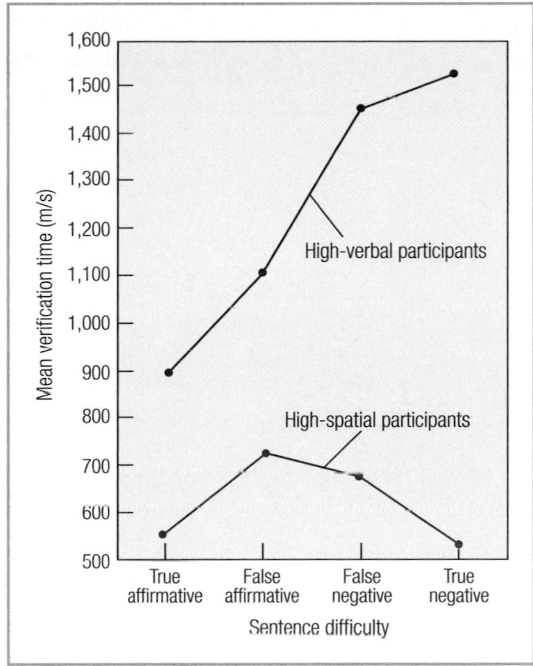

FIGURE 14.19 Mean time taken to judge a sentence as a function of sentence type for participants with high verbal ability compared with those with high spatial ability. (From MacLeod, Hunt, & Mathews, 1978.)

Reichle, Carpenter, and Just (2000) performed an fMRI brain-imaging study of the regions activated in these two strategies. They explicitly instructed participants to use either an imagery strategy or a verbal strategy to solve these problems. The participants instructed to use the imagery strategy were told:

> Carefully read each sentence and form a mental picture of the objects in the sentence and their arrangement. . . . After the picture appears, compare the picture to your mental image. (p. 268)

On the other hand, participants told to use the verbal strategy were told:

> Don't try to form a mental image of the objects in the sentence, but instead look at the sentence only long enough to remember it until the picture is presented. . . . After the picture appears, decide whether or not the sentence that you are remembering describes the picture. (p. 268)

They found that parietal regions associated with mental imagery tended to be activated in participants who were told to use the imagery strategy (see Figure 4.1), whereas regions associated with verbal processing tended to be activated in participants given the verbal strategy (see Figure 11.1). Interestingly, when told to use the imagery strategy, participants who had lower imagery ability showed greater activation in their imagery areas. Conversely, when told to use the verbal strategy, participants with lower verbal ability tended to show greater activation in their verbal regions. Thus, participants apparently have to engage in more neural effort when they are required to use their less favored strategy.

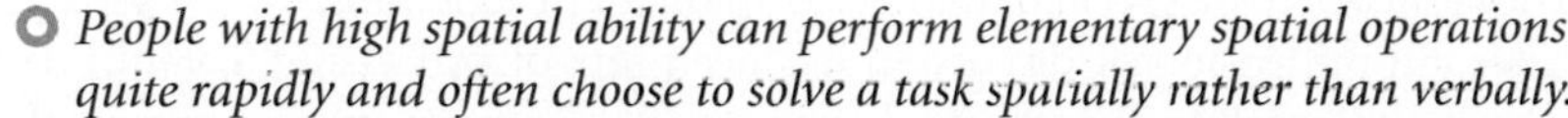

People with high spatial ability can perform elementary spatial operations quite rapidly and often choose to solve a task spatially rather than verbally.

Conclusions from Psychometric Studies

A major outcome of the research relating psychometric measures to cognitive tasks is to reinforce the distinction between verbal and spatial ability. A second conclusion of this research is that differences in an ability (reasoning, linguistic, or spatial) may result from differences in rates of processing and working-memory capacities. A number of researchers (e.g., Salthouse, 1992; Just & Carpenter, 1992) have argued that the working-memory differences may result from differences in processing speed, in that people can maintain more information in working memory when they can process it more rapidly.

As already mentioned, Reichle et al. (2000) suggested that more-able participants can solve problems with less expenditure of effort. An early study confirming this general relation was performed by Haier et al. (1988). These researchers looked at PET recordings taken during an abstract-reasoning task. They found that the better-performing participants showed less PET activity, again indicating that poorer-performing participants have to work harder at the same task. Like the information-processing work pointing to processing speed, this finding suggests that differences in intelligence may correspond to very basic processes. There is a tendency to see such results as favoring a nativist view, but in fact they are neutral to the nature-versus-nurture controversy. Some people may take longer and may need to expand more effort to solve a problem, either because they have practiced less or because they have inherently less efficient neural structures. We saw earlier in the chapter that, with practice, children could become faster than adults at processes such as mental rotation. Figure 9.1 illustrated how the activity of the brain decreases as participants become more practiced and faster at a task.

- *Individual differences in general factors such as verbal, reasoning, and spatial abilities appear to correspond to the speed and ease with which basic cognitive processes are performed.*

Conclusions

This concludes our consideration of human intelligence (this chapter) and human cognition (this book). A recurring theme throughout the book has been the diversity of the components of the mind. The first chapter reviewed evidence for different specializations in the nervous system. The early chapters reviewed the evidence for different levels of processing as the information entered the system. The different types of knowledge representation and the distinction between procedural and declarative knowledge were presented. Then, we considered the distinct status of language. Many of these distinctions have been reinforced in this chapter on individual differences. Throughout this book, different brain regions have been shown to be specialized to perform different functions.

A second dimension of discussion has been rate of processing. Latency data have been the most frequently used measure of cognitive functioning in this book. Often, error measures (the second most common dependent measure) were shown to be merely indications of slow processing. We have seen evidence in this chapter that individuals vary in their rate of processing, and this book has stressed that this rate can be increased with practice. Interestingly, the neuroscience evidence tends to associate faster processing with lower metabolic expenditure. The more efficient mind seems to perform its tasks faster and at less cost.

In addition to the quantitative component of speed, individual differences have a qualitative component. People can differ in where their strengths lie. They can also differ in their selection of strategies for solving problems. We saw evidence in Chapter 9 that one dimension of growing expertise is the development of more-effective strategies.

One might view the human mind as being analogous to a large corporation that consists of many interacting components. The differences among corporations are often due to the relative strengths of their components. With practice, different components tend to become more efficient at doing their tasks. Another way to achieve improvement is by strategic reorganizations of parts of the corporation. However, there is more to a successful company than just the sum of its parts. These pieces have to interact together smoothly to achieve the overall goals of the organization. Some researchers (e.g., Anderson et al., 2004; Newell, 1990) have complained about the rather fragmented picture of the human mind that emerges from current research in cognitive psychology. One agenda for future research will be to understand how all the pieces fit together to achieve a human mind.

Questions for Thought

1. Chapter 12 discussed data on child language acquisition. In learning a second language, younger children initially learn less rapidly, but there is evidence that they achieve higher levels of mastery. Discusses this phenomenon from the point of view of this chapter. Consider in particular Figure 12.8.
2. Most American presidents are between the ages of 50 and 59 when they are first elected as president. The youngest elected president was Kennedy (43 when he was first elected) and the oldest was Reagan (69 when he was first elected). The 2008 presidential election featured a contest between a 47-year-old Obama and a 72-year-old McCain. What are the implications of this chapter for an ideal age for an American president?
3. J. E. Hunter and R. F. Hunter (1984) report that ability measures like IQ are better predictors of job performance than academic grades. Why might be this be so? A potentially relevant fact is that the most commonly used measure of job performance is supervisor ratings.
4. The chapter reviewed a series of results indicating that higher ability people tended to perform basic information processing steps in less time. There is also a relationship between ability and perceived time it takes to perform a demanding task (Fink & Neubauer, 2005). Generally, the more difficult an intellectual task we perform, the more we tend to underestimate how long it took. Higher ability people tend to have more realistic estimates of the passage of time (i.e., they underestimate less). Why might they underestimate time less? How could this be related to the fact that they perform the task more rapidly?

Key Terms

concrete-operational stage
conservation
crystallized intelligence
factor analysis
fluid intelligence
formal-operational stage
intelligence quotient (IQ)
preoperational stage
psychometric test
sensory-motor stage

Glossary

2½-D sketch: Marr's proposal for a visual representation that identifies where surfaces are located in space relative to the viewer. (p. 40)

3-D model: Marr's proposal for an object-centered representation of a visual scene. (p. 40)

abstraction theory: A theory holding that concepts are represented as abstract descriptions of their central tendencies. Contrast with *instance theory.* (p. 140)

ACT (Adaptive Control of Thought): Anderson's theory of how *declarative knowledge* and *procedural knowledge* interact in complex cognitive processes. (p. 156)

action potential: The sudden change in electric potential that travels down the *axon* of a *neuron.* (p. 15)

activation: A state of memory traces that determines both the speed and the probability of access to a memory trace. (p. 156)

affirmation of the consequent: The logical fallacy that one can reason from the affirmation of the *consequent* of a *conditional statement* to the affirmation of its *antecedent*: *If A, then B* and *B is true* together can be thought (falsely) to imply *A is true.* (p. 276)

AI: See *artificial intelligence.*

allocentric representation: A representation of the environment according to a fixed coordinate system. Contrast with *egocentric representation.* (p. 107)

amnesia: A memory deficit due to brain damage. See also *anterograde amnesia; retrograde amnesia; Korsakoff syndrome.* (p. 200)

amodal hypothesis: The proposal that meaning is not represented in a particular modality. Contrast with multimodal hypothesis. (p. 130)

amodal symbol system: The proposal that information is represented by symbols that are not associated with a particular modality. Contrast with *perceptual symbol system.* (p. 127)

analogy: The process by which a problem solver maps the solution for one problem into a solution for another problem. (p. 218)

antecedent: The condition of a *conditional statement;* that is, the *A* in *If A, then B.* (p. 275)

anterior cingulate cortex (ACC): Medial portion of the *prefrontal cortex* important in control and dealing with conflict. (p. 89)

anterograde amnesia: Loss of the ability to learn new things after an injury. Contrast with *retrograde amnesia.* (pp. 146, 201)

aphasia: An impairment of speech that results from a brain injury. (p. 22)

apperceptive agnosia: A form of *visual agnosia* marked by the inability to recognize simple shapes such as circles and triangles. (p. 33)

arguments: An element of a *propositional representation* that corresponds to a time, place, person, or object. (p. 123)

articulatory loop: Baddeley's proposed system for rehearsing verbal information. (p. 153)

artificial intelligence (AI): A field of computer science that attempts to develop programs that will enable machines to display intelligent behavior. (p. 2)

associative agnosia: A form of *visual agnosia* marked by the inability to recognize complex objects such as an anchor, even though the patient can recognize simple shapes and can copy drawings of complex objects. (p. 33)

associative spreading: Facilitation in access to information when closely related items are presented. (p. 159)

associative stage: The second of Fitts's stages of skill acquisition, in which the declarative representation of a skill is converted into a procedural representation. (p. 241)

atmosphere hypothesis: The proposal by Woodworth and Sells that, when faced with a *categorical syllogism,* people tend to accept conclusions having the same quantifiers as those of the premises. (p. 283)

attention: The allocation of cognitive resources among ongoing processes. (p. 64)

attenuation theory: Treisman's theory of *attention,* which proposes that we weaken some incoming sensory signals on the basis of their physical characteristics. (p. 67)

attribute identification: The problem of determining what attributes are relevant to the formation of a hypothesis. See also *rule learning.* (p. 301)

auditory sensory store: A memory system that effectively holds all the information heard for a brief period of time. Also called *echoic memory.* (p. 149)

automaticity: The ability to perform a task with little or no central cognitive control. (p. 86)

autonomous stage: The third of Fitts's stages of skill acquisition, in which the performance of a skill becomes automated. (p. 241)

axon: The part of a *neuron* that carries information from one region of the brain to another. (p. 14)

backup avoidance: The tendency in problem solving to avoid *operators* that take one back to a *state* already visited. (p. 221)

backward inference: See *bridging inference.*

bar detectors: A cell in the visual cortex that responds most to bars in the visual field. Compare *edge detector.* (p. 38)

basal ganglia: Subcortical nuclei that play a critical role in the control of motor movement and cognition. (p. 20)

Bayes's theorem: A theorem that prescribes how to combine the *prior probability* of a hypothesis with the *conditional probability* of the evidence, given the hypothesis, to assess the *posterior probability* of the hypothesis, given the evidence. (p. 300)

behaviorism: The theory that psychology should be concerned only with behavior and should not refer to mental constructs underlying behavior. (p. 7)

binding problem: The question of how the brain determines which features in the visual field go together to form an object. (p. 75)

blood oxygen level dependent (BOLD) response: A measure obtained in *fMRI* studies of the amount of oxygen in the blood. (p. 28)

bottom-up processing: The processing of a stimulus in which information from a physical stimulus, rather than from general context, is used to help recognize the stimulus. Contrast with *top-down processing.* (p. 56)

bridging inference: In sentence comprehension, an inference that connects the sentence to the prior context. Contrast with *elaborative inference.* (p. 377)

Broca's area: A region in the left frontal cortex that is important for processing language, particularly *syntax* in speech. (p. 22)

categorical perception: The perception of stimuli being in distinct categories without gradual variations. (p. 54)

categorical syllogism: A *syllogism* consisting of statements that have *logical quantifiers* in which one premise relates *A* to *B*, another relates *B* to *C*, and the conclusion relates *A* to *C*. (p. 284)

center-embedded sentences: A sentence in which one clause is embedded within another; for example, *The boy whom the girl liked was sick.* (p. 365)

central bottleneck: The inability of central cognition to pursue multiple lines of thought simultaneously. Contrast with *perfect time-sharing.* (p. 85)

central executive: Baddeley's proposed system for controlling various slave rehearsal systems, such as the *articulatory loop* and the *visuospatial sketchpad.* (p. 152)

change blindness: The inability to detect a change in a scene when the change matches the context. (p. 60)

cognitive maps: A mental representation of the locations of objects and places in the environment. See also *route map; survey map.* (p. 106)

cognitive neuroscience: The study of the neural basis of cognition. (p. 12)

cognitive psychology: The scientific study of cognition. (p. 1)

cognitive stage: The first of Fitts's stages of skill acquisition, in which the declarative encoding of a skill is developed and used. (p. 241)

competence: A term in *linguistics* that refers to a person's abstract knowledge of a language, which is not always manifested in *performance.* (p. 327)

componential analyses: An approach to instruction that begins with an analysis of the individual elements that need to be learned. (p. 267)

concrete-operational stage: The third of Piaget's four stages of development, during which a child has systematic schemes for thinking about the physical world. (p. 393)

conditional probability: In the context of *Bayes's theorem,* the probability that a particular piece of evidence will be found if a hypothesis is true. (p. 301)

conditional statement: An assertion that, if an *antecedent* is true, then a *consequent* must be true: a statement of the form *If A, then B.* (p. 275)

confirmation bias: The tendency to seek evidence that is consistent with one's current hypothesis. (p. 303)

consequent: The result of a *conditional statement;* the *B* in *If A, then B.* (p. 275)

conservation: A term used by Piaget to refer to the particular properties of objects that are preserved under certain *transformations.* (p. 393)

consonantal feature: A consonant-like quality in a *phoneme.* (p. 52)

constituent: A subpattern that corresponds to a basic phrase, or unit, in a sentence's surface structure. (p. 360)

corpus callosum: A broad band of fibers that enables communication between the left and the right hemispheres of the brain. (p. 20)

crystallized intelligence: Cattell's term for the factor in intelligence that depends on acquired knowledge. (p. 413)

decay theory: The theory that forgetting is caused by the spontaneous decay of memory traces over time. Contrast with *interference theory.* (p. 181)

declarative memory: Explicit knowledge of various facts. Contrast with *procedural knowledge.* (p. 207)

deductive reasoning: Reasoning in which the conclusions can be determined to follow with certainty from the premises. (p. 274)

Deese-Roediger-McDermott paradigm: A paradigm for creating false memories of words by presenting associatively related words. (p. 194)

default values: A typical value for *slots* in a *schema* representation. (p. 135)

deliberate practice: The kind of practice that Ericsson postulated to be critical for the development of expertise. This practice is highly motivated and includes careful self-monitoring. (p. 263)

dendrite: The branching part of a *neuron* that receives *synapses* from the *axons* of other *neurons.* (p. 14)

denial of the antecedent: The logical fallacy that one can reason from the denial of the *antecedent* of a *conditional statement* to the denial of its *consequent: If A, then B* and *Not A* together are thought (falsely) to imply *Not B.* (p. 276)

depth of processing: The theory that memory for information is improved if the information is processed at deeper levels of analysis. (p. 151)

descriptive model: A model that states how people actually behave. Contrast with *prescriptive model.* (p. 302)

dichotic listening task: A task in which participants in an experiment are presented with two messages simultaneously, one to each ear, and are instructed to repeat back the words from only one of them. (p. 65)

difference reductions: The tendency in problem solving to select *operators* that eliminate a difference between the current *state* and the goal. (p. 221)

dissociations: A demonstration that a manipulation has an effect on performance of one task but not another. Such demonstrations are thought to be important in arguing for different cognitive systems. (p. 202)

dorsolateral prefrontal cortex (DLPFC): Upper portion of the *prefrontal cortex* thought to be important in cognitive control. (p. 89)

dual-code theory: Paivio's theory that there are separate visual and verbal representations for knowledge. (p. 127)

early-selection theory: A theory of *attention* stating that *serial bottlenecks* occur early in information processing. Contrast with *late-selection theory.* (p. 64)

echoic memory: Another term for *auditory sensory store.* (p. 149)

edge detectors: A cell in the visual cortex that responds most to edges in the visual field. Compare *bar detector.* (p. 37)

egocentric representation: A representation of the environment as it appears in a current view. Contrast with *allocentric representation.* (p. 107)

Einstellung effect: The term used by A. S. Luchins to refer to the *set effect,* in which people will repeat a solution that has worked for previous problems even when a simpler solution is possible. (p. 234)

elaborative inference: In sentence comprehension, an inference that connects a text to possible material not yet asserted. Contrast with *bridging inference.* (p. 377)

elaborative processing: The embellishment of a to-be-remembered item with additional information. (p. 166)

electroencephalography (EEG): Measurement of electrical activity of the brain, measured by electrodes on the scalp. (p. 25)

embodied cognition: The viewpoint that the mind can only be understood by taking into account the human body and how it interacts with the environment. (p. 129)

empiricism: The position that knowledge is acquired through experience in the world. Compare *nativism.* (p. 4)

encoding-specificity principle: Tulving's principle that memory is better when the encoding of an item at study matches the encoding at test. (p. 200)

epiphenomenon: A secondary mental event that has no functional role in the information processing. (p. 92)

event-related potential (ERP): Measurement of changes in electrical activity at the scalp in response to an external event. (p. 25)

excitatory synapse: A *synapse* in which the *neurotransmitters* decrease the potential difference across the membrane of the *neuron.* (p. 14)

executive control: The direction of central cognition, which is carried out mainly by prefrontal regions of the brain. (p. 88)

exemplar theory: A theory holding that we gain our knowledge of concepts by retrieving specific exemplars of the concepts. Contrast with *abstraction theory.* (p. 140)

explicit memory: Knowledge that we can consciously recall. Contrast with *implicit memory.* (p. 203)

factor analysis: In the context of intelligence tests, a statistical method that tries to find a set of factors that will account for performance across a range of tests. (p. 412)

false-memory syndrome: A term used to describe the condition of false memories of childhood abuse. (p. 193)

fan effect: The phenomenon that the retrieval of memories takes longer as more things are associated with the items composing the original memories. (p. 183)

feature analysis: A theory of pattern recognition that claims that we extract primitive features and then recognize their combinations. (p. 45)

feature-integration theory: Treisman's proposal that one must focus *attention* on a set of features before the individual features can be synthesized into a pattern. (p. 75)

feature maps: A representation of the spatial locations of a particular visual feature. (p. 39)

filter theory: Broadbent's *early-selection theory* of *attention,* which assumes that, when sensory information has to pass through a bottleneck, only some of the information is selected for further processing, on the basis of physical characteristics such as the pitch of a speaker's voice. (p. 66)

flashbulb memories: Particularly good memory for events that are very important and traumatic. (p. 172)

fluid intelligence: Cattell's term for the factor in intelligence that depends on the ability to reason or solve problems. (p. 413)

fMRI: See *functional magnetic resonance imaging.*

formal-operational stage: The fourth of Piaget's four stages of development, during which a child has abstract schemes for reasoning about the world. (p. 393)

forward inference: See *elaborative inference.*

fovea: The area of the retina with the greatest visual acuity. When we focus on an object, we move the eyes so that the image of the object falls on the fovea. (p. 35)

framing effects: The tendency for people to make different choices among the same alternatives, depending on the statement of the alternatives. (p. 314)

frontal lobe: The region at the front of the cerebral cortex that includes the motor cortex and the *prefrontal cortex.* (p. 19)

functional fixedness: The tendency to see objects only as serving conventional problem-solving functions and thus failing to see that they can serve novel functions. (p. 232)

functional magnetic resonance imaging (fMRI): A method for determining metabolic activity by measuring the magnetic field produced by the iron in oxygenated blood. (p. 25)

fusiform face area: A part of the temporal cortex that is special in fine discriminations, particularly of faces. (p. 102)

fusiform gyrus: A region in the temporal cortex involved in recognition of complex patterns like faces and words. (p. 50)

fuzzy logical model of perception (FLMP): Massaro's theory of perception, which states that stimulus features and context combine independently to determine perception. (p. 58)

gambler's fallacy: The belief that, if a string of probabilistic events has turned out one way, there is an increased probability that the next event will now turn out the other way. (p. 309)

garden-path sentences: A sentence with a *transient ambiguity* that causes us to make the wrong interpretation initially and then have to correct ourselves. (p. 370)

General Problem Solver (GPS): A problem-solving simulation program created by Newell and Simon that embodies *means-ends analysis.* (p. 224)

geons: One of Biederman's 36 primitive categories of subobjects that we combine to perceive larger objects. See also *recognition-by-components theory.* (p. 48)

gestalt principles of organization: Principles that determine how a scene is organized into components. The principles include proximity, similarity, good continuation, closure, and good form. (p. 41)

Gestalt psychology: An approach to psychology that emphasizes principles of organization that result in holistic properties of the brain that go beyond the activity of the parts. (p. 8)

goal-directed attention: Allocation of processing resources in response to one's goals. Contrast with *stimulus-driven attention.* (p. 64)

goal state: A *state* in a *problem space* in which the goal is satisfied. (p. 212)

grammar: A set of rules that prescribe all the acceptable utterances of a language. A grammar consists of *syntax, semantics,* and *phonology.* (p. 325)

gyrus: An outward fold on the brain. Contrast with *sulcus.* (p. 18)

hemodynamic response: The increased flow of oxygenated blood to a region of the brain that has greater activity—this is the basis of *fMRI* brain imaging. (p. 26)

hill climbing: The tendency to choose *operators* in problem solving that transform the current *state* into a new *state* more similar to the goal. (p. 222)

hippocampus: A structure within the temporal lobe that plays a critical role in the formation of permanent memories. (p. 19)

iconic memory: Another term for *visual sensory store.* (p. 149)

illusory conjunction: The illusion that features of different objects actually came from a single object. (p. 75)

immediacy of interpretation: The principle of language processing stating that people commit to an interpretation of a word and its role in a sentence as soon as they process the word. (p. 362)

implicit memory: Knowledge that we cannot consciously recall but that nonetheless manifests itself in our improved performance on some task. Contrast with *explicit memory.* (p. 203)

incubation effect: The phenomenon that sometimes a solution to a particular problem comes more easily after a period of time in which one has stopped trying to solve the problem. (p. 236)

inductive reasoning: Reasoning in which the conclusions follow only probabilistically from the premises. (p. 274)

information-processing approach: An analysis of human cognition into a set of steps in which abstract information is processed. (p. 16)

inhibition of return: The decreased ability to return our *attention* to a location or an object that we have already looked at. (p. 79)

inhibitory synapse: A *synapse* in which the *neurotransmitters* increase the potential difference across the membrane of a *neuron.* (p. 14)

insight problem: A problem in which the subject is not aware of being close to a solution. (p. 238)

intelligence quotient (IQ): A measure of general intellectual performance that is normed to have a mean of 100 and a standard deviation of 15. (p. 408)

intelligent tutoring system: A computer system that combines cognitive models with techniques from *artificial intelligence* to create instructional interactions with students. (p. 267)

interactive processing: The position that *semantic* and *syntactic* cues are simultaneously brought to bear in interpreting a sentence. Contrast with *modularity.* (p. 374)

interference theory: The theory that forgetting is caused by other memories interfering with the retention of the target memory. Contrast with *decay theory.* (p. 181)

introspection: A methodology much practiced at the turn of the 20th century in Germany that attempted to analyze thought into its components through self-analysis. (p. 6)

isa link: A particular *link* in a semantic network or *schema* that indicates the superset of the category. (p. 132)

Korsakoff syndrome: An *amnesia* resulting from chronic alcoholism and nutritional deficit. (p. 201)

language universal: A property that all *natural languages* satisfy. (p. 352)

late-selection Theory: A theory of *attention* stating that *serial bottlenecks* occur late in information processing. An example is Deutsch and Deutsch's theory, according to which all sensory information can be processed, but our ability to respond to that information has attentional limitations. Contrast with *early-selection theory.* (p. 64)

linguistic determinism: The proposal that the structure of one's language strongly influences the way in which one thinks. (p. 338)

linguistic intuitions: A judgment by the speaker of a language about whether a sentence is well formed and about other properties of the sentence. (p. 326)

linguistics: The study of the structure of language. (pp. 9, 324)

link: A connection between elements, or *nodes,* in a *propositional network.* (p. 126)

logical quantifiers: An element such as *all, no, some,* and *some not* that appears in such statements as *All A are B.* (p. 283)

long-term potentiation (LTP): The increase in responsiveness of a *neuron* as a function of past stimulation. (p. 163)

magnetoencephalography (MEG): Measurement of magnetic fields produced by electrical activity in the brain. (p. 25)

mastery learning: The effort to bring students to mastery of each element in a curriculum before promoting them to new material in the curriculum. (p. 267)

means-ends analysis: The creation of a new goal (end) to enable a problem-solving *operator* (means) to apply in achieving the old goal. (p. 222)

memory span: The amount of information that can be perfectly retained in an immediate test of memory. (p. 150)

mental imagery: The processing of perceptual-like information in the absence of an external source for the perceptual information. (p. 93)

mental model theory: Johnson-Laird's theory that participants judge a *syllogism* by imagining a world that satisfies the premises and seeing whether the conclusion is satisfied in that world. (p. 288)

mental rotation: The process of continuously transforming the orientation of a *mental image.* (p. 96)

method of loci: A *mnemonic technique* used to associate items to be remembered with locations along a well-known path. (p. 170)

mirror neurons: A *neuron* that fires both when the animal is performing the action and when it observes another animal performing the action. (p. 130)

mnemonic technique: A method for enhancing memory performance by giving the material to be remembered a meaningful interpretation. (p. 122)

modularity: The proposal that language is a component separate from the rest of cognition. It further argues that language comprehension has an initial phase in which only syntactic considerations are brought to bear. Contrast with *interactive processing.* (p. 342)

modus ponens: The rule of logic stating that, if a *conditional statement* is true and its *antecedent* is true, then its *consequent* must be true: Given both the *proposition If A, then B* and the *proposition A,* we can infer that *B* is true. (p. 275)

modus tollens: The rule of logic stating that, if a *conditional statement* is true and its *consequent* is false, then its *antecedent* must be false: Given the *proposition If A, then B* and the fact that *B is false,* we can infer that *A is false.* (p. 276)

mood congruence: The phenomenon that one's memory is better for studied material whose emotional content matches one's mood at test. (p. 197)

multimodal hypothesis: The theory that knowledge is represented in multiple perceptual and motor modalities. (p. 130)

N400: A negativity in the *event-related potential (ERP)* at about 400 ms after the processing of a semantically difficult word. (p. 368)

nativism: The position that children are born with a great deal of innate knowledge. Compare *empiricism.* (p. 4)

natural languages: A language that can be acquired and spoken by humans. (p. 353)

negative transfer: Poor learning of a second task as a function of having learned a first task. (p. 266)

neuron: The cell in the nervous system responsible for information processing. Neurons accumulate and transmit electrical activity. (p. 13)

neurotransmitter: A chemical that crosses the *synapse* from the *axon* of one *neuron* and alters the electric potential of the membrane of another *neuron.* (p. 14)

node: An element of a *propositional* or semantic *network.* (p. 126)

object-based attention: Allocation of *attention* to chunks of visual information corresponding to an object. Contrast with *space-based attention.* (p. 79)

occipital lobe: The region at the back of the cerebral cortex that controls vision. (p. 18)

operator: A term used in problem-solving research to refer to a particular action that will transform the problem *state* into another problem *state.* The solution of an overall problem is a sequence of these known operators. (p. 211)

P600: A positivity in the *event-related potential (ERP)* at about 600 ms after the processing of a syntactically difficult word. (p. 368)

parahippocampal place area (PPA): A region adjacent to the hippocampus that is active when people are perceiving places. (p. 102)

parameter setting: The proposal that children learn a language by learning the setting of 100 or so parameters that define a *natural language.* (p. 356)

parietal lobe: The region at the top of the cerebral cortex concerned with *attention* and higher level sensory functions. (p. 18)

parsing: The process by which the words in a linguistic message are transformed into a mental representation of their combined meaning. (p. 358)

partial-report procedure: An experimental procedure in which participants are cued to report only some of the items in a display. Contrast with *whole-report procedure.* (p. 148)

particular statements: Statements, frequently using the word *some,* that logicians interpret as meaning it is true about at least some members of a category. Contrast with *universal statements.* (p. 285)

perceptual symbol system: Barsalou's proposal that all knowledge is represented by information that is perceptual and tied to particular modalities. Contrast with *amodal symbol system.* (p. 127)

perfect time-sharing: The ability to pursue more than one task at the same time. Contrast with *central bottleneck.* (p. 83)

performance: A term in *linguistics* that refers to the way that a person speaks. This behavior is thought to be only an imperfect manifestation of that person's linguistic *competence.* (p. 327)

permission schema: An interpretation of a *conditional statement* in which the *antecedent* specifies the situations in which the *consequent* is permitted. (p. 279)

phonemes: The minimal unit of speech that can result in a difference in a spoken message. (p. 51)

phoneme-restoration effect: The tendency to hear *phonemes* that make sense in the speech context even if no such *phonemes* were spoken. (p. 59)

phonological loop: Baddeley's proposed system for rehearsing verbal information. Compare *visuospatial sketchpad.* (p. 152)

phonology: The study of the sound structure of languages. (p. 326)

phrase structure: The hierarchical organization of a sentence into a set of units called phrases, sometimes represented as a tree structure. (p. 328)

place of articulation: The place at which the vocal tract is closed or constricted in the production of a *phoneme.* (p. 52)

positron emission tomography (PET): A method for measuring metabolic activity in different regions of the brain with the use of a radioactive tracer. (p. 25)

posterior probability: In *Bayes's theorem,* the probability that a hypothesis is true after consideration of the evidence. (p. 301)

power function: A function in which the independent variable X is raised to a power to obtain the dependent variable Y, as in $Y = AX^b$. (p. 162)

power law of forgetting: The phenomenon that memory performance deteriorates as a *power function* of the retention interval. (p. 179)

power law of learning: The phenomenon that memory performance improves as a *power function* of practice. (p. 162)

prefrontal cortex: The region at the front of the frontal cortex that controls planning and other higher level cognition. (p. 19)

preoperational stage: The second of Piaget's four stages of development, during which a child has unsystematic schemes for thinking about the physical world. (p. 392)

prescriptive model: A model that specifies how people ought to behave to be considered rational. Contrast with *descriptive model.* (p. 302)

primal sketch: The level of visual processing in Marr's model in which the visual features have been extracted from a stimulus. (p. 61)

priming: The enhancement of the processing of a stimulus as a function of prior exposure. (p. 204)

principle of minimal attachment: A rule of *parsing* that interprets a sentence in a way that results in minimal complication of the *phrase structure.* (p. 371)

prior probability: In *Bayes's theorem,* the probability that a hypothesis is true before consideration of the evidence. (p. 300)

probability matching: The tendency to choose an alternative with a probability that matches the frequency with which that alternative occurs in experience. (p. 306)

problem space: A representation of the various sequences of problem-solving *operators* that lead among various *states* of a problem. Also called *state space.* (p. 212)

procedural knowledge: Knowledge of how to perform various tasks. Contrast with *declarative knowledge.* (p. 205)

proceduralization: The process by which *declarative knowledge* is converted into *procedural knowledge.* (p. 247)

productivity: Refers to the fact that *natural languages* have an infinite number of possible utterances. (p. 324)

proposition: The smallest unit of knowledge that can stand as a separate assertion. (p. 123)

propositional network: A *propositional representation* in which the *relation* and *arguments* of the *proposition* are linked in a network. (p. 125)

propositional representation: A representation of meaning as a set of *propositions.* (p. 123)

prosopagnosia: A neurological disorder characterized by the inability to recognize faces. (p. 50)

psychometric test: A test of various aspects of a person's intellectual performance. (p. 408)

rate of firing: The rate at which nerve impulses are generated along *axons.* (p. 15)

recognition-by-components theory: Biederman's theory stating that we recognize objects by first identifying the *geons* that correspond to their subobjects. (p. 47)

recognition heuristic: If one item is recognized and another is not, people view the recognized item to have a higher value on dimensions like size. (p. 310)

regularity: Refers to the fact that *natural languages* have systematic rules that determine the possible forms of utterances. (p. 324)

relation: The element that organizes the *arguments* of a *propositional representation.* (p. 123)

retrograde amnesia: Loss of memory for things that occurred before an injury. Contrast with *anterograde amnesia.* (p. 201)

route maps: A representation of the environment consisting of the paths between locations. Contrast with *survey map.* (p. 106)

rule learning: Determining how the features combine to make a hypothesis. (p. 301)

SAM (Search of Associative Memory): Shiffrin's theory of memory stating that the availability of memories is a function of their familiarity, which in turn is a function of their *strength* of association with cues in the environment. (p. 156)

schema: A representation of members of a category based on the type of objects that they are, the parts that they tend to have, and their typical properties. A *slot*-value structure is used to represent this information. (p. 134)

script: A *schema* representation proposed by Schank and Abelson for event concepts. (p. 138)

search: The process by which one finds a sequence of *operators* to solve a problem. (p. 212)

search tree: A representation of the set of *states* that can be reached by applying *operators* to an initial *state.* (p. 213)

selection task: A task in which a participant is given a *conditional statement* of the form *If A, then B* and must choose which situations among *A, B, Not A,* and *Not B* need to be checked to test the truth of the conditional. (p. 278)

semantics: The meaning structure of linguistic units. (p. 326)

sensory-motor stage: The first of Piaget's four stages of development, during which a child lacks basic schemes for thinking about the physical world and experiences it in terms of sensations and actions. (p. 392)

serial bottleneck: The point in the path from perception to action at which people cannot process all the incoming information in parallel. (p. 63)

set effect: The biasing of a solution to a problem as a result of past experiences in solving that kind of problem. (p. 233)

short-term memory: A proposed intermediate memory system that holds information as it travels from sensory memory to long-term memory. (p. 150)

situation model: A representation of the events and situations described in a text. (p. 387)

slot: An element of a *schema* that indicates different attributes of a concept. (p. 134)

space-based attention: Allocation of attention to visual information in a region of space. Contrast with *object-based attention.* (p. 79)

split-brain patients: A patient who has had surgery to sever the *corpus callosum,* which connects left and right hemispheres. (p. 21)

spreading activation: The proposal that *activation* spreads from items currently or recently processed to other parts of the memory network, activating the memory traces that reside there. (p. 159)

state: A term in problem solving used to refer to a representation of the problem in some degree of solution. (p. 212)

state-dependent learning: The phenomenon that memory performance is better when we are tested in the same emotional and physical state as we were in when we learned the material. (p. 198)

Sternberg paradigm: An experimental procedure in which participants are presented with a memory set consisting of a few items and must decide whether various probe items are in the memory set. (p. 10)

stimulus-driven attention: Allocation of processing resources in response to a salient stimulus. Contrast with *goal-directed attention.* (p. 64)

strategic learning: The learning of how to organize one's problem solving for a specific class of problems. Compare *tactical learning.* (p. 253)

strength: The property of a memory trace that determines how active the trace can become. Strength increases with practice and decays with time. (p. 161)

Stroop effect: A phenomenon in which the tendency to name a word will interfere with the ability to say the color in which the word is printed. (p. 87)

subgoal: A goal set in service of achieving a larger goal. (p. 211)

subjective probability: The probability people associate with an event, which need not be identical to the event's objective probability. (p. 313)

subjective utility: The value that someone places on something. (p. 312)

sulcus: An inward fold of the brain. Contrast with *gyrus.* (p. 18)

survey maps: A representation of the environment consisting of the position of locations in space. Contrast with *route map.* (p. 106)

syllogisms: A logical *argument* consisting of two premises and a conclusion. (p. 273)

synapse: The location at which the *axon* of one *neuron* almost makes contact with another *neuron.* (p. 14)

syntax: Grammatical rules for specifying correct word order and inflectional structure in a sentence. (p. 325)

tactical learning: The learning of sequences of actions that help solve a problem. Compare *strategic learning.* (p. 251)

template matching: A theory of pattern recognition stating that an object is recognized as a function of its overlap with various pattern templates stored in the brain. (p. 42)

temporal lobe: The region at the side of the cerebral cortex that contains the primary auditory areas and controls the recognition of objects. (p. 18)

theory of identical elements: The theory that there will be transfer from one skill to another only to the extent that the skills have the same knowledge elements in common. (p. 265)

top-down processing: The processing of a stimulus in which information from the general context is used to help recognize the stimulus. Contrast with *bottom-up processing.* (p. 56)

topographic organization: A principle of neural organization in which adjacent areas of the cortex process information from adjacent parts of the sensory field. (p. 22)

Tower of Hanoi problem: A problem-solving task in which disks are moved among pegs. (p. 226)

transcranial magnetic stimulation (TMS): A magnetic field is applied to the surface of the head to disrupt the neural processing in that region of brain. (p. 27)

transformation: A linguistic rule that moves a term from one part of a sentence to another part. (p. 333)

transient ambiguity: A temporary ambiguity within a sentence that is resolved by the end of the sentence. (p. 370)

universal statements: Statements, often involving words like *all* or *none,* that logicians interpret as having no exceptions. Contrast with *particular statements.* (p. 283)

utilization: The process by which language comprehenders respond to the meaning of a linguistic message. (p. 358)

ventromedial prefrontal cortex: The portion of the cortex in the front and center of the brain. It seems to be involved in decision making and self-regulation, including activities like gambling behavior. (p. 299)

visual agnosia: An inability to recognize visual objects that results neither from general intellectual loss nor from loss of basic sensory abilities. (p. 32)

visual sensory store: A memory system that effectively holds all the information in a visual array for a very brief period of time (about a second). Also called *iconic memory.* (p. 148)

visuospatial sketchpad: Baddeley's proposed system for rehearsing visual information. Compare *phonological loop.* (p. 152)

voicing: The property of a *phoneme* produced by vibration of the vocal cords. (p. 52)

Wernicke's area: A region of the left *temporal lobe* important to language, particularly the *semantic* content of speech. (p. 22)

whole-report procedure: A procedure in which participants are asked to report all the items of a display. Contrast with *partial-report procedure.* (p. 148)

word superiority effect: The superior recognition of letters presented in a word context than when the letters are presented alone. (p. 56)

working memory: The information that is currently available in memory for working on a problem. (p. 152)

References

Aaronson, D., & Scarborough, H. S. (1977). Performance theories for sentence coding: Some quantitative models. *Journal of Verbal Learning and Verbal Behavior, 16,* 277–304.

Adolphs, R. D., Tranel, A., Bechara, A., Damasio, H., & Damasio, A. R. (1996). Neuropsychological approaches to reasoning and decision-making. In A. R. Damasio, Y. Christen, & H. Damasio (Eds.), *Neurobiology of decision* (pp. 157–179). New York: Springer.

Ainsworth-Darnell, K., Shulman, H. G., & Boland, J. E. (1998). Dissociating brain responses to syntactic and semantic anomalies: Evidence from event-related potentials. *Journal of Memory and Language, 38,* 112–130.

Albert, M. L. (1973). A simple test of visual neglect. *Neurology, 23,* 658–664.

Allopenna, P. D., Magnuson, J. S., & Tanenhaus, M. K. (1998). Tracking the time course of spoken word recognition using eye movements: Evidence for continuous mapping models. *Journal of Memory and Language, 38,* 419–439.

Anderson, J. R. (1972). *Recognition confusions in sentence memory.* Unpublished manuscript.

Anderson, J. R. (1974a). Retrieval of propositional information from long-term memory. *Cognitive Psychology, 6,* 451–474.

Anderson, J. R. (1974b). Verbatim and propositional representation of sentences in immediate and long-term memory. *Journal of Verbal Learning and Verbal Behavior, 13,* 149–162.

Anderson, J. R. (1978b). Computer simulation of a language acquisition system: A second report. In D. LaBerge & S. J. Samuels (Eds.), *Perception and comprehension* (pp. 305–360). Hillsdale, NJ: Erlbaum.

Anderson, J. R. (1982). Acquisition of cognitive skill. *Psychological Review, 89,* 369–406.

Anderson, J. R. (1983). *The architecture of cognition.* Cambridge, MA: Harvard University Press.

Anderson, J. R. (1990). *The adaptive character of thought.* Hillsdale, NJ: Erlbaum.

Anderson, J. R. (1991). The adaptive nature of human categorization. *Psychological Review, 98,* 409–429.

Anderson, J. R. (1992). Intelligent tutoring and high school mathematics. *Proceedings of the Second International Conference on Intelligent Tutoring Systems* (pp. 1–10). Montreal: Springer-Verlag.

Anderson, J. R. (1993). *Rules of the mind.* Hillsdale, NJ: Erlbaum.

Anderson, J. R. (2000). *Learning and memory.* New York: Wiley.

Anderson, J. R. (2007). *How can the human mind occur in the physical universe?* New York: Oxford University Press.

Anderson, J. R., & Betz, J. (2001). A hybrid model of categorization. *Psychonomic Bulletin and Review, 8,* 629–647.

Anderson, J. R., Bothell, D., Lebiere, C., & Matessa, M. (1998). An integrated theory of list memory. *Journal of Memory and Language, 38,* 341–380.

Anderson, J. R., & Bower, G. H. (1972). Configural properties in sentence memory. *Journal of Verbal Learning and Verbal Behavior, 11,* 594–605.

Anderson, J. R., & Bower, G. H. (1973). *Human associative memory.* Washington, DC: Winston.

Anderson, J. R., Conrad, F. G., & Corbett, A. T. (1989). Skill acquisition and the LISP Tutor. *Cognitive Science, 13,* 467–506.

Anderson, J. R., Farrell, R., & Sauers, R. (1984). Learning to program in LISP. *Cognitive Science, 8,* 87–129.

Anderson, J. R., Kushmerick, N., & Lebiere, C. (1993). Navigation and conflict resolution. In J. R. Anderson (Ed.), *Rules of the mind* (pp. 93–120). Hillsdale, NJ: Erlbaum.

Anderson, J. R., & Lebiere, C. (Eds.). (1998). *Atomic components of thought.* Mahwah, NJ: Erlbaum.

Anderson, J. R., Reder, L. M., & Simon, H. (1998). Radical constructivism and cognitive psychology. In D. Ravitch (Ed.), *Brookings papers on education policy* (pp. 227–278). Washington, DC: Brookings Institute Press.

Anderson, J. R., & Reiser, B. J. (1985). The LISP tutor. *Byte, 10,* 159–175.

Angell, J. R. (1908). The doctrine of formal discipline in the light of the principles of general psychology. *Educational Review, 36,* 1–14.

Antell, S., & Keating, D. P. (1983). Perception of numerical invariance in neonates. *Child Development, 54,* 695–701.

Arrington, C. M., Carr, T. H., Mayer, A. R., & Rao, S. M. (2000). Neural mechanisms of visual attention: Object-based selection of a region in space. *Journal of Cognitive Neuroscience, 12*(Suppl. 2), 106–117.

Ashby, F. G., Alfonso-Reese, L. A., Turken, A. U., & Waldron, E. M. (1998). A neuropsychological theory of multiple systems in category learning. *Psychological Review, 107,* 442–481.

Ashby, F. G., Maddox, W. T. (2005). Human category learning. *Annual Review of Psychology, 56,* 149–178.

Atkinson, R. C., & Shiffrin, R. M. (1968). Human memory: A proposed system and its control processes. In K. Spence & J. Spence (Eds.), *The psychology of learning and motivation* (Vol. 2, pp. 89–195). New York: Academic Press.

Atwood, M. E., & Polson, P. G. (1976). A process model for water jug problems. *Cognitive Psychology, 8,* 191–216.

Ausubel, D. P. (1968). *Educational psychology: A cognitive view.* New York: Holt, Rinehart, & Winston.

Baars, B. J., Motley, M. T., & MacKay, D. G. (1975). Output editing for lexical status in artificially elicited slips of the tongue. *Journal of Verbal Learning and Verbal Behavior, 14,* 382–391.

Baddeley, A. D. (1976). *The psychology of memory.* New York: Basic Books.

Baddeley, A. D. (1986). *Working memory.* Oxford: Oxford University Press.

Baddeley, A. D., Thompson, N., & Buchanan, M. (1975). Word length and the structure of short-term memory. *Journal of Verbal Learning and Verbal Behavior, 14,* 575–589.

Bahrick, H. P. (1984). Semantic memory content in permastore: Fifty years of memory for Spanish learned in school. *Journal of Experimental Psychology: General, 113,* 1–24.

Bahrick, H. P. (circa 1993). Personal communication.

Barbizet, J. (1970). *Human memory and its pathology.* San Francisco: W. H. Freeman.

Barnes, C. A. (1979). Memory deficits associated with senescence: A neurophysiological and behavioral study in the rat. *Journal of Comparative Physiology, 43,* 74–104.

Baron-Cohen, S. (1995). *Mindblindness: An essay on autism and theory of mind.* Cambridge, MA: MIT Press.

Barsalou, L. W. (1999). Perceptual symbol systems. *Behavioral and Brain Sciences, 22,* 577–609.

Barsalou, L. W. (2003). Personal communication, March 12.

Barsalou, L. W. (2008). Grounded cognition. *Annual Review of Psychology, 59,* 617–645.

Barsalou, L. W., Simmons, W. K., Barbey, A., & Wilson, C. D. (2003). Grounding conceptual knowledge in modality-specific systems. *Trends in Cognitive Sciences, 7,* 84–91.

Bartlett, B. J. (1978). *Top-level structure as an organizational strategy for recall of classroom text.* Unpublished doctoral dissertation, Arizona State University.

Bartolomeo, P. (2002). The relationship between visual perception and visual mental imagery: A reappraisal of the neuropsychological evidence. *Cortex, 38,* 357–378.

Barton, R. A. (1998). Visual specialization and brain evolution in primates. *Proceedings of the Royal Society of London B, 265,* 1933–1937.

Bassok, M. (1990). Transfer of domain-specific problem-solving procedures. *Journal of Experimental Psychology: Learning, Memory, and Cognition, 16,* 522–533.

Bassok, M., & Holyoak, K. J. (1989). Interdomain transfer between isomorphic topics in algebra and physics. *Journal of Experimental Psychology: Learning, Memory, and Cognition, 15,* 153–166.

Bates, A., McNew, S., MacWhinney, B., Devesocvi, A., & Smith, S. (1982). Functional constraints on sentence processing: A cross-linguistic study. *Cognition, 11,* 245–299.

Baylis, G. C., Rolls, E. T., & Leonard, C. M. (1985). Selectivity between faces in the responses of a population of neurons in the cortex in the superior temporal sulcus of the monkey. *Brain Research, 342,* 91–102.

Bechara, A., Damasio, A. R., Damasio, H., & Anderson, S. W. (1994). Insensitivity to future consequences following damage to human prefrontal cortex. *Cognition, 50,* 7–15.

Bechara, A., Damasio, H., Tranel, D., & Damasio, A. R. (2005). The Iowa Gambling Task and the somatic marker hypothesis: Some questions and answers. *Trends in Cognitive Sciences, 9,* 159–162.

Beck, B. B. (1980). *Animal tool behavior: The use and manufacture of tools by animals.* New York: Garland STPM Press.

Beck, D. M., Rees, G., Frith, C. D., & Lavie, N. (2001). Neural correlates of change detection and change blindness. *Nature Neuroscience, 4,* 645–650.

Behrmann, M. (2000). The mind's eye mapped onto the brain's matter. *Current Psychological Science, 9,* 50–54.

Behrmann, M., & Moscovitch, M. (1994). Object-centered neglect in patients with unilateral neglect: Effects of left-right coordinates of objects. *Journal of Cognitive Neuroscience, 6,* 1–16.

Behrmann, M., Zemel, R. S., & Mozer, M. C. (1998). Object-based attention and occlusion: Evidence from normal participants and computational model. *Journal of Experimental Psychology: Human Perception and Performance, 24,* 1011–1036.

Beilock, S. L., Lyons, I. M., Mattarella-Micke, A., Nusbaum, H. C., & Small, S. L. (2008). Sports experience changes the neural processing of action language. *Proceedings of the National Academy of Sciences, USA, 105,* 13269–13273

Bellugi, U., Wang, P. P., & Jernigan, T. L. (1994). Williams syndrome: An unusual neuropsychological profile. In S. H. Broman & J. Grafman (Eds.), *Atypical cognitive deficits in developmental disorders implications for brain function* (pp. 23–56). Hillsdale, NJ: Erlbaum.

Benson, D. F., & Greenberg, J. P. (1969). Visual form agnosia. *Archives of Neurology, 20,* 82–89.

Berbaum, K., & Chung, C. P. (1981). Mueller-Lyer illusion induced by imagination. *Journal of Mental Imagery, 5,* 125–128.

Berlin, B., & Kay, P. (1969). *Basic color terms: Their universality and evolution.* Berkeley, CA: University of California Press.

Berntsen, D., & Rubin, D. C. (2002). Emotionally charged autobiographical memories across the life span: The recall of happy, sad, traumatic, and involuntary memories. *Psychology and Aging, 17,* 636–652.

Berry, D. C., & Broadbent, D. E. (1984). On the relationship between task performance and associated verbalizable knowledge. *Quarterly Journal of Experimental Psychology, 36A,* 209–231.

Biederman, I. (1987). Recognition-by-components: A theory of human image understanding. *Psychological Review, 94,* 115–147.

Biederman, I., Beiring, E., Ju, G., & Blickle, T. (1985). A *comparison of the perception of partial vs. degraded objects.* Unpublished manuscript, State University of New York at Buffalo.

Biederman, I., Glass, A. L., & Stacy, E. W. (1973). Searching for objects in real world scenes. *Journal of Experimental Psychology, 97,* 22–27.

Biederman, I., & Ju, G. (1988). Surface vs. edge-based determinants of visual recognition. *Cognitive Psychology, 20,* 38–64.

Black, J. B., & Bern, H. (1981). Causal coherence and memory for events in narratives. *Journal of Verbal Learning and Verbal Behavior, 20,* 267–275.

Blackburn, J. M. (1936). *Acquisition of skill: An analysis of learning curves.* IHRB Rep. No. 73.

Bloom, B. S. (1984). The 2 sigma problem: The search for methods of group instruction as effective as one-to-one tutoring. *Educational Researcher, 13,* 3–16.

Bloom, B. S. (Ed.). (1985a). *Developing talent in young people.* New York: Ballantine Books.

Bloom, B. S. (1985b). Generalizations about talent development. In B. S. Bloom (Ed.), *Developing talent in young people* (pp. 507–549). New York: Ballantine Books.

Bloom, R. (1994). Recent controversies in the study of language acquisition. In M. A. Gernsbacher (Ed.), *Handbook of psycholinguistics* (pp. 741–779). San Diego: Academic Press.

Boden, M. (2006). *Mind as machine.* Oxford: Oxford University Press.

Boer, L. C. (1991). Mental rotation in perspective problems. *Acta Psychologica, 76,* 1–9.

Boole, G. (1854). *An investigation of the laws of thought.* London: Walton and Maberly.

Boomer, D. S. (1965). Hesitation and grammatical encoding. *Language and Speech, 8,* 148–158.

Boring, E. G. (1950). *A history of experimental psychology.* New York: Appleton Century.

Boroditsky, L., Schmidt, L., & Phillips, W. (2003). *Sex, syntax, and semantics.* In D. Gentner & S. Goldin-Meadow (Eds.), *Language in mind: Advances in the study of language and cognition.* Cambridge, MA: MIT Press.

Bouchard, T. J. (1983). Do environmental similarities explain the similarity in intelligence of identical twins reared apart? *Intelligence, 7,* 175–184.

Bouchard, T. J., & McGue, M. (1981). Familial studies of intelligence: A review. *Science, 212,* 1055–1059.

Bower, G. H., Black, J. B., & Turner, T. J. (1979). Scripts in memory for text. *Cognitive Psychology, 11,* 177–220.

Bower, G. H., Karlin, M. B., & Dueck, A. (1975). Comprehension and memory for pictures. *Memory & Cognition, 3,* 216–220.

Bower, G. H., & Mayer, J. D. (1985). Failure to replicate mood-dependent retrieval. *Bulletin of the Psychonomic Society, 23,* 39–42.

Bower, G. H., Monteiro, K. P., & Gilligan, S. G. (1978). Emotional mood as a context for learning and recall. *Journal of Verbal Learning and Verbal Behavior, 17,* 573–587.

Bowerman, M. (1973). Structural relationships in children's utterances: Syntactic or semantic. In T. E. Moore (Ed.), *Cognitive development and the acquisition of language* (pp. 197–213). New York: Academic Press.

Bownds, M. D. (1999). *The biology of mind: Origins and structures of mind, brain, and consciousness.* Bethesda, MD: Fitzgerald Science Press.

Bradshaw, G. L., & Anderson, J. R. (1982). Elaborative encoding as an explanation of levels of processing. *Journal of Verbal Learning and Verbal Behavior, 21,* 165–174.

Brainerd, C. J. (1978). *Piaget's theory of intelligence.* Englewood Cliffs, NJ: Prentice-Hall.

Bransford, J. D., Barclay, J. R., & Franks, J. J. (1972). Sentence memory: A constructive versus interpretive approach. *Cognitive Psychology, 3,* 193–209.

Bransford, J. D., & Franks, J. J. (1971). The abstraction of linguistic ideas. *Cognitive Psychology, 2,* 331–380.

Brewer, J. B., Zhao, Z., Desmond, J. E., Glover, G. H., & Gabrieli, J. D. (1998). Making memories: Brain activity that predicts how well visual experience will be remembered. *Science, 281,* 118–120.

Brewer, W. F., & Treyens, J. C. (1981). Role of schemata in memory for places. *Cognitive Psychology, 13,* 207–230.

Broadbent, D. E. (1958). *Perception and communication.* New York: Pergamon.

Broadbent, D. E. (1975). The magical number seven after fifteen years. In R. A. Kennedy & A. Wilkes (Eds.), *Studies in long-term memory* (pp. 3–18). New York: Wiley.

Brodmann, K. (1960). On the comparative localization of the cortex. In G. von Bonin (Ed.), *Some papers on the cerebral cortex* (pp. 201–230). Springfield, IL: Charles C. Thomas. (Original work published 1909.)

Brooks, L. R. (1968). Spatial and verbal components of the act of recall. *Canadian Journal of Psychology, 22,* 349–368.

Brown, R. (1973). *A first language.* Cambridge, MA: Harvard University Press.

Brown, R., & Kulik, J. (1977). Flashbulb memories. *Cognition, 5,* 73–99.

Brown, R., & Lenneberg, E. H. (1954). A study in language and cognition. *Journal of Abnormal and Social Psychology, 49,* 454–462.

Bruce, C. J., Desimone, R., & Gross, C. G. (1981). Visual properties of neurons in a polysensory area in superior temporal sulcus of the macaque. *Neurophysiology, 46,* 369–384.

Bruner, J. S. (1964). The course of cognitive growth. *American Psychologist, 19,* 1–15.

Bruner, J. S., Goodnow, J. J., & Austin, G. A. (1956). *A study of thinking.* New York: NY Science Editions.

Buckner, R. L. (1998). Personal communication.

Burgess, N. (2006). Spatial memory: How egocentric and allocentric combine. *Trends in Cognitive Sciences, 10,* 551–557.

Buxhoeveden, D. P., & Casanova, M. F. (2002). The minicolumn hypothesis in neuroscience. *Brain, 125,* 935–951.

Byrne, M. D., & Anderson, J. R. (2001). Serial modules in parallel: The psychological refractory period and perfect time-sharing. *Psychological Review, 108,* 847–869.

Cabeza, R., Rao, S. M., Wagner, A. D., Mayer, A. R., & Schacter, D. L. (2001). Can medial temporal lobe regions distinguish true from false? An event-related fMRI study of veridical and illusory recognition memory. *Proceedings of the National Academy of Sciences, USA, 98,* 4805–4810.

Camerer, C., Loewenstein, G., & Prelec, D. (2005). Neuroeconomics: How neuroscience can inform economics. *Journal of Economic Literature, 43,* 9–64.

Caplan, D. (1972). Clause boundaries and recognition latencies for words in sentences. *Perception and Psychophysics, 12,* 73–76.

Caplan, D., Alpert, N., Waters, G., & Olivieri, A. (2000). Activation of Broca's area by syntactic processing under conditions of concurrent articulation. *Human Brain Mapping, 9,* 65–71.

Caramazza, A. (2000). The organization of conceptual knowledge in the brain. In M. S. Gazzaniga (Ed.), *The cognitive neurosciences* (2nd ed., pp. 1037–1046). Cambridge, MA: MIT Press.

Card, S. K., Moran, T. P., & Newell, A. (1983). *The psychology of human-computer interaction.* Hillsdale, NJ: Erlbaum.

Carey, S. (1978). The child as word learner. In M. Halle, J. Bresnan, & G. Miller (Eds.), *Linguistic theory and psychological reality* (pp. 264–293). Cambridge, MA: MIT Press.

Carey, S. (1985). *Conceptual change in childhood.* Cambridge, MA: MIT Press.

Carpenter, P. A., & Just, M. A. (1975). Sentence comprehension: A psycholinguistic processing model of verification. *Psychological Review, 82,* 45–73.

Carpenter, P. A., & Just, M. A. (1977). Reading comprehension as eyes see it. In M. A. Just & P. A. Carpenter (Eds.), *Cognitive processes in comprehension* (pp. 109–140). Hillsdale, NJ: Erlbaum.

Carpenter, T. P., & Moser, J. M. (1982). The development of addition and subtraction problem-solving skills. In T. P. Carpenter, J. M. Moser, & T. Romberg (Eds.), *Addition and subtraction: A cognitive perspective* (pp. 10–24). Hillsdale, NJ: Erlbaum.

Carraher, T. N., Carraher, D. W., & Schliemann, A. D. (1985). Mathematics in the streets and in the schools. *British Journal of Developmental Psychology, 3,* 21–29.

Carroll, J. B. (1993). *Human cognitive abilities: A survey of factor-analytic studies.* Cambridge, England: Cambridge University Press.

Case, R. (1978). Intellectual development from birth to adulthood: A neo-Piagetian approach. In R. S. Siegler (Ed.), *Children's thinking: What develops?* (pp. 37–71). Hillsdale, NJ: Erlbaum.

Case, R. (1985). *Intellectual development: A systematic reinterpretation.* New York: Academic Press.

Casey, B. J., Trainor, R., Giedd, J. N., Vauss, Y., Vaituzis, C. K., et al. (1997a). The role of the anterior cingulate in automatic and controlled processes: A developmental neuroanatomical study. *Developmental Psychobiology, 30,* 61–69.

Casey, B. J., Trainor, R. J., Orendi, J. L., Schubert, A. B., Nystrom, L. E., et al. (1997b). A pediatric functional MRI study of prefrontal activation during performance of a Go-No-Go task. *Journal of Cognitive Neuroscience, 9,* 835–847.

Cattell, R. B. (1963). Theory of fluid and crystallized intelligence: A critical experiment. *Journal of Educational Psychology, 54,* 1–22.

Ceci, S. J. (1991). How much does schooling influence general intelligence and its cognitive components? A reassessment of the evidence. *Developmental Psychology, 27,* 703–722.

Ceci, S. J., & Liker, J. K. (1986). A day at the races: A study of IQ, expertise, and cognitive complexity. *Journal of Experimental Psychology: General, 115,* 255–266.

Ceci, S. J., Loftus, E. F., Leichtman, M. D., & Bruck, M. (1994). The possible role of source misattributions in the creation of false beliefs among preschoolers. *International Journal of Clinical and Experimental Hypnosis, 42,* 304–320.

Chambers, D., & Reisberg, D. (1985). Can mental images be ambiguous? *Journal of Experimental Psychology: Human Perception and Performance, 11,* 317–328.

Charness, N. (1976). Memory for chess positions: Resistance to interference. *Journal of Experimental Psychology: Human Learning and Memory, 2,* 641–653.

Charness, N. (1979). Components of skill in bridge. *Canadian Journal of Psychology, 33,* 1–16.

Charness, N. (1981). Search in chess: Age and skill differences. *Journal of Experimental Psychology: Human Perception and Performance, 7,* 467–476.

Chase, W. G., & Clark, H. H. (1972). Mental operations in the comparisons of sentences and pictures. In L. W. Gregg (Ed.), *Cognition in learning and memory* (pp. 205–232). New York: Wiley.

Chase, W. G., & Ericsson, K. A. (1982). Skill and working memory. In G. H. Bower (Ed.), *The psychology of learning and motivation* (Vol. 16, pp. 1–58). New York: Academic Press.

Chase, W. G., & Simon, H. A. (1973). The mind's eye in chess. In W. G. Chase (Ed.), *Visual information processing* (pp. 215–281). New York: Academic Press.

Cheng, P. W., & Holyoak, K. J. (1985). Pragmatic reasoning schemas. *Cognitive Psychology, 17,* 391–416.

Cheng, P. W., Holyoak, K. J., Nisbett, R. E., & Oliver, L. M. (1986). Pragmatic versus syntactic approaches to training deductive reasoning. *Cognitive Psychology, 18,* 293–328.

Cherry, E. C. (1953). Some experiments on the recognition of speech with one and with two ears. *Journal of the Acoustical Society of America, 25,* 975–979.

Chi, M. T. H. (1978). Knowledge structures and memory development. In R. S. Siegler (Ed.), *Children's thinking: What develops?* (pp. 76–93). Hillsdale, NJ: Erlbaum.

Chi, M. T. H., Bassok, M., Lewis, M., Reimann, P., & Glaser, R. (1989). Self-explanations: How students study and use examples in learning to solve problems. *Cognitive Science, 13,* 145–182.

Chi, M. T. H., Feltovich, P. J., & Glaser, R. (1981). Categorization and representation of physics problems by experts and novices. *Cognitive Science, 5,* 121–152.

Chomsky, C. (1970). *The acquisition of syntax in children from 5 to 10.* Cambridge, MA: MIT Press.

Chomsky, N. (1965). *Aspects of the theory of syntax.* Cambridge, MA: MIT Press.

Chomsky, N. (1980). Rules and representations. *Behavioral and Brain Sciences, 3,* 1–61.

Chomsky, N., & Halle, M. (1968). *The sound pattern of English.* New York: Harper.

Christen, F., & Bjork, R. A. (1976). *On updating the loci in the method of loci.* Paper presented at the 17th annual meeting of the Psychonomic Society, St. Louis, MO.

Christensen, B. T., & Schunn, C. D. (2007). The relationship of analogical distance to analogical function and pre-inventive structure: The case of engineering design. *Memory & Cognition, 35,* 29–38.

Christianson, K., Hollingworth, A., Halliwell J., & Ferreira, F. (2001). Thematic roles assigned along the garden path linger. *Cognitive Psychology, 42,* 368–407.

Christoff, K., Prabhakaran, V., Dorfman, J., Zhao, Z., Kroger, J. K., et al. (2001). Rostrolateral prefrontal cortex involvement in relational integration during reasoning. *Neuroimage, 14,* 1136–1149.

Church, A. (1956). *Introduction to mathematical logic.* Princeton, NJ: Princeton University Press.

Clark, E. V. (1983). Meanings and concepts. In P. H. Mussen (Ed.), *Handbook of child psychology* (pp. 787–840). New York: Wiley.

Clark, H. H. (1974). Semantics and comprehension. In R. A. Sebeok (Ed.), *Current trends in linguistics* (Vol. 12, pp. 1291–1428). The Hague: Mouton.

Clark, H. H., & Chase, W. G. (1972). On the process of comparing sentences against pictures. *Cognitive Psychology, 3,* 472–517.

Clark, H. H., & Clark, E. V. (1977). *Psychology and language.* New York: Harcourt Brace Jovanovich.

Clark, H. H., & Fox Tree, J. E. (2002). Using uh and um in spontaneous speech. *Cognition, 84,* 73–111.

Clifton, C., Jr., & Duffy, S. (2001). Sentence comprehension: Roles of linguistic structure. *Annual Review of Psychology, 52,* 167–196.

Cohen J. D., & Servan-Schreiber, D. (1992). Context, cortex and dopamine: A connectionist approach to behavior and biology in schizophrenia. *Psychological Review, 99,* 45–77.

Cohen, M. R., & Nagel, E. (1934). *An introduction to logic and scientific method.* New York: Harcourt Brace.

Cohen, J. T., & Graham, J. D. (2003). A revised economic analysis of restrictions on the use of cell phones while driving. *Risk Analysis, 23,* 5–17.

Cole, M., & D'Andrade, R. (1982). The influence of schooling on concept formation: Some preliminary conclusions. *Quarterly Newsletter of the Laboratory of Comparative Human Cognition, 4,* 19–26.

Cole, M., Gay, J., Glick, J., & Sharp, D. (1971). *The cultural context of learning and thinking.* New York: Basic Books.

Collins, A. M., & Quillian, M. R. (1969). Retrieval time from semantic memory. *Journal of Verbal Learning and Verbal Behavior, 8,* 240–247.

Conrad, C. (1972). Cognitive economy in semantic memory. *Journal of Experimental Psychology, 92,* 149–154.

Conrad, R. (1964). Acoustic confusions in immediate memory. *British Journal of Psychology, 55,* 75–84.

Conway, M. A., Anderson, S. J., Larsen, S. F., Donnelly, C. M., McDaniel, M. A., et al. (1994). The formation of flashbulb memories. *Memory & Cognition, 22,* 326–343.

Cooper, W. E., & Paccia-Cooper, J. (1980). *Syntax and speech.* Cambridge, MA: Harvard University Press.

Corbett, A. T., & Anderson, J. R. (1990). The effect of feedback control on learning to program with the LISP tutor. *Proceedings of the 12th Annual Conference of the Cognitive Science Society,* 796–803.

Corbett, A. T., & Chang, F. R. (1983). Pronoun disambiguation: Accessing potential antecedents. *Memory & Cognition, 11,* 283–294.

Corbetta, M., & Shulman, G. L. (2002). Control of goal-directed and stimulus-driven attention in the brain. *Nature Reviews Neuroscience, 3,* 201–215.

Cosmides, L. (1989). The logic of social exchange: Has natural selection shaped how humans reason? Studies with the Wason selection task. *Cognition, 31,* 187–276.

Cowart, W. (1983). *Reference relations and syntactic processing: Evidence of pronoun's influence on a syntactic decision that affects naming.* Indiana University Linguistics Club.

Craik, F. I. M., & Lockhart, R. S. (1972). Levels of processing: A framework for memory research. *Journal of Verbal Learning and Verbal Behavior, 11,* 671–684.

Crick, F. H. C., & Asanuma, C. (1986). Certain aspects of the anatomy and physiology of the cerebral cortex. In J. L. McClelland & D. E. Rumelhart (Eds.), *Parallel distributed processing: Explorations in the microstructure of cognition* (Vol. 2, pp. 331–371). Cambridge, MA: MIT Press/Bradford Books.

Crossman, E. R. F. W. (1959). A theory of the acquisition of speed-skill. *Ergonomics, 2,* 153–166.

Curran, T. (1995). On the neural mechanisms of sequence learning. *Psyche, 2*(12). Available at http://psyche.cs.monash.edu.au/volume2-1/psyche-95-2-12-sequence-1-curran.html.

Damasio, H., Grabowski, T., Frank, R., Galaburda, A. M., & Damasio, A. R. (1994). The return of Phineas Gage: Clues about the brain from the skull of a famous patient. *Science, 264,* 1102–1105.

Daneman, M., & Carpenter, P. A. (1980). Individual differences in working memory and reading. *Journal of Verbal Learning and Verbal Behavior, 19,* 450–466.

Darwin, G. J., Turvey, M. T., & Crowder, R. G. (1972). An auditory analogue of the Sperling Partial Report Procedure: Evidence for brief auditory storage. *Cognitive Psychology, 3,* 255–267.

Daugherty, K. G., MacDonald, M. C., Petersen, A. S., & Seidenberg, M. S. (1993). Why no mere mortal has ever flown out to center field but people often say they do. *Proceedings of the 15th Annual Conference of the Cognitive Science Society,* 383–388.

Daw, N. D., Niv, Y., and Dayan, P. (2005). Uncertainty-based competition between prefrontal and dorsolateral striatal systems for behavioral control. *Nature Neuroscience, 8,* 1704–1711.

de Beer, G. R. (1959). Paedomorphesis. *Proceedings of the 15th International Congress of Zoology,* 927–930.

Deese, J. (1959). On the prediction of occurrence of particular verbal intrusions in immediate recall. *Journal of Experimental Psychology, 58,* 17–22.

de Groot, A. D. (1965). *Thought and choice in chess.* The Hague: Mouton.

de Groot, A. D. (1966). Perception and memory versus thought. In B. Kleinmuntz (Ed.), *Problem-solving* (pp. 19–50). New York: Wiley.

Dehaene, S. (2000). Cerebral bases of number processing and calculation. In M. Gazzaniga (Ed.), *The new cognitive neurosciences* (pp. 987–998). Cambridge, MA: MIT Press.

Dennett, D. C. (1969). *Content and consciousness.* London: Routledge.

Desimone, R., Albright, T. D., Gross, C. G., & Bruce, C. (1984). Stimulus-selective properties of inferior temporal neurons in the macaque. *Neuroscience, 4,* 2051–2062.

Deutsch, J. A., & Deutsch, D. (1963). Attention: Some theoretical considerations. *Psychological Review, 70,* 80–90.

de Valois, R. L., & Jacobs, G. H. (1968). Primate color vision. *Science, 162,* 533–540.

Diamond, A. (1991). Frontal lobe involvement in cognitive changes during the first year of life. In K. R. Gibson & A. C. Petersen (Eds.), *Brain maturation and cognitive development: Comparative and cross-cultural perspectives* (pp. 127–180). New York: Aldine de Gruyter.

Dickstein, L. S. (1978). The effect of figure on syllogistic reasoning. *Memory & Cognition, 6,* 76–83.

Diehl, R. L., Lotto, A. J., & Holt, L. L. (2004). Speech perception. *Annual Review of Psychology, 55,* 149–179.

Dodson, C. S., & Schacter, D. L. (2002a). Aging and strategic retrieval processes: Reducing false memories with a distinctiveness heuristic. *Psychology and Aging, 17,* 405–415.

Dodson, C. S., & Schacter, D. L. (2002b). When false recognition meets metacognition: The distinctiveness heuristic. *Journal of Memory and Language, 46,* 782–803.

Dooling, D. J., & Christiaansen, R. E. (1977). Episodic and semantic aspects of memory for prose. *Journal of Experimental Psychology: Human Learning and Memory, 3,* 428–436.

Driver, J., Baylis, G. C., Goodrich, S., & Rafal, R. D. (1994). Axis-based neglect of visual shape. *Neuropsychologia, 32,* 1353–1365.

Dronkers, N., Redfern, B., & Knight, R. (2000). The neural architecture of language disorders. In M. Gazzaniga (Ed.), *The cognitive neurosciences* (2nd ed., pp. 949–958). Cambridge, MA: MIT Press.

Dunbar, K. (1993). Concept discovery in a scientific domain. *Cognitive Science, 17,* 397–434.

Dunbar, K. (1997). How scientists think: Online creativity and conceptual change in science. In T. B. Ward, S. M. Smith, & S. Vaid (Eds.), *Conceptual structures and processes: Emergence, discovery and change.* Washington, DC: APA Press.

Dunbar, K., & Blanchette, I. (2001). The in vivo/in vitro approach to cognition: The case of analogy. *Trends in Cognitive Sciences, 5,* 334–339.

Dunbar, K., & MacLeod, C. M. (1984). A horse race of a different color: Stroop interference patterns with transformed words. *Journal of Experimental Psychology: Human Perception and Performance, 10,* 622–639.

Duncker, K. (1945). On problem-solving. (L. S. Lees, Trans.). *Psychological Monographs, 58.*

Dunning, D., & Sherman, D. A. (1997). Stereotypes and tacit inference. *Journal of Personality and Social Psychology, 73,* 459–471.

Easton, R. D., & Sholl, M. J. (1995). Object-array structure, frames of reference, and retrieval of spatial knowledge. *Journal of Experimental Psychology: Learning, Memory, and Cognition, 21,* 483–500.

Edwards, W. (1968). Conservatism in human information processing. In B. Kleinmuntz (Ed.), *Formal representations of human judgment* (pp. 17–52). New York: Wiley.

Egan, D. E., & Schwartz, B. J. (1979). Chunking in recall of symbolic drawings. *Memory & Cognition, 7,* 149–158.

Egly, R., Driver, J., & Rafal, R. D. (1994). Shifting visual attention between objects and locations: Evidence from normal and parietal lesion subjects. *Journal of Experimental Psychology: General, 123,* 161–177.

Ehrlich, K., & Rayner, K. (1983). Pronoun assignment and semantic integration during reading: Eye movements and immediacy of processing. *Journal of Verbal Learning and Verbal Behavior, 22,* 75–87.

Eich, E. (1985). Context, memory, and integrated item/context imagery. *Journal of Experimental Psychology: Learning, Memory, and Cognition, 11,* 764–770.

Eich, E., & Metcalfe, J. (1989). Mood dependent memory for internal versus external events. *Journal of Experimental Psychology: Learning, Memory, and Cognition, 15,* 443–455.

Eich, J., Weingartner, H., Stillman, R. C., & Gillin, J. C. (1975). State-dependent accessibility of retrieval cues in the retention of a categorized list. *Journal of Verbal Learning and Verbal Behavior, 14,* 408–417.

Eichenbaum, H., Dudchenko, P., Wood, E., Shapiro, M., & Tanila, H. (1999). The hippocampus, memory, and place cells: Is it spatial memory or a memory space? *Neuron, 23,* 209–226.

Eimas, P. D., & Corbit, J. (1973). Selective adaptation of linguistic feature detectors. *Cognitive Psychology, 4,* 99–109.

Ekstrand, B. R. (1972). To sleep, perchance to dream. In C. P. Duncan, L. Sechrest, & A. W. Melton (Eds.), *Human memory: Festschrift in honor of Benton J. Underwood* (pp. 58–82). New York: Appleton-Century Crofts.

Ekstrom, A. D., Kahana, M. J., Caplan, J. B., Fields, T. A., Isham, E. A., et al. (2003). Cellular networks underlying human spatial navigation. *Nature, 425,* 184–188.

Elbert, T., Pantev, C., Wienbruch, C., Rockstroh, B., & Taub, E. (1995). Increased use of the left hand in string players associated with increased cortical representation of the fingers. *Science, 270,* 305–307.

Elio, R., & Anderson, J. R. (1981). The effects of category generalizations and instance similarity on schema abstraction. *Journal of Experimental Psychology: Human Learning and Memory, 7,* 397–417.

Ellis, A. W., & Young, A. W. (1988). *Human cognitive neuropsychology.* Hillsdale, NJ: Erlbaum.

Elman, J. L., Bates, E., Johnson, M. H., Karmiloff-Smith, A., Parisi, D., et al. (1996). *Rethinking innateness: A connectionist perspective on development.* Cambridge, MA: MIT Press.

Enard, W., Przeworski, M., Fisher, S., Lai, C., Wiebe, V., et al. (2002). Molecular evolution of FOXP2, a gene involved in speech and language. *Nature, 418,* 869–872.

Engle, R. W., & Bukstel, L. (1978). Memory processes among bridge players of differing expertise. *American Journal of Psychology, 91,* 673–689.

Erickson, M. A., & Kruschke, J. K. (1998). Rules and exemplars in category learning. *Journal of Experimental Psychology: General, 127,* 107–140.

Erickson, T. A., & Matteson, M. E. (1981). From words to meanings: A semantic illusion. *Journal of Verbal Learning and Verbal Behavior, 20,* 540–552.

Ericsson, K. A., Krampe, R. T., & Tesch-Römer, C. (1993). The role of deliberate practice in the acquisition of expert performance. *Psychological Review, 100,* 363–406.

Ernst, G., & Newell, A. (1969). *GPS: A case study in generality and problem solving.* New York: Academic Press.

Ervin-Tripp, S. M. (1974). Is second language learning like the first? *TESOL Quarterly, 8,* 111–127.

Evans, J. St. B. T., Handley, S. J., & Harper, C. (2001). Necessity, possibility and belief: A study of syllogistic reasoning. *Quarterly Journal of Experimental Psychology, 54A,* 935–958.

Farah, M. J. (1990). *Visual agnosia: Disorders of object recognition and what they tell us about normal vision.* Cambridge, MA: MIT Press.

Farah, M. J., Hammond, K. M., Levine, D. N., & Calvanio, R. (1988). Visual and spatial mental imagery: Dissociable systems of representation. *Cognitive Psychology, 20,* 439–462.

Farah, M. J., & McClelland, J. (1991). A computational model of semantic memory impairment: Modality specificity and emergent category specificity. *Journal of Experimental Psychology: General, 120,* 339–357.

Farah, M. J., Stowe, R. M., & Levinson, K. L. (1996). Phonological dyslexia: Loss of a reading-specific component of the cognitive architecture? *Cognitive Neuropsychology, 13,* 849–868.

Fernandez, A., & Glenberg, A. M. (1985). Changing environmental context does not reliably affect memory. *Memory & Cognition, 13,* 333–345.

Ferreira, F., & Clifton, C. (1986). The independence of syntactic processing. *Journal of Memory and Language, 25,* 348–368.

Ferreira, F., & Henderson, J. M. (1991). Recovery from misanalyses of garden-path sentences. *Journal of Memory and Language, 25,* 725–745.

Ferreira, F., & Patson, N. (2007). The good enough approach to language comprehension. *Language and Linguistics Compass, 1,* 71–83.

Fillenbaum, S. (1971). On coping with ordered and unordered conjunctive sentences. *Journal of Experimental Psychology, 87,* 93–98.

Fillenbaum, S. (1974). Pragmatic normalization: Further results for some conjunctive and disjunctive sentences. *Journal of Experimental Psychology, 103,* 913–921.

Fincham, J. M., Carter, C. S., van Veen, V., Stenger, V. A., & Anderson, J. R. (2002). Neural mechanisms of planning: A computational analysis using event-related fMRI. *Proceedings of the National Academy of Sciences, USA, 99,* 3346–3351.

Fink, G. R., Halligan, P. H., Marshall, J. C., Frith, C. D., Frackowiack, R. S. J., et al. (1996). Where in the brain does visual attention select the forest and the trees? *Nature, 382,* 626–628.

Fink, A., & Neubauer, A. C. (2005). Individual differences in time estimation related to cognitive ability, speed of information processing and working memory. *Intelligence, 33,* 5–26.

Finke, R. A., Pinker, S., & Farah, M. J. (1989). Reinterpreting visual patterns in mental imagery. *Cognitive Science, 13,* 51–78.

Fischer, K. W. (1980). A theory of cognitive development: The control and construction of hierarchies of skills. *Psychological Review, 87,* 477–531.

Fischhoff, B. (2008). Assessing adolescent decision-making competence. *Developmental Review, 28,* 12–28.

Fischhoff, B., & Beyth-Marom, R. (1983). Hypothesis evaluation from a Bayesian perspective. *Psychological Review, 90,* 239–260.

Fitts, P. M., & Posner, M. I. (1967). *Human performance.* Belmont, CA: Brooks Cole.

Flavell, J. H. (1978). Comment. In R. S. Siegler (Ed.), *Children's thinking: What develops?* (pp. 97–105). Hillsdale, NJ: Erlbaum.

Flavell, J. H. (1985). *Cognitive development.* Englewood Cliffs, NJ: Prentice-Hall.

Flege, J., Yeni-Komshian, G., & Liu, S. (1999). Age constraints on second language learning. *Journal of Memory and Language, 41,* 78–104.

Flynn, J. R. (1987). Massive IQ gains in 14 nations: What IQ tests really measure. *Psychological Bulletin, 101,* 171–191.

Fodor, J. A. (1983). *The modularity of mind.* Cambridge, MA: MIT Press/Bradford Books.

Fong, G. T., Krantz, D. H., & Nisbett, R. E. (1986). The effects of statistical training on thinking about everyday problems. *Cognitive Psychology, 18,* 253–292.

Forward, S., & Buck, C. (1988). *Betrayal of innocence: Incest and its devastation.* New York: Penguin Books.

Franklin, N., & Tversky, B. (1990). Searching imagined environments. *Journal of Experimental Psychology: General, 119,* 63–76.

Frase, L. T. (1975). Prose processing. In G. H. Bower (Ed.), *The psychology of learning and motivation* (Vol. 9, pp. 1–47). New York: Academic Press.

Friedman-Hill, S., Robertson, L. C., & Treisman, A. (1995). Parietal contributions to visual feature binding: Evidence from a patient with bilateral lesions. *Science, 269,* 853–855.

Frisch, S., Schlesewsky, M., Saddy, D., & Alpermann, A. (2002). The P600 as an indicator of syntactic ambiguity. *Cognition, 85,* B83–B92.

Fromkin, V. (1971). The non-anomalous nature of anomalous utterances. *Languages, 47,* 27–52.

Fromkin, V. (1973). *Speech errors as linguistic evidence.* The Hague: Mouton.

Fugelsang, J., & Dunbar, K. (2005). Brain-based mechanisms underlying complex causal thinking. *Neuropsychologia, 43,* 1204–1213.

Funahashi, S., Bruce, C. J., & Goldman-Rakic, P. S. (1993). Dorsolateral prefrontal lesions and oculomotor delayed-response performance: Evidence for mnemonic "scotomas." *Journal of Neuroscience, 13,* 1479–1497.

Funahashi, S., Bruce, C. J., & Goldman-Rakic, P. S. (1991). Neural activity related to saccadic eye movements in the monkey's dorsolateral prefrontal cortex. *Journal of Neurophysiology, 65,* 1464–1483.

Fuster, J. M. (1989). *The prefrontal cortex: Anatomy, physiology, and neuropsychology of the frontal lobe.* New York: Raven Press.

Gabrieli, J. D. E. (2001). Functional neuroimaging of episodic memory. In R. Cabeza & A. Lingstone (Eds.), *Handbook of functional neuroimaging of cognition* (pp. 253–292). Cambridge, MA: MIT Press.

Gagné, E., Yekovich, C. W., & Yekovich, F. R. (1993). *The cognitive psychology of school learning.* New York: HarperCollins.

Gardner, H. (1975). *The shattered mind: The person after brain damage.* New York: Knopf.

Gardner, R. A., & Gardner, B. T. (1969). Teaching sign language to a chimpanzee. *Science, 165,* 664–672.

Garrett, M. F. (1975). The analysis of sentence production. In G. H. Bower (Ed.), *The psychology of learning and motivation* (Vol. 9, pp. 133–177). New York: Academic Press.

Garrett, M. F. (1980). Levels of processing in sentence production. In B. Butterworth (Ed.), *Language production* (Vol. 1, pp. 177–220). London: Academic Press.

Garrett, M. F. (1990). Sentence processing. In D. N. Osherson & H. Lasnik (Eds.), *Language: An invitation to cognition science* (Vol. 1, pp. 133–175). Cambridge, MA: MIT Press.

Garro, L. (1986). Language, memory, and focality: A reexamination. *American Anthropologist, 88,* 128–136.

Gauthier, I., Skudlarski, P., Gore, J. C., & Anderson, A. W. (2000). Expertise for cars and birds recruits brain areas involved in face recognition. *Nature Neuroscience, 3,* 191–197.

Gauthier, I., Tarr, M. J., Anderson, A. W., Skudlarski, P., & Gore, J. C. (1999). Activation of the middle fusiform "face area" increases with expertise in recognizing novel objects. *Nature Neuroscience, 2,* 568–573.

Gazzaniga, M. S., Ivry, R. B., & Mangun, G. R. (1998). *Cognitive neuroscience: The biology of the mind.* New York: W. W. Norton.

Gazzaniga, M. S., Ivry, R. B., & Mangun, G. R. (2002). *Cognitive neuroscience: The biology of the mind* (2nd ed.). New York: W. W. Norton.

Gee, J. P., & Grosjean, F. (1983). Performance structures: A psycholinguistic and linguistic appraisal. *Cognitive Psychology, 15,* 411–458.

Geiselman, E. R., Fisher, R. P., MacKinnon, D. P., & Holland, H. L. (1985). Eyewitness memory enhancement in the police interview: Cognitive retrieval mnemonics versus hypnosis. *Journal of Applied Psychology, 70,* 401–412.

Geison, G. L. (1995). *The private science of Louis Pasteur.* Princeton, NJ: Princeton University Press.

Gelman, S. A. (1988). The development of induction within natural kind and artifact categories. *Cognitive Psychology, 20,* 65–95.

Gentner, D. (1983). Structure-mapping: A theoretical framework for analogy. *Cognitive Science, 7,* 155–170.

Georgopoulos, A. P., Lurito, J. T., Petrides, M., Schwartz, A. B., & Massey, J. T. (1989). Mental rotation of the neuronal population vector. *Science, 243,* 234–236.

Gernsbacher, M. A. (1985). Surface information loss in comprehension. *Cognitive Psychology, 17,* 324–363.

Geschwind, N. (1980). Neurological knowledge and complex behaviors. *Cognitive Science, 4,* 185–194.

Gibson, E. J. (1969). *Principles of learning and development.* New York: Meredith.

Gibson, J. J. (1950). *Perception of the visual world.* Boston: Houghton Mifflin.

Gick, M. L., & Holyoak, K. J. (1980). Analogical problem solving. *Cognitive Psychology, 12,* 306–355.

Gigerenzer, G., & Hoffrage, U. (1995). How to improve Bayesian reasoning without instruction: Frequency formats. *Psychological Review, 102,* 684–704.

Gigerenzer, G., & Hug, K. (1992). Domain-specific reasoning: Social contracts, cheating, and perspective change. *Cognition, 43,* 127–171.

Gigerenzer, G., Swijtink, Z., Porter, T., Daston, L., Beatty, J., et al. (1989). *The empire of chance: How probability changed science and everyday life.* Cambridge, England: Cambridge University Press.

Gigerenzer, G., Todd, P. M., & ABC Research Group. (1999). *Simple heuristics that make us smart.* New York: Oxford University Press.

Gilbert, S. J., Spengler, S., Simons, J. S., Frith, C. D., & Burgess, P. W. (2006). Differential functions of lateral and medial rostral prefrontal cortex (area 10) revealed by brain-behaviour correlations. *Cerebral Cortex, 16,* 1783–1789.

Gillund, G., & Shiffrin, R. M. (1984). A retrieval model for both recognition and recall. *Psychological Review, 91,* 1–67.

Ginsburg, H. J., & Opper, S. (1980). *Piaget's theory of intellectual development.* Englewood Cliffs, NJ: Prentice-Hall.

Gleitman, L. R., Newport, E. L., & Gleitman, H. (1984). The current status of the motherese hypothesis. *Journal of Child Language, 11,* 43–80.

Glenberg, A. M. (2007). Language and action: Creating sensible combinations of ideas. In G. Gaskell (Ed.), *The Oxford handbook of psycholinguistics* (pp. 361–370). Oxford, UK: Oxford University Press.

Glenberg, A. M., Smith, S. M., & Green, C. (1977). Type I rehearsal: Maintenance and more. *Journal of Verbal Learning and Verbal Behavior, 16,* 339–352.

Gluck, M. A., & Bower, G. H. (1988). From conditioning to category learning: An adaptive network model. *Journal of Experimental Psychology: General, 117,* 227–247.

Gluck, M. A., Mercado, E., & Myers, C. E. (2008). *Learning and memory: From brain to behavior.* New York: Worth.

Glucksberg, S., & Cowan, G. N., Jr. (1970). Memory for nonattended auditory material. *Cognitive Psychology, 1,* 149–156.

Glucksberg, S., & Weisberg, R. W. (1966). Verbal behavior and problem solving: Some effects of labeling in a functional fixedness problem. *Journal of Experimental Psychology, 71,* 659–666.

Gobet, F., Richman, H., Staszewski, J., & Simon, H. A. (1997). Goals, representations, and strategies in a concept attainment task: The EPAM model. In D. L. Medin (Ed.), *The psychology of learning and motivation* (Vol. 37, pp. 265–290). San Diego: Academic Press.

Godden, D. R., & Baddeley, A. D. (1975). Context-dependent memory in two natural environments: On land and under water. *British Journal of Psychology, 66,* 325–331.

Goel, V., Buchel, C., Frith, C., & Dolan, R. (2000). Dissociation of mechanisms underlying syllogistic reasoning. *Neuroimage, 12,* 504–514.

Goel, V., & Grafman, J. (1995). Are the frontal lobes implicated in "planning" functions? Interpreting data from the Tower of Hanoi. *Neuropsychologica, 33,* 623–642.

Goel, V., & Grafman, J. (2000). The role of the right prefrontal cortex in ill-structured problem solving. *Cognitive Neuropsychology, 17,* 415–436.

Goldberg, R. A., Schwartz, S., & Stewart, M. (1977). Individual differences in cognitive processes. *Journal of Educational Psychology, 69,* 9–14.

Goldin-Meadow, S. (2003). *The resilience of language: What gesture creation in deaf children can tell us about how all children learn language.* New York: Psychology Press.

Goldman-Rakic, P. S. (1987). Circuitry of primate prefrontal cortex and regulation of behavior by representational memory. In *Handbook of physiology. The nervous system: Vol. 5. Higher functions of the brain* (pp. 373–417). Bethesda, MD: American Physiology Society.

Goldman-Rakic, P. S. (1988). Topography of cognition: Parallel distributed networks in primate association cortex. *Annual Review of Neuroscience, 11,* 137–156.

Goldman-Rakic, P. S. (1992). Working memory and mind. *Scientific American, 267,* 111–117.

Goldstein, D. G., & Gigerenzer, G. (1999). The recognition heuristic: How ignorance makes us smart. In G. Gigerenzer, P. M. Todd, & ABC Research Group (Eds.), *Simple heuristics that make us smart* (pp. 37–58). New York: Oxford University Press.

Goldstein, D. G., & Gigerenzer, G. (2002). Models of ecological rationality: The recognition heuristic. *Psychological Review, 109,* 75–90.

Goldstein, M. N. (1974). Auditory agnosia for speech ("pure word deafness"): A historical review with current implications. *Brain and Language, 1,* 195–204.

Goodale, M. A., Milner, A. D., Jakobson, L. S., & Carey, D. P. (1991). A neurological dissociation between perceiving objects and grasping them. *Nature, 349,* 154–156.

Gould, E., & Gross, C. G. (2002). Neurogenesis in adult mammals: Some progress and problems. *Journal of Neuroscience, 22,* 619–623.

Gould, S. J. (1977). *Ontogeny and phylogeny.* Cambridge, MA: Belknap.

Graesser, A. C., Singer, M., & Trabasso, T. (1994). Constructing inferences during narrative text comprehension. *Psychological Review, 101,* 371–395.

Graf, P., Squire, L. R., & Mandler, G. (1984). The information that amnesic patients do not forget. *Journal of Experimental Psychology: Learning, Memory, and Cognition, 10,* 164–178.

Graf, P., & Torrey, J. W. (1966). Perception of phrase structure in written language. *American Psychological Association Convention Proceedings,* 83–88.

Granrud, C. E. (1986). Binocular vision and spatial perception in 4- and 5-month-old infants. *Journal of Experimental Psychology: Human Perception and Performance, 12,* 36–49.

Granrud, C. E. (1987). Visual size constancy in newborn infants. *Investigative Ophthalmology & Visual Science, 28* (Suppl. 5).

Gray, J. A., & Wedderburn, A. A. I. (1960). Grouping strategies with simultaneous stimuli. *Quarterly Journal of Experimental Psychology, 12,* 180–184.

Greenberg, J. H. (1963). Some universals of grammar with particular reference to the order of meaningful elements. In J. H. Greenberg (Ed.), *Universals of language* (pp. 73–113). Cambridge, MA: MIT Press.

Greene, J. D., Sommerville, R. B., Nystrom, L. E., Darley, J. M., & Cohen, J. D. (2001). An fMRI investigation of emotional engagement in moral judgment. *Science, 293,* 2105–2108.

Greeno, J. G. (1974). Hobbits and orcs: Acquisition of a sequential concept. *Cognitive Psychology, 6,* 270–292.

Griggs, R. A., & Cox, J. R. (1982). The elusive thematic-materials effect in Wason's selection task. *British Journal of Psychology, 73,* 407–420.

Gron, G., Wunderlich, A. P., Spitzer, M., Tomczak, R., & Riepe, M. W. (2000). Brain activation during human navigation: Gender different neural networks as substrate of performance. *Nature Neuroscience, 3,* 404–408.

Grosjean, F., Grosjean, L., & Lane, H. (1979). The patterns of silence: Performance structures in sentence production. *Cognitive Psychology, 11,* 58–81.

Gross, C. G. (2000). Neurogenesis in the adult brain: Death of a dogma. *Nature Review, 1,* 67–73.

Gugerty, L., deBoom, D., Jenkins, J. C., & Morley, R. (2000). Keeping north in mind: How navigators reason about cardinal directions. In *Proceedings of the Human Factors and Ergonomics Society 2000 Congress* (pp. I148–I151). Santa Monica, CA: Human Factors and Ergonomics Society.

Guilford, J. P. (1982). Cognitive psychology's ambiguities: Some suggested remedies. *Psychological Review, 89,* 48–59.

Gunzelmann, G., & Anderson, J. R. (2002). Strategic differences in the coordination of different views of space. In W. D. Gray & C. D. Schunn (Eds.), *Proceedings of the Twenty-Fourth Annual Conference of the Cognitive Science Society* (pp. 387–392). Mahwah, NJ: Erlbaum.

Guskey, T. R., & Gates, S. (1986). Synthesis of research on the effects of mastery learning in elementary and secondary classrooms. *Educational Leadership, 43,* 73–80.

Haesler, S., Rochefort, C., Georgi, B., Licznerski, P., Osten, P., et al. (2007). Incomplete and inaccurate vocal imitation after knockdown of FoxP2 in songbird basal ganglia nucleus area X. *PLoS Biology, 5,* 2885–2897.

Haier, R. J., Siegel, B. V., Jr., Nuechterlein, K. H., Hazlett, E., Wu, J. C., et al. (1988). Cortical glucose metabolic rate correlates of abstract reasoning and attention studied with positron emission tomography. *Intelligence, 12,* 199–217.

Hakes, D. T. (1972). Effects of reducing complement constructions on sentence comprehension. *Journal of Verbal Learning and Verbal Behavior, 11,* 278–286.

Hakes, D. T., & Foss, D. J. (1970). Decision processes during sentence comprehension: Effects of surface structure reconsidered. *Perception and Psychophysics, 8,* 413–416.

Halford, G. S. (1982). *The development of thought.* Hillsdale, NJ: Erlbaum.

Halford, G. S. (1992). Analogical reasoning and conceptual complexity in cognitive development. *Human Development, 35,* 193–217.

Hammerton, M. (1973). A case of radical probability estimation. *Journal of Experimental Psychology, 101,* 252–254.

Harlow, J. M. (1868). Recovery from a passage of an iron bar through the head. *Publications of the Massachusetts Medical Society, 2,* 327–347.

Harris, R. J. (1977). Comprehension of pragmatic implications in advertising. *Journal of Applied Psychology, 62,* 603–608.

Hart, R. A., & Moore, G. I. (1973). The development of spatial cognition: A review. In R. M. Downs & D. Stea (Eds.). *Image and environment* (pp. 246–288). Chicago: Aldine.

Hartley, T., Maguire, E. A., Spiers, H. J., & Burgess, N. (2003). The well-worn route and the path less traveled: Distinct neural bases of route following and wayfinding in humans. *Neuron, 37,* 877–888.

Hauk, O., Johnsrude, I., & Pulvermuller, F. (2004). Somatotopic representation of action words in human motor and premotor cortex. *Neuron, 41,* 301–307.

Haviland, S. E., & Clark, H. H. (1974). What's new? Acquiring new information as a process in comprehension. *Journal of Verbal Learning and Verbal Behavior, 13,* 512–521.

Haxby, J. V., Ungerleider, L. G., Clark, V. P., Schouten, J. L., Hoffman, E. A., et al. (1999). The effect of face inversion on activity in human neural systems for face and object perception. *Neuron, 22,* 189–199.

Hayes, C. (1951). *The ape in our house.* New York: Harper.

Hayes, J. R. (1984). *Problem solving techniques.* Philadelphia: Franklin Institute Press.

Hayes, J. R. (1985). Three problems in teaching general skills. In J. Segal, S. Chipman, & R. Glaser (Eds.), *Thinking and learning* (Vol. 2, pp. 391–406). Hillsdale, NJ: Erlbaum.

Hayes-Roth, B., & Hayes-Roth, F. (1977). Concept learning and the recognition and classification of exemplars. *Journal of Verbal Learning and Verbal Behavior, 16,* 321–338.

Haygood, R. C., & Bourne, L. E. (1965). Attribute and rule-learning aspects of conceptual behavior. *Psychological Review, 72,* 175–195.

Heath, S. B. (1983). *Ways with words: Language, life and work in communities and classrooms.* New York: Cambridge University Press.

Heider, E. (1972). Universals of color naming and memory. *Journal of Experimental Psychology, 93,* 10–20.

Henkel, L. A., Johnson, M. K., & DeLeonardis, D. M. (1998). Aging and source monitoring: Cognitive processes and neuropsychological correlates. *Journal of Experimental Psychology: General, 127,* 251–268.

Henson, R. N., Burgess, N., & Frith, C. D. (2000). Recoding, storage, rehearsal and grouping in verbal short-term memory: An fMRI study. *Neuropsychologia, 38,* 426–440.

Hilgard, E. R. (1968). *The experience of hypnosis.* New York: Harcourt Brace Jovanovich.

Hinton, G. E. (1979). Some demonstrations of the effects of structural descriptions in mental imagery. *Cognitive Science, 3,* 231–250.

Hintzman, D. L., O'Dell, C. S., & Arndt, D. R. (1981). Orientation in cognitive maps. *Cognitive Psychology, 13,* 149–206.

Hirshman, E., Passannante, A., & Arndt, J. (2001). Midazolam amnesia and conceptual processing in implicit memory. *Journal of Experimental Psychology: General, 130,* 453–465.

Hockett, C. F. (1960). The origin of speech. *Scientific American, 203,* 89–96.

Hockey, G. R. J., Davies, S., & Gray, M. M. (1972). Forgetting as a function of sleep at different times of day. *Experimental Psychology, 24,* 386–393.

Hoffman, D. D., & Richards, W. (1985). Parts of recognition. *Cognition, 18,* 65–96.

Holding, D. H. (1992). Theories of chess skill. *Psychological Research, 54,* 10–16.

Holmes, J. B., Waters, H. S., & Rajaram, S. (1998). The phenomenology of false memories: Episodic content and confidence. *Journal of Experimental Psychology: Learning, Memory, and Cognition, 24,* 1026–1040.

Horn, J. L. (1968). Organization of abilities and the development of intelligence. *Psychological Review, 75,* 242–259.

Horn, J. L., & Stankov, L. (1982). Auditory and visual intelligence. *Intelligence, 6,* 165–185.

Horton, J. C. (1984). Cytochrome oxidase patches: A new cytoarchitectonic feature of monkey visual cortex. *Philosophical Transactions of the Royal Society of London, 304,* 199–253.

Hsu, F.-H. (2002). Behind Deep Blue. Princeton N. J. Princeton University Press.

Hubel, D. H., & Wiesel, T. N. (1962). Receptive fields, binocular interaction, and functional architecture in the cat's visual cortex. *Journal of Physiology, 166,* 106–154.

Hubel, D. H., & Wiesel, T. N. (1977). Functional architecture of macaque monkey visual cortex. *Philosophical Transactions of the Royal Society of London, 198,* 1–59.

Hunt, E. B. (1985). Verbal ability. In R. J. Sternberg (Ed.), *Human abilities: An information-processing approach* (pp. 144–162). New York: W. H. Freeman.

Hunt, E. B., Davidson, J., & Lansman, M. (1981). Individual differences in long-term memory access. *Memory & Cognition, 9,* 599–608.

Hunter, J. E., & Hunter, R. F. (1984). Validity and utility of alternative predictors of job performance. *Psychological Bulletin, 96,* 72–98.

Huttenlocher, P. R. (1994). Synaptogenesis in human cerebral cortex. In G. Dawson & K. W. Fischer (Eds.), *Human behavior and the developing brain* (pp. 137–152). New York: Guilford Press.

Hyams, N. M. (1986). *Language acquisition and the theory of parameters.* Dordrecht: D. Reidel.

Hyde, T. S., & Jenkins, J. J. (1973). Recall for words as a function of semantic, graphic, and syntactic orienting tasks. *Journal of Verbal Learning and Verbal Behavior, 12,* 471–480.

Iacoboni, M., Woods, R. P., Brass, M., Bekkering, H., Mazziotta, J. C., et al. (1999). Cortical mechanisms of human imitation. *Science, 286,* 2526–2528.

Ishai, A., Ungerleider, L. G., Martin, A., Maisog, J. M., & Haxby, J. V. (1997). fMRI reveals differential activation in the ventral object vision pathway during the perception of faces, houses, and chairs. *Neuroimage, 5,* S149.

Jacobsen, C. F. (1935). Functions of frontal association areas in primates. *Archives of Neurology & Psychiatry, 33,* 558–560.

Jacobsen, C. F. (1936). Studies of cerebral functions in primates. I. The function of the frontal association areas in monkeys. *Comparative Psychology Monographs, 13,* 1–60.

Jacoby, L. L. (1983). Remembering the data: Analyzing interactive processes in reading. *Journal of Verbal Learning and Verbal Behavior, 22,* 485–508.

Jacoby, L. L., & Witherspoon, D. (1982). Remembering without awareness. *Canadian Journal of Psychology, 36,* 300–324.

Jaeger, J. J., Lockwood, A. H., Kemmerer, D. L., Van Valin, R. D., Jr., Murphy, B. W., et al. (1996). A positron emission tomographic study of regular and irregular verb morphology in English. *Language, 72,* 451–497.

James, W. (1890). *The principles of psychology* (Vols. 1 and 2). New York: Holt.

Janer, K. W., & Pardo, J. V. (1991). Deficits in selective attention following bilateral anterior cingulotomy. *Journal of Cognitive Neuroscience, 3,* 231–241.

Jarvella, R. J. (1971). Syntactic processing of connected speech. *Journal of Verbal Learning and Verbal Behavior, 10,* 409–416.

Jeffries, R. P., Polson, P. G., Razran, L., & Atwood, M. E. (1977). A process model for missionaries: Cannibals and other river-crossing problems. *Cognitive Psychology, 9,* 412–440.

Jeffries, R. P., Turner, A. A., Polson, P. G., & Atwood, M. E. (1981). The processes involved in designing software. In J. R. Anderson (Ed.), *Cognitive skills and their acquisition* (pp. 225–283). Hillsdale, NJ: Erlbaum.

Jenkins, I. H., Brooks, D. J., Nixon, P. D., Frackowiak, R. S. J., & Passingham, R. E. (1994). Motor sequence learning: A study with positron emission tomography. *Journal of Neuroscience, 14,* 3775–3790.

Johnson, D. M. (1939). Confidence and speed in the two-category judgment. *Archives of Psychology, 241,* 1–52.

Johnson, J. S., & Newport, E. L. (1989). Critical period effects in second language learning: The influence of maturational state on the acquisition of English as a second language. *Cognitive Psychology, 21,* 60–99.

Johnson-Laird, P. N. (1983). *Mental models.* Cambridge, MA: Harvard University Press.

Johnson-Laird, P. N. (1995). Mental models, deductive reasoning, and the brain. In M. S. Gazzaniga (Ed.), *The cognitive neurosciences* (pp. 999–1008). Cambridge, MA; MIT Press.

Johnson-Laird, P. N. (2003). Personal communication.

Johnson-Laird, P. N., & Goldvarg, Y. (1997). How to make the impossible seem possible. *Proceedings of the Nineteenth Annual Conference of the Cognitive Science Society*, 354–357.

Johnson-Laird, P. N., & Steedman, M. (1978). The psychology of syllogisms. *Cognitive Psychology, 10,* 64–99.

Johnston, W. A., & Heinz, S. P. (1978). Flexibility and capacity demands of attention. *Journal of Experimental Psychology: General, 107,* 420–435.

Jones, L., Rothbart, M. K., & Posner, M. I. (2003). Development of inhibitory control in preschool children. *Developmental Science, 6,* 498–504.

Jonides, J., Schumacher, E. H., Smith, E. E., Koeppe, R. A., Awh, E., et al. (1998). The role of parietal cortex in verbal working memory. *Journal of Neuroscience, 18,* 5026–5034.

Jung-Beeman, M., Bowden, E. M., Haberman, J., Frymiare, J. L., Arambel-Liu, S., et al. (2004). Neural activity when people solve verbal problems with insight. *Public Library of Science Biology, 2,* 500–510.

Just, M. A., & Carpenter, P. A. (1980). A theory of reading: From eye fixations to comprehension. *Psychological Review, 87,* 329–354.

Just, M. A., & Carpenter, P. A. (1985). Cognitive coordinate systems: Accounts of mental rotation and individual differences in spatial ability. *Psychological Review, 92,* 137–172.

Just, M. A., & Carpenter, P. A. (1987). *The psychology of reading and language comprehension.* Boston: Allyn & Bacon.

Just, M. A., & Carpenter, P. A. (1992). A capacity theory of comprehension: Individual differences in working memory. *Psychological Review, 99,* 122–149.

Kahn, I., & Wagner, A. D. (2002). Diminished medial temporal lobe activation with expanding retrieval practice. *Journal of Cognitive Neuroscience, D71* (Suppl., Cognitive Neuroscience Society Ninth Annual Meeting).

Kahneman, D., & Tversky, A. (1979). Prospect theory: An analysis of decisions under risk. *Econometrica, 97,* 263–291.

Kahneman, D., & Tversky, A. (1984). Choices, values, and frames. *American Psychologist, 80,* 341–350.

Kahneman, D., & Tversky, A. (1996). On the reality of cognitive illusions. *Psychological Review, 103,* 582–591.

Kail, R. (1988). Developmental functions for speeds of cognitive processes. *Journal of Experimental Child Psychology, 45,* 339–364.

Kail, R., & Park, Y. (1990). Impact of practice on speed of mental rotation. *Journal of Experimental Child Psychology, 49,* 227–244.

Kamin, L. J. (1974). *The science and politics of IQ.* Potomac, MD: Erlbaum.

Kandel, E. R., & Schwartz, J. H. (1984). *Principles of neural science* (2nd ed.). New York: Elsevier.

Kandel, E. R., Schwartz, J. H., & Jessell, T. M. (1991). *Principles of neural science* (3rd ed.). New York: Elsevier.

Kanwisher, N., McDermott, J., & Chun, M. M. (1997). The fusiform face area: A module in human extra-striate cortex specialized for face perception. *Journal of Neuroscience, 17,* 4302–4311.

Kanwisher, N. J., Tong, F, & Nakayama, K. (1998). The effect of face inversion on the human fusiform face area. *Cognition, 68,* B1–B11.

Kanwisher, N. J., & Wojciulik, E. (2000). Visual attention: Insights from brain imaging. *Nature Review Neuroscience, 1,* 91–100.

Kaplan, C. A. (1989). Hatching a theory of incubation: Does putting a problem aside really help? If so, why? Unpublished doctoral dissertation, Carnegie Mellon University, Pittsburgh, PA.

Kaplan, C. A., & Simon, H. A. (1990). In search of insight. *Cognitive Psychology, 22,* 374–419.

Kapur, S., Craik, F. I. M., Tulving, E., Wilson, A. A., Houle, S., et al. (1994). Neuroanatomical correlates of encoding in episodic memory: Levels of processing effect. *Proceedings of National Academy of Sciences, USA, 91,* 2008–2011.

Kastner, S., DeWeerd, P., Desimone, R., & Ungerleider, L. G. (1998). Mechanisms of directed attention in ventral extrastriate cortex as revealed by functional MRI. *Science, 282,* 108–111.

Katz, B. (1952). The nerve impulse. *Scientific American, 187,* 55–64.

Kay, P., & Regier, T. (2006). Language, thought, and color. *Recent developments. Trends in Cognitive Sciences, 10,* 51–54.

Keenan, J. M., Baillet, S. D., & Brown, P. (1984). The effects of causal cohesion on comprehension and memory. *Journal of Verbal Learning and Verbal Behavior, 23,* 115–126.

Keeney, T. J., Cannizzo, S. R., & Flavell, J. H. (1967). Spontaneous and induced verbal rehearsal in a recall task. *Child Development, 38,* 953–966.

Keeton, W. T. (1980). *Biological science.* New York: W. W. Norton.

Kellogg, W. N., & Kellogg, L. A. (1933). *The ape and the child.* New York: McGraw-Hill.

Keppel, G. (1968). Retroactive and proactive inhibition. In T. R. Dixon & D. L. Horton (Eds.), *Verbal behavior and general behavior theory* (pp. 172–213). Englewood Cliffs, NJ: Prentice-Hall.

Kershaw, T. C., & Ohlsson, S. (2001). Training for insight: The case of the nine-dot problem. In J. D. Moore & K. Stenning (Eds.), *Proceedings of the Twenty-Third Annual Conference of the Cognitive Science Society* (pp. 489–493). Mahwah, NJ: Erlbaum.

Kinney, G. C., Marsetta, M., & Showman, D. J. (1966). *Studies in display symbol legibility. Part XXI. The legibility of alphanumeric symbols for digitized television* (ESD-TR-66–117). Bedford, MA: The Mitre Corporation.

Kintsch, W. (1974). *The representation of meaning in memory.* Hillsdale, NJ: Erlbaum.

Kintsch, W. (1998). *Comprehension: A paradigm for cognition.* Cambridge, England: Cambridge University Press.

Kintsch, W., Welsch, D. M., Schmalhofer, F., & Zimny, S. (1990). Sentence memory: A theoretical analysis. *Journal of Memory and Language, 29,* 133–159.

Kirsh, D., & Maglio, P. (1994). On distinguishing epistemic from pragmatic action. *Cognitive Science, 18,* 513–549.

Klahr, D., & Dunbar, K. (1988). Dual space search during scientific reasoning. *Cognitive Science, 12,* 1–4.

Klatzky, R. L. (1975). *Human memory.* New York: W. H. Freeman.

Klayman, J., & Ha, Y.-W. (1987). Confirmation, disconfirmation, and information in hypothesis testing. *Psychological Review, 94,* 211–228.

Knutson, B., Taylor, J., Kaufman, M., Peterson, R., & Glover, G. (2005). Distributed neural representation of expected value. *Journal of Neuroscience, 25,* 4806–4812.

Koedinger, K. R., & Corbett, A. T. (2006). Cognitive tutors: Technology bringing learning science to the classroom. In R. K. Sawyer (Ed.), *Handbook of the learning sciences* (pp. 61–78). New York: Cambridge University Press.

Koestler, A. (1964). *The action of creation.* London: Hutchinson.

Köhler, W. (1927). *The mentality of apes.* New York: Harcourt Brace.

Köhler, W. (1956). *The mentality of apes.* London: Routledge & Kegan Paul.

Kolb, B., & Wishaw, I. Q. (1996). Fundamentals of human neuropsychology (4th ed.). New York: W. H. Freeman.

Kolers, P. A. (1976). Reading a year later. *Journal of Experimental Psychology: Human Learning and Memory, 2,* 554–565.

Kolers, P. A. (1979). A pattern analyzing basis of recognition. In L. S. Cermak & F. I. M. Craik (Eds.), *Levels of processing in human memory* (pp. 363–384). Hillsdale, NJ: Erlbaum.

Kolers, P. A., & Perkins, P. N. (1975). Spatial and ordinal components of form perception and literacy. *Cognitive Psychology, 7,* 228–267.

Körkel, J. (1987). *Die Entwicklung von Gedächtnis- und Metagedächtnisleistungen in Abhängigkeit von bereichsspezifischen Vorkenntnissen.* Frankfurt: Lang.

Kosslyn, S. M., Alpert, N. M., Thompson, W. I., Maljkovic, V., Weise, S. B., et al. (1993). Visual mental imagery activates topographically organized visual cortex: PET investigation. *Journal of Cognitive Neuroscience, 5,* 263–287.

Kosslyn, S. M., DiGirolamo, G., Thompson, W. L., & Alpert, N. M. (1998). Mental rotation of objects versus hands: Neural mechanisms revealed by positron emission tomography. *Psychophysiology, 35,* 151–161.

Kosslyn, S. M., Pascual-Leone, A., Felician, O., Camposano, S., Keenan, J. P., et al. (1999). The role of area 17 in visual imagery: Convergent evidence from PET and rTMS. *Science, 284,* 167–170.

Kosslyn, S. M., & Thompson, W. L. (2003). When is early visual cortex activated during visual mental imagery? *Psychological Bulletin, 129,* 723–746.

Kotovsky, K., Hayes, J. R., & Simon, H. A. (1985). Why are some problems hard? Evidence from Tower of Hanoi. *Cognitive Psychology, 17,* 248–294.

Koutstaal, W., Wagner, A. D., Rotte, M., Maril, A., Buckner, R. L., et al. (2001). Perceptual specificity in visual object priming: fMRI evidence for a laterality difference in fusiform cortex. *Neuropsychologia, 39,* 184–199.

Kroger, J. K, Nystrom, L. E., Cohen, J. D., & Johnson-Laird, P. N. (2008). Distinct neural substrates for deductive and mathematical processing. *Brain Research, 1243,* 83–103.

Krause, J., Lalueza-Fox, C., Orlando L., Enard W., Green, R. E., et al. (2007). The derived FOXP2 variant of modern humans was shared with Neandertals. *Current Biology, 17,* 1908–1912.

Kroll, J. F., & De Groot, A. M. B. (Eds.). (2005). *Handbook of bilingualism: Psycholinguistic approaches.* Oxford: Oxford University Press.

Kuffler, S. W. (1953). Discharge pattern and functional organization of mammalian retina. *Journal of Neurophysiology, 16,* 37–68.

Kuhl, P. K. (1987). The special mechanisms debate in speech research: Categorization tests on animals and infants. In S. Harnad (Ed.), *Categorical perception: The groundwork of cognition.* (pp. 355–386). Cambridge, England: Cambridge University Press.

Kulik, C., Kulik, J., & Bangert-Downs, R. (1986). *Effects of testing for mastery on student learning.* Paper presented at the annual meeting of the American Educational Research Association, San Francisco.

Kutas, M., & Federmeier, K. D. (2000). Electrophysiology reveals semantic memory use in language comprehension. *Trends in Cognitive Sciences, 4,* 463–470.

Kutas, M., & Hillyard, S. A. (1980b). Event-related brain potentials to semantically inappropriate and surprisingly large words. *Biological Psychology, 11,* 539–550.

Labov, W. (1973). The boundaries of words and their meanings. In C.-J. N. Bailey & R. W. Shuy (Eds.), *New ways of analyzing variations in English* (pp. 340–373). Washington, DC: Georgetown University Press.

Lakoff, G. (1971). On generative semantics. In D. Steinberg & L. Jakobovits (Eds.), *Semantics: An interdisciplinary reader in philosophy, linguistics, anthropology, and psychology.* London: Cambridge University Press.

Landauer, T. K., Foltz, P. W., & Laham, D. (1998). Introduction to latent semantic analysis. *Discourse Processes, 25,* 259–284.

Langley, P. W., Simon, H. A., Bradshaw, G. L., & Zytkow, J. (1987). *Scientific discovery: Computational explorations of the cognitive processes.* Cambridge, MA: MIT Press.

Larkin, J. H. (1981). Enriching formal knowledge: A model for learning to solve textbook physics problems. In J. R. Anderson (Ed.), *Cognitive skills and their acquisition* (pp. 311–335). Hillsdale, NJ: Erlbaum.

Lee, D. W., Miyasato, L. E., & Clayton, N. S. (1998). Neurobiological bases of spatial learning in the natural environment: Neurogenesis and growth in the avian and mammalian hippocampus. *Neuroreport, 9,* R15–R27.

Lehman, H. G. (1953). *Age and achievement.* Princeton, NJ: Princeton University Press.

Lenneberg, E. H. (1967). *Biological foundations of language.* New York: Wiley.

Lesgold, A., Rubinson, H., Feltovich, P., Glaser, R., Klopfer, D., et al. (1988). Expertise in a complex skill: Diagnosing X-ray pictures. In M. T. H. Chi, R. Glaser, & M. J. Farr (Eds.), *The nature of expertise* (pp. 311–342). Hillsdale, NJ: Erlbaum.

Levine, D. N., Warach, J., & Farah, M. (1985). Two visual systems in mental imagery: Dissociation of "what" and "where" in imagery disorders due to bilateral posterior cerebral lesions. *Neurology, 35,* 1010–1018.

Lewis, C. H., & Anderson, J. R. (1976). Interference with real world knowledge. *Cognitive Psychology, 7*, 311–335.

Lewis, M. W. (1985). *Context effects on cognitive skill acquisition.* Unpublished doctoral dissertation, Carnegie-Mellon University.

Liberman, A. M. (1970). The grammars of speech and language. *Cognitive Psychology, 1*, 301–323.

Liberman, A. M., & Mattingly, I. G. (1985). The motor theory of speech perception revised. *Cognition, 21*, 1–36.

Lieberman, P. (1984). *The biology and evolution of language.* Cambridge, MA: Harvard University Press.

Linden, E. (1974). *Apes, men, and language.* New York: Saturday Review Press.

Lindsay, P. H., & Norman, D. A. (1977). *Human information processing.* New York: Academic Press.

Lisker, L., & Abramson, A. (1970). The voicing dimension: Some experiments in comparative phonetics. *Proceedings of Sixth International Congress of Phonetic Sciences, Prague, 1967.* Prague: Academia.

Livingstone, M., & Hubel, D. (1988). Segregation of form, color, movement, and depth: Anatomy, physiology, and perception. *Science, 240*, 740–749.

Loftus, E. F. (1974). Activation of semantic memory. *American Journal of Psychology, 86*, 331–337.

Loftus, E. F. (1975). Leading questions and the eyewitness report. *Cognitive Psychology, 7*, 560–572.

Loftus, E. F. (1996). *Eyewitness testimony.* Cambridge, MA: Harvard University Press.

Loftus, E. F., Miller, D. G., & Burns, H. J. (1978). Misinformation and memory: The creation of new memories. *Journal of Experimental Psychology: General, 118*, 100–104.

Loftus, E. F., & Pickerall, J. (1995). The formation of false memories. *Psychiatric Annals, 25*, 720–725.

Loftus, E. F., & Zanni, G. (1975). Eyewitness testimony: The influence of the wording of a question. *Bulletin of the Psychonomic Society, 5*, 86–88.

Logan, G. D. (1988). Toward an instance theory of automatization. *Psychological Review, 95*, 492–527.

Logan, G. D., & Klapp, S. T. (1991). Automatizing alphabet arithmetic. I. Is extended practice necessary to produce automaticity? *Journal of Experimental Psychology: Learning, Memory, and Cognition, 17*, 179–195.

Long, D. L., Golding, J. M., & Graesser, A. C. (1992). A test of the on-line status of goal-related elaborative inferences. *Journal of Memory and Language, 31*, 634–647.

Luchins, A. S. (1942). Mechanization in problem solving. *Psychological Monographs, 54*(No. 248).

Luchins, A. S., & Luchins, E. H. (1959). *Rigidity of behavior: A variational approach to the effects of Einstellung.* Eugene, OR: University of Oregon Books.

Luck, S. J., Chelazzi, L., Hillyard, S. A. & Desimone, R. (1977). Neural mechanisms of spatial selective attention in areas V1, V2, and V4 of macaque visual cortex. *Journal of Neurophysiology, 77*, 24–42.

Lucy, J., & Shweder, R. (1979). Whorf and his critics: Linguistic and non-linguistic influences on color memory. *American Anthropologist, 81*, 581–615.

Lucy, J., & Shweder, R. (1988). The effect of incidental conversation on memory for focal colors. *American Anthropologist, 90*, 923–931.

Luria, A. R. (1961). *The role of speech in the regulation of normal and abnormal behavior.* New York: Liveright.

Luria, A. R. (1987). *The mind of a mnemonist: A little book about a vast memory.* (L. Solotaroff, Trans.). Cambridge, MA: Harvard University Press.

Lynch, G., & Baudry, M. (1984). The biochemistry of memory: A new and specific hypothesis. *Science, 224*, 1057–1063.

Lynn, S. J., Lock, T., Myers, B., & Payne, D. G. (1997). Recalling the unrecallable: Should hypnosis be used for memory recovery in psychotherapy? *Current Directions in Psychological Science, 6*, 79–83.

Maclay, H., & Osgood, C. E. (1959). Hesitation phenomena in spontaneous speech. *Word, 15*, 19–44.

MacLeod, C. M., & Dunbar, K. (1988). Training and Stroop-like interferences: Evidence for a continuum of automaticity. *Journal of Experimental Psychology: Learning, Memory, and Cognition, 14*, 126–135.

MacLeod, C. M., Hunt, E. B., & Matthews, N. N. (1978). Individual differences in the verification of sentence-picture relationships. *Journal of Verbal Learning and Verbal Behavior, 17*, 493–507.

Macmillan, M. (2000). *An odd kind of fame. Stories of Phineas Gage.* Cambridge, MA: MIT Press.

MacWhinney, B., & Leinbach, J. (1991). Implementations are not conceptualizations: Revising the verb learning model. *Cognition, 29*, 121–157.

Maguire, E. A., Burgess, N., Donnett, J. G., Frackowiak, R. S. J., Frith, C. D., et al. (1998). Knowing where and getting there: A human navigation week. *Science, 280*, 921–924.

Maguire, E. A., Gadian, D. G., Johnsrude, I. S., Good, C. D., Ashburner J., et al. (2000). Navigation-related structural change in the hippocampi of taxi-drivers. *Proceedings of the National Academy of Sciences, USA, 97*, 4398–4403.

Maguire, E. A., Spiers, H. J., Good C. D., Hartley, T., Frackowiak, R. S. J., et al. (2003). Navigation expertise and the human hippocampus: A structural brain imaging analysis. *Hippocampus, 13*, 208–217.

Maier, N. R. F. (1931). Reasoning in humans. II. The solution of a problem and its appearance in consciousness. *Journal of Comparative Psychology, 12*, 181–194.

Mandler, J. M., & Johnson, N. S. (1977). Remembrance of things parsed: Story structure and recall. *Cognitive Psychology, 9*, 111–151.

Mandler, J. M., & Ritchey, G. H. (1977). Long-term memory for pictures. *Journal of Experimental Psychology: Human Learning and Memory, 3*, 386–396.

Mangun, G. R., Hillyard, S. A., & Luck, S. J. (1993). Electrocortical substrates of visual selective attention. In D. Meyer & S. Kornblum (Eds.), *Attention and performance* (Vol. 14, pp. 219–243). Cambridge, MA: MIT Press.

Marcus, G. F., Brinkman, U., Clahsen, H., Wiese, R., Woest, A., et al. (1995). German inflection: The exception that proves the rule. *Cognitive Psychology, 29*, 189–256.

Marler, P. (1967). Animal communication signals. *Science, 157,* 764–774.

Marr, D. (1982). *Vision.* San Francisco: W. H. Freeman.

Marr, D., & Nishihara, H. K. (1978). Representation and recognition of the spatial organization of three-dimensional shapes. *Proceedings of the Royal Society of London B, 200,* 269–294.

Marslen-Wilson, W., & Tyler, L. K. (1987). Against modularity. In J. L. Garfield (Ed.), *Modularity in knowledge representation and natural-language understanding* (pp. 37–62). Cambridge, MA: MIT Press.

Marslen-Wilson, W., & Tyler, L. K. (1998). Rules, representations, and the English past tense. *Trends in Cognitive Science, 2,* 428–435.

Martin, A. (2001). Functional neuroimaging of semantic memory. In R. Cabeza & A. Lingstone (Eds.), *Handbook of functional neuroimaging of cognition* (pp. 153–186). Cambridge, MA: MIT Press.

Martin, L. (1986). Eskimo words for snow: A case study on the genesis and decay of an anthropological example. *American Anthropologist, 88,* 418–423.

Martin, R. C. (2003). Language processing: Functional organization and neuroanatomical basis. *Annual Review of Psychology, 54,* 55–89.

Martinez, A., Moses, P., Frank, L., Buxton, R., Wong, E., et al. (1997). Hemispheric asymmetries in global and local processing: Evidence from fMRI. *Neuroreport, 8,* 1685–1689.

Mason, R. A., & Just, M. A. (2006). Neuroimaging contributions to the understanding of discourse processes. In M. Traxler & M. A. Gernsbacher (Eds.), *Handbook of psycholinguistics* (pp. 765–799). Amsterdam: Elsevier.

Mason, R. A., Just, M. A., Keller, T. A., & Carpenter, P. A. (2003). Ambiguity in the brain: How syntactically ambiguous sentences are processed. *Journal of Experimental Psychology: Learning, Memory, and Cognition, 29,* 1319–1338.

Massaro, D. W. (1979). Letter information and orthographic context in word perception. *Journal of Experimental Psychology: Human Perception and Performance, 5,* 595–609.

Massaro, D. W. (1992). Broadening the domain of the fuzzy logical model of perception. In H. L. Pick, Jr., P. Van den Broek, & D. C. Knill (Eds.), *Cognition: Conceptual and methodological issues* (pp. 51–84). Washington, DC: American Psychological Association.

Massaro, D. W. (1996). Modeling multiple influences in speech perception. In A. Dijkstra & K. de Smedt (Eds.), *Computational psycholinguistics: AI and connectionist models of human language processing* (pp. 85–113). London: Taylor and Francis.

Masson, M. E. J., & MacLeod, C. M. (1992). Reenacting the route to interpretation: Enhanced identification without prior perception. *Journal of Experimental Psychology: General, 121,* 145–176.

Mayer, A., & Orth, I. (1901). Zur qualitativen Untersuchung der Association. *Zeitschrift für Psychologie, 26,* 1–13.

Mayer, R. E. (2008). *Learning and instruction* (2nd ed.). Upper Saddle River, NJ: Merrill Prentice-Hall.

Mazoyer, B. M., Tzourio, N., Frak, V., Syrota, A., Murayama, N., et al. (1993). The cortical representation of speech. *Journal of Cognitive Neuroscience, 5,* 467–479.

McCarthy, G., Puce, A., Gore, J. C., & Allison, T. (1997). Face-specific processing in the human fusiform gyrus. *Journal of Cognitive Neuroscience, 9,* 604–609.

McCarthy, J. (1996). From here to human-level intelligence. Unpublished memo, Department of Computer Science, Stanford University, Stanford, CA. Available at www.formal.stanford.edu/jmc/human.html.

McCloskey, M., & Glucksberg, S. (1978). Natural categories: Well-defined or fuzzy sets? *Memory & Cognition, 6,* 462–472.

McCloskey, M., Wible, C. G., & Cohen, N. J. (1988). Is there a special flashbulb-memory mechanism? *Journal of Experimental Psychology: General, 117,* 171–181.

McConkie, G. W., & Currie, C. B. (1996). Visual stability across saccades while viewing complex pictures. *Journal of Experimental Psychology: Human Perception and Performance, 22,* 563–581.

McDonald, J. L. (1984). *The mapping of semantic and syntactic processing cues by first and second language learners of English, Dutch, and German.* Unpublished doctoral dissertation, Carnegie-Mellon University.

McGaugh, J. L., & Roozendaal, B. (2002). Role of adrenal stress hormones in forming lasting memories in the brain. *Current Opinion in Neurobiology, 12,* 205–210.

McKeithen, K. B., Reitman, J. S., Rueter, H. H., & Hirtle, S. C. (1981). Knowledge organization and skill differences in computer programmers. *Cognitive Psychology, 13,* 307–325.

McLaughlin, B. (1978). *Second-language acquisition in childhood.* Hillsdale, NJ: Erlbaum.

McNeil, B. J., Pauker, S. G., Cox, H. C., Jr., & Tversky, A. (1982). On the elicitation of preferences for alternative therapies. *New England Journal of Medicine, 306,* 1259–1262.

McNeill, D. (1966). Developmental psycholinguistics. In F. Smith & G. A. Miller (Eds.), *The genesis of language: A psycholinguistic approach.* Cambridge, MA: MIT Press.

McRae, K., Spivey-Knowlton, M. J., & Tannehaus, M. K. (1998). Modeling the influence of thematic fit (and other constraints) in on-line sentence comprehension. *Journal of Memory and Language, 38,* 283–312.

Medin, D. L., & Schaffer, M. M. (1978). A context theory of classification learning. *Psychological Review, 85,* 207–238.

Mednick, S. A. (1962). The associative basis of the creative process. *Psychological Review, 69,* 220–232.

Metcalfe, J., & Wiebe, D. (1987). Intuition in insight and non-insight problem solving. *Memory & Cognition, 15,* 238–246.

Metzler, J., & Shepard, R. N. (1974). Transformational studies of the internal representations of three-dimensional objects. In R. L. Solso (Ed.), *Theories of cognitive psychology: The Loyola Symposium* (pp. 147–201). Hillsdale, NJ: Erlbaum.

Meyer, B. J. F. (1974). *The organization of prose and its effect on recall.* Unpublished doctoral dissertation, Cornell University.

Meyer, B. J. F., Brandt, D. M., & Bluth, G. J. (1978). *Use of author's textual schema: Key for ninth-grader's comprehension.* Paper presented at the annual conference of the American Educational Research Association, Toronto.

Meyer, D. E., & Schvaneveldt, R. W. (1971). Facilitation in recognizing pairs of words: Evidence of a dependence between retrieval operations. *Journal of Experimental Psychology, 90,* 227–234.

Middleton, F. A., & Strick, P. L. (1994). Anatomical evidence for cerebellar and basal ganglia involvement in higher cognitive function. *Science, 266,* 458–461.

Miller, G. A., & Nicely, P. (1955). An analysis of perceptual confusions among some English consonants. *Journal of the Acoustical Society of America, 27,* 338–352.

Milner, A. D., & Goodale, M. A. (1995). *The visual brain in action.* Oxford: Oxford University Press.

Milner, B. (1962). Les troubles de la memoire accompagnant des lesions hippocampiques bilaterales. In P. Passonant (Ed.), *Physiologie de l'hippocampe* (pp. 257–262). Paris: Centre National de la Recherche Scientifique.

Miyachi, S., Hikosaka O., Miyashita K., Karadi, Z., & Rand, M. K. (1997). Differential roles of monkey striatum in learning of sequential hand movement. *Experimental Brain Research, 115,* 1–5.

Moll, M., & Miikkulainen, R. (1997). Convergence-zone episodic memory: Analysis and simulations. *Neural Networks, 10,* 1017.

Monsell, S. (2003). Task switching. *Trends in Cognitive Science, 7,* 134–140.

Moray, N. (1959). Attention in dichotic listening: Affective cues and the influence of instructions. *Quarterly Journal of Experimental Psychology, 9,* 56–90.

Moray, N., Bates, A., & Barnett, T. (1965). Experiments on the four-eared man. *Journal of the Acoustical Society of America, 38,* 196–201.

Mori, G., & Malik, M. J. (2003). Recognizing objects in adversarial clutter: Breaking a visual CAPTCHA. *IEEE Conference on Computer Vision and Pattern Recognition,* 134–141.

Motley, M. T., Camden, C. T., & Baars, B. J. (1982). Covert formulation and editing of anomalies in speech production: Evidence from experimentally elicited slips of the tongue. *Journal of Verbal Learning and Verbal Behavior, 21,* 578–594.

Moyer, R. S. (1973). Comparing objects in memory: Evidence suggesting an internal psychophysics. *Perception and Psychophysics, 13,* 180–184.

Murray, J. D., & Burke, K. A. (2003). Activation and encoding of predictive inferences: The role of reading skill. *Discourse Processes, 35,* 81–102.

Näätänen, R. (1992). *Attention and brain function.* Hillsdale, NJ: Erlbaum.

Neisser, U. (1964). Visual search. *Scientific American, 210,* 94–102.

Neisser, U. (1967). *Cognitive psychology.* New York: Appleton.

Neisser, U. (1981). John Dean's memory: A case study. *Cognition, 9,* 1–22.

Neisser, U., & Becklen, R. (1975). Selective looking: Attending to visually specified events. *Cognitive Psychology, 7,* 480–494.

Neisser, U., Boodoo, G., Bouchard, T., Boykin, A. W., Brody, N., et al. (1996). Intelligence: Knowns and unknowns. *American Psychologist, 51,* 77–101.

Neisser, U., & Harsch, N. (1992). Phantom flashbulbs: False recollections of hearing the news about *Challenger.* In E. Winogrand & U. Neisser (Eds.), *Affect and accuracy in recall: Studies of "flashbulb" memories* (pp. 9–33). Cambridge, England: Cambridge University Press.

Neisser, U., Winograd, E., Bergman, E. T., Schreiber, C., Palmer, S., et al. (1996). Remembering the earthquake: Direct experience versus hearing the news. *Memory, 4,* 337–357.

Nelson, D. L. (1979). Remembering pictures and words: Appearance, significance, and name. In L. S. Cermak & F. I. M. Craik (Eds.), *Levels of processing in human memory* (pp. 45–76). Hillsdale, NJ: Erlbaum.

Nelson, T. O. (1971). Savings and forgetting from long-term memory. *Journal of Verbal Learning and Verbal Behavior, 10,* 568–576.

Nelson, T. O. (1976). Reinforcement and human memory. In W. K. Estes (Ed.), *Handbook of learning and cognitive processes* (Vol. 3, pp. 207–246). Hillsdale, NJ: Erlbaum.

Nelson, T. O. (1978). Detecting small amounts of information in memory: Savings for nonrecognized items. *Journal of Experimental Psychology: Human Learning and Memory, 4,* 453–468.

Neves, D. M., & Anderson, J. R. (1981). Knowledge compilation: Mechanisms for the automatization of cognitive skills. In J. R. Anderson (Ed.), *Cognitive skills and their acquisition* (pp. 57–84). Hillsdale, NJ: Erlbaum.

Newell, A. (1990). *Unified theories of cognition.* Cambridge, MA: Harvard University Press.

Newell, A., & Rosenbloom, P. S. (1981). Mechanisms of skill acquisition and the law of practice. In J. R. Anderson (Ed.), *Cognitive skills and their acquisition* (pp. 1–55). Hillsdale, NJ: Erlbaum.

Newell, A., & Simon, H. (1972). *Human problem solving.* Englewood Cliffs, NJ: Prentice-Hall.

Newport, E. L. (1986). *The effect of maturational state on the acquisition of language.* Paper presented at the Eleventh Annual Boston University Conference on Language Development, October 17–19.

Newport, E. L., & Supalla, T. (1990). *A critical period effect in the acquisition of a primary language.* Unpublished manuscript, University of Rochester, Rochester, NY.

Nickerson, R. S. (1998). Confirmation bias: A ubiquitous phenomenon in many guises. *Review of General Psychology, 2,* 175–220.

Nida, E. A. (1971). Sociopsychological problems in language mastery and retention. In P. Pimsleur & T. Quinn (Eds.), *The psychology of second language acquisition* (pp. 59–66). London: Cambridge University Press.

Nilsson, L.-G., & Gardiner, J. M. (1993). Identifying exceptions in a database of recognition failure studies from 1973 to 1992. *Memory & Cognition, 21,* 397–410.

Nilsson, N. J. (1971). *Problem-solving methods in artificial intelligence.* New York: McGraw-Hill.

Nilsson, N. J. (2005). Human-level artificial intelligence? Be serious! *AI Maganine, 26,* 68–75.

Nissen, M. J., & Bullemer, P. (1987). Attentional requirements of learning: Evidence from performance measures. *Cognitive Psychology, 19,* 1–32.

Noelting, G. (1975). *Stages and mechanisms in the development of the concept of proportion in the child and adolescent.* Paper presented at the First Interdisciplinary Seminar on Piagetian Theory and Its Implications for the Helping Professions, University of Southern California, Los Angeles.

Nosofsky, R. M. (1986). Attention, similarity, and the identification-categorization relationship. *Journal of Experimental Psychology: General, 115,* 39–57.

Nosofsky, R. M. (1991). Tests of an exemplar model for relating perceptual classification and recognition in memory. *Journal of Experimental Psychology: Human Perception and Performance, 17,* 3–27.

Oaksford, M., & Chater, N. (1994). A rational analysis of the selection task as optimal data selection. *Psychological Review, 101,* 608–631.

Oaksford, M., & Wakefield, M. (2003). Data selection and natural sampling: Probabilities do matter. *Memory & Cognition, 31,* 143–154.

O'Craven, K. M., Downing, P., & Kanwisher, N. K. (1999). fMRI evidence for objects as the units of attentional selection. *Nature, 401,* 584–587.

O'Craven, K., & Kanwisher, N. (2000). Mental imagery of faces and places activates corresponding stimulus-specific brain regions. *Journal of Cognitive Neuroscience, 12,* 1013–1023.

Oden, D. L., Thompson, R. K. R., & Premack, D. (2001). Can an ape reason analogically? Comprehension and production of analogical problems by Sarah, a chimpanzee (Pan troglodytes). In D. Gentner, K. J. Holyoak, & B. N. Kokinov (Eds.), *Analogy: Theory and phenomena* (pp. 472–497). Cambridge, MA: MIT Press.

Ohlsson, S. (1992). The learning curve for writing books: Evidence from Professor Asimov. *Psychological Science, 3,* 380–382.

Okada, S., Hanada, M., Hattori, H., & Shoyama, T. (1963). A case of pure word-deafness. *Studia Phonologica, 3,* 58–65.

Okada, T., & Simon, H. A. (1997). Collaborative discovery in a scientific domain. *Cognitive Science, 21,* 109–146.

O'Keefe, J., & Dostrovsky, J. (1971). The hippocampus as a spatial map: Preliminary evidence from unit activity in the freely moving rat. *Experimental Brain Research, 34,* 171–175.

Olds, J., & Milner, P. (1954). Positive reinforcement produced by electrical stimulation of septal area and other regions of rat brain. *Journal of Comparative and Physiological Psychology, 47,* 419–427.

Osterhout, L., & Holcomb, P. J. (1992). Event-related potentials elicited by syntactic anomaly. *Journal of Memory and Language, 31,* 785–806.

Otten, L. J., Henson, R. N., & Rugg, M. D. (2001). Depth of processing effects on neural correlates of memory encoding: Relationship between findings from across- and within-task comparisons. *Brain, 124,* 399–412.

Owens, J., Bower, G. H., & Black, J. B. (1979). The "soap opera" effect in story recall. *Memory & Cognition, 7,* 185–191.

Oyama, S. (1978). The sensitive period and comprehension of speech. *Working Papers on Bilingualism, 16,* 1–17.

Paivio, A. (1971). *Imagery and verbal processes.* New York: Holt, Rinehart, & Winston.

Paivio, A. (1986). *Mental representations: A dual coding approach.* New York: Oxford University Press.

Palinscar, A. S., & Brown, A. L. (1984). Reciprocal teaching of comprehension monitoring activities. *Cognition and Instruction, 1,* 117–175.

Paller, K. A., & Wagner, A. D. (2002). Observing the transformation of experience into memory. *Trends in Cognitive Science, 6,* 93–102.

Palmer, S. E. (1977). Hierarchical structure in perceptual representation. *Cognitive Psychology, 9,* 441–474.

Palmer, S. E., Schreiber, G., & Fox., C. (1991, November 22–24). *Remembering the earthquake: "Flashbulb" memory of experienced versus reported events.* Paper presented at the 32nd annual meeting of the Psychonomic Society, San Francisco.

Palmeri, T. J., & Johansen, M. K. (1999). Prototypes, rules, and instances in category learning. In *Proceedings of the Psychonomic Society,* Los Angeles, CA.

Pardo, J. V., Pardo, P. J., Janer, K. W., & Raichle, M. E. (1990). The anterior cingulate cortex mediates processing selection in the Stroop attentional conflict paradigm. *Proceedings of the National Academy of Sciences, USA, 87,* 256–259.

Paris, S. C., & Lindauer, B. K. (1976). The role of interference in children's comprehension and memory for sentences. *Cognitive Psychology, 8,* 217–227.

Parker, E. S., Birnbaum, I. M., & Noble, E. P. (1976). Alcohol and memory: Storage and state dependency. *Journal of Verbal Learning and Verbal Behavior, 15,* 691–702.

Parker, E. S., Cahill, L., & McGaugh, J. L. (2006). A case of unusual autobiographical remembering. *Neurocase, 12,* 35–49.

Parsons, L. M., & Osherson, D. (2001). New evidence for distinct right and left brain systems for deductive vs. probabilistic reasoning. *Cerebral Cortex, 11,* 954–965.

Pascual-Leone, A., Gomez-Tortosa, E., Grafman, J., Always, D., Nichelli, P., et al. (1994). Induction of visual extinction by rapid-rate transcranial magnetic stimulation of parietal lobe. *Neurology, 44,* 494–498.

Pascual-Leone, J. (1980). Constructive problems for constructive theories: The current relevance of Piaget's work and a critique of information-processing psychology. In R. H. Kluwe & H. Spada (Eds.), *Developmental models of thinking* (pp. 263–296). New York: Academic Press.

Pashler, H. E. (1995). Attention and visual perception: Analyzing divided attention. In S. M. Kosslyn & N. D. Osherson (Eds.), *Visual cognition* (pp. 71–100). Cambridge, MA: MIT Press.

Penfield, W. (1959). The interpretive cortex. *Science, 129,* 1719 1725.

Penfield, W., & Jasper, H. (1954). *Epilepsy and the functional anatomy of the human brain.* Boston: Little, Brown.

Perlmutter, M., Kaplan, M., & Nyquist, L. (1990). Development of adaptive competence in adulthood. *Human Development, 33,* 185–197.

Perrett, D. I., Rolls, E. T., & Caan, W. (1982). Visual neurons responsive to faces in the monkey temporal cortex. *Experimental Brain Research, 47,* 329–342.

Peterson, M. A., Kihlstrom, J. F., Rose, P. M., & Gilsky, M. L. (1992). Mental images can be ambiguous: Reconstruals and reference-frame reversals. *Memory & Cognition, 20,* 107–123.

Peterson, S. B., & Potts, G. R. (1982). Global and specific components of information integration. *Journal of Verbal Learning and Verbal Behavior, 21,* 403–420.

Peterson, S. E., Robinson, D. L., & Morris, J. D. (1987). Contributions of the pulvinar to visual spatial attention. *Neuropsychologia, 25,* 97–105.

Petrides, M., Alvisatos, B., Evans, A. C., & Meyer, E. (1993). Dissociation of human mid-dorsolateral from posterior dorsolateral frontal cortex in memory processing. *Proceedings of the National Academy of Sciences, USA, 90,* 873–877.

Phelps, E. A. (1989). *Cognitive skill learning in amnesiacs.* Doctoral dissertation, Princeton University.

Phelps, E. A. (2004). Human emotion and memory: Interactions of the amygdala and hippocampal complex. *Current Opinion in Neurobiology, 14,* 198–202.

Picton, T. W., & Hillyard, S. A. (1974). Human auditory evoked potentials. II. Effects of attention. *Electroencephalography and Clinical Neurophysiology, 36,* 191–199.

Pillsbury, W. B. (1908). The effects of training on memory. *Educational Review, 36,* 15–27.

Pine, D. S., Grun, J., Maguire, E. A., Burgess, N., Zarahn, E., et al. (2002). Neurodevelopmental aspects of spatial navigation: A virtual reality fMRI study. *Neuroimage, 15,* 396–406.

Pinker, S. (1994b). *The language instinct.* New York: HarperCollins.

Pinker, S., & Prince, A. (1988). On language and connectionism: Analysis of a parallel distributed processing model of language acquisition. *Cognition, 28,* 73–193.

Pirolli, P. L., & Anderson, J. R. (1985). The role of practice in fact retrieval. *Journal of Experimental Psychology: Learning, Memory, and Cognition, 11,* 136–153.

Pirolli, P. L., & Card, S. K. (1999). Information foraging. *Psychological Review, 106,* 643–675.

Pisoni, D. B. (1977). Identification and discrimination of the relative onset time of two component tones: Implications for voicing perception in stops. *Journal of the Acoustical Society of America, 61,* 1352–1361.

Pizlo, Z., Stefanov, E., Saalweachter, J., Li, Z., Haxhimusa, Y., et al. (2006). Traveling salesman problem: A foveating pyramid model. *Journal of Problem Solving, 1,* 83–101.

Pohl, W. (1973). Dissociation of spatial discrimination deficits following frontal and parietal lesions in monkeys. *Journal of Comparative and Physiological Psychology, 82,* 227–239.

Poincaré, H. (1929). *The foundations of science.* New York: Science House.

Poldrack, R. A., & Gabrieli, J. D. E. (2001). Characterizing the neural mechanisms of skill learning and repetition priming: Evidence from mirror reading. *Brain, 124,* 67–82.

Poldrack, R. A., Prabhakaran, V., Seger, C., Desmond, J. E., Glover, G. H., et al. (1999). Striatal activation during acquisition of a cognitive skill learning. *Neuropsychology, 13,* 564–574.

Polson, P. G., Muncher, E., & Kieras, D. E. (1987). *Transfer of skills between inconsistent editors.* Austin, TX: Microelectronics and Computer Technology Corporation. (MCC Technical Report Number ACA-HI-395-87.)

Polster, M., McCarthy, R., O'Sullivan, G., Gray, P., & Park, G. (1993). Midazolam-induced amnesia: Implications for the implicit/explicit memory distinction. *Brain & Cognition, 22,* 244–265.

Pope, K. S. (1996). Memory, abuse, and science: Questioning claims about the false memory syndrome epidemic (author's reprint). *American Psychologist, 51,* 957–974.

Posner, M. I. (1988). Structures and functions of selective attention. In T. Boll & B. Bryant (Eds.), *Master lectures in clinical neuropsychology* (pp. 173–202). Washington, DC: American Psychological Association.

Posner, M. I., Cohen, Y., & Rafal, R. D. (1982). Neural systems control of spatial orienting. *Philosophical Transactions of the Royal Society of London B, 298,* 187–198.

Posner, M. I., Nissen, M. J., & Ogden, W. C. (1978). Attended and unattended processing modes: The role of set for spatial location. In H. L. Pick, Jr., & I. J. Saltzman (Eds.), *Modes of perceiving and processing information* (pp. 137–157). Hillsdale, NJ: Erlbaum.

Posner, M. I., Peterson, S. E., Fox, P. T., & Raichle, M. E. (1988). Localization of cognitive operations in the human brain. *Science, 240,* 1627–1631.

Posner, M. I., Rafal, R. D., Chaote, L. S., & Vaughn, J. (1985). Inhibition of return: Neural basis and function. *Cognitive Neuropsychology, 2,* 211–228.

Posner, M. I., Snyder, C. R. R., & Davidson, B. J. (1980). Attention and the detection of signals. *Journal of Experimental Psychology: General, 109,* 160–174.

Posner, M. I., Walker, J. A., Friederich, F. J., & Rafal, R. D. (1984). Effects of parietal injury on covert orienting of attention. *Journal of Neuroscience, 4,* 1863–1874.

Postman, L. (1964). Short-term memory and incidental learning. In A. W. Melton (Ed.), *Categories of human learning* (pp. 146–201). New York: Academic Press.

Premack, D. (1976). *Intelligence in ape and man.* Hillsdale, NJ: Erlbaum.

Premack, D., & Premack, A. J. (1983). *The mind of an ape.* New York: W. W. Norton.

Pressley, M., McDaniel, M. A., Turnure, J. E., Wood, E., & Ahmad, M. (1987). Generation and precision of elaboration: Effects on intentional and incidental learning. *Journal of Experimental Psychology: Learning, Memory, and Cognition, 13,* 291–300.

Price, J. (2008). *The woman who can't forget.* New York, NY: Simon & Schuster.

Priest, A. G., & Lindsay, R. O. (1992). New light on novice-expert differences in physics problem solving. *British Journal of Psychology, 83,* 389–405.

Pritchard, R. M. (1961). Stabilized images on the retina. *Scientific American, 204,* 72–78.

Pullman, G. K. (1989). The great Eskimo vocabulary hoax. *National Language and Linguistic Theory, 7,* 275–281.

Pylyshyn, Z. W. (1973). What the mind's eye tells the mind's brain: A critique of mental imagery. *Psychological Bulletin, 80,* 1–24.

Qin, Y., Anderson, J. R., Silk, E., Stenger, V. A., & Carter, C. S. (2004). The change of the brain activation patterns along with the children's practice in algebra equation solving. *Proceedings of the National Academy of Sciences, USA, 101,* 5686–5691.

Qin, Y., Sohn, M.-H., Anderson, J. R., Stenger, V. A., Fissell, K., et al. (2003). Predicting the practice effects on the blood oxygenation level-dependent (BOLD) function of fMRI in a symbolic manipulation task. *Proceedings of the National Academy of Sciences, USA, 100,* 4951–4956.

Quillian, M. R. (1966). *Semantic memory.* Cambridge, MA: Bolt, Beranak and Newman.

Raaijmakers, J. G. W., & Shiffrin, R. M. (1981). Search of associative memory. *Psychological Review, 88,* 93–134.

Rabinowitz, M., & Goldberg, N. (1995). Evaluating the structure-process hypothesis. In F. E. Weinert & W. Schneider (Eds.), *Memory performance and competencies: Issues in growth and development* (pp. 225–242). Hillsdale, NJ: Erlbaum.

Ratcliff, R. A., & McKoon, G. (1978). Priming in item recognition: Evidence for the propositional structure of sentences. *Journal of Verbal Learning and Verbal Behavior, 17,* 403–417.

Ratcliff, G., & Newcombe, F. (1982). Object recognition: Some deductions from the clinical evidence. In A. W. Ellis (Ed.), *Normality and pathology in cognitive functions* (pp. 147–171). London: Academic Press.

Ratiu, P., Talos, I. F., Haker, S., Lieberman, S., & Everett, P. (2004). The tale of Phineas Gage, digitally remastered. *Journal of Neurotrauma, 21,* 637–643.

Raymond, C. R., & Redman, S. J. (2006). Spatial segregation of neuronal calcium signals encodes different forms of LTP in rat hippocampus. *J. Physiol. 570,* 97–111.

Reder, L. M. (1982). Plausibility judgment versus fact retrieval: Alternative strategies for sentence verification. *Psychological Review, 89,* 250–280.

Reder, L. M., & Kusbit, G. W. (1991). Locus of the Moses illusion: Imperfect encoding, retrieval or match? *Journal of Memory and Language, 30,* 385–406.

Reder, L. M., Park, H., & Keiffaber, P. (2009). Memory systems do not divide on consciousness: Reinterpreting memory in terms of activation and binding. *Psychological Bulletin, 135,* 23–49.

Reder, L. M., & Ross, B. H. (1983). Integrated knowledge in different tasks: Positive and negative fan effects. *Journal of Experimental Psychology: Human Learning and Memory, 8,* 55–72.

Reed, S. K. (1972). Pattern recognition and categorization. *Cognitive Psychology, 3,* 382–407.

Reed, S. K. (1987). A structure-mapping model for word problems. *Journal of Experimental Psychology: Learning, Memory, and Cognition, 13,* 124–139.

Reed, S. K., & Bolstad, C. A. (1991). Use of examples and procedures in problem solving. *Journal of Experimental Psychology: Learning, Memory, and Cognition, 17,* 753–766.

Reicher, G. (1969). Perceptual recognition as a function of meaningfulness of stimulus material. *Journal of Experimental Psychology, 81,* 275–280.

Reichle, E. D., Carpenter, P. A., & Just, M. A. (2000). The neural basis of strategy and skill in sentence-picture verification. *Cognitive Psychology, 40,* 261–295.

Reitman, J. (1976). Skilled perception in GO: Deducing memory structures from interresponse times. *Cognitive Psychology, 8,* 336–356.

Reyna, V. F., & Farley, F. (2006). Risk and rationality in adolescent decision making: Implications for theory, practice, and public policy. *Psychological Science in the Public Interest, 7,* 1–44.

Richardson-Klavehn, A., & Bjork, R. A. (1988). Measures of memory. *Annual Review of Psychology, 39,* 475–543.

Richter, T., & Späth, P. (2006). Recognition is used as one cue among others in judgment and decision making. *Journal of Experimental Psychology: Learning, Memory & Cognition, 32,* 150–162.

Rist, R. S. (1989). Schema creation in programming. *Cognitive Science, 13,* 67–96.

Ritter, S., Anderson, J. R., Koedinger, K. R., & Corbett, A. (2007). Cognitive tutor: Applied research in mathematics education. *Psychonomic Bulletin & Review, 14,* 249–255.

Rizzolatti, G., & Craighero, L. (2004). The mirror-neuron system. *Annual Review of Neuroscience, 27,* 169–192.

Roberson, D., Davies I., & Davidoff, J. (2000). Colour categories are not universal: Replications and new evidence from a stone-age culture. *Journal of Experimental Psychology: General, 129,* 369–398.

Roberts, R. J., Hager, L. D., & Heron, C. (1994). Prefrontal cognitive processes: Working memory and inhibition in the antisaccade task. *Journal of Experimental Psychology: General, 123,* 374–393.

Robertson, L. C., & Lamb, M. R. (1991). Neuropsychological contributions to theories of part/whole organization. *Cognitive Psychology, 23,* 299–330.

Robertson, L. C., & Rafal, R. (2000). Disorders of visual attention. In M. Gazzaniga (Ed.), *The new cognitive neuroscience* (2nd ed., pp. 633–650). Cambridge, MA: MIT Press.

Robinson, G. H. (1964). Continuous estimation of a time-varying probability. *Ergonomics, 7,* 7–21.

Roediger, H. L., & Guynn, M. J. (1996). Retrieval processes. In E. L. Bjork & R. A. Bjork (Eds.), *Human Memory* (pp. 197–236). San Diego: Academic Press.

Roediger, H. L., & McDermott, K. B. (1995). Creating false memories: Remembering words not presented in lists. *Journal of Experimental Psychology: Learning, Memory, and Cognition, 21,* 803–814.

Roelfsema, P. R., Lamme, V. A. F., & Spekreijse, H. (1998). Object-based attention in the primary visual cortex of the macaque monkey. *Nature, 395,* 376–381.

Roland, P. E., Eriksson, L., Stone-Elander, S., & Widen, L. (1987). Does mental activity change the oxidative metabolism of the brain? *Journal of Neuroscience, 7,* 2373–2389.

Roland, P. E., & Friberg, L. (1985). Localization of cortical areas activated by thinking. *Journal of Neurophysiology, 53,* 1219–1243.

Rolls, E. T. (1992). Neurophysiological mechanisms underlying face processing within and beyond the temporal cortical visual areas. *Philosophical Transactions of the Royal Society of London B, 335,* 11–21.

Roring, R. W. (2008). Reviewing expert chess performance: A production-based theory of chess skill. Unpublished Ph.D. thesis, Florida State University.

Rosch, E. (1973). On the internal structure of perceptual and semantic categories. In T. E. Moore (Ed.), *Cognitive development and the acquisition of language* (pp. 111–144). New York: Academic Press.

Rosch, E. (1975). Cognitive representations of semantic categories. *Journal of Experimental Psychology: General, 104,* 192–223.

Rosch, E. (1977). Human categorization. In N. Warren (Ed.), *Advances in cross-cultural psychology* (Vol. 1, pp. 1–49). London: Academic Press.

Ross, B. H. (1984). Remindings and their effects in learning a cognitive skill. *Cognitive Psychology, 16,* 371–416.

Ross, B. H. (1987). This is like that: The use of earlier problems and the separation of similarity effects. *Journal of Experimental Psychology: Learning, Memory, and Cognition, 13,* 629–639.

Ross, J., & Lawrence, K. A. (1968). Some observations on memory artifice. *Psychonomic Science, 13,* 107–108.

Rossi, S., Cappa, S. F., Babiloni, C., Pasqualetti, P., Miniussi, C., et al. (2001). Prefrontal cortex in long-term memory: An "interference" approach using magnetic stimulation. *Natural Neuroscience, 4,* 948–952.

Rossi, S., Pasqualetti, P., Zito, G., Vecchio, F., Cappa, S. F., et al. (2006). Prefrontal and parietal cortex in human episodic memory: An interference study by repetitive transcranial magnetic stimulation. *European Journal of Neuroscience, 23,* 793–800.

Rothkopf, E. Z. (1966). Learning from written instruction materials: An explanation of the control of inspection behavior by test-like events. *American Educational Research Journal, 3,* 241–249.

Ruiz, D. (1987). Learning and problem solving: What is learned while solving the Tower of Hanoi? Doctoral dissertation, Stanford University, 1986. *Dissertation Abstracts International, 42,* 3438B.

Rumelhart, D. E., & McClelland, J. L. (1986a). On learning the past tenses of English verbs. In J. L. McClelland & D. E. Rumelhart (Eds.), *Parallel distributed processing: Explorations in the microstructure of cognition* (Vol. 2, pp. 216–271). Cambridge, MA: MIT Press/Bradford Books.

Rumelhart, D. E., & Ortony, A. (1976). The representation of knowledge in memory. In R. C. Anderson, R. J. Spiro, & W. E. Montague (Eds.), *Semantic factors in cognition* (pp. 99–135). Hillsdale, NJ: Erlbaum.

Rumelhart, D. E., & Siple, P. (1974). Process of recognizing tachistoscopically presented words. *Psychological Review, 81,* 99–118.

Rundus, D. J. (1971). Analysis of rehearsal processes in free recall. *Journal of Experimental Psychology, 89,* 63–77.

Russell, S., & Norvig, P. (2002). *Artificial intelligence: A modern approach* (2nd ed.). Upper Saddle River, NJ: Prentice-Hall.

Sacks, O. W. (1985). *The man who mistook his wife for a hat and other clinical tales.* New York: Summit Books.

Saffran, E. M., & Schwartz, M. F. (1994). Of cabbages and things: Semantic memory from a neuropsychological perspective—a tutorial review. In C. Umilta & M. Moscovitch (Eds.), *Attention and performance XV* (pp. 507–536). Hove and London: Churchill Livingstone.

Safren, M. A. (1962). Associations, set, and the solution of word problems. *Journal of Experimental Psychology, 64,* 40–45.

Salamy, A. (1978). Commissural transmission: Maturational changes in humans. *Science, 200,* 1409–1411.

Salthouse, T. A. (1985). Anticipatory processes in transcription typing. *Journal of Applied Psychology, 70,* 264–271.

Salthouse, T. A. (1986). Perceptual, cognitive, and motoric aspects of transcription typing. *Psychological Bulletin, 99,* 303–319.

Salthouse, T. A. (1992). *Mechanisms of age-cognition relations in adulthood.* Hillsdale, NJ: Erlbaum.

Sams, M., Hari, R., Rif, J., & Knuutila, J. (1993). The human auditory sensory memory trace persists about 10 s: Neuromagnetic evidence. *Journal of Cognitive Neuroscience, 5,* 363–370.

Sanfey, A. G., Hastie, R., Colvin, M. K., & Grafman, J. (2003). Phineas gauged: Decision-making and the frontal lobes. *Neuropsychologia, 41,* 1218–1229.

Santa, J. L. (1977). Spatial transformations of words and pictures. *Journal of Experimental Psychology: Human Learning and Memory, 3,* 418–427.

Santrock, J. W., & Yussen, S. R. (1989). *Child development—An introduction.* Dubuque, IA: Wm. C. Brown.

Sarason, S. B., & Doris, J. (1979). *Educational handicap, public policy, and social history.* New York: Free Press.

Saufley, W. H., Otaka, S. R., & Bavaresco, J. L. (1985). Context effects: Classroom tests and context independence. *Memory & Cognition, 13,* 522–528.

Savage-Rumbaugh, E. S., Murphy, J., Sevik, R. A., Brakke, K. E., Williams, S. L., et al. (1993). Language comprehension in ape and child. *Monographs of the Society for Research in Child Development, 58*(Serial No. 233).

Sayers, D. L. (1968). *Five red herrings.* New York: Avon.

Schacter, D. L. (1987). Implicit memory: History and current status. *Journal of Experimental Psychology: Learning, Memory, and Cognition, 13,* 501–518.

Schacter, D. L. (2001). *The seven sins of memory: How the mind forgets and remembers.* Boston: Houghton Mifflin.

Schacter, D. L., & Badgaiyan, R. D. (2001). Neuroimaging of priming: New perspectives on implicit and explicit memory. *Current Directions in Psychological Science, 10,* 1–4.

Schacter, D. L., Cooper, L. A., Delaney, S. M., Peterson, M. A., & Tharan, M. (1991). Implicit memory for possible and impossible objects: Constraints on the construction of structural descriptions. *Journal of Experimental Psychology: Learning, Memory, and Cognition, 17,* 3–19.

Schaie, K. W. (1996). Intellectual development in adulthood. In J. Birren & K. W. Schaie (Eds.), *Handbook of the psychology of aging* (4th ed., pp. 266–286). San Diego: Academic Press.

Schank, R. C., & Abelson, R. (1977). *Scripts, plans, goals, and understanding.* Hillsdale, NJ: Erlbaum.

Scheines, R., & Sieg, W. (1994). Computer environments for proof construction. *Interactive Learning Environments, 4,* 159–169.

Schieffelin, B. (1979). *How Kaluli children learn what to say, what to do, and how to feel: An ethnographic study of the development of communicative competence.* Unpublished doctoral dissertation, Columbia University.

Schmidt, R. A. (1988). Motor and action perspectives on motor behavior. In O. G. Meijer & K. Rother (Eds.), *Complete movement behavior: The motor-action controversy* (pp. 3–44). Amsterdam: Elsevier.

Schneider, W., Körkel, J., & Weinert, F. E. (1988, July 6–8). *Expert knowledge, general abilities, and text processing.* Paper presented at the Workshop on Interactions among Aptitudes, Strategies, and Knowledge in Cognitive Performance.

Schneiderman, B. (1976). Exploratory experiments in programmer behavior. *International Journal of Computer and Information Sciences, 5,* 123–143.

Schoenfeld, A. H., & Herrmann, D. J. (1982). Problem perception and knowledge structure in expert and novice mathematical problem solvers. *Journal of Experimental Psychology: Learning, Memory, and Cognition, 8,* 484–494.

Schumacher, E. H., Seymour, T. L., Glass, J. M., Fencsik, D. E., Lauber, E. J., et al. (2001). Virtually perfect time sharing in dual-task performance: Uncorking the central cognitive bottleneck. *Psychological Science, 12,* 101–108.

Selfridge, O. G. (1955). Pattern recognition and modern computers. *Proceedings of the Western Joint Computer Conference.* New York: Institute of Electrical and Electronics Engineers.

Selkoe, D. J. (1992). Aging brain, aging mind. *Scientific American, 267*(3), 135–142.

Semendeferi, K., Armstrong, E., Schleicher, A., Zilles, K., & Van Hoesen, G. W. (2001). Prefrontal cortex in humans and apes: A comparative study of area 10. *American Journal of Physical Anthropology, 114,* 224–241.

Shafir, E. (1993). Choosing versus rejecting: Why some opinions are both better and worse than others. *Memory & Cognition, 21,* 546–556.

Sharot, T. Martorella, E. A., Delgado, M. R., & Phelps, E. A. (2007). How personal experience modulates the neural circuitry of memories of September 11. *Proceedings of the National Academy of Sciences, USA, 104,* 389–394.

Shelton, A. L., & Gabrieli, J. D. (2002). Neural correlates of encoding space from route and survey perspectives. *Journal of Neuroscience, 22,* 2711–2717.

Shepard, R. N. (1967). Recognition memory for words, sentences, and pictures. *Journal of Verbal Learning and Verbal Behavior, 6,* 156–163.

Shepard, R. N., & Metzler, J. (1971). Mental rotation of three-dimensional objects. *Science, 171,* 701–703.

Shepard, R. N., & Teghtsoonian, M. (1961). Retention of information under conditions approaching a steady state. *Journal of Experimental Psychology, 62,* 302–309.

Shortliffe E. H. (1976). *Computer based medical consultations: MYCIN.* New York: Elsevier.

Shuford, E. H. (1961). Percentage estimation of proportion as a function of element type, exposure time, and task. *Journal of Experimental Psychology, 61,* 430–436.

Siegler, R. S. (1996). *Emerging minds: The process of change in children's thinking.* New York: Oxford University Press.

Siegler, R. S. (1998). *Children's thinking* (3rd ed). Upper Saddle River, NJ: Prentice-Hall.

Silveira, J. (1971). *Incubation: The effect of interruption timing and length on problem solution and quality of problem processing.* Unpublished doctoral dissertation, University of Oregon.

Silver, E. A. (1979). Student perceptions of relatedness among mathematical verbal problems. *Journal for Research in Mathematics Education, 12,* 54–64.

Simester, D., & Drazen, P. (2001). Always leave home without it: A further investigation of the credit card effect on willingness to pay. *Marketing Letters, 12,* 5–12.

Simon, H. A. (1989). The scientist as a problem solver. In D. Klahr & K. Kotovsky (Eds.), *Complex information processing: The impact of Herbert Simon* (pp. 375–398). Hillsdale, NJ: Erlbaum.

Simon, H. A., & Gilmartin, K. (1973). A simulation of memory for chess positions. *Cognitive Psychology, 5,* 29–46.

Simon, H., & Lea, G. (1974). Problem solving and rule induction. In H. Simon (Ed.), *Models of thought.* New Haven, CT: Yale University Press.

Simon, T. J., Hespos, S. J., & Rochat, P. (1995). Do infants understand simple arithmetic? A replication of Wynn (1992). *Cognitive Development, 10,* 253–269.

Simons, D. J., & Chabris, C. F. (1999). Gorillas in our midst: Sustained inattentional blindness for dynamic events. *Perception, 28,* 1059–1074.

Simons, D. J., & Levin, D. T. (1998). Failure to detect changes to people in a real-world interaction. *Psychonomic Bulletin and Review, 5,* 644–649.

Singer, M. (1994). Discourse inference processes. In M. A. Gernsbacher (Ed.), *Handbook of psycholinguistics* (pp. 479–515). San Diego: Academic Press.

Singley, K., & Anderson, J. R. (1989). *The transfer of cognitive skill.* Cambridge, MA: Harvard University Press.

Sivers, H., Schooler, J., Freyd, J. J. (2002). Recovered memories. In V. S. Ramachandran (Ed.), *Encyclopedia of the human brain* (Vol. 4., pp 169–184). San Diego, CA, and London: Academic Press.

Skoyles, J. R. (1999). Expertise vs. general problem solving abilities in human evolution: Reply to Overskeid on brain-expertise. *Psycoloquy, 10,* 1–14.

Slamecka, N. J., & Graf, P. (1978). The generation effect: Delineation of a phenomenon. *Journal of Experimental Psychology: Human Learning and Memory, 4,* 592–604.

Sleeman, D., & Brown, J. S. (Eds.). (1982). *Intelligent tutoring systems.* New York: Academic Press.

Smith, E. E., & Jonides, J. (1995). Working memory in humans: Neuropsychological evidence. In M. S. Gazzaniga (Ed.), *The cognitive neurosciences* (pp. 1009–1020). Cambridge, MA: MIT Press.

Smith, E. E., & Grossman, M. (2008). Multiple systems for category learning. *Neuroscience and Biobehavioral Reviews, 32,* 249–264.

Smith, E. E., Patalano, A., & Jonides, J. (1998). Alternative strategies of categorization. *Cognition, 65,* 167–196.

Smith, J. D., & Minda, J. P. (1998). Prototypes in the mist: The early epochs of category learning. *Journal of Experimental Psychology: Learning, Memory & Cognition, 24,* 1411–1436.

Smith, M. (1982). *Hypnotic memory enhancement of witnesses: Does it work?* Paper presented at the meeting of the Psychonomic Society, Minneapolis.

Smith, S. M., & Blakenship, S. E. (1989). Incubation effects. *Bulletin of the Psychonomic Society, 27,* 311–314.

Smith, S. M., & Blakenship, S. E. (1991). Incubation and the persistence of fixation in problem solving. *American Journal of Psychology, 104,* 61–87.

Smith, S. M., Brown, H. O., Toman, J. E. P., & Goodman, L. S. (1947). The lack of cerebral effects of d-tubercurarine. *Anesthesiology, 8,* 1–14.

Smith, S. M., Glenberg, A., & Bjork, R. A. (1978). Environmental context and human memory. *Memory & Cognition, 6,* 342–353.

Snow, C., & Ferguson, C. (Eds.). (1977). *Talking to children: Language input and acquisition (Papers from a conference sponsored by the Committee on Sociolinguistics of the Social Science Research Council).* New York: Cambridge University Press.

Sohn, M.-H., Goode, A., Stenger, V. A, Carter, C. S., & Anderson, J. R. (2003). Competition and representation during memory retrieval: Roles of the prefrontal cortex and the posterior parietal cortex. *Proceedings of National Academy of Sciences, USA, 100,* 7412–7417.

Spearman, C. (1904). The proof and measurement of association between two things. *American Journal of Psychology, 15,* 72–101.

Spelke, E., Hirst, W., & Neisser, U. (1976). Skills of divided attention. *Cognition, 4,* 215–230.

Sperling, G. A. (1960). The information available in brief visual presentation. *Psychological Monographs, 74*(Whole No. 498).

Sperling, G. A. (1967). Successive approximations to a model for short-term memory. *Acta Psychologica, 27,* 285–292.

Spiro, R. J. (1977). Constructing a theory of reconstructive memory: The state of the schema approach. In R. C. Anderson, R. J. Spiro, & W. E. Montague (Eds.), *Schooling and the acquisition of knowledge* (pp. 137–166). Hillsdale, NJ: Erlbaum.

Squire, L. R. (1987). *Memory and brain.* New York: Oxford University Press.

Squire, L. R. (1992). Memory and the hippocampus: A synthesis from findings with rats, monkeys, and humans. *Psychological Review, 99,* 195–232.

Standing, L. (1973). Learning 10,000 pictures. *Quarterly Journal of Experimental Psychology, 25,* 207–222.

Stanfield, R. A., & Zwaan, R. A. (2001). The effect of implied orientation derived from verbal context on picture recognition. *Psychological Science, 12,* 153–156.

Starkey, P., Spelke, E. S., & Gelman, R. (1990). Numerical abstraction by human infants. *Cognition, 36,* 97–127.

Stein, B. S., & Bransford, J. D. (1979). Constraints on effective elaboration: Effects of precision and subject generation. *Journal of Verbal Learning and Verbal Behavior, 18,* 769–777.

Stein, N. L., & Trabasso, T. (1981). What's in a story? Critical issues in comprehension and instruction. In R. Glaser (Ed.), *Advances in the psychology of instruction* (Vol. 2, pp. 213–268). Hillsdale, NJ: Erlbaum.

Sternberg, R. J. (1977). *Intelligence, information processing, and analogical reasoning.* Hillsdale, NJ: Erlbaum.

Sternberg, R. J. (1998). Personal communication.

Sternberg, R. J., & Gardner, M. K. (1983). Unities in inductive reasoning. *Journal of Experimental Psychology: General, 112,* 80–116.

Sternberg, S. (1966). High-speed scanning in human memory. *Science, 153,* 652–654.

Sternberg, S. (1969). Memory scanning: Mental processes revealed by reaction time experiments. *American Scientist, 57,* 421–457.

Stevens, A., & Coupe, P. (1978). Distortions in judged spatial relations. *Cognitive Psychology, 10,* 422–437.

Stillings, N. A., Feinstein, M. H., Garfield, J. L., Rissland, E. L., Rosenbaum, D. A., et al. (1987). *Cognitive science: An introduction.* Cambridge, MA: MIT Press.

Strangman, G., Boas, D. A., & Sutton, J. P. (2002). Non-invasive neuroimaging using near-infrared light. *Biological Psychiatry, 52,* 679–693.

Stratton, G. M. (1922). *Developing mental power.* New York: Houghton Mifflin.

Strayer, D. L., & Drews, F. A. (2007). Cell-phone-induced driver distraction. *Current Directions in Psychological Science, 16,* 128–131.

Strohner, H., & Nelson, K. E. (1974). The young child's development of sentence comprehension: Influence of event probability, nonverbal context, syntactic form, and strategies. *Child Development, 45,* 567–576.

Stromswold, K. (2000). The cognitive neuroscience of language acquisition. In M. Gazzaniga (Ed.), *The cognitive neurosciences* (2nd ed., pp. 909–932). Cambridge, MA: MIT Press.

Stroop, J. R. (1935). Studies of interference in serial verbal reactions. *Journal of Experimental Psychology, 18,* 643–662.

Studdert-Kennedy, M. (1976). Speech perception. In N. J. Lass (Ed.), *Contemporary issues in experimental phonetics* (pp. 243–293). Springfield, IL: Charles C. Thomas.

Sulin, R. A., & Dooling, D. J. (1974). Intrusion of a thematic idea in retention of prose. *Journal of Experimental Psychology, 103,* 255–262.

Swinney, D. A. (1979). Lexical access during sentence comprehension: (Re)consideration of context effects. *Journal of Verbal Learning and Verbal Behavior, 18,* 645–659.

Szameitat, A. J., Schubert, T., Muller, K., & von Cramon, D. Y. (2002). Localization of executive functions in dual-task performance with fMRI. *Journal of Cognitive Neuroscience, 14,* 1184–1199.

Talarico, J. M., & Rubin, D. C. (2003). Confidence, not consistency, characterizes flashbulb memories. *Psychological Science, 14,* 455–461.

Tanaka, J. W., & Farah, M. (1993). Parts and wholes in face recognition. *Quarterly Journal of Experimental Psychology, 46A,* 225–245.

Taylor, H. A., & Tversky, B. (1992). Spatial mental models derived from survey and route descriptions. *Journal of Memory and Language, 31,* 261–292.

Teasdale, J. D., & Russell, M. L. (1983). Differential effects of induced mood on the recall of positive, negative and neutral words. *British Journal of Clinical Psychology, 22,* 163–171.

Terman, L. M., & Merrill, M. A. (1973). *Stanford-Binet intelligence scales: 1973 norms edition.* Boston: Houghton Mifflin.

Terrace, H. S., Pettito, L. A., Sanders, R. J., & Bever, T. G. (1979). Can an ape create a sentence? *Science, 206,* 891–902.

Thelen, E. (2000). Grounded in the world: Developmental origins of the embodied mind. *Infancy, 1,* 3–30.

Thomas, E. L., & Robinson, H. A. (1972). *Improving reading in every class: A sourcebook for teachers.* Boston: Allyn & Bacon.

Thompson, D. M. (1972). Context effects on recognition memory. *Journal of Verbal Learning and Verbal Behavior, 11,* 497–511.

Thompson, M. C., & Massaro, D. W. (1973). Visual information and redundancy in reading. *Journal of Experimental Psychology, 98,* 49–54.

Thompson, W. L., & Kosslyn, S. M. (2000). In A. W. Toga & J. C. Mazziotta (Eds), *Brain mapping II: The systems* (pp. 535–560). San Diego: Academic Press.

Thorndike, E. L. (1898). Animal intelligence: An experimental study of the associative processes in animals. *Psychological Monographs, 2*(Whole No. 8).

Thorndike, E. L. (1906). *Principles of teaching.* New York: A. G. Seiler.

Thorndike, E. L., & Woodworth, R. S. (1901). The influence of improvement in one mental function upon the efficiency of other functions. *Psychological Review, 9,* 374–382.

Thorndyke, P. W. (1977). Cognitive structures in comprehension and memory in narrative discourse. *Cognitive Psychology, 9,* 77–110.

Thorndyke, P. W., & Hayes-Roth, B. (1982). Differences in spatial knowledge acquired from maps and navigation. *Cognitive Psychology, 14,* 560–589.

Thurstone, L. L. (1938). *Primary mental abilities.* Chicago: University of Chicago Press.

Tipper, S. P., Driver, J., & Weaver, B. (1991). Object-centered inhibition of return of visual attention. *Quarterly Journal of Experimental Psychology, 43A,* 289–298.

Tomasello, M., & Call, J. (1997). *Primate cognition.* New York: Oxford University Press.

Tootell, R. B. H., Silverman, M. S., Switkes, E., & DeValois, R. L. (1982). Deoxyglucose analysis of retinotopic organization in primate striate cortex. *Science, 218,* 902–904.

Townsend, D. J., & Bever, T. G. (1982). Natural units interact during language comprehension. *Journal of Verbal Learning and Verbal Behavior, 28,* 681–703.

Trabasso, T. R., Rollins, H., & Shaughnessy, E. (1971). Storage and verification stages in processing concepts. *Cognitive Psychology, 2,* 239–289.

Trabasso, T. R., Secco, T., & van den Broek, P. (1984). Causal cohesion and story coherence. In H. Mandl (Ed.), *Learning and comprehension of text* (pp. 83–111). Hillsdale, NJ: Erlbaum.

Treisman, A. M. (1960). Verbal cues, language, and meaning in selective attention. *Quarterly Journal of Experimental Psychology, 12,* 242–248.

Treisman, A. M. (1964). Monitoring and storage of irrelevant messages and selective attention. *Journal of Verbal Learning and Verbal Behavior, 3,* 449–459.

Treisman, A. M. (1978). Personal communication.

Treisman, A. M., & Geffen, G. (1967). Selective attention: Perception or response? *Quarterly Journal of Experimental Psychology, 19,* 1–17.

Treisman, A. M., & Gelade, G. (1980). A feature-integration theory of attention. *Cognitive Psychology, 12,* 97–136.

Treisman, A. M., & Riley, J. (1969). Is selective attention selective perception or selective response? A further test. *Journal of Experimental Psychology, 79,* 27–34.

Treisman, A. M., & Schmidt, H. (1982). Illusory conjunction in the perception of objects. *Cognitive Psychology, 14,* 107–141.

Treves, A., & Rolls, E. T. (1994). A computational analysis of the role of the hippocampus in memory. *Hippocampus, 4,* 374–392.

Trueswell, J. C., Tannehaus, M. K., & Garnsey, S. M. (1994). Semantic influences on parsing: Use of thematic role information in syntactic ambiguity resolution. *Journal of Memory and Language, 33,* 285–318.

Tsushima, T., Takizawa, O., Sasaki M., Siraki S., Nishi K., et al. (1994). *Discrimination of English /r-l/ and /w-y/ by Japanese infants at 6–12 months: Language specific developmental changes in speech perception abilities.* Paper presented at the International Conference on Spoken Language Processing 4. Yokohama.

Tulving, E., & Pearlstone, Z. (1966). Availability versus accessibility of information in memory for words. *Journal of Verbal Learning and Verbal Behavior, 5,* 381–391.

Tulving, E., & Thompson, D. M. (1973). Encoding specificity and retrieval processes in episodic memory. *Psychological Review, 80,* 352–373.

Turing, A. M. (1950). Computing machinery and intelligence. *Mind, 59,* 433–460.

Tversky, A., & Kahneman, D. (1974). Judgments under uncertainty: Heuristics and biases. *Science, 185,* 1124–1131.

Tweney, R. D. (1989). A framework for the cognitive psychology of science. In B. Gholson, A. Houts, R. A. Neimeyer, & W. Shadish (Eds.), *Psychology of science and metascience* (pp. 342–366). Cambridge, England: Cambridge University Press.

Tyler, R., & Marslen-Wilson, W. (1977). The on-line effects of semantic context on syntactic processing. *Journal of Verbal Learning and Verbal Behavior, 16,* 683–692.

Ullman, S. (1996). *High-level vision.* Cambridge, MA: MIT Press.

Ullman, S. (2006). Object recognition and segmentation by a fragment-based hierarchy. *Trends in Cognitive Science, 11,* 58–64.

Ultan, R. (1969). Some general characteristics of interrogative systems. *Working Papers in Language Universals (Stanford University), 1,* 41–63.

Underwood, G. (1974). Moray vs. the rest: The effect of extended shadowing practice. *Quarterly Journal of Experimental Psychology, 26,* 368–372.

Ungerleider, L. G., & Brody, B. A. (1977). Extrapersonal spatial orientation: The role of posterior parietal, anterior frontal and inferotemporal cortex. *Experimental Neurology, 56,* 265–280.

Ungerleider, L. G., & Miskin, M. (1982). Two visual pathways. In D. J. Ingle, M. A. Goodale, & R. J. W. Mansfield (Eds.), *Analysis of visual behavior.* (pp. 549–586). Cambridge, MA: MIT Press.

Vallar, G., & Baddeley, A. D. (1982). Short-term forgetting and the articulatory loop. *Quarterly Journal of Experimental Psychology, 34,* 53–60.

Vallar, G., Di Betta, A. M., & Silveri, M. C. (1997). The phonological short-term store-rehearsal system: Patterns of impairment and neural correlates. *Neuropsychologia, 35,* 795–812.

Van Berkum, J. J. A., Hagoort, P., & Brown, C. M. (1999). Semantic integration in sentences and discourse: Evidence from the N400. *Journal of Cognitive Neuroscience, 11,* 657–671.

Van Essen, D. C., & DeYoe, E. A. (1995). Concurrent processing in the primitive visual cortex. In M. S. Gazzaniga (Ed.), *The cognitive neurosciences* (pp. 383–400). Cambridge, MA: MIT Press.

Van Loosbroek, E., & Smitsman, A. W. (1992). Visual perception of numerosity in infancy. *Developmental Psychology, 26,* 916–922.

Vargha-Khadem, F., Watkins, K., Alcock, K., Fletcher, P., & Passingham, R. (1995). Praxic and nonverbal cognitive deficits in a large family with a genetically transmitted speech and language disorder. *Proceedings of the National Academy of Sciences, USA, 92,* 930–933.

Von Ahn, L., Blum, M., & Langford, J. (2002). Telling humans and computers apart (automatically). *Carnegie Mellon University Tech Report.*

Von Frisch, K. (1967). *The dance language and orientation of bees.* (C. E. Chadwick, Trans.). Cambridge, MA: Belknap Press.

Von Neumann, J., & Morgenstern, O. (1944). *Theory of games and economic behavior.* New York: Wiley.

Wade, N. (2003). Early voices: The leap to language. *New York Times,* July 15, F1.

Wagner, A. D., Bunge, S. A., & Badre, D. (2004). Cognitive control, semantic memory, and priming: Contributions from prefrontal cortex. M. S. Gazzaniga (Ed.), *The cognitive neurosciences* (3rd ed.). Cambridge, MA: MIT Press.

Wagner, A. D., Schacter, D. L., Rotte, M., Koutstaal, W., Maril, A., et al. (1998). Building memories: Remembering and forgetting of verbal experiences as predicted by brain activity. *Science, 281,* 1188–1191.

Wallace, B. (1984). Apparent equivalence between perception and imagery in the production of various illusions. *Memory & Cognition, 12,* 156–162.

Wanner, H. E. (1968). *On remembering, forgetting, and understanding sentences: A study of the deep structure hypothesis.* Unpublished doctoral dissertation, Harvard University, Cambridge, MA.

Warren, R. M. (1970). Perceptual restorations of missing speech sounds. *Science, 167,* 392–393.

Warren, R. M., & Warren, R. P. (1970). Auditory illusions and confusions. *Scientific American, 223,* 30–36.

Warrington, E. K., & Shallice, T. (1984). Category specific semantic impairments. *Brain, 197,* 829–854.

Washburn, D. A. (1994). Stroop-like effects for monkeys and humans: Processing speed or strength of association? *Psychological Science, 5,* 375–379.

Wason, P. C. (1960). On the failure to eliminate hypotheses in a conceptual task. *Quarterly Journal of Experimental Psychology, 12,* 129–140.

Wason, P. C. (1968). On the failure to eliminate hypotheses—A second look. In P. C. Wason & P. N. Johnson-Laird (Eds.), *Thinking and reasoning* (pp. 165–174). Baltimore: Penguin.

Wason, P. C., & Johnson-Laird, P. N. (1972). *Psychology of reasoning: Structure and content.* Cambridge, MA: Harvard University Press.

Wason, P., & Reich, S. S. (1979). A verbal illusion. *Quarterly Journal of Experimental Psychology, 31,* 591–597.

Wasow, T. (1989). Grammatical theory. In M. I. Posner (Ed.), *Foundations of cognitive science* (pp. 161–205). Cambridge, MA: MIT Press.

Watkins, M. J., & Tulving, E. (1975). Episodic memory: When recognition fails. *Journal of Experimental Psychology: General, 104,* 5–29.

Watson, J. (1930). *Behaviorism.* New York: W. W. Norton.

Waugh, N. C., & Norman, D. A. (1965). Primary memory. *Psychological Review, 72,* 89–104.

Weber, E., Böckenholt, U., Hilton, D., & Wallace, B. (1993). Determinants of diagnostic hypothesis generation: Effects of information, base rates and experience. *Journal of Experimental Psychology: Learning, Memory, and Cognition, 19,* 1151–1164.

Weber-Fox, C., & Neville, H. J. (1996). Maturational constraints on functional specializations for language processing: ERP and behavioral evidence in bilingual speakers. *Journal of Cognitive Neuroscience, 8,* 231–256.

Weisberg, R. W. (1969). Sentence processing assessed through intrasentence word associations. *Journal of Experimental Psychology, 82,* 332–338.

Weisberg, R. W. (1986). *Creativity: Genius and other myths.* New York: W. H. Freeman.

Weiser, M., & Shertz, J. (1983). Programming problem representation in novice and expert programmers. *International Journal of Man-Machine Studies, 19,* 391–398.

Werker, J. F., & Tees, R. C. (1999). Experiential influences on infant speech processing: Toward a new synthesis. *Annual Review of Psychology, 50,* 509–535.

Wertheimer, M. (1912/1932). Experimentelle Studien über das Sehen von Beuegung. *Zeitschrift für Psychologie, 61,* 161–265.

Wheeler, D. D. (1970). Processes in word recognition. *Cognitive Psychology, 1,* 59–85.

Whorf, B. L. (1956). *Language, thought, and reality.* Cambridge, MA: MIT Press.

Wickelgren, W. A. (1974). *How to solve problems.* New York: W. H. Freeman.

Wickelgren, W. A. (1975). Alcoholic intoxication and memory storage dynamics. *Memory & Cognition, 3,* 385–389.

Whitaker, C. F. (1990). [Letter]. Ask Marilyn column. *Parade Magazine,* 16.

Wikman, A. S., Nieminen, T., & Summala, H. (1998). Driving experience and time-sharing during in-car tasks on roads of different width. *Ergonomics, 41,* 358–372.

Windes, J. D. (1968). Reaction time for numerical coding and naming numerals. *Journal of Experimental Psychology, 78,* 318–322.

Winston, P. H. (1970). *Learning structural descriptions from examples* (Tech. Rep. No. 231). Cambridge, MA: MIT, AI Laboratory.

Wixted, J. T., & Ebbesen, E. B. (1991). On the form of forgetting. *Psychological Science, 2,* 409–415.

Woldorff, M. G., Gallen, C. C., Hampson, S. A., Hillyard, S. A., Pantev, C., et al. (1993). Modulation of early sensory processing in human auditory cortex during auditory selective attention. *Proceedings of the National Academy of Sciences, USA, 90,* 8722–8726.

Wolfe, J. M. (1994). Guided search 2.0: A revised model of visual search. *Psychonomic Bulletin and Review, 1,* 202–238.

Woodrow, H. (1927). The effect of the type of training upon transference. *Journal of Educational Psychology, 18,* 159–172.

Woodworth, R. S., & Sells, S. B. (1935). An atmospheric effect in formal syllogistic reasoning. *Journal of Experimental Psychology, 18,* 451–460.

Wurtz, R. H., Goldberg, M. E., & Robinson, D. L. (1980). Behavioral modulation of visual responses in the monkey: Stimulus selection for attention and movement. *Progress in Psychobiology, Physiology and Psychology, 9,* 43–83.

Wynn, K. (1992). Addition and subtraction by human infants. *Nature, 358,* 749–750.

Yin, R. K. (1969). Looking at upside-down faces. *Journal of Experimental Psychology, 81,* 141–145.

Zaehle, T., Jordan, K., Wüstenberg, T., Baudewig, J., Dechent, P., et al. (2007). The neural basis of the egocentric and allocentric spatial frame of reference. *Brain Research, 1137,* 92–103.

Zatorre, R. J., Mondor, T. A. & Evans, A. C. (1999). Auditory attention to space and frequency activates similar cerebral systems. *Neuroimage, 10,* 544–554.

Name Index

Subject Index

D

E

W